Social Vulnerability to DISASTERS

Social Vulnerability to DISASTERS

Edited by
Brenda D. Phillips
Deborah S.K. Thomas
Alice Fothergill
Lynn Blinn-Pike

CRC Press
Taylor & Francis Group
Boca Raton London New York

CRC Press is an imprint of the
Taylor & Francis Group, an **informa** business

CRC Press
Taylor & Francis Group
6000 Broken Sound Parkway NW, Suite 300
Boca Raton, FL 33487-2742

© 2010 by Taylor and Francis Group, LLC
CRC Press is an imprint of Taylor & Francis Group, an Informa business

No claim to original U.S. Government works

Printed in the United States of America on acid-free paper
10 9 8 7 6 5 4 3 2 1

International Standard Book Number: 978-1-4200-7856-5 (Hardback)

Library of Congress Cataloging-in-Publication Data

Social vulnerability to disasters / editors, Brenda Phillips ... [et al.].
    p. cm.
  Includes bibliographical references and index.
  ISBN 978-1-4200-7856-5 (hbk. : alk. paper)
  1. Disasters--Social aspects. 2. Risk assessment. I. Phillips, Brenda. II. Title.

HV553.S586 2010
363.34'2--dc22
                                                      2009024408

Visit the Taylor & Francis Web site at
http://www.taylorandfrancis.com

and the CRC Press Web site at
http://www.crcpress.com

This volume is dedicated to

Mary Fran Myers

(1952–2004)

For many years, Mary Fran Myers served as the codirector of the Natural Hazards Research and Applications Information Center at the University of Colorado at Boulder. Many authors in this volume first met through Mary Fran, an individual dedicated to reducing vulnerability. In 1997, she received the Association of State Floodplain Managers' Goddard-White Award for her efforts, their highest award. In 2002, the Gender and Disaster Network established the Mary Fran Myers Award for her work to advance women's careers and to promote research on gender issues. In 2003, colleagues, family, and friends created the Mary Fran Myers Scholarship. Funds bring under-represented individuals to the annual Boulder Hazards Workshop. Mary Fran is the person most responsible for weaving together the network of authors in this volume. We dedicate our work to her memory.

All proceeds from this book are donated to the
Mary Fran Myers Scholarship Fund.

Contents

SECTION I   Understanding Social Vulnerability

SECTION II   Socially Vulnerable Groups

SECTION III   Building Capacity

Preface

In 2004 and 2005, the world watched in horror as the Indian Ocean tsunami claimed 300,000 lives across 13 nations and then as Hurricane Katrina stranded thousands on rooftops across the U.S. Gulf Coast. About 80% of the tsunami victims were women and children. Close to 75% of the Hurricane Katrina victims were elderly, many with some type of disability; in New Orleans the majority was African American. In both circumstances, women and girls faced difficult post-disaster choices that too many times exposed them to violence. And in all nations affected by these events, children orphaned or separated from their families required help to find safety. Both of these disasters clearly revealed how social structure and roles produced extensive human suffering and differential impacts. These are just a few recent events that highlight the need for a comprehensive book that explicitly focuses on the social construction of disasters, acknowledging that the characteristics of an event alone do not create the tragedies that unfurl.

Simultaneously, people historically vulnerable stepped up time and time again. Women created rescue efforts and opened shelters. Poor people shared local knowledge that inspired environmentally friendly or "green rebuilding." People presumed to bear disabilities launched cleanup efforts and located missing family members. In other words, those "vulnerable" also have a great deal of capacity.

The primary purpose of this book is to help readers understand why such vulnerabilities exist and what can be done in order to foster change, and ultimately to reduce vulnerabilities and build capacity. We dedicate this volume to all those who have suffered from natural and technological events. Most importantly, we hope that it will inspire those who work in all aspects of emergency management to directly incorporate social vulnerability as a fundamental principle and goal.

The editing team for *Social Vulnerability to Disasters* gratefully acknowledges the contributions of a number of people who made this book possible. First, the book is based on materials originally created for the Federal Emergency Management (FEMA) Higher Education Program, directed by Dr. B. Wayne Blanchard. We appreciate his vision that fostered a network of experts to create materials supporting the teaching of emergency management. His initiative brought together a number of teams who created college-level materials, including the authors of the original material that launched this book. The original materials can be found at http://www.training.fema.gov/EMIWeb/edu/sovul.asp (access date July 17, 2008). FEMA graciously provided those materials to assist in the creation of this book. The content of the book, however, remains the responsibility of the authors and editors and does not necessarily reflect the views of FEMA or its staff.

The creators of the FEMA course on Social Vulnerability to Disasters included lead course developer Dr. Elaine Enarson, who was supported by Dr. Cheryl Childers, Dr. Betty Hearn Morrow, Dr. Deborah Thomas, and Dr. Ben Wisner. Dr. Robert C. Bolin, Lorna Jarrett, Dr. David McEntire, and Dr. Brenda Phillips served as volunteer consultants on the development of those materials.

FEMA, through Dr. Blanchard's efforts, offers an annual Higher Education Conference. At one of those conferences CRC Press editor Mark Listewnik realized the potential of bringing together a team of writers to create a book that could truly make a difference in the lives of those at risk. Through his encouragement, an editing and writing team came together to produce this volume. We very much appreciate the support, guidance, and encouragement that he provided. Our many phone conversations and e-mails spurred us on to write, edit, and share our expertise and hope for a safer world. He is an important part of that effort. Stephanie Morkert, Taylor & Francis Production Coordinator, proved to be our best friend on the project by answering both routine and extremely detailed questions regarding formatting. We thank her and the Taylor & Francis production team (especially those at CRC Press and particularly Prudy Taylor Board) for the many hours that went in and for their high level of professionalism in producing this volume.

The editors are grateful for the efforts of the chapter authors who took time from already busy schedules to write. Authors of original course materials returned for a number of chapters along with additional experts in their respective fields. We engaged authors with reputations for producing materials with scholarly depth and practical applications. They also brought a heightened sense of compassion to the work at hand, to reduce vulnerability among those most likely to be affected. Not only did they bring keen minds to bear on the problem, but equally important, they brought strong, caring hearts to the work as well. The combination produced compelling chapters that are visionary in what the applications might render.

As a person who worked tirelessly to integrate issues of vulnerability into emergency management, we dedicate this book to our friend, colleague, and mentor Mary Fran Myers of the Natural Hazards Research and Applications Information Center at the University of Colorado at Boulder. The editors and authors associated with this book benefited professionally from both direct and indirect association with Mary Fran. She built our network; invited us to meetings; helped us to secure grants; offered writing, publishing, and speaking opportunities; and made a difference with her life. We would not have been able to write this book unless she had connected and inspired us. We miss her so much, but carry on in the spirit and professionalism that she demonstrated.

All proceeds from the sale of this book will go to the Mary Fran Myers Scholarship Fund, which recognizes "outstanding individuals who share Mary Fran's commitment to disaster research and practice and who have the potential to make a lasting contribution to reducing disaster vulnerability." By purchasing this volume or adopting it for a class, you are helping to extend her legacy. Past scholarship recipients have come from Honduras, Australia, France, China, Pakistan, Nigeria, Guatemala, India, and the United States. Their work includes Katrina relief, land use planning, sustainable development, mitigation, floodplains, social and economic impacts, university safety, community outreach, poverty, vulnerability reduction, and public education. Dollars spent for this volume will go far. For more information on the scholarship, please visit http://www.colorado.edu/hazards/awards/myers-scholarship.html (access date July 17, 2008).

Since the Indian Ocean tsunami and Hurricane Katrina, more events have claimed those vulnerable to disaster. The Burma/Myanmar cyclone and the China earthquake in 2008 are only two such events. May you find the chapters in this volume enlightening guides to a safer, more humane world. *Our work is not done.*

Brenda D. Phillips
Oklahoma State University

Deborah S. K. Thomas
University of Colorado Denver

Alice Fothergill
University of Vermont

Lynn Blinn-Pike
Indiana University–Purdue University Indianapolis

Contributors

Lynn Blinn-Pike, PhD
Department of Sociology
Indiana University–Purdue University
Indianapolis, Indiana

John Brett, PhD
Department of Anthropology
University of Colorado Denver
Denver, Colorado

Alan Clive, PhD (deceased)
Equal Rights Office
Federal Emergency Management Agency
Washington, D.C.

Nicole Dash, PhD
Department of Sociology
University of North Texas
Denton, Texas

Elizabeth A. Davis, JD, MEd
EAD & Associates, LLC
Brooklyn, New York

Elaine Enarson, PhD
Independent Sociologist
Boulder, Colorado

Maureen Fordham, PhD
Divisions of Geography & Environmental
   Management
University of Northumbria
Northumbria, United Kingdom

Alice Fothergill, PhD
Department of Sociology
University of Vermont
Burlington, Vermont

Jennifer Goldsmith, Graduate Student
University of Colorado Denver
Denver, Colorado

Eve Gruntfest, PhD
Social Science Woven into Meteorology
   (SSWIM)
University of Oklahoma
Norman, Oklahoma

Rebecca Hansen, MSW
EAD & Associates, LLC
Brooklyn, New York

Alison Herring, Graduate Student
University of North Texas
Denton, Texas

Pamela Jenkins, PhD
Department of Sociology
University of New Orleans
New Orleans, Louisiana

William E. Lovekamp, PhD
Department of Sociology & Anthropology
Eastern Illinois University
Charleston, Illinois

Brenda G. McCoy, Assistant Professor
Sociology Program
University of North Texas Dallas Campus
Dallas, Texas

Jennifer Mincin, ABD
International Rescue Committee
New York City, New York

Betty Hearn Morrow, PhD, Emeritus
Florida International University
Miami, Florida

Katie Oviatt, Graduate Student
University of Colorado Denver
Denver, Colorado

Eve Passerini, PhD
Department of Sociology
Regis University
Denver, Colorado

Lori Peek, PhD
Department of Sociology
Colorado State University
Fort Collins, Colorado

Brenda D. Phillips, PhD
Center for the Study of Disasters and Extreme
    Events
Oklahoma State University
Stillwater, Oklahoma

Jean Scandlyn, PhD
Departments of Anthropology and Health &
    Behavioral Sciences
University of Colorado Denver
Denver, Colorado

Carrie N. Simon, Graduate Student
Colorado School of Public Health
Denver, Colorado

Pamela K. Stephens, Graduate Student
University of Colorado Denver
Denver, Colorado

Deborah S.K. Thomas, PhD
Department of Geography & Environmental
    Sciences
University of Colorado Denver
Denver, Colorado

1 Introduction

Brenda D. Phillips and Maureen Fordham

CONTENTS

1.1 CHAPTER PURPOSE

This opening chapter provides an overview of why understanding social vulnerability matters for the practice of disaster management. The chapter content contrasts the historically dominant hazards approach with that of social vulnerability and concludes with an overview of upcoming sections and chapters.

1.2 OBJECTIVES

At the conclusion of this chapter, readers should be able to

1. Understand basic terms relevant to social vulnerability.
2. Understand the dominant view of hazards.

3. Identify the shortcomings of the dominant view.
4. Trace the historical development of a social vulnerability approach.
5. Understand the general framework of a social vulnerability approach.
6. Appreciate why considering social vulnerability is necessary in order to reduce risk.

1.3   INTRODUCTION

For many of us, the images of people dying in the Indian Ocean Tsunami (2004) or of those awaiting rescue on the rooftops of New Orleans after Hurricane Katrina (2005) mark a point in time when we understood the extent of human vulnerability in disaster situations (Figure 1.1). The stark images also raised deeper questions. Why were people in harm's way? What could have been done to prevent such loss of life? How could we have prevented the tragedies from happening? What became of those affected? Were they able to return to their homes, recover psychologically, find another source of employment, reunite their families?

The study of social vulnerability to disasters is compelling. For anyone who wondered why so many people were on the rooftops in New Orleans and why so many died, the answers are in this volume; for those who practice professions designed to reduce that same vulnerability, current

FIGURE 1.1   FEMA Urban Search and Rescue team evacuates nursing home residents from New Orleans on September 2, 2005. *Source*: Jocelyn Augustino/FEMA news photo.

practices are critically reviewed. This book is designed to make a difference in our understanding of and efforts to reduce conditions that threaten life safety, personal property, as well as our neighborhoods and communities. We invite you to be part of the solution.

Researchers have been studying and writing about human vulnerability to disasters for decades. Yet, much of that promising body of knowledge has not made its way into the practice of disaster management. Far too frequently, efforts to reduce vulnerability occur only after a major event has claimed lives and destroyed family assets, including homes, businesses, and savings. Measures to reduce vulnerability tend to rely on assessing established practices, analyzing current policies, and revising already-existing plans, but recent research on vulnerability has much to offer managers and practitioners in disaster risk reduction. Consider, for example, the following issues:

- *Class*. Lower income families and households tend to live in housing that suffers disproportionately during disasters. Disaster managers should recognize such inequitable circumstances and act to even the odds (Mileti 1999).
- *Race and ethnicity*. Warning messages tend to be issued in the dominant language with an expectation that people will take the recommended action immediately. Research indicates that culture influences how people may receive and interpret warnings and how they may respond (Lindell and Perry 2004).
- *Gender*. Domestic violence appears to increase after a disaster, yet few communities include women's advocates in their emergency operations planning (Jenkins and Phillips 2009). Further, though women tend to be the ones most likely to secure relief aid for the family, they are under-represented and under-used in recovery efforts (Enarson and Morrow 2000).
- *Age*. Senior citizens are reluctant to secure aid after a disaster out of concern they may lose their independence (Bolin and Klenow 1982; Fernandez et al. 2002). As a consequence, they tend to under-use relief programs and experience delays in returning to their homes.
- *Disability*. People with disabilities experience considerable problems in securing adequate transportation to evacuate as well as appropriate, accessible shelters and post-disaster housing (U.S. Governmental Accountability Office 2006).
- *Health*. Disasters can disrupt access to health care particularly for the poor, the elderly, and people with disabilities. Individuals dependent on health services such as dialysis or cancer treatment experience life-threatening circumstances. Disasters can also create conditions that worsen health conditions, such as debris, mold, and chemicals that cause or aggravate respiratory conditions (Lin et al. 2005; Malievskaya, Rosenberg, and Markowitz 2002).
- *Literacy*. Most emergency preparedness materials are available in written form. Few options exist to inform and prepare people with low reading levels, despite the potential for such materials to help people across literacy levels, language barriers, cognitive abilities, and age ranges (U.S. Department of Justice 2008).
- *Families and Households*. Families provide an important unit in which people can care for each other as they rebound from disasters. Yet many programs fail to address the diversity of families, including households of unrelated individuals. People who cohabit, renters, roommates, and couples who are lesbian, gay, bisexual, or transgendered may experience difficulty in securing aid or the comfort of people who care about them (Eads 2002; Morrow 2000).

Despite these problems, people who live within and across these population groups, or whose circumstances have not been adequately recognized also bring valuable assets to the process of reducing risks. Consider, for example, that Presidential Executive Order 13347 advises the inclusion of people with disabilities in all phases of disaster management. By doing so, we bring fresh perspectives to the planning table and invite a wider partnership. Doing so yields fresh perspectives, insights, networks, and linkages that can help disaster managers to address transportation and evacuation problems, issues in shelters and long-term housing, and strategies for preparing populations in harm's way.

In this work, knowledgeable authors present up-to-date information on the various ways in which some populations experience higher risks than others, and offer practical strategies to reduce that vulnerability. To set the stage for this volume, this chapter introduces you to understanding vulnerability by first providing an overview of key terms. The chapter then addresses and contrasts two perspectives that have the potential to influence disaster management and how social groups experience crisis occasions.

1.3.1 UNDERSTANDING VULNERABILITY

The term "vulnerability" means different things to varying agencies and organizations and can be conceptualized in several ways. To illustrate, some agencies may use the term to mean physical rather than social vulnerability. For example, the U.S. Geological Survey conducts work on coastal vulnerability to sea level rise. In contrast, the U.S. Department of Homeland Security sees vulnerability as produced via the political intentions of terrorists. As another example, the U.S. Governmental Accountability Office (2006) describes some vulnerable populations as "transportation disadvantaged." Disaster managers at the local level understand vulnerability in both its physical and social dimensions as they see neighborhoods inundated by floodwaters and work to help residents recover.

In this text, we concentrate on social vulnerability, which results from differential social relations among groups in a given society. As Bankoff (2006) notes,

> [b]y the 1980s, it was apparent in both the developed and the developing world that to be "at risk" was not just a question of being in the wrong place at the wrong time, and of regarding disasters as purely physical happenings requiring largely technological solutions. Disasters were more properly viewed as primarily the result of human actions; that while hazards are natural, disasters are not. Social systems generate unequal exposure to risk by making some people more prone to disaster than others and these inequalities are largely a function of the power relations (class, age, gender and ethnicity among others) operative in every society.

Vulnerability results from multiple conditions and circumstances that could include health, disability, age, literacy, or immigration status (Wisner 2006). However, it is not disability or literacy alone that produces vulnerability. Rather, it is the failure of society to recognize that a condition such as poverty means you cannot mitigate risk, live in a safer location, or afford to evacuate when told to do so. When disaster managers and political leaders fail to design warning systems that reach people who are deaf or to provide paratransit systems to evacuate a wheelchair user, society bears responsibility for the consequences. Social vulnerability thus results from social inequalities and historic patterns of social relations that manifest as deeply embedded social structural barriers that are resistant to change:

> Race and class are certainly factors that help explain the social vulnerability in the South, while ethnicity plays an additional role in many cities. When the middle classes (both White and Black) abandon a city, the disparities between the very rich and the very poor expand. Add to this an increasing elderly population, the homeless, transients (including tourists), and other special needs populations, and the prospects for evacuating a city during times of emergencies becomes a daunting challenge for most American cities (Cutter 2006).

Vulnerability is "embedded in complex social relations and processes" (Hilhorst and Bankoff 2004, 5) and is best viewed as a social problem that requires social solutions. Doing so requires us to address how complex the problem really is, because it is not just that a hurricane approaches or an earthquake shakes the ground. Rather, the problem stems from an "interface of society and

FIGURE 1.2 An overpass in New Orleans after Hurricane Katrina. Photo by Pam Jenkins and Barbara Davidson. With permission.

environment" (Oliver-Smith 2002) that is a pre-existing condition (Cutter 1996). That interface requires that we "unpack" the idea of vulnerability not only as it affects various social groups but in how we inherently participate in continuation of the disparities that produce risk more for some than for others.

Risk is thus socially produced and is not inherent to the hazard. Disasters, which result from a misfit between human systems, the built environment, and the physical world, tend to reveal clearly the social problems that make response and recovery difficult at the individual and family levels (Mileti 1999; Barton 1969). Risk can be thought of as "the probability of an event or condition occurring" (Mileti 1999, 106). When people are exposed to a risk, they may experience vulnerability as a result of social, economic, and political conditions, many of which are beyond their control. Children who are born into poverty will experience difficulty in climbing into another socioeconomic level. People with disabilities experience incomes far lower than people without disabilities. One third of female-headed single-parent families fall below the poverty line as well. Tens of thousands of elderly Americans attempt to survive solely on social security checks that fall at minimal levels. When an event like Hurricane Katrina occurs before the end of the month when paychecks, social security income, and entitlement funds arrive, evacuation is virtually unaffordable. These socioeconomic realities, which represent real social problems, can be addressed through evacuation planning (Figure 1.2). Or, as done before the 2008 hurricanes that struck the Gulf Coast, entitlement checks like veterans' and social security checks can be released early to spur departures. By recognizing the nature of vulnerability, we can design solutions and reduce consequences. Because power relations underlie much of the economic, social, and political segregations that marginalize social groups and increase risk, the solution also lies in empowering those most vulnerable, in short, a political solution as well as a social solution (Hilhorst and Bankoff 2004).

This text attempts to elucidate the notion of vulnerability for various social groups, culminating in an understanding of how we might transform vulnerability and disaster management. We start first by examining a historic approach to the practice of disaster management and then expand on the relevance of a social vulnerability approach for disasters.

1.3.2 PERSPECTIVES

In this section, we examine perspectives that try to explain why people experience disaster risks differently. Perspectives provide a means for outlining the assumptions that underlie disaster

TABLE 1.1
The Dominant View of Disasters

Key Questions	Dominant Paradigm
How is nature viewed?	Extreme events in nature are seen as the primary causes of disaster. Nature and extreme events in nature are seen as external to society.
How are chance and time viewed?	Disasters are seen as accidents and freak events. Disasters are seen as operating outside of human history and as break in the normal flow of time.
How are science and technology viewed?	Science and technology are seen as the primary means available to deal with natural hazards. Providing the technological fix has become a major industry in the United States.
How are individuals understood?	People are viewed as having "bounded rationality," inadequate information and ability to make sound choices in the face or risk. People are viewed as having to be instructed and led.
How is society understood?	Political, social, and economic relations are viewed as not involved in causing disasters but only in modifying the impacts of extreme natural events. Social change in the direction of increasing hierarchy and complexity and increasing wealth and technological capacity is seen as the necessary and sufficient condition for reducing risk of disasters.
Who believes and applies the framework?	The traditional emergency manager. Physical scientists.
What are the shortcomings?	Failure to consider all social, economic, and political conditions that may foster vulnerability.
	Failure to consider the full range of people's capacities as well as their vulnerabilities.

Source: Excerpted verbatim from Wisner, B. Session 2: Development of social vulnerability analysis. In *A social vulnerability approach to disasters.* FEMA course, Higher Education Project. Full session is available at http://training.fema.gov/emiweb/edu/completeCourses.asp. Reprinted courtesy of FEMA.

management approaches and the consequences those approaches produce. For example, approaches that assume we are at the mercy of nature suggest that little can be done to reduce human vulnerability. Conversely, a perspective that assumes human agency can offer strategies for incorporating any given population appropriately into response plans. By digging into how various perspectives frame our understanding of vulnerability, we can offer tools for change. Perspectives, with the support of empirical research, can inform the practice of emergency management, social work, and trauma counseling, as well as the work of first responders, health care workers, volunteers, and local officials. Consequently, we begin this volume with two paradigms that frame our understanding of risk and influence the solutions we pursue.

1.3.3   UNDERSTANDING THE DOMINANT VIEW OF HAZARDS

We first explore the dominant view of hazards, which has generally been the most common approach taken by most disaster researchers and practitioners (although not all), even today. To do so, we examine how the dominant view understands nature, chance, time, science, technology, people, and society. Following this overview, we then discuss the implications of the dominant view before we identify its shortcomings, and finally turn to an alternative and more recent perspective, the social vulnerability approach. For an overview of this section, see Table 1.1.

1.3.3.1   How Does the Dominant View Understand Nature, Chance, and Time?

The dominant view understands nature as the agent that causes the disaster to occur. While this may seem obvious, the view merits fuller interpretation. As described by Tobin and Montz (1997, 8):

[t]he traditional view of natural hazards has ascribed all or almost all responsibility for them to the processes of the geophysical world. The approach has meant that the root cause of large-scale death and destruction has been attributed to the extremes of nature rather than encompassing the human world. Frequently, disaster victims have been viewed as unfortunates who could do little but react to physical processes. The physical world, then, has been seen as an external force, separate from human forces.

The dominant view explains disasters as the result of nature impinging upon human society but there is little that can be done to change the situation. In the dominant view, then, nature is the cause, the condition, and the propelling force that damages, destroys, and kills. Nature, unharnessed, is to blame. Hewitt (1983, 5) explains:

> Conceptual preambles and the development of "risk assessment" appear to have swept away the old unpalatable causality of environmental determinism … [but] [t]he sense of causality or the direction of explanation still runs from the physical environment to its social impacts.

The dominant view has, for a long time, simply been accepted as the way to understand disasters. It interprets the hazards that society faces as an attack on the functioning and stability of social systems. Communities are perceived as subject to what the storm will bring to bear on their abilities to survive. The dominant perspective has powerfully influenced both research and practice. E. L. Quarantelli (1998, 266), the cofounder of the Disaster Research Center, now at the University of Delaware, writes, "the earliest workers in the area, including myself, with little conscious thought and accepting common sense views, initially accepted as a prototype model the notion that disasters were an outside attack upon social systems that 'broke down' in the face of such an assault from outside." Disasters must be managed, placed under human control and influence where possible, in contrast to approaches that integrate human activity with natural systems and honor ecological integrity.

Disasters are thus viewed as horrendous tragedies, as accidents or even as freak events. Because they are so conceived, in many locations and cultures it is assumed that there is little one can do to prevent their occurrence and consequently their effects. Risk is the result of chance, of being in the wrong location at the wrong time. Society simply cannot do much about such events because they occur naturally and seemingly without prediction. We are at the mercy of nature. Steinberg (2000, xix), in his historical perspective on disasters, illuminates this barrier between society and nature:

> These events are understood by scientists, the media, and technocrats as primarily accidents—unexpected, unpredictable happenings that are the price of doing business on this planet. Seen as freak events cut off from people's everyday interactions with the environment, they are positioned outside the moral compass of our culture.

Disasters, as disruptive influences, are viewed as operating outside of human history and as a "break" in the "normal" flow of time. They are an "other," an "outsider" to the way in which we view our normal relations, and thus represent the untoward. In the 2008 tragedies that befell Myanmar/Burma and the People's Republic of China, both media commentators and experts in the field used the dominant view to explain "donor fatigue," meaning that people had reduced their financial contributions to charitable organizations: "it might be more accurately described as disaster fatigue—the sense that these events are never-ending, uncontrollable and overwhelming. Experts say it is the one reason Americans have contributed relatively little so far" (Tolin 2008). Hewitt elaborates (1983, 10):

> The language of discourse is often a good indicator of basic assumptions. In hazards work one can see how language is used to maintain a sense of *discontinuity* or *otherness*, which severs these problems from the rest of man-environment relations and social life. That is most obvious in the recurrent use of words stressing the "*un*"-ness of the problem. Disasters are *un*managed phenomena. They are the *un*expected, the *un*precedented. They derive from natural processes or events that are highly *un*certain.

*Un*awareness and *un*readiness are said to typify the condition of their human victims. Even the common use of the word [disaster] "event" can reinforce the idea of a discrete unit in time and space. In the official-sounding euphemism for disasters in North America, they are "*un*scheduled events."

Accepting the dominant view implies that little can be done to prevent catastrophe from striking (Steinberg 2000, xix). Even the word "disaster" implies a discontinuity with normal, routine events (Hewitt 1983, 10). Time stops while we gather the injured and dead and pick up the pieces so as to move on. To recover from disaster then means to restore a sense of normal time, to bring back a routine order, and to provide social stability and functioning.

1.3.3.2   How Does the Dominant View Understand Science and Technology?

If we are at the mercy of nature and unexpected events, how are we to safeguard the stability and functioning of our social systems? How should we move to manage the presumably unmanageable in order to thwart the effects of such disruptions on our time? The dominant view sees science and technology as the main tools available to address disasters. To manage the seeming unpredictability of earthquakes, we place seismic monitoring devices around the planet, hoping to ascertain the connection between foreshocks and main shocks. In the aftermath of the 2004 Indian Ocean Tsunami, nations worked collaboratively to place wave detection systems across vast waterway expanses. Across the United States, dams and levees have been erected to ward off floodwaters and storm surges.

In short, the dominant view prescribes an engineering solution to many hazards, even those that do not emanate from the natural world. Further, disasters usually fall into three general categories: natural (hurricanes, floods, tornadoes), technological (hazardous materials accidents, oil spills, nuclear accidents), and terrorism. It is clear that the dominant view and its emphasis on scientific or technological management is the preferred solution. For example, after September 11th, efforts focused on reinforcing buildings through integrating breakthroughs in "blast performance research." Tremendous amounts of funding were diverted toward "hardening" targets, especially buildings, with far less funding directed toward evacuation planning, particularly for people with disabilities, seniors, and those lacking transportation. The harsh reality of Hurricane Katrina revealed the consequences of applying the dominant approach. Although new funding and initiatives have addressed human vulnerability to a greater extent than before the storm, far more funding and effort have targeted rebuilding the massive levee system. Environmentally friendly approaches that would restore coastal integrity to stem storm surge and replenish endangered ecosystems have fared badly; in the dominant view, coastal restoration, as a natural means to stem storm surge, is deemed too expensive.

Finally, turning to the practical application of science and technology offers an approach consistent with, and supportive of, a capitalist economy. As Alexander (2000, 25) indicates, "structural mitigation is preferred for obvious reasons by the construction and economic growth lobbies. Technological hardware production ... has offered ever more complex, expensive and sophisticated solutions to the problem of hazards." Thus, because technology is seen as a near-panacea for the problems produced by disasters of all kinds, engineering and "hard science" applications receive funding far in excess of social science research. The dominant view, then, does not consider solutions that might work in concert with nature. Rather, "the most expensive actions and the most formidable scientific literature, recommending action are concerned mainly with geophysical monitoring, forecasting and direct engineering or land-use planning in relation to natural agents" (Hewitt 1983, 5). Science and technology in this sense serve a perceived need to command and control nature. In fact, command and control is the preferred form of dealing with people too, as we discuss next.

1.3.3.3   How Does the Dominant View Understand People?

The dominant view sees human beings as unable to make good decisions regarding disasters. Conceptually, the term "bounded rationality" means that people lack sufficient information to make well-informed decisions regarding their risks. Although "behavior is generally rational or logical" it is "limited by perception and prior knowledge" (Tobin and Montz 1997, 5). According to the dominant view, for instance (although the social vulnerability approach would argue differently), the tragedy of the cyclone in Myanmar in 2008 was attributable to such limitations. Local people lacked information or understanding regarding the impending cyclone and thus could not or did not make evacuation decisions. The dominant view also assumes that, even with sufficient information, people would not necessarily process the knowledge adequately and thus would choose from a bounded set of options. The dominant view has been used most recently to explain why so many failed to leave New Orleans despite clear warnings to do so. Burton, Kates, and White (1978, 52) concur:

> It is rare indeed that individuals have access to full information in appraising either natural events or alternative courses of action. Even if they were to have such information, they would have trouble processing it, and in many instances they would have goals quite different than maximizing the expected utility. The bounds on rational choice in dealing with natural hazards, as with all human decisions, are numerous.

In many disaster studies, people serve as the individualized focus of inquiry. Researchers "ask how people respond to forecasts, requests to conserve water and hazard zone legislation. They examine how people 'cope' when the volcano erupts or when a crop is destroyed" (Hewitt 1983, 7). Such research focuses squarely on the event as a disruptive extreme that causes even seasonal events, such as agricultural production, to cease. Although the intent of the research seems reasonable, it misses "the main sources of social influence over hazards" (Hewitt 1983, 7).

Consequently, the conclusion has been that people must be instructed, led, and managed. Often, this is experienced as a top-down, hierarchical model designed to "command and control" events, as if the disaster itself could be herded into submission. For emergency managers who subscribe to this view, the differential responses of people to hazards and subsequent "orders" seem chaotic and nonsensical. People appear to have lost their way, to have behaved out of compliance with the clear-headed thinking of those in authority.

1.3.3.4 How Does the Dominant View Understand Society?

If nature is at fault, then surely the disaster is not the result of political, social, or economic systems or the misfit of interactions among these systems. Such systems, and the actors within them, are viewed as only modifying the disaster and its effects, and thus the ability of society to respond is obviously limited (Hewitt 1983, 6):

> In the dominant view, then, disaster is itself attributed to nature. There is, however, an equally strong conviction that something can be done about disaster by society. But that something is viewed as strictly a matter of public policy backed up by the most advanced geophysical, geotechnical and managerial capacity. There is a strong sense, even among social scientists for whom it is a major interest, that everyday or "ordinary" human activity can do little except make the problem worse by default. In other words, the structure of the problem is seen to depend upon the ratios between given forces of nature and the "advanced" institutional and technical counterforce.

Yet changes within social systems, according to the dominant view, can provide solutions. Consistent with the use of science, technological fixes and engineering solutions are viewed as the means by which to engage in risk reduction. Individuals cannot bear the risk because of limited means. Accordingly, measures consistent with economic interests that distribute risk will emerge. Insurance policies, for example, distribute risk when everyone buys in and shoulders the cost of an event. Burton, Kates, and White (1978, 219) describe the shared solution: "[T]he construction of dams, irrigation systems, or seawalls, and the design or monitoring, forecasting, and warning systems with complex equipment would be clearly beyond the scope of individual action." Socially shared risk, embedded within existing scientific and economic systems, affords a measure of security to stabilize the functioning of social systems. However, as Burton, Kates, and White (1978, 219) point out, "these favored adjustments require interlocking and interdependent social organization, and they tend to be uniform in application, inflexible and difficult to change."

1.3.3.5 Who Believes and Applies the Dominant View?

The implications of the dominant view can be profound, influencing not only how we view nature, time, people, and society but also the means for solving problems associated with disaster. Who would believe in and apply the dominant view? Blanchard (2000) has identified two general groups of emergency managers in the United States, separated typically by age, race, and gender. The older group of emergency managers is more likely to adopt practices based on the dominant approach. Characterized by Waugh (1999) as part of the old-school "air raid wardens," the older group seems more likely to believe in bounded rationality and to follow a command and control approach (Dynes 1990).

In contrast, people who have entered the emergency management profession more recently are a more diverse group in terms of gender, race/ethnicity, training/education, and professional experience. The newer group is also more likely to belong to professional associations and to recognize issues of social vulnerability. This separation implies a generational difference that is associated with clear periods of social and political change, as well as the increasing professionalization of the practice of emergency management.

The more recent cohort appears to be influencing governmental agencies, in part by challenging the assumptions of the dominant view. For example, some government agencies have acknowledged and incorporated a social vulnerability approach, although it frequently remains in the position of an "add-on" while mainstream thinking, practice, and funding continue to be driven by the more traditional missions of the agencies. To illustrate, only recently has a special journal issue been published on social vulnerability and warning systems. As noted by Lazo and Peacock (2007, 43), "Hurricane Katrina illustrated that even with the improvements in forecasts and warnings, societal factors still exist that can lead to large loss of life" (see also Phillips and Morrow 2007).

In the United States, presidential administrations can also dramatically influence agency approaches through their presidential appointees. For example, President Bill Clinton appointed James Lee Witt to direct FEMA, which subsequently addressed physical vulnerability in its mitigation activities and included social solutions as well. For example, Project Impact included outreach to communities and operated at the grassroots level, where physical and social vulnerability is typically experienced and, according to the advice of authors in this volume, best addressed. Unfortunately, Project Impact was discontinued under the next presidential administration. Organizationally, nongovernmental organizations (NGOs) are more likely to spurn the dominant view in favor of vulnerability approaches, although such adoption is not consistent across organizations. Groups that operate on Cold War assumptions tend toward civil defense assumptions consonant with the dominant view (e.g., see http://www.tacda.org). Faith-based organizations (FBOs), on the other hand, tend toward the social vulnerability approach and situate their disaster efforts squarely in an understanding of how race, income, gender, age, and disability can influence life chances, personal safety, and property loss (e.g., see http://www.cwserp.org/; http://www.afsc.org/ematasst.htm).

1.3.3.6 Shortcomings of the Dominant View

A number of shortcomings of the dominant view have been identified. For example, the dominant view does not consider all causes of disasters. Carr (1932, 221) noted that people and societies survive disasters all the time. What is important is that "as long as the levees hold, there is no disaster. It is the collapse of the cultural protection that constitutes the disaster proper." Given that Carr spoke these words 73 years before Hurricane Katrina, his words seem prophetic. The category 5 storm surge that pushed into New Orleans occurred in large part because of the decimation of natural coastal protections, coupled with engineer-driven levee solutions that were unable to withstand storms exceeding a category 3 level.

Indeed, the dominant view relies heavily on understanding physical processes to the neglect of social forces. Hewitt (1983) emphasized this in his work. First, too much causality has been attributed to geophysical forces. In contrast, Mileti (1999) identified disasters as the result of a misfit of three systems: the physical world, the built environment, and human systems. Second, disasters occur because society lacks effective measures to reduce the impact; such measures reflect the values and institutions of the society. Whether or not a mitigation measure has been instigated will have much to do with economic and political will. Trailer parks, for example, are continually approved without requiring congregate sheltering facilities. Such homes routinely fail in the lowest levels of tornadic activity. Third, disasters consequently result from social rather than geophysical activity (Tobin and Montz 1997, 11–12).

Overall, critics argue that vulnerability occurs because of the ways in which social systems are constructed, choices are made, and groups are (or sometimes not) protected. In many locations, populations remain vulnerable because we have failed collectively to address the social conditions, such as inferior housing that fails to provide adequate protection. Disasters thus "bring to the surface the poverty which characterizes the lives of so many inhabitants" (Hardoy and Satterthwaite 1989, 203). The assumption (or claim) that the geophysical world is the originator of risk is called into question; critics argue instead that risk stems from "the risks, pressures, uncertainties that bear upon awareness of and preparedness for natural fluctuations [that] flow mainly from what is called 'ordinary life,' rather than from the rareness and scale of those fluctuations" (Hewitt 1983, 25).

The dominant view is also accused of failing to consider all effects of disasters. Death, injuries and property loss are not the only consequences,

[t]hey can also redirect the character of social institutions, result in permanent new and costly regulations for future generations, alter ecosystems, and even disturb the stability of political regimes. Costs like these rarely, if ever, are counted as part of the disaster impacts (Mileti 1999, 90).

The dominant view also promotes an emphasis on preparedness and response rather than understanding how to reduce risk through mitigation and adaptation, a common critique levied at the U.S. Department of Homeland Security and FEMA priorities. Mileti (1999, 237–38) and a panel of experts in the United States recognized this disparity and wrote,

[a]chieving patterns of rebuilding that generally keep people and property out of harm's way is increasingly viewed as an essential element of any disaster recovery program. Rebuilding that fails to acknowledge the location of high-hazard areas is not sustainable, nor is housing that is not built to withstand predictable physical forces. Indeed, disasters should be viewed as providing unique opportunities for change—not only to building local capability for recovery—but for long-term sustainable development as well.

To illustrate, the Northridge, California, earthquake generated $2.5 billion in direct losses with an estimated total loss of $44 billion. Over 20,000 people experienced displacement from their homes, and over 681,000 requested federal assistance totaling approximately $11 billion in individual and public assistance. Bolin and Stanford (1999, 104–5) found that all dimensions of recovery were influenced by one's location in the social system:

From the individual's standpoint, relief accessibility is complex and takes up issues of personal knowledge of federal programs, cultural and language skills, and physical location, with the mediating effects of social class, ethnicity, and gender. It is here that language, cultural and residency barriers may hinder households in access to resources for recovery. In Fillmore, with its history of an Anglo-dominated power structure and exclusionary practices aimed at farm-workers (and lower-income Latinos in general), local political culture compounded resource access problems for Latino disaster victims.

The dominant view also is charged with failing to take advantage of the full range of solutions and measures to address risk. Disasters are considered opportunities when "swift action" can be taken to "develop or implement measures" (Blaikie et al. 1994, 224), but the dominant view does not deem those at risk to be possible partners in creating safer conditions. For instance,

[w]omen are pivotal in the intersection between household and community recovery. While their needs and experiences are in many respects gender specific, as well as deeply influenced by class and ethnicity, they also provide critical insights into neglected, yet central, problems, processes, and mechanisms of household and community recovery. We conclude that a gendered analysis is crucial to understanding and mitigating against future impacts of disasters on families and communities (Enarson and Morrow 1997, 135–36).

Churches and other bodies form the centres for citizen response to economic dislocation and crisis. Food banks, community kitchens, and pantries have sprung up all over the US and in many Latin American countries to assist and involve poor and hungry people. People's health centres and public health movements have also emerged in the slums of many of the world's mega-cities from Brooklyn and the Bronx to Rio de Janeiro, Mexico City and Manila. Such formal and informal organizations are woefully underutilized by authorities responsible for disaster mitigation. Non-governmental organizations have been quicker to recognize the potential of such groups (Blaikie et al. 1994, 236).

The dominant perspective provides a limited view of the causes of, and solutions to, disasters and fails, in particular, to recognize the true nature of vulnerability and the capacity that related populations bring to bear on their own risk as well as that of the larger society. We turn next to consideration of an alternative perspective, the social vulnerability approach.

1.3.4 THE SOCIAL VULNERABILITY VIEW

Disaster management is a relatively recent profession. Most writers trace the early days of the occupation to the days of "civil defense" in the 1950s and 1960s. Disaster managers were initially viewed as "air raid wardens" who would sound an alert when an attack came from outside the United States, presumably from what used to be the Union of Soviet Socialist Republics (Waugh 1999; Waugh and Tierney 2007). Concern over the use of nuclear powers prompted air raid drills, the creation of bomb shelters, and the possibility of an external threat. It was assumed that people would respond in panic and shock. However, a series of pivotal studies conducted by the Disaster Research Center (founded at the Ohio State University, now at the University of Delaware) demonstrated that socio-behavioral response in disaster varied from the set of assumptions under which civil defense operated. For instance, altruism and other forms of pro-social behavior were found to be normative, rather than those irrational antisocial responses such as panic and looting. The Disaster Research Center prompted further inquiry into socio-behavioral responses to disaster—looking at organizational response, for instance—in order to arrive at a better understanding of the broader social, economic, and policy conditions that influenced disaster management.

Over time, an increasing awareness of some of the limitations of the dominant paradigm resulted in the incorporation of the concept of social vulnerability into increased research and practice (for a comparison of the two approaches, see Table 1.2). Several historically influential social or political movements began to raise questions about social vulnerability in disasters and produced new ways of thinking about various populations. In the 1930s, spatial concentrations of rural poverty were observed which came to be known as the "other America" (Harrington 1962). These observations laid the foundation for the development of various federally funded entitlement programs, including social security for senior citizens and even large-scale regional development projects like the Tennessee Valley Authority. These "New Deal" era programs recognized that despite their best efforts, people experienced considerable difficulty in securing housing, employment, health care, education, and more. The struggles of people at varying socioeconomic levels to secure scarce resources generated new perspectives for the scientific study of people affected by disasters.

Another major trend in the United States prompted even deeper insights. During the 1950s and 1960s, multiple social movements emerged to promote the rights of various populations. The civil rights movement, for example, conducted concerted efforts to retract segregation, push educational reforms, and extend voting rights for African Americans (Morris 1984). A massive

TABLE 1.2
The Dominant versus Vulnerability View of Disaster

Dominant View	Vulnerability View
The dominant view concentrates on the physical processes of the hazard.	The vulnerability view addresses socioeconomic and political influences.
Management style emphasizes problem solving through hierarchies and authorities.	Management style emphasizes a decentralized approach that involves community-based problem solving.
A top-down approach.	A grassroots or bottom-up approach.
Uses technology, engineering, and science to address the hazard.	Uses local knowledge, networks, imagination, and creativity to address the hazard.
The goal is to reduce physical damage.	The goal is to reduce social vulnerability of people.
The general philosophical approach is utilitarian and the conquest of nature.	The general philosophical approach is equitable approaches to reduce vulnerability and working in concert with nature.
Emphasizes bounded systems.	Emphasizes open systems and complexity.

Source: Enarson et al. Social Vulnerability to Disasters (Course Materials).

women's rights campaign in the 1960s and 1970s expressed concern over political representation, economic rights, health and reproductive care, education, and more (Ferree and Hess 1985). Similarly, a Latino rights movement pursued issues ranging from agricultural labor concerns to more broadly based political representation (Gutierrez 2006). A grassroots environmental movement pushed for recognition of environmental damage (Carson 1962). Gay rights efforts attempted to secure basic human respect and laid a foundation for broader struggles in ensuing decades. In the 1980s, an environmental justice movement linked pollution and pesticides, as one example, to detrimental health effects within marginalized communities (Bullard 1990). Disability rights advocates organized and promoted inclusion and accommodation (Christiansen 1995; Barnartt and Scotch 2001). Senior advocates and senior citizens created a "gray panther" movement that leveraged growing numbers of baby boomers into a more powerful lobby group, recognizing a broad spectrum of issues including health care, elder abuse, crime, and social stereotyping (Kuhn 1978). In short, several decades of social and political organizing raised awareness of issues facing various populations and the ways in which they were historically marginalized. Organized social movements advocated for inclusion and change and, in so doing, laid a foundation to question the dominant view.

Research by social scientists worldwide has revealed strong evidence that social vulnerability to disasters is deeply rooted in a people's history; vulnerability is related to major social structural factors such as the lack of access to political power and the uneven distribution of income. The characteristics of a disaster resilient society—or the lack thereof—are noticeable in these studies. For example, over 8000 people died in 1974 when Hurricane Fifi devastated northeastern Honduras. Farmers, who had been displaced from rich valley land due to the establishment of banana plantations, had cleared steep slopes to grow meager crops. Fifi's torrential rains caused the slopes to fail, leading to significant numbers of deaths and the loss of a means to feed families.

Proponents of the vulnerability approach point out that the assumptions of the dominant view fail to explain the Honduran deaths (Mileti 1999, 28):

Although the "bounded rationality" model of human choice explicitly recognizes the existence of constraining social, political, and economic forces and cultural values, recognizing those boundaries apparently has not helped to break through them to reduce losses. It is possible, in fact, that those forces are much more powerful than previously thought.

Concurrent, then, with the evolution of social and political rights movements in the United States, research on vulnerable groups began to appear in publications and professional meetings in the 1980s. Disaster researchers reported evidence of race, class, age, and gender discrimination and differentiation in the effects of disasters throughout all phases of disasters (e.g., Glass et al. 1980; Bolin 1982; Perry, Hawkins, and Neal 1983; Bolin and Bolton 1986; Bolin and Klenow 1988).

It became even more clear that technological means were insufficient to prevent major damage in the United States as a result of events such as Hurricane Hugo, which tore apart South Carolina in 1989; the Loma Prieta earthquake, which badly damaged the homes of Latino agricultural workers and low-income seniors that same year; Hurricane Andrew, which ripped through south Florida's ethnically diverse communities in 1992; the far-ranging Mississippi River floods of 1993 that affected over a dozen states; and the Northridge, California, earthquake in 1994. Bureaucratic procedures clearly failed when trying to reach historically vulnerable populations as described by one Northridge survivor (personal communication to author):

> I was not wearing my hearing aids that morning, of course, it was 4:31 in the morning. When my foot hit the floor, my bare feet felt every piece of glass that had broken. My husband was out of town, I was alone and extremely scared; my husband is profoundly deaf, no one even told him there had been an earthquake. I went to FEMA [and] there was no interpreter. Someone later suggested I call my congresswoman. Almost nine months passed before I got my FEMA check.

FEMA, the American Red Cross, and other organizations who are among the more visible relief agencies in the United States, endured criticism for not taking diversity into consideration. Simultaneously, the economic costs of disasters began to escalate rapidly, a fact that was confirmed by the U.S. insurance industry's recognition of increasing insured losses. Internationally, the 1995 earthquake in Kobe, Japan, reinforced doubts of a technological panacea. Despite the world's best engineering, many structures collapsed, the fire fighting system failed, and more than 6000 people died. Over 50% of the dead were over 60 years of age, and 1.5 times as many women died as men (Seager 2006). In 1991, flooding in Bangladesh killed five times more women than men (Seager 2006), demonstrating that social factors clearly affect life safety.

We should not be surprised, then, that over 70% of the dead in Hurricane Katrina were over the age of 65 and that African Americans died in numbers disproportionately to whites and to their local population numbers (Sharkey 2007). Nor should we be surprised that the Indian Ocean Tsunami claimed over 300,000 lives, including about 240,000 women and children (MacDonald 2005). Such deaths are predictable and, with adequate preparation, their numbers are reducible. New perspectives and practices, accordingly, have been deemed overdue and more than appropriate.

In the 1990s, the United Nations launched the International Decade for Natural Disaster Reduction, a decade-long effort to reduce vulnerability. That effort continues to the present day as the International Strategy for Disaster Reduction. In 1995 the United Nations convened a mid-decade conference in Yokohama, Japan, at which "a strong case was made by many representatives that more needed to be done to understand and to tap the local knowledge of ordinary people and to understand and address social vulnerability" (Wisner 2003).

In the 1990s, a major assessment of disaster research took place in the United States (Mileti 1999). This major undertaking involved over 100 scientists and experts who reviewed the extant literature and evaluated its meaning. The report recommended the adoption of a social vulnerability approach in distinct contrast to the dominant view (Mileti 1999). Several key principles were recommended by researchers as a means to transform the circumstances of socially vulnerable populations. First, a participatory approach that involves and includes stakeholders must be adopted, in contrast to the assumptions of a bounded rationality approach where people must be led or directed. Second, social and intergenerational equity issues must be addressed, to insure that all stakeholders enjoy the right to survive. Third, economic vitality must be considered, including the full range of businesses that employ from all socioeconomic levels including home-based work, agriculture labor, retail, and industrial employment. Fourth, quality of life issues, as identified by those local stakeholders, must be considered rather than imposed from outside. Fifth, environmental quality must be retained and even enhanced, including rebuilding in ways that reduce impact on marginalized populations and nonrenewable resources. Overall, the vulnerability approach understands that disaster-resilient communities stem from more than the geophysical world, and takes into consideration the full range of social institutions and populations that comprise a richly diverse human system. It is the involvement of those marginalized groups that can produce insights and perspectives to change vulnerability, an emphasis addressed by this text.

1.3.4.1   The Framework of the Social Vulnerability Approach

The social vulnerability approach is not sufficient alone to plan for disasters and must be understood as part of a larger, broader approach that includes understanding geophysical hazards and technological solutions. Vulnerability assessment thus incorporates insights from the physical world but emphasizes the roles of social, economic, and political relations in the creation of hazardous situations in a specific place. Vulnerability analysis examines the social distribution of risk and why some populations bear disproportionate levels of risk to disasters. Research for a number of years has examined the notion that (Blaikie et al. 1994, 9)

> [s]ome groups in society are more prone than others to damage, loss, and suffering in the context of differing hazards. Key characteristics of these variations of impact include class, caste, ethnicity, gender, disability, age, or seniority.

Social vulnerability reflects the "classic political economy problem of the allocation of scarce resources among competing individuals, groups and classes," that is, the problem of differential vulnerability for people "by virtue of where they live, work, or own property" (Boyce 2000). People working at lower waged jobs, as well as those unable to work or those experiencing underemployment, live in housing that fails to withstand high winds, seismic activity, or flood risk. Seniors and people with disabilities lacking accessible public transportation cannot evacuate. Home-based businesses that disasters destroy undermine important incomes especially for low-income households. Yet government programs provide only loans to businesses, not grants. When disasters destroy domestic violence shelters, as they did in three Louisiana parishes, survivors may desperately resort to living with offenders. In short, in a society with scarce resources, there are winners and losers. As Barton argued as far back as 1969, "disasters lay bare the social problems of a society." It is in understanding those social problems that we can find places of intervention that reduce risk. International humanitarian Fred Cuny wrote (1983), "The most basic issues in disasters are their impact on the poor and the links between poverty and vulnerability to a disaster … we must address the question of how to reduce poverty … if we hope to reduce suffering and to make a true contribution to recovery." For Cuny, the solutions will be found in tackling issues of social justice and social change.

From the vulnerability perspective, it is necessary to understand both the physical impact of disasters and the social conditions that underlie differential outcomes. The degree to which people receive transportation, shelter, warning, and protective action, or are safe from injury, loss of life, or property damage, depends on their level of income, quality of housing, type of employment, and on whether or not they are subject to discrimination and prejudice. Thus, the vulnerability approach seeks to understand how social, economic, and political relations influence, create, worsen, or can potentially reduce hazards in a given geographic location. The vulnerability approach also appreciates the importance of context, meaning that the time, place, and circumstances in which people live matters. For example, historic patterns of race relations may have resulted in segregated neighborhoods or in situations where entire towns remain situated in hazardous locations (Cutter 2006). Gendered patterns of political representation may mean that women remain excluded from policymaking positions that influence the practice of disaster management. Socioeconomic and political contexts will also differ significantly across geographic locations. Urban populations, for example, will include considerable numbers of seniors and people with disabilities that may overstretch organizational response capacities. Rural areas, or historically impoverished states, may suffer from a lack of funding to assess and plan for those at risk. In a political context, where some hazards are deemed more important to fund than others, local repetitive hazards may fail to be addressed. Coastal areas like the states affected by Hurricane Katrina will feature diverse forms of employment from corporate settings to fishing villages. Understanding the social distribution of risk in those settings vis-à-vis the local socioeconomic context can identify those at risk and locate community resources, which would help ensure a safer environment.

Social vulnerability approaches can be used to inform a reinvigorated risk assessment and planning process. By assuming that social vulnerability exists, key questions can be identified to reveal areas of concern and action items. Most disaster managers, for example, rely on a four-phase life cycle of disaster management that organizes activities around preparedness, response, recovery, and mitigation.

Concern for social vulnerability in the preparedness phase, for example, might look at the types of materials developed to educate the public:

- What language are they written in?
- Do they address concerns with literacy levels?
- Are they accessible to people with visual or hearing challenges?
- Are they relevant for the variety of social groups present in a given community?
- Can they be understood by people of varying ages including children?

The response phase, from a social vulnerability perspective, might suggest that appropriate questions would include

- Are there sufficient numbers of paratransit vehicles to move people from nursing homes or to assist people with disabilities?
- Are first responders trained in basic words in local languages, including American Sign Language, which could help with rescue efforts and emergency medical care?
- Are shelters ready to accept a wide range of cultures, faiths, and ages with different nutritional requirements?

In recovery, social vulnerability perspectives can be applied to identify areas of need and plan accordingly:

- Are sufficient numbers of local units or mobile homes available that are accessible to the local population, including veterans, people with disabilities, and seniors?
- What is the local housing stock like? How old is it and who lives in it? Where is the housing situated vis-à-vis local hazards, and how will that housing fare in a disaster?
- Does the recovery plan address the full range of employment and businesses that need to be supported so that people can return to work?

Mitigation measures offer a means through which risk can be reduced, such as through strengthening a levee or building a safe room. From a social vulnerability perspective, it would be prudent to find out

- Whether there are populations that require assistance in putting up mitigation measures like shutters in hurricane areas, including single parents and seniors.
- Whether local hazards threaten congregate facilities, such as nursing homes, or facilities for people with cognitive disabilities, and whether such facilities can be afforded greater protection.

- Whether some mitigation measures like insurance remain unaffordable and whether local organizations might plan for the needs of those likely to suffer significant losses.

Social vulnerability approaches also emphasize the ways in which local populations bring capacities and capabilities to the disaster management process, which are largely untapped. Hurricane Katrina clearly demonstrated vulnerability through the sheer numbers of people lacking transportation and who were subsequently trapped in the flooded city of New Orleans. Few people heard stories of the tremendous efforts that were brought to aid those in need, including students and staff from the Louisiana School for the Deaf who helped with translation, the building of shelters, debris removal, and distributing donations. Experienced community organizers also pointed out that impoverished groups, though dramatically impacted by the storm, also brought coping methods to their experience by sharing what they had, including food, clothing, and homes. Families doubled and tripled up, took in strangers, and provided comfort. Children, even those separated traumatically from their families, proved resilient in forming new social bonds with peers and shelter workers.

The social vulnerability approach also assumes that local resources can be tapped to address the problems noted in this text. Communities include voluntary, faith-based, community, and civic organizations with track records of assisting those at risk in both nondisaster and disaster situations. Post-disaster, it is also likely that a number of emergent groups will form to address unmet needs. Organizations external to the community will also arrive in many disasters and target those who suffer disproportionately. Though disasters are not equal opportunity events, the human capacity to assist pro-socially exists in abundance. Disaster managers, social service providers, health care staff, voluntary organizations, and others concerned with socially vulnerable populations, then, must tap into these grassroots resources and fulfill their potential for change.

The social vulnerability approach, in concert with one that provides effective means for mitigating the physical consequences of storms, earthquakes, and terrorist attacks, can significantly reduce losses and enhance outcomes for a wider set of those at risk. The goal of this text, therefore, is to reduce human suffering by applying an empirically supported social vulnerability perspective with practical solutions that change disaster circumstances. It is clear, though, that a selective focus on just disaster contexts remains insufficient. As Cuny (1983) understood, "Ultimately, addressing vulnerability means committing to social justice and social change."

1.4 OVERVIEW OF COMING CHAPTERS

This text adopts a social vulnerability approach that recognizes differential impacts as well as the potential to tap into the capacities of those at risk. Throughout this text, readers will find realistic, empirical assessments of socially vulnerable populations. You will also find practical solutions to the raw circumstances in which too many people find themselves before, during, and after disaster. This text thus aims to provide both insight and solutions. You are invited to be a part of the transformative vision these authors promote and to join us in building a safer, more equitable society for all.

1.4.1 Section I: Understanding Social Vulnerability

This text unfolds in several sections. In the first section, the following two chapters teach us about key theories and concepts. These chapters also globalize the concerns about social vulnerability. In Chapter 2, "Theoretical Framing of World Views, Values, and Structural Dimensions of Disasters," Drs. Jean Scandlyn, Deb Thomas, and John Brett (University of Colorado Denver), and graduate student Carrie Simon (Colorado School of Public Health) expand from Chapter 1 on social vulnerability theories and perspectives. Their work helps us to understand how disaster is viewed by disaster planners, individuals, and communities and how we might reduce risks from disasters. In Chapter 3, "The Intrinsic Link of Vulnerability to Sustainable Development," Kate Oviatt (a graduate student at the University of Colorado Denver) along with John Brett (UC Denver) help us identify the root causes for disaster losses. Their work then situates this text in an understanding of sustainable development and its links to vulnerability, resiliency, and capacity—themes that will resonate throughout the remainder of the text. Their work helps us to grasp the sustainable liveli-hoods approach, which is addressed later in the text in Chapter 14.

1.4.2 SECTION II: SOCIALLY VULNERABLE GROUPS

The second section of the text looks at social groups, primarily within the U.S. context, which is the primary audience for this text, by examining the vulnerabilities they experience and the capacities that exist or can be developed for each. Each chapter presents a demographic overview of the social group of concern followed by a summary of relevant scientific literature. Findings are organized into sections that correspond to key disaster management activities. Content first covers warning, evacuation, and response, and then addresses how disasters impact those groups and how they fare during recovery periods. A concluding section discusses implications for action by addressing practical and policy considerations to reduce vulnerability as well as specific suggestions to build capacity. Each chapter offers key books, videos, and Web sites to provide further understanding and practical strategies. Section II includes Chapters 4 through 12 on issues of class, race and ethnicity, gender, age, disability, health, literacy, family and households, and violence.

In Chapter 4, Dr. Nicole Dash, along with graduate students Brenda McCoy and Alison Herring, all from the University of North Texas, examine the influence of socioeconomic circumstances on abilities to prepare for, respond to, and recover from disaster. This chapter helps us to understand the demographic distribution of social class in the United States and how social class influences people's life chances. A connection is made between class and disaster vulnerability through case studies and scenarios that bring the content to life. A concluding section describes practical strate-gies for addressing vulnerability as experienced at lower income levels.

Dr. Dash continues her work in Chapter 5 on issues of race and ethnicity. She begins by conceptu-alizing race and ethnicity as socially constructed attributes that differentially influence opportunity. Dr. Dash pursues an understanding of the structural effects of race and ethnicity on U.S. society. This chapter reviews the racial and ethnic composition of the United States, specifically examining the role of race during Hurricane Katrina, and suggests ways to ameliorate existing conditions.

In Chapter 6, Dr. Elaine Enarson, an independent sociologist and the lead author of the FEMA course materials used here, addresses gendered vulnerability. Dr. Enarson focuses on understand-ing how gender differentiation can influence life safety, abilities to respond, and experiences in recovery for both men and women. It is clear, though, that research finds vulnerability higher for women in most circumstances, and it is to this concern that Dr. Enarson addresses the bulk of the chapter content.

Dr. Lori Peek, from Colorado State University, offers insights into issues of age including chil-dren and the elderly in Chapter 7. First, she defines children and the elderly and explains why we should distinguish between various groups of each. Disaster experiences, for example, differ between young children and adolescents as well as those who are older or may be frail elderly. Dr. Peek then provides a demographic profile of youth and elderly populations and helps us to understand how those populations vary by age, race, class, and gender. We then learn about the experiences and risks faced by children and the elderly and what factors increase their vulnerabil-ity. Finally, Dr. Peek gives practical ideas and approaches to reduce vulnerability of our children, nieces, nephews, grandchildren, parents, grandparents, aunts, uncles, and friends.

A team of authors provides insights on disability issues in Chapter 8. Authors include Elizabeth Davis, Alan Clive, Jennifer Mincin, and Rebecca Hansen. Davis and Hansen both work out of EAD & Associates, LLC, a consulting firm that specializes in emergency prepared-ness and people with disabilities. Sadly, Alan Clive passed away just before publication of this book. His lifetime of work as the civil rights program manager for the U.S. Federal Emergency

Management Agency serves as a tangible reminder of the dedication required to reduce vulner-ability. Mincin, formerly of EAD & Associates, LLC, is now with the International Rescue Committee where she links refugees with relocation services. Their collective expertise is lev-eraged to understand specific conditions that contribute to increased risk for the full range of people with disabilities. This chapter also informs us about terminology and concepts used to understand and frame disability. We next move through the life cycle of disasters to understand disability issues for warning, evacuation, response, and recovery. A comprehensive set of strate-gies and resources are offered to promote resiliency within the disability community and for practical use by disaster managers.

Dr. Deborah Thomas returns in Chapter 9 to present issues on health and medical care along with colleagues Elizabeth Davis and Alan Clive. Disasters disrupt access to medical care and reveal long-standing social problems that underlie and exacerbate health concerns. Her work serves as a reminder that social institutions are not invulnerable to the effects of disaster or societal neglect. This chapter reveals vulnerabilities tied to health concerns and the necessity of preparing this critical part of our disaster response and recovery infrastructure, particularly for those with low incomes, disabilities, and challenging medical conditions.

Dr. Betty Hearn Morrow, an emeritus faculty member from Florida International University and an original author of the FEMA course materials used for this book, looks at language literacy issues in Chapter 10. She starts by presenting disaster cases where language or literacy issues mat-tered, such as with warning messages or delivering relief. We then learn of the prevalence of lan-guage and literacy issues across the United States and their relevance for disaster management such as preparedness materials. Dr. Morrow subsequently presents and explains tools and strategies that help to translate materials into language- and literacy-appropriate resources.

Dr. Lynn Blinn-Pike, Indiana University-Purdue University of Indiana, examines families and households in Chapter 11. She begins by explaining current household and family composition in the United States and the implications for disaster response. Various studies then help us to under-stand how household and family characteristics, as well as their related resources, are tied to how well they may be able to prepare for, respond to, and recover from disasters. High-risk households and families are discussed along with strategies for reaching out to these units in an effort to reduce the effects of disasters.

Dr. Brenda Phillips, Oklahoma State University, along with Dr. Pam Jenkins, University of New Orleans, and independent sociologist Dr. Elaine Enarson, work through the rarely examined topic of post-disaster violence in Chapter 12. This chapter explains how various kinds of violence dif-ferentially impact social groups in the United States. These authors explain why it is important to understand violence in disaster situations and what can be done prior to an event to build partner-ships that anticipate and potentially reduce aggression, hostility, brutality, and cruelty.

1.4.3 Section III: Building Capacity

The final chapters of the book fall into a section that promotes capacity building in various ways. In Chapter 13, Dr. Eve Passerini, Regis University, provides insights into how the social capital and other community resources can be leveraged. Her work reveals the value of what the full set of com-munity members, regardless of income or dis/ability, can bring to the table when responding to and recovering from disaster effects. Dr. Deborah Thomas, along with University of Colorado Denver students Pamela Stephens and Jennifer Goldsmith, reveal practical strategies for community vulner-ability analysis (CVA) in Chapter 14. CVA allows emergency managers and planners (among others) to identify, analyze, monitor, and integrate social vulnerability into the full life cycle of emergency management: preparedness, response, recovery, and mitigation. Their work includes explaining how geographical information systems can help us to map vulnerability. The chapter also includes discussion of participatory mechanisms for increasing community input for vulnerability analysis as well as discussion of how to foster more sustainable communities.

Dr. Eve Gruntfest, director of the Social Science Woven into Meteorology (SWWIM) Initiative at the University of Oklahoma and codirector of the WAS * IS (Weather and Society Integrated Studies) movement, offers new ideas for disaster managers, social service providers, voluntary organizations, and others concerned with changing social vulnerability in Chapter 15. She works with Drs. Elaine Enarson, Brenda Phillips, and Deborah Thomas to present fresh ideas that promote transformative and inspiring insights. This unique and innovative chapter challenges us to remain current in the field in order to move forward our efforts to reduce vulnerability.

Finally, Dr. Bill Lovekamp, Eastern Illinois University, thoroughly covers ideas and strategies for empowerment in Chapter 16. He starts by walking us through how social change and empowerment take place. Next, we understand how community-based organizations and nongovernmental organizations can play pivotal roles in leveraging social capital found in social groups. He also helps us to grasp how disasters can influence social change and specifically examines those effects after September 11th and Hurricane Katrina.

1.5   SUMMARY

This chapter introduced the idea of social vulnerability to disasters, which is deemed to be a pre-existing condition deeply embedded in social, economic, and political relations among groups of people. The problem of social vulnerability requires social solutions that redress deeply embedded social problems that require concentrated effort, not only from disaster managers, but from the broader society as well. Such solutions require significant manifestations of political will and social effort. Because these social problems remain resistant to change, disaster managers, social service providers, elected officials, and others concerned with vulnerability and risk must design realistic strategies that impact at the individual, family, household, and community levels. This text sets out to understand how various social groups experience vulnerability and to design practical solutions that can, at least, serve as interim measures. As such, this book takes to heart the Maori proverb, "*Ha aha te mea nui? He tangata, he tangata, he tangata.*" "What is the most important thing? The people, the people, the people."

1.6   DISCUSSION QUESTIONS

1. Why is there such a strong bias toward technology in the dominant view of disasters?
2. What is the role of "chance" or "random" events in your own life? Describe a "freak occurrence" you've experienced.
3. Describe the key elements of the dominant and vulnerability perspectives.
4. What are the strong points of the dominant view of disasters, in your opinion? Explain and justify your views. What critiques make sense to you?
5. Discuss the notion that a disaster is "an act of God." The dominant view does not explicitly invoke divine causation or agency any more, but do you think there is still some legacy of this earlier view to be found in the dominant approach? Why? Why not?
6. Discuss and explain the deaths that occurred during the Indian Ocean Tsunami (2004), Hurricane Katrina (2005), the Myanmar cyclone (2008), or the Chinese (2008) earthquake from both the dominant and vulnerability perspectives.
7. What are the strong points of the vulnerability view of disasters, in your opinion? Explain and justify your views. What critiques make sense to you?
8. Are there social groups in your community that may experience higher vulnerability to disaster than others? Who are they and why do you believe them to be vulnerable?
9. How might an emergency manager approach warning and evacuation from the dominant and vulnerability perspectives?
10. Using the dominant and then the vulnerability perspectives, how might an emergency manager develop a recovery effort?

ACKNOWLEDGMENTS

The authors are indebted to Dr. Ben Wisner, the original author of the FEMA course materials session on social vulnerability analysis on which this chapter is based, as well as to the full team of course developers who contributed, including Drs. Elaine Enarson, Betty Morrow, Cheryl Childers, and Deborah Thomas. We have taken special care to honor their original intent by following their original outline, perspectives, references, and at times their wording. However, the interpretations and conclusions are those of the authors and do not necessarily represent those of the original team or author. Materials are used courtesy of FEMA's Higher Education Project, which is directed by Dr. Wayne Blanchard.

REFERENCES

Alexander, D. 2000. *Confronting catastrophe.* New York: Oxford University Press.

Bankoff, G. 2006. The tale of the three pigs: Taking another look at vulnerability in light of the Indian Ocean Tsunami and Hurricane Katrina. http://understandingkatrina.ssrc.org/Bankoff/ (accessed November 18, 2008).

Barnartt, S., and R. Scotch. 2001. *Disability protests.* Washington, DC: Gallaudet University Press.

Barton, A. 1969. *Communities in disaster.* New York: Doubleday.

Blanchard, W. 2000. Higher Education Project presentation. Emergency Management Institute, Emmitsburg, MD, (July).

Bolin, R. 1982. *Long-term recovery from disaster.* Boulder, CO: Institute of Behavioral Science.

Bolin, R., and P. Bolton. 1986. *Race, religion, and ethnicity in disaster recovery.* Boulder, CO: University of Colorado.

Bolin, R., and D. Klenow. 1982. Response of the elderly to disaster: An age stratified analysis. *International Journal of Aging and Human Development* 16 (4): 283–96.

Bolin, R., and L. Stanford. 1999. Constructing vulnerability in the first world: The Northridge earthquake in Southern California, 1994. In *The angry earth: Disasters in anthropological perspective*, ed. A. Oliver-Smith and S. Hoffman, 89–112. New York: Routledge.

Boyce, J. K. 2000. Let them eat risk? *Disasters* 24 (3): 254–61.

Bullard, R. 1990. *Dumping in Dixie.* Boulder, CO: Westview Press.

Burton, I., and R. Kates. 1964. The perception of natural hazards in resource management. *Natural Resources Journal* 3:412–14.

Carr, L. 1932. Disasters and the sequence-pattern concept of social change. *American Journal of Sociology* 38 (2):207–18.

Carson, R. 1962. *Silent spring.* Boston: Houghton Mifflin Co.

Christiansen, J. 1995. *Deaf president now!* Washington, DC: Gallaudet University Press.

Cuny, F. 1983. *Disasters and development.* Dallas, TX: Intertech.

Cutter, S. 1996. Vulnerability to environmental hazards. *Progress in Human Geography* 20 (4): 529–39.

———. 2006. The geography of social vulnerability: Race, class and catastrophe. http://understandingkatrina.ssrc.org/ (accessed November 17, 2008).

Dynes, R. 1990. Community emergency planning. http://dspace.udel.edu:8080/dspace/handle/19716/517 (accessed November 17, 2008).

Eads, M. 2002. Marginalized groups in times of crisis: Identity, needs and response. Quick Response Report #152. Boulder, CO: Natural Hazards Center.

Enarson, E. 1999. Violence against women in disasters. *Violence Against Women* 5 (7): 742–68.

Enarson, E., and B. Morrow. 2000. A gendered perspective: Voices of women. In *Hurricane Andrew*, eds. W. Peacock, B. H. Morrow, and H. Gladwin, 116–40. Miami, FL: International Hurricane Center.

Enarson, E., B. Morrow, D. Thomas, B. Wisner, and C. Childers. 2006. A Social Vulnerability Approach to Disaster. Emmittsburg, MD: FEMA Higher Education Course.

Fernandez, L. S., D. Byard, C.-C. Lin, S. Benson, and J. A. Barbera. 2002. Frail elderly as disaster victims: Emergency management strategies. *Prehospital and Disaster Management* 17 (2): 67–74.

Ferree, M. M., and B. Hess. 1985. *Controversy and coalition: The new feminist movement.* Boston: G. K. Hall.

Free 1996 (death penalty African American men citation/reference)

Glass, R. I., R. B. Craven, D. J. Bregman, B. J. Stroll, P. Kerndt Horowitz, and J. Winkle. 1980. Injuries from Wichita Falls tornado: Implications for prevention. *Science* 207:734–38.

Gutierrez, R. A. 2006. The Chicano movement. In *Latinas in the United States*, eds. V. Ruiz and V. Sanchez, 151–55. Bloomington: Indiana University Press.

Hardoy, J., and D. Satterthwaite. 1989. *Squatter citizen: Life in the urban third world*. London: Earthscan.

Harrington, M. 1962. *The other America: Poverty in the U.S.* New York: Simon and Schuster.

Hewitt, K. 1983. The idea of calamity in a technocratic age. In *Interpretations of calamity*, ed. K. Hewitt, 3–32. Boston: Allen and Unwin.

Hilhorst, D., and G. Bankoff. 2004. Introduction: mapping vulnerability. In *Mapping vulnerability: Disasters, development and people*, eds. G. Bankoff, G. Frerks, and D. Hilhorst, 1–9. London: Earthscan.

Jenkins, P., and B. D. Phillips. 2009. Battered women, catastrophe and the context of safety. *NWSA Journal* 20 (3): 49–68.

Krug, E., M.-J. Kresnow, J. Peddicord, L. Dahlberg, K. Powell, A. Crosby, and J. Annest. 1998. "Suicide After Natural Disasters." *New England Journal of Medicine* 338 (6): 373–378.

Kuhn, M. 1978. Insights on aging. *Journal of Home Economics* 70 (4): 18–20.

Lazo, J., and W. Peacock. 2007. Social science research needs for the hurricane forecast and warning system: An introduction. *Natural Hazards Review* 8 (3): 43–44.

Lin, S., J. Reibman, J. A. Bowers, S.-A. Hwang, A. Hoerning, M. I. Gomez, and E. F. Fitzgerald. 2005. Upper respiratory symptoms and other health effects among residents living near the World Trade Center after September 11, 2001. *American Journal of Epidemiology* 162 (16): 499–507.

Lindell, M., and R. Perry. 2004. *Communicating risk in multi-ethnic communities*. Thousand Oaks, CA: Sage.

MacDonald, M. 2005. How women were affected by the tsunami. PloS Med 2 (6): e.178. http://www.pubmed-central.nih.gov (accessed November 17, 2008).

Malievskaya, E., N. Rosenberg, and S. Markowitz. 2002. Assessing the health of immigrant workers near Ground Zero: Preliminary results of the World Trade Center day laborer medical monitoring project. *American Journal of Industrial Medicine* 42 (6): 548–40.

Mileti, D. 1999. *Disasters by design: A reassessment of natural hazards in the United States*. Washington, DC: Joseph Henry Press.

Morris, A. 1984. *Origins of the civil rights movement*. New York: Free Press.

Morrow, B. 2000. Stretching the bonds: The families of Andrew. In *Hurricane Andrew*, eds. W. Peacock, B. H. Morrow, and H. Gladwin, 141–70. Miami, FL: International Hurricane Center.

Oliver-Smith, A. 2002. Theorizing disasters: Nature, power, and culture. In *Catastrophe and culture: The anthropology of disaster*, eds. S. Hoffman and A. Oliver-Smith, 23–47. Santa Fe: School of American Research Press.

Perry, J. B., R. Hawkins, and D. M. Neal. 1983. Giving and receiving aid. *International Journal of Mass Emergencies and Disasters* 1:171–88.

Phillips, B., and B. H. Morrow. 2007. Social vulnerability, forecasts and warnings. *Natural Hazards Review* 8 (3): 61–68.

Quarantelli, E. L. 1998. Epilogue. In *What is a disaster?* ed. E. L. Quarantelli, 226–28. London: Routledge.

Seager, J. 2006. Noticing gender (or not) in disasters. *Geoforum* 37 (1): 2–3.

Sharkey, P. 2007. Survival and death in New Orleans. *Journal of Black Studies* 37 (4): 482–501.

Steinberg, T. 2000. *Acts of God: The unnatural history of natural disaster in America*. New York: Oxford University Press.

Tobin, G., and B. Montz. 1997. *Natural hazards*. New York: Guilford.

Tolin, L. May 19, 2008. Americans suffering from 'disaster fatigue.' *Intelligencer Journal* (Associated Press).

United States Department of Justice. 2008. Executive order 131661: Improving access to services for persons with limited English proficiency. http://www.usdoj.gov/crt/cor/Pubs/eolep.htm (accessed May 25, 2008).

United States Government Accountability Office. 2006. Disaster preparedness: Preliminary observations on the evacuation of hospitals and nursing homes due to hurricanes. GAO-06-790T.

Waugh, W. 1999. *Living with hazards, dealing with disasters*. Armonk, NY: M. E. Sharpe.

Waugh, W., and K. Tierney. 2007. *Emergency management: Principles and practice for local government*. 2nd ed. Washington, DC: ICMA Press.

Wisner, B. 1993. Disaster vulnerability: Scale, power, and daily life. *GeoJournal* 30 (2): 127–40.

———. 2003. Disaster risk reduction in megacities. In *Building safer cities*, eds. A. Kreimer, M. Arnold, and A. Carlin, 181–96. Washington, DC: The World Bank.

———. 2006. *At risk*. London: Routledge.

RESOURCES

- A powerpoint presentation is available at the original FEMA materials Web site for this chapter, http://www.training.fema.gov/EMIWeb/edu/sovul.asp (access date July 18, 2008).
- A series of papers including many from the vulnerability perspective can be found at the Social Science Research Council Web site, Understanding Katrina, at http://understandingkatrina.ssrc.org/ (access date July 18, 2008). An additional set of papers on a broader array of disasters can be found at the Radix Web site, http://www.radixonline.org/resources_papers.htm.
- For a community-based examination of the vulnerability perspective, visit the Greater New Orleans Community Data Center at http://www.gnocdc.org (access date July 18, 2008).

Section I

Understanding Social Vulnerability

2 Theoretical Framing of Worldviews, Values, and Structural Dimensions of Disasters

Jean Scandlyn, Carrie N. Simon,
Deborah S. K. Thomas, and John Brett

CONTENTS

2.1 CHAPTER PURPOSE

This chapter explores the fundamental and significant ways that our worldviews—our representations and assumptions about the world—frame our understanding of and response to hazards and disasters. We begin by defining theory, the formal, explicit, and systematic worldviews that provide the foundation for the scientific analysis of hazards and disasters and for disaster planning and mitigation. This is followed by a discussion of the shift in theory from framing hazards and disasters as primarily natural and unexpected events to framing them as expected outcomes of human and environment interaction. This theoretical shift has led to a focus on social vulnerability: why some individuals, groups, communities, and nations are more vulnerable to hazards and disasters than

others. We then discuss how critical and conflict theories contribute to a comprehensive understanding and analysis of vulnerability at multiple levels of analysis. Because these theories focus
primarily on social structure, the structure and agency perspective is introduced to examine how
vulnerable individuals and communities view and respond to hazards and disasters within a given
social structure. Finally, systems theory, specifically, political ecology theory, provides a practical
analytic framework to understand and evaluate social vulnerability and reduce vulnerability by
linking it to sustainable development and social justice.

2.2 OBJECTIVES

At the conclusion of this chapter, readers should be able to:

1. Understand what theory is and how it contributes to framing social vulnerability in a way
   that illuminates the critical elements of this complex issue.
2. Define critical and conflict theories and explain how they contribute to understanding vulnerability in a more comprehensive fashion.
3. Appreciate how structure and agency interplay in the creation of vulnerability.
4. Explain how theory leads to an explanation of worldviews and values that in turn influences how disasters are viewed by disaster planners and by individuals and communities
   who are vulnerable to hazards and disasters.
5. Appreciate how the theoretical framing of structure and agency illuminate how worldviews and values affect our approaches to tackling disaster reduction.
6. Discuss how systems theory guides a mechanism for understanding and evaluating vulnerability, also linking to sustainable development.

2.3 INTRODUCTION

On February 19, 2002, a severe rainstorm "pummeled" La Paz, the capital of Bolivia, "killing 60,
injuring 100 and leaving over 500 homeless. Hailstorms, heavy rains and flash floods tore through the
region, destroying homes, washing away bridges and ripping up road surfaces and brick walls." The
mayor of La Paz, Juan del Granado, estimated damages at $60 million (Steen 2002). Bolivia's president,
Jorge Quiroga, declared a state of emergency, and volunteers joined the city's emergency staff and the
Bolivian Red Cross to provide relief to the injured and homeless, stabilize buildings, and search for
missing persons (Enever 2002; Steen 2002).

Why include a chapter on theory in a book about vulnerability to natural disasters? What role can
theory possibly play in understanding or responding to a disaster such as the flood that occurred in
La Paz in 2002? In this account of a flood disaster, which is presented as a simple recounting of a
current event, theory plays a critical, though unstated role. It identifies the agents or actors in the
story, explains the results of their actions, provides direction for appropriate response, and predicts
what will happen if appropriate responses are (or are not) made. Theories help us to understand
the world around us, but they can also limit what we see and how we perceive it. Consequently,
if we want to minimize the human, environmental, and social losses from hazards and disasters,
it is critical that we are aware of, and deliberate in, our use of theory. Like formalized scientific
theories, worldviews also provide us with explanations of how the world works and what motivates
and directs human behavior—explanations that are based in shared assumptions and values about
human character and our relationship with the natural environment. As much or more than the
scientific theories espoused by disaster managers and planners, our various worldviews and values,
shaped by history, the physical environment, and social institutions, affect our responses to hazards
and disasters.

This chapter defines theory and the role it plays in framing social vulnerability to identify and
illuminate the various dimensions of this complex issue. We then discuss the emerging focus on

social vulnerability and the two major theories—conflict and systems theory—that have been used to understand hazards and disasters from this perspective. Critical and conflict theory explain how differential access to resources and power, embedded in social institutions or social structure, and the actions or agency of individuals and groups interact to create vulnerability (Box 2.1). In addition, these theories explain why some groups are more vulnerable to hazards and disasters than others and also contribute to understanding the worldviews and values that direct how disasters and hazards are viewed in various communities. Systems theory is valuable in analyzing the interaction of critical variables, e.g., the physical environment, human societies and institutions, and animal and plant species. Because systems theory makes it possible to view these phenomena as interdependent components of an encompassing world system, it permits the integration and application of theory and knowledge from many disciplines, including geography, geology, sociology, engineering, biology, political science, among numerous others.

2.4 WHAT IS THEORY?

"At a basic level, though, theory is just a version of some aspect of reality" (Perry 2003, 2). In science, theory is elaborated, can be explicitly stated, and is frequently associated with an individual who first set it out in a formal manner, for example, Darwin's theory of natural selection or Einstein's theory of relativity. Scientific theories are rarely the product of one person's thought or work; they emerge from a body of observation and experiment and scholarly exchange that has accumulated over time. For example, contemporary geologists use plate tectonic theory to understand earthquakes, volcanoes, and other changes in the earth's surface. Plate tectonics theory defines the relevant agents of geologic events: magma, oceanic crust, ocean ridges and trenches, and tectonic plates. It defines the processes that drive the movement of plates: radioactive decay at the earth's core that creates convection currents in the molten magma beneath the earth's surface that move the plates in different directions. And it explains and predicts what results from the interaction of plates: earthquakes, volcanoes, and mountain ranges. Understanding the characteristics and movements of tectonic plates and their boundaries allows geologists to explain past events such as the formation of the Himalayas in Asia and the Great Rift Valley in Africa and to predict, at least to some extent, where earthquakes and volcanic eruptions are likely to occur in the future. This theory, which was formulated in the 1960s and 1970s, transformed geology by bringing together findings from studies of fossils, the earth's magnetism, and the distribution of earthquakes and volcanoes and explaining them with one set of unified concepts and principles. Plate tectonics is an excellent example of scientific theory.

Plate tectonic theory and others like it form the foundation of scientific inquiry. Because they define the relevant agents, conditions, and relationships of a given aspect of reality, they determine the questions that we ask, how we ask them, and how we interpret the answers we obtain. Consider the case of earthquakes. Because plate tectonics is so powerful in explaining geologic events, investigations into the causes and processes of natural disasters are framed by that theory. After the tsunami in Southeast Asia in 2005, scientists focused their attention on how the earthquake generated the tsunami, the pattern of where it struck land, and how to augment and improve warning systems to prevent loss of life from tsunamis in the future. In other words, many scientists assumed that the cause of the disaster was a natural event and that plate tectonics could explain its occurrence. Many did not consider as readily the patterns of human settlement and land use that placed people, animals, and property in the wave's path as equally significant causes.

Not all theories are as well developed or explicitly stated as plate tectonics. We use theory, in the more informal sense of worldview, to understand and respond to common events in our everyday lives. For example, there are theories about who is safe (friends and family) and who is potentially or actually dangerous (strangers and enemies). Although not usually labeled "theory," these worldviews or common sense theories, like formal theories, are nonetheless versions of reality that contain the same elements—assumptions, concepts, and propositions—as scientific theory. Like

BOX 2.1   CASE STUDY: POLITICS AND PUBLIC IMAGE IN DISASTER RELIEF

Cyclone Nargis, which passed over the Irrawaddy Delta region of Myanmar (Burma) on May 2, 2008, illustrates how disasters can highlight internal and external political conflicts. It also demonstrates the importance of considering individual and collective agency in providing resilience to hazards and disasters.

The cyclone, a category 4 storm, affected over 10,000 square kilometers and 2.4 million people (Figure 2.1). The UN estimates deaths at 63,000–101,000 with 220,000 persons missing (http://www.iht.com/articles/2008/06/17/asia/myanmar.php). Myanmar is one of the poorest countries in Southeast Asia. Although it has reduced child mortality since 1990, it ranks 40th among nations for under-5 child mortality, life expectancy is 59 years for men and 61 for women, and 32% of children under 5 are moderately or severely underweight (UNICEF 2008). Malnutrition and food security are major concerns for the entire population. Consequently, Myanmar's population is vulnerable to a host of potential problems in the face of an event like Cyclone Nargis: measles outbreaks among children who have not been adequately vaccinated, diarrhea and other waterborne diseases from damaged sewage and potable water systems, and outbreaks of malaria and dengue fever from increased exposure to mosquitoes as homes are damaged and people must spend more time outdoors. As a press release from Johns Hopkins' Bloomberg School of Public Health observes, "Disease outbreaks have not occurred following the majority of tropical cyclones in the past several decades, primarily because of timely humanitarian response … (Beyrer, Doocy, and Robinson 2008, 3).

Myanmar has been under military rule since 1962 under Senior General Than Shwe since 1992. In the fall of 2007 Buddhist monks led a series of protests against the military government's decision to double the price of fuel; the government responded with a violent suppression of monasteries that evoked strong international censure. The military government responded with increased control over the media and isolation (http://news.bbc.co.uk/2/hi/asia-pacific/7016608.stm). Government statistics on the scale of deaths and destruction from Cyclone Nargis reflect the government's desire to control foreign perceptions of the emergency. In contrast to UN statistics, official sources in Myanmar listed the death toll at 29,000 with 42,000 persons missing and 1.5 million persons displaced (Beyrer, Doocy, and Robinson 2008). Several days passed before General Shwe agreed to allow foreign aid agencies to provide relief and initially restricted relief to supplies and food, but not personnel. Journalist Gavin Hewett, reported from Myanmar:

> Among the senior officers there is a fear that foreigners will undermine their power. The military regime hopes, bizarrely, that this crisis might even enhance their prestige. Much of the aid is transferred to army trucks. They want the people to see Burmese soldiers saving the people (http://news.bbc.co.uk/2/hi/asia-pacific/7416952.stm).

International aid workers' feared that the delay in providing aid, both supplies and skilled personnel, would lead to widespread deaths from infectious diseases and starvation and were publicly critical of the government's response.

Despite these fears, an article in the International Herald Tribune six weeks after the storm reported that survivors were recovering slowly. "The Burmese people are used to getting nothing. They just did the best they could," said Shari Villarosa, the highest-ranking U.S. diplomat in Myanmar, formerly known as Burma. "I'm not getting the sense that there have been a lot of deaths as a result of the delay" (http://www.iht.com/articles/2008/06/17/asia/myanmar.php). In the face of widespread poverty and a government slow to respond, the people of Myanmar demonstrated resilience, providing food and shelter to survivors and some actively protesting for allowing more foreign aid workers to enter the country. Yet, how much additional mortality, illness, and economic loss occurred because of a tightly controlled and slow response?

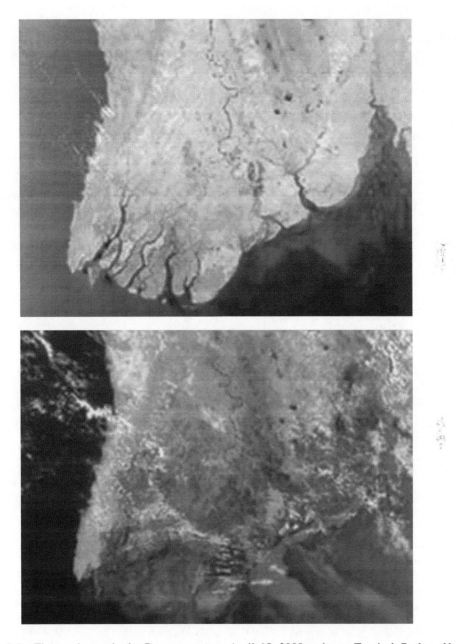

FIGURE 2.1   The top image is the Burma coast on April 15, 2008, prior to Tropical Cyclone Nargis and the bottom image is the same coastline on May 5, 2008, showing the extensive flooding caused by the cyclone. *Source*: NASA/MODIS Rapid Response Team. http://www.nasa.gov/topics/earth/features/nargis_floods.html.

scientific theories, worldviews offer shared explanations and predictions about the world around us. For the most part our experience supports these theories (or we ignore it when it does not), which we learn as part of our cultural and historical heritage, and they remain largely unstated and unconscious. Unlike formal theory, worldviews are not subjected to rigorous and systematic testing, and their assumptions, concepts, and propositions may contain contradictions and logical inconsistencies not present (at least not intentionally) in scientific theories. But occasionally events contradict our theories in ways that we cannot ignore or easily dismiss. For example, an enemy performs an act of kindness, a stranger says "hello," or a family member betrays or hurts us. This may cause us to revise our theories or to reject the evidence as an outlier to the general theory, the "exception that proves the rule."

2.5   HAZARDS AND DISASTERS: THE DOMINANT VIEW

Returning to the case of the flood in La Paz, in the immediate aftermath of an event like this, we rely on the commonly shared theory that disasters are "natural events," the result of "extremes of nature." Media accounts of the flood in La Paz depict the rainstorm as the active agent of the disaster: it "pummels" the city, kills 60 people, and destroys property. It is an unusual event that disrupts the normal order. Reporting on the flood in La Paz, Steen (2002) noted that "[t]he Bolivian National Meteorological Service said that the city has not had such an intense rain in the 50 years it has kept records." Humans are passive victims swept away by the rushing torrents of water despite their efforts to cling to branches and other fixed objects. Responses to the disaster are technological, dictated by accommodating natural forces: removing people from the rushing water, repairing buildings, and restoring damaged systems. Prevention of future disasters requires shoring up structures to withstand the pressure of the water, or, as noted in a UN report issued after the flood in La Paz, creating a system to warn people when water levels rise rapidly and dangerously (UN/ISDR 2007).

The way the story of the 2002 flood in La Paz is told illustrates what Hewitt (1983) calls the dominant or scientific view of hazards as described at length in Chapter 1. Scholars who approach the study of hazards and disasters from the perspective of social vulnerability criticize the dominant view as being based in common sense theories or worldview. The following quotation by Quarantelli illustrates the unconsciously accepted character of this theory:

> The earliest workers in the area, including myself, with little conscious thought and accepting common sense views, initially accepted as a prototype model the notion that disasters were an outside attack upon social systems that "broke down" in the face of such an assault from outside (Quarentelli 1998, 266) [emphasis added].

Tobin and Montz criticize the dominant view for failing to incorporate human action as a root cause of hazards and disasters:

> The traditional view of natural hazards has ascribed all or almost all responsibility for them to the processes of the geophysical world. The approach has meant that the root cause of large-scale death and destruction has been attributed to the extremes of nature rather than encompassing the human world. Frequently, disaster victims have been viewed as unfortunates who could do little but react to physical processes. The physical world, then, has been seen as an external force, separate from human forces. For example Burton and Kates (1964), defined natural hazards as those elements of the physical environment harmful to man and caused by forces external to him (Tobin and Montz 1997, 8) [emphasis added].

Although scientific theory is supposed to be a model of universal and timeless laws and processes, and therefore objective and impartial, in reality theory arises within specific historical and cultural contexts. McEnaney (2000) argues that the dominant approach to disasters formed during the Cold War, a time when the nation focused on having a strong civil defense system to protect against attack from external enemies. This civil defense model, argues McEnaney, was applied to disasters and hazards, which were conceived of as attacks by natural forces. Watts (1983) traces the dominant approach to hazards and disasters to the positivist science of the Enlightenment in which nature can be studied and observed empirically and objectively, but human behavior and society are vague and metaphysical and therefore outside the domain of science (1983, 233). Thus logically, a scientific and technological approach to hazards and disasters must examine their natural rather human causes.

Scientific theories, especially those that involve human beings and social phenomena, are also shaped by the social position and power of those who propound them (see discussion of Gramsci's concept of hegemony and Foucault's ideas of knowledge and power in section 2.8.1). To view natural disasters as isolated events or accidents of nature keeps us from recognizing both the regularity with which they occur and the human decisions and actions that place some, but not all, people in the way of natural forces or create changes in the environment that place them at risk. For example, a United Nations environment report on the flood in La Paz notes:

> Floods and mudslides are recurrent disasters in La Paz. The Bolivian city lies along a narrow valley crossed by more than two hundred rivers, including subterranean rivers, and suffers from unstable geological conditions. The rapid growth of the city has forced many people to live in flood plains and high slope hills, making them particularly vulnerable to floods and mudslides during the rainy season (December to March) (UN/ISDR 2007).

This statement challenges the dominant model in several ways and raises many important questions. First, floods and mudslides are not uncommon in La Paz; the area is geologically unstable with major water drainage (Figure 2.2). Second, people as much as nature are in the center of this situation of risk and vulnerability (Figure 2.3).

This description raises a series of important questions about the social causes of the "natural" hazard of floods in La Paz. Why is Bolivia's capital built in a geologically unstable area? Who in La Paz is most at risk from floods and mudslides? Who or what "forces" or requires that people live in flood plains and on high, unstable slopes?

FIGURE 2.2   La Paz, Bolivia, showing development and building practices with flood and landslide risk. *Source*: Photo by John Brett, with permission.

FIGURE 2.3   Street vendors along a shopping street in La Paz, Bolivia. *Source*: Photo by Jean Scandlyn, with permission.

2.6   CHALLENGING THE DOMINANT VIEW: SOCIAL VULNERABILITY

In the 1960s and 1970s, the Civil Rights Movement, the War on Poverty, and the emerging environmental movement provided conditions that stimulated emergency managers, social scientists, and those affected by disasters and hazards to question the assumptions of the dominant view (see Chapter 1). Additionally, fieldwork in disaster research beginning in the 1970s revealed complex social structural factors contributing to disasters. For example, agricultural development in northeastern Honduras provides an illustrative case. During the early to mid 20th century, many subsistence farmers in this region sold their land in valley bottoms to companies that used the land for large-scale commercial banana plantations. The displaced farmers subsequently cleared land on hillside plots above the valleys for their subsistence farming, a process that destabilized the soil on these steep slopes. In 1974, when Hurricane Fifi struck Honduras, heavy rains produced major landslides and the collapse of an irrigation dam in which 8000 people died and the banana crop was largely destroyed (Pielke et al. 2003). Was this only a natural disaster?

In the 1980s and 1990s technological approaches to disaster and hazard mitigation in the United States failed to prevent widespread destruction from events such as Hurricane Hugo in 1989, the Loma Prieta earthquake also in 1989, the Northridge earthquake in 1994, Hurricane Andrew in 1992, and floods in Mississippi in 1993. Despite the world's most advanced structural engineering, in the earthquake in Kobe, Japan, in 1995, 6000 people died and many buildings collapsed. At the same time, increasing recognition of the differential effect of disasters on populations based on race, class, age, disability, and gender raised questions of unequal exposure to risks and hazards.

During the same period, anthropologists and other social scientists accumulated evidence that people were usually very knowledgeable about recurrent risks and hazards in their environment and had often developed means to mitigate their risk. An important feature of the human species is its ability to adapt to a wide variety of physical and social environments. Successful adaptation requires balancing competing needs, e.g., the need to be close to sources of water and food and the need to minimize risk from floods (Oliver-Smith 1999). For example, rice farmers in Bangladesh deliberately live concentrated in the floodplain of the Ganges and depend upon predictable annual floods to replenish rice crops and fish harvests. Moving from flooded land; obtaining assistance from extended kin; selling land, livestock, and belongings; and spending savings are all regular, accepted ways that Bangladeshis mitigate risks from floods (Zaman 1999). Yet social changes, especially those that increase poverty or undermine local power, may make it difficult for people to act on their knowledge of hazards and disasters and usual patterns of response. After a particularly severe flood in Bangladesh in 1998, the initial proposals of aid agencies such as the United Nations Development Program (UNDP) and South Asian Association for Regional Cooperation (SAARC) to permanently reduce risks from floods included "expensive structural engineering 'megaplans' that called for construction of massive embankments on major rivers throughout the country and the dredging of rivers to obtain lower water levels" (Zaman 1999, 203). Following evaluation of the plans these technological solutions were replaced with programs to improve long-term economic development and welfare to enhance residents' ability to recover from flood damage and losses.

These historical and intellectual developments stimulated the search for new perspectives and theories about hazards and disasters that would take social factors, local knowledge, and inequity in exposure to risk into account. Vulnerability or social vulnerability was the concept that emerged to redirect research and analysis. The United Nations International Strategy for Disaster Reduction defines vulnerability as "[t]he conditions determined by physical, social, economic and environmental factors or processes, which increase the susceptibility of a community to the impact of hazards." Wisner, Blaikie, and Cannon expand the definition to include "… capacity to anticipate, cope with, resist and recover" (2004, 11). There are many definitions of this term, but they all include considerations of individual and collective susceptibility to natural events and the capacity to respond to those events, often linked to the concept of resilience. Drawing from a number of sources, Birkmann provides the following definition of resilience: "Generally, a common ground can be seen in the understanding that resilience describes the capability of a system to maintain its basic functions and structures in a time of shocks and perturbations" (2006, 15–16). Resilience is closely related to the concept of adaptation, mentioned previously and discussed in relation to systems theory later in this chapter: the ability to adjust material culture to varying environments, both physical and social, and to changes in those environments over time.

Those working within the framework of vulnerability further recognize that vulnerability occurs on many levels of analysis, i.e., individual, community, regional, national, and global, and that vulnerability is determined by a host of social as well as physical factors such as gender, race, ethnicity, age, and social class. As Hewitt (1983) notes, one of the most important developments of the social vulnerability approach is to view disasters not as exceptional events, but as the product of normal or usual processes. Consequently, a theory that can describe, explain, and predict social vulnerability to disasters must take into account social as well as environmental determinants, analyze causality at multiple scales or levels, and view disasters as resulting from normal or usual and not exceptional events and processes (see Chapter 3 for a discussion of the sustainable livelihoods approach that seeks to accomplish this).

Finally, the concept of social vulnerability raises questions of social justice. With few exceptions, the poor and marginalized are most vulnerable to disasters, whether they occur in rich or poor nations, and are less able to act upon their knowledge and awareness of risks and hazards. A notable example is coastal real estate development. Although both types of property owners are exposed to risk from hurricanes, the meaning and implications of risk for a wealthy individual who builds a second home on beachfront property are quite different from those of the individual from a commercial fishing village whose family has lived and worked there for several generations.

This discussion underscores not only the importance of theory in understanding and responding to disasters and hazards, but the need to make the theories we use explicit if we are to:

- Understand the differential effects of hazards and disasters on individuals, communities, regions, and nations
- Understand how human actions, knowledge, and beliefs affect vulnerability and resilience to hazards and disasters
- Decrease inequities in risk and exposure within and across populations and increase capacity and resilience in all kinds of communities (social justice)
- Develop more flexible, locally adaptable interventions and approaches

2.7   CONFLICT AND CRITICAL THEORY

Why are some people more vulnerable to hazards and disasters than others? In the case of the 2002 street floods in La Paz, street vendors, the majority of whom were women, bore the highest risk and exposure. Although that particular flood was a relatively rare event, those women who survived the flood returned to sell their goods in the same locations. How do we understand this response and the processes that created it? Social scientists have applied two major theoretical perspectives to understanding social vulnerability: political economy and systems theory and their combination in political ecology.

Strictly speaking, political economy is a not a theory, but a perspective from which several distinct social theories have developed. During the European Enlightenment, social philosophers began to investigate the origin, nature, and relationships between nation-states and their colonial holdings. Swiss philosopher Jean-Jacques Rousseau was the first to use the phrase "political economy" in his *A Discourse on Political Economy* published in 1755. Rousseau defined the general or "political economy" as an extension of the "particular economy," that is, "the wise and legitimate government of the house for the common good of the whole family" to "that great family, the State" (Rousseau 1973, 128). Just as in a household, the state had an *economy*, the production and exchange of goods and services, and *politics*, the just (ideally) use of power and legitimate authority to allocate goods and benefits, set policy, protect rights, and resolve disputes. A key aspect of this perspective is the link between politics and economics. Although often separated into distinct areas of study in subsequent eras, i.e., political science and economics, Enlightenment era theorists saw them as inextricably linked. Political power and processes supported the national economy through the creation and protection of institutions such as private property and taxation. The economy, through tax revenues, enabled the state to establish its authority internally and expand it externally through wars of conquest and colonization, setting domestic and foreign policies favorable to economic development and supporting them by force when necessary.

At the same time that the political economy perspective emerged, the critical tradition that developed in Europe in the 17th century and involved critical analysis of texts such as the Bible was expanded and applied to a critical assessment of and need for reform of government, law, and other social institutions to improve the human condition (Therborn 1996). The convergence of political economy and the critical tradition yielded conflict theory, expressed most fundamentally in Karl Marx' critique of political economy in *Capital* (1990 [1867]). Conflict theory rests on the assumption that conflict and contradiction are inherent in human social life and that this conflict produces historical changes, sometimes violent and revolutionary, that generate progress in social organization and life. For example, in the capitalist political economy or mode of production, conflict and contradiction are inherent in control over the means of production: those physical resources, e.g., raw materials, electricity, or machinery, necessary for the production of goods and services by a given class of people. Those who control or own the means of production, the capitalist class, are in conflict with those who do not, the laboring or working class, who must sell their labor to sustain themselves and their families. Whereas Marx acknowledged that capitalism is a powerful engine of production and technological innovation that could benefit the state and that would ultimately become the dominant form of political economy globally, he also argued that class conflict inevitably creates inequality, exploitation, and oppression both within and among nations.

Within capitalist societies, inequality becomes institutionalized through various forms of capital: human, social, cultural, institutional, financial, and political. For example, human capital is the attainment of valued skills and knowledge by individuals through training and education. In the United States, lawyers, doctors, and engineers have high human capital; they speak English and perhaps other languages, are literate, and have mastery and expertise of a professional body of knowledge and related skills that are highly valued in the society and the market. A CEO of a large corporation, if she or he owns stock in the company, may have a great deal of financial capital as well as institutional capital, the power that comes from holding an official position of leadership in an established financial entity supported by the laws of the state. These forms of capital can be translated into power to affect the social and physical environment, power that is often subtly exercised to maintain prestige and wealth. But not everyone has an equal chance of obtaining various forms of capital, nor do all forms of capital provide the same kinds of resources for responding to hazards and disasters. Opportunity is highly structured, even in a nation like the United States that values equality, freedom, and self-determination.

Globally, the division between capitalists and laborers was recreated among nations and regions of the world through colonialism. European nations extracted raw materials from their colonies using slave labor from Africa or the forced labor of indigenous people in South America and Asia, but retained a monopoly on manufacturing and processing of those raw materials in Europe. Investment in all kinds of infrastructure, from courts of law to schools to roads and railways, was concentrated in Europe, with only those resources necessary to meet the needs of extracting raw materials invested in the colonies. As Rodney (1982) noted in Africa over 30 years ago, "African economies are integrated in the very structure of the developed capitalist economies; and they are integrated in a manner that is unfavorable to Africa and insures that Africa is dependent on the big capitalist countries" (1982, 25). Postcolonial nations still lack the infrastructure and wealth to prepare for and mitigate the effects of disasters and suffer higher losses of life when disasters occur (Dilley et al. 2005; Wisner, Blaikie, and Cannon 2004).

2.8 STRUCTURE AND AGENCY

In conflict theory, inequality is viewed as an inherent part of the social *structure*. Elements of social structure include the institutions that form the context of our daily lives: schools, religions, courts of law, financial markets, professions, government agencies, the police and military, businesses and corporations and their regulation, hospitals and clinics, and marriage and the family. This structure largely determines the conditions within which an individual lives his or her life and the resources available to her or him. Schools in poor neighborhoods receive less funding, have larger average class sizes, have higher rates of absenteeism and change in their student populations, and have a harder time recruiting and retaining high quality teachers than those in affluent suburbs. Thus, children growing up in poor neighborhoods and attending these schools are at an educational disadvantage from the day they enter kindergarten (Kozol 1991). The result of the institutionalization of inequality results in *structural violence*. As Farmer notes, "Structural violence is violence exerted systematically—that is, indirectly—by everyone who belongs to a certain social order ..." (2005, 307). For example, the systematic neglect of levees that protected poor neighborhoods of New Orleans left African Americans disproportionately vulnerable to loss of life and property from Hurricane Katrina. Their vulnerability was compounded by their reliance on public transportation to leave the city and their mistrust of public institutions' willingness to help them or to provide accurate information about evacuation based on long-standing racism (Elder et al. 2007).

Some social observers view globalization as a process that can reduce inequality within and among nations and regions by increasing "transnational flows of capital/goods, information/ideas, and people" (Kalb 2000, cited in Lewellen 2002, 8). As more of the world's people participate in the production and exchange of goods and services, ideas and values, standards of living, life expectancy, and quality of life will improve everywhere. Rapley argues that the economic policies of neoliberalism underlying globalization "have had the effect of raising aggregate income but skewing its distribution" (2004, 6). In other words, average incomes have risen but the gap between rich and poor has widened. Whereas there is greater economic integration globally at the macro level of nations and regions, at the local level of families and communities inequalities in the ability to participate in global processes persist (Lewellen 2002). Although cell phones have increased access to global communication for many people in poorer countries, computers and the Internet remain beyond the reach of the majority of the world's population (Chinn and Fairlie 2007). In the 1960s and 1970s, large multinational banks actively marketed loans to governments in Africa and Latin America for economic development—loans that those governments readily secured. When they could not keep up with repayment, the IMF and World Bank mandated restructuring of the loans and demanded "austerity measures" to ensure their adherence to the terms of restructuring. Many of these measures required that governments of debtor nations make massive cuts in spending on health care, infrastructure, education, agricultural development, and other social programs that increased the vulnerability of their citizens to a variety of hazards and disasters and eroded the state's ability to provide assistance in times of need (Gill 2000; von Braun, Teklue, and Webb 1998).

2.8.1 UNDERSTANDING VULNERABILITY

How does this theory help us to understand social vulnerability to disasters? Various forms and amounts of capital affect where people live, work, travel, how many children they have, the resources in their social networks, and thus both their exposure to risk and their ability to respond to a hazard or disaster. Although wealthy individuals who own waterfront or coastal property (high financial capital) are at high risk from floods and storms, they usually have the means to leave the area when conditions threaten and can purchase insurance to protect them against some if not all of the damage to their property. They have the social connections (social capital) and skills (human capital) to ensure that their claims are processed quickly and successfully and that their livelihoods are less likely to be fully at risk (Wisner, Blaikie, and Cannon 2004). The purchase of insurance is evidence that those individuals who purchase it understand that their property is at risk. Those who are poor (low financial capital) may be just as aware of the risks they face from storms and floods, but they usually have fewer choices of where they can live and the quality of their housing, and may not be able to afford insurance or feel that more personal forms of insurance, such as sharing resources among family members, are more reliable. The family whose livelihood depends on commercial or subsistence fishing needs to live on the coast, where both their homes and their business are at risk from storms, flooding, and other hazards. Furthermore, residents in a fishing village in Southeast Asia are more vulnerable to loss of life and property than those living in coastal villages in Australia or Europe. Although the concepts and principles of conflict theory are relatively simple, their application suggests the complex interplay of social, economic, and historical factors that contribute to differences in risk and vulnerability to disasters and hazards for different populations within countries and for different countries and regions globally.

So far we have considered the *material* aspects of social structure and power as discussed by conflict theorists. Material aspects include, among others, control over natural resources; the accumulation of wealth; investment in roads, buildings, and manufacturing capacity; the creation of universities and research facilities; and the development of technology and science. Other theorists working within this paradigm have focused on how *nonmaterial* elements of social structure—symbols, beliefs, values, and knowledge itself—play a critical role in maintaining and reproducing inequality and exercising power. One of the key questions that conflict theorists must answer is how one class of people can not only be exploited and dominated by a much smaller class of people without the constant use or threat of force and violence, but may actively embrace and uphold the structures of power that dominate them. Most contemporary capitalist societies do not rely primarily on organized religion to support the power of the state and many actively espouse values such as freedom, individual rights and civil liberties, and popular participation in government. Gramsci (1971), discussed aspects of the role of ideology in social structure through his development of the concept of hegemony. Hegemony, Gramsci argues, is the exercise of power indirectly by the use of ideas, ideology, and a view of life that supports the social structure and those in power. This process is complex and contradictory, with various groups vying to dominate popular thought and media. Nonetheless, an overarching set of values becomes those that the majority of a society's members internalize.

The dominant view of disasters may be viewed as having hegemonic aspects or qualities. By viewing disasters as events caused by natural forces and processes outside human history and beyond human control, governments and other powerful organizations can deflect criticism for inadequate enforcement of building codes, lack of investment in warning systems and disaster planning, and for allowing some communities to suffer higher costs than others when disasters occur. Because this view also infuses media accounts of disasters and hazards and appears in disaster management literature and courses, it is accepted as "common sense" and is therefore sometimes difficult to effectively challenge. Thus, the focus in the accounts of the flood in La Paz focus on its rarity and unusual strength rather than on the social and economic structure that compels many people to live on unstable hillsides every day and sit literally in the streets trying to sell something to provide income to feed and clothe their families.

Foucault examined the ways in which we internalize the dominant views of the powerful both in social institutions and in our bodies through scientific discourse and knowledge. Under capitalism, Foucault argues, science supplants religion as the primary means of determining truth in most societies. "Truth is linked in a circular relation with systems of power which produce and sustain it, and to effects of power which it induces and which extend it. A '"régime' of truth" (1980, 133). Consequently, those who control the production of scientific knowledge and its applications through technology also control our conversations or discourse and thus can affect in important ways how we view, study, and respond to phenomena such as disasters and hazards. Jason Corburn (2005) describes how discourse can affect planning for development:

> For example, Tauxe (1995), in a study of a development process in western North Dakota, shows how community voices were marginalized by planners who attended more closely to technical styles of discourse. Community voices were marginalized despite public efforts to involve residents. Even when local residents managed to gain an audience, they had little impact on development decisions in part because planners and residents did not speak the same language and understand each other's politics (Tauxe quoted in Corburn 2005, 147–48).

Charts, tables, and lengthy written documents often carry more weight in such public conversations than do the evidence of what Corburn calls "street science" or what anthropologists call "local knowledge," which may be presented in the form of stories or oral history that appears anecdotal even if it condenses years of accumulated empirical observation and experience (Corburn 2005). Control of discourse reinforces inequalities among and within nations in understanding and responding to disasters and hazards. Because the dominant view of disasters sees them as products of nature, natural and earth sciences have, until recently, received the majority of funding for research and the focus of mitigation has been on technology instead of social issues.

According to Foucault, an important aspect of the power of truth through science is how it internalizes social control within the individual members of a society. Biology and psychology, applied through organized medicine and psychiatry and communicated through schools and mass media, define what is considered normal behavior or a normal body. We internalize these standards of normality and discipline our behavior to achieve them. Bourdieu (1998) called this embodiment of social standards and scientific knowledge "habitus." Habitus is internalized social structure: an individuals' habitus consists of the largely unconscious patterns of thinking, feeling, and acting that she or he exhibits in daily life. According to Bourdieu, habitus not only incorporates mainstream or dominant standards of behavior and physical qualities and values, but those that are particular to an individual's location in the social structure, i.e., his or her class status. Because local knowledge is so frequently dismissed as unscientific or anecdotal, community members, particularly those with little formal education, may dismiss the authority of their own knowledge and experience at least in discussions with those identified as experts. At the same time, when internalized shared worldviews or habitus include a sense of futility or powerlessness in the face of social injustice, it can represent a barrier to effective social and political action to mitigate hazards and disasters.

Just as those working within the dominant view of hazards can focus too much attention on natural causes of disasters, so conflict theorists can focus too much on the constraints and dominance of social structure and fail to recognize the role of individual and human action to generate change that can affect social life and the physical environment. For Foucault and Bourdieu, structure, external and internalized, does not completely determine individual and collective behavior and action. Individual and collective action or agency also affects social structure. Foucault acknowledged that alternative sources of knowledge and understanding and models for action exist outside mainstream images and institutions (Moore and Sanders 2006, 13), for example, in the coded opposition to power of the Brer Rabbit stories of rural blacks in the United States (Kushnick 1998) or in local forms of resistance such as seasonal workers in Malaysia delaying the harvest of crops of landowners who have overly exploited or mistreated them (Scott 1985). For Bourdieu, habitus is not only the product of what we receive and are taught, but also of our everyday actions and social encounters or practice, and thus is subject to innovation and change.

2.9 SYSTEMS THEORY AND SOCIAL VULNERABILITY

The whole is more than the sum of its parts.

—Aristotle (384–322 BC)

General systems theory is another major theory, also frequently implicit, that underlies social vulnerability approaches to understanding hazards and disasters. As we will discuss later in the chapter, it is often combined with political economy in *political ecology* and with culture in *cultural ecology*. Historically, the scientific approach that developed during the Enlightenment in Western Europe was based on the assumption that a phenomenon (whole) consisted only as a sum of its smallest identifiable parts. To understand a phenomenon, for example, the human body, it is necessary to determine its smallest parts, i.e., the cell, and understand their characteristics and behavior. Once these are understood, individual organs and whole bodies could be understood as well. This breaking down, or reductionism, is evident in different scientific disciplines: biologists break down living organisms into their smallest units, cells; chemists break down matter into atoms and molecules; and physicists break atoms further into subatomic particles and waves. By the early 20th century the various scientific disciplines worked largely independently of each other, each examining the parts of the world that formed the object of their study.

In the 1930s, biologist Ludwig von Bertalanffy (1950) reacted against scientific fragmentation and reductionism, arguing that a more holistic approach was needed. Understanding the genetic basis of a particular cancer is important, but by itself this knowledge is insufficient to design interventions to prevent cancer. Instead, to combat cancer, the disease must be understood at the genetic, cellular, biological, economic, and social levels. Writing in 1956, Boulding described the consequences of reductionism: "[T]he more science breaks into sub-groups, and the less communication is possible among the disciplines, however, the greater chance there is that the total growth of knowledge is being slowed down by the loss of relevant communications" (1956, 198–99). General systems theory provides a way to increase communication among scientific disciplines through the concept of the system. Though the origin of the fundamental idea behind systems theory can be traced to scientists and philosophers such as Aristotle, Descartes, and Galileo, its contemporary incorporation into general systems theory is generally credited to Ludwig von Bertalanffy (1972).

2.9.1 WHAT IS A SYSTEM?

Although the definition of system might seem obvious, it is important to examine its elements. By definition a system is composed of at least two interrelated parts or elements (Kast and Rosenzweig 1972). A more applicable definition is "a collection of interacting or independent entities that produces a unified functional whole, whose properties or behaviors cannot be predicted from a separate understanding of each individual level component" (Dale et al. 2004). Systems theory is based on the assumption that wholes are not merely a collection of different parts, but are organized, distinct phenomena that have characteristics, qualities, and behavior unique to them and different from the qualities of their component parts. This principle, known as *emergentism* (the character of the whole *emerges* from its parts) is fundamental to systems theory and distinguishes it from reductive approaches. What makes the whole unique is how the parts are linked to one another through organizing functions, the tasks or jobs that various parts of the system perform. Whereas some parts may perform more than one job, and many systems have redundant parts, the whole is dependent upon its parts working together in unity. Changes in one part of system generate responses and changes in other parts of the system.

An important feature of systems is whether they are open or closed. Closed systems have impermeable boundaries and so do not exchange energy or materials from their surrounding environment but must regulate themselves internally. Open systems, on the other hand, have permeable boundaries and freely exchange energy and materials with other systems in their environment. These are relative qualities: most systems are more or less open or closed. Culture, for example, is a relatively open system that exchanges materials and energy through human interactions with the physical environment, plants, and animals. In turn, those systems are also altered by the exchange.

2.9.2 ECOLOGICAL SYSTEMS

> An ecosystem is greater than the sum of its parts.
>
> **—Eugene P. Odum (1913–2002)**

Von Bertalanffy applied general systems theory to biological organisms such as the human body, but in the 1970s it was adopted by the emerging science of ecology. Odum presented the idea of the "new ecology" in 1964 in an article by that title in which he links ecology, the study of the inter-action between organisms and their environment, with general systems theory. Because it identi-fies the similarities among phenomena of different disciplines, general systems theory provided a common ground to link the study of physical geography with biology and human geography, par-ticularly the interaction between human individuals and communities and their environment, both living and nonliving. The new ecology recognized that explaining structure and function at only one level of analysis could not explain the whole picture. For example, understanding the effect of building a dam on the price and availability of electricity will not explain its effects on human communities displaced by the dam or the increased burden of parasitic, waterborne diseases in humans who live above the dam. In addition, the new ecology acknowledged that descriptive research is not enough to link the layers of scientific research. For example, studying the descrip-tive nature of plant growth and nutrient cycling will not produce larger crop yields. However, if the functions of these two phenomena are studied together, common denominators can be determined leading to an understanding of their interactions. Odum describes the ecosystem concept as a basic unit of structure and function that must be dealt with: "The new ecology is thus a systems ecology" (Odum 1964).

The power of systems theory lies in its ability to examine complex interrelationships at mul-tiple levels and thus analyze vulnerability to disasters and hazards as well as identifying ways to mitigate them. In the case of the flood disaster in La Paz, for example, multiple systems were affected by the rushing water: transportation systems in the city, sewer systems that contain waste and keep it from contaminating drinking water, communication systems where utility and phone lines are damaged, power systems that supply electricity to homes and businesses, but also to police, fire, and rescue departments, and health care systems that must cope with multiple victims during the flood and patients who present with waterborne diseases from contaminated drinking water after the waters subside. Additionally, the political and economic system means that many poor Bolivians, particularly women, must sit on city streets to sell their goods and remain with those goods even as flood waters rush down the streets. The failure of the government to build and maintain roads, drainage ditches, and enforce building codes, coupled with migration of the rural poor to the city's unstable hillsides, all increase the vulnerability of the poor to flood disasters. With few options and resources, and low value placed on public safety by the state, La Paz's poor street vendors have little choice but to adopt the worldview that a flood disaster is "God's will" and to return to the streets.

The emergence of ecological systems perspective was a significant scientific and theoretical development that arose from increasing awareness of environmental pollution and its effect on health, increasing human population and the demand on natural resources, and the extinction of plants and animals resulting from human actions (Holling and Chambers 1973). Within this context, ecological systems theory represents a shift in scientific and popular (in those areas of the world where Western science is dominant) conceptions of the relationship between humans and nature.

2.9.3 CRITIQUE OF ECOLOGICAL SYSTEMS: POLITICAL ECOLOGY

Although ecological systems theory provides an excellent framework for describing the "what's" and "how's" of these relationships and the social vulnerabilities that exist within these systems, they tend to focus on equilibrium and balance instead of conflict and change. Within the ecological sys-tems view it is hard to see disasters as anything other than extreme natural events or disturbances to the system with resilience as a systems' ability to recover from external forces (Wilcox and Horwitz 2005). Political ecology, which combines ecological systems theory with political economy per-spectives, most notably those of conflict theorists such as Wolf (1982), Frank (1969), and Wallerstein (1974), became an important framework for examining the role of power, inequalities and inequities in the distribution of resources, and global capitalism on ecological changes at local, regional, and global levels of analysis (Walker 2005). "Whereas cultural ecology and systems theory emphasized adaptation and homeostasis, political ecology emphasized the role of political economy as a force of maladaptation and instability (Walker 2005, 74).

The creation of large dams to harness hydroelectric power in many developing countries in the 1960s and 1970s are a case in point. The dams did generate power, but in creating large freshwater lakes they also greatly increased the habitat for freshwater snails and altered patterns of human agriculture, fishing, transportation to increase settlement near the lakes, and human contact with the water. Thus, the stage was set for the rapid spread of schistosomiasis, a debilitating, chronic parasitic infection, throughout the world's tropical regions (Desowitz 1976). In India, despite decades-long protests from people threatened with displacement from dam projects, the government has built 4300 large dams that "have submerged about 37,500 square kilometers—an area almost the size of Switzerland—and displaced tens of millions of people" (International Rivers 2008). Underlying the decisions to build these dams and the responses to their construction and the changes they brought were several competing worldviews and values.

2.10   WHAT ARE WORLDVIEWS?

Worldview, from the German *weltanschauung*, refers to ways of thinking about the world and its events that are more or less shared by a group of people. Worldviews provide answers to questions about the meaning of life and death and what the appropriate human response to those events should be. Implied in the concept of worldview is a direct relationship between the way an individual or group views the world and their behavior. Worldviews are learned through social interactions with parents, friends, and others in one's community from early childhood. They may be expressed through religion or philosophy, or they may be implicit in the structure, norms, and values of institutions such as public schools or medical clinics. Worldviews are largely unconscious and may guide our actions without our awareness. The concept of worldview is conceptually problematic in that worldviews are only "more or less" shared among members of a society or social group; like habitus, worldviews vary by an individual's or a community's position within the social structure and by their unique experiences. The world may look very different if you are a small landholder working to produce food your family than if you are a commercial fisherman who supplies fish for sushi on the global market or an investment banker on Wall Street. For this reason, many contemporary anthropologists prefer ideology or habitus to worldview.

Worldviews respond to questions about human relationship with nature, and thus to understand vulnerability and response to hazards and disasters it is critical to take worldviews into account. Broadly speaking, there are three ways of understanding the society-nature relation:

* People under nature (nature's theory): humans are at nature's mercy
* People with nature: humans live their collective lives in harmony with nature
* People over nature (human's theory): humans dominate nature through manipulation of the natural world

Under the first worldview, an earthquake or tornado might be seen as an "act of nature" or as an "act of God" if God is accepted as the creator of nature. The response might be to accept it as an unavoidable though unfortunate event and to rebuild damaged structures. Under the second worldview, the same event might be viewed as something to which human society must adapt and for which it must plan by understanding weather patterns, building structures and locating cities on stable ground and away from common tornado pathways, and using knowledge and cooperation to provide safe places of refuge. Under the third worldview, damage to structures or lives lost result from human failure to master nature and the response is to design and build structures that can better withstand the forces of earthquakes or learn to predict and warn against tornados.

The relationship between a society's political, economic, and social structure and its view of the relationship between humans and nature has been a subject of debate among anthropologists. Some, like Harris (1979), argue that a society's material, economic bases, i.e., how its members obtain their needs from nature or mode of production, determines their worldview. Thus, a society based on hunting and gathering in which success depends on an intimate knowledge of the local environment and its plants and animals will tend to have a worldview of people with nature. A society based on industrial technology where most people live far removed from nature will tend to have a worldview of people over nature. And a society or community that has few resources and whose members have little control over where they live and how they make a living are likely to adopt the worldview of people under nature. Most social scientists would agree the relationship between environment, mode of production, and view of nature is complex and can work in both directions: our view of nature can change.

2.11 WORLDVIEWS AND VALUES

Values are guidelines for action (behavior) and decisions that are generally consistent with and derived from worldviews. For example, in the general worldview of human over nature, life is valued over that of other species. The human need or desire to increase crop yields through the application of pesticides is justified through this value, even though it may never be stated unless someone challenges that decision and its underlying value. Values address questions of morality, of right and wrong action, and what is good and desirable. Like worldviews, they may be explicitly stated or unconscious and implicit in the form of "gut feelings" that a given action or decision is the "right" or "wrong" thing to do.

Values express equity or fairness, justice, and the relationship of the individual to society. What do I owe a stranger simply because that person is a human being in need? How much should my individual opinion or need or desire count in society? What is "consent," and how should it be expressed? Philosophers distinguish between intrinsic values, those things that are good, desirable, or important in and of themselves without relation to any other thing, and extrinsic values, those things that are valuable because they are a means to obtaining, enjoying, or protecting something that is intrinsically good (Flew 1979, 365). Intrinsic and extrinsic values are considered when we invoke the sacredness of the earth as part of creation (Hayden 1995; Khalid with O'Brien 1992) or assign monetary value to a unique geological feature or to preserving remote areas so that humans can experience wilderness (Foster 1997). Values also guide discussions of which risks can be mitigated and for whom, and which risks are acceptable and at what level. For example, are the risks from landslides and earthquakes viewed as impossible to manage, whereas nuclear power accidents or terrorist attacks must be prevented at any cost?

Values exist and affect decisions and behaviors at various levels and through various systems, and they often come into conflict with one another. For instance, disaster managers and economic planners in a city may believe that they should provide protection from disasters equally across the entire population; thus, equality is valued. They probably also want to achieve this by using scarce or limited resources wisely; thus, efficiency is valued. If there is a small population of the city that is very hard to protect, it may not be efficient to spend 90% of the resources to protect only 10% of the population. The issue becomes more problematic if that small group is also an ethnic, racial, or occupational minority group. Many planners and officials believe that historically marginalized or deprived groups should receive assistance in greater proportion than their strictly equal share—the value of equity.

Returning to the example of dams in India, the worldview embraced by the Indian government is one of humans over nature, expressed in its willingness to use technical solutions—dams—to solve human needs for energy. The government also values economic development more than the possible harm or disruption caused to the millions of people displaced by the dams. The worldview embraced by the protestors, in contrast, is one of nature with humans, expressed in the desire for economic development that values environmentally sustainable solutions to the need for power and that value local community needs over national needs or special interests.

2.12 COMMUNITY-BASED APPROACHES AND SOCIAL AND ENVIRONMENTAL JUSTICE

Conflict theory forces us to acknowledge social inequity as a source of vulnerability to disasters and to redefine hazards to include not only extreme events such as earthquakes and volcanic eruptions, but conditions that millions of people live with daily: contaminated water, lack of sanitary facilities, unsafe roads, and inadequate food and nutrition. These theories also direct us to consider different approaches to mitigating hazards and disasters that incorporate social justice and participatory approaches to research and planning.

Freire (1970) examined how individuals and groups could challenge structures of power and inequality through literacy and *conscientização* or critical consciousness. Freire observed that becoming literate, i.e., learning to read and write especially as taught in schools, is a process whereby society inculcates dominant values and views. It is thus dehumanizing and oppressive for poor and marginalized members of society. Learning to read and write can, however, be a process of humanization and liberation if it is taught in a way that demonstrates the power embedded in language and if teachers work in equal partnership with the person learning to read to control that power her- or himself (Freire 1970).

Analogously, research on hazards and disasters can be a process that empowers residents of communities at high risk. Participatory Rural Appraisal or Assessment (PRA) and Community Based Participatory Research (CBPR) (Israel 2005) rest on principles that emphasize the knowledge and strengths of local communities and their members and strive to equalize the power between researchers or technical experts and those they are studying:

> PRA depends on facilitators acting as convenors and catalysts, but without dominating the process. Many find this difficult. They must take time, show respect, be open and self-critical, and learn not to interrupt. They need to have confidence that local people, whether they are literate or not, women or men, rich or poor, are capable of carrying out their own analysis (Weiss 2000, 4).

The sustainable livelihoods approach (SLA), described in Chapter 3, uses PRA in assessing a community's vulnerability and resilience to hazards and disasters.

These are lofty ideals, and PRA and CBPR projects often fall short of truly equal partnership and collaboration. Nonetheless, these models offer an approach that values local knowledge of the physical and social environment and has the potential to recognize and incorporate indigenous ways of living with hazards and disasters that may prove more sustainable than purely technological approaches (Zaman 1999). Although this knowledge and participation could be extracted and used for top-down programs and interventions imposed by government or civic agencies and institutions outside the community, these approaches are guided by the view that community members must be equal partners in all aspects of research, program design, implementation, and evaluation and that this process should be used to empower local communities. Consequently, PRA and CBPR have been used to directly respond to issues of social and environmental justice (Shepard et al. 2002) such as pesticide exposure among farm workers (Arcury, Quandt, and Dearry 2001). "Fundamentally, *street science* is about the pursuit of environmental-health justice. Mobilizing local knowledge helps disadvantaged communities organize and educate themselves, as well as increases control over the decisions that impact their lives" (emphasis original) (Corburn 2005, 216). Thus, these frameworks support the position that communities have the right to know about local hazards and a right to protection from disasters.

Discussion of human rights and social justice returns us to the power of conflict and critical theory in analyzing inequities in social vulnerability. Conflict and critical theory proposes that a society's dominant or hegemonic worldview and underlying values, and its institutions and policies regarding those factors that govern human and environmental interactions are mutually reinforcing. In other words, if a society's economic system of production is based on exploiting natural resources and human labor and exchanging its products in a free market, its social structure will incorporate unequal access to and control over productive resources. Its worldview will be one of humans over nature; its core values will support efficiency over equity; and the view that hazards and disasters are uncontrollable natural events will predominate. These structures and values will generate policies that result in differential social vulnerability to hazards and disasters based on a variety of factors including race, gender, age, ethnicity, and social class.

But to focus solely on structure and hegemony denies the power of individual and collective agents to change their interaction with the environment and the values and worldview that guide those interactions. Through concerted action in a variety of scientific disciplines, in social policy, and in hazard and disaster management, the dominant view of hazards and disasters is slowly being transformed. The application of conflict and critical theory forces attention on the role of social structure, worldview, and values on social vulnerability. The concept of sustainability forces us to consider the real costs of the inequalities and inequities that result from a worldview of humans over nature and points to the value of local knowledge in creating sustainable interactions with the environment. As Oliver-Smith notes, "In effect, if a society cannot withstand without major damage and destruction a predictable feature of its environment, that society has not developed in a sustainable way" (1996, 2). Finally, attention to agency through participatory research and planning offers the promise of empowering those who are disproportionately at risk to demand equity in mitigation and planning.

2.12 SUMMARY

Theory is critical to our scientific approach to hazards and disasters. To view hazards and disasters as extraordinary natural events or as basic features of human environmental systems is more than a matter of semantics; it represents critical choices in how we study and respond to these events that affect our environment and millions of lives every day. Disasters such as Hurricane Katrina and the La Paz flooding demonstrate that risk and vulnerability are not distributed equally within a society. Critical and conflict theory explain these inequalities and inequities as the product of social structure, worldviews, and values. Combined with systems theory, the political ecology framework provides a powerful mechanism to analyze the complex interplay of variables that result in disasters like the earthquake in Sichuan, China (2008), in which 69,000 people perished (IFRCS 2008). Adding the concept of human agency and using participatory approaches to research creates the possibility of changes in hazard and disaster planning, mitigation, and prevention that can decrease social vulnerability and promote sustainable human-environment interactions.

2.13 DISCUSSION QUESTIONS

1. Using a conflict and critical theory approach, how do the zoning policies and building codes in your local community affect social vulnerability to hazards and disasters?
2. What individuals or organizations can you identify at the local, national, and international level that have succeeded in changing worldviews and values that directly affect disaster planning and mitigation? How have they achieved these changes?
3. How do you see institutions responsible for disaster planning and mitigation responding to the use of participatory approaches to research and planning in your community? Should community members and organizations be full and equal partners? Why or why not? How do you determine who should be included and which voices should be heard?
4. Analyze media reports for a disaster or hazard. What values and worldview guide how the event is reported? What is the view of hazards and disasters they present? How might you go about informing journalists and media representatives about alternative ways of viewing these events?
5. How does the concept of sustainability challenge the view of hazards and disasters as natural events? What does it tell us about the costs of social vulnerability? What worldview of the relationship of humans to nature does it support?
6. Is protection from hazards and disasters a human right?

REFERENCES

Arcury, T. A., S. A. Quandt, and A. Dearry. 2001. Farmworker pesticide exposure and community-based participatory research: Rationale and practical applications. *Environmental Health Perspectives* 109 (3): 429–34.

Beyrer, C., S. Doocy, and C. Robinson. 2008. Cyclone Nargis: 3.2 million Burmese affected, limited humanitarian assistance poses health threat as conditions worsen. Johns Hopkins Bloomberg School of Public Health Press Release, May 13.

Birkmann, J. 2006. Measuring vulnerability to promote disaster-resilient societies: Conceptual frameworks and definitions. In *Measuring vulnerability to natural hazards: Towards disaster resilient societies,* ed. Jörn Birkmann, 9–54. Tokyo: United Nations University Press.

Boulding, K. E. 1956. General systems theory—The skeleton of science. *Management Science* 2 (3): 197–208.

Bourdieu, P. 1998. *Practical reason: On the theory of action.* Stanford, CA: Stanford University Press.

Burton, I., and R. Kates. 1964. The perception of natural hazards in resource management. *Natural Resources Journal* 3:412–14.

Chinn, M. D., and R. W. Fairlie. 2007. Determinants of the global digital divide: A cross-country analysis of computer and Internet penetration. *Oxford Economic Papers* 59 (1): 16–44.

Corburn, J. 2005. *Street science: Community knowledge and environmental health justice.* Cambridge, MA: MIT Press.

Dale, V., S. Bartell, R. Brothers, and J. Sorensen. 2004. Systems approach to environmental security. *EcoHealth* 1:119–23.

Desowitz, R. S. 1976. *New Guinea tapeworms and Jewish grandmothers.* New York: W.W. Norton & Company.

Dilley, M., R. S. Chen, U. Deichmann, A. L. Lerner-Lam, and M. Arnold. 2005. Natural disaster hotspots: A global risk analysis, synthesis report. New York: International Bank for Reconstruction and Development, The World Bank, and Columbia University. http://sedac.ciesin.columbia.edu/hazards/hotspots/synthesis-report.pdf (accessed July 20, 2008).

Elder, K., S. Xrasagar, N. Miller, S. A. Bowen, S. Glover, and C. Piper. 2007. African Americans' decisions not to evacuate New Orleans before Hurricane Katrina: A qualitative study. *AJPH* 97 (suppl 1): S124–29.

Enever, A. 2002. Fifty dead in shock Bolivian flood. *BBC News.* http://news.bbc.co.uk/2/hi/americas/1833002.stm (accessed July 10, 2008).

———. 2005. *Pathologies of power: Health, human rights, and the new war on the poor.* Berkeley, CA: University of California Press.

Flew, A., ed. consultant. 1979. *A dictionary of philosophy.* New York: St. Martin's.

Foster, H. D. 1997. *The Ozymandias principles: Thirty-one strategies for surviving change.* Victoria, BC: Southdowne Press.

Foucault, M. 1980. *Power/knowledge: Selected interviews and other writings 1972–1977.* Ed. C. Gordon. New York: Pantheon Books.

Frank, A. G. 1969. *Capitalism and underdevelopment in Latin America: Historical studies of Chile and Brazil.* New York: Monthly Review Press.

Freire, P. 1970. *Pedagogy of the oppressed,* trans. M. B. Ramos. New York: Seabury Press.

Gill, L. 2000. *Teetering on the rim: Global restructuring, daily life, and the armed retreat of the Bolivian state.* New York: Columbia University.

Gramsci, A. 1971. *Selections from the prison notebooks.* Trans. and eds. Q. Hoare and G. N. Smith. New York: International Publishers.

Harris, M. 1979. *Cultural materialism: The struggle for a science of culture.* New York: Random House.

Hayden, D. 1995. *The power of place: Urban landscapes as public history.* Cambridge, MA: MIT Press.

Hewitt, K. 1983. The idea of calamity in a technocratic age. In *Interpretations of calamity,* ed. K. Hewitt, 3–32. Boston: Allen & Unwin, Inc.

Holling, C. S., and A. D. Chambers. 1973. Resource science: The nurture of an infant. *BioScience* 23 (1): 13–20.

IFRCS (International Federation of Red Cross and Red Crescent Societies). 2008. China—Sichuan earthquake facts and figures. August 20. http://www.ifrc.org/Docs/pubs/disasters/sichuan-earthquake/ff120808.pdf (accessed November 17, 2008).

International Rivers. 2008. India. http://www.internationalrivers.org/en/south-asia/india (accessed September 22, 2008).

Israel, B. A. 2005. Community-based participatory research: Lessons learned from the centers for children's environmental health and disease prevention research. *Environmental Health Perspectives* 113 (10): 1463–71.

Kalb, D. 2000. Localizing flows: Power, paths, institutions, and networks. In *The ends of globalization: Bringing society back,* eds. D. van der Land, M. Staring, R. van Steenbergen, B. Wilterdink, and N. Kalb. Lanham, MD: Rowman and Littlefield. Quoted in T. C. Lewellen. *The anthropology of globalization: Cultural anthropology enters the 21st century* (Westport, CT: Bergin and Garvey, 2002), 8.

Kast, F. E., and J. E. Rosenzweig. 1972. General systems theory: Applications for organization and management. *The Academy of Management Journal* 15 (4): 447–65.

Khalid, F. M., ed. with J. O'Brien. 1992. *Islam and ecology*. New York: Cassell.

Kozol, J. 1991. *Savage inequalities: Children in America's schools*. New York: Crown Publishers.

Kushnick, L. 1998. Review of the Norton anthology of African American literature, the Norton companion to African American literature, and the Oxford book of the American South. *Race & Class* 39 (3): 105–108.

Lewellen, T. C. 2002. *The anthropology of globalization: Cultural anthropology enters the 21st century*. Westport, CT: Bergin and Garvey.

Marx, K. 1990 [1867]. *Capital: A critique of political economy*. Trans. B. Fowkes. New York: Penguin Books.

McEnaney, L. 2000. *Civil defense begins at home: Militarization meets everyday life in the fifties*. Princeton, NJ: Princeton University Press.

Moore, H. L., and T. Sanders. 2006. Anthropology and epistemology. In *Anthropology in theory: Issues in epistemology*, ed. H. L. Moore and T. Sanders, 1–21. Malden, MA: Blackwell Publishing.

Odum, E. P. 1964. The new ecology. *BioScience* 14 (7): 14–16.

Oliver-Smith, A. 1996. Anthropological research on hazards and disasters. *Annual Review of Anthropology* 25:303–28.

———. 1999. What is a disaster?: Anthropological perspectives on a persistent question. In *The angry earth: Disaster in anthropological perspective,* ed. A. Oliver-Smith and S. M. Hoffman, 18–34. New York: Routledge.

Perry, R. J. 2003. *Five key concepts in anthropological thinking*. Upper Saddle River, NJ: Prentice Hall.

Pielke, R. A., Jr., J. Rubiera, C. Landsea, M. L. Fernández, and R. Klein. 2003. Hurricane vulnerability in Latin America and the Caribbean: Normalized damage and loss potentials. *Natural Hazards Review* 4 (3): 101–14.

Quarentelli, E., ed. 1998. *What is a disaster?* New York: Routledge.

Rapley, J. 2004. *Globalization and inequality: Neoliberalism's downward spiral*. Boulder: Lynne Reiner Publishers.

Rodney, W. 1982. *How Europe underdeveloped Africa*. Washington, DC: Howard University Press.

Rousseau, J. 1973. A discourse on political economy. In *The social contract and the discourses,* trans. G. D. H. Cole, 128–68. London: David Campbell Publishers Ltd.

Scott, J. C. 1985. *Weapons of the weak: Everyday forms of peasant resistance*. New Haven: Yale University Press.

Shepard, P. M., M. E. Northridge, S. Prakesh, and G. Stover. 2002. Preface: Advancing environmental justice through community-based participatory research. *Environmental Health Perspectives* 110 (2): 139–40.

Steen, R. 2002. Bolivian floods kill 60, over 500 homeless. *Red Cross*. http://www.redcross.org/news/in/flood/020222boliviafloods.html (accessed July, 10, 2008).

Tauxe, C. S. 1995. Marginalizing public participation in local planning: An ethnographic account. *Journal American Planning Association* 61 (4): 471–81. Quoted in J. Corburn. *Street science: Community knowledge and environmental health justice* (Cambridge, MA: MIT Press, 2005), 147–48.

Therborn, G. 1996. Dialectics of modernity, on critical theory and the legacy of 20th century Marxism. In *A companion to social theory*, ed. B. S. Turner. Oxford: Blackwell.

Tobin, G. A., and B. E. Montz. 1997. *Natural hazards: Explanation and integration*. New York: Guilford Press.

UNICEF. 2008. At a glance: Myanmar. http://www.unicef.org/infobycountry/myanmar_statistics.html#51 (accessed November 17, 2008).

UN/ISDR. 2007. Bolivia: Flood early warning system projected for La Paz. http://www.reliefweb.int/ochaunep/edr/Boliviafloods.pdf (accessed July 10, 2008).

von Bertalanffy, L. 1950. An outline of general systems theory. *The British Journal for the Philosophy of Science* 1 (2): 134–65.

———. 1972. The history and status of general systems theory. *The Academy of Management Journal* 15 (4): 407–26.

von Braun, J., T. Teklue, and P. Webb. 1998. *Famine in Africa: Causes, responses and prevention*. Baltimore: Johns Hopkins University Press.

Walker, P. A. 2005. Political ecology: Where is the ecology? *Progress in Human Geography* 29 (1): 73–82.

Wallerstein, I. 1974. *The modern world-system: Capitalist agriculture and the origins of the European world economy in the sixteenth century.* New York: Academic Press.

Watts, M. 1983. On the poverty of theory: Natural hazards research in context. In *Interpretations of calamity,* ed. K. Hewitt, 231–62. Boston: Allen & Unwin, Inc.

Weiss, B. 2000. Rapid assessment procedures (RAP): Addressing the perceived needs of refugees and internally displaced persons through participatory learning and action. Draft report. http://www.certi.org/news_events/year1_workshop/draft(2)_072100.PDF (accessed November 16, 2008).

Wilcox, B. A., and P. Horwitz. 2005. The tsunami: Rethinking disasters. *EcoHealth* 2:89–90.

Wisner, B., P. Blaikie, and T. Cannon. 2004. *At risk: Natural hazards, people's vulnerability and disasters.* 2nd ed. London: Routledge.

Wolf, E. 1982. *Europe and the people without history.* Berkeley, CA: University of California Press.

Zaman, M. Q. 1999. Vulnerability, disaster, and survival in Bangladesh: Three case studies. In *The angry Earth: Disaster in anthropological perspective,* eds. A. Oliver-Smith and S. M. Hoffman, 192–212. New York: Routledge.

RESOURCES

National Institute of Environmental Health Science, Environmental Science, and Community-Based Participatory Research. http://www.niehs.nih.gov/research/supported/programs/justice/ (accessed November 16, 2008).

Office of the United Nations High Commissioner for Human Rights. Issues in focus: Natural disasters and internal displacement. http://www.allacademic.com//meta/p_mla_apa_research_citation/2/7/2/4/8/pages272483/p272483-1.php (accessed November 16, 2008).

Participatory Planning Monitoring and Evaluation (PPM&E). http://portals.wi.wur.nl/ppme/ (accessed November 16, 2008).

3 The Intrinsic Link of Vulnerability to Sustainable Development

Katie Oviatt and John Brett

CONTENTS

3.1 CHAPTER PURPOSE

This chapter explores a variety of perspectives around the argument that sustainable development (SD) can reduce vulnerability to natural hazards and enhance resilience among vulnerable populations to the consequences of natural hazard events. We first review the relationship between development, especially focusing on various aspects of poverty reduction, and vulnerability, followed by a discussion of the core principles of sustainable development and its promises. The concepts of sustainable development are often abstract so we introduce the sustainable livelihoods approach (SLA), which creates an explicit model and process of development, allowing planners and practitioners to identify areas of vulnerability and resiliency and to develop specific approaches for addressing vulnerabilities and enhancing resilience. This is followed by a discussion of sustainability and vulnerability, and sustainability and resiliency. We develop a detailed case example drawn from the authors' research in a rural tropical region of northern Ecuador.

3.2 OBJECTIVES

At the conclusion of this chapter, readers should be able to:

1. Understand the need for addressing "root causes" for disaster loss reduction.
2. Explain the basic elements of sustainable development and why it makes sense to integrate disaster planning/emergency management with this framework.
3. Elaborate on the explicit links among vulnerability and resilience and sustainable development, understanding how taking a sustainable development approach can increase resiliency and capacity.
4. Gain an appreciation for the sustainable livelihoods approach (SLA) and how it addresses root causes of vulnerability.

3.3 INTRODUCTION

According to Didier Cherpitel, secretary general of the International Federation of Red Cross and Red Crescent Societies (IFRC), "Disasters are first and foremost a major threat to development, and specifically to the development of the poorest and most marginalized people in the world. *Disasters seek out the poor and ensure they stay poor*" (emphasis added) (Twigg 2004, 9). This is an important sentiment; however, following the arguments on root causes and alternative perspectives on vulnerability presented in Chapter 2, it neglects an extremely important distinction: disasters do not "seek out" the poor; rather, social and political-economic processes ultimately create the conditions that preferentially expose the poor to hazards and minimize capabilities for responding to and recovering from hazard events. The cause lies only partly in the event; it is the social and political-economic conditions that often have deep historical roots and increase risk of a disaster, generally impacting subsets of the population disproportionately when a hazard event occurs.

Because the root causes of vulnerability arise primarily through inequality, power structures, worldviews, and belief systems, changing them in meaningful ways is extremely challenging. A bridge can be relatively easily repaired in the aftermath of an earthquake or can be strengthened prior to an event, but addressing poverty, gender inequality, ethnicity, etc., is significantly more complicated. Twigg (2004, 2) argues that disaster planning has too often been considered part of a humanitarian aid orientation rather than being part of overall (sustainable) development efforts. Humanitarian aid, although necessary, provides only immediate and temporary assistance after an event, but does not address root causes. This lack of integration between development and disaster planning can, and has, perpetuated an increase in disaster vulnerability. A single disaster is capable of destroying years of development work. Likewise, development projects that fail to consider disaster risk can increase both the effects and the likelihood of a disaster (UW-DMC 1997).

Unfortunately, because the political-economic and social contributors are more complex, the result can be inaction. Some might even argue that issues of vulnerability do not belong in the emergency management realm, but nothing could be further from the truth if the goal is actually disaster loss reduction. By directly incorporating disaster planning and emergency management with explicit vulnerability reduction approaches into sustainable development programs in the United States and internationally, we can potentially reduce vulnerability and enhance resilience. Sustainable development (SD), with its integration of environmental, economic, and social issues, is becoming a significant theme within discussions on disaster vulnerability reduction. There is an increasing recognition that "the social and the economic are closely linked with the environmental sphere" (Birkmann 2006, 44). These elements are intrinsically linked to reducing disaster vulnerability, and yet Birkmann (2006) argues that rarely are these frameworks used in conjunction with one another in practice, although a few examples exist (see Twigg 2004, 5; and Cannon, Twigg, and Rowell 2003 for case examples).

In this chapter, we explore how sustainable development approaches can potentially decrease vulnerability to disasters, explicitly focusing on the sustainable livelihoods approach (SLA) as a model to operationalize sustainability and vulnerability reduction. This chapter explores the direct associations between SD and vulnerability, both conceptually and through a focused review of the literature on these links. To illustrate some of these elements and processes, we present data from the lowland Ecuador community of Mondaña, which is actively developing and implementing sustainable practices. We begin with a short review of the concept and principles of SD followed by a discussion on how sustainable development, as conceptualized and practiced through SLA, can provide a model for considering both sustainable development and vulnerability reduction in the same planning processes. The steps in assessing SLA will be taken up in more detail in Chapter 14 ("Measuring and Conveying Social Vulnerability").

3.4 DEVELOPMENT AND VULNERABILITY

Around the world, a growing share of the devastation triggered by "natural" disasters stems from ecologically destructive practices and from putting ourselves in harm's way. Many ecosystems have been frayed to the point where they are no longer resilient and able to withstand natural disturbances, setting the stage for "unnatural disasters"—those made more frequent or more severe due to human actions. By degrading forests, engineering rivers, filling in wetlands, and destabilizing the climate, we are unraveling the strands of a complex ecological safety net (Abramovitz cited in UNISDR 2004, 27).

The relationship between disaster vulnerability and development is a complicated one (Figure 3.1). Disasters have often been considered deviations or interruptions from "normal" human activity or development (UNDP 2004). Within moments a hazardous event can undo years of development gains. However, it is increasingly recognized that the relationship between disasters and development

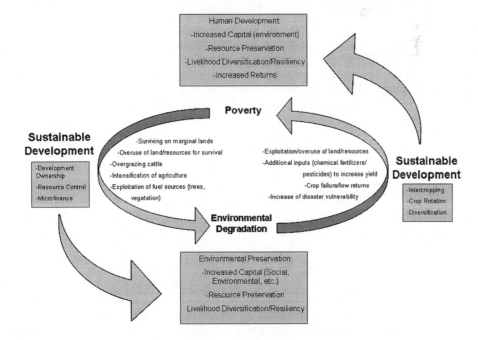

FIGURE 3.1   Relationship of development and sustainable development. *Source*: Kate Oviatt and John Brett, with permission.

is not one-way. Poorly planned, narrowly defined, and inadequately executed development practices themselves can increase the likelihood and the effects of a disaster, directly influencing and shaping disaster risk (UW-DMC 1997; UNDP 2004). It is often the consequences of development that result in environmental degradation, rapid population growth, and urbanization that create the disaster, rather than the actual hazardous event (UW-DMC 1997). The Brundtland Commission recognized this relationship, commenting eloquently on the 1980s droughts in Africa:

> The recent crisis in Africa best and most tragically illustrates the ways in which economics and ecology can interact destructively and trip into disaster. Triggered by drought, its real causes lie deeper. They are to be found in part in national policies that gave too little attention, too late, to the needs of small-holder agriculture and to the threats posed by rapidly rising populations. Their roots extend also to a global economic system that takes more out of a poor continent than it puts in. Debts that they cannot pay force African nations relying on commodity sales to overuse their fragile soils, thus turning good land to desert (Brundtland Commission 1987).

To reduce disaster vulnerability, both the impacts of natural hazards on development efforts and the impacts of development on natural hazards risk must be considered. Both loss of infrastructure, such as roads, bridges, communication lines, energy sources, etc., and loss of people, through death, disablement, and migration, can have devastating effects on local, regional, and national economic and social development (UNDP 2004). Such losses usually have a much greater net effect in less-developed countries with less robust economies. For example, in 2001, both the United States and El Salvador experienced roughly US$2 billion in losses due to damage from earthquakes. Whereas the United States could accommodate such expenses without difficulty, such a loss accounted for 15% of El Salvador's annual gross domestic product (UNDP 2004). The effects of a single hazard event can have lasting repercussions on an area by undoing years of development gains, setting back both social and economic development.

Although less obvious than a disaster's impacts on development, the impact that development can have on disaster vulnerability is extremely important. There are many ways in which development can increase disaster vulnerability, most notably by failing to incorporate hazards planning into development strategies. In areas that are prone to certain hazards, the impacts can be mitigated if the relationships between hazards, vulnerability and development are considered throughout the planning process. Development that fails to consider the hazard risk of an area can directly increase the population's vulnerability. The 1992 earthquake in Cairo, Egypt, exemplifies this. The earthquake, which measured 5.2 on the Richter scale, an event that would be considered small to moderate in the United States or Western Europe, caused massive damage with over 500 deaths and 4000 injuries. Failure to account for earthquake risk in construction of older as well as newer buildings resulted in tremendous loss of life and property damage from a relatively minor earthquake. Over 2500 houses were completely destroyed, 1087 schools had to be closed, and 5780 more required extensive repairs (UW-DMC 1997, 34). Similarly, the 2008 Sichuan, China, earthquake graphically illustrated the importance of consistent planning and policy implementation. Although official policy required building to earthquake standards, the codes were not enforced for many buildings, including schools. As a consequence, these poorly designed and built buildings collapsed in much greater numbers than those properly designed and built, disproportionately contributing to the very high death toll. Had the existing earthquake building requirements been implemented during the construction of these houses and schools, the loss of life and damage would undoubtedly have been lower.

Development increases disaster vulnerability through unintended consequences that weaken either the "ecological safety net" or a society's ability to cope with hazard events when they occur (resilience). Population growth, migration, the introduction of new production/consumption patterns, the implementation of new technologies, etc., can alter existing social and environmental relationships, which in turn can lead to either shifting, increasing, or possibly decreasing vulnerability. Such changes can result in severe environmental degradation due to increased pressure on environmental resources, the creation of more waste and pollutants, and the use of marginal lands (UW-DMC 1997). "Environmental degradation increases the intensity of natural hazards and is often the factor that transforms the hazard into a disaster" (UNISDR 2004, 27). An explicit example of these interactions can be seen on many Caribbean islands where bananas and other crops for export were planted on fertile valley bottom lands, a practice which forces subsistence farmers up onto steep slopes. Widespread forest clearing and short fallow cycles expose broad areas to erosion. When heavier than usual rains occur, extensive erosion and landslides are the inevitable result, leading to down-slope pollution, loss of life, and property damage (UN ISDR 2003). Current economic models encourage consumption and production practices that largely ignore environmental constraints, often leading to an increase in vulnerability (see section 3.5.2 for further details).

The 1984–1985 famine in Sudan is a clear example of how the unintended consequences of development increase vulnerability. Before the 1970s, Sudanese farmers largely practiced subsistence farming and employed techniques such as crop rotation, migratory grazing, and leaving land fallow to protect and maintain soil fertility. Beginning in the 1970s, industrial agricultural techniques were introduced to boost the nation's agricultural export economy. Industrial agriculture requires more land per farm than traditional agriculture and is focused on producing cash export crops rather than food for local consumption. The expansion of industrial agriculture, coupled with increasing population pressures, reduced the land available for subsistence farming and displaced many people from their land. The cumulative effect of this was an overall increase in vulnerability: social networks were destroyed, traditional farming techniques and coping mechanisms were abandoned, and those who still had land farmed it more intensively to produce enough food to survive, leading to an increase in deforestation and soil degradation. With the emphasis on cash crops, people became more vulnerable to fluctuations in market prices and job availability. Drought is a common hazard in Sudan, but the introduction of industrial agriculture reduced the effectiveness of traditional coping mechanisms and resulted in an increase of vulnerability. When the drought began in the early 1980s, traditional methods of coping proved ineffective and nearly 25,000 people were gravely affected (UW-DMC 1997, 35).

3.5 THE SUSTAINABLE DEVELOPMENT FRAMEWORK

In 1987 the United Nation's Commission on Environment and Development met to discuss issues of poverty, population growth, and environmental degradation. The commission, commonly known as the Brundtland Commission (named after the chairwoman, Gro Harlem Bruntland), recognized the importance of integrating economic development with environmental issues. The commission codified a long-standing critique that traditional approaches to development had left an "increasing number of people poor and vulnerable, while at the same time degrading the environment" (Brundtland Commission 1987). (See the Sustainable Development Timeline for the antecedent events and discussions leading up to the commission [International Institute for Sustainable Development 2007].)

The Brundtland Commission emphasized the concept of sustainable development as a way to bridge the gap between economic development and the environment. The commission recognized that development and the environment are tightly linked; development orientations and practices that erode environmental resources will ultimately undermine and inhibit economic development (Brundtland Commission 1987).

The commission defined sustainable development as

> development that can meet the needs of the present without compromising the ability of future generations to meet their own needs (Brundtland Commission 1987).

The sustainable development orientation seeks to improve people's quality of life without undermining the environmental resource base. It considers longer-term ramifications of development and practices in such a way that the natural resource base is preserved for future generations. In various ways, practitioners consider environmental, economic, and social factors (Kates, Parris, and Leiserowitz 2005; Kates et al. 2001). The challenge of sustainable development is to understand how these three components, the "sustainability triad," interact and affect one another through development, and to consider each in development planning.

3.5.1 ENVIRONMENT

It was felt that the sky was so vast and clear that nothing could ever change its colour, our rivers so big and their water so plentiful that no amount of human activity could ever change their quality, and there were trees and natural forests so plentiful that we will never finish them. ... Today we should know better.
                       —**Hon. Victoria Chitepo, Minister of Natural Resources and Tourism, Government of
                            Zimbabwe on the Industrial Revolution (Brundtland Commision 1987)**

The primary foundation for sustainable development is the recognition that human social and economic activities are tightly linked to the environment. Maintaining the "resilience and robustness of biological and physical systems" is a central component of sustainable development (Rogers, Jalal, and Boyd 2006, 23). Current economic practices favor wasteful consumption and production patterns, resulting in loss of environmental diversity and economic production potential. Environmental degradation is occurring on an unprecedented global scale; some estimate that the Brazilian rainforest is being deforested at a rate of four football fields a minute, a rate that is equal to 5760 football fields a day. Industrial agriculture practices reduce the amount of arable land through soil erosion and land degradation. Global climate change, exacerbated by human economic activity, is significantly affecting ecosystems throughout the world (Horrigan, Lawrence, and Walker 2002; Raskin et al. 1998; NRDC 2000). While ultimate outcomes are unknowable, a range of dramatic impacts on human populations and global ecosystems is likely if the intimate relationships of environmental, economic, and social well-being are not adequately addressed.

Lasting and stable social and economic development requires reframing the use of environmental resources and services in terms of long-term use versus immediate consumption. Environmental sustainability means that resources are not depleted beyond their ability to regenerate (Brundtland Commission 1987). Diverse biological systems, clean air and water, and productive soil are all limited resources upon which human well-being depends. Environmental, or ecosystem, service is an emerging economic consideration regarding environmental sustainability where natural processes, that in many cases literally make life possible, are attributed an explicit value, examples of which include the production of soil (upon which all agriculture depends), the hydrologic cycle that provides regular supplies of fresh water, and the dilution and breakdown of many toxic substances. Efforts to place a value on these ecosystem services have demonstrated that if we had to pay for them, the costs would be astronomical, lending weight to the argument that it is better to preserve the function of these ecosystem services than to have to replace them (Constanza et al. 1997). Approaches to begin acknowledging ecosystem services include clean, renewable energy sources, the production and consumption of durable, nontoxic materials, and sustainable agricultural.

3.5.2 ECONOMIC FACTORS

The Brundtland definition stresses meeting the needs of the present as an essential element of sustainable development. This involves improving living standards for people throughout the world. Despite significant improvements in global food production, education, and overall health, populations worldwide still suffer from crushing poverty. Roughly 20% of the world's population (1.3 billion people) lives in extreme poverty, defined by the World Bank as living on US$1 or less a day.

People experiencing this extreme degree of poverty are chronically malnourished, lack safe drinking water and sanitation, cannot afford education for their children, and lack access to basic health care (Sachs 2005a). An additional three billion people, roughly half of the world's population, live in moderate poverty, defined as living off merely US$2 or less a day (Rogers, Jalal, and Boyd 2006). Under these conditions basic needs are barely met.

Addressing the income gap is a central social justice component in the sustainable development argument. Additionally, poverty has important implications for environmental resource use. Approximately 700 million people live in ecologically fragile environments (IDL Group 2008). Faced with limited economic opportunities, overexploitation of environmental resources is often necessary for basic survival (Rogers, Jalal, and Boyd 2006). Such exploitation of already degraded and at-risk environments keeps populations impoverished through consumption of vital resources needed for basic survival. Poverty and environmental degradation create a complex cycle, making both poverty alleviation and environmental protection difficult. Thus, improving living standards is requisite for successful sustainable development, which can only occur by increasing the availability of essential needs such as food, water, sanitation, health care, and education (World Bank Development Web 2001).

Although it is the cornerstone to SD, the full integration of environmental and economic considerations issues is extremely challenging. Critics contend that economic interests are inherently at odds with environmental interests. Current economic development models are based on assumptions of continuous growth and ever-increasing consumption, largely ignoring environmental limitations (Osorio, Lobato, and del Castillo 2005).

Given that the current economic approaches are not sustainable, how are economic issues to be incorporated into sustainable development? Here it is important to distinguish between economic growth and economic development. Daly notes, "When something grows it gets bigger. When something develops it transforms into something different. The earth ecosystem develops (evolves), but does not grow. … [T]he economy must eventually stop growing, but can continue to develop" (Daly 1993). Continual economic growth is an impossibility considering inherent environmental limitations. However, the economy can continue to develop, to change. One of the challenges of sustainable development is to foster this development and change by designing and implementing innovative economic practices that are consistent with environmental and social goals. It is into this conundrum that Paul Hawken, Amory Lovins, and Hunter Lovins stepped in the late 1990s with their concept of "natural capitalism." They argue that four interlocking business principles can create financially profitable and ecologically sustainable business: (1) dramatically increase the productivity of natural resources, (2) shift to biologically inspired production models, (3) move to solutions-based business model, and (4) reinvest in natural capital. They argue that adopting "some very simple changes to the way we run our businesses can yield startling benefits for today's shareholders and for future generations" (Lovins, Lovins, and Hawken 1999, 146). (See also Hawken, Lovins, and Lovins [1999] for an extended treatment of the concept.)

Sustainable economic practices consider both social and environmental issues. They enhance the welfare of individuals while simultaneously considering environmental resource limitations. Ideally sustainable economic practices incorporate the regenerative capacity of natural resources, and do not use more resources or create more waste than can be renewed or assimilated by the environment (Rogers, Jalal, and Boyd 2006). Pollution can be reduced by producing and selling goods locally. Goods can be produced that are durable, repairable, recyclable, or biodegradable, thus reducing unnecessary waste. Through improvements in technology, efficiency, and resource management, economic practices can be made more sustainable. In addition to environmental concerns, sustainable economic practices consider social ramifications and strive to improve human well-being.

Making business decisions and changes that bring an enterprise in line with available environmental resources must make good "business sense" if it is to occur in a highly competitive international business climate. While "greening" a business or manufacturing process may be the "right thing to do," few enterprises can justify major capital outlays without concomitant increases in efficiency and capacity. As research and practice advance, it is becoming increasingly clear that building green is only marginally more expensive than standard approaches when long-term cost savings are factored in.

3.5.3 SOCIAL FACTORS

While economic and environmental factors are obvious concerns in any consideration of sustainable development, social conditions are no less important. A population that is inadequately nourished, that does not have access to basic health care and clean water, or lacks educational resources is constrained in its ability to develop viable livelihoods that would reduce vulnerability to environmental shocks and increase its resilience when confronted with a hazard event. Beyond merely meeting the basic needs of people, many practitioners of sustainable development place significant emphasis on issues of equity, participation, empowerment, and cultural preservation (Kates, Parris, and Leiserowitz 2005). Quality of life requires that more than just basic survival needs be met; people deserve to preserve their cultural identity and be part of the process of their development (Brundtland Commission 1987).

One of the primary social concerns of sustainable development is equity. Equity is considered in terms of both intra- and intergenerational equity. Intragenerational equity, as indicated by the Brundtland's definition, is "meeting the needs of the present" (Brundtland Commission 1987). As discussed within section 3.5.2 on economic factors, there exists an enormous gap between the rich and the poor of this world. The basic needs of many people are simply not being met, while others live extravagantly luxurious lifestyles. Nearly one billion people lack access to clean drinking water; a child in a developing country is over 13 times more likely to die before the age of five than a child in a developed country; malnutrition is rising globally, and now affects nearly one billion people (Food and Agriculture Organization 2008; United Nations 2008). Addressing such disparities is imperative, as "everyone has the right to a standard of living adequate for health and well-being," including food, clothing, housing, and medical care, according to the United Nations Universal Declaration of Human Rights (United Nations 2008 [1948]). Furthermore, as previously discussed, poverty and environmental degradation are often related. Thus, addressing poverty is a requisite part of sustainable development.

Similarly, intergenerational equity requires that the development of the current generation be practiced in a way that does not compromise "the ability of future generations to meet their own needs" (Brundtland Commission 1987). This concept is founded on the belief that current populations have an obligation to maintain the well-being of the environment for future generations. Our actions today should not negatively influence the welfare of future generations. Thus, preserving environmental resources is of chief importance for intergenerational equity. "[E]nvironmental quality is not something that can be swapped for other goods without a loss of welfare" (Beder 2000). Meeting the needs of both the present generations and those to come is fundamental to sustainable development.

Gender and gender equity have long been recognized as central components in any consideration of sustainable development, beginning with explicit statements in the Brundtland report and reinforced in each of the subsequent efforts. The importance of gender and gender relations lies in the fact that men and women have different relationships to livelihoods, the environment, and the economy. Women in most societies have primary responsibility for the household and are generally the most direct link between the household and the broader environment, whether in rural or urban areas; limits on access to water, education, health care, and food often fall heaviest on women and children. A failure to examine and understand these relationships necessarily means a failure to involve the majority of the population in development efforts (women and children). A major focus on women and sustainable development has been central to discussion of sustainable development for decades and much has been accomplished, but much more remains (Dankelman 2004).

3.5.4 POST-BRUNDTLAND

Since the Brundtland Commission in 1987, sustainable development has emerged as a widely held paradigm shift and is a major concern of nongovernmental organizations (NGOs), development organizations, governments, and communities throughout the world. In the years since the Brundtland Commission, the core concepts of sustainable development have remained relatively unchanged, but significant effort has been devoted to identifying specific meanings and mechanisms for implementation at local, regional, and global levels.

In 1992, people from 178 countries gathered in Rio de Janeiro, Brazil, for the United Nations Conference on Environment and Development (UNCED). Also known as the Earth Summit, this conference was hailed as the largest international conference ever held (Reid 1995). The focus of the Earth Summit was to develop agreements and plans on addressing issues such as climate change and conservation of biodiversity. One of the central documents to emerge from the Rio conference was Agenda 21 (United Nations 2005a). Basically a plan of action for sustainable development, Agenda 21 develops four primary points: social and economic development, conservation and management of resources for development, strengthening the roles of major groups involved in sustainable development, and the means of implementation (Reid 1995). It discusses specific actions for implementing the sustainable use of natural resources and provides concrete measures for confronting poverty, population growth, and destructive environmental practices (Sitarz 1993), and so has become one of the leading documents regarding sustainable development.

Ten years after the Earth Summit in Rio, world leaders and NGOs met again for the World Summit on Sustainable Development in Johannesburg, South Africa, to discuss both the successes and failures since Rio, and to refine and redefine plans of action. During this conference, commonly called the Johannesburg Summit, a new document called the Plan of Implementation was written, which provided specific commitments regarding issues such as water, sanitation, energy, health, agriculture, and biodiversity (Middleton and O'Keefe 2003; United Nations 2005b). Although frustration surrounded the lack of progress since Rio, the Johannesburg Summit reaffirmed the principles of the original Earth Summit and supported the further implementation of Agenda 21 (United Nations 2002).

In 2000, world leaders met at the United Nations Millennium Summit and defined the Millennium Development Goals (MDGs). The underlying rationale of the MDGs is to provide an agreed-upon blueprint on how to proceed in addressing the needs of the world's poorest populations. This broad consensus was made concrete through the UN Millennium Project, published in 2005 (Sachs 2005b), which took the broad framework and broke it into operational goals and recommendations around which specific plans and targets could be built. The first seven goals aim at a monumental decrease in poverty, disease, and environmental degradation, all of which contribute to vulnerability, while simultaneously calling for significant improvements in education and gender equality by the year 2015. The eighth goal is significant in that it requires a partnership between developed and developing nations, and demands commitment from developed nations to assist developing countries in their struggles (Sachs 2005a). Through goal 7 (ensure environmental sustainability), target 9 of the UN Millennium Project, sustainable development is linked directly with the other goals and targets by "[i]ntegrat[ing] the principles of sustainable development into country policies and programs and revers[ing] the loss of environmental resources" (Sachs 2005b). Adequate food, water, shelter, health care, and education are basic to development and are essential in any sustainable development effort. A healthy and educated population will be more productive and more able to invest in environmental considerations.

3.5.5 THE PROMISE AND SHORTCOMINGS/LIMITATIONS OF SUSTAINABLE DEVELOPMENT

The integration of the social, economic, and environmental factors is what differentiates sustainable development from previous development approaches. Common development practices have focused primarily on economic development, assuming social and environmental problems will be addressed when a certain level of economic development has been reached. Furthermore, as identified by the Brundtland Commission and subsequent research and practice, the processes of economic development often have negative social and environmental effects. In contrast, sustainable development seeks to maximize economic gains in relation to social and environmental concerns. Sustainable approaches seek to synthesize the three areas and find solutions that are environmentally, economically, and socially viable.

Although it is the most cited and widely known definition of sustainable development, the Brundtland Commission definition has shortcomings. A primary criticism of this definition is its ambiguity, only partially addressed in subsequent efforts. How does sustainable development actually integrate development and the environment? Critics claim that such vagueness enables current consumption-oriented development, which is inherently at odds with environmental protection, to continue under the guise of sustainability (Jabareen 2008; Osorio, Lobato, and del Castillo 2005). Furthermore, the vague use of the word "needs" is problematic. What are needs? Are needs merely basic food, water, and shelter, the things indispensable for survival? What about education, health care, cultural identity, security, and quality of life? Are these needs or wants? Moreover, who gets to define needs? Another criticism of sustainable development is that it is a Western approach, and that it is Westerners who define and guide the process (Osorio, Lobato, and del Castillo 2005). These issues have been partly addressed through the Millennium Development Goals process.

3.6 SUSTAINABLE LIVELIHOODS APPROACH

An alternative approach that integrates sustainability and development and addresses some of the limitations inherent in global definitions and approaches advocated by the Brundtland Commission, Rio, and Johannesburg summits is the sustainable livelihoods approach (SLA) and related approaches (DFID 1999; Ashley and Carney 1999; Carney 2002; Frankenberger et al. 2002). The SLA offers a less abstract, more practical framework for understanding development and sustainability at the local level. Its primary goal is poverty reduction, which it tackles through regional, people-centered, and participatory means. A livelihood is defined as "the capabilities, assets (both material and social), and activities required for a means of living," and is considered sustainable when "it can cope with and recover from stresses and shocks and maintain or enhance its capabilities and assets both now and in the future without undermining the natural resource base" (DFID 1999).

More concrete and process oriented than the more abstract definitions of sustainable development, the SLA explicitly accepts the triad of social, economic, and environment factors, but places people and their livelihoods as the essential outcomes of development processes. It recognizes that the need for a secure and sustainable livelihood is a central priority for most individuals, and anchors development projects in the day-to-day reality of local populations and their environmental context (Carney 2002).

The "translation" of the sustainability triad developed through the Bruntland Commission Report in the sustainable livelihoods approach is achieved through an exploration of five primary assets to which people have access (Figure 3.2). Through the planning process these assets are evaluated and developed to reduce their vulnerability and increase livelihood security. These assets are defined as different kinds of "capital": human, social, physical, financial, and natural (DFID 1999). Similar to the triad concept of sustainable development, these capitals represent the environmental, economic, and social factors that affect people's livelihood security.

3.6.1 SUSTAINABLE LIVELIHOODS APPROACH ASSETS DEFINED

Much less ambiguous than the definition of sustainable development, the SLA clearly identifies its main objective as poverty reduction. As SLA is necessarily local, or at most regional, it is important to acknowledge that it does not replace broader-scale planning efforts that are likely more

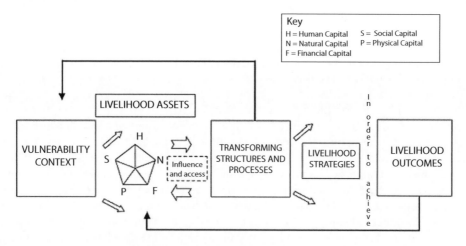

FIGURE 3.2 Sustainable livelihoods. *Source*: DFID 1999.

quantitative and macro-level (e.g., Estrategia Andina para la Prevención y Atención de Desatres 2008). Furthermore, by placing people at the center of development, the sustainable livelihoods approach focuses on understanding what most directly impacts local populations. When the needs, perspectives, and strengths of local communities are understood and given priority, poverty reduction initiatives become more compatible with local strategies, and will be more effective (DFID 1999). Participatory approaches identify local priorities and strategies, putting control of development into the hands of the people, rather than outsiders. The types of capital are defined as

- *Human capital*: The skills, knowledge, ability to labor, and good health that enable people to achieve their livelihood objectives.
- *Social capital*: The social networks, group membership, and relationships upon which people can draw.
- *Physical capital*: The basic infrastructure needed to support a viable livelihood, including affordable transportation, adequate shelter, clean water supply, and adequate sanitation.
- *Financial capital*: The financial resources people can access, including cash, livestock, income, pensions, and remittances.
- *Natural capital*: The natural resource base from which people derive their livelihoods, and which provide basic environmental services such as water and air purification, erosion protection, and hazard defense (DFID 1999).

3.6.2 SUSTAINABLE LIVELIHOODS AND VULNERABILITY

The sustainable livelihoods approach integrated with the vulnerability paradigm provides a comprehensive process for reducing vulnerability and ultimately decreasing loss. Where the "vulnerability approach" drives the orientation of this volume, we are talking in this chapter about what could be called a "resiliency approach" (Folke et al. 2002). The vulnerability approach acknowledges that political-economic, historic, and social factors make certain individuals, populations, or segments of populations more vulnerable to hazard events; these people then disproportionately suffer the consequences of disasters. For example, Blaikie at al. (1994) state,

> The essence of the vulnerability approach is to investigate the role of social, economic, and political relations in the creation of hazardous situations in a specific place. It also investigates the social distribution of risk in that place (that is: which social groups are more or less at risk to one or another of an array of hazards).

Furthermore, quoting Blaikie,

> Some groups in society are more prone than others to damage, loss, and suffering in the context of differing hazards. Key characteristics of these variations of impact include class, caste, ethnicity, gender, disability, age, or seniority (Blaikie et al. 1994, 9).

In current thinking, taking these factors into account is necessary for disaster loss reduction. Thus, considering vulnerability to hazard risk in the context of sustainable livelihoods development projects offers a greater opportunity to tackle the difficult challenges of broader social, political-economic, and historical forces. A failure to acknowledge these factors at the local level during a planning effort potentially loses important opportunities for change, decreases the impact of interventions, or puts the project at risk. Additionally, there may be opportunities to reduce vulnerability and enhance resiliency at the macro level, if attention is paid to the possibility in planning process.

Instead of just acknowledging "root causes," coupling an SLA with community vulnerability assessment (CVA) truly attends to them by enhancing livelihoods, reducing vulnerability, and increasing resiliency. "Of particular importance is the idea of a 'chain of causation' that goes from 'root causes' through 'dynamic pressures' in the production of 'unsafe conditions'" (Blaikie et al. 1994; Wisner, Blaikie, and Cannon 2004). This "chain of causation" analysis process is much the same as the ecological modeling proposed in sustainable livelihood approaches, and so could be easily adapted to consider livelihoods as a component of this chain of causation analysis (for more on a similar approach see Kohler, Jülich, and Bloemertz 2004). Instead of simply asking, "What can be done?" in the context of reducing vulnerability to a particular hazard or set of hazards, with SLA we can begin to ask, "What can be done?" in the context of sustainable development efforts to address the kinds of factors that put populations, or segments of populations, at greater risk in the first place. In the context of comprehensive planning and the systems theory modeling that underlies both emerging disaster planning approaches and the sustainable livelihoods approach, it could be possible to address both issues at once, realizing benefits for both livelihoods and vulnerability reduction. Increasing livelihood options, almost by definition, should lead to reduced vulnerability and enhanced resiliency, while on the other hand working to reduce vulnerability should enhance livelihood opportunities, if for no other reason than the reduction of loss through various natural phenomena.

The central connection between SLA and CVA concerns the factors that make households, segments of populations, or regions vulnerable to income shocks (threats to livelihoods), which are strikingly similar to ones that place them at higher risk to natural hazard events. It is the constellation of natural, socioeconomic, and political forces that limit livelihoods, thus decreasing resilience while increasing vulnerability (see Chapter 14, section 14.5.3, for a further discussion of SLA and vulnerability assessment).

3.7   SUSTAINABILITY AND RESILIENCY

Recognizing that it is often inappropriate, inadequate, or misguided development activities that create vulnerability to disasters, much can be gained by incorporating risk and disaster considerations into comprehensive development planning. Consideration of the relationships between development and hazards can help identify possible interactions among development plans and existing risks and vulnerabilities. Sustainable development is increasingly recognized as an important perspective in disaster research and planning (Birkman 2006; UNISDR 2004). As opposed to traditional development, the more holistic framework of sustainable development considers the relationship between environmental, economic, and social issues. By understanding these relationships, and by identifying the best use of available connections, sustainability can contribute to a reduction of disaster vulnerability (UNISDR 2004).

In this section, resiliency and vulnerability are considered as opposite poles of a spectrum with an inverse relationship (Folke et al. 2002). Sustainable development acts as the "slider" or the motive

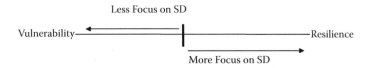

FIGURE 3.3 Relationship of vulnerability, resilience, and sustainability. *Source*: Kate Oviatt and John Brett, with permission.

force that moves a population from more vulnerable to more resilient (Figure 3.3). As in the SLA, sustainable development and vulnerability reduction do not have particular end points; rather, they are processes over time that enhance resiliency and reduce vulnerability. While this is conceptually obvious, in practice it is, of course, much more difficult.

Environmental degradation can significantly influence disaster vulnerability because a weakened environment is much more susceptible to disasters. The short term, "one way" use of natural resources characteristic of much market-oriented development frequently exacerbates risk and heightens vulnerabilities. A central tenet of sustainable development holds that development initiatives must operate within environmental limits. This ensures that resources are not used beyond their capacity to regenerate, thus providing longer-term economic benefits, and maintaining hazard protections and buffering capacities that come from an intact natural environment. Sustainable use of natural resources "will increase the resilience of communities to disasters by reversing current trends of environmental degradation" (UNISDR 2003, 9).

In much of the developing world, careful consideration of land use strategies are especially important in sustainable development to help lower disaster vulnerability. The growing demand for food, timber, and other resources has placed increased pressure on the earth's ecosystems. Land that has been overworked, through intensive agriculture, deforestation, and other forms of resource exploitation, is more prone to erosion, desertification, and landslides (Raskin et al. 1998). An important consideration in any sustainable development process is to avoid romantic engagement with some mythic past where everyone had enough to eat, was happy, and suffered less. Equally, pie-in-the-sky schemes on "saving the planet" are of little value. The central consideration in sustainable development is maximization of social and economic output while minimizing negative environmental consequences that increase vulnerability over the long term. This holistic approach to planning requires a change in focus for planning. There can be, for example, little argument that agricultural intensification is inevitable given population increases and rising incomes internationally (wealthier people consume more food resources than poorer ones). Conventional agricultural intensification considers available markets, necessary agricultural inputs, highest producing varieties, land ownership that inhibits intensification, and related factors with the aim of maximum return relative to inputs. The focus is nearly always on near-term benefits of increased production and income. The wider perspective of sustainable development considers all of these same factors but in the context of social and environmental outcomes with the aim of long-term benefits across the economic, social, and environmental spectrum. SD does not preclude using particular agricultural methods of intensification (e.g., improved seed varieties, fertilizers, tractors, etc.). Rather, what it does is weigh those against the desired longer-term outcomes.

While the consequences of ecological practices are perhaps the easiest to see, social and economic aspects of development play an equally important role in reducing vulnerability. Economic practices that encourage environmental and social welfare can potentially decrease disaster vulnerability by creating more diverse opportunities for populations in disaster prone regions. The practice of mixed-cropping is not only environmentally beneficial, but can also enhance household income security in at least two ways: First, it decreases household agricultural expenses by reducing the need for expensive chemical pesticides and fertilizers, enabling farmers to grow more of their own food as part of an integrated, mixed use "agroecological system." Second, growing multiple crops helps protect against major losses due to fluctuations in international market prices (Horrigan,

Lawrence, and Walker 2002; Twigg 2004). If the market value of one crop (e.g., coffee, cacao) decreases, farmers who practice mono-cropping will experience more severe economic losses than those who rely on a mixture of crops.

Fair trade practices can also decrease disaster vulnerability through income enhancement by offering prices that more accurately reflect the underlying labor inputs. Offering prices above minimum market rates seeks to empower all partners involved (UNDP 2004). Despite market fluctuations in the value of agricultural products, primary producers receive a superior price. Access to increased and more stable income can help decrease disaster vulnerability. Fair trade efforts also often try to identify value added processes that can further increase local income (e.g., selling processed cacao paste vs. the raw beans). Beyond economic benefits, fair trade promotes "collaborative decision-making and the setting aside of resources [for] enhancing social development or ecological protection" (UNDP 2004, 68). Such broad-based empowerment can increase the ability to withstand and respond to disasters.

Education and empowerment are elements of sustainable development, and are also important for reducing vulnerability. An educated population has a wider range of income generation options and has a wider exposure to the world outside their home community, and is thus better able to understand both the risks and vulnerabilities they face, and their options for addressing them. Empowerment though community participation has become a focus for sustainable development, and is increasingly being recognized as an important element for vulnerability reduction (Twigg 2004). Planning for both development and disasters has traditionally been a top-down approach, generally lacking locally relevant information about the context as residents understand it. Community-based planning efforts are increasingly being utilized as a way to gain a thorough and more accurate understanding of the situation at the local level. Local talent, abilities, and resources are used and communities become engaged participants rather than passive recipients of development (UW-DMC 1997). A more educated and empowered population will likely be able to cope with a disaster more effectively. Thus, these two elements are important for both sustainable development and disaster vulnerability reduction.

3.8   SUSTAINABLE DEVELOPMENT AND VULNERABILITY: THE CASE OF MONDAÑA, ECUADOR

Many of the abstract concepts discussed above can be illustrated through a case example using findings from research conducted by the authors in a lowland tropical region of northern Ecuador around the rural town of Mondaña, on the Napo River roughly 70 km south of the Colombian border. The focus of the research is sustainable development and health, conducted in the context of a multi-year field school through the Departments of Anthropology and Health & Behavioral Sciences, University of Colorado Denver.

3.8.1   POVERTY IN THE MONDAÑA AREA

Mondaña, like much of tropical America, is characterized by poverty and relative lack of opportunity. The Napo River basin is one of the primary oil producing regions in Ecuador, providing limited opportunities to local populations for unskilled labor jobs. The majority of the population relies on agriculture, working as laborers on large farms, or producing subsistence crops, and cacao and coffee for sale in international markets. Prices and production for coffee and cacao fluctuate annually, sometimes dramatically, resulting in very uneven income and uncertainty.

Tropical soils typically have low levels of nutrients and so tend to be relatively unproductive over the long term or require intensive and expensive agricultural inputs (fertilizer, pesticides) to maintain the production cycle. Most people in the area live on 5-hectare plots granted to them by the government beginning in the 1970s. Five hectares was deemed adequate for subsistence and cash crop production with an initial emphasis on coffee. While coffee prices were maintained at relatively high levels through international price agreements, those largely ended in the mid 1990s, drastically reducing cash income and imperiling already fragile livelihoods. As prices fell, people planted more and more coffee in an effort to maintain income, meaning less and less land was available for subsistence crops. In consequence people had to buy more produce and staples from markets than before, further reducing available cash. People also turned to "wildcat" logging, taking out high value trees from the forest, receiving $10 for logs that have a value of thousands of dollars on the international markets. This destabilizes forest resources as much of this illegal harvesting is from public lands.

3.8.2 Education and Practice at Colegio Técnico Yachana

One of the central components in sustainable development in the Mondaña region is an innovative educational program being developed by the Yachana Foundation. The Colegio Técnico Yachana (CTY) is a private not-for-profit high school dedicated to creating sustainable livelihoods through innovative, quality education that seeks to provide students with a range of skills usable in the regional economy. As a technical high school the curriculum is a mix of academic and practice-based education broadly focused on sustainable agriculture, micro-enterprise, and eco-tourism. The goal is to provide students with knowledge and a range of practical and leadership skills that will facilitate their becoming the center of an emerging sustainable economy in the region.

An important aspect of the overall training program at the CTY is the diffusion of what students learn in school throughout the region. The school is residential, meaning students come from a wide area. One of their requirements when they are visiting their home communities is to create demonstration agricultural projects to diffuse knowledge across the region.

3.8.3 Sustainable Agriculture

A major effort on the part of CTY faculty and students is the development and testing of a sustainable agriculture system for the region. The sustainable agriculture effort has three major goals: (1) produce food for students and teachers at the CTY; (2) produce food products for sale in the local markets and to the nearby Yachana Lodge; (3) serve as a testing and demonstration project on what is possible in the region. Collectively, these goals are designed to enhance agricultural and livelihood sustainability, thereby reducing vulnerability to economic shocks and environmental hazards. Practices put into place and resulting findings include using a mixed cropping approach (Figure 3.4), which takes advantage of different plant habits, allowing more production in same area for roughly the same amount of work. Because different crops mature at different times, it is possible, for example, to plant corn (maize), manioc, and bananas/plantains, which begin yielding at about 4 months (corn), continuing with manioc at about 9 months, followed by plantain, which matures in 18 months and continues for several years.

Using a system of crop rotation allows repeated harvests from the same land before requiring a fallow (rest) period. Most tropical soils require a fallow period every few years, which allows them to recover soil nutrients lost to crop growth, but if crops are carefully rotated through fields, soil fertility can be maintained for longer periods. Crops that use large quantities of nitrogen can be rotated with crops that use more potassium and crops that replace soil nitrogen (legumes). Tropical soils do not contain many nutrients and generally have a very poor structure. In order to maintain fertility and improve structure for gardening and agriculture, organic matter through composting can be highly beneficial (Figure 3.5) The CTY has created a composting operation that uses all of the organic material produced by the kitchens at the lodge and at the school. This compost is added to raised beds created for intensive vegetable production. Intensive production of vegetables through raised beds can yield large quantities of fresh produce, which reduces the amount of imported fresh vegetables local populations need to buy and with the potential of producing surpluses for sale.

FIGURE 3.4   Sustainable practices: mixed planting of plantains, cassava, and maize in Mandaña, Ecuador. *Source*: Photo by John Brett, with permission.

A very important aspect of reducing vulnerability to natural hazards is planting according to the landscape. Local knowledge of soils, flood conditions, and wet and dry seasons are well established and can be used to reduce vulnerability. A 10-meter buffer of trees next to the river slows annual flood waters while allowing the accumulation of high quality soil over fields next to the river. Planting of certain tree crops that can better withstand annual flooding near the river allows for production in an area otherwise at risk from flooding hazard. While flooding can be damaging to crops and farmsteads near the river, it also brings important nutrients to area soils. The intercropping of annual crops (e.g., pineapple, maize) between flood-tolerant tree crops in riverside fields takes advantage of annual soil renewal.

FIGURE 3.5 Sustainable practices: composting in Mandaña, Ecuador. *Source*: Photo by John Brett, with permission.

Tree crops (cacao, coffee) are planted to mimic forest structure with an understory of commercial crops (e.g., ginger), and an overstory to provide shade, restore soil nutrients, and provide fruit. If the overstory trees are leguminous, they add nitrogen to the soil, reducing the need for fertilizer. The use of a variety of plants in the same area reduces insect damage and disease incidence because plant diversity creates a less ideal environment for insect and disease pests. This in turn reduces the need for pesticides, thus reducing costs and potential environmental damages.

Much feed for farm animals is produced locally, reducing the need to spend scarce cash on imported feed. Chickens (for eggs and meat), pigs, and tilapia (a tropical fish well adapted to farm production) can be incorporated into a comprehensive production system. A variety of crops are easily grown that can provide much of the feed for local animals, and animal waste in turn can be incorporated into the composting program.

3.8.4 FAIR TRADE CACAO PROJECTS

Cacao, the primary raw ingredient for chocolate, is native to tropical South America and so is well adapted to and grows well in these conditions. Among the problems in growing primary agricultural products is that they are subject to tremendous price fluctuations according to world markets. Even under the best of circumstances, the prices paid are generally very low, dramatically limiting income relative to labor input. One of the major international efforts directed toward social and economic sustainability is the fair trade movement where people are paid a higher than market price for their agricultural products. This generally allows growers to produce a higher quality product through organic production, and in many cases to create value-added products (locally packaged coffee, processed chocolate, etc.) that are less susceptible to price fluctuations on international markets. Beginning in the late 1990s, the US–Ecuadorian nongovernmental organization FUNEDESIN (now the Yachana Foundation) began organizing cacao growers into cooperatives, offering technical assistance to improve quality and yield (improved varieties and production processes). As quality increased and many farms became organic, FUNEDESIN was able to begin a fair trade program, thus reinforcing the value of producing a superior crop. While their price also fluctuates, it is

**BOX 3.1   HURRICANE MITCH, SUSTAINABILITY,
AND DISASTER VULNERABILITY**

Hurricane Mitch provided an excellent example of how environmentally sustainable practices can lower disaster vulnerability. In 1998 Hurricane Mitch devastated the countries of Nicaragua, Honduras, and Guatemala, causing massive landslides and flooding. Over 10,000 people died, nearly 20,000 people were missing, and 2.5 million required emergency aid (Twigg 2004). After the event, members of the Farmer to Farmer network, a grassroots sustainable agricultural movement, noticed that the hurricane had varying effects on "conventional" farms and "agroecological" farms. Conventional farms were farms that employed standard agricultural methods. They practiced clear-cutting and burning of fields before planting, and planted over very wide areas. They used high levels of chemical fertilizers, pesticides, herbicides, and hybrid seeds. In contrast, agroecological farms used much more ecologically oriented methods that were designed with sustainability in mind. Between crop cycles they planted cover crops to protect soil quality and prevent erosion. They practiced integrated pest management, which involves a variety of strategies to lower insect damage, and used organic fertilizers. Such practices mimicked the local ecology, thus encouraging resource conservation and regeneration (Twigg 2004; World Neighbors 2000).

To understand the varying effects the hurricane had on these two different types of farms, the members from the Farmer to Farmer network conducted research in collaboration with the NGO World Neighbors. Comparing variations in topsoil depth, moisture content, and surface erosion, their study found that the farms using sustainable methods fared better than the conventional farms. Plots that had been sustainably farmed retained 28%–38% more topsoil than conventional farms, had 3%–15% more soil moisture, lost 18% less arable land to landslides, and had a 49% lower incidence of landslides (Twigg 2004; Holt-Giménez 2001; World Neighbors 2001). Soil erosion was much greater on conventional farms, with agroecological farms suffering 58% less surface erosion in Honduras, 70% less in Nicaragua, and an astounding 99% less in Guatemala (World Neighbors 2000).

Although damage from Hurricane Mitch was widespread and inevitable, the Farmer to Farmer and World Neighbor study clearly shows how the use of sustainable methods can decrease disaster vulnerability. Those whose losses were fewer were almost by definition more resilient. Relatively intact agricultural resources allow for more rapid replanting and return to productivity, thus requiring less "disaster aid" over a shorter period of time.

generally about 15% above international prices, reflecting the higher quality product. It is important to note these are not "subsidies" in any sense, but higher prices paid for higher quality products.

This "package" of educational and agricultural activities is beginning to create a more stable, ecologically sound economy in the region, thus reducing vulnerability and enhancing resilience. (For another example, see Box 3.1). By developing systems of sustainable agriculture through an innovative education program that takes advantage of tropical conditions while working to accommodate to the limitations inherent in the region, crops will be at less risk from natural events (especially heavy rains and flooding), agriculture outputs will increase in yield and quality, and incomes will rise. Creating a cadre of well-educated young people with job skills applicable to the local economy creates opportunities that reduce the need for young people to migrate to urban areas in search of work. Having a motivated, skilled workforce with training as micro-entrepreneurs, ecotourism and sustainable agriculture has the potential to develop the local economy in ways that no single intervention can. Similarly, the requirement that students apply what they learn in school in their home communities diffuses the core knowledge throughout the region, thus increasing the impact to a much larger area than the immediate surrounding community.

3.9 SUMMARY

After more than 20 years since the Brundtland Commission published its report, nearly half of humanity lives in significant poverty (<US$2 a day), the global population is an astonishing 6.5 billion and growing, and environmental emergencies range from tropical forest destruction and air pollution to worldwide climate change (Rogers et al. 2002; UNFPA 2005). In this context, disasters appear ever more devastating, with damage and death largely attributable to development factors, rather than an increase in hazard events (Hurricane Katrina [2005], recent earthquakes Pakistan, Turkey, China [2008], Indian Ocean Tsunami [2004], and Typhoon Nargis in Myanmar [2008]). In the face of these seemingly insurmountable problems, the necessity for merging sustainable practices with vulnerability reduction efforts is arguably more important than ever.

3.10 DISCUSSION QUESTIONS

1. What is the sustainability triad and why is it so difficult to achieve?
2. Choosing specific cases for analysis, discuss how sustainable development interrelates with vulnerability?
3. What is the sustainable livelihoods approach? How does it interact with the vulnerability paradigm?
4. How might attending to root causes reduce vulnerability to disasters?

REFERENCES

Ashley, C. and D. Carney. 1999. Sustainable livelihoods: Lessons from early experience. UK Department for International Development, London.

Beder, S. 2000. Costing the earth: Equity, sustainable development and environmental economics. *New Zealand Journal of Environmental Law* 4: 227–43.

Birkmann, J. ed. 2006. *Measuring vulnerability to natural hazards: Toward disaster resilient societies.* New York: United Nationals University Press.

Blaikie, P., T. Cannon, I. Davis, and B. Wisner. 1994. *At risk: Natural hazards, people's vulnerability and disasters.* London: Routledge.

Brundtland Commission (The World Commission on Environment and Development). 1987. *Our common future.* New York: Oxford University Press.

Cannon, T., J. Twigg, and J. Rowell. 2003. Social vulnerability, sustainable livelihoods and disasters. Report to DFID, Conflict and Humanitarian Assistance Department (CHAD) and Sustainable Livelihoods Support Office. Livelihoods and Institutions Group, Natural Resources Institute, Department of International Development, University of Greenwich, UK. (pp. 1–63). http://www.proventionconsortium.org/themes/default/pdfs/CRA/DFIDSocialvulnerability.pdf; www.livelihoods.org/info/docs/vulnerability.doc (accessed October 30, 2008).

Carney, D. 2002. Sustainable livelihood approaches: Progress and possibilities for change. UK Department for International Development, London.

Chambers, R., and G. Conway. 1991. Sustainable rural livelihoods: Practical concepts for the 21st century. Institute of Development Studies discussion paper 296.

Costanza, R., R. d'Arge, R. de Groot, S. Farber, M. Grasso, B. Hannon, K. Limburg, S. Naeem, R. V. O'Neill, J. Paruelo, R. G. Raskin, P. Sutton, and M. van den Belt. 1997. The value of the world's ecosystem services and natural capital. *Nature* 387 (15): 253–60.

Daly, H. E. 1993. Sustainable growth: An impossible theorem. In *Valuing the earth: Economics, ecology, ethics*, eds. H. E. Daly and K. N. Townsend, 267–73. Cambridge: MIT Press.

Dankelman, I. 2004. *Women and the environment.* United Nations Environment Program, Policy Series.

DFID (Department for International Development). 1999. *Sustainable livelihoods guidance sheets.* London: Department for International Development.

Estrategia Andina para la Prevención y Atención de Desatres. 2008. UNDP. Electronic document. http://obd.descentralizacion.gov.bo/index.php?option=com_remository&Itemid=86&func=fileinfo&id=19 (accessed October 8, 2008).

Folke, C., S. Carpenter, T. Elmqvist, L. Gunderson, C. S. Holling, B. Walker, J. Bengtsson, F. Berkes, J. Colding, K. Danell, M. Falkenmark, L. Gordon, R. Kasperson, N. Kautsky, A. Kinzig, S. Levin, K.-G. Mäler, F. Moberg, L. Ohlsson, P. Olsson, E. Ostrom, W. Reid, J. Rockström, H. Savenije, and U. Svedin. 2002. Resilience and sustainable development: Building adaptive capacity in a world of transformations. Scientific background paper on resilience for the process of the World Summit on sustainable development on behalf of the Environmental Advisory Council to the Swedish Government. http://www.resalliance.org/files/1144440669_resilience_and_sustainable_development.pdf (accessed October 8, 2008).

Food and Agriculture Organization. 2008. Hunger on the Rise. September 18. http://www.fao.org/newsroom/en/news/2008/1000923/index.html (accessed October 8, 2008).

Frankenberger, T., K. Luther, J. Becht, and M. K. McCaston. 2002. *Household livelihood security assessments: A toolkit for practitioners.* United States: CARE.

Hawken, P., A. B. Lovins, and L. H. Lovins. 1999. *Natural capitalism: Creating the next industrial revolution.* Boston: Little-Brown.

Holt-Giménez, E. 2002. *Measuring farmers' agroecological resistance to Hurricane Mitch in Central America: Participatory action research for sustainable agricultural development.* London: International Institute for Environment and Development.

Horrigan, L., R. S. Lawrence, and P. Walker. 2002. How sustainable agriculture can address the environmental and human health harms of industrial agriculture. *Environmental Health Perspectives* 110 (5): 445–56.

IDL Group. 2008. http://www.theidlgroup.com/portfolios/environment-natural-resources.html (accessed May 11, 2009).

International Institute for Sustainable Development. 2007. The sustainable development timeline—2007. http://www.iisd.org/publications/pub.aspx?pno=894 (accessed November 2008).

Jabareen, Y. 2008. A new conceptual framework for sustainable development. *Environment, Development, and Sustainability* 10: 179–92.

Kates, R., T. M. Parris, and A. A. Leiserowitz. 2005. What is sustainable development? Goals, indicators, values, and practice. *Environment* 47 (3): 8–21.

Kates, R. W., W. C. Clark, R. Corell, J. M. Hall, C. C. Jaeger, I. Lowe, J. J. McCarthy, H. J. Schellnhuber, B. Bolin, N. M. Dickson, S. Faucheux, G. C. Gallopin, A. Grübler, B. Huntley, J. Jäger, N. S. Jodha, R. E. Kasperson, A. Mabogunje, P. Matson, H. Mooney, B. Moore III, T. O'Riordan, and U. Svedin. 2001. Environment and development: Sustainability science. *Science* 292 (5517): 641–42.

Kohler, A., S. Jülich, and L. Bloemertz. 2004. Guidelines: Risk analysis—a basis for disaster risk management. Deutsche Gesellschaft für Technische Zusammenarbeit (GTZ). http://www.proventionconsortium.org/themes/default/pdfs/CRA/GTZ2004_meth.pdf (accessed October 8, 2008).

Lovins, A. B., L. H. Lovins, and P. Hawken. 1999. A road map for natural capitalism. *Harvard Business Review* May–June.

Middleton, N., and P. O'Keefe. 2003. *Rio plus ten: Politics, poverty and the environment.* Ann Arbor: University of Michigan Press.

NRDC (Natural Resources Defense Council). 2008. Global warming basics. http://www.nrdc.org/globalWarming/f101.asp (accessed October 8, 2008).

Osorio, L. A. R., M. O. Lobato, and X. Á. del Castillo. 2005. Debates on sustainable development: Towards a holistic view of reality. *Environment, Development and Sustainability* 7 (4): 501–18.

Raskin, P., G. Gallopin, P. Gutman, A. Hammond, and R. Swart. 1998. Bending the curve: Toward global sustainability. Report to Global Scenario Group. Stockholm Environment Institute, PoleStar Series Report no. 8.

Reid, D. 1995. *Sustainable development: An introductory guide.* London: Earthscan Publications Ltd.

Rogers, P. P., K. F. Jalal, and J. A. Boyd. 2006. *An introduction to sustainable development.* Cambridge, Massachusetts: Harvard University Press.

Sachs, J. 2005a. *The end of poverty: Economic possibilities for our time.* New York: Penguin Press.

———. 2005b. Investing in development: A practical plan to achieve the Millennium Development Goals. http://www.unmillenniumproject.org/reports/fullreport.htm (accessed October 8, 2008).

Sitarz, D. 1993. *Agenda 21: The earth summit strategy to save our planet.* Boulder: Earthpress.

Twigg, J. 2004. Disaster risk reduction: Mitigation and preparedness in development and emergency planning. *Humanitarian Practice Network, Good Practice Review*, no. 9.

UNDP (United Nations Development Programme). 2004. *Reducing disaster risk: A challenge for development.* United Nations Development Programme, Bureau for Crisis Prevention and Recovery.

UNFPA (United Nations Population Fund). 2008. http://www.unfpa.org/pds/trends.htm (accessed May 11, 2009).

UNISDR (United Nations International Strategy for Disaster Reduction). 2003. *Disaster reduction and sustainable development: Understanding the links between vulnerability and risks to disasters related to development and environment*. Geneva, Switzerland: UNISDR.

———. 2004. *Living with risk: A global review of disaster reduction initiatives*. Geneva, Switzerland: UNISDR.

United Nations. 2002. *Report of the world summit on sustainable development*. New York: United Nations.

———. 2005a. Agenda 21. http://www.un.org/esa/sustdev/documents/agenda21/index.htm (accessed November 9, 2008).

———. 2005b. Johannesburg Plan of Implementation. http://www.un.org/esa/sustdev/documents/WSSD_POI_PD/English/POIToc.htm (accessed November 9, 2008).

———. 2008. Millennium Development Goals. http://www.un.org/millenniumgoals/index.shtml (accessed October 8, 2008).

———. 2008 (1948). Universal Declaration of Human Rights. http://www.un.org/Overview/rights.html (accessed October 8, 2008).

UW-DMC (University of Wisconsin–Disaster Management Center). 1997. *Disasters and development, study guide and course text*. Madison, WI: University of Wisconsin–Disaster Management Center.

Wisner, B., P. Blaikie, and T. Cannon. 2004. *At risk: Natural hazards, people's vulnerability and disasters*, 2nd ed. London: Routledge.

World Bank Development Web. 2001. What is sustainable development? http://worldbank.org/depweb/english/sd.html (accessed August 20, 2008).

World Neighbors. 2000. Reasons for resiliency: Toward a sustainable recovery after Hurricane Mitch. Research Report, World Neighbors, Oklahoma, USA. http://www.wn.org/Mitch.pdf (accessed October 20, 2008).

RESOURCES

Chiwaka, E., and R. Yates. Participatory vulnerability analysis: A step–by–step guide for field staff. 2005. http://www.proventionconsortium.org/themes/default/pdfs/CRA/PVA_ActionAid2005.pdf (accessed November 15, 2008).

International Federation of Red Cross and Red Crescent Societies (IFRC). What is VCA? An introduction to vulnerability and capacity assessment. Geneva, Switzerland: IFRC. 2006. http://www.ifrc.org/Docs/pubs/disasters/resources/preparing-disasters/vca/whats-vca-en.pdf (accessed October 30, 2008).

International Federation of Red Cross and Red Crescent Societies (IFRC). How to do a VCA: A practical step-by-step guide for Red Cross Red Crescent staff and volunteers. 2007. http://www.proventionconsortium.org/themes/default/pdfs/CRA/how-to-do-VCA-en_meth.pdf (accessed October 30, 2008).

Rodríguez, H., and J. Barnshaw. The social construction of disasters: From heat waves to worst-case scenarios. *Contemporary Sociology* 35, no. 3 (2006): 218–23.

Rodríguez, H., and D. Marks. Disasters, vulnerability, and governmental response: Where (how) have we gone so wrong? *Corporate Finance Review* 10, no. 6 (2006): 5–14.

Rodríquez, H., and C. N. Russell. Understanding disasters: Vulnerability, sustainable development, and resiliency. In *Public sociologies reader*, eds. J. R. Blau and K. E. I. Smith. Lanham MD: Rowman & Littlefield Publishing, 2006.

Sustainable Livelihoods. http://www.livelihoods.org/ (accessed August 20, 2008). This is a very rich site. While the roots of the sustainable livelihoods approach go back to the early 1990s (Chambers and Conway 1991), DFID and other organizations (CARE, OXFAM, UNDP) took the central concepts and tried, tested, and revised the approach over a number of years. Much of that information is at this very in-depth site.

Section II

Socially Vulnerable Groups

4 Class

Nicole Dash, Brenda G. McCoy, and Alison Herring

CONTENTS

4.1 CHAPTER PURPOSE

One of the key features of social life in the United States is the stratification of the population into different social classes. Social class includes both material resources such as money and nonmaterial resources such as power. This chapter first explains the complex nature of social class, particularly in the United States, and then illustrates how social class impacts disaster vulnerability.

4.2 OBJECTIVES

As a result of reading this chapter, the reader should be able to

1. Define "social class" and describe its component attributes.
2. Describe the demographic distribution of social class in the United States.
3. Explain how "social class" structures people's life chances and opportunities.

4. Articulate the connections between social class and disaster vulnerability.
5. Apply your knowledge of social class and vulnerability to both disaster case studies and disaster scenarios.
6. Describe ways in which emergency management can help to address vulnerability issues associated with lower class status.

4.3   INTRODUCTION

The ability to prepare for and respond to a disaster or hazardous event and to reduce its impact on our lives in the aftermath depends largely on our personal resources. Common wisdom (and lots of research) suggests that people who have more resources are better prepared, respond more quickly, and recover faster than those who have less. But exactly what resources are we talking about? Obviously, money is important and often the only thing considered. However, economic assets are not the only ones that people draw from—especially in the face of a catastrophic event. A person's knowledge, skill, and social connections may be just as important as money, or even more important, depending on the crisis. Taken as a whole, these resources are considered a person's social class. This chapter describes the types of resources most commonly employed by individuals who must cope with a disaster and how these resources are distributed among individuals in the United States. It also specifically examines how inadequate resources may result in increased vulnerability of individuals and communities in the face of disaster and the ways emergency management operations can reduce the harm to these segments of the population.

4.4   UNDERSTANDING SOCIAL CLASS

Social scientists use the concept of *social class* to categorize people who share similar levels of economic and social resources. People within a specific social class tend to have similar amounts of financial resources, education, and opportunities for achievement. Beyond this rather general definition, there is not a lot of consensus among scholars about how to group people into distinctive class groups. Some scholars break the upper class into two separate groups—the super rich and the rich—and use one broad category for the middle class and two other categories for the working class and the poor (e.g., Beeghley 2008). Others may have only one category for the upper class, and multiple categories for the middle class, working class, and the poor (e.g., Gilbert 2002). The grouping process is far more complex than it might seem at first glance. Exploring the problems associated with grouping people into classes is beyond the scope of this chapter. Instead, our consideration will focus on the fundamental attributes of social class, including wealth, income, education, occupation, and social networks; the interconnected nature of these resources; and how these resources are distributed across the U.S. population.

Researchers typically determine a person's social class or *socioeconomic status* (SES) based on the amount of the person's income, level of education, and type of occupation. These three indicators are obviously related. For example, having a good education generally is an important factor in securing a good job, and a good job, in turn, typically helps an individual earn more money. Likewise, having money clearly can help a person get a good education and a satisfying lifestyle during the process.

Max Weber (1922) was perhaps the first to describe the interplay between financial resources and lifestyle. For Weber, *life style* is a product of a person's *life chances* and *life conduct*. Life style is the visible element of social class and involves a person's patterns of expenditure and consumption like the size and location of a home or the make and model of his or her car. Life chances refer to the probability that a person will be able to get what he or she wants and needs in life and are largely, but not exclusively, rooted in financial strength. Life conduct involves personal choice and self-direction. In other words, Weber believed that an individual's lifestyle was a product of both life chances and life conduct.

For the majority of the U.S. population, social class is ascribed at birth, yet part of what we learn as the "American dream" is that class systems are fluid and that with enough work (and perhaps a little luck) we can achieve a higher-class position. While most believe this, there is, in actuality, very little class movement in the United States. However, unlike other class-based structures, such as the caste system in India, there are opportunities for class mobility even though the likelihood is low. Social class affects our life styles, the life chances we have available to us, and the neighborhoods we live in. (For an illustration of these effects, see Box 4.1) It affects the education we receive, the schools we attend, and our occupations. Yet for as important as class is in our lives, we tend to have very unrealistic beliefs regarding the class system.

Despite what people believe, however, the United States has the highest "wealth gap" and poverty rates in all industrialized countries. In other words, the difference between those at the top and those at the bottom is quite large. One way economists measure this gap is by comparing a CEO's pay to that of an average worker. In 1999 in the United States, CEOs earned 458 times as much as the average worker (Lanzarotta 2001). And if this difference was not enough to illustrate the significant gap between the "haves" and "have nots," the poverty rate in the United States also emphasizes class differences. In 2006, according to the U.S. Census, the poverty rate in the United States was 13.3%, up from 12.4% in 2000. Considering the economic crisis currently in the United States, the rate will probably continue to rise. And yet, as the average American struggles with mortgage payments and rising debt, those at the top continue to gain wealth, income, occupational prestige, and important social networks. The next section explains these critical components of social class, and highlights their demographic distribution in the United States.

4.5 DEMOGRAPHIC OVERVIEW—SOCIAL CLASS IN THE UNITED STATES

Considering the complicated nature of social class, it is not surprising that most Americans do not understand its meaning or its nature. The following sections will do two things. First, they will explain the different components of social class such as wealth, income, and education, and second, they will describe and analyze the demographic patterns in the United States.

4.5.1 WEALTH

Wealth is a major determinant of social class and a person's life chances. Its importance to the concept of social class has long been recognized. Karl Marx (1845/1978) first distinguished between capitalists—the holders of sufficient wealth to own the means of production—and workers, who had only their labor to sell. Since Marx, numerous social theorists have refined the notion of social class to include other dimensions, but all have maintained that wealth is a crucial component.

Even though wealth is an important feature of social class, it is often ignored in social research. This is partly because of the difficulty in computing a person's wealth. For example, many people own assets such as stocks that may change value frequently. Wealth may also be ignored by researchers because of commonly held beliefs about class in America. Dalton Conley (1999) asserts that the three indicators of socioeconomic status—income, education, and occupation—"fit nicely with our image of a fair society in which everyone gets a fair shot to succeed according to his or her own merits" (p. 14). Other scholars echo this argument and have suggested that many Americans believe that the United States is fundamentally a classless society or that the United States is a nation largely composed of a middle class (Mantsios 2001). The resistance to examining wealth, however, does not eliminate its importance.

Wealth consists of the total *net value* of a person's cash assets and savings, housing and other real estate, investments, the surrender value of life insurance, and pension plans. In short, wealth consists of any financial resources that a person has left over after all his or her debts have been paid. The computation of wealth does not include income, which will be discussed in detail in a later section. People who have earnings from jobs and/or investments that exceed their requirements for

BOX 4.1   STRATIFIED MONOPOLY

Often it is hard for us to put ourselves in the position of others. In other words, in the context of social class, those of us who are middle or upper class find it difficult to imagine what it is like to be lower or working class, and those of us who grew up lower or working class find it hard to imagine what it is like to be middle or upper class. Huge stereotypes about the poor, in particular, exist in American society. Some of these stereotypes include "poor people choose to be poor and if they only worked harder they would be able to earn more money." These stereotypes are based on the idea that everyone has the same opportunity to pull himself up by his bootstraps, and those who do not make it simply are not working hard enough. The reality, however, is very different. As the beginning of this chapter emphasized, class mobility is very challenging. If you are not born into a certain level of wealth, the playing field is unequal from the beginning. Your life chances are affected and part of those chances is opportunity. The game Monopoly can be used to illustrate the effects of a class-based stratification system. Using a regular Monopoly board we can slightly change the rules to illustrate the challenges to class mobility. To play, you and five others should set up the game as instructed in the game directions. However, do not hand out any starting money. Once the game is ready, each person playing should count off from one to six. Once each player has a starting number, distribute money based on the following: player 1, $900; player 2, $3750; player 3, $0; player 4, $1500; player 5, $200; and player 6, $450. Play the game for an hour just as the directions describe except for one deviation. The rules indicate that a person who has no money is bankrupt, and no longer plays the game. In this version, instead of being bankrupt, players who lose all their money (or start with none) may borrow from other players willing to make loans. Players should keep track of how much money is owed to them or they owe others. As you will see when playing the game, those who started with little money find it challenging to increase their wealth. They may have some limited cash in their hands, but they are less likely to own property, homes, and hotels. What you will find, however, is that it is not impossible for players to improve their position, but it is difficult. Seeing how difficult this is, imagine how challenging it would be if you changed a few parameters. What if someone had no source of income so that every time they passed go, they received nothing? What if you designated some people as female, and those who were female received less money each time they passed go? As you can imagine, modeling different life experiences in the game would lead to different results. But what becomes clear during this exercise is that when the playing field from the beginning is not equal, those with fewer resources struggle more. Before you put the game away, make sure you record the following information for each player so we can use it later: cash on hand, how much money is owed to you, how much money you owe others, value of properties you own, and value of houses and hotels.

Without access to resources, individuals, families, and even poor communities face challenges when trying to mitigate against and prepare for hazardous events. Poor health and education levels also play a critical role in hazard outcomes by rendering some more vulnerable than others. The key to this vulnerability is the structural impediment resulting from limited access to material and nonmaterial resources. Likewise, poor communities have similar issues with increased vulnerability as they also, as a community, have less ability to garner resources needed for disaster.

everyday living may choose to build their personal wealth by saving or investing a portion of their income. However, simply having a sizeable income is no guarantee that a person will accumulate wealth. Moreover, income streams may be interrupted through the loss of a job or by making a poor investment decision. In contrast, wealth is a pool of stored financial value that is available when needed and thus is a good reflection of material comfort and well-being.

Contrary to what many Americans believe, wealth is far from evenly distributed in the United States and most of it is *not* controlled by a large middle class. In 2004, over a third (34.3%) of the wealth in the United States was concentrated in the hands of 1% of the most affluent Americans (Wolff 2007). Moreover, the wealthiest 10% in the country controlled almost three quarters (71.2%) of the country's total wealth. Viewed from another perspective, the richest 1% of Americans had more wealth at their disposal (34.3%) than the bottom 90% (29.8%).

Actual dollar figures provide greater insight into the financial reserves that may or may not be available to many Americans. In 2004, 17% of the population possessed no wealth at all or their debts exceeded the total value of their assets. Just over one out of four Americans (26.8%) possessed less than $5000 in wealth, and 30% had less than $10,000 (Wolff 2007).

In the United States in 2004, median wealth was $77,900. In other words, half of the population had more than $77,900 in financial resources or wealth and half had less. For many Americans, equity in their homes constitutes a considerable portion of their wealth. Home equity, while valuable, is *illiquid*. It takes longer to convert it to cash than other types of investments. Homeowners must either wait until their home is sold to gain access to their net equity, or go through the process of securing a home equity loan. Because of this, Edward Wolff (2007) argues that a computation of wealth that excludes net equity in an owner-occupied house more accurately reflects financial resources that are immediately available for expenditure. By his estimation, median non-home wealth in the United States in 2004 was only $18,200.

This lopsided distribution of wealth in the United States has important implications. One of the most important is that those who are wealthy have considerable power—political and otherwise. They populate the ranks of the decision makers and shape public policy. In contrast, nearly three out of four Americans have either minimal or no personal financial reserves that they can rely on in the event of an emergency. Most people simply live from paycheck to paycheck and hope that nothing happens to disrupt their regular source of income. Unfortunately, many disasters or catastrophes destroy businesses and the jobs associated with those businesses.

4.5.2   INCOME

Income is another indicator of social class. Income typically consists of receipts in the form of salary, wages, or pension payments. It also includes earnings, if any, from investments or from other nonlabor sources such as child support, disability, and unemployment insurance. Most researchers examine *household income* rather than individual income because most people live with other earners and share their financial burdens as well as rewards. In most cases, households consist of people related by blood. However, many nonrelated people share the same residence and the expenses associated with running that household. While they may or may not share their income, researchers assume that they share similar economic circumstances. Nonfamily households accounted for 32% of all U.S. households in 2006 (U.S. Census Bureau 2007).

As with wealth, *median income* is more commonly reported by researchers than average income because of the magnitude of the difference between the lowest incomes (zero) in the United States and the very highest. In addition, because the highest earners account for a disproportionately large share of the aggregate earnings in the United States, use of average income would produce a distorted picture.

In 2006, median household income in the United States was $48,201—an increase of 0.7% over 2005, but still lower than the 1999 peak of $49,244 (U.S. Census Bureau 2007). Thus, members of the middle-ranked household in the United States would have had approximately $4000 per month

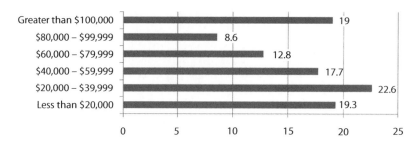

FIGURE 4.1 Percent of U.S. households by income group, 2006. *Source*: U.S. Census Bureau, 2007.

in income before payment of taxes, leaving some amount less than that to pay for housing, groceries, clothing, transportation, other necessities, and any leisure activities or nonessential items.

Median household income, like wealth but not to the same extreme, varies dramatically in the United States. In order to study income distribution, researchers first sort all the households in the United States from the highest gross earnings to the lowest. The sorted households are then divided into five equal groups, which are referred to as *quintiles*.

As is the case with wealth, most income is earned by a fairly small portion of the population. In 2006, households in the top quintile earned half (50.5%) of all personal income in America, while the top 5% made 22.3%. Households in the top quintile had earnings in excess of $97,030 annually. The second highest quintile accounted for 22.9% of the country's aggregate income with receipts of at least $60,000 per year. In other words, the top 40% of U.S. households earned nearly three out of every four dollars. In contrast, the lowest quintile garnered only 3.4% of all income and made less than $20,032 per year (U.S. Census Bureau 2007).

An examination of the percentage of households in various income groups provides another perspective on the distribution of income in America (Figure 4.1). In 2006, just less than 2% of households reported earnings in excess of $250,000 per year while 7.5% of households struggled to manage on less than $10,000 annually. Another 30% or so of American households had combined incomes ranging from $40,000 to $80,000 annually. Households in this range could be considered part of the "middle"; however, the differences in living standards among these households could be significant depending on the number and age of people in the household. Approximately 19% of American households reported income of over $100,000. Unfortunately, a near equal percentage of households had total earnings that were less than $20,000 per year.

4.5.3 Low Income and Poverty

According to the federal government, a household with four members who together earned less than $20,000 per year in 2006 was classified officially as poor (U.S. Department of Health and Human Services 2006). In that year, an individual who earned less than $9,800 annually was defined as poor, and 13.3% of all Americans fell into that category. Nearly one out of every ten (9.8%) families was considered poor (U.S. Census Bureau 2007).

Many Americans believe that the poor are people who are simply unwilling to work, or who do not work hard enough. And that may be true for some individuals. However, the majority of poor people in the United States work very hard—sometimes at more than one job. The problem is that they do not make enough money at their jobs to pay for essential goods and services. To protect workers from being exploited by their employers, the U.S. Congress passed the Fair Labor Standards Act in 1938, which banned child labor, established the 40-hour workweek, and set a minimum wage threshold. Despite its name, many workers are not covered by the provisions of this law. Regardless of the government's intentions, having a federally mandated minimum wage does not necessarily ensure a livable wage.

TABLE 4.1
Poverty Rates for 10 Major U.S. Cities with Hazard Risks in 2006

City	Poverty Rate (%)	Type of Event	City	Poverty Rate (%)	Type of Event
Brownsville, TX	40.6	Hurricanes	Memphis, TN	23.5	Earthquakes
Dallas, TX	22.1	Tornados	Miami, FL	26.9	Hurricanes
Fayetteville, AR	16.4	Tornados	North Charleston, SC	27.6	Hurricanes
Fresno, CA	22.8	Earthquakes	Oklahoma City, OK	17.1	Tornados
Los Angeles, CA	19.0	Earthquakes	Pensacola, FL	16.1[a]	Hurricanes

Source: U.S. Census Bureau, 2007.
[a] 2000 Census data; 2006 estimate not available.

In 2006, the federal minimum wage was $5.15 per hour—a rate that had remained unchanged for nearly a decade. In July 2007, the minimum wage rate was raised to $5.85 per hour and was increased again in July 2008 to $6.55 per hour (U.S. Department of Labor 2008). A person who earned minimum wage in 2006 and worked full-time made $206 per week, $824 per month, or $10,712 per year (at 52 weeks with no time off and before paying taxes). It is important to note that this person would not be considered officially poor by the federal government if he or she were single and living alone. After taxes, this single woman or man would have had approximately $23.54 per day to pay for housing, food, and other essentials. However, if this individual was a single mother supporting a child she would have qualified as poor since her yearly wages were less than $13,200—the poverty threshold for a household with two people (U.S. Department of Health and Human Services 2006). She might have had a few more after-tax dollars if she were a mom since she would have gotten another deduction and possibly other tax benefits with a child. But in neither case would she have had funds available to purchase such things as flashlights, batteries, nonperishable foods, and bottled water to prepare for a potential disaster or hazardous event. All of her income is required for day-to-day survival. In 2006, an estimated 1.7 million workers earned the minimum wage or less (U.S. Department of Labor 2007).

Neighborhoods tend to reflect the strength or weakness of the financial resources of the residents. This has important emergency planning implications. Poorer neighborhoods and communities tend to have a higher percentage of substandard housing and bad roads, more crime, fewer grocery stores and retail outlets, and less access to doctors, health care facilities, and pharmacies. These areas also typically have fewer employment opportunities, and the people who live in them tend to be more dependent on public transportation to get to work elsewhere. In 2006, many cities in the United States had poverty rates that far exceeded the national average of 13.3%. Some of these cities are considered by emergency planners to be at higher risk for some type of hazardous event (Table 4.1). Preparing for, mitigating against, and responding to disasters or hazardous events in cities or areas with large, vulnerable populations is a serious and ongoing challenge for emergency planners.

4.5.4 EDUCATION

Level of education is another major indicator of social class because it is a fairly consistent predictor of a person's earnings capability. People who have completed more formal education tend to earn more than those who have not. In 2006, the median earnings for men with a college degree ($55,446) were about 75% higher than the median income of men with only a high school diploma ($31,715) and well over double that of a high school dropout ($22,151) (Figure 4.2). The median income of women follows the same trend even though women's earnings fall significantly below

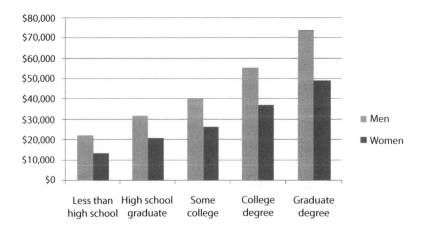

FIGURE 4.2   Median earning by level of education, 2006. (Includes both full-time and part-time workers over 25 years of age.) *Source*: U.S. Census Bureau, 2007.

men's. The disparity in income evident between women and men irrespective of education level is explained in part by the tendency of caregiving responsibilities for children, elderly parents, or sick family members to fall on women. As a result, many women work part time in order to accommodate family needs.

Examination of household income provides a slightly different perspective on the relationship between education and earnings capability. In 2006, 59% of the households with incomes of $100,000 or more had at least one household member with a college degree or higher. In contrast, only 11% of households with earnings less than $20,000 included a person with those educational credentials (U.S. Census Bureau 2007). Moreover, among the households with annual earnings of less than $20,000, educational levels were substantially lower with 13% having less than a ninth grade education, 18% having finished some high school, and only 37% having actually received a high school diploma.

Many Americans believe with good reason that getting a good education is a key to success. However, they often overlook the role that having financial resources to begin with plays in getting a good education. Numerous studies show that getting a good education is as much about opportunity and mentorship as it is about basic intelligence. For example, parents with money are able to pay to enhance their children's educational experiences and shape their children's educational choices. The children of parents with financial resources have the opportunity to study more and work less and they do not tend to be shackled with repaying student loans after graduation.

Educational attainment is also affected by structural factors such as the tendency of people to live in close proximity to others with similar economic resources. Because public schools are frequently financed with taxes based on property values, schools located in poorer areas often do not have the same resources as those located in more expensive neighborhoods. Moreover, children who live in poorer neighborhoods are often exposed to environmental hazards or have health issues that impede academic performance. For these reasons and others, many scholars believe that children from working class families are prevented from attaining levels of education that would improve their class position (Blau and Duncan 1967; Conley 1999).

Education, however, also possesses intrinsic qualities that transcend its economic value. People who have low levels of education may have lower self-esteem. They may have difficulty reading and with verbal communication, which makes it harder for them to access other resources or social assistance. It also complicates their ability to recognize health risks and follow the instructions of health care providers. Lower levels of education serve to narrow the lens through which people see their world. It constrains where and how people get information—an issue of vital importance to emergency planners.

4.5.5   OCCUPATION AND PRESTIGE

A person's occupation—another indicator of social class—is closely related to a person's level of education. Even though the U.S. Bureau of Labor Statistics classifies workers into 820 different occupations, jobs are often grouped into two broad categories: white collar and blue collar. Jobs believed to require greater skill and training and that are typically held by people with college or professional degrees are referred to as "white collar." These occupations are associated with higher levels of prestige, higher pay, and are usually conducted indoors or in more pleasant surroundings. Blue-collar jobs, in contrast, are believed to require less mental skill and tend to be more physically labor intensive.

In 2006, the largest proportion of blue-collar workers earning minimum wage or less were employed in service-related occupations—most often those associated with leisure and hospitality (U.S. Department of Labor 2007). In an effort to study the problems and challenges facing this type of worker, Barbara Ehrenreich took jobs in different parts of the country as a waitress, hotel maid, house cleaner, nursing home aide, and Wal-Mart salesperson. Her experiences are recorded in her best-selling classic, *Nickel and Dimed*, first published in 2001. Ehrenreich, who holds a PhD, reported that her first discovery was that "no job, no matter how lowly, is truly 'unskilled.' Every one of the jobs … required concentration, and most demanded that [she] master new terms, new tools, and new skills …" (p. 193). She also noted that the often physically demanding nature of these jobs—some even damaging—rarely provided health insurance benefits.

Ehrenreich made other important observations about minimum- and low-wage work. Compared to white-collar workers, low-wage blue-collar workers tend to have very little control over their schedule or how they work. They are more closely monitored than white-collar workers and must be more careful about taking breaks and making or receiving personal phone calls. Low-wage workers often find it much more difficult to take time off from work for personal appointments such as meeting with a child's teacher or going to the doctor. Many of these workers have more than one job in order to make enough money to meet expenses. In 2006, 7.6 million Americans—5.3% of all employed workers—held more than one job (U.S. Department of Labor 2007). While many white-collar workers work longer than 40-hour weeks, they are often able to afford help at home in the form of a housekeeper or lawn service. White-collar workers also have more flexibility in determining when they will work longer hours. These issues are especially pertinent for emergency planners. Many people have jobs that they feel little freedom to leave—even in the face of a pending disaster or hazardous event—because they believe that, if they elect to do so, their job is at risk. Moreover, people working long hours or two jobs may have little time to consider or prepare for a potential disaster. Unfortunately, people working long hours and earning low wages often have fewer people in their lives that they can turn to for help.

4.6   RELEVANCE

As we have seen, social class or socioeconomic status is a complicated, yet important feature of society. Our social class plays a role both on a micro (individual) level and a macro (community) level. In the following section, we will discuss some of the ways in which social class impacts our lives. What should be clear is that social class is a hindrance for those on the bottom and a great benefit for those on the top of the class hierarchy.

One of the ways that social class is important involves our connections with other people. Many social scientists refer to the interpersonal networks of family members, friends, coworkers, neighbors, and other voluntary associations as *social capital*. The term social capital implies that our social networks have economic value in addition to the emotional support, advice, companionship, and other forms of assistance we typically associate with interpersonal relationships. In fact, most people have either received material support in the form of a gift, loan, or other goods such as food from others in their network, or have rendered this type of aid to others. Moreover, assistance either to or from others may also take the form of some service that would otherwise need to be purchased such as home repair or child care.

Another way that social capital is translated into economic value involves the types of relationships that people have in their networks. For example, those individuals who have powerful contacts in the work world are often able to use those connections to find a job or to get a better job either for themselves or for someone else in their network. Similarly, people may have contacts who have political power and who are able to influence the types and amounts of governmental or other resources that are made available to a business, neighborhood, community, or city. Studies show that the size of people's social networks is positively related to their socioeconomic status. In other words, people with more money and prestige tend to have more extensive and more frequent contact with their personal networks than people who are poor (Thoits 1995). Employment status and age also affect the size of an individual's social network. People who are younger and those who are employed tend to have larger personal networks to draw support from than the unemployed or elderly.

For many, a person's spouse is considered a critical component of his or her social network, helping to provide financial, emotional, and other forms of basic assistance. Unfortunately, those most in need of the support associated with marriage are also the least likely to have it. In 2006, less than half (41%) of all households with combined earnings under $20,000 annually were family households, and among these family households, only 44% were comprised of married couples (U.S. Census Bureau 2007). However, 87% of households reporting combined incomes of $100,000 per year or higher were family households. These households were more than twice as likely to contain married couples (91%). Households with lower combined incomes also tend to have fewer members. Over half (56%) of households that reported under $20,000 per year in earnings consisted of only one person. In contrast, 55% of households with incomes of $100,000 or more annually consisted of two to three people.

People's social capital is a vital consideration for emergency planners. It affects how people get information about potential hazardous situations and how that information is perceived, since we often consult with those closest to us about important matters. Level of social capital is also reflective of the "people resources" available to an individual to prepare, respond, or attempt to recover from a disaster or hazardous event. Social capital and the other components of social class—wealth, income, education, and occupation—are inextricably linked. People with fewer of these resources are far and away more vulnerable to disasters and other hazardous events than those who possess more. More detail on this topic can be found in the next section of this chapter.

As we have seen, there is considerable variation in social class in the United States, and as a result variation in "life chances" of individuals. Social class structures people's access to life chances. The lower your social class, the more challenging life chances are to achieve (Mantsios 2001). At the same time, social class impacts the lifestyles we live. Examples of lifestyles include the types of leisure activities we engage in, the social networks we are a part of, our diet and cuisine, the type of housing we have, and the type of car we drive. In other words, social class increases or decreases the chance for individuals to experience events or circumstances that enhance quality of life (Mantsios 2001). Research has found that social class plays a significant role in health in a variety of different ways. Those with less access to wealth, for example, are more likely to have health-related issues. The barriers to maintain good health are the problem; in other words, the structures that create inequality are at fault, not the individual. Those with less access to money, for example, are more likely to be malnourished as money for food may quickly run out for poor families. In fact, according to Sullivan (2000) in a report published by the Center on Hunger and Poverty, over 15% of poor families are malnourished. For many poor children, the only consistent meals they get are those they receive as part of the free breakfast and lunch program at public schools. For those who have enough resources for some meals, these meals tend to be very high in carbohydrates since pasta and rice tend to be less expensive than fruits and vegetables. Poverty, then, may also be correlated with obesity and other conditions. And to make matters worse, over 15.8% (or about 47 million people) of Americans had no health insurance in 2006, and the likelihood of being without coverage increased as socioeconomic status decreased (DeNavas-Walt, Proctor, and Smith 2007). The health insurance crisis also goes much deeper with many middle class families reporting being under insured. As a result, many treatable health conditions such as diabetes worsen until they become acute and critical. Health care that we often take for granted, such as prenatal care, is frequently absent for the poor. The consequence of this is that the infant mortality rate for poor families is twice as high as the national average, and for families considered in extreme poverty the rate is four times the national average (Macionis 2002).

Beyond infant mortality rates being higher, members of poor families also have lower overall life expectancies than those in non-poor families (Williams 1990). This disparity exists for a variety of reasons. First, as discussed earlier, people who are poor are less likely to have health insurance, and as a result, less likely to have access to preventative medical care. In addition, when ill, they are less likely to seek treatment. Without health insurance, often illnesses accelerate to acute status. Coupled with limited access to insurance is the fact that poor families are more likely than non-poor families to live in hazardous or toxic environments (Syme and Berkman 1997). For the working poor, they often work in jobs that are more hazardous as well, and thus, their life expectancy is lower due to the more dangerous nature of their employment (Syme and Berkman 1997). The genesis of their health problems, however, is less important than the consequences of them. As we will investigate later, their ability to prepare for, respond to, and recover from disaster is compromised. Those with more wealth are more likely to have better health overall through better access to resources. These same resources impact the type and location of housing the poor can obtain.

One of the most significant consequences of social class is its impact on housing. For those with wealth or in a higher social class, access to almost any type of housing that they desire is possible. With enough money, they can buy or build homes in the best neighborhoods with the strictest safety standards. For those with little financial resources, their housing options are much more limited. Most significant is that the poor are less likely to own their own homes, and the extreme poor are more likely to live in public housing. The poor spend a greater proportion of their income on housing, thus limiting the amount of money they have for other necessities. For example, approximately 82% of poor renter households spent more than 30% of their household income on rent and utilities in 1995 (Daskal 1998, 12), and this percentage no doubt has increased as prices for oil and other commodities increased significantly in the United States during the late 1990s into the 2000s. For some, the percent of their income they spend on housing is even greater, with 60% of poor renters spending more than 50% of their household income on housing in 1995. Of those who earn more than 200% of the poverty line, only 3% spend over 50% of their income on housing (Daskal 1998). As a result, those with more income are more likely (but not guaranteed) to have more discretionary income available for other necessities and emergencies. For those who receive no subsidized housing, Daskal (1998, 2) argues that the typical poor spent about 77% of their household income on housing in 1995.

More significant is that available affordable housing for low-income renters becomes more challenging to find. In its annual report on "worst-case housing needs," the U.S. Department of Housing and Development (2005, 4) reported that "there continues to be a shortage of affordable housing that is available to very-low-income and, more significantly, extremely-low-income renters. In 2003, there were 78 rental units affordable to extremely-low-income renters for every 100 such households, but only 44 were available for these households (the remainder being occupied by higher-income households)." This lack of affordable housing is a major reason why poor often end up homeless. In addition, there is significant concern that this housing may be substandard and greatly at risk. In 1998, Daskal (1998, 22) found that approximately 14% of poor renters lived in housing with moderate or severe physical problems, while about 40% of poor homeowners lived in poor quality housing in 1995. As we will see later when we discuss vulnerability across the disaster life cycle, quality of housing plays a significant role in hazard vulnerability. The need to find affordable housing restricts housing options. When such a significant percentage of one's income is going to housing, even when safety is a goal, price dominates housing decisions. As a result, many financially marginal families and individuals live in housing that is at the greatest risk.

In addition to the challenges to find housing, social class also impacts access to and quality of education. Children from poor families are more likely than children from non-poor families to attend schools with inadequate funding (Kozol 1991). Significant consequences result from poorly funded schools. Poorly funded schools are more likely to have fewer teachers, larger class sizes, inadequate instructional materials such as books and computers, and often dangerous building structures. These same children are less likely to finish high school than non-poor families (Shanahan, Miech, and Elder 1998), and poor and working-class children are more likely to be tracked into general or vocational programs in schools, while children from higher classes are more likely to be tracked into college-preparatory programs (Oakes 1985). As a result, class becomes a vicious cycle where kids born into low income or working-class families find it difficult to improve their class position. Their opportunities, regardless of intelligence and ability, are limited because of structural impediments to success. With less education, they are more likely to have low-paying jobs with limited, if any, benefits. Thus, the system itself creates replicating channels of vulnerability by limiting opportunities to move to higher social classes where access to resources such as money and power reduces vulnerability across the disaster lifecycle (Box 4.1).

4.7 VULNERABILITY ACROSS THE DISASTER LIFE CYCLE

How does social class impact disaster vulnerability? In this section, we will examine this question by looking at how limited access to both material and nonmaterial resources affects vulnerability across the disaster life cycle. Researchers are in general agreement that the poor lose relatively more in disasters (Beatley 1989; Dash, Peacock, and Morrow 1997; Fothergill and Peek 2004; Wisner et al. 2004). The most devastating disasters in the 20th century are believed to have had the greatest impact on relatively poor populations (Beatley 1989). This is not to say that absolute dollar loss has been highest among the poor, but rather that the poor proportionately lose more during disasters, and likewise have a more challenging time recovering. In other words, the vulnerability of the poor is greater as they have less ability to withstand their losses. During Hurricane Andrew in 1992, for example, one family living on Miami Beach had $60,000 worth of damage to their home while a family in Florida City lost $40,000. On the surface, we might conclude that the home in Miami Beach had the greater loss, but in reality the impact of that loss was much less. The Miami Beach home was valued at over $1 million whereas the Florida City home was valued at only $55,000. The family in Miami Beach simply lost things like awnings or had damage to their pool, while the Florida City family lost almost their entire home. The Florida City family was displaced after the storm for over a year, while the family in Miami Beach was able to continue living in their home. So, as you can see, looking at just the absolute dollar amount of loss does not reflect the true reality of who is bearing the brunt of the cost of disaster. Nor does it reflect the challenges the poor face in all phases of disaster.

4.7.1 WARNING/EVACUATION/RESPONSE

Warning, evacuation, and response all belong to what is considered the preparedness phase of the disaster cycle. For some types of hazards such as earthquakes, there is little or no warning phase, and as a result, often few options for evacuation. Other hazards such as hurricanes often have lengthy warning phases that offer opportunities for pre-impact protective action such as evacuation. While on the surface this seems like an easy concept to understand, the reality is that warning and evacuation are complex social processes that require individuals to understand and process the information they receive. Social class impacts this process in multiple ways. Social class may impact how people understand the information they receive, whom they receive information from, and the options people have once they understand the dangers. During warnings, social class plays a role in perceptions of danger. Think of social class as a type of lens in which information is filtered. One's experiences at the bottom of the class hierarchy or at the top will impact how that information is filtered.

One of the lenses that impacts whether people recognize danger is education. Education impacts vulnerability in that those who have more exposure to education about hazards are better able to recognize danger and consequently prepare for the hazards. School systems in wealthier neighborhoods are more likely to have some educational opportunities for education about area hazards. For example, in some parts of North Texas, school children regularly attend programs that introduce them to how tornadoes are formed, and what types of things they can do when tornado warnings are issued. These children then take this information home to parents, and ultimately the household knows, generally, what to do in case a tornado is in the area. These programs are more likely to exist in middle-class and wealthy communities where the school district has financial resources for things like transportation to off-campus programs. In addition, with the emphasis of the federal government's "No Child Left Behind" educational program, where school funding is tied to student performance on standardized tests, even less school time is available to explore hazards as it takes away time from teachers' preparing students for state mandated testing. As a result, students from particularly poor school districts are even less likely to learn about earthquakes, floods, tornadoes, hurricanes, and wildfires. With less knowledge, they are less likely to perceive danger.

What is interesting is that the empirical evidence on the impact of social class is somewhat mixed, with some research finding that those with lower socioeconomic status are more likely to perceive risks while others have found little or no support for this finding (White 1974; Flynn, Slovic, and Mertz 1994). Some empirical research has found a connection between the type of employment someone has and their risk perception, with those with riskier jobs being less likely to perceive dangers related to hazards since they have to cope with dangers every day. And as we discussed earlier, people with lower SES are more likely to work in riskier jobs. Inaccurate risk perception puts people in greater danger since most people will not act on warnings, for example, without recognizing that they are in danger. As a result, those who do not perceive the danger are less likely to take preparedness measures such as gathering supplies, putting up hurricane shutters, or evacuating at-risk areas. Likewise, those who live more dangerous lives, such as the homeless, are often more likely to underestimate their risk since their everyday existence constantly requires them to negotiate dangerous situations, and as a result, they may not take warnings seriously (Mileti, Drabek, and Hass 1975). Hazard vulnerability, then, is greater since they are less likely to recognize the extraordinary dangers the hazard may pose to them or their families. However, even when those with lower socioeconomic status do recognize their risk, their options for protective action are limited. (For an illustration of these effects, see Box 4.2.)

Consider the advice that is often given by response agencies such as FEMA and the American Red Cross. Both agencies believe that households are responsible for having survival supplies (water, food, radio, flashlight, etc.) to last a family for at least three days. In other words, all of us should have these supplies on hand all the time in our "disaster" kit so that we are prepared for any type of event, whether it has a warning phase or not. While this is sound advice for the majority of Americans, it poses somewhat of a problem for those who are the most financially marginal. Think back to our discussion of housing earlier—the most extreme poor may spend up to 77% of their income on housing, leaving a relatively small amount left for transportation and food. Many of the extreme poor, in fact, do not have enough money in a month to cover all their expenses and often, as the health data indicate, the poor do not have enough money to eat. If this is the reality for some, how do we expect them to use the limited resources they have to stockpile water and food for an event that may or may not happen when right at that moment they or their children are hungry? Often the assumption is that people simply refuse to prepare themselves for hazardous events, but the reality is that many simply cannot. Their inability to have the resources needed to have supplies on hand renders them more vulnerable. The wealthy, in comparison, have the resources to invest in food and water that they may never need; the poor do not have this luxury, even if they clearly recognize the need. Similarly, lack of resources negatively impacts the poor's ability to take other protective measures such as evacuation.

Significant research has focused on understanding evacuation and evacuation decision making. In their summary of evacuation research, Sorensen and Vogt Sorensen (2006) summarize some of

BOX 4.2   STRATIFIED MONOPOLY AND DISASTER

Earlier, we played a game of stratified Monopoly where the playing field was not even for everyone in the game. After the game, you recorded how much money and assets you gained while playing the game. Take all of those assets and add them up. This is your current level of wealth. If you ended up with a negative amount, this means that you are overwhelmed with debt. Using the information you know about disaster and vulnerability, the rules outlined below, and the assets and debt you earned while playing stratified Monopoly, prepare for the following disaster. You must consider each individual and their attributes, and all individuals as a community (those playing the game with you). Discuss and outline what each individual would do and what limitations you would have. Here are some of the things you can consider: What would you need to be prepared? Would you have what you need to prepare? Would you need to evacuate? Would you be able to evacuate? Where are your children? What would you do first in this scenario? If you survived, do you believe your home would still be standing? Would you be able to live at your home? If not, where would you go? How long would it take for you to recover? What would your community look like? Would the community be the same or different 2 years post event?

RULES (the amounts here are general guidelines as the amount of money you will acquire will vary based upon how long you play the game):

The disaster happens three days before the end of the month.

- If you earned less than $450, you do not own a car.
- If you earned less than $1000, you do not own a house, you rent. Any property you own is where you would like to build a house, but you have not been able to get enough money together yet to build on it.
- If you earned less than $1600 you have no money in the bank at the end of the month. All cash goes to your daily living expenses.
- If you earned more than $650, but less than $1600, you have done no mitigation (no shutters for hurricanes, no tying down of roof, no earthquake or flood protection).
- If you have less than $250 of total assets, you are homeless.
- Ultimately, at least one person playing the game will be homeless, one or two will not have cars, and about half will be renters.

Disaster Scenario: You live in a city in the Midwest, population about 100,000. The downtown area is thriving with commercial and residential activity. Many people who live in the downtown area do not have cars because everything they need is there. There is some public transportation around the city but nothing that leaves the city. There are two major highways running through the city with many minor arteries that feed into the major highways. Few people consider the area to be at risk despite the fact that a major fault line runs through the area. Very few tremors have been experienced, and while there is some public education on the risk, it is usually focused on yearly announcements on grocery bags at one of the major food stores in the city. Earthquake drills are not routine in the school system. New, more expensive homes have some earthquake mitigation built in to the structures such as pipes and hot water heaters being secured, but older, inexpensive homes were built before mitigation measures were thought to be important. Out of the blue, the U.S. Geological Survey (USGS) issues a prediction for a major earthquake (7.0 or greater) to strike the city within the month. The suggestion from the USGS is that people begin preparations immediately by securing their homes, developing a disaster kit, and having an evacuation plan in place should there be significant damage in the area when the earthquake happens. Within a week, the city begins to feel some minor earthquake shocks. As the shocks get stronger, buildings begin to show significant signs of structural damage. Some housing in the poorer area of town begins to crumble. Not knowing what to do at this point, the mayor calls for an immediate citywide evacuation. Are you prepared? How do you get out of the city? Where will you go? After the earthquake strikes, what do you think you will find when you come back to your home? What happens then? You and your community (those playing the game with you) should work together to develop these answers. Develop a response and recovery plan for you and your community.

the key factors that have been examined in evacuation research. They conclude that overall higher socioeconomic status yields higher evacuation rates and that the empirical support for this finding is high (p. 191). Those with more resources have more options for evacuation. They are more likely to have transportation and the financial resources needed to protect themselves and their families. For example, think back to our earlier discussion of social networks. People on the upper end of the social class hierarchy are more likely to have wider social networks. As a result, middle and upper class families are more likely to have people outside of the evacuation zone with which to stay, and if not, they are more likely to have the financial means to stay at a hotel. Those who are poorer, on the other hand, are less likely to have the same options. As a result, those who are poorer are more likely to evacuate to public shelters or remain in their homes (Gladwin and Peacock 1997). The homeless have even fewer options as shelters often require identification for entrance, which the homeless often cannot provide. In addition, shelter locations are often reported through radio or television media, which are not readily available to the homeless.

In addition, renters and poor homeowners are less likely to have hazards insurance. Poor homeowners often have no or inadequate insurance covering both their home's structure and personal property; renters often have no coverage at all for the contents of their apartments. Although renter's insurance is considered affordable by many, it is often out of reach for those who are even minimally financially marginal since renter's insurance often requires adequate credit. For those who are poor or who have struggled out of poverty, their credit history is often spotty, if not worse. Without an adequate credit score, insurance underwriters often assume the individual is a risk, and will deny coverage. Thus, the poor, who cannot afford to lose and replace their belongings, are often the most exposed to losses. Similarly, homeowners face the same dangers when they are underinsured, as will be discussed later in this chapter.

4.7.2 Impacts

As discussed earlier, it is often the poor who bear the greatest costs during a disaster. While these costs may not be higher in absolute dollars, they are much higher in proportional losses. One of the reasons that the poor have a greater vulnerability to disaster impacts is their limited housing opportunities. People in the lower part of the social class hierarchy are more likely than people in the higher part of the social class hierarchy to live in substandard housing. Substandard housing includes a variety of different issues. These issues include, but are not limited, to the following: housing in bad repair; housing located in hazardous areas, but not built to building codes; manufactured housing (mobile homes); older housing that has not been retrofitted to meet newer building codes; rental housing and poorly constructed housing. Homes that are built more poorly are more likely to be damaged during disasters. Since the poor are more likely to live in this type of housing, they are more susceptible to losses. In addition, as discussed earlier, the poor are more likely to be renters, and as renters they have little, if any, control over the structural soundness of their homes. They have few options for mitigation even when they themselves are willing to invest in the cost. For example, in areas with high hurricane risks, renters are often not allowed to put up their own window protection for threatening storms since to do so would require them to drill into the building itself, which they do not own. As a result, in areas with a large number of renters, you often see most windows of multi-unit structures with taped Xs on them. The tape is believed to help during high wind events, but the reality is that the tape offers no additional protection at all.

If the poor, then, are living in more dangerous housing to start with, it is no wonder that research has found that they are more likely to have significant disaster losses (Dash, Peacock, and Morrow 1997; Perry and Mushkatel 1986; Cochrane 1975). In earthquakes, unreinforced masonry buildings are at the greatest risk, and they are most likely to be inhabited by the poor (see Fothergill and Peek 2004), and in wind events such as tornadoes and hurricanes, manufactured housing (mobile homes) are at the greatest risk. While today, new manufactured housing is built for the specific wind zone in which it will be placed, prior to 1994 wind standards were not considered in the manufacture of the units. Prior to 1976, no structural standards were in place at all. In 1976, the U.S. Housing and Urban Development Agency began to oversee the building of manufactured housing, and at that time, imposed minimum guidelines for structural soundness. However, most of the guidelines were to mitigate fire risk and not wind dangers (Dash 2005). And while it is hard to believe, older mobile homes do not leave the housing stock; instead, it appears that these units simply get sold to those who are even more financially marginal. In other words, some of the most financially vulnerable populations live in the most physically vulnerable housing. While data for the entire United States is a challenge to gather, Florida can be used as a case study. As of 2005, the state of Florida's building stock included over 300,000 pre-1976 mobile homes and in excess of 643,000 manufactured housing units built between then and the middle of 1994 (Dash 2005). In a small study of residents who live in the oldest, most vulnerable mobile homes in Florida (sample size about 500), Dash (2005) found that about 20% of those living in pre-1976 mobile homes have annual incomes of $10,000 or less, with another 32% reporting household incomes between $10,000 and $20,000. During Hurricane Andrew, out of 6600 mobile homes in south Florida before the storm, only nine remained afterward (Morrow 1997). Clearly, the poor are more vulnerable due to the type of housing they inhabit. As a result, the poor are more vulnerable to injuries and fatalities. In the 1992 Chicago heat wave, for example, the poor were more likely than the wealthy to perish from the extreme heat (Klinenberg 2003). Their health beforehand was more tenuous, thus putting them more at risk to feel the effects of the heat, and their physical locations (in urban areas where the heat concentrates, for example) were more dangerous as well.

Vulnerability, then, emerges for the poor due to the limited choices they have in housing location. Vulnerable land is increasingly used as locations to build affordable housing for lower-income families (Tierney 1989). Consequently, people in the lower half of the social class hierarchy are more likely than those in higher social classes to live on vulnerable land. This dangerous combination of socially vulnerable people on physically vulnerable land is seen when analyzing damage from Hurricane Andrew. Nearly all of the state and federal public housing in the hardest hit area of south Florida was severely damaged (Yelvington 1997), leaving many either living in damaged units without power for months or in tent cities set up by the Army. Despite the danger of mobile homes in hurricane-prone areas, FEMA's alternate solution was to move the poor into small mobile homes. While this may have been a feasible short-term solution, many, due to their poverty status or family size, ended up living in these units for years. As a result, the poor who lost everything remained at increased risk through the very policies that were being used to help them recover from the storm.

While much of the previous discussion has focused on individuals and families, it is important to note that poor communities also bear a significant burden in disaster. As discussed earlier, the poor are more likely to have limited social networks and to live geographically close in poor communities. Poor communities in larger urban ecological networks are more likely to be ignored and underserved even during periods without disaster, thus creating what some have called a "cycle of poverty" (Logan and Molotch 1987, 197). Poorer communities are more likely to have less organized local governments who, even when trying their best, do not have resources to protect their community. As a result, in addition to the damage that households in poor communities experience, the communities themselves often suffer significant damage. One of the poorest communities in the impact area of Hurricane Andrew, Florida City, not only had significant damage to its housing stock (see Box 4.3 for a case study), but all the city structures were also completely damaged. City Hall, for example, was a complete loss, and during the storm city workers who stayed in the building in order to meet community needs during the storm literally tied themselves to support columns during the storm in order to survive. The ultimate consequence, however, is that those who most need community support and assistance (the poor) are unable to receive it when the community itself loses all of its structures. Local government, then, must figure out ways for its own recovery as its residents attempt the same. In fact, it is during recovery from disaster that the most significant vulnerability of the poor surfaces.

4.7.3 SHORT- AND LONG-TERM RECOVERY

Clearly, we have seen that the poor are more vulnerable to hazards in both the preparedness/warning stage of a disaster and during impact. The reasons for this increased vulnerability lie not in any flaw of the individual or family, but rather in the systems of stratification of society that put them at greater risk. However, as challenging as it is for the poor in the first two phases of disaster, their most significant challenges appear during the recovery phase of disaster (Bolin 1986; Bolin and Bolton 1986; Bolin and Stanford 1991; Phillips 1993). In part, recovery is challenging because of the significant impacts that they experience, but more than the impacts, their vulnerability arises from social structures that make it more difficult for them to garner the necessary resources for recovery. The most major short-term recovery need for the poor is often housing. While permanent housing is the most important long-term recovery goal, temporary housing or sheltering is the most significant short-term issue. Without financial resources, the options for the poor are often limited. Renting hotel rooms requires access to credit cards with available credit as well as transportation to the site. We often forget that the poor are not likely to have credit cards or access to significant amounts of cash. Research has found that those with higher incomes were more likely to stay at hotels and motels, while those with lower incomes stayed with family (Morrow 1997). In addition, the length of time for those who stay with family is higher for the poor than others. Morrow (1997) found that the poor were three times more likely to still be staying with family three months after Hurricane Andrew than higher income groups. In some situations, few options for the poor exist, and the federal government may step in to shelter poor families. After Hurricane Andrew, the Army built tent cities to house the poor. While this was considered temporary sheltering, it lasted for over six weeks and was an important step in being able to keep families together in the area (Yelvington 1997). Without the development of the tent cities, recovery for the poor may have been even more retarded, with a high likelihood of displacement out of the south Florida area similar to that of the poor after Hurricane Katrina. As of now, how New Orleans recovers, particularly the poor, is still being written, but the process is clearly complicated with the displacement of residents throughout the United States. This displacement began when the poor were sheltered significant distances outside of the city with little opportunity to easily return. In addition, social networks during recovery are extremely important for the poor. Earlier we emphasized that the wealthy have more elaborate social networks—networks that are geographically wider and politically more powerful. For the wealthy these social networks help during all phases of a disaster. Recovery of the social networks, however, is of particular importance for the poor. Poor families use their networks for child care, food, transportation, and support. Displacement destroys these networks and makes recovery much more challenging for the poor. For those who were displaced from New Orleans during Hurricane Katrina, for example, returning to New Orleans was difficult without the support and assistance of their former social networks. Likewise, being displaced is problematic as the networks that people had relied on at home do not exist in their new towns or cities. As a result of these complicated social processes, measuring recovery is challenging as some people continue to struggle to return to their homes and a city that they believe is not getting enough resources for long-term recovery.

Indeed, it is during the long-term recovery phase that a community's ability to wield power in larger sociopolitical structures makes a significant difference in long-term recovery. As Peacock and Ragsdale (1997) point out, the recovery process requires different political structures within a community network to compete for limited recovery resources. Those "systems" that can best compete will get the most resources. For the poor, in particular, recovery is a combination of what little resources they can garner on their own, but more importantly, the resources a community receives to aid them during the process, such as grants. Communities that are well developed and wealthy with strong leadership are the communities most likely to succeed during the very competitive recovery period (Klinteberg 1979; Rubin 1985). Long-term recovery, then, is impacted by resources on both a personal level and a community level.

The case of Florida City (Box 4.3) emphasizes that community structures play a vital role in recovery processes; however, there is no doubt that adequacy of other types of resources also play a major role in recovery. Families in the lower half of the social class hierarchy have fewer internal and external resources for recovery than families in the higher social classes. As mentioned earlier when discussing preparedness, the poor are more likely than others to have substandard insurance. When they do have insurance it is often with smaller insurance agencies that are less likely to make adequate settlements (Peacock and Girard 1997). Without insurance, individuals and families must rely on their own personal resources to recovery; however, the poor are less likely to have these resources available. To complicate matters, most disaster assistance is readily available for homeowners, with renters less likely to receive aid.

As a result of limited ability to access resources, poor families recover at a slower rate than do non-poor families. For families of all social classes, the quicker they can return to permanent housing the quicker they recover. However, returning to permanent housing is particularly challenging for the poor. In a summary of housing recovery following disaster, Peacock, Dash and Zhang (2006) highlighted that housing recovery in the United States is a market-driven process, and as such, pre-disaster inequalities tend to be replicated during post-disaster recovery. Unless recovery plans give attention to the additional needs of the poor, a market-based solution, by nature, benefits those who have the power and wealth to access the resources necessary to rebuild and repair. Those with adequate resources are more quickly able to find contractors, acquire building materials, and navigate the complicated system of city/county permitting and rules. Those with fewer resources may attempt to do repairs themselves or find a less expensive contractor who may not have the same skills as those selected by those with more wealth. Thus, even with some resources, those who are poorer may find the rebuilding process lengthier. The need for long-term temporary housing, then, becomes more critical for poor homeowners, but finding permanent post-disaster housing for renters is even more of a challenge. Many of the same challenges they have finding housing in a pre-disaster context continue post-disaster. Of particular concern is that the stock of affordable permanent housing is often limited after disasters. Rent, for example, often significantly increases after a disaster as landlords attempt to benefit from the limited nondamaged housing stock. Under the best of conditions there is no surplus of housing for low-income families, and this is exacerbated in a post-disaster environment (Bolin and Stanford 1991), as the limited rental housing pool is reduced even further by landlords who choose not to rebuild or repair (Childers et al. 1998).

In addition, poor families receive less aid than non-poor families (Bolin and Stanford 1991; Phillips 1993; Dash, Peacock, and Morrow 1997), which makes recovery even more challenging considering that their own internal resources will be significantly limited. The reason for this inequality is twofold. One reason for this disparity is that low-interest loans are an important factor in family recovery after disaster, and the poor are less likely to be able to qualify for such loans (Bolin and Bolton 1986; Bolin 1986; Tierney 1989). For homeowners with no or limited insurance, the primary government form of aid is SBA loans (Peacock, Dash, and Zhang 2006). Since this is not a grant program, but rather a loan program, the application process is more complicated and

BOX 4.3   CASE STUDY: FLORIDA CITY AND HURRICANE ANDREW

Hurricane Andrew made landfall August 24, 1992, in the southernmost portion of Florida after a quick strengthening as it spun in the Atlantic basin. The storm came ashore as a category 5 hurricane with sustained winds over 145 mph and gusts over 175 mph. The winds were so severe that they blew the measuring instruments off the roof of the National Hurricane Center's building on the campus of the University of Miami. Andrew's storm track was significant for two critical reasons. First, it went south of downtown Miami, where population was denser and losses were expected to be even greater than they were. And second, the eye of the hurricane tracked near Florida City—one of the poorest incorporated cities in south Florida, if not the country. According to the 1990 U.S. Census, Florida City had a population of about 5800 with a median household income of $15,917 as compared to a U.S. median of $30,056. Thirty-seven percent of the population in 1990 fell below the poverty line compared to 13.5% in the United States as a whole. In addition, 55% of housing units were renter occupied. Clearly, Florida City was a poor community, and in the larger context of the area as a whole, it wielded very little political power as both citizens and as an incorporated community. It had a weak government that was somewhat unorganized before the storm, and even more so afterward, and as a community it had very little power in the larger county government. Using property tax data from the county, analysis showed that Florida City single-family homes lost 81% of their value as a result of the hurricane. While the dollar amount lost may not have been as significant as it was in other areas, nowhere was the proportional loss greater.

In fact, its neighboring incorporated city, Homestead, lost only 47% of its single-family housing value. But overall, Homestead was not as economically marginal as Florida City. Its median household income was higher, although lower than the United States as a whole, and its poverty rate was similarly lower. Home values, however, were over $10,000 higher, and more important, as a community Homestead wielded more power in the larger context of the county. Homestead also had a strong city government that was more organized and able to garner resources for the community. Nowhere can the effects of this been seen more then in an analysis of long-term single-family housing recovery. Florida City's single-family property values did not reach their pre-impact level until about seven to eight years after the hurricane, whereas Homestead reached pre-Andrew levels within two assessments of Hurricane Andrew, or about two years.

More significant is looking at the long-term patterns in both of these communities. The 2000 U.S. Census occurred about seven to eight years after Hurricane Andrew, and illustrates how disaster can exacerbate inequality. In 2000, Florida City's median household income actually fell to $14,923 while Homestead's increased to $26,775, and the United States as a whole increased to $41,994. Poverty rates in Florida City increased in 2000 to 43.3% while the United States as a whole fell to 12.4%. While it is hard to attribute all these negative changes to Hurricane Andrew, it is clear that the hurricane played some role. Decisions made by community leaders and the relocation of agriculture out of the area as a result of the storm all played a role in making a poor community even poorer in the wake of a major disaster (Dash and Peacock 2003).

requires a level of approval not usually necessary for grant-based programs. Applications for SBA loans are initially subjected to an income-level test, and if applicants pass this test, they are then subjected to an analysis of "ability to repay loan." As a result, loan approvals are more likely for moderate to higher income families who appear to be less of a risk. Other FEMA programs tend to only focus on short-term emergency repairs so that no further damage occurs. As a result, when poor families fail to qualify for SBA loans they often cannot repair their homes. In the end, they end up with very few options. They can try to sell their damaged home without repairs; however, if the amount they receive is lower than the amount they owe on their mortgage, they must continue to pay the difference. More often what happens is that families abandon their homes unrepaired, and those with mortgages are foreclosed upon. In addition, the state or local government may come in and secure homes that are not repaired. Once this is done homeowners are often given a period of time in which to repair the home. If it is not repaired, the state may take ownership of it. This was a significant issue after Hurricane Andrew for the poorest and hardest hit families, and continues to be an issue in the poorest areas of New Orleans after Hurricane Katrina.

Perhaps understanding the issues would be easier if we could simply argue that the poor are denied aid, such as loans, more than those who are wealthier. If all we had to consider were the complexities of post-disaster loans, then perhaps the solution to the problem would be more readily evident. The problem, however, is that the issue of aid is complicated by the fact that the poor simply apply for aid at lower rates than those who are wealthier (Dash, Peacock, and Morrow 1997).

The poor, for example, are less likely to have documentation of residence, which is required for aid. Without such documentation, they cannot apply for aid. The poor are also more likely to live "doubled up" in a house. In other words, more than one family may live in the same "house." In these cases, only one head of household may apply for aid, and as a result, an entire family may get no assistance. Although this is problematic in many disasters, FEMA rules have not changed. And as discussed earlier, most federal aid goes to homeowners over renters (Bolin and Stanford 1991), and since the poor are more likely to be renters, they are often left relying on charitable organizations for recovery assistance. Clearly, without aid the recovery process is stymied.

Social class, then, plays a significant role in generating vulnerability for those on the bottom of the social class hierarchy in each phase of the disaster cycle. Whether it is having limited resources for preparedness or more structurally dangerous housing or little political power during the recovery period, the poor disproportionately feel the effects of disaster. As individuals, they have little ability to garner the financial means necessary to withstand hazards, and ultimately, even less to recover from them. Yet, even knowing this, as a society we have yet to fully address the needs of this population. In many ways, this should not be surprising since as a society we tend to want the poor to be and stay invisible. We close our eyes to the homeless every day and fail to recognize the everyday threats the truly poor and disadvantaged face in trying to meet their material needs in a non-disaster context. Yet, when disasters strike, political leaders, in particular, continue to consider them "acts of God" or equal opportunity events, and they fail to recognize that planning for the poor before a disaster happens ultimately saves money in the long run. Disaster after disaster we see these differential impacts and effects, yet as much as we talk about "lessons learned," these lessons seem to rarely be implemented (see Box 4.2).

4.8   IMPLICATIONS FOR ACTION

While much of what we have discussed in this chapter results from structural features of society, there are some ways emergency management can address the needs of those in the lower social classes. Focusing planning on the issues outlined in this chapter is the first step in minimizing the vulnerability that the poor experience during hazardous events. Through programs focused on this population, they may be able to develop their capacity for resilience. The key when thinking about resilience for this group is to understand that this capacity will not develop without assistance. The vulnerability that exists for this group, whether in terms of health, education, housing, or disaster, in part reflects a laissez faire attitude toward the poor. As long as people believe the poor deserve to be poor or that everyone has equal opportunity, we as a society will continue to fail the groups that need our help the most. Changing attitudes, then, is the first thing that must be done to begin to address the specific needs and issues of the poor. While attitudes in general need altering, specific programs of education for emergency managers are needed in order to bring poverty to the forefront as a planning issue.

4.8.1   RECOGNIZE THAT DISASTERS WORSEN SOCIAL INEQUALITIES

One of the first things that needs to happen is emergency managers must recognize that disasters can exacerbate already existing inequalities within the community. While disasters in general bring communities together, this altruistic state where stratification and inequality issues disappear is very short lived. As we saw with the case study of Florida City, disasters often make the divide between those who have and those who do not even greater. To address this, emergency managers need programs in place before disaster strikes that address the needs of the poor. Programs that recognize that those who are poor may not be able to have a disaster kit on hand will begin to address some of these needs. In addition, considering that poorer families will have a harder time evacuating and finding shelter, emergency managers need to go into their communities and learn what the needs are from those who live in the community. Programs that have local community-based town hall meetings to discuss disaster preparedness and evacuation may be one way to address needs. These programs must be held where the poor live and work in order for them to participate. Programs that require travel to attend will not help those who do not have the means to get to the locations. Furthermore, communities must recognize the power that they have and how much citizens rely on them. During interviews with Hurricane Katrina survivors, many poor minority residents reported that they waited for the mayor to call for a mandatory evacuation. Until the mandatory evacuation was called, they did not think the danger was significant, and once he did call it, they felt it was too late to leave. Those with more wealth and income were able to leave earlier as they had less to risk and more resources with which to go. The working poor could not leave until they were allowed to leave and not report back to work. As expensive as evacuation is for a community, leaders must learn to make the hard decisions earlier in order to allow all residents to have an equal opportunity to get out.

4.8.2   DEVELOP MITIGATION PROGRAMS THAT TARGET LOWER SOCIAL CLASSES

Another significant way emergency management can address the needs of the poor is to not only implement, but also encourage participation in mitigation programs targeting lower social classes. In order to do this, some fundamental shifts in mitigation methodology may be required. Most mitigation projects are funded based upon the completion of a cost-benefit analysis. This analysis estimates the cost of a mitigation project, and then the benefits that can be expected once the project is completed. The inherent problem with this type of analysis for the poor is that it is often very hard to get a cost–benefit ratio which is the required threshold to meet. This inability to meet the threshold is a direct result of using only specific costs (such as the cost of retrofit material) and specific benefits (i.e., the amount of damage that is avoided). However, as we know, avoiding damage has other significant benefits as well that can not always be quantified, particularly for the poor. New methods then need to be developed that consider the nonmonetary benefits of mitigation. Programs for mitigation of private structures have been attempted (such as Florida's RCMP program in the early 1990s–1998); however, the biggest criticism of these programs is that they often mitigate the homes of the rich, as their cost-benefit ratios are highest. However, those on the upper end of the social class hierarchy are also the ones most capable of investing in mitigation without government assistance. Grant programs that qualify households based on factors other than cost-benefit ratios are needed to address the structural vulnerabilities of the housing of the poor. Considering that those on the lower end of the hierarchy tend to bear the highest burden during disaster, investment in mitigation must be based on more than the traditional costs and benefits (see the H. John Heinz III Center for Science, Economics, and the Environment 1999 report on the hidden costs of coastal hazards). In order to target appropriate structures, mapping of housing located on vulnerable land and socioeconomic demographics is necessary. By combining social and geographical data, emergency managers can assess locations that are the most physically and socially vulnerable, and target mitigation projects in those areas. To be successful, emergency managers must work with community leaders who are trusted by the citizens most in need. Without these partnerships, the poor will be skeptical of the intentions of the program. By working with community leaders (not necessarily politicians) to explain the program and recruit participants, the likelihood of success grows.

4.8.3   Include Community Members in Disaster Planning

Including members of lower social classes in disaster planning and development meetings is a key to developing programs that pay particular attention to the needs of community members. By engaging community members, particularly those in the lower half of the social class hierarchy, in developing education programs on disaster mitigation and preparedness, the particular needs of the poor will be integrated. Again, think of the issue of disaster kits. As we discussed, the poor may recognize the need for a disaster kit, but simply not have the resources necessary to have the supplies on hand. Educational programs that focus on disaster kits alienate those who simply cannot have the items available. This is not to suggest that disaster kits and supplies should not be consistently mentioned in disaster education; however, limitations of the poor must be recognized and alternatives recommended. If your target audience feels left out from the beginning, they will not listen or participate in the effective plans that might come later. Members of planning committees representing the poor can offer insight into what types of things will be successful in poorer communities. As long as we continue to impose "one size fits all" emergency plans on all parts of a community, we fail to address the special needs of those that bear the greatest burden in disaster.

4.8.4   Recognize the Unique Needs of the Poor

Recognizing that lower social classes have unique needs that are not often met by federal, state, and local disaster aid policies, emergency managers need to be proactive by identifying specific sources of disaster relief before any type of event occurs. Planning for recovery is vital for success during recovery for everyone. If you know before a disaster occurs that the poor will have less opportunity for traditional aid, then knowing what alternate sources are available will be key to their recovery. If you wait until after a disaster occurs to compile a list of resources, then those who most need the information and help will already be negatively impacted during the recovery phase. The key is for emergency managers to plan ahead for the challenges that the poor will face. These challenges include struggles to find new, safe affordable housing, and emergency managers must plan ahead for this challenge. Quick damage assessments and availability of the stockpile of affordable housing in a community after disaster allow for a more rapid needs assessment for those who have lost their homes. Understanding the extent of the problem will help to address it. Since affordable housing options are critical for the poor to begin the long-term recovery process, then clearly programs that help motivate owners of these properties to rebuild quickly are necessary. Incentives should be used to restore and repair these units with guarantees from the owners that rents will remain affordable. Similarly, just as most communities have laws that prevent price gouging for pre- and post-disaster supplies such as water, ice, and wood, programs need to be developed that offer property owners incentives to keep rents in disaster impacted areas reasonable. Issues related to housing may be some of the most challenging to address since housing recovery is allowed to be market driven; however, without intervention, the poor will continue to struggle in the aftermath of disaster.

4.9   SUMMARY

The problems highlighted in this chapter focus on ways the poor, in particular, are more vulnerable to disaster due to their inability to be able to garner resources. These resources may be obvious, such as money or housing, or much more subtle, such as political will and power. Without all of these things, the poor bear the greatest burden during disaster. While their absolute losses may not be as high as those in the upper classes, their proportional losses are often greater. In addition, they are less likely to have the necessary resources to recover from these losses. Those who find themselves at the lower end of the class structure often find themselves struggling more in the wake of disaster. In other words, disaster exacerbates inequality; the gap between those considered the "haves" and those considered the "have nots" increases. The inherent problem, however, is that to reduce the effects of disaster on this population requires structural changes to U.S. society that address class issues. In other words, to best reduce vulnerability of the poor, we must eliminate poverty. Clearly this is easier said than done in the United States. But it would be a mistake to think that these issues are endemic to the United States. only. In fact, if you look at international disasters such as the 2005 tsunami or any earthquake or tropical weather system in the developing world, the poor clearly bear the brunt of the losses. Ultimately, while emergency managers can develop programs as discussed above to minimize the impact of class on disaster impact and recovery, the reality is that within our current social structure what is required are more programs addressing poverty in and of itself. Until society as a whole recognizes this, unfortunately disasters will continue to significantly impact the poor. The job of emergency managers is to recognize this and minimize the effects as much as possible.

4.10 DISCUSSION QUESTIONS

1. Define social class and explain its attributes.
2. Discuss the demographic distribution of social class and its attributes.
3. Explain the connection between social class and life chances and life styles.
4. What are some of the ways in which social class affects vulnerability to disaster across the disaster life cycle?
5. Play stratified Monopoly with your classmates (or friends). Was everybody able to prepare for the disaster scenario? What did you learn from the exercise?
6. Develop strategies for your local community to meet the unique needs of those on the lower end of the social class hierarchy. What types of programs would be the most useful?

ACKNOWLEDGMENTS

This chapter is modeled on Session 7 of the FEMA Higher Education Course titled, *A Social Vulnerability Approach to Disaster*, originally designed by Cheryl Childers. The authors thank Dr. Childers for the work she did that made this chapter possible.

REFERENCES

Beatley, T. 1989. Toward a moral philosophy of natural disaster mitigation. *International Journal of Mass Emergencies and Disasters*. 7 (1): 5–32.

Beeghley, L. 2008. *The structure of social stratification in the U.S.*, 5th ed. Boston: Pearson Allyn & Bacon.

Blau, P., and O. Duncan. 1967. *The American occupational structure*. New York: Free Press.

Bolin, R. C. 1986. Disaster impact and recovery: A comparison of black and white victims. *International Journal for Mass Emergencies and Disasters* 4 (1): 35–50.

Bolin, R. and L. Stanford. 1991. "Shelter, Housing and Recovery: A Comparison of U.S. Disasters." *Disasters* 15(1):24–34.

Bolin, R. C., and P. Bolton. 1986. *Race, religion and ethnicity in disaster recovery*. Boulder, CO: University of Colorado Press.

Bolin, R. C., and L. Stanford. 1998. *The Northridge earthquake: Vulnerability and disaster*. London: Routledge.

Childers, C., B. Phillips, A. Herring, and C. Garcia. 1998. Defining and applying sustainability after disaster: The experience of Arkadelphia, Arkansas (USA). Paper presented at the Sustainability, Globalisation and Hazards: Enhancing Community Resilience Conference, London, England.

Cochrane, H. C. 1975. *Natural disasters and their distributive effects*. Boulder, CO: University of Colorado Press.

Conley, D. 1999. *Being black, living in the red*. Berkeley, CA: University of California Press.

Dash, N. Analysis of Non-Recommended RCMP Homeowners. 1999. Submitted to Florida Department of Community Affairs as part of a year end report by the International Hurricane Center, Florida International University.

Dash, N. 2005. Mobile home replacement program in Florida: What we know today and where we should go in the future. In *Final Report*. Submitted to the International Hurricane Research Center.

Dash, N., and W. G. Peacock. 2003. Long-term recovery from Hurricane Andrew: A comparison of two ethnically diverse communities. Presentation at the 2003 Southwest Sociological Conference Meetings, San Antonio, TX, April 16–19.

Dash, N., W. G. Peacock, and B. H. Morrow. 1997. And the poor get poorer. In *Hurricane Andrew: Ethnicity, gender, and the sociology of disasters*, eds. W. G. Peacock, B. H. Morrow, and H. Gladwin, 206–25. New York: Routledge.

Daskal, J. 1998. In search of shelter: The growing shortage of affordable rental housing. Center on Budget and Policy Priorities. http://www.cbpp.org/615hous.pdf (accessed May 29, 2008).

DeNavas-Walt, C., B. D. Proctor, and J. Smith. 2007. Income, poverty and health insurance coverage in the U.S.: 2006. Current Population Reports. U.S. Census Bureau. http://www.census.gov/prod/2007pubs/p60-233.pdf.

Ehrenreich, B. 2001. *Nickel and dimed*. New York: Henry Holt and Company.

Flynn, J., P. Slovic, and C. K. Mertz. 1994. Gender, race, and perception of environmental health risks. *Risk Analysis* 14 (6): 1101–8.

Fothergill, A., and L. A. Peek. 2004. Poverty and disasters in the U.S.: A review of the recent sociological findings. *Natural Hazards* 32 (1): 89–110.

Gilbert, D. 2002. *The American class structure in an age of growing inequality*. Belmont: Wadsworth.

Gladwin, H., and W. G. Peacock. 1997. Warning and evacuation: A night for hard houses. In *Hurricane Andrew: Ethnicity, gender, and the sociology of disasters*, eds. W. G. Peacock, B. H. Morrow, and H. Gladwin, 52–74. New York: Routledge.

H. John Heinz III Center for Science, Economics, and the Environment. 1999. *The Hidden Costs of Coastal Hazards: Implications for Risk Assessment and Mitigation*. Island Press.

Klinenberg, E. 2002. *Heat wave: A social autopsy of disaster in Chicago*. Chicago: The University of Chicago Press.

Klinteberg, R. 1979. Management of disaster victims and rehabilitation of uprooted communities. *Disasters* 3 (1): 67–70.

Kozol, J. 1991. *Savage inequalities*. New York: Crown.

Lanzarotta, M. 2001. *Across the great divide: The wealth gap challenges American ideals*. http://www.impact-press.com/articles/augsep01/divide80901.html (accessed June 14, 2008).

Logan, J., and H. L. Molotch. 1987. *Urban fortunes: The political economy of place*. Berkeley, CA: University of California Press.

Macionis, J. J. 2002. *Social problems*. Upper Saddle River, NJ: Prentice Hall.

Mantsios, G. 2001. Class in America: Myths and realities. In *Race, class, and gender in the U.S.*, 5th ed., ed. P. S. Rothenberg, 168–82. New York: Worth.

Marx, K. (1845/1978). The German ideology. In *The Marx Engels reader*, 2nd ed., ed. R. Tucker, 146–200. New York: W. W. Norton.

Mileti, D., T. E. Drabek, and J. Eugene Hass. 1975. *Human systems in extreme environments: A sociological perspective*. Program on Environment and Behavior monograph no. 21. Boulder, CO: University of Colorado, Institute of Behavioral Science, Natural Hazards Research and Applications Information Center.

Morrow, B. H. 1997. Disaster in the first person. In *Hurricane Andrew: Ethnicity, gender, and the sociology of disasters*, eds. W. G. Peacock, B. H. Morrow, and H. Gladwin, 1–19. New York: Routledge.

Oakes, J. 1985. The reproduction of inequality: The content of secondary school tracking. *The Urban Review* 14 (2): 107–20.

Peacock, W. G., N. Dash, and Y. Zhang. 2006. Sheltering and housing recovery following disaster. In *Handbook of disaster research*, eds. H. Rodriguez, E. L. Quarantelli, and R. Dynes, 258–74. New York: Springer.

Peacock, W. G., and C. Girard. 1997. Ethnic and racial inequalities in hurricane damage and insurance settlements. In *Hurricane Andrew: Ethnicity, gender, and the sociology of disasters*, eds. W. G. Peacock, B. H. Morrow, and H. Gladwin, 171–90. New York: Routledge.

Peacock, W. G., and A. K. Ragsdale. 1997. Social systems, ecological networks and disasters: Toward a sociopolitical ecology of disasters. In *Hurricane Andrew: Ethnicity, gender, and the sociology of disasters*, eds. W. G. Peacock, B. H. Morrow, and H. Gladwin, 20–35. New York: Routledge.

Perry, R. W., and A. H. Mushkatel. 1986. *Minority citizens in disaster*. Athens, GA: University of Georgia Press.

Phillips, B. 1993. Cultural diversity within disasters: Sheltering, housing and long-term recovery. *International Journal of Mass Emergencies and Disaster* 11 (1): 99–110.

Rubin, C. B. 1985. The community recovery process in the U.S. after a major disaster. *International Journal of Mass Emergencies and Disasters* 3 (2): 9–28.

Shanahan, M. J., R. A. Miech, and G. H. Elder, Jr. 1998. Changing pathways to attainment in men's lives: Historical patterns of school, work, and social class. *Social Forces* 77 (1): 231–56.

Sorenson, J., and B. Vogt Sorenson. 2006. Community processes: Warning and evacuation. In *Handbook of disaster research*, eds. H. Rodriguez, E. L. Quarantelli, and R. Dynes, 183–99. New York: Springer.

Sullivan, A. F. 2000. Hunger in the U.S.: A summary of recent studies on hunger and emergency food demand. Report by the Center on Hunger and Poverty, Boston, MA.

Syme, S. L., and L. F. Berkman. 1997. Social class, susceptibility, and sickness. In *Sociology of health and illness*, 5th ed., ed. P. Conrad, 29–35. New York: St. Martin's.

Thoits, P. 1995. Stress, coping, and social support processes: Where are we? What next? *Journal of Health and Social Behavior* 35 (extra issue): 53–79.

Tierney, K. 1989. Improving theory and research on hazard mitigation: Political economy and organizational perspectives. *International Journal of Mass Emergencies and Disasters* 7 (3): 367–96.

U.S. Department of Health and Human Services. 2006. The 2006 HHS Poverty Guidelines. http://aspe.hhs.gov/POVERTY/06poverty.shtml (accessed July 25, 2008).

U.S. Department of Housing and Urban Development. 2005. Affordable housing needs: A report to Congress on the significant need for housing. http://www.huduser.org/publications/affhsg/affhsgneed.html (accessed September 2, 2008).

U.S. Department of Labor, Bureau of Labor Statistics. 2007. Characteristics of minimum wage workers. http://www.bls.gov/cps/minwage2006.htm (accessed July 25, 2008).

U.S. Department of Labor, Bureau of Labor Statistics. Characteristics of Minimum Wage Workers: 2007. http://www.bls.gov/cps/minwage2006.htm. (Accessed July 25, 2008).

U.S. Department of Labor, Bureau of Labor Statistics. Characteristics of Minimum Wage Workers: 2008. http://www.bls.gov/cps/minwage2007.htm. (Accessed May 7, 2009).

U.S. Department of Labor, Bureau of Labor Statistics. Characteristics of Minimum Wage Workers: 2009. http://www.bls.gov/cps/minwage2008.htm. (Accessed May 7, 2009).

Weber, M. 1922. *Economy and society*. Tubingen, Germany: Mohr.

Webster, B., A. Bishaw, and U.S. Census Bureau. 2007. American Community Survey Reports, ACS-08, *Income, earnings, and poverty data from the 2006 American community survey*. Washington, DC: U.S. Government Printing Office.

White, G. F. 1974. *Natural hazards: local, national, global*. New York: Oxford University Press.

Williams, D. R. 1990. Socioeconomic differentials in health: A review and redirection. *Social Psychology Quarterly* 53 (2): 81–99.

Wisner, B., P. Blaikie, T. Cannon, and I. Davis. 2004. *At risk: Natural hazards, people's vulnerability and disasters*. London: Routledge.

Wolff, E. N. 2007. Recent trends in household wealth in the U.S.: Rising debt and the middle-class squeeze. Working paper no. 502. New York: The Levy Economics Institute of Bard College.

Yelvington, K. 1997. Coping in a temporary way: The tent cities. In *Hurricane Andrew: Ethnicity, gender, and the sociology of disasters*, eds. W. G. Peacock, B. H. Morrow, and H. Gladwin, 92–115. New York: Routledge.

RESOURCES

SOCIAL CLASS IN THE UNITED STATES

Barr, D. *Health disparities in the U.S.: Social class, race, ethnicity, and health*. Baltimore: Johns Hopkins University Press, 2008.

Center on Budget and Policy Priorities. Census data show increases in extent and severity of poverty and decline in household income. 2002. http://www.cbpp.org/9-24-02pov.htm (accessed November 18, 2008).

Keister, L. A., and S. Moller. Wealth inequality in the U.S. *Annual Review of Sociology* 26 (2000): 63–81.

Rubin, L. B. *Families on the fault line: America's working class speaks about the family, the economy, race, and ethnicity*. New York: HarperCollins, 1994.

Wikipedia. Social class in the United States. http://en.wikipedia.org/wiki/Social_class_in_the_United_States (accessed May 6, 2009).

Social Class and Disaster Vulnerability

Anderson, M. B. Vulnerability to disaster and sustainable development: A general framework for assessing vulnerability. In *Disaster prevention for sustainable development: Economic and policy issues*, eds. M. Munasinghe and C. Clarke, 41–50. Washington, DC: The World Bank, 1995.

Morrow-Jones, H. A., and C. R. Morrow-Jones. Mobility due to natural disaster: Theoretical considerations and preliminary analysis. *Disasters* 15, no. 2 (1991): 126–32.

Phillips, B. D. 1998. Sheltering and housing of low-income and minority groups in Santa Cruz County after the Loma Prieta earthquake. In *The Loma Prieta, California, earthquake of October 17, 1989—Recovery, mitigation, and reconstruction*. Professional paper 1533-D, U.S. Geological Survey (1998): 17–18.

Westgate, K. Land-use planning, vulnerability and the low-income dwelling. *Disasters* 3, no. 3 (1979): 244–48.

5 Race and Ethnicity

Nicole Dash

CONTENTS

5.1 CHAPTER PURPOSE

This chapter focuses on key features of social vulnerability to disaster: race and ethnicity. The chapter explains the nature of race and ethnicity in the United States and ways in which they impact vulnerability to disaster.

5.2 OBJECTIVES

As a result of reading this chapter, the reader should be able to:

1. Conceptualize race and ethnicity as socially constructed attributes.
2. Understand the racial and ethnic makeup of the United States.
3. Examine the structural effects of race and ethnicity on U.S. society.
4. Analyze the extent to which white privilege continues in the United States today.
5. Describe ways in which race and ethnicity results in hazards vulnerability across the disaster life cycle.
6. Understand the role that race played in Hurricane Katrina.
7. Suggest ways to address the vulnerability of racial and ethnic minorities with emergency and mitigation measures.

5.3 INTRODUCTION

When Hurricane Katrina struck the United States in 2005, the intersection of race and ethnicity and disasters became headline news. While disaster researchers long knew that race and ethnicity were issues in the experience of and recovery from disasters (Bolin and Bolton 1986; Philips 1993; Dash, Peacock, and Morrow 1997; Fothergill, Maestas, and Darlington 1999; Wisner et al. 2004), the relationship became more evident in the aftermath of the storm as damage, displacement, and death for minorities in New Orleans became headline news. This chapter attempts to illustrate how social structures of race and ethnicity generate increased vulnerability for minorities in disasters in the United States. The chapter focuses on four broad issues: (1) What are race and ethnicity and how are these structured in the United States?; (2) How do race and ethnicity create vulnerability?; (3) What are the consequences of this vulnerability in the experience of disaster?; and (4) What types of actions can be taken to address the increased vulnerability of racial and ethnic minorities?

5.4 UNDERSTANDING RACE AND ETHNICITY

Race and ethnicity are often taken for granted. Not the race or ethnicity of an individual per se, but what it means when we use the terms. Most people when thinking about the ideas of race and ethnicity simply draw upon common usage to understand the concepts. The reality is that most people's conceptions of race and ethnicity are based on incorrect assumptions and stereotypes. And while both have similar consequences in disaster, the two ideas are not the same or interchangeable. Ethnicity is based on a shared culture such as language, religion, or common norms and practices, rather than specific physical traits. On the other hand, people often assume that race is genetically based biological differences that manifest themselves as different physical characteristics. While members of different races have different physical attributes such as different skin tone or eye shape, people of different races are not inherently genetically different in the sense of creating biological subspecies (Sykes 2001). In other words, people with lighter skin tones are biologically categorized the same as those with darker skin tones. In fact, unlike other animal species who have a variety of subspecies, there is only one type of human.

If race is not necessarily genetically based, then what is it? Race is primarily a social construction. In other words, it is an arbitrary way to organize people based upon easily distinguishable physical features. The categories, however, are not part of some natural biological order, but rather are created and imposed by members of society. Race as an idea and concept and the racial categories that go along with it are culturally defined. Not every culture uses physical characteristics as a way of organizing and defining their populations. In this chapter, when speaking of race, the issues discussed are very specific to the United States where we commonly use three racial categories: white, black and Asian. However, according to the U.S. Census, the agency that counts the population in the United States, there are five races: white, black, American Indian or Alaska Native, Asian, and Native Hawaiian or Pacific Islander. In fact, the U.S. Census even has an option for "other race," once again illustrating the arbitrary nature of the categories. Starting with the 2000 census, individuals were given the option to choose membership in multiple racial categories. In addition, the categories used in the United States illustrate how specific racial grouping is to specific cultures. The categories used in the United States, for example, would not help delineate populations in other parts of the world. Race, then, is rooted in society's need to categorize people based upon easily noticeable physical differences. The origins of these differences are less important than the consequences of them.

One of the categories missing from the discussion of race is Hispanic. As discussed earlier, race and ethnicity are often confused as the same. When thinking of Hispanics, people commonly consider Hispanics a different racial group, but in actuality, being Hispanic is considered an ethnicity. People from Spanish-speaking cultures can be any race, although most in the United States have Latin American roots and are likely to be considered "people of color" even though they are not designated as being in a racial category by the U.S. Census. When completing the census, individuals are asked first to designate their race, and then second, to designate whether they are Hispanic. And similar to race, ethnic issues in the United States are very different from those in other parts of the world. How ethnicity is defined is different in different geographical areas. In the United States, for example, we focus on groups such as Hispanics, Italian Americans, and Irish Americans where people within the groups have a shared identity based on either genealogical country of origin, language, or religion. Ethnic categories in other parts of the world are different and may be based on dialect, religious beliefs, or other cultural features. Just like racial categories, they are socially constructed and culturally defined. And while in theory race and ethnicity are different, in practice these groups are often merged together. For example, in social science research when looking at differences among groups, the most common groups considered are white, black, and Hispanic. The key is that regardless of whether considering race or ethnicity, different traits of an individual tend to create trait generalizations, such as intelligence or work ethic, where individuals are assumed to have specific characteristics based upon their race or ethnicity. So, if the categories are arbitrary and socially constructed, why do race and ethnicity receive so much attention?

One of the reasons race is a significant feature of society is that physical attributes serve as visual markers designating one person different from another. With visual markers we can more easily create the notion of the "other." In other words, physical differences allow us to separate "us" from "them." This notion is significant for how society is structured. If you see society as a social system structured by power, then it is easy to give those that look like "us" power. What ultimately happens is the creation of majority and minority populations, where the majority has power and the minority does not. Once these power dynamics are integrated into society then physical difference gives us a convenient system to segregate, isolate, and discriminate. Those in the majority separate themselves from the minority, and as a consequence, structures of inequality are formed that have significant consequences and benefits for minority and majority populations. Because some are benefiting from the system, changing the system is difficult. And while race and ethnicity can be markers for group membership that offers pride and identity, for the most part in society today they serve mainly as a basis for prejudice and discrimination. Thus, it is not race or ethnicity that inherently creates increased disaster vulnerability for groups of people, but rather, it is how race and ethnicity are interpreted by society, and the structures surrounding race and ethnicity that relate to vulnerability, as we will discuss later in the chapter.

5.5 DEMOGRAPHIC OVERVIEW—RACE AND ETHNICITY IN THE UNITED STATES

As discussed earlier, the U.S. Census is the agency responsible for collecting race and ethnicity data in the United States. The categories used to collect race and ethnicity data in the 2000 census were determined by the Office of Management and Budget (OMB) in October of 1997 (Grieco and Cassidy 2001). For the first time in the 2000 census, respondents were able to designate more than one racial category. In other words, they could choose both white and black (or any other combination) to reflect a multiracial family of origin. Racial categories according to the U.S. Census have very specific definitions. The following are brief definitions of the five racial categories according to the U.S. Census (Grieco and Cassidy 2001, 2):

- "White" — people having origins in any of the original peoples of Europe, the Middle East, or North Africa
- "Black or African American" — people having origins in any of the black racial groups of Africa
- "American Indian and Alaska Native" — people having origins in any of the original peoples of North and South America (including Central America) and who maintain tribal affiliation or community attachment

- "Asian" — people having origins in any of the original peoples of the Far East, Southeast Asia, or the Indian subcontinent
- "Native Hawaiian or other Pacific Islander" — people having origins in any of the original peoples of Hawaii, Guam, Samoa, or other Pacific Islands
- "Other Race" — included for respondents who were unable to identify with the five OMB race categories

Again, these categories are very specific to the United States. In fact, when looking at the Canadian Census Web site (http://www12.statcan.ca/english/census/index.cfm), data is not organized by race at all. The Canadian census presents data for "population groups" that include 12 different groups including black, Latino, and Chinese, as examples. Race, thus, is not as significant of a notion there as it is in the United States.

The majority of the population in the United States is white. Table 5.1 shows the racial composition of the United States in 2006. A little less than three fourths of the population is white. Of the remaining population, a little less than half are black. Two significant features of the data are that they do not include a separate category for Hispanics, so Hispanics are included in each of the categories and those who selected more than one race are included as a separate category. In addition, Table 5.1 shows a significant number of people who consider themselves "some other race." One of the reasons this number is so high is the confusion by the general public of race and ethnicity. Many Hispanics do not consider themselves white or black; rather, they see themselves as a different racial category. Therefore, many Hispanics either choose other as their racial category or they write in that they are Hispanic, which is included in the "other" category.

As the categories of race are arbitrary, we can also look at the composition of the United States in an attempt to capture a clearer majority–minority picture. To do this, we can recreate the data to include a category for Hispanic. Each of the other categories in Table 5.2, then, do not include those who consider themselves Hispanic. Whites and blacks, for example, are now non-Hispanic whites and non-Hispanic blacks. Table 5.2 illustrates the population percentages with the new category configuration. One of the most significant changes is in the number and percent in the "other race" category. When including Hispanic as its own category the "other race" category becomes rather insignificant. This change highlights our earlier discussion of the confusion between race and ethnicity. Although the difference between race and ethnicity may be important to the U.S. government, the difference is not widely understood by its citizens. For its citizens, difference in general seems to be the more important feature of how people categorize themselves. For the population, what makes someone a minority (race or ethnicity) appears less important than the acknowledgment of

TABLE 5.1
Racial Composition of the United States Population, 2006

Race	Number	Percent
White	221,331,507	73.93
Black or African American	37,051,483	12.38
American Indian or Alaska Native	2,369,431	0.79
Asian	13,100,095	4.38
Native Hawaiian or Pacific Islander	426,194	0.14
Other race	19,007,129	6.35
Two or more races	6,112,646	2.04
Total	299,398,485	

Source: U.S. Census Bureau, American Community Survey 2006.

TABLE 5.2
**Racial and Hispanic Composition of the United
States Population, 2006**

Race	Number	Percent
White	198,176,991	66.19
Black or African American	36,434,530	12.17
Hispanic	44,252,278	14.78
American Indian or Alaska Native	2,035,551	0.68
Asian	12,945,401	4.32
Native Hawaiian or Pacific Islander	387,230	0.13
Other race	768,782	0.26
Two or more races	4,397,722	1.47
Total	299,398,485	

Source: U.S. Census Bureau, American Community Survey 2006.

the difference. Hispanics clearly recognize themselves as different from whites in the United States, and as a result, are less likely to report themselves as white. Because of the "othering" that occurs to those who are not part of the majority, the following discussion of the consequences of being "minority" applies to both racial and ethnic groups.

5.6 RELEVANCE

Society is structured, to some degree, based on status or the position someone holds in society. These positions come with social roles and expectations. In other words, when we know someone is a daughter, student, doctor, or black woman, we use our knowledge and experience of society to define what and how we expect a person to act. Everyone has a variety of achieved and ascribed statuses. Achieved status is earned through activities and includes student, doctor, lawyer, or president. Others are inherited, or ascribed, to us at birth. These include gender and race. But while each individual has a variety of these statuses, they are not all equal in the eyes of the individual or society. As individuals we tend to value our achieved statuses, while society tends to focus on ascribed status. A female doctor, for example, tends to be seen as a woman first in society and as a doctor second. Gender, then, is a master status—what people see and judge first. Race is also a master status; it is what people notice first, and thus how they judge the individual. While some would like to argue that society is "color blind," people in the United States tend to be very aware of skin color. Along with this comes a strong tendency for nonwhite or minority status to take precedence over other statuses. This is particularly true for blacks and Hispanics in certain parts of the country. An individual, then, is seen first by race and ethnicity and second by achieved statuses, and thus interactions are dominated by the assumptions or stereotypes people have of the members of these groups.

Stereotypes are a set of oversimplified generalizations about a group based upon either observed or perceived qualities of the group members. Stereotypes may be positive or negative, but negative stereotypes have the greatest consequence for life experiences, particularly for minorities. Negative stereotypes are hard to eliminate from society because the stereotype itself, while often false, reinforces the ideas contained within it. Consider the following examples where stereotypes create a vicious cycle:

- Teacher does not expect as much from black students, and as a result black students do not perform as well.

- Boss does not expect Hispanic employees to think for themselves, and as a result Hispanics are less likely to take on leadership roles at work that require decision making.
- Disaster worker does not think black victims' losses are great enough to qualify for assistance, and the workers make this opinion known to people. As a result, black victims will file fewer applications for aid than might be expected because they believe their losses are not large enough.

Because individuals are treated based upon a stereotypical expectation, they often reinforce the stereotypes themselves. Life chances, then, are altered because what people assume about a group of people is applied to every individual of that group as well. The stereotypes perpetuate themselves because of the limited opportunities and the cycle begins anew. But it is a fallacy to think that all assumptions about race are negative. For those in the majority, the assumptions are often positive, which offer everyone in the group added opportunity. These positive opportunities or experiences are often called privilege. Privilege is the opportunity one has simply because of membership into a specific majority group such as whites or males. The tendency is to think that prejudice always puts someone at a disadvantage, but the other side of it is that it creates advantages. Privilege is not easy to see because it is taken for granted. Some examples of white privilege include not being regularly viewed with suspicion, not being asked to speak for your entire race, and dealing with people in authority who are similar to you. As a result, opportunities and experiences are completely different for those in the majority when compared to those in the minority. This institutional racism, racism that is embedded in social structure and social systems, is reflected in residential segregation in the United States, ghettoization, and political marginalization. Segregation and ghettoization restrict where minorities live, and political marginalization limits the voice minorities have in policy making. As a result minorities, racial minorities in particular, are more vulnerable in every phase of the disaster cycle. However, before a discussion of the specific phases of disaster, a general discussion of how race impacts vulnerability is needed.

Wisner et. al. (2004, 7) argues that vulnerability emerges from "social, economic and political processes that influence how hazards affect people in varying ways and with differing intensities." In their model of understanding disasters, they focus on societal features that generate more vulnerability for minority members of the population. These structural forces shape the experience of disasters. Segregation, ghettoization, and political marginalization restrict access to resources in a variety of ways. And while this chapter focuses on the relationship of race and ethnicity to disaster, it should be noted that disentangling race and ethnicity from issues of social class and gender is challenging. Social systems, whether race or gender, for example, are interrelated, and as a result vulnerability is not uniform for everyone. While vulnerability has specific outcomes within the disaster cycle, we first need to understand the connections between race and vulnerability more broadly. However, much of what comes into play when considering how race and ethnicity impact vulnerability centers on limits of opportunity as a result of issues like segregation. Ultimately, issues or race and ethnicity are environmental justice issues. Environmental justice focuses on the equitable distribution of environmental risks and dangers across racial and ethnic groups, as well as social classes.

Environmental decision making and policies often mirror the power arrangements of the dominant society and its institutions. Environmental racism disadvantages people of color while providing advantages or privileges for whites. A form of illegal "exaction" forces people of color to pay costs of environmental benefits for the public at large by living on marginal lands most proximate to risk. The question of who pays and who benefits from the current environmental and industrial policies is central to this analysis of environmental racism and other systems of domination and exploitation. Racism influences the likelihood of exposure to environmental and health risks as well as accessibility to health care. Some examples:

- *Landfills and Their Correlation with Racial and Economic Status of Surrounding Communities* reports a study that revealed that three out of four of the off-site, commercial hazardous waste landfills in one federal region (which comprises eight states in the South) were located in predominantly black communities, although blacks made up only 20% of the region's population (U.S. General Accounting Office 1983).

- *Toxic Waste and Race in the United States* was the first national study to correlate waste facility sites and demographic characteristics. Race was found to be the most potent variable in predicting where these facilities were located—more powerful than poverty, land values, and home ownership (Lee 1987).
- *Dumping in Dixie: Race, Class, and Environmental Quality* (Bullard 2000) chronicled the convergence of two social movements—social justice and environmental movements— into the environmental justice movement. This book highlighted blacks' environmental activism in the South, the same region that gave birth to the modern civil rights movement. What started out as local and often isolated community-based struggles against toxics and facility siting blossomed into a multi-issue, multi-ethnic, and multi-regional movement (Environmental Justice Resource Center, www.ejrc.cau.edu).
- Stretesky and Hogan (1998) found that census tracts with higher percentages of minorities, specifically blacks and Hispanics, are more likely to be located in census tracts with a Superfund site (a property with significant chemical contamination that the U.S. Environmental Protection Agency designated for cleanup).

While these examples focus on toxic contamination, the same issues hold true across other types of hazardous locations. While the land is problematic in and of itself, the broader issue is the social systems that contribute to minorities living in these locations. Vulnerability, then, is not simply due to being minority, but rather it is due to social conditions that marginalize minorities to dangerous locations. Some would question why minorities choose to live in these risky locations, but such questions fail to recognize structural forces that limit agency. Societal conditions also impact vulnerability by limiting not only land choices but housing choices as well.

As a consequence of segregation and racism, ethnic and racial minorities have limited housing options. Research has found that racial and ethnic minorities tend to live in more marginal or low-quality housing (Logan and Molotch 1987; South and Crowder 1997). Vulnerability is generated through a greater likelihood that the homes are poorly maintained and built with older building codes and poorer construction materials (Bolin 1994; Bolin and Stanford 1998; Peacock and Girard 1997). This is particularly problematic for renters who have little control over structural maintenance and mitigation. With about 54% of all blacks living in rental housing (compared to 34% of whites) in 2000 (McKinnon and Bennett 2005), the instability of poor black communities dominated by rental housing and unsupported infrastructure significantly contributes to increased vulnerability. In addition, Klinenberg (2002, 91), in his study of the 1995 Chicago heat wave, found that increased vulnerability to extreme heat was not simply a function of poverty. In comparing two poor communities, one predominantly white and the other predominantly black, he found that "the dangerous ecology of abandoned buildings, open spaces, commercial depletion, violent crime, degraded infrastructure, low population density, and family dispersion" creates an atmosphere of increased vulnerability." His findings underscore the role that race plays in creating structural conditions that generate vulnerability.

Race, then, is a social construction with arbitrary categories based on specific time and place. The importance of race is not that it exists as differential categories, but rather the significance of race is the consequences of racial structures in the United States. Race is not inherently problematic in its existence; it is problematic in its use as a mechanism for discrimination. Racism, and thus discrimination, are the inherent problems as they create structural conditions that impact the ability for minority groups to garner the necessary resources (money and power, for example) to prepare for and respond to hazardous events. If structural conditions were different, race would not, in and of itself, create vulnerability. This distinction is important. Vulnerability, while often applied on a micro or individual level, is actually about the macro or structural level. What puts people at greater risk is the structural elements of society that place minorities in positions of greater vulnerability through features such as segregation that limit free selection of housing options. Institutional racism built into the structural system of the United States and accompanying stereotypes and expectations from individuals creates an environment where the experiences of racial and ethnic minorities in disaster are significantly different from those of whites. These differences hold true across the disaster life cycle (for related content, see Box 5.1).

As stated earlier, minority populations are more likely to live on marginal lands. According to The Brookings Institute (2005, 16), almost three fourths of minority residents and a little over half of renters lived in the flood plain. The areas of the city with the lowest minority residents did not flood, while those areas with the highest number of minority residents did flood. Those in the majority have the power to live on lands that are at lesser physical risk. Racial minorities have fewer options for housing, and as a result live on lands that are least desirable, such as lands in or closer to the flood zone. Beyond having a greater flooding risk, minorities were less likely to have evacuated during the storm. While some question why people would choose not to evacuate, the reality for many is that they did not have the resources to evacuate.

First, it is estimated that over 100,000 people in the New Orleans area did not have access to a car before the storm hit, and that a little over half of poor blacks had no access as compared to 17% of poor whites (Center for Social Inclusion n.d.). Without transportation, leaving the area was difficult, if not impossible. As a result, many blacks in the area wound up in the refuge of last resort, the Superdome. As more and more people found their way to one of the only known locations of safety, conditions at the Superdome continued to deteriorate both as a consequence of the damage it received during the storm and overcapacity of the shelter. Some estimates suggest that 30,000 people evacuated to the Superdome—the majority being black.

Second, even those who evacuated the storm often had no home to return to, and as a result, tens of thousands of residents were bused and flown all over the country in the days and weeks after the storm. Large numbers of people went to the Houston, San Antonio, and Dallas areas in Texas, while still others were flown to areas as far as Denver, CO, and Atlanta, GA. In the process of relocating, families were often split up—with one member on a bus to Dallas while another was on a plane to Atlanta, for example. Parents were separated from their children, and little record keeping made it a challenge to reunite families. In the longer term, while areas of New Orleans recovered quickly, such as the French Quarter, not surprisingly, predominantly poor black neighborhoods continue to struggle. With significant rental property destroyed, rents in the area skyrocketed, leaving many unable to afford to return back to the city. In addition, FEMA has given little assistance to help people return.

Hurricane Katrina was not an equal opportunity event. The example of Hurricane Katrina and the metropolitan New Orleans area emphasizes how segregation and institutionalized racism generate differing vulnerabilities for racial and ethnic minorities. While still a majority, 2006 population estimates suggest that fewer blacks live in New Orleans. The 2006 American Community Study shows that the black population is now at a little less than 59%. However, poverty estimates remain about the same. These changing demographics, in part, result from displaced residents not being able or not wanting to return to the city. In addition, there is a sense that some parts of the area are being gentrified as developers purchase destroyed low-income properties and redevelop them into more high-rent districts with vastly different social landscapes. Similarly, HUD is destroying many of the public housing projects in the city, making it even harder for many to return home. Driving through the city today tells the story of two different Americas, one in which those with power and money (the "haves") experience less storm impact and recover faster than those without power and money (the "have nots"), who continue to struggle. In New Orleans, the "have nots" are racial and ethnic minorities, and thus it is this group that faces an unknown future. The complete story of Hurricane Katrina and the city of New Orleans has yet to be told as the city continues to struggle to recover, but the glaring vulnerability of minority communities cannot be denied.

BOX 5.1   HURRICANE KATRINA CASE STUDY

Hurricane Katrina made landfall as a category 3 (winds approximately 125 mph) hurricane on the Gulf Coast of the United States on Monday, August 29, 2005, with the eye of the storm coming ashore between New Orleans, LA, and Biloxi, MS. While the storm impacted a variety of communities along the Gulf Coast, the storm's impact in New Orleans illustrates the consequences of the increased vulnerability of a predominantly black community in the United States. As the storm approached the Gulf Coast, its strongest winds approached category 5 wind speeds of about 175 mph. A hurricane, as the storm spins toward the coast, creates a storm surge. The total height of the surge is a combination of the water pushed by the force of the winds combined with normal tide. As Hurricane Katrina made landfall, it is believed that the storm surge in the New Orleans area was between 15 and 19 feet in the eastern area and 10 to 14 feet in the western portion of the city (Knabb, Rhome, and Brown 2005). New Orleans, built below sea level, was inundated with water as the surge breached the levee system and flooded the city. In the end, over 1450 people lost their lives in Louisiana, the majority in the New Orleans area, with still hundreds missing. While no one knows exact numbers, tens of thousands of people in New Orleans remained in the city as the storm made landfall. Estimates suggest that 30,000 to 40,000 made their way to the Superdome and convention center in New Orleans either shortly before the storm made land-fall or in its aftermath. While there are no good statistics on the racial composition of the evacuees in the Superdome and convention center, media images suggest that the majority were black. Of these, many were rescued by helicopter as the water continued to rise and stranded people on their roofs or in their attics with few options. While not the strongest hur-ricane in U.S. history, Hurricane Katrina clearly had one of the greatest impacts not only in the damage it created, but in the disruption to the lives of many of its residents. If Hurricane Katrina was not the strongest storm in U.S. history, then why was it one of the most damag-ing, particularly in New Orleans?

The city of New Orleans, well known for its French Quarter and jazz music, is also known for its poverty. According to the U.S. Census, 22.9% of all individuals in the city lived below the poverty level as compared to 12.4% of the United States as a whole. However, to argue that poverty was the cause of the disaster is to ignore another significant feature of the area—the significant racial stratification. The New Orleans metropolitan area is much larger than the city of New Orleans. Census 2000 figures show about 1.3 million people in the metropolitan area with about 485,000 in the city of New Orleans (The Brookings Institute 2005). While the city accounted for only 36% of the region's population, about two thirds of the metropolitan area's black population lived in the city (The Brookings Institute 2005). New Orleans itself is a city that is majority minority with a little over 67% of its population being black. However, according to The Brooking Institute's 2005 report, *New Orleans after the Storm*, while the city always had a large population of blacks, by 2000 the city had become extremely segregated with most blacks living in neighborhoods that were more than 75% black (The Brookings Institute 2005, 6). With these clear geographic divisions along racial lines came concentrated levels of poverty as well. Some of their most significant findings illustrating the significant racial segregation in the community include (pp. 7–8):

- 84% of the poor population was black.
- Median income for blacks was half that of whites.
- Poverty rate for blacks was three times higher than white poverty rate.
- Poor blacks were five times as likely to live in areas of extreme poverty.

- College attainment was four times lower for blacks than for whites.
- Only 41% of black households owned their own homes as compared to 56% of whites.

What is evident is that the pre-Katrina experiences of black New Orleans was completely different from that of white New Orleans, and thus their experience with Hurricane Katrina was significantly different as well.

5.7 VULNERABILITY ACROSS THE DISASTER LIFE CYCLE

The effects of vulnerability are not similar across the different stages of the disaster life cycles. While the vulnerability is rooted in the same structural systems discussed earlier, the actual outcome of that vulnerability will vary based upon the actual processes that occur at changing points of time during the buildup toward, the outcome of, and the recovery from disaster. During the warning, evacuation, and response stages, race plays a role in how individuals process and respond to information given to them. Race also plays a role in the options available when the risk is recognized. While many of the effects may appear to be due to economics, it is challenging to disentangle the two issues in the United States. However, minorities receive, interpret, and process warning information differently for a variety of reasons. In addition, minorities are more likely to be more impacted by disaster events both in terms of causalities and damage. The same social systems that generate vulnerability also impact short-term and long-term recovery by limiting access to recovery aid, emergency sheltering, and long-term housing options.

5.7.1 WARNING/EVACUATION/RESPONSE

Warnings for disaster are social processes. This idea sometimes is not an easy one to understand. Most people think that a warning is issued and people simply act in response to it. But in reality, warning is a process in which the receiver of the warning goes through a series of steps, or processes, before a decision is made. Warnings have multiple actors (such as the giver of the warning and the receiver) involved and numerous feedback cycles where one thing is decided and then feeds back into the larger picture. The complexity of these intertwined processes reflects many social factors. Race and ethnicity are two factors that influence not only how warning is processed, but also what types of protective measures are taken.

How does increased vulnerability resulting from race and ethnicity impact the warning process? One of the ways to impact that process centers on the channels of communication to disseminate the warning. The same social structures that isolate minority populations in segregated communities also impact the warning messages they receive. For example, minorities are more likely to rely on family and social networks for disaster information (Perry and Mushkatel 1986; Perry and Lindell 1991), rather than official sources such as local emergency managers. These same friends and family are likely to be living in the same geographic area, and as a result are just as likely as the respondent to not have accurate information. If everyone in the social network is relying on each other for information and no one has accurate information, then many people within an at-risk area may make decisions based on false information. However, even when information is received from official sources, there is no guarantee that those are trusted sources. Racial and ethnic minorities may not automatically see police, news media, or emergency management personnel, for example, as trusted sources, as experiences with them prior to the hazard event may influence perceptions. Thus, individuals interpret warnings differently based upon who they are, whom they are with, who and what they see or do not see, and what they hear (Mileti et al. 1975, 43). As a result, even "fire" yelled in a large university classroom will be heard, understood, interpreted, and reacted to differently by individuals who hear it. Warnings for any kind of hazard are filtered through experience, and this experience influences the interpretation of the messages. Being a minority does not inherently mean people interpret things differently; rather, it is the social experiences of being a minority that influence that interpretation. Ultimately, warnings are part of a process that leads to risk perception where an individual actually recognizes danger. Without recognizing the danger of a hazardous event, people usually fail to take protective measures for the hazard.

Recognizing risk before or after a disaster is critical for people to take precaution. And while perceiving danger is often a necessary condition for taking protective measures, it is not a sufficient condition as other social factors may influence the ability to protect oneself regardless of the amount of danger one perceives. One argument for why racial and ethnic minorities may not recognize their risk to the same extent as others is that the hazard or disaster agent seems no more dangerous than their everyday social conditions. Ghettoized neighborhoods to which racial and ethnic minorities are often socially confined may be extremely dangerous with high crime rates. Klinenberg (2002) focuses on some of these everyday dangers in his study of the 1995 Chicago heat wave. In areas that were considered particularly dangerous, such as Cabrini Green (at the time one of the most dangerous public housing developments in the country), people were afraid to open their windows to mitigate the heat. One of the things that can be concluded is that individuals who find themselves in everyday dangerous situations may be less likely to perceive risk of a hazard. Consequently, ethnic and racial minorities may also respond differently to dangers. These differing responses may be a result of limited risk recognition or may be a consequence of structural impediments that restrict options.

Some of these restricted options are due to cultural factors, while others are due to economic factors. While the role of class or economic factors was discussed earlier in Chapter 4, it cannot simply be dismissed when discussing racial and ethnic minorities due to how inexplicitly race and class structures are tied together in the United States. While this is true, this section will attempt to focus on some of the unique characteristics of race and ethnicity. Think back to what you read earlier about Hurricane Katrina (see Box 5.1); the problems that arose were not singularly a result of class issues. Rather, the significant issue was how race and class intersected to create more danger for some individuals. In addition, those who were both black and poor were more likely to live in dangerous locations. This type of development pattern holds true across hazards. As a result, minorities are often in areas that need to be evacuated. Research on how race and ethnicity impact evacuation is somewhat mixed in its results, with some studies finding that it is a significant predictor of evacuation and others finding that it is not (Drabek and Boggs 1968; Perry and Mushkatel 1986; Gladwin and Peacock 1997).

Gladwin and Peacock (1997), in particular, found that black households during Hurricane Andrew that resided in an evacuation zone were less likely to evacuate. Compared to whites they were two-thirds less likely to evacuate. In coming to this conclusion, however, Gladwin and Peacock failed to examine the role of risk perception in evacuation behavior. Thus, the question remains as to whether those who did not evacuate did so due to decreased risk perception or simply because they chose not to act upon the danger they recognized. One of the things we do know that impacts evacuation compliance is whether those asked to evacuate have an evacuation destination. While for most hazards and disasters evacuation shelters are opened, public shelters are considered a last resort by most evacuees. The majority of those who leave before a storm go to the homes of family and friends. However, minority evacuees overwhelmingly use public shelters. This increased use of shelters may result from a variety of different vulnerabilities.

First, family members are more likely to also live in evacuation zones. Second, as racial and ethnic minorities continue to process warning information and determine their risk, it is possible that they simply wait too long to go to any other type of safe location. Third, in areas where race and ethnicity intersect with poverty, transportation may be a significant issue. Many communities will provide public transportation to people trying to evacuate to a public shelter. However, no transportation assistance is afforded to those who try to evacuate to nonpublic shelters. Fourth, evacuation may be costly, thus restricting minority evacuees from traveling longer distances for shelter. In addition, once the initial hazard passes, minorities may react differently to continuing dangers.

For example, after earthquakes, ethnic minorities are believed to be less willing to reenter their homes regardless of the level of damage that the structure sustained. Fears such as these result from a shared ethnic culture in which past experiences may be remembered. Mexicans in California, for example, may remember stories they were told of previous earthquakes in Mexico during which aftershocks caused further damage or injury. Therefore, the key to how race and ethnicity generate vulnerability during the warning/evacuation/response phase of a disaster lies in how experiences as a minority impact the social lenses that one uses to interpret warnings and perceive risk. Then, in conjunction with how warnings are interpreted, evacuation is impacted by limited access to evacuation options in part due to the intersection of race and class. This connection between race and class also plays a key role in the impact stage of disaster.

5.7.2 IMPACTS

In disasters, it is often minorities and the poor who bear the brunt of the disaster impact. They bear this cost not in absolute dollars, but rather in their proportional losses. In other words, minorities are more likely to lose more of their home and belongings even when the dollar amount of that loss is less. To illustrate, imagine a home whose structure is valued at $150,000 being in an earthquake zone and sustaining $50,000 worth of damage. While this is a significant amount of damage, the home itself may be inhabitable and relatively easy to repair. Now consider a home worth $60,000 that sustains $50,000 worth of damage. This home is not inhabitable, nor is it easy to repair. It is possible that all that remains is the foundation and some plumbing. Both homes sustained the same dollar amount of damage; however, the consequences of that damage are completely different. One received damage equivalent to 83% of its value (the second example) while the other lost the equivalent of 33% of its value. As a result, not only are the impacts of the earthquake different in terms of loss, but also, as we will see later, they also affect the recovery process. The question that needs to be answered is why minorities are more likely to have greater proportional losses. The answer to this question is not an easy one since, similar to the issues that impact the warning phase of a disaster, impact is influenced by both class and race or ethnicity. In addition, impacts are influenced by societal features such as racism and segregation.

As discussed earlier, one of the consequences of the institutional racism that exists in the United States is residential housing segregation, and this segregation significantly affects how disasters impact racial and ethnic minorities. Minority populations live in less desirable locations, and as a result they are often concentrated geographically. Disasters occur in geographic space. Whether earthquakes, tornados, hurricanes, fires, or nuclear power plant accidents, the extent of the impact area may be narrow or wide, but more important than the extent of the damage is the population that lives in those areas. Because space is, for the most part in the United States, racially and ethnically segregated, disasters may impact a concentrated population. For an illustration, Figure 5.1 is a census tract map for Tarrant County, TX, illustrating the locations of census tracts where the population is over 50% minority. As you can see, minority populations are, for the most part, concentrated in contiguous areas, with the southern part of the county having the highest concentration. However, other locations in the county also illustrate minority population concentrations. Since we know that minority populations are more likely to live in more vulnerable locations, we can see why impacts may be worse for minorities depending on where a disaster event occurs.

Even when disasters hit areas with equal amounts of minority populations, minorities still experience more proportional losses, as discussed earlier. When Hurricane Andrew struck south Florida during the early morning hours of August 24, 1992, the strongest category 5 winds crossed over the cities of Homestead and Florida City. Yet, even though these areas suffered similar hurricane-force winds, damage was more significant in Florida City. According to the 1990 census, Florida City's population was 61% black, while Homestead's population was only 23% black. In addition, Florida City's population was considerably poorer with a median income about $5,000 lower than that of Homestead. So in this context, with storm experience being very similar, Florida City's single-

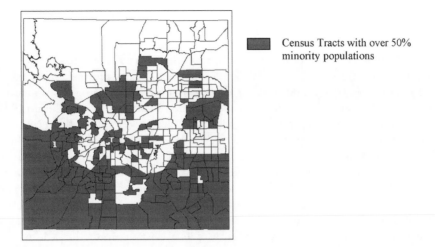

Census Tracts with over 50%
minority populations

FIGURE 5.1   Segregation in Tarrant County, TX. *Source*: Data from 2000 U.S. Census.

family homes lost 81% of their value as a result of Hurricane Andrew, while Homestead's lost only 47%. While both were significant, Florida City clearly experienced a greater impact. Again, the dual impact of class and race placed this community more at risk.

In addition to increased risk to physical structures, some research has also found that mortality rates often are higher among minorities (Moore 1958; Bolin and Bolton 1986). In his study of the Chicago heat wave, Klinenberg (2002) found that blacks had the highest proportional death rate compared to any other ethnic or racial group, while Hispanics had a relatively low mortality rate. He argues, in part, that the increased vulnerability of blacks stemmed from the locations where they lived in the Chicago area. For example, blacks were more likely to be living in locations with high crime rates and isolated streets. As a result, the level of fear in these areas was higher, and people's willingness to open windows was lower, putting them at greater risk for high temperatures in their homes. Minorities living in public housing were at particular risk because most of the units were without air conditioning. In addition, older black men were more likely to be socially isolated—the leading cause of death during the heat wave according to Klinenberg. While analysis is still under way, it is believed that the majority of deaths in Hurricane Katrina will be minorities as well. This is not surprising considering the racial composition of New Orleans, but it does illustrate the consequences of living in riskier areas.

5.7.3   SHORT- AND LONG-TERM RECOVERY

Trying to demonstrate the effects of vulnerability in these three distinct phases of disaster is challenging as the phases themselves are interconnected. Research finds that minority communities struggle more during recovery (Bolin 1986; Bolin and Bolton 1986; Bolin and Stanford 1998; Phillips 1993). While these studies have highlighted the challenges minorities face in the aftermath of disaster, they are less clear on how discriminatory structures impact the recovery process. As we have discussed, one of the reasons race and ethnicity play a significant role in disaster is their connection to social class or economics in the United States. This also remains true when discussing recovery from disaster. The ability to garner resources in the wake of disaster is one of the keys to recovery, and racial and ethnic minorities often have limited access to necessary resources. And while this clearly does include financial resources, in the recovery stage the issues are broader, and also include the ability to leverage political power for the benefit of the community. Minority communities often have little political power in the larger political context, and as a result, after disaster, they are often least likely to get assistance. Likewise, homes in minority areas are often less likely to have adequate insurance coverage. Since there is a direct correlation between insurance coverage and recovery, limited insurance resources negatively impacts minority homeowners' ability to recover. Recovery then is a complicated process that involves both the individual's ability to garner resources and the community's ability to compete for required resources. (See Peacock and Ragsdale 1997 for more information on community competition.) Without adequate resources, recovery is slowed.

Looking at resources on the individual or household level first, research finds that minorities often have inadequate insurance coverage (Bolin and Bolton 1986; Peacock and Girard 1997). Since recovery, for the most part, is market driven, insurance plays a key role in the recovery process. Without adequate coverage, recovery is slowed. Peacock and Girard (1997) analyzed the connection between race and ethnicity and insurance coverage in the wake of Hurricane Andrew. While most households had some insurance coverage, blacks and non-Cuban Hispanics had the greatest likelihood of not having coverage. Likewise, non-Cuban Hispanics and blacks were more likely than non-Hispanic whites and Cubans to report that their insurance companies were not adequately covering their losses. To try to understand the significant difference between these racial and ethnic groups, Peacock and Gladwin (1997) analyzed insurance coverage in the hardest hit area. They found that those without sufficient coverage were more likely to not be insured with one of three major insurance companies (State Farm, Allstate, or Prudential). Ultimately, they found that of the homeowners who were not insured by one of the major carriers, black homeowners were four times more likely than whites to report insufficient coverage, whereas no racial differences emerged for the group who were insured by one of the major insurance agencies (Peacock and Gladwin 1997, 183–184). In their attempt to understand this pattern, they found that black households were half as likely as white households to be insured by one of the big three companies. Their ultimate conclusion is that "residential segregation deters blacks, but not Hispanics, from obtaining a policy from a top insurance company" (Peacock and Girard 1997, 187). Thus, if insurance is the cornerstone of disaster recovery in the United States, and blacks, in particular, are less likely to have adequate coverage due to structural impediments against attaining insurance from a top insurance company, then it is clear that recovery will be significantly impacted.

Minority communities are also less likely to have the political power to garner necessary resources within larger social systems. Recovery is often seen as a competitive process where different segments of a larger community fight for limited resources (Peacock and Ragsdale 1997). Segments of the population that can wield more power are more likely to garner the resources they need in the aftermath of disaster. Local governments that are strong and well organized with strong leaders and a readiness to act are more likely to quickly and adequately recover (Rubin 1985; Dash, Peacock, and Morrow 1997). Minority communities often have little power in larger political systems such as county or state level government, and often they struggle both organizationally and financially. As a result, recovery is delayed due to the inability to fight for limited resources. In addition, these weaker local governments may be more susceptible to power elites who push and pressure them into making decisions that may not be in the best interest of their communities. Minority communities, both the property within the community and the inhabitants, are often forgotten by those with power, and what often results is a cycle in which the community members themselves are blamed for poor community conditions which resulted from not getting adequate resources in the first place (Logan and Molotch 1987). As a result, the distribution of aid to minority neighborhoods is often inadequate, resulting in both short-term and long-term recovery struggles. Examples of this effect can be seen in recovery efforts from both Hurricanes Andrew and Katrina.

5.8 IMPLICATIONS FOR ACTION

Race and ethnicity generate vulnerability not simply through cultural differences, although those play a role. Beyond cultural differences, racism embedded in the structural foundations of the United States limits opportunity and mobility, and this plays the larger role in vulnerability to disaster. The problem with this connection is not that we recognize its existence, but rather that we are limited in many ways in our response to it. As argued in the previous chapter, the best way to mitigate vulnerability of the poor to disaster is to eliminate poverty in the first place. And while this is a simple answer to a complex problem, it is not a solution that can be implemented without major changes and alterations to American culture and society. Similarly, the best option to reverse the vulnerability to disaster for racial and ethnic minorities is to eliminate racism and its accompanying ethnic and racial stereotypes. The problem with such a needed solution is that it too requires significant societal change. This is not to say that it cannot or will not happen, but it is not a practical response that can immediately alter the disaster experiences of minority groups. The following section outlines a variety of actions emergency personnel can immediately take to address the increased vulnerability of racial and ethnic minorities.

5.8.1 Understanding Stratification

While the profession of emergency management continues to professionalize, more work needs to be done to educate emergency leaders of the impact of race and ethnicity on the disaster experience. Books like this one represent a good first step in understanding the structural inequalities that exist in the United States. As this chapter shows, it is not always easy for those in the majority to recognize the experiences of those in the minority. From the outside it is not always easy to see how stratified social systems like the United States results in overt and institutionalized discrimination. Acknowledging this structure is the first step to reducing vulnerability; without it, emergency management professions cannot meet the specialized needs of these groups.

To develop a better understanding of the issues, students of emergency management should consider taking classes that focus on racial, ethnicity, and culture. Classes that focus on these issues are available in both anthropology and sociology departments at most colleges and universities. These classes can be taken as electives while completing emergency management programs, or emergency managers already in the field can take classes as non-degree-seeking students at local colleges and universities. To understand the effects disasters have on communities and their citizens, it is vital to first understand the structure of society itself. Understanding how race or ethnicity impacts individuals and communities in non-disaster times will help emergency managers better meet the needs of minority populations during disasters. Along with this general knowledge, reducing vulnerability also includes emergency personnel knowing their own communities.

5.8.2 Know Your Community

With the professionalization of the field of emergency management comes more relocation of personnel. In other words, people with degrees in emergency management programs with qualified faculty may find available positions in Seattle, Washington, or Bangor, Maine. To best meet the needs of community members, emergency management personnel, then, need to first know their communities. One of the ways to do this is to make sure that social vulnerability is included in community vulnerability maps. While it is important to know the locations of nuclear power plants, hospitals, and schools, it is just as important to know where racial and ethnic minorities live. With vulnerability maps, analysis can help illustrate where the greatest needs may be after disaster.

By overlaying a variety of different coverages in a geographic information system (GIS), emergency managers can actually understand and recognize the added vulnerabilities of minority groups. For example, known flood zones can be integrated with census data to understand whether racial and ethnic minorities are more likely to be at flood risk. Similarly, data can be integrated to analyze whether shelters and emergency transportation routes meet the needs of minority populations.

Part of understanding the community is learning to ask the right questions. To know what those questions should be, emergency managers need to become active in their communities beyond emergency management. This is particularly important in understanding minority populations. The issues will vary from community to community, and understanding these complexities may be aided by subscribing to community newspapers and newsletters that will help emergency managers understand the specific social structure of their communities. For example, in south Florida there is a major difference between Cubans and non-Cuban Hispanics. In areas in the Pacific Northwest, understanding Asian American issues may be key to reducing vulnerability. To best understand the community, emergency managers can proactively attend community meetings, particularly those centered on minority issues. Through this involvement not only do emergency managers learn more about their communities, but communities also get the opportunity to meet and engage with emergency managers. For marginal populations who often feel on the fringe, direct involvement with emergency personnel helps build trust that may play an important role during the warning and evacuation phase of a disaster. In addition to building trust, emergency managers should engage minority populations as active members in the planning process.

By effectively using the human and cultural capital of minority community members, emergency managers can develop plans that take into account specific cultural issues often not considered. Minority groups often are excluded in disaster planning and preparation processes (Bolin and Bolton 1986; Aguirre 1988; Phillips 1993), and as a result, risk increases for these groups. A good example of this is what occurred during Hurricane Andrew with a sect of Orthodox Jews. Even though Miami Beach was under a mandatory evacuation order, this sect refused to evacuate because their leader in Israel felt they would be safe remaining in their homes. Before the evacuation call, no one in emergency management knew that this sect would seek guidance from their spiritual leader in Israel, and thus with the storm approaching there was little that could be done to motivate evacuation compliance.

If Hurricane Andrew had stayed on its original predicted path, Miami Beach would have received a direct hit by the storm's eye and the accompanying storm surge. Luckily for this group, the storm tracked about 25 miles to the south. In the years following Hurricane Andrew, considerable effort was made to develop a relationship with this group. Ultimately, this effort paid off and led to the development of an evacuation plan that met both the needs of the group and the county. The heightened risk this sect experienced during Andrew would have been diminished had members of this community been part of the planning process in the first place. This example highlights the importance of incorporating minority leaders into emergency management advisory boards. Diverse advisory boards create environments where both the special needs and talents of under-represented populations can be heard and utilized. In addition, initiatives to help employ people from minority groups also help to increase diversity within emergency management organizations, which will keep minority issues in the forefront.

Members of minority communities will know the best ways to engage with their citizens and will be aware of different cultural events that serve as ideal venues for community outreach. To help promote hazard awareness, emergency organizations can take advantage of strong traditions and institutions within these minority communities, such as religious organizations and cultural events. For example, in some areas Cinco de Mayo festivals are ideal ways to reach Hispanics, and partnerships with black churches lend themselves to be conduits of reaching black citizens. To reach minority populations, emergency managers must not assume that one channel of communication will reach all citizens. Proactively engaging minority leaders in the process helps create a symbiotic relationship between emergency personnel and community members, where both are assisting the other to develop culturally appropriate and successful hazard planning.

5.8.4 PUBLIC EDUCATION

Recognizing that effective information varies based upon the target audience, emergency managers need to develop appropriate materials and delivery systems. Programs targeted toward racial and ethnic minorities must be a priority for emergency managers in all communities. Pamphlets and materials need to represent minority members through the use of minority actors in ad campaigns and appropriate language (Figure 5.2). Educational materials must focus on the information

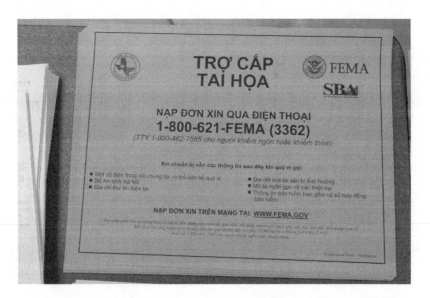

FIGURE 5.2 FEMA distributes information in local languages. *Source*: Photo by Leif Skoogfers/FEMA news photo.

minorities most need to reduce their exposure. Information such as who needs to evacuate, transportation options, and shelter locations best serve minority populations. In conjunction with the materials, delivery methods geared toward minority populations are vital. Often hazard information is disseminated to the public at major grocery store chains. During specific periods of time, campaigns are designed that print hazards information on grocery bags. Such campaigns hope to reach the general public through a mechanism that they frequently use.

The problem with such campaigns for minorities is that the large grocery chains that participate in these programs often do not exist in minority neighborhoods. Small, independently owned grocery stores are more likely to be in minority neighborhoods, and such stores do not necessarily have the resources to engage in hazard education campaigns. As a result, minorities are less likely than others to receive the information. To reach minorities, then, emergency managers must think beyond traditional educational campaigns. Options include programs in adult education venues as well as public schools. Partnering with public schools in inner cities, for example, emergency managers can help develop materials that provide hazards education while fulfilling other academic requirements. Students can develop their reading, for example, with age-appropriate hazards stories. History and science lessons can likewise integrate information focusing on hazard mitigation and preparedness. Young minority children, then, are exposed to the language of hazards and methods of preparedness from a young age; it becomes part of culture. They bring the information home to their parents, but more than that, they become adults who are aware of dangers and ways to reduce their risk. While such programs are important for all, they are particularly important for minorities who have limited access to other types of programs and information. To ameliorate vulnerability, education programs are particularly effective during the warning/evacuation/response phase. Other programs need to be developed to reduce the effects of vulnerability during other disaster stages.

5.8.5 PLANNING WITH MINORITY COMMUNITIES

Education clearly reduces the probability of increased damage and mortality; however, it does not eliminate the increased risk of minority citizens. Once emergency managers know their communities, they need to develop plans that address the community's specific needs (Figure 5.3). Time and time again we see that plans often fail to recognize the needs of the community. One of the things

FIGURE 5.3 Thirty-five Arizona tribal emergency personnel participate in a four-day class in Phoenix. *Source*: Photo by Lynne Carrier/FEMA photo

that is often overlooked are plans for short- and long-term sheltering and displacement. The majority of high-level emergency planners in the United States are part of the racial and ethnic majority, and plans are often based on their experience. As a result, the interconnectedness of some racial and ethnic groups is not recognized. This is particularly important during large-scale disasters where populations are displaced. Hurricane Katrina highlights the significance of this failure.

Racial and ethnic minorities are often more connected to each other than whites (Morrow 1997). They are more likely to be part of the informal economy, and thus be tied to their fellow community members in ways that are often not recognized. Displacing people without understanding their social landscapes results in additional trauma. Moving Hispanic families, for example, to locations with little Latino culture fails to recognize the importance of not only language, but the richness of their specific ways of life. After the 1972 Buffalo Creek flood in West Virginia, the U.S. Department of Housing and Urban Development (HUD) responded by setting up mobile homes in the hard hit area. However, when placing families in this temporary housing, they failed to understand the importance of social networks among the population, and as a result, families were displaced from their usual social networks, which caused additional trauma during the recovery period (see Erikson 1976).

One of the things displaced New Orleans residents miss the most is the food. While it seems like a trivial issue in the big picture, for those experiencing long-term displacement from their homes, these seemingly unimportant things makes a huge difference in the quality of their "new" lives. Displacing people long term reshapes their social landscapes. The social networks they relied on for transportation, child care, and entertainment, to name a few, are now gone (Litt 2008). Where people are relocated to and how they are accepted in their new communities is a critical, and often forgotten, aspect of emergency planning. Displaced whites tend to move to communities where people look like them and accept them. This is not always the case for minorities. In fact, many Katrina evacuees felt unwelcome in their new communities. Reports of increased crime in areas with significant numbers of evacuees such as Houston, for example, led many evacuees to feel uncomfortable in their new surroundings. Cultural sensitivity embedded within plans can minimize additive effects of poor plans on minority communities.

5.8.6 BUILDING CAPACITY

While it is extremely important for emergency managers to integrate minority leaders into planning and create education programs that target minority populations, it is even more crucial for minority leaders to help their own communities develop and build capacity. In conjunction with this, the key is developing ways in which communities themselves can build their own capacity from the ground up. While the prior discussion focuses on how community members can help emergency managers plan better, we can likewise see ways that minority communities can help themselves prepare better.

Minority communities can develop teams within their own communities that focus on emergency preparedness. By creating both informal and formal ties with each other, they can avoid problems that stem from not trusting external power structures. Imagine a situation where you have a minority leader involved with emergency management. The leader learns that a flood warning is going to be issued to the community. The community can create a network where the leader contacts key citizens, and then those citizens alert others within their network. The idea is that those who are designated to communicate the information to the rest of the community are trained to give proper information and recommendations for response. Since minorities are more likely to use kin and social networks, training community members can mitigate the danger of passing on poor information. These trained community members become conduits of education as well. They can pass on information that is developed specifically for their community or information developed for their racial or ethnic group. Specific information geared toward their population group considers culture in its development, and as a result is more likely to be utilized. FEMA's Citizen Corps program promotes community level training for citizens. For such programs to succeed in minority communities, minority leaders must embrace them and promote involvement. One final way to build capacity in minority communities is to teach people that emergency management is a viable career option. Universities that offer emergency management training should actively recruit from under-represented populations. Graduating trained minority emergency management personnel will create an environment where needs are more readily met.

5.9 SUMMARY

One of the reasons that addressing issues of vulnerability connected to race and ethnicity is challenging is because minority status in the United States is tied to issues of poverty and social class. In other words, separating the source of increased vulnerability is difficult. However, even with the complex nature of the problem, this chapter highlighted ways in which race and ethnicity, in the United States, generates vulnerability. At the root of the problem lies a societal system rife with racism and discrimination. This system creates a social structure in which racial and ethnic minorities are segregated and ghettoized onto marginal lands and into dangerous housing. Experiences of racism shape how minorities see the world, and thus these social lenses shape how hazard warnings are filtered and understood. Response to warnings and thus evacuations, for example, are different. While poor whites have some similar problems such as lack of resources for evacuation, minorities' experiences are different as they struggle to not only garner monetary resources, but political resources as well in a system that historically marginalizes them. And while there seems to be little that can be done when the problem is rooted in the structure of society itself, there are some clear suggestions that can be implemented to reduce the increased risk of minorities. One of the most important things that must be done is for more emergency personnel to recognize the increased vulnerability of minority populations in the first place. With clear recognition, solutions to the problem can begin to be addressed. Without an understanding of the unique experience of racial and ethnic minorities, vulnerability will continue to rise, and future Hurricane Katrinas are inevitable.

5.10 DISCUSSION QUESTIONS

1. Explain why we argue that race and ethnicity are social constructions.
2. What is the racial and ethnic composition of the United States? (Remember, for current figures go to the U.S. Census Web page: http://www.census.gov.)

3. Explain why race is considered so important by Americans and discuss its role in American society today.
4. How does racism affect whites or those in the majority?
5. Explain at least five ways that racism affects the vulnerability of racial and ethnic minorities to hazards.
6. Discuss ways in which race played a role in the Hurricane Katrina disaster.
7. Develop a plan for addressing the social vulnerability of racial and ethnic minorities in your community.

ACKNOWLEDGMENTS

I would like to thank Dr. Betty Morrow for allowing me use of her original work she developed for the FEMA Higher Education Course on this topic. In addition, I would like to thank all the editors for their hard work and ever-present patience during this process.

REFERENCES

Aguirre, B. E. 1988. The lack of warnings before the Saragosa tornado. *International Journal of Mass Emergencies and Disasters* 6: 65–74.
Bolin, R. C. 1986. Disaster impact and recovery: A comparison of black and white victims. *International Journal for Mass Emergencies and Disasters* 4: 35–50.
———. 1994. *Household and community recovery after disaster*, mongraph no. 56. Boulder, CO: Program on Environment and Behavior, Institute of Behavioral Science, University of Colorado.
Bolin, R. C., and P. Bolton. 1986. *Race, religion and ethnicity in disaster recovery*. Boulder, CO: University of Colorado Press.
Bolin, R. C., and L. Stanford. 1998. *The Northridge earthquake: Vulnerability and disaster*. London: Routledge.
The Brookings Institute. 2005. New Orleans after the storm: Lessons from the past, plans for the future. http://www.brookings.edu/~/media/Files/rc/reports/2005/10metropolitanpolicy_fixauthorname/20051012_NewOrleans.pdf (accessed June 4, 2008).
Bullard, R. D. 2000. *Dumping in Dixie: Race, class and environmental quality*. Boulder, CO: Westview Press.
Center for Social Inclusion. n.d. Hurricane Katrina fact sheet: Promoting opportunity for all Americans. http://www.centerforsocialinclusion.org/PDF/katrina_fact_sheet.pdf (accessed June 3, 2008).
Dash, N., W. G. Peacock, and B. H. Morrow. 1997. And the poor get poorer. In *Hurricane Andrew: Ethnicity, gender, and the sociology of disasters*, eds. W. G. Peacock, B. H. Morrow, and H. Gladwin, 206–25. New York: Routledge.
Drabek, T. E., and K. S. Boggs. 1968. Families in disaster: Reactions and relatives. *Journal of Marriage and the Family* 30: 443–51.
Erikson, K. 1976. *Everything in its path*. New York: Simon and Schuster.
Fothergill, A., E. Maestas, and J. Darlington. 1999. Race, ethnicity and disasters in the United States: A review of the literature. *Disasters* 23 (2): 156–73.
Gladwin, H., and W. G. Peacock. 1997. Warning and evacuation: A night for hard houses. In *Hurricane Andrew: Ethnicity, gender, and the sociology of disasters*, eds. W. G. Peacock, B. H. Morrow, and H. Gladwin, 52–74. New York: Routledge.
Greico, E. M., and R. C. Cassidy. 2001. *Overview of race and Hispanic origin: Census 2000 brief*. U.S. Department of Commerce, Economics and Statistics Administration, Census Bureau.
Klinenberg, E. 2002. *Heat wave: A social autopsy of disaster in Chicago*. Chicago: The University of Chicago Press.
Knabb, R. D., J. R. Rhome, and D. P. Brown. 2005. Tropical cyclone report: Hurricane Katrina 23–30 August 2005. National Hurricane Center, updated August 2006. http://www.nhc.noaa.gov/pdf/TCR-AL122005_Katrina.pdf (accessed June 3, 2008).
Lee, C. 1987. *Toxic waste and race in the United States*. New York: United Church of Christ Commission for Racial Justice.
Litt, J. 2008. New Orleans: Gender, the meaning of place, and the politics of displacement. *National Women's Studies Journal*.
Logan, J. R., and H. L. Molotch. 1987. *Urban fortunes: The political economy of race*. Berkeley, CA: University of California Press.

McKinnon, J. D., and C. E. Bennett. 2005. *We the people: Blacks in the United States*. Census 2000 Special Reports. U.S. Department of Commerce, Economics and Statistics Administration, U.S. Census.

Mileti, D. S., T. E. Drabek, and J. E. Haas. 1975. *Human systems in extreme environments*. Boulder, CO: University of Colorado, Institute of Behavioral Science, Program on Environment and Behavior.

Moore, H. E. 1958. *Tornadoes over Texas*. Austin: University of Texas Press.

Morrow, B. H. 1997. Stretching the bonds: Families of Andrew. In *Hurricane Andrew: Ethnicity, gender, and the sociology of disasters*, eds. W. G. Peacock, B. H. Morrow, and H. Gladwin, 141–70. New York: Routledge.

Peacock, W. G., and C. Girard. 1997. Ethnic and racial inequalities in hurricane damage and insurance settlements. In *Hurricane Andrew: Ethnicity, gender, and the sociology of disasters*, eds. W. G. Peacock, B. H. Morrow, and H. Gladwin, 171–90. New York: Routledge.

Peacock, W. G., and H. Gladwin. 1997. Ethnic and racial inequalities in hurricane damage and insurance settlements. In *Hurricane Andrew: Ethnicity, gender, and the sociology of disasters*, eds. W. G. Peacock, B. H. Morrow, and H. Gladwin, 171–90. New York: Routledge.

Peacock, W. G., and A. K. Ragsdale. 1997. Social systems, ecological networks and disasters: Toward a socio-political ecology of disasters. In *Hurricane Andrew: Ethnicity, gender, and the sociology of disasters*, eds. W. G. Peacock, B. H. Morrow, and H. Gladwin, 20–35. New York: Routledge.

Perry, R. W., and M. K. Lindell. 1991. The effects of ethnicity on evacuation. *International Journal of Mass Emergencies and Disasters* 9: 47–68.

Perry, R. W., and A. H. Mushkatel. 1986. *Minority citizens in disaster*. Athens, GA: University of Gerogia Press.

Phillips, B. 1993. Cultural diversity within disasters: Sheltering, housing and long-term recovery. *International Journal of Mass Emergencies and Disaster* 11 (1): 99–110.

Rubin, C. 1985. The community recovery process in the United States after a major natural disaster. *International Journal of Mass Emergencies and Disasters* 3 (2): 9–28.

South, S. J., and K. D. Crowder. 1997. Escaping distressed neighborhoods: Individual, community and metro-politan influences. *American Journal of Sociology* 102 (4): 1040–84.

Stretesky, P., and M. J. Hogan. 1998. Environmental justice: An analysis of Superfund sites in Florida. *Social Problems* 45 (2): 268–87.

Sykes, B. 2001. *The seven daughters of Eve*. New York: W. W. Norton.

U.S. General Accounting Office. 1983. *Siting of hazardous waste landfills and their correlation with racial and economic status of surrounding communities*. Washington, DC: Government Printing Office.

Wisner, B., P. Blaikie, T. Cannon, and I. Davis. 2004. *At risk: Natural hazards, people's vulnerability and disasters*. London: Routledge.

RESOURCES

BOOKS

Dyson, M. E. *Come hell or high water: Hurricane Katrina and the color of disaster*. New York: Basic Civitas Books, 2007. (Paperback)

Horne, J. *Breach of faith: Hurricane Katrina and the near death of a great American city*. New York: Random House Trade Paperbacks, 2008.

FILMS

American Apartheid. Princeton, NJ: Films for the Humanities and Sciences, 1998 (37 min).

Race—The World's Most Dangerous Myth. New York: Insight Media, 1993 (59 min).

Understanding Race. Princeton, NJ: Films for the Humanities and Sciences, 1999 (52 min).

When the Levees Broke: A Requiem in Four Acts. HBO Documentary Films, 2006 (directed and produced by Spike Lee, http://www.hbo.com/docs/programs/whentheleveesbroke/index.html) (accessed May 11, 2009).

WEB SITES

PBS. What is race? http://www.pbs.org/race/001_WhatIsRace/001_00-home.htm (accessed May 11, 2009).

Social Science Research Council. Hurricane Katrina research hub. http://katrinaresearchhub.ssrc.org (accessed May 11, 2009).

U.S. Census data in your area: http://www.census.gov/main/www/cen2000.html (accessed May 11, 2009).

6 Gender

Elaine Enarson

CONTENTS

6.1   CHAPTER PURPOSE

What does gender have to do with disaster? And why focus on women and girls? Are women's and men's lives so different in a disaster? If so, why is this and what does it mean for emergency management? To help answer these questions, the chapter first presents a conceptual framework for gender analysis and a statistical snapshot of gender relations in the contemporary United States. Then, the relevance of gender for disaster vulnerability is examined with respect to health and safety, livelihood, housing and transportation, and decision making. In the following section, gender concerns are examined through the life cycle of disasters, drawing mainly on events in the United States. The chapter concludes with practical steps toward more effective and equitable emergency management.

6.2 OBJECTIVES

As a result of reading this chapter, the reader should be able to

1. Understand the definition of gender.
2. Appreciate how gender relations affect people's everyday lives.
3. Reflect on gender inequalities affecting women in disasters.
4. Explain how gender relations affect women and men in disaster contexts.
5. Relate gender to other social dynamics affecting disaster resilience.
6. Understand the relevance of gender to a social vulnerability approach.
7. Compare gender vulnerability in the United States with other cultures.
8. Identify action steps for mainstreaming gender in emergency management.

6.3 INTRODUCTION

So what does gender have to do with disasters? Everything. Think back to your favorite disaster movie. What does it convey about people and their environment, the private lives of emergency managers and first responders—and women and men in crisis? Though gender stereotypes are vividly on display (men lead and women follow; men are stoic and women emotional), these are rarely confirmed by case studies of actual disasters. Later in this chapter we will see how gender actually plays out in disasters and shapes the working culture of emergency management.

6.4 DEMOGRAPHIC OVERVIEW

The implications of sex and gender in disasters are difficult to capture statistically, especially when used simply to note the relative numbers of women and men, for example, in a workplace or in a census tract. Yet census data and other statistical indicators are indispensable tools for social vulnerability analysis. As you will see in Box 6.1, many demographic indicators hint at broader social dynamics that position women and men differently in disasters. Most American women live longer than men, for example, and hence are more likely to experience physical limitations that matter in emergencies. Especially in older age, they are more likely than older men to live alone and experience poverty. Clearly, ethnicity interacts with sex so census data regularly indicate higher levels of poverty in households headed by African American women and women from other marginalized ethnic groups. Across ethnic groups, men are more likely than women to be homeowners and to have more secure income through employment, both factors that can be protective in disasters. At the same time, men are more likely than women to be homeless and living on the street when emergencies or disasters occur. American men, especially those in disadvantaged ethnic communities, also experience high levels of interpersonal violence, which can undermine their ability to access neighborhood resources in disaster contexts. Women's high exposure to domestic violence and sexual assault has the same effect. The historic trend toward female employment changes the family context in which emergencies unfold and raises pressing issues related to child care and dual-career couples in emergency roles. When preparing for the unexpected, and especially in the aftermath, the historic caregiving responsibilities of women across the life span should be especially noted by emergency planners. As you read on, you will want to reflect on other demographic patterns and trends that can be captured statistically and guide emergency planners.

BOX 6.1   DEMOGRAPHIC PROFILE

- Percent of all households comprised of married couples: 53% (Spraggins 2005). Percent of older women who are married: 43% (vs. 75% male) (Gist and Hetzel 2004).
- Percent of women in the labor force: 58% (vs. 71% male) (Clark and Weismantle 2003).
- Percent employed full-time: 75% (U.S. Department of Labor 2007).
- Percent of older women who are married: 43% (vs. 75% male). Percent widowed: 45% female, 14% male (Gist and Hetzel 2004).
- Percent of women 65 and older who lived alone in 1970: 32% (vs. 15% male), and in 2000: 36% (vs. 17% male) (Spraggins 2005).
- Percent of women age 80 or older living alone: 51% (Family Caregiver Alliance n.d.).
- Family households maintained by women with no husband present numbered 12.9 million, almost three times the number maintained by men with no wife present (4.4 million) (Spraggins 2005).
- Percent of families maintained by women without spouses who are homeowners: 49.6% (vs. 55.4% male) (Simmons and O'Neill 2001).
- Percent of female older persons ages 75+ who needed assistance with activities of daily living in 1997: 70% (U.S. Department of Health and Human Services 2008).
- Percent of women among adults aged 25–29 who are college graduates: 32% (vs. 27% men) (U.S. Department of Education 2005).
- Percent of women living below poverty in 2001: 22.9% (vs. 17.7% male). Women accounted for 58.2% of unrelated individuals in poverty in 2002 (Proctor and Dalaker 2003).
- Percent of women 85 and over living below the poverty line: 16.9% (vs. 9.6% male) (Gist and Hetzel 2004).
- Percent of single African American women ages 65+ who are poor: 41%; of elderly Hispanic women, 49% (Family Caregiver Alliance n.d.).
- Percent of women aged 25 years and older with a bachelor's degree or higher in 2007: 28% (vs. 30% male) (U.S. Department of Labor 2007).
- Female-to-male earnings ratio at the median for year-round, full-time workers in 2002: 77% (up by 5% since 1999) (Weinberg 2004).
- Percent increase expected in female employment of women age 55 and older between 2000 and 2010: 52%, from 6.4 million to 10.1 million (U.S. Department of Health and Human Services 2008).
- Percent of single women in homeless population: 17% (vs. 51% male). Families, single mothers, and children make up the largest group of people of the rural homeless (National Coalition for the Homeless 2007).
- Percent of women reporting rape and/or physical assault by a current or former spouse, cohabiting partner, or date in their lifetimes: 25% (vs. 8% male) (Antiviolence Resource Guide 2000).
- Percent of the U.S. median income earned by women with physical disabilities: 77% (Baylor College of Medicine, n.d., Characteristics).
- Percent of women living with a disability or residing in a nursing home: 24.4% (26 million) (Baylor College of Medicine, n.d., Demographics).
- Percent of family or informal caregivers who are women: 75% (U.S. Department of Health and Human Services 2008).

- Average caregiver profile: age 46, female, married, and working outside the home earning an annual income of $35,000. Women may spend as much as 50% more time providing care than male caregivers (U.S. Department of Health and Human Services 2008).
- Percent of female caregivers with one or more chronic health conditions: 54% (vs. 41% non-caregivers) and percent with symptoms of depression: 51% (vs. 38% non-caregivers) (Family Caregiver Alliance n.d.).

6.5   DEFINITIONS AND CONCEPTS

"Gender" is shorthand for a very complex and changing set of factors based on difference and inequality with respect to biology (reproduction, health, sexuality), the gender identities to which we are socialized (personality, interaction, gender norms), and the dominant gender relations of the societies we inhabit (life chances, opportunities for personal security, achievement, self-determination). Though sex, sexuality, gender identity, and gender relations are distinct, all are powerful forces in our lives. Gender, like race, is a "master status" that trumps other parts of ourselves such as our actual roles at work, in the kitchen, or in the bedroom—whether we resist this or not, and we often do. Women's and men's different family and job responsibilities, how and when they use public spaces such as parks or city streets, their modes of transportation—these and host of other gender patterns put women and men in different places at different times during the day and week. This is true in affluent societies and poorer nations, and cuts across all cultures, faiths, and social groups.

Arguably, sex and gender stereotypes are still such a strong part of advertising, schooling, and family discipline because these norms are not "natural" at all, but must be carefully taught, much as racial identity is. When parents of young children observe that boys gravitate toward fire trucks, are they observing anything more than that children are "hard wired" to be highly sensitive to social cues of approval? When a young boy grows up to be a fire fighter active in disaster relief, is he any more "manly" than his brother the counselor? Each generation and culture has different expectations of women and men, boys and girls, just as they have different values and approaches to the natural and built environment. Gender norms attached to interaction between women and men, and among women and men, are often quite diverse in a complex society like the United States. Consider how your own relationships have changed as you matured, or how differently couples live now (and lived in the past) in your own hometown. Relationships may also change or be challenged by crisis, as we see below. Are you a leader or follower? In control or under control? Women and men may have very different degrees of comfort reaching out for help from a counselor, taking directions from a first responder, or speaking out in a community meeting about reconstruction.

Gender is a powerful marker of inequality, as well as difference. Resources critical to people's ability to anticipate, prepare for, cope with, respond to, and recover from disasters, including transportation, safe housing, secure income, time, good health, and political voice (Wisner et al. 2004), are not equally available to women and men in any society. The World Economic Forum produces an annual *Gender Gap Report* based on such statistical indicators as employment status, education, health, and exposure to violence to capture these inequalities between women and men, boys and girls as they change. Notwithstanding women's access to undergraduate college education, the (slowly) narrowing gender gap in electoral politics, or the access of women and men to occupations traditionally considered "wrong" for them, the report indicates that significant gender equality gaps persist in the United States (World Economic Forum 2007). As in every society today, social power accrues more to men than to women, not because "biology is destiny" but because *gender stratification* distributes social rewards and power in ways that privilege most boys and men. It is also important to recall how long women and their male supporters have struggled for autonomy and self-determination from the straightjacket of gender.

FIGURE 6.1   Male-dominated professions may put men differentially at risk, as is the case with many first responder professions. *Source*: Leif Skoogfors/FEMA news photo.

Is gender really all about women and women's vulnerability? As we will see, gender can endanger the health and well-being of boys and men in disasters (and see Mishra, 2009, for an international perspective). While gender is never irrelevant in human life, it is never by itself a determinative factor of disaster vulnerability, any more than ethnicity or age are. Gender is certainly not an automatic indicator of disadvantage, nor does it shape all women's disaster experiences equally or identically (Fordham 2004, 1999; Cupples 2007). All people are inescapably defined at once by their sex, sexuality, gender, age, race, or ethnicity, and their physical bodies at any point in time. The concept of *vulnerability bundling* highlights intersecting social patterns that, taken together, increase or reduce people's relative vulnerability and capacity in the face of hazards and disasters.

Gender can be a *root cause of social vulnerability* based on gender differences or inequalities or both (Enarson, Fothergill, and Peek 2006; Enarson and Phillips 2008; Bolin, Jackson, and Crist 1998). For example, women have specific needs in late pregnancy, their domestic work is generally discounted, and they are at increased risk of abuse post-disaster; men are at risk in male-dominated relief occupations (Figure 6.1), may feel it "unmanly" to ask for counseling, and suffer the effects of unmanageable stress or substance abuse. Gender can also be a cross-cutting factor in social vulnerability. Some population groups such as the poor or the elderly are more heavily "feminized" than would be expected if women and men were distributed equally across all populations. This can arise due to differences (for example, women living long enough to be old and frail) or can relate back to inequality (being employed in low-wage occupations). Cultural context is vital, too (Enarson and Meyreles 2004). In many wealthy nations, poor women and others living at increased risk may nonetheless be more resilient to the effects of a disaster than either women or men in low-income developing nations. Practitioners and others should pay particular attention to how income, disability, violence, age, homelessness, single parenting, social isolation, minority status, immigrant status, and widowhood may affect women's differential vulnerability. Marginal or transitional sexualities and gender indentities can also increase vulnerability (e.g., Eads 2002).

Gender, age, race, and class were all significant "facts of life" when Hurricane Katrina struck the Gulf Coast: one in four women residing in the city of New Orleans lived below the poverty line; more than half (56%) of families with children were headed by women and two fifths of these lived in poverty; over a third (35%) of African American women in Louisiana were officially poor, the worst record in the region and nation; and over half (61%) of the poor people over 65 in the city of New

Orleans were women (Gault et al. 2005). The stubbornly gender-neutral interpretation of this catastrophe ignores these pre-existing patterns of social vulnerability and what transpired as a consequence.

This chapter draws from case studies illustrating how differently women are affected by disasters, reinforcing the need for a more multidimensional or intersectional approach to the study of gender and disaster. Which women in your community are most at risk—and how do you know? Which men and why? All lives are precious, but the exposure of an affluent woman who resides in a high-rise condo on Miami's coast cannot be equated to that of her nanny or domestic worker whose wages sent home to the Dominican Republic help educate and protect her own children, to take just one example. Similarly, gender does not confer the same advantage automatically to all men—consider the male executive and the male gardener he employs (what ethnicity do you ascribe to each?) or the risks to men known not to be heterosexual.

Social vulnerability analysis also directs our attention to change. How will changes in American life affect the people you love in our increasingly hazardous future? Climate change is a powerful force bringing more extreme and uncertain weather events in its wake, and women and men are not exposed in the same ways or with the same effects. The same can be said of terrorism and such technological hazards as toxic contamination of water supplies. Household and family lives are also changing. The percentage of female-headed households continues to increase, and women who are heads of households live in poverty at twice the rate of male heads of households; these women are also disproportionately from marginalized racial and ethnic groups. Owing to maternal poverty and related factors, the children from these homes often live in substandard housing with caregivers who may lack jobs with secure benefits, not to mention reliable transportation in a disaster. High rates of child poverty in the nation also mean that growing numbers of children lack health insurance and therefore are without regular health care, so they are often facing the uncertainties of hazards and disasters while in poor health. The national shift away from state-supported social services especially affects families dependent on the social safety net in the best of times. As described in the demographic section, these and related trends and patterns are highlighted as factors affecting disaster vulnerability in our nation at the turn of the century. Gender relations matter in disasters in subtle as well as self-evident ways, and throughout the life course of a disaster (Fothergill 1998). They are an important, if neglected, aspect of good vulnerability analysis (Laska and Morrow 2006/2007).

6.6   GENDER CONCERNS THROUGH THE DISASTER CYCLE

Today's emergency managers have gender-sensitive research to guide them rather than the kind of "myths of male superiority" that Scanlon (1999) documented in his study of the 1917 explosion in Halifax, Nova Scotia. What a marked contrast there was between how observers saw women and men respond, and how novelists and journalists told the story later. In this section, we review some of the major empirical conclusions drawn about gender relations in warning, evacuation, impact, response, and recovery by researchers who have studied recent U.S. disasters, drawing attention to the practical implications for emergency managers.

6.6.1   Risk Communication and Response to Warnings

Concern for the safety of their families is a strong motive underlying women's well-documented involvement in environmental protection movements and neighborhood emergency preparedness campaigns (Krauss 1993; Erikson 1994; Neal and Phillips 1990). Even the best designed and delivered warnings come to "receivers" who are human and draw on their own judgment, experience, and networks before responding—or not. Who is listening when emergency managers try to alert the public, and who is more likely to act? This is a complex subject, but researchers have demonstrated that gender relations are one part of the answer (Cutter 1992). Men, on balance, are more risk tolerant than women, which translates into being less likely to take self-protective action in disaster contexts. In their study of Californians responding to earthquake aftershocks, for instance, O'Brien

---

BOX 6.2   GENDERED RESPONSES TO FLOODING

[W]hen we heard that Lincoln dike had broke, we all called my sister to say we'd come over and get trucks and we would move everything out of their home. And [my brother-in-law] just refused. He said, "It's *not* going to flood. We're all right." He just abso-lutely—and she had a business down in her basement and she wanted to get all that stuff and he just, he refused … And I think when it hit, [he] was very closed. You couldn't get him to talk. He would go off and walk by himself a lot, just not talk to anyone and I think he felt really guilty that—"What if I would have done this, we wouldn't have lost all of our furniture, [her] business" (Enarson 1998).

---

and Atchison (1998) found that women responded more positively to aftershock warnings on virtu-ally every indicator, from seeking out more information to securing household items and developing family emergency plans. This finding was echoed in a second study of gendered responses to warn-ings following the New Madrid earthquake (Major 1999; Blanchard-Boehm 1997). The difference can be devastating for both women and men in the aftermath (see Box 6.2).

Women's pivotal roles in family life and their extensive social networks based on neighborhood, parenting, school, work, and faith put them at the center of the process of interpreting and assessing warnings. They are also key actors in mobilizing response to warnings as families generally take action as a unit; as household managers, women are instrumental in drawing the extended family together to assess the credibility of warnings and determine a course of action. This is especially important when large ethnic families and complex multigenerational households must be gathered to assess warnings, share information, and chart a course of action (Phillips and Morrow 2007; and see Litt, 2008, on women's social networks in Katrina evacuations).

Women are strong risk communicators in their capacity as volunteers and staff in local social service groups and community agencies, and active participants in community-based preparedness and mitigation campaigns (Turner, Nigg, and Paz 1986). Reaching community members through women's associations and clubs can be highly effective. In an innovative project involving inter-national exchanges between women in Ukraine and Oregon, Weidner (2004) and her colleagues helped raise women's awareness about hazards and train women in first aid techniques. Women are also dominant figures in the everyday activities of most religions, supporting the call to communi-cate to vulnerable groups through faith-based organizations, for example, in the wake of Hurricane Katrina (Eisenman et al. 2007). As men may find official warnings more credible and rely more on mass media than informal conversation (Major 1999), outreach through the workplace may reach men best.

Gender can constrain women's access to emergency preparedness information and critically needed warnings and forecasts (for international examples, see Fordham 2001). The "digital divide" in cyberspace (unequal access to computers and the Internet) is a limiting factor in many cultures, still including the United States in some respects (Papadakis 2000). Low-income women less famil-iar with the Internet or those with less time or access to computers are disadvantaged by Web-based awareness and preparedness campaigns. Similarly, deaf or blind women and non-English speaking women cannot be reached unless alternative media and languages are used to convey potentially life-saving information. Women's networks come into play as "[t]hey are more likely to know what's going on in their neighborhoods, including the presence of an elderly man down the street who needs extra help in an emergency" (Morrow 2006, 40)

A "one size fits all" approach to emergency risk communications targeting "the public" with very general messages may miss both a male audience in need of persuasion and women who face specific barriers and their specific communication networks. Effective disaster risk communication means reaching out creatively to different subpopulations, including high-risk women whose own safety and those of the dependents in their care may depend on good information at the right time in the right way.

6.6.2 EVACUATION

When waters rise or the air thickens with wildfire smoke, women are reportedly among the first to act. In some studies, men have interpreted this desire to act as "panic" and women report being frustrated by lack of social power or funds to make decisions for the household. Gender is, indeed, a good predictor of evacuation behavior, especially when children are present (Gladwin and Peacock 1997). When children and other dependents must be evacuated, women generally accompany them so evacuation orders are implicitly gendered. Gender can also be the basis for mandatory evacuation orders. As floodwaters approached the border, nearly all women from a small Canadian community were evacuated; the six women allowed to stay all worked in service roles supportive of male emergency responders (Enarson and Scanlon 1998).

Most families evacuate together, but it is not uncommon for the sons and fathers of families facing evacuation to resist due to a strong sense of self as family provider and in the hopes of safeguarding property. As one Katrina survivor explained from a Houston shelter, "They were already robbing. And my dad, he had to stay behind because we had a lot of tools and belongings there" (Eisenman et al. 2007, S111). Women food producers whose income supports their families in developing nations make the same decision and often pay with their lives (Ikeda 1995).

Women and men may simply have different capacities to act on their intentions. This was suggested in a multivariate analysis by researchers who studied evacuation behavior when Hurricane Bonnie approached the coast of North Carolina in 1998. They found that women were more likely to evacuate due to "underlying gender difference in caregiving roles, evacuation preparation, their greater exposure to certain objective risks [such as living in a mobile home], and their more acute perception of subjective risk" (Bateman and Edwards 2002, 116). Who decides when to leave? Their study suggested that when men (like women) were in caregiving roles for dependents with special medical needs (or lived in mobile homes or in storm surge zones), they were more likely than women to evacuate. Gender power at the household level meant that men could realize their own intentions more effectively. Men who are physically absent can also be a powerful force in women's evacuation decisions. When Proudley (2008) talked to women who remained at home with youngsters during an Australian bushfire, she found that husbands away on Australia's voluntary firefighting crews made key decisions which women came to regret: "I wanted my husband's decision. I regret what I did. I should never have gone," recalled one wife (p. 41).

Women's well-established roles in the family and workplace as caregivers for the young, old, ill, and disabled mean many stay who would like to leave. One woman described a tense evening shortly after her husband had undergone major surgery in Grand Forks. Awake in the early hours, she heard radio warnings urging evacuation ("our area was specifically named") but could not persuade her husband or grown son to leave when she awoke them at 5 am. "It took me until the afternoon on Saturday to convince [him] that we should leave. All medical services were down, and I didn't want to have to worry about getting him to medical help if he should need it in an area where none was available" (Enarson 2001, 6). Her son refused to leave. The debate is a familiar one in many households faced with evaluating warnings and making difficult decisions about evacuation.

The faces of those left stranded on rooftops fighting to stay above Katrina's floodwaters are forever a grim reminder to the nation of unequal resources and lack of understanding of how and under what conditions people make fateful decisions in disasters. Though other factors were in play, lack of access to functional cars and money for gasoline forced many low-income African Americans to stay, as interviewers learned when they queried survivors in a Houston shelter (Elder et al. 2007; Eisenman et al. 2007). The sheer capacity to leave cannot be overestimated: "You have to be able to feed your children when you leave. You have to be able to have a place to stay, you have to have gas money, you have to have rental car money. I couldn't afford to do that," explained one single mother (Eisenman et al. 2007, S112).

6.6.3 Impacts and Crisis Response

Men in search and rescue roles, strong male leaders, and men in construction jobs represent the most respected forms of immediate response. Women's work is far less visible (Fordham 1998; Enarson 2001) though their web of social relationships serves the family and community very well. At one extreme, the fictive kin bonds created by women in the camps of Nazi Germany were literally life-saving, especially for women; while men received more food they were less connected to "family" and survived for shorter periods of time in Clason's study (1983).

It was found early on that, in the immediate aftermath, men are more likely to make their way to the center of damage to assist strangers, while women tend to help family and kin first (Wenger and James 1994). This reflects the competing obligations of women to dependents as well as health status such as pregnancy. Lack of child care is also a barrier to professional women and men in response roles (Dobson 1994; Scanlon 1998). When family obligations and health permit, women and teenaged girls do help prepare their homes and communities. Photographers tell the story when they capture on film the many mixed-sex crews of sandbaggers, animal rescuers, kitchen crews, and emergency medical teams. Women's presence is, of course, hard to miss in the lower levels of all Red Cross disaster activities (Gibbs 1990) and other disaster relief agencies. Even in societies such as Iran, with strict segregation of the sexes in rural areas, the Red Cross and Red Crescent Society employ women to reach women unable to move freely in their community but likely to be hard hit in an earthquake or flood (Oxlee 2000). With respect to formal emergency response roles, the picture is decidedly more masculine. Formal emergency response roles and agencies are highly gendered and gender segregated around the world, and in the United States as well, as discussed below. On balance, women's response to crisis is more inside and backstage, while men's is more outside and frontstage (Enarson 2001; Alway, Belgrave, and Smith 1998).

6.6.3.1 Life, Safety, and Health

This chapter focuses primarily on how gender difference and inequality put women and girls at increased risk. With respect to disaster fatalities, gender is clearly a factor endangering the lives of boys and men, too. Measuring disaster impacts is a contested and complex task in which mortality data figure large, though these are very rarely reliable or sex specific. There are contradictory results on gender fatalities in U.S. tornadoes (Schmidlin 1997; Ono 2002). But it is noteworthy that when Central America was hit by hurricane Mitch, some researchers found higher fatality rates among men who responded incautiously or operated unfamiliar power tools (Buvinić 1999). A study on the children of Katrina suggests that more boys than girls died (Zahran, Peek, and Brody 2008), echoing other evidence that elderly, poor, African American men suffered disproportionately high fatalities in this storm relative to their presence in the population most affected (Sharkey 2007). This supports Klinenberg's (2002) conclusion from his "social autopsy" of Chicago's 1995 heat wave that 80% of the unclaimed bodies were those of African American men who were old, poor, and residing in a highly vulnerable neighborhood. Controlling for age, men were more than twice as likely to die in the same age group, a finding he relates to "the gender of isolation" reflecting masculinity norms of detachment and independence that result in more tenuous ties to family.

Nonetheless, in studies of major destructive events in the developing world, girls and women are highly vulnerable to the effects of environmental disasters and are the majority of those killed (Anderson 2000; Cutter 1995; Rivers 1982; Ikeda 1995). A recent statistical study of disaster-related gendered gaps in life expectancy concludes that women more than men die at an earlier age than would be expected in developing nations than are struck by natural disasters (Neumayer and Plümper 2007). In addition to family care, physical health, and reproductive status, the gendered division of labor is a powerful explanation, for this puts adult women and men in physically different locations; to take just one example, when the extraordinarily powerful Indian Ocean Tsunami wave came ashore in many Sri Lankan villages, men out fishing survived more often than women waiting on the beach to prepare and market the day's catch (Oxfam International 2005).

Overall, more women are likely to have died in the drawn-out *wake* of Hurricane Katrina, too, for women predominate among the frail elderly population, among the poor, among those dependent upon personal care in nursing homes and similar facilities, among those with disabilities, and among those employed as caretakers for those with functional limitations. Significant threats to the life and safety of women and girls also arise from *gender violence*, which is discussed further in Chapter 12. The question of gender mortality in disasters cannot readily be answered and is, for emergency managers, the wrong question. All human life is to be equally valued and all gender-based vulnerabilities are significant.

Poor living conditions, overcrowding, lack of access to services, constraints on breast feeding, and limited access to birth control were among the problems noted by health researchers in the aftermath of Katrina (Callaghan et al. 2007). Like the Centers for Disaster Control, which included a fact sheet for pregnant women in materials distributed to evacuees, they emphasize the need for practitioners to include pregnancy status in medical intakes of displaced women and consider their specific contraceptive needs. Without access to reliable birth control, women may be faced with unintended pregnancies, so resilient family planning services are essential. Indeed, in the first half year following Katrina, 17% of 55 young women (aged 16–24) in New Orleans told researchers they needed but were not able to obtain health care, a third found it difficult to practice their usual birth control method, and four in five had not used birth control (Kissinger et al. 2007).

The immediate needs of *pregnant women* should certainly be part of emergency planning. More than 1.1 million women of reproductive age (15–44 years) are believed to have resided in the affected areas before Hurricane Katrina, and they were disproportionately at risk of adverse outcomes related to poor nutrition, lack of services, and poverty before the storm; not surprisingly, the rate of low-weight births among the children they gave birth to after the storm was significantly higher than the U.S. norm (Callaghan et al. 2007). African American women whose health was jeopardized by years of neglect and an eroding safety net lived in the paths of these storms, so negative effects on their health and well-being and their infants born after the storm were easily predicted (Bennett 2005).

In a study from Quebec, Canada, of a prolonged ice storm, prenatal maternal stress increased and the cognitive development and language development of the unborn children were negatively affected (King and Laplante 2005). This may be an indicator of future reproductive health risks related to stressful changes in weather events—or deliberate destruction such as occurred in the World Trade Center attacks. The ratio of female to male live births increased in the wake of these attacks as well as the 1995 Kobe earthquake, leading to speculation about how disasters and other stressors affect fetal viability, especially among male fetuses (Catalanol et al. 2006). Clearly the reproductive health of both men and women can be affected by exposure to toxic chemicals, so it is vital to mitigate exposure to contaminants arising from toxic spills or explosions, contaminated water, or unhealthy living conditions in temporary accommodations.

Gender differences in disaster-related stress have been well documented by U.S. researchers (among others, see Van Willigen 2001). The interaction of social class, life stage, family size, and family structure generally put women at greater risk of *post-disaster stress*. A major review of this literature based on case studies from the United States and elsewhere (Norris et al. 2002) determined that being married is a risk factor for women, while being somewhat more protective for men. Additionally, as Ollenburger and Tobin (1998) noted in their study of stress after three U.S. floods, "Older women are also more likely to suffer from health and mobility limitations, increasing their disaster vulnerability. In addition divorced women are more likely to be heading households with two or more residents and women usually have custody of the children following a divorce" (p. 106).

Studies from the Exxon Valdez oil spill also point to more self-destructive coping strategies such as substance abuse or fighting among men (Palinkas et al. 1993). Coping with the emotional needs of male partners is an added challenge to women who are "shock absorbers" for so many of the effects of disasters. Acting as sounding boards for men may also be part of the job of women in first-responder roles, as this firefighter who responded to the World Trade Center recalled:

> Guys will come into my office and cry to me who aren't going in to the office and crying to my lieutenants. As women, I think we've got a big burden. The burden has always been on the women, because we're in a fishbowl (Hagen and Carouba 2002, 179).

Following the 1997 Red River flood, this college-educated Native American woman described her husband's emotional withdrawal from the family (Enarson and Fordham 2001):

> He was not the strong one any more because he had such a difficult time, thinking, not only did he lose his home but his parents' home. … The first three or four months he was, he stayed away. He was real distant and kind of did his own thing … He said the most difficult thing for him was the fact that he is supposed to take care of his family and he had nowhere to bring that family (p. 14).

Interviewed a year and a half after the flood, and newly settled into a new job and new house, she felt ready for counseling, but free counseling was no longer available. The highly feminized mental health care system and lack of attention to the specific gender issues that arise for boys and men constitute an invisible gender barrier to men and to the full recovery of families hit by disasters around the world (Fordham and Ketteridge 1998).

Finally, women's often tenuous *access to health care* before disasters can deteriorate further in the aftermath, as was reported of low-income Katrina survivors who depended upon diabetes clinics, maternal and infant care programs, and community clinics serving those living with HIV/AIDS or other chronic diseases (Jones-DeWeever 2007). This same report noted that rising numbers of undocumented Latinas moving to the area for work put pressure on emergency rooms as they deferred prenatal care due to fear of authorities. Home and community health care systems need more attention in disaster emergency medicine as they are staffed predominantly by women and serve predominantly female populations such as the frail elderly, the chronically ill, patients needing reproductive health care, and those subject to intimate partner abuse.

6.6.3.2   Shelter and Housing

Low-income women living alone may not get needed assistance preparing their homes, as was found among African American women living in a state of disrepair in public housing in South Miami. As Hurricane Andrew approached, they reported that male managers ignored their requests for plywood and nails to cover apartment windows (Morrow and Enarson 1996). When forced to relocate during the emergency period, affluent women move their families to out-of-town cabins, fly to the home of distant family members, or check into hotels instead of shelters. Strong credit records and savings help them recover or hire other women to help. But housing issues during evacuation, relocation, and resettlement are an ongoing struggle for most women.

Temporary shelters, which often house displaced residents for months or even years, are rarely sited near major employers of women, public transportation lines, or child care centers, making it all the more difficult for women to earn income and help their families start anew. *Home-based work* can be both a liability and an opportunity in disasters. In the United States as around the world, self-employed women engaged in micro-enterprise or operating small businesses struggle to collapse family and paid work into cramped workspaces with greatly diminished resources (Enarson 2000a).

6.6.3.3   Care Work

The emotional and physical needs of male partners, children, aged relatives, the ill or disabled, and other dependents are met predominantly by women before, during, and after disasters. These responsibilities tend to increase dramatically, even as newer forms of disaster work arise and women seek income-generating jobs. Not only is it more difficult to meet the immediate needs of family members (e.g., lacking transportation, stores, money), but they may have new needs as well, from new housing and clothing to help relocating, school supplies, and perhaps long-term medical or psychological care.

After a disaster, when family life resumes under very different conditions, lack of facilities, equipment, supplies, space, and time clearly expand women's domestic labor, magnifying the demands of those who hold down paid jobs while also managing the household and (in the middle-aged "sandwich generation") caring both for the young and the old. This is especially true of low-income women unable to purchase such replacement services as child or elder care, restaurant meals, domestic help, or dry cleaning. Often, households expand in size as women able to do so offer space and personal services (cooking, laundry, child care, emotional support) to kin, coworkers, friends, and evacuated families not known to them personally.

During their long stays in temporary accommodations of all sorts, women's day-to-day efforts to cook, clean, and care for their families, often in combination with paid jobs and unpaid community work, are complicated by the physical limitations of temporary accommodations, e.g., lack of privacy, few play spaces for children or activities for teens, insufficient laundry facilities, social isolation. In Miami's FEMA trailer camps a decade ago, interviewers (Morrow and Enarson 1996) found women were often isolated, fearful for their personal safety, lacked needed mental and reproductive health services and reliable transportation, and were unable to access needed community services. There was no child care, elder care, or family respite care consistently provided in public spaces to support women with dependents in their efforts to repair homes, search for new housing, or access relief services. These themes are echoed in studies of the Red River flood and mothers displaced by Gulf Coast storms.

Care work falls more to women in the best of times and in the wake of disasters, too, as they strive to create and recreate a sense of security for children in makeshift shelters or temporary houses. The routine and exceptional demands of daily life are more time-consuming and difficult in temporary accommodations, but also an essential part of rebuilding home and hearth (Fothergill 2004). Kin work such as celebrating birthdays, religious holidays, and anniversaries, home visits to older relatives, and care for the ill does not stop during relocation, and generally falls to the women of the family.

Caring for children in temporary housing, or the back rooms of distant kin or host families, can be extremely difficult (Enarson and Scanlon 1999; Peek and Fothergill, 2009). New child care issues arise including conflicts with grandparents, disrupted nursing schedules and toilet training, more sibling conflict, and unfamiliar child care providers. In a study of 19 adult and elderly women evacuated from New Orleans to trailer parks in nearby states and cities, women described caring for elderly mothers who now saw their daughters as the only source of stability in their lives; the storm had undermined their independence and taken their precious cooking pots "which they had cooked so many meals in for so many people. The pots were a chronicling of the lives women had led" (Mason 2007, 4).

Sociologists who have followed single mothers displaced by the Gulf Coast storms report that "mothering became much more difficult and complicated, largely due to the separation from fathers and from extended family networks" (Peek and Fothergill, 2009). While a few of the single mothers spoke of "absent fathers," most of the single mothers in our study informed the researchers that their children's fathers had played important roles in their children's lives before the storm. In fact, many of the single mothers reported that even though they did not live together, these fathers still spent time with their children and shared in at least some parental duties. This support system was another direct impact women faced and also complicated decisions about relocation. The dominant political discourse blamed the victim, especially in diatribes against black single mothers who in turn felt abandoned:

> Four people died around me. Four. Diabetes. I am a diabetic and I survived it, by the grace of God. … Look, I was on top of the Interstate. Five days, okay? … People do leave a dog in a house, but they do leave him food and water. They didn't do that (Ransby 2006, 217).

6.6.3.4 Income-Generating Work

Temporary relocation (which may last a very long time) impinges directly and indirectly on women's ability to earn income. Female labor force participation rates in New Orleans after the storms declined along with their average wages, the opposite of men's experience; further, it is female-dominated sectors that decline most dramatically, for example, in service work and in health and education (Jones-DeWeever 2007). This was also observed after the Red River flood when the state job service reported employment declines of 14.7% in retail trade and 15.9% in service jobs (Enarson 2001). Women's income declines due to secondary unemployment, too. Domestic workers, for instance, may well lose both homes and jobs when their middle-class employers relocate with insurance checks to await housing repairs or relocate altogether.

The "financial fallout" for women after the 1997 Red River flood meant downward mobility for many when women lost income due to business closures and cutbacks and increased debt (Fothergill 2004). Older women sometimes took early retirement from heavily impacted businesses, or were forced to postpone planned retirements and continue working, and counselors and child care workers lost money while free or subsidized services were available to flood survivors (Enarson 2001). Flexplace/time policies and continuous salary and benefits helped women do their jobs and still complete the flood of paperwork, meet insurance adjusters at home, or take children to see counselors. However, this support was more available to professional women in universities and other large bureaucratic organizations than to working-class women in low-wage manual jobs, part-time workers, and women in the informal sector.

Informal and formal child care systems enable women's employment but are highly susceptible to disruption. The immediate loss of 5000 licensed child care slots in Grand Forks is a case in point, affecting both providers and employed mothers when licensed child care slots were closed in just one day due to flooding (Enarson 1998). As one child care advocate reported, "It really opened their eyes! It took 53 feet of water for them to realize—oh, family child care is an issue. And then we were getting calls from the business community. 'Well, what are you going to do about it? How are you going to fix it?'" (p. 4). More than two and a half years after Hurricane Katrina, just 117 child care centers were operating compared to 275 before the storm, and only one fifth as many public buses were available for employed women without private transport (Agenda for Children 2008; The New Orleans Index 2008). Organizations such as the Mennonite Economic Development Association are responding with training for child care workers and micro-economic loans.

Like the families they serve, child care providers are hard hit when they lose their working space, equipment, supplies, and clientele. Child care providers affected by the Red River flood reported that they earned on average one third of the family income, so theirs is a significant loss (Enarson 2001). Yet disaster relief policies can make it difficult for self-employed child care workers to claim losses to home space or equipment used by clients and family alike.

Women who work in agricultural jobs or are owner/operators of family farms suffer both income loss and severe degradation of the natural world around them, in rich and poor societies alike. Women with *resource-dependent livelihoods* are impacted in complex ways when these resources are degraded (among others, see Stehlik, Lawrence, and Gray 2000 for a study of women and drought in Australia). A qualitative study from rural Manitoba, Canada, found many women deeply affected by the threat posed by "mad cow disease," due both to restrictions in cross-border trade and to social contamination (Reinsch, 2009). The photographs taken by women of their life with this "creeping disaster" captured their alienation from husbands, unmet standards for care of home and hearth, and their sorrow at the great loss of the family farm, their most precious inheritance from the past and legacy to their children. The diffuse effects on women's livelihoods in the face of global warming warrant much closer attention as snow decreases, decline of species availability, more variability in weather patterns, and related effects of climate change are linked both to climate change and to women's health and sustainable livelihoods, for example, by Owens (2005) in her study from Labrador in Canada's north.

6.6.4 RECOVERY NEEDS AND RESPONSES

The following section offers a short review of gender issues throughout the recovery process, with selected examples of how women individually and collectively step into action to help themselves, their families, and their communities. One clear "lesson" to be learned from gender-focused research on vulnerability and impact in U.S. disasters is that, whatever the contours or cultural location of the next disaster or catastrophe, women will be leaders in the long walk forward to the "new normal" while struggling with their own unmet recovery issues.

6.6.4.1 Help Seeking

Extensive care work is a significant barrier to women's recovery, both because this work conflicts with income-generating work, and because it asks so much of women who may themselves be left bereaved, ill, unemployed, deserted by male partners, landless, or without support for their many conflicting roles. As noted, men are highly visible frontline responders in their jobs as firefighters, elected officials, or certified emergency managers, and other socially visible relief roles. Domestic work and child care keep many women home so they cannot as readily participate in post-event meetings, as this elderly woman from a small Canadian town recalled after a flood:

> After we moved back, my husband would go to the [disaster relief centre] and find out what was happening. He also went there to eat meals from time to time. I didn't. I stayed here to eat so I could keep working. There was so much cleaning to do" (Enarson and Scanlon 1999, 115).

Like the men in their families, women generally resist asking for emergency assistance from government and private relief agencies because of the "stigma of charity" (Fothergill 2004). Yet they must put aside these feelings, for researchers around the globe find that the *"second disaster" of paperwork* falls disproportionately to them. Like so many others with family responsibilities, this Native American mother of a young daughter had no choice:

> I had a hard time going to, like, Red Cross or anything like that. I had a very difficult time. And I don't know if it was a pride thing or what. My Dad would not go. [And your husband?] Oh, there's no way. No. And when we were [evacuated] out there, I had to go. I had nothing for my daughter (Enarson 1998, 3).

Wives and daughters interviewed in case studies typically report that it is they who register the household for assistance before evacuation, deal in person and by telephone with a range of agencies to pursue damage claims, and otherwise pursue the frustrating "treasure search" for any and all relief and recovery resources. Predictably, women at increased risk before disasters are slow to recover. For instance, poor health kept many elderly widows from returning promptly after their evacuation from flooded Grand Forks in 1997. Because they were not in town to arrange for cleanup and repairs before construction work slowed for the winter, repairs were not initiated and they returned to depressing living conditions in damaged homes. Widows living alone on deteriorating family farms in a region with a strong ethic of self-reliance were reluctant to ask for help; they lived instead in substandard housing "with their basements collapsing" after the flood (Enarson 1999). In other cases, fraudulent contractors seemed to target older, non-English-speaking women (Morrow and Enarson 1996).

6.6.4.2 Relocation

Women's economic status and family roles are formidable barriers in the race for affordable housing, making women *more dependent on temporary accommodations*. One year after the Red River flood, a housing specialist in Grand Forks estimated that 30% to 40% of FEMA trailer residents were women, often single mothers with large families, on public assistance, or marginally employed (Enarson 1999). In Miami after Hurricane Andrew, women were the majority of those long-time residents of "temporary" FEMA housing, especially non-English-speaking women heading multi-generational families (Morrow and Enarson 1996), a pattern repeating in the wake of the 2005 Gulf Coast storms.

Women are far more likely than men to be household heads who rely on their own low incomes or modest government assistance, so the national shortage of affordable housing (Joint Center for Housing Studies of Harvard University 2004; Habitat for Humanity n.d.) can become a personal crisis. More likely than men to be renters, women cannot afford escalating rental rates, for example, in New Orleans where rents nearly doubled after Hurricane Katrina and 80% of the housing units destroyed were considered affordable or low-income housing. The demolition of thousands of public housing units helps explain why 83% of single mothers were still unable to return to their own communities two years after the storms:

"The same people who were left behind during the storm have been left behind in rebuilding it. The elderly, the young, single mothers" (Jones-DeWeever 2007, 10).

Lack of affordable permanent housing has many ramifications. In Grand Forks, women interviewed 18 months after the flood spoke of behavioral problems with children in crowded living quarters, health problems, and pressure to take in ex-partners who had no living space. Ten years later, very similar problems haunt Katrina's displaced mothers two years after the storms (Peek and Fothergill, 2009). As discussed in a later chapter, overcrowding resulting from lack of affordable alternatives may well increase the risk to children of family sexual assault, and abused women may be forced back into violent relationships.

The material and emotional tasks of resettling a household and making houses into homes again generally falls more to women, who express especially *strong ties to place* (Phillips 1995; Fordham and Ketteridge 1998). They recall destroyed or damaged homes as places of personal growth where babies were born, family rituals enacted, gardens tended, and emotional and physical lives constructed under their care. The loss of household possessions was the loss of family history and personal identity: "Every box of my life was just floating around," one Grand Forks woman remembered feeling as she surveyed her flooded basement (Fothergill 2004, 196).

Men, of course, also struggle with strong emotions, especially if the homes they built themselves or worked on are damaged. A member of the disaster outreach team touring Grand Forks reported from an affluent flooded-out neighborhood:

We had a lady call us and say, "Just come, I'll show you." We go down there and the guy got out of the car and he stopped at the end of the driveway and he sobbed and he sobbed. And she goes, "This is what he does every time. We can't even talk. He's a wreck and I have to hold everything together" (Enarson 1999, 52).

Down the road, a Latina wife and mother noted that most support groups and counseling that were made available targeted women—not cultural bias but gender bias led to her husband's increasing sense of isolation and depression, she felt (Enarson and Fordham 2001). Another close observer is critical of "heroism for its own sake" for its unhealthy effects, especially among men, adding that prolonged inattention to contrary feelings of defeat or loss "works like duct tape, holding things together but only for awhile" (Twohey 1998, 13).

Couples may also struggle with *conflicting priorities* when making decisions about whether, when, and where to relocate, and about repair and rebuilding priorities. Flood-affected women in the Midwestern United States objected when men's interests took priority in home reconstruction and repairs to home-business space, laundry rooms, or play spaces used predominantly by women and children were delayed: "I was just furious," one woman told an interviewer (Fothergill 2004). "It was as if my work was worthless" (Enarson 2001, 139).

6.6.4.3 Marginalization

Gender bias in *recovery programs* may also deter women's recovery. Childers' study of several flooded communities in Louisiana (1999) found that low-income elderly women were disproportionately in need of economic assistance but less likely to receive it. Women who owned small businesses in a flooded Midwestern community experienced disproportionately high failure rates (Staples and Stubbings 1998), perhaps because their work was often based in the home (bookkeeping, beauty salons, arts and crafts, professional typing). Yet women were found in an earlier study to be disadvantaged in federal disaster relief programs for small businesses (Nigg and Tierney 1990). If small loan programs targeting women do not include feasibility studies, job training, and other social supports, they may sap women's resources without advancing their long-term recovery.

Barriers to women in post-disaster *work relief programs* are often reported in developing nations. In the reconstruction boom post-Katrina, too, women were less often employed in housing construction than men; undocumented women who did find construction work were reportedly vulnerable to abuse, sometimes not receiving pay for completed work, and yet unable to object due to fear of deportation or other retribution (Jones-DeWeever 2007). Targeting relief funds to male-dominated employment projects in construction, debris removal, or landscaping supports the economic recovery of teenaged and adult men but disadvantages women and girls who also need income support. Good disaster relief jobs often go to middle-class women with formal credentials, job experience, and professional networks (Krajeski and Peterson 1997); these are women who also have such private assets as out-of-town cabins or credit for hotel rooms, savings accounts for refurnishing homes, and cash for hiring lower-income women to help them muck out their homes, as was evident following the 1997 Red River flood (Enarson and Fordham 2001, and see Peterson 1997).

Lack of voice is another barrier to girls and women. With challenges at home and work and often lacking transportation and childcare, it can be especially difficult for women to make their needs known and help shape the rebuilding process, as this woman recalls of Grand Forks: "The flood response committee. How many people are free at six o'clock Wednesday night to go do that? I mean, I taught a class 'til six. I'd run over there. I'd try and spend time with my kids" (Enarson 2001, 14). As women are primary users of relief systems and resources and those who seek public assistance have few other resources, it is especially important that recovery planning be gender sensitive.

Gender bias in disaster recovery arises from normative expectations about whose voice matters, how a "family" looks or acts, stereotypes about the passions and skills of women and men, and lack of knowledge about the challenges and dangers faced by girls and women. A Latina social service administrator dealing with flood-affected migrant families criticized traditional recovery strategies, asking for more community engagement with high-risk women: "It doesn't address what happens right after, it doesn't address the healing part. Women tend to pick up the brunt of that" (Enarson and Fordham 2001, 51). She also objected that emergency managers fail to consult those most knowledgeable about vulnerable populations, among them migrant workers:

> [F]ew community planners would go to [a migrant worker like her] and say, "How do we plan for migrant families coming in? What do we need?" And I think here's where you have the ... understanding, the knowledge of the community and the knowledge of the client.

6.6.4.4 Women Working Collectively

Typecast as hapless victims, women are actively involved in resolving problems before, during, and after a disaster. As mothers and wives, community volunteers, and social service workers, they secure and distribute much-needed disaster relief assistance and are the lifeline for the emotional recovery of children and other dependents. Mental health counselors, antiviolence crisis workers, primary school teachers, and personal care workers in nursing homes or halfway homes for the disabled are among the legions of women drawn into recovery work by the nature of their professions. A study of visiting home health nurses during a Canadian ice storm, for instance (Sibbald 1998), found these women to be a vital link to isolated, old, and frail residents otherwise out of sight. Across the border in the United States, part-time nurses in a local hospice program worked overtime during the Red River flood without child care or other support systems to provide uninterrupted medication and support to terminally ill patients in hard-to-reach flooded areas (Enarson 2001). Women do what needs doing at home and at work:

> I never knew when I walked in my door who was coming out of my shower, who was using my laundry, or how many people I was going to feed that night when I came home. I had people in and out. … [The men] were tired by the time they came back, so I always had the meals ready to go, not knowing what time they were coming—and I never knew when they were going to be there (Enarson 1998, 4).

At another level, women are highly involved in emergent post-disaster organizations. From the ashes of the Berkeley/Oakland fires, women architects formed a women's group that met for over three years, fearful that local women would be disenfranchised in the process of their own "recovery." Informally structured, the group "provided so much courage it saw almost full attendance every Monday night for three years" (Hoffman 1998, 60). In Miami, too, women built their own relief group (Enarson and Morrow 1998b) when the male-dominated group distributing relief monies failed to address the needs of women and children. Women Will Rebuild, a coalition of over 40 women's organizations, mobilized for a place on the executive board and urged that 10% of all donated funds be redirected to women's economic recovery, antiviolence services, youth recreation, child care, and affordable housing. The solidarity they demonstrated is their legacy to disaster resilience along this hazardous coastline.

Women family members led survivor groups seeking redress after the attacks of September 11, 2001; six years later, their interfaith responses have been documented (Radcliff Institute for Advanced Study 2007). Predictably, women's groups swung into action after the 2005 Gulf Coast storms (Pyles and Lewis 2007). The women's caucus of the Common Ground Collective built a women's room and offered health services for low-income women and children, and many African American women worked through ACORN for affordable and secure housing. A resource handbook was developed by Katrina Warriors to help women and promote their safety, while Women of the Storm, a network of elite women, lobbied at a state and national level for government leadership (David, 2008). The Ms. Foundation, Soroptimists, and many other women's sporting, business, and professional organizations quickly stepped in to support women and their families and women's groups working for transparent, participatory, and environmentally sustainable recovery (Vaill 2006). Over a century earlier, women "good government" reformers in Galveston had done the same in the wake of their own devastating hurricane (Turner 1997). Women's collective recovery work in the United States parallels international organizing for sustainable mitigation and recovery (Yonder, Ackar, and Gopalan 2005; Figure 6.2).

Community celebrations of survival and resilience are critical to recovery and here, too, women's leadership is evident (Krajeski and Peterson 1997): they

> They understand the "symbolic" nature of recovery and the importance of community ritual and symbols. They are the keepers of traditions and celebrations, and thus the providers of meaning and hope. They not only survive, they sustain themselves, their families and—given the opportunity—their communities (p. 126).

Haitian women in Miami, for instance, organized a spring cultural celebration six months after Hurricane Andrew devastated their Miami neighborhood (Morrow and Enarson 1996). Quilters, artists, musicians, and writers used the arts to help others make sense of the 1997 Red River flood (Enarson 2000b) just as the women from the Berkeley/Oakland hills who lost their homes "tatted back neighborhoods like so much lace" (Hoffman 1998, 61). Though the daughters, mothers, wives, and grandmothers of Katrina are still in limbo, they will do the same over time.

The constraints to recovery reviewed above reflect and reinforce male dominance in the practice of emergency management as well. When a work culture is dominated by the norms of traditionally male-dominated occupations and the life experiences of men more than women, gender bias

FIGURE 6.2   A volunteer from the First Presbyterian Church, Stillwater, Oklahoma, rebuilds a damaged home in New Orleans. *Source*: Photo by Tim Schlais, with permission.

follows—no surprise in emergency management given its origins and evolution. Organizational gender norms are usually examined with respect to women, for example, in Phillips' pioneering study of gender bias in emergency management (1990), which explained how women's exclusion from the "old boys' network" deprives emergency management organizations of much-needed sensitivity to the socio-emotional needs of survivors. A decade later, Wilson found (1999) that just 10 of the 67 Florida counties that employed Office of Emergency Management directors employed women in professional roles. Predictably, these same dynamics are in evidence around the world at the professional level (for Australia, see Childs 2006 and Wraith 1997). In contrast, masculinity norms are rarely examined. Competing notions of manliness were found to affect working relationships in a study of firefighters (structural and wildfire) in British Columbia (Pacholok 2005); similar dynamics were found in a study of decision makers launching the ill-fated Challenger (Maier 1997).

Box 6.3 tells the story of just one woman in emergency management in the recent past. But there is also enormous potential for personal and organizational growth as women and men pursue

---

BOX 6.3   WOMEN'S EMPOWERMENT IN A DISASTER

But the frustrations brought tremendous change in me. The heat, the workload, the sorrow at seeing such destruction began to release in me an adrenalin that forced me to stand on my own two feet. If once I had been the woman who never said no, now I was developing my own voice and it was plenty pissed off. I began to argue with males or authority figures for the first time in my life. I asserted my rights with contractors, roofers, adjusters, even my bosses at work. The more I practiced, the better it felt. No longer would I sit back and wait. When the insurance office called a security guard to stand by as I ranted and raved about the promised check that could not be found once again, I realized someone was actually *afraid* of me. This was an incredible feeling of empowerment—the first time I ever felt that way. ... In the aftermath of the hurricane I found a source of strength and power of survival that I hold within myself and because of that I am a stronger person today (Colina 1998).

> ## BOX 6.4   A FEMALE EMERGENCY MANAGER LOOKS BACK
>
> When I began emergency planning, I entered into a profession historically dominated by retired military men or men from the public safety field. … It is my observation that public service personnel progress through the ranks depending on how well they fit into the "good old boy" culture. Most of the women I know in the field of emergency management got their start as public educators and do not seem to be as motivated by whistles and red lights. Like myself, these women tend to emphasize the basics of emergency management—preparedness, mitigation, response and recovery. Perhaps when more women are employed in fire departments, law enforcement and the military, women in emergency management will be accepted more readily. In the meantime, women who work in this male-dominated profession will continue to experience gender bias and will have limited access to upper management. As one example, when emergency management is part of the fire department women who are not "sworn" fire personnel do not advance up the career ladder (Barnecut 1998).

common goals. In a recent workshop on gender and disaster, it was evident that men, too, must want and promote gender mainstreaming for it to succeed (see Box 6.4 for practical recommendations). In the same vein, a recent publication of the International Association of Emergency Managers (IAEM 2005) highlighted the changing roles of women, many of whom applauded male champions and mentors.

6.7   DO GENDER RELATIONS CHANGE IN DISASTERS?

Like any crisis, a disaster can be a pivotal moment for self-knowledge and personal growth. When women's consciousness changes—and future researchers will certainly explore how disasters impact men's identities, too—a foundation is built for collective action for change. At the individual level, those who live through disasters often speak of how the event changed their expectations of themselves and others, if only in the short term (few disaster studies consider change of any kind over the long term). Generally, these changes support traditional patterns of interaction between and among women and men.

Writing about Katrina, researchers observed that:

> the pressures and expectations of paid employment often pushed fathers in the direction of the provider role (which subsequently meant that, generally speaking, men were not involved in hurricane preparations because they were required to work), while mothers were often pulled into the homemaker role because of the lack of reliable childcare and the fact that their schedules were typically more flexible or their incomes more expendable (Peek and Fothergill, 2009).

Similarly, when the firestorm struck the Berkeley/Oakland hills, men returned more quickly to employment; coveted space in crowded rental homes was allocated to their computers and other necessities while wives quit their jobs to care for the children; insurance companies did their part by issuing checks in the names of their husbands. In this context, a "fifty year setback" was observed:

> Men launched into command and took action. Assuming the family helm, they proceeded to exercise autonomous decision. With the domicile *gone,* women on the other hand found themselves thrown into utter domesticity. Whether they worked in the outside world or not, women drowned in a veritable sea of intestine, homely detail, towels, toothbrushes, underwear, Spaghetti-O's. Women further fell unwittingly into old habits of compliance. As men picked rental houses and very often commandeered the design of new houses, even down to the kitchens, women retreated in silence and acquiesced (Hoffman 1998, 57).

BOX 6.5   MEN AND GENDER MAINSTREAMING

Men participating in a breakout session of the 2004 Gender Equality and Disaster Risk Reduction Workshop in Honolulu made these strategic recommendations for change.

- Men need to advocate for gender equality.
- Men need to deliver gender mainstreaming messages to other men.
- Men need to be full partners in gender sensitivity training.
- Men as leaders need to be committed to bringing gender equity results within their own organizations.
- Men need to confront gender stereotyping, and create opportunities for personal and institutional transformation.
- Men need to recognize that women have lots of personal knowledge and skills in coping with disasters, and that more women need to be trained as first responders.
- Tools are needed to sensitize and empower men to implement gender equality.
- A separate workshop on men's role in gender equality/gender mainstreaming is needed, and sessions should be held at upcoming meetings.
- The Gender and Disaster Network should be used to share ideas, tools, and best practices.

Other case studies suggest just as dramatically that restrictive gender norms can be overcome (see Box 6.5). Women surprise themselves by negotiating with insurance adjusters, coping with divorce in the midst of a storm, stepping into leadership roles, or simply speaking their minds when it really mattered. Some leave abusive relationships behind, too: "I'm starting a new life. So, I'm going to take that flood, and all that abuse, and when the flood waters left Grand Forks, well that was my old life leaving" (Fothergill 2004, 166). For other women, liberation meant developing new skills as they worked alongside husbands to repair the damage done by Hurricane Andrew: "I can do wire now! Changed all my outlets and I can put up lights" (Enarson 1999, 52). Men, too, have recounted their surprise at being drawn into more egalitarian and nontraditional roles through disaster work (Fothergill 2004).

6.8   WORKING WITH WOMEN TO BUILD COMMUNITY RESILIENCE: STRATEGIC AND PRACTICAL STEPS

In an era of climate change and increasing hazards and disasters, gender sensitivity is not a luxury but an essential quality of effective disaster risk management. Without the skills and knowledge of both women and men, the scarce resources available for reducing risk and responding to disasters will not reach those most in need, or in the long run build true community resilience. In this spirit, Box 6.6 summarizes some of the practical implications of the preceding discussion, and frames the specific initiatives discussed in the concluding section below.

6.8.1   DEVELOPING PARTNERSHIPS TO BUILD CAPACITY

Partnering with women's groups and agencies that know both the needs and the resources of local women opens new possibilities for local emergency managers to increase community resilience. Some examples are working with women's groups to design appropriate disaster exercises and scenarios, sharing mailing lists for newsletters and other emergency communications, revising emergency resource handbooks to include these groups, and soliciting interns or seasonal hires from women's colleges or traditionally female programs of study at the local college or university.

BOX 6.6   SOME PRACTICAL SUGGESTIONS FOR PRACTITIONERS AND ADVOCATES

AWARENESS AND PREPAREDNESS

Nontraditional outlets should be used and gender-sensitive messaging developed in consultation with diverse local women's groups to include: targeting messages through different outlets; household preparedness information printed on grocery bags, for example, or distributed through sports clubs and religious activities attracting women or men, respectively. Awareness can also be increased by targeting radio stations or television programs popular with local women, including messages integrated into "soap opera" style programs as has been done successfully to reach grassroots women internationally.

EVACUATION

Transportation assistance may be needed for low-income women who often both provide and need special care, and advance planning to evacuate the caregivers as well as dependents in community facilities and private homes. Gender-specific evacuation messages should be used to explicitly address family-based obstacles, with special attention to men who may place property protection over their own safety. Online preparedness guides can be illustrated with vignettes from qualitative studies of how couples make evacuation decisions and what the consequences are.

CRISIS RESPONSE

Opportunities should be created for male and female children, youth, and adults to participate to the degree feasible in all facets of emergency response and preparedness programs at the local level. Evaluations should be conducted to identify unintended barriers and gender stereotypes restricting the roles of women and men in training for crisis response. Advance planning for family support of emergency relief workers, including child care arrangements, is a step often recommended to support all parent practitioners. The capacities for emergency response of local women's groups should be assessed and training offered through both women's and men's groups at the local level.

ECONOMIC RECOVERY

Emergency managers should be aware of employment trends and patterns for both women and men with special attention to women who are insecurely employed or self-employed. Hazard and risk assessments should include sex-specific data on the likely economic effects of different disaster events for women and men, respectively, including loss of child and elder care systems. Outreach to employers to promote service and business continuity should target women's employers and encourage flexible work policies post-disaster, and additional support can be planned to forestall more severe effects on women's small businesses. Outreach to rural communities should be sensitive to the impacts on women farmers as well as men when disasters threaten rural livelihoods.

COMMUNITY PARTNERSHIPS

Capacity building is needed for women's and community organizations that serve high-risk families to ensure service continuity and realistic opportunities to help shape community recovery plans. Family-friendly assistance made available over the long term to women is vital. Strong partnerships are needed between emergency managers and local, state, and tribal women's groups and networks to identify the long-term recovery concerns of high-risk women and men, respectively, and gender-sensitive indicators used to measure their long-term recovery. Women's organizations should be directly solicited to help design and evaluate community-based long-term recovery planning.

Capacity building is needed for crisis shelters, family assistance centers, community clinics, child-care centers, and other organizations that will be called upon by those least able to help themselves. This may include direct assistance to help low-budget agencies develop and test tailor-made emergency preparedness plans and helping them secure the resources needed to implement these. Pilot programs can be funded and then scaled up to help foster a gender-sensitive culture of prevention at the grassroots level. Regional or national templates for capacity building in women's agencies can be developed and circulated, with culturally specific approaches appropriate to different organizational environments. Training workshops bringing emergency management issues into the forefront of operational planning in grassroots women's groups is essential, as is including these organizations, coalitions, and groups in scenario-based exercises. These organizations are a critical *social* infrastructure in all communities, so enhancing organizational resilience is an important investment in public safety.

Bringing women's and community groups into the mainstream of emergency management as valued and long-term stakeholders and partners is the foundation for asking and answering the right questions about sex and gender in disaster contexts.

6.8.2 RISK MAPPING

Gender-sensitive risk mapping is vital. Multidimensional risk maps now show at a glance what population groups are most exposed to particular hazards, and where critical facilities and lifelines are located. The complexities of gender identity and gender relations cannot be mapped in any simple way as a ratio of women to men in a given census block or year, but the statistical profile developed in the demographic section of this chapter suggests important indicators of vulnerability and capacity to monitor.

Practitioners should use census data if possible but also ask community planning agencies to gather or provide gender data directly, or solicit this information from nonprofit organizations serving women and other high-risk populations or local universities and colleges; in the process, they will forge new links with future disaster researchers and volunteers and potential new emergency managers. Planners will learn about gender as a planning issue by connecting with women's groups across cultural and age groups and asking, among other questions:

- What is the age distribution of the local female population? How many women are of child-bearing age?
- How many single mothers and single fathers live here? How large are their households?
- How many local women earn income at home? How many own their own businesses?
- How many women here are employed full time? Part time? What is their average income?
- What are the region's major employers of men and women, boys and girls?
- How many widows and widowers reside here?
- What is the poverty rate for women and men? What proportion of single mothers live below the poverty line here?
- How many women here live with what kinds of disabilities, and how many are employed as caregivers to persons with disabilities?
- What kinds of child care are used by local families?
- How many homeless women and men live in this area? Where do they reside?

- How many women with school-aged children are employed full-time, and how many have access to personal cars?
- What proportion of women in this community rent or own their own homes? How many people here live in public housing units?
- What is the dominant language spoken by senior women and men? What is the literacy rate of women and men?
- How many family day care associations, women's business networks, women's trade union groups, service clubs, faith-based auxiliaries, youth agencies, and similar organizations can be located? What is their contact information, and are their resources included in assessments of community resilience?
- How many crisis shelters are there, and local organizations serving women at increased risk (e.g., women with disabilities, new immigrant women, lesbian women)? How many have solicited and/or received assistance preparing emergency plans?
- Where are the child care centers, schools, health care facilities, parks, community centers, domestic violence shelters, homeless shelters, adult day care homes, halfway homes, and other places where outreach to women could be effective?

6.8.3 Gender-Sensitive Programming and Planning

Gender-sensitive programming should include specific gender indicators, benchmarks, and targets in all aspects of project design, implementation, monitoring, and evaluation. Policy reviews are useful for identifying systemic gender bias that may disadvantage women or men, respectively, for example, in the design of psychosocial services or economic recovery programs. It is also vital that the public face of local, state, and national emergency management reflect the "gendered terrain of disaster" in Web site content and illustration, public education materials, emergency management conference planning, and community outreach (for recommended action steps from a Canadian perspective, see Enarson 2008).

Guidelines for gender sensitive planning are readily available through international sources (visit the Web site hosting the Gender and Disaster Sourcebook as listed in the Resources section).

Implementing gender guidelines, many developed and tested by humanitarian relief agencies, save emergency managers' time. Why reinvent the wheel? The resource section of this chapter includes Web sites that offer, among other tools, gender-sensitive risk mapping templates; self-assessment guides for women's organizations about emergency preparedness; self-assessment guides for emergency management agencies about gender; sector-based guidelines for responding to women and men, boys and girls; and emergency preparedness guides for domestic violence shelters. Gender-sensitive indicators of effective disaster recovery, to take one example, might include such steps as:

- Consulting with local women's groups to plan and evaluate recovery services, including opportunities for affected women to fully participate in decision making
- Targeting economic recovery programs to include home-based workers, women's small businesses, part-time employees in small companies, and those who derive income from natural resources
- Building community capacity for continuous, affordable, and culturally appropriate child care and dependent care for others who rely on family members and paid caregivers
- Giving priority to low-income and high-risk women seeking affordable and appropriate low-cost permanent housing, including rental rebates and loan assistance
- Targeting senior women, women with disabilities, low-income single mothers, and other high-risk women in programs for debris removal and housing rehabilitation assistance
- Providing continuous accessible health care facilities including mobile reproductive services and infant and maternal care

- Building community capacity for timely and culturally appropriate mental health services with sensitivity to the specific challenges faced by women and men
- Collaborating with women's antiviolence agencies to increase public awareness of the increased risk of abuse or assault in the aftermath of disasters
- Providing practical support to women and their families as they seek emergency and recovery assistance, such as supervised youth recreation and safe community spaces for women and children

Gender-based assessments of emergency plans relating to particular issues are also needed. For example, a recent Canadian study found nurses were critical frontline responders to SARS, when this public health threat shut down Toronto area hospitals and brought international travel to a standstill in Canada (Amaratunga and O'Sullivan 2006). Interviewed later, the predominantly female group reported a range of factors that would undermine the nation's surge capacity by deterring them from reporting to work in a future crisis of this sort. Much more attention to work and family conflicts is warranted. While the traditional family support system helped past generations put work first in an emergency, this cannot be assumed in the context of dual career families and women's entry into first-response professions. Dual-career families in the population raise special concerns for emergency management agencies, principally around child care (Scanlon 1998):

> Who stays and who reports for duty when one parent is a police officer and the other a nurse? What happens when one is a chemist with knowledge of hazardous chemicals, the other a teacher, and an incident occurs when children are at school? ... Access to emergency child care may need to become part of emergency plans (p. 50).

Provisions for protecting reproductive health should also be in place for both women and men in planning responses to hazardous materials events. Human resource policies and procedures should be reviewed to identify family needs and potential conflicts, and internal human resource management strategies revised as needed. Plans should be reviewed with sensitivity to gender concerns during daytime and night events.

Assessing emergency plans for gender sensitivity can become a routine part of organizational self-assessments. Planners might ask, among other questions:

- Are women's networks utilized to reach families with information about household preparedness, cleanup, and repair? Do your emergency warnings specifically target men who may be reluctant to prepare for disasters?
- Do you know which women in your area are most likely to need assistance before, during, and after the emergency? Which women will need what kinds of long-term assistance?
- Have you budgeted for on-site child care and other services improving women's access to your resources after a disaster? Do your mental health programs and publications target women caregivers and men unable to ask for help?
- Do your mental health programs and publications identify gender-specific sources of stress specifically arising for women? Can you support women who host evacuees and those who head evacuated households?
- Have you analyzed the vulnerabilities and capacities of local child care and family support systems in the event of a disaster? Do you target child-care centers and family day homes in emergency preparedness initiatives?
- Are funding provisions in place to help local crisis centers respond to increased violence against women? Have shelters been identified as critical care facilities? Are women's antiviolence organizations included in community emergency plan exercises?
- Is antiracist training provided to those in emergency relief roles? Have you assessed the race-specific impacts of your emergency response procedures and policies? Do your staff and volunteers reflect the diversity of your community?

BOX 6.7   COMMUNITY OUTREACH TO ETHNIC WOMEN

The issue is that the Vietnamese women are not apt to voice their concerns. Vietnamese, in general, don't like to ask for help. [They are] very proud. With the women, it's hard to convince them why they need to participate more in community meetings. … And so to have our organization and our staff who are able to identify with them on a cultural level has been really instrumental in getting the Vietnamese community, and women in particular, to start saying, "We need this, we need this for our community" (Social Policy Research Associates 2006).

- Are sex-specific data available on women's economic status in your community? Can you monitor the economic impacts of disasters on women employees, business owners, farmers, and homemakers? Do women's primary employers have disaster plans in place supporting the work and family roles of employees in emergencies?
- Are women's organizations in your area networked with direct-service agencies serving other vulnerable populations? Is emergency preparedness on their agenda?
- Are women integrated into all levels of emergency management in your community? Have you educated local media about the complex roles women take on in disasters?

6.8.4   PUBLIC EDUCATION

Gender-sensitive awareness campaigns are equally important. Risk communicators should determine what television stations or community language radio stations are most popular with high-risk women and men, and plan how to reach the hard-to-reach, whether these are women lacking easy access to the Internet or male farmers unlikely to seek out post-disaster counseling. Every community is different, so risk communication projects must include messaging and outlets suitable to reach women in a Mennonite community, a trailer park dominated by seniors, Aboriginal youth living off reservation, or the personal care attendants of people living with disabilities. Consulting with local women journalists and communications experts is a good beginning. Students can be enlisted to evaluate existing materials and propose alternatives. Local media contact sheets should also include newsletters and occasional publications put out by women's and community groups. Partnering with ethnic women's networks provides important communication avenues for two-way communication about the concerns of marginalized women and how they can protect themselves (see Box 6.7).

6.8.5   INTEGRATING WOMEN INTO EMERGENCY MANAGEMENT

Build a stronger organization with a broad base that reflects the diversity of the nation and its future. Actively recruiting women, who may not have considered jobs in emergency management, at high levels or in nontraditional roles is essential. The professionalization of emergency management will open the door to highly educated women, but recruiting and mentoring women and men whose life experiences have taught them about social vulnerabilities and the hazards of everyday life is equally important. Emergency managers can invite high school students to job shadow emergency managers in nontraditional roles, and mentor young women and men who first enter the organization as student interns and temporary hires from under-represented groups. Recruiting through an expanded and grassroots stakeholder network will encourage applications from Native American, Asian, Latina, and African American women; women with connections to different disability communities; older women with years of volunteer experience; and low-income women knowledgeable about handling crises. Outreach to students of environmental studies, ethnic studies, gerontology, social work, and gender studies is another important step. Targeted emergency management internships or study grants can be created to increase interest among women in studying emergency management and among men in studying disaster-relevant fields such as social work and psychology. Organizational self-assessments should be routinely used to monitor race, class, and gender patterns of employment, training, and promotion. In-house training programs presenting gender and diversity as positive organizational development should be part of the learning curve in every private and public agency that contributes in some way to building community resilience to disaster.

6.9 SUMMARY

This chapter began by inviting attention to how sex and gender interact with other social dynamics in our everyday lives, often to increase vulnerability but also as a foundation for resilience. Gender concerns through the disaster cycle were illuminated through reports from many of the nation's most destructive recent natural disasters, including those based on the division of labor and differences in risk perception and those based on gender power and the gender-based inequalities that jeopardize the safety and well-being of women and girls especially. Practical issues arising for women and men, respectively, during preparedness, evacuation, emergency response, and recovery were discussed with attention to livelihood, housing, violence, and possible gender bias in programming. This led to a concluding section with action steps to more fully integrate gender into the routine practices and the overarching policies of emergency management, with grassroots women's groups at the center of this process.

For emergency managers, who know too well how many hands are needed, the outstanding challenge is to engage us all in practical efforts to reduce risk and respond to disasters in ways that will leave our communities safe and stronger. As indicated by the many case studies reviewed here, an important platform for change is to tackle the gender inequalities that increase vulnerability and undermine the resilience of all people to hazards and disasters. Overcoming all the social fault lines that divide us in the new America is the first step toward a true culture of prevention.

6.10 DISCUSSION QUESTIONS

1. Take the role of any emergency manager or first responder you have seen in your favorite disaster movie and reverse the gender. What difference do you think it would make if this person were a women (or man) instead and why? Think about other practitioners, members of the public, family members, elected officials, etc.
2. Do you think men's or women's lives change more during a disaster? In what ways and why? What about in the recovery period?
3. Is it the job of an emergency manager to consider "private" issues such as domestic violence, sexual preference, child care arrangements, or relationship stress? Why or why not?
4. Thinking of any emergency or disaster you have been involved with, what did you observe about the behavior of women and men? What do you think explains this?
5. What are the three most significant barriers to community resilience that gender inequalities or differences raise, in your view? How might each be addressed and minimized?
6. What do you think are the most significant barriers to girls or women on the basis of their sex and gender identity? What about boys and men?
7. How could a disastrous flood, fire, explosion, or health emergency in your community be a catalyst for change in family, community, or emergency organizations during the post-event "window of opportunity"?
8. What obstacles to gender mainstreaming have you identified through personal experience in emergency management? What changes have you seen in this respect in workplace cultures today?

ACKNOWLEDGMENTS

It is a pleasure to recognize the women and men who have helped develop and strengthen these ideas, both my colleagues who worked with me on the original FEMA Higher Education Project course and those I know only "virtually" though the Gender and Disaster Network. I thank you all for helping me think through these issues and for prompting new questions.

REFERENCES

Agenda for Children. 2008. Greater New Orleans Community Data Center. Open child care facilities in Orleans Parish as of April 28, 2008. http://www.gnocdc.org/maps/orleans_child_care.pdf (accessed June 16, 2008).

Alway, J., L. L. Belgrave, and K. Smith. 1998. Back to normal: Gender and disaster. *Symbolic Interaction* 21 (2): 175–95.

Amaratunga, C., and T. O'Sullivan. 2006. In the path of disasters: Psychosocial issues for preparedness, response, and recovery. *Prehospital Disaster Medicine* 21 (3): 149–55.

Anderson, W. 2000. Women and children in disasters. In *Managing disaster risk in emerging economies*, eds. A. Kreimer and M. Arnold, 85–90. Washington, DC: World Bank.

Anti-violence Resource Guide. 2000. *Facts about violence.* Data based on the Full Report of the Prevalence, Incidence, and Consequences of Violence Against Women, Findings from the National Violence Against Women Survey, November 2000. http://www.feminist.com/antiviolence/facts.html. Accessed May 7, 2009.

Barnecut, C. 1998. Disaster prone: Reflections of a female permanent disaster volunteer. In *The gendered terrain of disaster: Through women's eyes*, eds. E. Enarson and B. H. Morrow, 151–159. Westport, CT: Greenwood Publications.

Bateman, J., and R. Edwards. 2002. Gender and evacuation: A closer look at why women are more likely to evacuate for hurricanes. *Natural Hazards Review* 3 (3): 107–17.

Baylor College of Medicine. n.d. *Characteristics of the U.S. population of women with disabilities.* Center for Research on Women with Disabilities. http://www.bcm.edu/crowd/?PMID=1330 (accessed June 17, 2008).

Baylor College of Medicine. n.d. *Demographics: Income and poverty.* Center for Research on Women with Disabilities. http://www.bcm.edu/crowd/?pmid=1584 (accessed June 17, 2008).

Bennett, T. 2005. Women's health: After the fall. *Women's Health Issues* 15:237–39.

Blanchard-Boehm, D. 1997. Risk communication in Southern California: Ethnic and gender response to 1995 revised, upgraded earthquake probabilities. University of Colorado Natural Hazards Center, Quick Response Report #94. http://www.colorado.edu/hazards/qr/qr94.html (accessed June 16, 2008).

Bolin R., M. Jackson, and A. Crist. 1998. Gender inequality, vulnerability and disaster: Issues in theory and research. In *The gendered terrain of disaster: Through women's eyes*, eds. E. Enarson and B. H. Morrow, 27–44. Westport, CT: Greenwood Publications.

Buvinić, M. 1999. Hurricane Mitch: Women's needs and contributions. Inter-American Development Bank, Sustainable Development Department.

Callaghan, W., S. Rasmussen, D. Jamieson, S. Ventura, S. L. Farr, P. D. Sutton, T. J. Mathews, B.E. Hamilton, K. R. Shealy, D. Brantley, and S. Posner. 2007. Health concerns of women and infants in times of natural disasters: Lessons learned from Hurricane Katrina. *Maternal and Child Health* 11:307–11.

Catalanol, R, T. Bruckner, A. R. Marks, and B. Eskenazi. 2006. Exogenous shocks to the human sex ratio: The case of September 11, 2001 in New York City. *Human Reproduction* 21 (12): 3127–31.

Childers, C. 1999. Elderly female-headed households in the disaster loan process. *International Journal of Mass Emergencies and Disasters* 17 (1): 99–110.

Childs, M. 2006. Counting women in the Australian fire services. *Australian Journal of Emergency Management* 21 (2): 29–34.

Clark, S., and M. Weismantle. 2003. *Employment status 2000.* U.S. Census 2000 Brief. http://www.census.gov/prod/2003pubs/c2kbr-18.pdf (accessed June 17, 2008).

Clason, C. 1983. The family as a life-saver in disaster. *International Journal of Mass Emergencies and Disasters* 1 (1): 43–62.

Colina, D. 1998. Reflections from a teacher and survivor. In *The gendered terrain of disaster: Through women's eyes*, eds. E. Enarson and B. H. Morrow, 181–183. Westport, CT: Greenwood Publications.

Cupples, J. 2007. Gender and Hurricane Mitch: Reconstructing subjectivities after disaster. *Disasters* 31 (2): 155–75.

Cutter, S. 1992. Engendered fears: Femininity and technological risk perception. *Industrial Crisis Quarterly* 6:5–22.

———. 1995. The forgotten casualties: Women, children, and environmental change. *Global Environmental Change* 5 (3): 181–94.

David, E. 2008. Cultural trauma, memory, and gendered collective action: The case of women of the storm following Hurricane Katrina. *National Women's Studies Journal* 20 (3): 138–62.

Dobson, N. 1994. From under the mud-pack: Women and the Charleville floods. *Australian Journal of Emergency Management* 9 (2): 11–13.

Eads, M. 2002. Marginalized groups in times of crisis: Identity, needs, and response. University of Colorado, Natural Hazards Center, Quick Response Report #152. http://www.colorado.edu/hazards/qr/qr152/qr152.html (accessed June 16, 2008).

Eisenman, D., K. M. Cordasco, S. Asch, J. F. Golden, and D. Glik. 2007. Communication with vulnerable communities: Lessons from Hurricane Katrina. *American Journal of Public Health* 97 (S1): S109–15.

Elder, K., S. Xirasagar, N. Miller, S. A. Bowen, S. Glover, and C. Piper. 2007. African Americans' decisions not to evacuate New Orleans before Hurricane Katrina: A qualitative study. *American Journal of Public Health* 97 (S1): S124–29.

Enarson, E. 1998. Women, work, and family in the 1997 Red River Valley flood: Ten lessons learned. Unpublished community report. http://www.crid.or.cr/digitalizacion/pdf/eng/doc13585/doc13585.pdf (accessed June 16, 2008).

———. 1999. Women and housing issues in two US disasters. *International Journal of Mass Emergencies and Disasters* 17 (1): 39–63.

———. 2000a. 'We will make meaning out of this': Women's cultural responses to the Red River Valley flood. *International Journal of Mass Emergencies and Disasters* 18 (1): 39–62

———. 2000b. Gender and natural disasters. International Labour Organization, InFocus Programme on Crisis and Reconstruction, working paper no. 1. http://www.ilo.org/public/english/employment/recon/crisis/gender.htm (accessed June 16, 2008).

———. 2001. What women do: Gendered labor in the Red River Valley flood. *Environmental Hazards* 3 (1): 1–18.

———. 2008. Gender mainstreaming in emergency management: Opportunities for building community resilience in Canada. Paper prepared for the Public Health Agency of Canada. http://www.gdnonline.org/ (accessed June 19, 2008).

Enarson, E., and M. Fordham. 2001. Lines that divide, ties that bind: Race, class, and gender in women's flood recovery in the US and UK. *Australian Journal of Emergency Management* 15 (4): 43–53.

Enarson, E., A. Fothergill, and L. Peek. 2006. Gender and disaster: Foundations and possibilities. In *Handbook of disaster research*, eds. H. Rodriguez, H. L. Quarantelli, and R. Dynes, 130–46. New York: Springer.

Enarson, E., and L. Meyreles. 2004. International perspectives on gender and disaster: Differences and possibilities. *International Journal of Sociology and Social Policy* 14 (10): 49–92.

Enarson, E., and B. H. Morrow, eds. 1998a. *The gendered terrain of disaster: Through women's eyes*. Westport, CT: Greenwood Publications.

Enarson, E., and B. H. Morrow. 1998b. Women will rebuild Miami: A case study of feminist response to disaster. In *The gendered terrain of disaster: Through women's eyes*, eds. E. Enarson and B. H. Morrow, 185–200. Westport, CT: Greenwood Publications.

Enarson, E., and B. Phillips. 2008. Invitation to a new feminist disaster sociology: Integrating feminist theory and methods. In *Women in disaster*, eds. B. Phillips and B. H. Morrow, 41–74. Xlibris Publications.

Enarson, E., and J. Scanlon. 1999. Gender patterns in a flood evacuation: A case study of couples in Canada's Red River Valley. *Applied Behavioral Science Review* 7 (2): 103–24.

Erikson, K. 1994. *A new species of trouble: The human experience of modern disasters*. New York: W. W. Norton.

Family Caregiver Alliance. n.d. Women and caregiving: Facts and figures. National Center on Caregiving. http://www.caregiver.org/caregiver/jsp/content_node.jsp?nodeid=892 (accessed June 17, 2008).

Fordham, M. 1998. Making women visible in disasters: Problematising the private domain. *Disasters* 22 (2): 126–43.

———. 1999. The intersection of gender and social class in disaster: Balancing resilience and vulnerability. *International Journal of Mass Emergencies and Disasters* 17 (1): 15–36.

Fordham, M. 2001. Challenging boundaries: A gender perspective on early warning in disaster and environmental management. Paper prepared for the Expert Working Group meeting, Ankara, Turkey. Available through the UN Division for the Advancement of Women: www.un.org/womenwatch/daw/csw/env_manage/documents.html.

———. 2004. Gendering vulnerability analysis: Toward a more nuanced approach. In *Mapping vulnerability: Disasters, development, and people*, eds. G. Bankoff, G. Frerks, and D. Hillhorst, 174–82. London: Earthscan.

Fordham, M., and A. Ketteridge. 1998. 'Men must work and women must weep': Examining gender stereotypes in disasters. In *The gendered terrain of disaster: Through women's eyes*, eds. E. Enarson and B. H. Morrow, 81–94.Westport, CT: Greenwood Publications.

Fothergill, A. 1998. The neglect of gender in disaster work: An overview of the literature. In *The gendered terrain of disaster: Through women's eyes*, eds. E. Enarson and B. H. Morrow, 11–25. Westport, CT: Greenwood Publications.

———. 1999. Women's roles in a disaster. *Applied Behavioral Science Review* 7 (2): 125–43.

———. 2004. *Heads above water: Gender, class and family in the Grand Forks flood*. Ithaca, NY: SUNY Press.

Gault, B., H. Hartmann, A. Jones-DeWeever, M. Werschkul, and E. Williams. 2005. The women of New Orleans and the Gulf Coast: Multiple disadvantages and key assets for recovery. Institute for Women's Policy Briefing, Part One. http://www.iwpr.org/pdf/D464.pdf (accessed June 16, 2008).

Gender Equality and Disaster Risk Reduction Workshop. 2004. Executive summary. http://www.ssri.hawaii.edu/research/GDWwebsite/pages/exec_summary.html (accessed June 5, 2008).

Gibbs, S. 1990. *Women's role in the Red Cross/Red Crescent*. Geneva: Henry Dunant Institute.

Gist, Y., and L. Hetzel. 2004. *We the people: Aging in the US*. U.S. Census 2000 Special Report. http://www.census.gov/prod/2004pubs/censr-19.pdf (accessed June 17, 2008).

Gladwin, H., and W. G. Peacock. 1997. Warning and evacuation: A night for hard horses. In *Hurricane Andrew: Ethnicity, gender and the sociology of disasters*, eds. W. G. Peacock, B. H. Morrow, and H. Gladwin, 52–74. New York: Routledge.

Habitat for Humanity. n.d. Affordable housing statistics. http://www.habitat.org/how/stats.aspx (accessed June 16, 2008).

Hagen, S., and Carouba, M., eds. 2002. *Women at Ground Zero: Stories of courage and compassion*. Indianapolis, IN: Alpha Books.

Hoffman, S. 1998. Eve and Adam among the embers: Gender patterns after the Oakland Berkeley firestorm. In *The gendered terrain of disaster: Through women's eyes*, eds. E. Enarson and B. H. Morrow, 55–61. Westport, CT: Greenwood Publications.

Ikeda, K. 1995. Gender differences in human loss and vulnerability in natural disasters: A case study from Bangladesh. *Indian Journal of Gender Studies* 2 (2): 171–93.

International Association of Emergency Managers. 2005. Special focus issue: Women in emergency management. *IAEM Bulletin* 22, no. 9. http://www.iaem.com/publications/Bulletin/documents/200509bulletinonline.pdf (accessed June 16, 2008).

Joint Center for Housing Studies of Harvard University. 2004. The state of the nation's housing. http://www.jchs.harvard.edu/publications/markets/son2004.pdf (accessed June 16, 2008).

Jones-DeWeever, A. 2007. Women in the wake of the storm: Examining the post-Katrina realities of the women of New Orleans and the Gulf Coast. Institute for Women's Policy Report Briefing, Part Three. http://www.iwpr.org/pdf/D481.pdf (accessed June 18, 2008).

King, S., and D. P. Laplante. 2005. The effects of prenatal maternal stress on children's cognitive development: Project ice storm. *Stress* 8 (1): 35–45.

Kissinger, P., N. Schmidt, C. Sanders, and N. Liddon. 2007. The effect of the Hurricane Katrina disaster on sexual behavior and access to reproductive care for young women in New Orleans. *Sexually Transmitted Diseases* 34 (11): 883–86.

Klinenberg, E. 2002. *Heat wave: A social autopsy of disaster in Chicago*. Chicago: University of Chicago Press.

Krajeski, R., and K. Peterson. 1997. 'But she is a woman and this is a man's job': Lessons for participatory research and participatory recovery. *International Journal of Mass Emergencies and Disasters* 17 (1): 123–30.

Krauss, C. 1993. Women and toxic waste protests: Race, class and gender as sources of resistance. *Qualitative Sociology* 16 (3): 247–62.

Laska, S., and B. H. Morrow. 2006/2007. Social vulnerabilities and Hurricane Katrina: An unnatural disaster in New Orleans. *Marine Technology Society Journal* 40 (4): 6–26.

Litt, J. 2008. "Getting Out or Staying Put: An African American Women's Network in Evacuation from Katrina." *National Women's Studies Journal* 20 (3): 32–48.

Maier, M. 1997. Gender equity, organizational transformation and Challenger. *Journal of Business Ethics* 16 (9): 943–62.

Major, A. M. 1999. Gender differences in risk and communication behavior: Responses to the New Madrid earthquake prediction. *International Journal of Mass Emergencies and Disasters* 17 (3): 313–38.

Mason, B. 2007. Hurricane Katrina, women, and the process of multiple victimizations. *The Consortium on Race, Gender and Ethnicity, Research Connections, University of Maryland* (Spring): 3–4.

Mishra, P. 2009. Let's share the stage: Inclusion of men in gender risk reduction. In *Women, gender and disaster: Global issues and initiatives*, eds. E. Enarson and D. Chakrabarti.

Morrow, B. H. 2006. Women: An organizational resource. *Emergency Management Canada* 4:40–41.

Morrow, B. H., and E. Enarson. 1996. Hurricane Andrew through women's eyes: Issues and recommendations. *International Journal of Mass Emergencies and Disasters* 14 (1): 1–22.

National Coalition for the Homeless. 2007. Who is the homeless? http://www.nationalhomeless.org/publications/facts/Whois.pdf (accessed June 17, 2008).

Neal, D., and B. Phillips. 1990. Female-dominated local social movement organizations in disaster-threat situations. In *Women and social protest*, eds. G. West and R. Blumberg, 243–55. New York: Oxford.

Neumayer, E., and T. Plümper. 2007. The gendered nature of natural disasters: The impact of catastrophic events on the gender gap in life expectancy, 1981–2002. *Annals of the Association of American Geographers* 97 (3): 551–66.

The New Orleans Index. 2008 (April 16). Tracking recovery of New Orleans and the metro area. http://www.gnocdc.org/NOLAIndex/NOLAIndex.pdf (accessed June 16, 2008).

Nigg, J., and K. Tierney. 1990. Explaining differential outcomes in the small business disaster loan application process. Preliminary paper #156. University of Delaware: Disaster Research Center.

Norris, F., M. Friedman, P. Watson, C. M. Byrne, E. Diaz, and K. Kaniasty. 2002. 60,000 disaster victims speak: Parts 1 and 2. *Psychiatry* 65 (3): 207–60.

O'Brien, P., and P. Atchison. 1998. Gender differentiation and aftershock warning response. In *The gendered terrain of disaster: Through women's eyes*, eds. E. Enarson and B. H. Morrow, 161–72. Westport, CT: Greenwood Publications.

Ollenburger, J., and G. Tobin. 1998. Women and postdisaster stress. In *The gendered terrain of disaster: Through women's eyes,* eds. E. Enarson and B. H. Morrow, 95–108. Westport, CT: Greenwood Publications.

Ono, Y. 2002. Risk factors for death in the 8 April 1998 Alabama tornadoes. Quick Response Report #145. Boulder, CO: University of Colorado, Natural Hazard Center.

Owens, S. 2005. Climate change and health: A project with women of Labrador. Santé Communautaire. MSc Thesis. Université Laval.

Oxfam International. 2005. Gender and the tsunami. Oxfam briefing note. http://www.oxfamamerica.org/news-andpublications/publications/briefing_papers/briefing_note.2005-03-30.6547801151/bn_tsunami_gender033005.pdf (accessed June 16, 2008).

Oxlee, C. 2000. Beyond the veil: Women in Islamic national societies. *IFRC Magazine* 1. http://www.redcross.int/EN/mag/magazine2000_1/voile_en.html (accessed June 16, 2008).

Pacholok, S. 2005. Masculinities in crisis: A case study of the Okanagan Mountain Park fire. Paper presented at the annual meeting of the American Sociological Association, Philadelphia.

Palinkas, L., M. A. Downs, J. S. Petterson, and J. Russell. 1993. Social, cultural, and psychological impacts of the Exxon Valdez oil spill. *Human Organization* 52 (1): 1–13.

Papadakis, M. 2000. Complex picture of computer use in the home emerges. Division of Science Resources Studies, NSF Issue Brief. http://www.nsf.gov/statistics/issuebrf/sib00314.htm (accessed June 16, 2008).

Peacock, W. G., B. H. Morrow, and H. Gladwin, eds. 1997. *Hurricane Andrew: Ethnicity, gender and the sociology of disasters.* New York: Routledge.

Peek, L., and A. Fothergill. 2009. Parenting in the wake of disaster: Mothers and fathers respond to Hurricane Katrina. In *Women, gender and disaster: Global issues and initiatives*, eds. E. Enarson and D. Chakrabarti.

Peterson, K. 1997. From the field: Gender issues in disaster response and recovery. *Natural Hazards Observer* 21 (5): 3–4.

Phillips, B. 1990. Gender as a variable in emergency response. In *The Loma Prieta earthquake*, ed. R. Bolin, 83–90. Boulder, CO: University of Colorado, Institute for Behavioral Science.

———. 1995. Creating, sustaining and losing place: Homelessness in the context of disaster. *Humanity and Society* 19 (4): 94–101.

Phillips, B., and B. H. Morrow. 2007. Social science research needs: Focus on vulnerable populations, forecasting, and warnings. *Natural Hazards Review* 8 (3): 61–68.

Phillips, B., and B. H. Morrow, eds. 2008. *Women and disasters: From theory to practice.* Xlibris Publications.

Proctor, B., and J. Dalaker. 2003. *Poverty in the United States: 2002.* Current Population Report. http://www.census.gov/prod/2003pubs/p60-222.pdf (accessed June 17, 2008).

Proudley, M. 2008. Fire, families and decisions. *Australian Journal of Emergency Management* 23 (1): 37–43.

Pyles, L., and J. Lewis. 2007. Women of the Storm: Advocacy and organizing in post-Katrina New Orleans. *Affilia: Journal of Women and Social Work* 22 (4): 385–89.

Radcliffe Institute for Advanced Study. 2007. Women's interfaith initiatives after 9/11. http://www.pluralism. org/events/womeninterfaith/index.php (accessed June 18, 2008).

Ransby, B. 2006. Katrina, black women, and the deadly discourse on black poverty in America. *Du Bois Review* 3 (1): 215–22.

Reinsch, S. 2009. 'A part of me had left': Learning from women about disaster stress in rural Canada. In *Women, gender and disaster: Global issues and initiatives*, eds. E. Enarson and D. Chakrabarti.

Rivers, J. P. W. 1982. Women and children last: An essay on sex discrimination in disasters. *Disasters* 6 (4): 256–67.

Robertson, D. 1998. Women in emergency management: An Australian perspective. In *The gendered terrain of disaster: Through women's eyes*, eds. E. Enarson and B. H. Morrow, 201–16. Westport, CT: Greenwood Publications.

Scanlon, J. 1998. The perspective of gender: A missing element in disaster response. In *The gendered terrain of disaster: Through women's eyes*, eds. E. Enarson and B. H. Morrow, 45–51. Westport, CT: Greenwood Publications.

———. 1999. Myths of male and military superiority: Fictional accounts of the 1917 Halifax explosion. *English Studies in Canada* 24:1001–25.

Schmidlin, T. 1997. Risk factors for death in the 1 March 1997 Arkansas tornadoes. Quick Response Report #98. Boulder, CO: University of Colorado, Natural Hazard Center.

Sharkey, P. 2007. Survival and death in New Orleans: An empirical look at the human impact of Katrina. *Journal of Black Studies* 37 (4): 482–501.

Sibbald, B. 1998. RNs unsung heroes during ice storm '98. *The Canadian Nurse* 94 (4): 18–21.

Simmons, T., and G. O'Neill. 2001. *Households and families 2000*. U.S. Census 2000 brief. http://www.census. gov/prod/2001pubs/c2kbr01-8.pdf (accessed June 17, 2008).

Social Policy Research Associates. 2006. Redefining the parameters for rebuilding: Evaluation of the Katrina Women's Response Fund. http://www.ms.foundation.org/user-assets/PDF/Program/KatrinaFinalReport. pdf (accessed June 16, 2008).

Spraggins, R. 2005. *We the people: Women and men in the US*. U.S. Census 2000 Special Report 2005. http:// www.census.gov/prod/2005pubs/censr-20.pdf (accessed June 18, 2008).

Staples, C., and K. Stubbings. 1998. Gender inequality in business recovery following the Grand Forks flood. Paper presented to the Midwest Sociological Society, Kansas City, MO.

Stehlik, D., G. Lawrence, and I. Gray. 2000. Gender and drought: Experiences of Australian women in the drought of the 1990s. *Disasters* 24 (1): 38–53.

Turner, E. H. 1997. After the storm: Women, public policy, and power. In *Women, culture, and community: Religion and reform in Galveston, 1880–1920*, 187–227. New York: Oxford University Press.

Turner, R. H., J. M. Nigg, and D. H. Paz. 1986. *Waiting for disaster: Earthquake watch in California*. Berkeley: University of California Press.

Twohey, D. 1998. Don't be ashamed if you're heartbroken: Men and depression. *Society for the Psychological Study of Men and Masculinity Bulletin*. 3 (3): 13–14.

U.S. Department of Education, National Center for Education Statistics. 2005. *Trends in educational equity of girls and women, 2004*. http://nces.ed.gov/pubs2005/equity/Section9.asp (accessed June 17, 2008).

U.S. Department of Health and Human Services. 2008. Women'shealth.gov. *Caregiver stress*. http:// www.4woman.gov/FAQ/caregiver.htm#b (accessed June 17, 2008).

U.S. Department of Labor, Women's Bureau. 2007. *Quick stats 2007*. http://www.dol.gov/wb/stats/main.htm (accessed June 17, 2008).

Vaill. S. 2006. The calm in the storm: Women leaders in Gulf Coast recovery. Briefing paper for the Women's Funding Network and the MS Foundation for Women. http://www.ms.foundation.org/user-assets/PDF/ WFNMFWkatrina_report_1.pdf (accessed June 16, 2008).

Van Willigen, M. 2001. Do disasters affect individuals' psychological well-being? An over-time analysis of the effect of Hurricane Floyd on men and women in Eastern North Carolina. *International Journal of Mass Emergencies and Disasters* 19 (1): 40–65.

Weidner, N. 2004. Neighborhood emergency networks in Corvallis, Oregon, and Uzhhorod, Ukraine. Paper presented at the Gender Equality and Disaster Risk Reduction Workshop. *http://www.ssri.hawaii.edu/ research/GDWwebsite/pages/proceeding.html* (accessed June 16, 2008).

Weinberg, D. 2004. *Evidence from census 2000 about earnings by detailed occupation for men and women.* Census 2000 Special Reports. http://www.census.gov/prod/2004pubs/censr-15.pdf (accessed June 17, 2008).

Wenger, D., and T. James. 1994. The convergence of volunteers in a consensus crisis: The case of the 1985 Mexico City earthquake. In *Disasters, collective behavior, and social organization,* eds. R. Dynes and K. Tierney, 229–43. Newark: University of Delaware Press.

Wilson, J. 1999. Professionalization and gender in local emergency management. *International Journal of Mass Emergencies and Disasters* 17 (1): 111–22.

Wisner, B., P. Blaikie, T. Cannon, and I. Davis. 2004. *At risk: Natural hazards, people's vulnerability and disasters.* 2nd ed. London: Routledge.

World Economic Forum. 2007. The global gender gap report. http://www.weforum.org/en/initiatives/gcp/Gender%20Gap/index.htm (accessed June 16, 2008).

Yonder, A., with S. Ackar, and P. Gopalan. 2005 .Women's participation in disaster relief and recovery. Pamphlet #2, SEEDS. http://www.popcouncil.org/pdfs/seeds/Seeds22.pdf pdf (accessed June 16, 2008).

Zahran, S., L. Peek, and S. D. Brody. 2008. Youth mortality by forces of nature. *Children, Youth and Environments* 18 (1): 371–88. http://www.colorado.edu/journals/cye (accessed June 18, 2008).

RESOURCES

- *Gender and Disaster Network [GDN],* international network of policy makers, professionals and practitioners: http://www.gdnonline.org.
- *Gender and Disaster Sourcebook,* international compilation of practical tools, research, and background papers: http://www.gdnonline.org/sourcebook/index.htm.
- *Disaster Watch,* Web site sponsored by the Huairou Commission and GROOTS International featuring grassroots women's organizations active in disasters: http://www.disasterwatch.net/.
- *Empower,* emergency management professional organization for women: http://www.empower-women.com/mc/page.do?sitePageId=46823&orgId=emp.
- Gender Broadsheet: Six Principles For Engendered Relief And Reconstruction, GDN response to the 2004 Indian Ocean tsunami: http://www.gdnonline.org/resources/genderbroadsheet.doc.
- Honolulu Call to Action, one outcome of the 2004 Gender Equality and Disaster Risk Reduction Workshop: http://www.ssri.hawaii.edu/research/GDWwebsite/.
- *Gender Perspective: Good Practices and Lessons Learned, 2007,* ISDR: http://www.unisdr.org/eng/about_isdr/isdr-publications/09-gender-good-practices/gender-good-practices.pdf.
- *Still Waiting: Life After Katrina,* PBS documentary on a displaced extended family: http://www.stillwaiting.colostate.edu/dvd.html.
- *From Chaos to Creativity,* short video on global women's disaster responses: http://www.disasterwatch.net/resources.htm#film1.
- *Katrina Warriors,* antiviolence coalition active in the Gulf South: http://www.katrinawarriors.net/.
- *Sociologists for Women in Society Fact Sheet on Women and Disaster,* E. Enarson: http://www.socwomen.org/socactivism/factdisaster.pdf.
- *World Disaster Report 2006,* Chapter 6 ("Please don't raise gender now, we're in an emergency!"): http://www.redcross.ca/article.asp?id=20509&tid=001.
- *World Disaster Report 2007,* Chapter 5 ("The urgency of equality"): http://www.ifrc.org/Docs/pubs/disasters/wdr2007/WDR2007-English-5.pdf.
- *Making Risky Environments Safer: Women Building Sustainable and Disaster-Resilient Communities, 2004,* E. Enarson. UN Division for the Advancement of Women, Women 2000 and Beyond, April: http://www.un.org/womenwatch/daw/public/w2000.html.

7 Age

Lori Peek

CONTENTS

7.1 CHAPTER PURPOSE

The length of time that someone has lived can significantly affect that person's ability to prepare for, respond to, and recover from disaster. Indeed, age is correlated with a number of factors associated with one's likelihood of withstanding a disaster event. For example, age in many ways influences cognitive development, physical ability and mobility, socioeconomic status, access to resources, assumed responsibility for disaster preparedness and response activities, and levels of social integration or isolation. Thus, it is clear that age alone does not make a person vulnerable. Instead age interacts with many other factors to result in the increased vulnerability of some members of our population, particularly the very young and the old. As such, this chapter focuses specifically on the vulnerabilities of children and the elderly in disaster.

7.2 OBJECTIVES

As a result of reading this chapter, readers should be able to

1. Offer definitions for "children" and "the elderly" based on chronological age.
2. Explain why it is important to understand the distinctions between different groups of children (e.g., infants and very young children, young children, and adolescents) and the elderly (e.g., young old, aged, oldest old, and frail elderly).
3. Provide demographic overviews of the youth and elderly populations in the United States, and highlight important variations by age, race, class, and gender.
4. Explain the specific risks that children face across the disaster life cycle, and identify the factors most likely to increase their vulnerability during the warning, evacuation, response, impact, and recovery phases.
5. Explain the specific risks that the elderly face across the disaster life cycle, and identify the factors most likely to increase their vulnerability during the warning, evacuation, response, impact, and recovery phases.
6. Describe several possible approaches for addressing the vulnerability of children and the elderly before and after disaster.

7.3 INTRODUCTION

Social definitions for both childhood and the elderly vary considerably across cultures and contexts and are only loosely linked with chronological age (Boyden 2003; Friedsam 1962). However, for the sake of clarity, in this chapter I refer to children as those individuals age 18 or younger. This is in accordance with the United Nations Convention on the Rights of the Child, although of course the diversity of young people must be recognized and captured in age-disaggregated data. For that reason and where possible, I distinguish between "infants and very young children" (0–5 years of age), "young children" (6–11 years of age), and "adolescents" (12–18 years of age). An elderly person typically is defined as someone who is 65 years of age or older. Further distinction is made between the "young old" (65–74 years of age), the "aged" (75–84 years of age), the "oldest old" (85 years of age or older), and the "frail elderly" (65 years of age or greater, with physical or mental infirmities) (He et al. 2005; Ngo 2001). It is important to understand the distinctions among these age groups because there are clearly differences *among* the elderly, as well as differences *between* older and younger persons in terms of health, function, and interaction in society (Friedsam 1962; Ngo 2001). The following section offers a general demographic description of youth and elderly in the United States, which illustrates the diversity of these populations.

7.4 DEMOGRAPHIC OVERVIEW

Over 300 million persons live in the United States, which is the third most populous and one of the most diverse nations in the world. Almost 25% of the U.S. population is made up of children age 18 or younger, while persons age 65 and over represent 12.4% of the population (U.S. Census Bureau 2006).* Below, I offer a brief overview of the demographic characteristics of American children and the elderly, with a specific focus on sex, racial and ethnic diversity, and poverty rates. It is important to consider the intersections between age and these other characteristics because these factors all influence experiences in disasters, as will be further considered in later sections of this chapter and in other chapters of this book.

---

* Unless indicated otherwise, all figures included in this section of the chapter come from the U.S. Census Bureau, 2006 American Community Survey data, which are available online at http://www.census.gov/.

7.4.1 Children

In 2006, 73.5 million children lived in the United States. These children were divided proportionately by age group, with about one third of the child population in each of the very young (0–5 years), young (6–11 years), and adolescent (12–18 years) categories. Also, there was basically an even distribution of boys and girls across each age category.

Approximately 96% of children in the United States were born here, while the remaining 4% were born outside the country (about 12.5% of the entire U.S. population is foreign born). Children are actually more racially and ethnically diverse than their adult counterparts. Just over 57% of American children are non-Hispanic white,* while 20% of children are Hispanic or Latino; 15% are African American; 4% are Asian, Native Hawaiian, or Pacific Islander; almost 1% are American Indian; and 8.5% of children identify as some other race.† The child population is a reflection of the growing diversity of the American population, as well as an indicator of the probable further diversification of the nation over the next several decades.

The number of children living in poverty in the United States grew steadily throughout the first decade of the 21st century. Well over 13 million American children live in families with incomes below the federal poverty level, which in 2008 was $21,200 for a family of four (U.S. Department of Health and Human Services 2008). A higher percentage of children in the United States live in poverty (18.3%) than the population as a whole (13.3%). These numbers do not bode well for the future of many of America's youth, and they are even more troubling given that the federal poverty measure is widely viewed as a flawed metric of economic hardship. Research consistently shows that families need an income of about *twice* the federal poverty level to make ends meet. Children living in families with incomes below this level are referred to as low income, and almost 40% of the nation's children live in low-income households (Fass and Cauthen 2007). These "near poor" children and their families are often overlooked and are not eligible to receive public assistance, yet live in incredibly precarious situations nonetheless (Newman and Chen 2007). Poor and low-income children, for example, are much more likely to experience food insecurity, lack health insurance and access to regular health care, struggle as a result of unaffordable housing costs, and attend lower quality schools and thus experience lower educational attainment (Fass and Cauthen 2007; Kozol 1991, 2005).

The percent of children living below the federal poverty level varies significantly by geographic location, with higher concentrations of poverty in the southern United States. Areas with the highest rates of child poverty include the District of Columbia (32.6%), Mississippi (29.5%), Louisiana (27.8%), New Mexico (25.6%), West Virginia (25.2%), Arkansas (24.3%), Oklahoma (24.3%), and Texas (23.9%). These figures can be compared to states with much lower child poverty rates, such as New Hampshire (9.6%) and Maryland (9.7%).

Minority youth are disproportionately poor in the United States. In 2006, 40% of American Indian children, 33% of black children, 27% of Latino children, and 12% of Asian children lived in poor families (Fass and Cauthen 2007; also see Children's Defense Fund 2006). A lower percentage of white children live in poverty (10%), yet white children comprise the largest group of poor children because they represent a larger proportion of the overall population. Having immigrant parents increases a child's chances of being poor, with approximately one in four children with immigrant parents living in poverty (Fass and Cauthen 2007).

Family structure affects access to resources and economic well-being for children as well. Children in single-parent households are among the poorest groups in the nation, with 44% of

---

* This can be compared with the overall U.S. population, which is about 70% non-Hispanic white. The term non-Hispanic white is used to refer to people who report being white and no other race and who are not Hispanic.

† These numbers do not add up to 100% because of the way the Census Bureau measures race and ethnicity, which has become more complicated over past decades due to the increasing diversity of the population, rising rates of immigration, and the number of interracial marriages. In particular, persons of Hispanic or Latino origin may be of any race, and since the year 2000, parents or guardians are allowed to mark more than one race for those in the household.

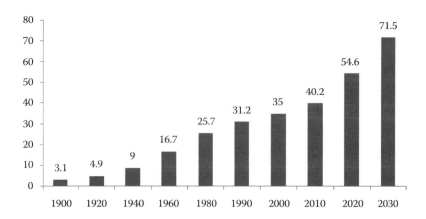

FIGURE 7.1 Number of persons 65 and older, 1900–2030 (numbers in millions). *Source*: U.S. Department of Health and Human Services. Administration on Aging. A profile of older Americans: 2006. Washington, DC, 2006.

children in female-headed households ("no husband present") living in poverty. Comparatively, 22% of children in male-headed households ("no wife present") live below the poverty line, while 8.6% of children in married-couple families are poor.

7.4.2 ELDERLY

In 2006, about 37 million Americans were age 65 or older, representing 12.4% of the total population. Among the older population, approximately 18 million were aged 65–74 years, 14 million were aged 75–84 years, and 5 million were 85 and older. According to U.S. Census Bureau projections, a substantial increase in the number of older people will occur when the baby boom generation (people born after World War II and between 1946 and 1964) begins to turn 65 in 2011. The older population is projected to double to 71.5 million in 2030, and to increase to 20% of the entire population in the same time period as seen in Figure 7.1 (He et al. 2005, 6). Significantly, the oldest-old population—those aged 85 and above—is also projected to double over the next several decades, to 9.6 million by 2030, and to double again to 20.9 million by 2050 (He et al. 2005, 6).

There is more sex ratio imbalance between older adults than among the rest of the population, with women comprising 58% of the elderly, and men representing only 42% of those over 65 years of age. This is largely because women live longer, on average, than men. Older men are much more likely to be married than older women—72% of men versus 42% of women. The proportion of elderly people living alone has soared since 1950. Almost one in three, or 10.6 million, non-institutionalized older persons live alone, and half of all women over the age of 75 live alone. A relatively small number (about 1.56 million) and percentage (4.5%) of persons over age 65 lived in nursing homes in 2000. However, the percentage increases significantly with age, with about 1.1% of the young old, 4.7% of the aged, and 18.2% of the oldest old living in nursing homes. In addition, about 5% of the elderly live in senior housing or assisted living facilities of some type (U.S. Department of Health and Human Services 2006).

The distribution of older persons varies considerably by state. In 2005, just over half (51.6%) of persons 65 and older lived in nine states: California (3.9 million), Florida (3 million), New York (2.5 million), Texas (2.3 million), Pennsylvania (1.9 million), and Illinois, Ohio, Michigan, and New Jersey each had well over one million elderly residents (U.S. Department of Health and Human Services 2006, 6). Most older persons in the United States live in metropolitan areas, and the elderly are less likely to change residence than other groups (U.S. Department of Health and Human Services 2006; He et al. 2005).

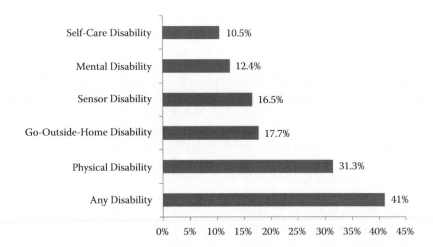

FIGURE 7.2   Disability characteristics among persons 65 and older, 2006. *Source*: U.S. Census Bureau. 2006 American Community Survey data. http://www.census.gov/ (accessed February 1, 2008).

Older persons are less racially and ethnically diverse than other segments of the American population. However, the elderly are expected to grow more diverse over the next several decades, largely reflecting demographic changes in the U.S. population as a whole. In 2006, the elderly population was 81.1% non-Hispanic white, 8.3% black, 6.3% Hispanic or Latino, 3.2% Asian, 0.5% American Indian, and 0.6% of the elderly identified as some other race.

In 2005, the median income of older persons was $21,784 for males and $12,495 for females (U.S. Department of Health and Human Services 2006). Major sources of income for older persons were Social Security (reported by 89% of older persons); income from assets (reported by 55%); private pensions (reported by 29%); earnings (reported by 24%); and government employee pensions (reported by 14%). About 3.5 million older adults (10%) were living in poverty in 2006, which was slightly lower than the national average. People aged 65–74 had a poverty rate of 9%, compared with 12% of those aged 75 and older. Older women were more likely than older men to live in poverty (13% compared to 7%). Non-Hispanic whites (8%) were less likely than older blacks (24%) and older Hispanics (20%) to be living in poverty. Among older women living alone in 2003, poverty rates were 17% for non-Hispanic white women and about 40% for black women and Hispanic women (He et al. 2005).

Limitations of mobility and chronic poor health are difficulties common to older people around the world (International Federation of Red Cross and Red Crescent Societies 2007). In the United States, about 80% of seniors have at least one chronic health condition and 50% have at least two (He et al. 2005). Arthritis, hypertension, heart disease, diabetes, and respiratory disorders are some of the leading causes of activity limitation among older people (He et al. 2005), and these health conditions are exacerbated by poverty and lack of access to affordable and reliable health care. In 2006, 41% of the elderly, representing more than 14.5 million persons, had some type of disability and many seniors reported having two or more disabilities (Figure 7.2; for related information see Chapter 8 on disability). Older women (43%) were more likely than older men (38.2%) to experience disability. And the disabled elderly were more likely to be living in poverty than their non-disabled counterparts.

7.5   VULNERABILITY ACROSS THE DISASTER LIFE CYCLE

Recent disaster events in the United States and around the globe tragically illustrate the vulnerability of children and the elderly during times of disaster. The 2004 Indian Ocean earthquake and tsunami claimed the lives of at least 60,000 children, most of who lived in the hardest hit regions of Indonesia, Sri Lanka, India, and Thailand (Oxfam International 2005). Over 18,000 children perished in the 2005 Pakistan earthquake, largely as a result of the collapse of more than 10,000 school buildings (Hewitt 2007). In 2008, a deadly earthquake struck Sichuan Province in China and caused an estimated 10,000 child fatalities. Schools where predominantly poor children attended were especially hard hit, and many of the youngest victims died in their classrooms (Jacobs 2008). Following Hurricane Katrina, over 160,000 children from Louisiana and Mississippi were displaced from their homes and schools, and this population has subsequently suffered from high rates of emotional and behavioral problems, chronic health conditions, and poor access to medical care (Abramson and Garfield 2006; Abramson et al. 2007; Lauten and Lietz 2008). Old age was the single most important factor in determining who died in Hurricane Katrina. Among the over 1,300 persons who died in New Orleans, 67% were at least 65 years old, although this group represented only about 12% of the pre-storm population (Sharkey 2007). The 1995 Chicago heat wave claimed more than 700 lives, and 73% of the heat-related deaths were among persons over 65 years of age (Klinenberg 2002). The 2003 European heat wave resulted in more than 52,000 deaths, most of which were concentrated among the elderly (Larsen 2006). In the 1995 Kobe earthquake, 53% of the fatalities were among older persons and 10% of the victims were children (Hewitt 2007).

When certain segments of the population suffer disproportionately during times of disaster, it is important to consider what factors place these groups at particular risk before, during, and after the event. The following sections attempt to do just that by drawing on published research literature and agency reports that address the experiences of children and the elderly in disaster. The sections are organized by three major stages of the disaster life cycle: (1) warnings, evacuation, and response; (2) impacts; and (3) short- and long-term recovery (see Fothergill 1996; Fothergill, Maestas, and Darlington 1999; Fothergill and Peek 2004). I begin by discussing issues that children face across the disaster life cycle. Then I consider factors that contribute to the vulnerability of older persons. The chapter concludes with a discussion of the implications of these findings for practice.

7.5.1 CHILDREN—WARNING, EVACUATION, AND RESPONSE

This phase of the disaster life cycle entails receiving formal warning signals, such as emergency broadcasts and flood sirens or other risk communication of an immediate danger, and taking action with some type of response to the warning, such as evacuating or sheltering in place. To date, very little social science research has focused on how children receive, interpret, or respond to forecasts and warnings (Phillips and Morrow 2007). Dominant models of risk communication do not include youth as either sources or recipients of risk information (Mitchell et al. 2008). Instead it is commonly assumed that parents will inform, warn, and protect their children in the event of a disaster (Adams 1995). The lack of focus on children's understanding of risk and warnings represents a serious gap in knowledge considering that (1) children are often separated from their parents, such as when they are in school, day care, or with their friends; (2) there are an estimated one million homeless and street youth in the United States who totally lack familial support (Unger, Simon, and Newman 1998); and (3) more than 1.6 million American children are home alone every day each year (Phillips and Hewett 2005).

Although children can contribute in meaningful ways during the warning and emergency response phase of disasters, it is important to acknowledge that they do not have the same level of independence or resources available as adults (see Mitchell et al. 2008). In homes, child-care centers, and schools, for example, adults are primarily responsible for making evacuation decisions, providing vital resources, securing shelter, and establishing routine (Peek and Fothergill 2008). Moreover, children and adolescents often turn to the important adults in their lives to help them understand and make sense of uncertain or frightening situations (Prinstein et al. 1996). According to Phillips and Morrow (2007), children model their behavioral response to disaster on the reactions of adults around them. Parents, teachers, and child-care workers give useful clues on how to respond given that children lack a behavioral repertoire or even a reference framework for disaster situations (Phillips and Morrow 2007, 63).

A number of studies have examined the effect of having children on the evacuation decisions of adults. This work reveals that adults with children are more likely to respond to disaster warnings and evacuation messages than people without children (Carter, Kendall, and Clark 1983; Dash and Gladwin 2007; Edwards 1993; Fischer et al. 1995; Houts et al. 1984; Lindell, Lu, and Prater 2005). This suggests that parents and other caregivers of children would be receptive to hazards education materials that highlight the age- and hazard-specific risks children face, particularly if these materials draw on the principles of sound risk communication and include clear, consistent, and precise messages that are delivered through multiple channels (Mileti and Darlington 1997; Mileti and Fitzpatrick 1992; Mileti and O'Brien 1992).

While adults with children are more likely to respond to evacuation orders, a lack of resources may hinder the ability of low-income families to take recommended protective measures (Dash and Gladwin 2007). In Hurricane Katrina, poor and working-class mothers who were not able to leave New Orleans before the levee system failed faced dangerous and stressful evacuations with their children, as they were forced to wade through the floodwaters or be rescued by helicopter or boat (Fothergill and Peek 2006). In some cases, young people assisted directly with the evacuation of elderly and disabled family members by placing them on mattresses and helping them to float through the flooded city (Kirschke and van Vliet 2005).

Families with pets may also face particular challenges in evacuation. A study by Heath, Voeks, and Glickman (2000) explored evacuation and pet rescue in two communities—one in California that was under an evacuation notice due to flooding, and a second community in Wisconsin that evacuated in response to a hazardous chemical spill. Approximately 20% of pet-owning households in the California disaster and 50% of pet-owning households in the Wisconsin disaster evacuated without their pets. An estimated 80% of persons who reentered the evacuated areas did so to rescue their pet, and attempts to rescue a pet were most common among households with children. The authors posit that children may have become distressed over the abandonment of a pet and, therefore, put pressure on their parents to rescue it. This study demonstrates that pet rescues can endanger the health and well-being of animals and families, especially families with children.

The limited research available on children and emergency response primarily focuses on the household context and the decisions that adults make. But what happens when children are not at home when disaster strikes? Or when parents are separated from their children? Are schools and child-care centers adequately prepared? What factors shape evacuation planning and decision making among school administrators and day-care staff? These questions certainly warrant further consideration. On any given weekday during the academic year, there are approximately 55 million children in public and private schools across the United States (U.S. Census Bureau 2006). In addition to school-age youth, millions more infants and very young children are cared for in licensed child-care centers and in-home day cares.

Research on emergency response has highlighted the importance of household members being able to account for one another before taking recommended protective actions such as sheltering in place or evacuating (see Tierney, Lindell, and Perry 2001). Parents, in particular, are highly unlikely to leave a threatened area until they are reunited with their children or certain that their children have been safely evacuated. Research conducted in the aftermath of the September 11 attacks emphasized the many problems that parents with children attending schools in lower Manhattan faced (Bartlett and Patrarca 2002). For example, because phone service was limited or nonexistent, parents were unable to contact the school to learn more about the situation or their spouses to coordinate who was picking up the child. In several cases, parents could not access their children's school because of the shutdown of public transportation services and street closings, which led to a delay in reuniting families.

Some research has focused on the ability or willingness of teachers and other school personnel to participate in the evacuation of students in the event of an emergency. Johnson (1985) surveyed 232 teachers at 29 public schools located near a nuclear power plant in California. Nearly one third of the teachers indicated that they would not assist in an evacuation effort in the event of a radiological emergency, owing largely to a strong sense of obligation to their families and concerns for personal safety. An additional 10% of teachers qualified their responses by stating that their participation in evacuation efforts would be contingent upon being able to contact their own family members by telephone, limited to a specified length of time, or restricted to the evacuation of their class only. A survey of bus drivers in Suffolk County, New York, indicated that 66% would not report promptly to transport school children to destinations outside of the designated danger zone in the event of a nuclear accident (cited in Johnson 1985, 88). Bus drivers most often specified concern for family as the reason why they would not fulfill their duties. It is important to note that both studies—of teachers in California and bus drivers in New York—were based on hypothetical incidents. Nonetheless, this research raises important questions about the role conflict that school personnel are likely to face as they attempt to care for the children in their schools while also trying to ensure the safety of their own families. Bartlett and Patrarca (2002) and Johnson (1985) recommend that school districts recruit backup emergency personnel who could assist in the event of a major crisis.

Only two studies have explored preparedness and response capabilities among child-care centers. Wilson and Kershaw (2008) surveyed child-care providers in hurricane-prone regions of Florida. Most of the 67 child-care centers included in the sample had experienced a hurricane (83%) or had closed due to hurricane-related concerns (92%) over the past five years. Despite the high-risk area in which these centers were located, only about two thirds of the respondents indicated that their center had a written hurricane response plan (and in about half of these cases, the plans were not frequently reviewed by center staff). Roughly 70% of respondents were either in the process of or had completed assembling a "hurricane kit" (including vital contact numbers, business papers, insurance, and medications). The authors also found that about 40% of the centers had a contingency plan in place in the event that their facility became uninhabitable following a hurricane. Junn and Guerin (1996) examined levels of earthquake preparedness among child-care centers in a seismically active region of Southern California. They found that over half of the 25 centers studied did not have an earthquake plan on file; those that did often failed to share their plan with teachers, staff, parents, or local emergency response agencies. Almost half of the centers lacked basic essentials, such as food or water, which would be necessary to cope comfortably in the aftermath of a major earthquake. In addition, approximately one third of the center directors believed incorrectly that emergency response agencies would evacuate children from child-care facilities for relocation within 24 hours after a disaster. The authors conclude that, at best, only half of the day-care facilities were even minimally equipped to handle the crises associated with a major earthquake.

When evacuation is necessary, families typically seek refuge in the homes of relatives or friends or stay in hotels (Tierney, Lindell, and Perry 2001). Children who do stay in shelters may face special risks, and there is evidence that the United States is ill-prepared to handle disasters that involve large numbers of injured or displaced children (Markenson and Redlener 2004). When shelters first open, they may not have necessary supplies such as diapers, baby wipes, formula, soap, or prescription medicines to support the health and well-being of children, and infants may be especially vulnerable (Garrett et al. 2007). Also, children with disabilities or chronic health conditions may be particularly prone to adverse effects of evacuation and disruption of support systems and routines (Peek and Stough forthcoming; Rath et al. 2007). Brandenburg and colleagues (2006) identified numerous child injury hazards at a National Guard center in Oklahoma that had been converted to a temporary shelter for Katrina evacuees. Risks to children resulted from both preexisting conditions of the facility (e.g., open electrical outlets, lack of smoke detectors, insecure window screens), and hazards created as a result of the relief efforts and influx of evacuees and volunteers (e.g., unsafe toys, open containers of chemicals and cleaning materials, open tubs of water). Children are also at higher risk of acquiring respiratory and gastrointestinal diseases due to unsanitary conditions in shelters (Garrett et al. 2007).

Shelter workers and local volunteers often play crucial roles in helping to minimize the threats to children's physical safety and emotional well-being. For example, Fothergill and Peek (2006) found that after Hurricane Katrina shelter workers organized tutoring programs, play areas, and child drop-off locations that helped children stay active, while giving parents the opportunity to rest or to take care of other important responsibilities. The Church of the Brethren Children's Disaster Services program trains and mobilizes volunteers in the immediate aftermath of disaster and provides free child care to families affected by disasters of all types (Peek, Sutton, and Gump 2008). After the 2007 California wildfires, Save the Children partnered with Children's Disaster Services and the American Red Cross to set up "Safe Spaces" in evacuation centers (Smith 2008). The goal of Safe Spaces was to allow children to play in a secure and structured environment. Save the Children also recently implemented a program in evacuation centers called Resilient and Ready. This program, which is workshop-based, allows children an opportunity to discuss their feelings of worry or concern, and also teaches them what to do in an emergency situation. After the children complete the workshop, they are given a backpack with emergency evacuation supplies.

7.5.2　Children—Impacts

Over the past two decades, an increasing amount of scholarly attention has been devoted to the psychological impact of disasters on children. This literature examines children's responses to natural and technological disasters, as well as to terrorism and other forms of violent conflict (see Weissbecker et al. 2008). The most widely studied reaction to disasters has been that of post-traumatic stress disorder (PTSD) or related symptoms (La Greca et al. 2002; Norris et al. 2002). This work has shown that a significant proportion of children show reactions following exposure to disasters that can substantially interfere with or impair their daily living and can cause distress to them and their families (La Greca et al. 2002). In their review of the literature on the psychosocial consequences of disaster, Norris and colleagues (2002) found that youth were more likely to be severely affected by disasters than adults, with 48% of school-age samples suffering from moderate post-disaster impairment and 52% experiencing severe or very severe effects in communities that had suffered a major natural disaster. Udwin (1993, 124) notes that there is a growing body of evidence to show that most children react adversely after exposure to traumatic events, and that a significant proportion of child survivors of disasters (possibly 30%–50%) are likely to develop PTSD symptoms, which may persist for long periods of time.

Disaster impacts on children vary by age group, prior experiences, and stage of physical and mental development. For very young children, problems include clinginess, dependence, nightmares, refusing to sleep alone, irritability and temper tantrums, aggressive behavior, incontinence, hyperactivity, and separation anxiety (Norris et al. 2002). Older children may exhibit marked reactions of fear and anxiety, increased hostility with siblings, somatic complaints, sleep disorders, problems with school performance, social withdrawal, apathy, re-enactment through play, PTSD, and anxiety (Mandalakas, Torjesen, and Olness 1999). Adolescents may experience decreased interest in social activities and school, rebellion and other behavioral problems, sleep and eating disorders, somatic complaints, increased or decreased physical activity, confusion, lack of concentration, a decline in responsible behaviors; engage in risk-taking behaviors; suffer from PTSD; and be at increased risk for alcohol or drug misuse after disaster (Mandalakas, Torjesen, and Olness 1999; Reijneveld et al. 2005; Shannon et al. 1994).

Several factors influence children's psychological and emotional reactions to traumatic events (see Green et al. 1991; La Greca, Silverman, and Wasserstein 1998; Vernberg et al. 1996). One of the most critical predictors of children's post-disaster distress is the *extent and intensity of exposure* to the traumatic event. Children who experience life threat, become separated from family members, lose a loved one, suffer extensive damage to their homes and communities, or witness scenes of disaster destruction either directly or through media intake are at particular risk for developing PTSD, anxiety, or depression (Lengua et al. 2005; McFarlane 1987; Pfefferbaum et al. 1999; Saylor

et al. 2003; Shannon et al. 1994). The *characteristics of the child,* including demographic characteristics and pre-disaster functioning, also influence children's reactions to disaster. Girls, racial and
ethnic minorities, and children from lower-socioeconomic backgrounds seem to be at increased risk
for psychological impairment after disaster, although results are not always consistent (Lonigan et
al. 1994; Shannon et al. 1994; Vogel and Vernberg 1993). Children with poorer behavioral and academic functioning prior to disaster are also likely to suffer higher rates of post-disaster impairment
(La Greca, Silverman, and Wasserstein 1998). *Characteristics of the post-disaster environment,*
including parental distress, lack of access to social support, and the occurrence of additional life
stressors (abuse, poverty, divorce, death or illness of a family member) have been linked to children's adverse mental health outcomes and behavioral problems in the aftermath of disaster (Maida,
Gordon, and Strauss 1993; Stuber et al. 2005; Swenson et al. 1996; Warheit et al. 1996; Wasserstein
and La Greca 1998). Finally, the *coping skills of the child* and *the coping assistance received* also
influence children's ability to adapt and respond to highly traumatic events (Jeney-Gammon et al.
1993; Prinstein et al. 1996).

Compared to the number of studies that examine the mental health effects of disasters on children, much less research has explored children's risk for physical injury or loss of life in disasters of
various types. The research that is available has examined the rates of injuries and fatalities among
children in particular disaster events (Glass et al. 1977; Ikeda 1995; Parasuraman 1995; Ramirez
et al. 2005). Most of this work has focused on developing countries because they are much more
prone to large-scale natural catastrophes that cause extensive loss of life. In contrast to developing
countries, the risk of child mortality by forces of nature in the United States is relatively low. The
Centers for Disease Control and Prevention (2004) recorded 6108 deaths caused by natural disaster
events between 1999 and 2003. Of the persons killed, 530 were children and youth between the ages
of 0 and 24 years.

Researchers have identified several social and environmental factors that contribute to children
being at risk for death or injury in disaster. These include residing in poorer countries and communities (Sapir and Lechat 1986), living in and going to school in substandard structures (Hewitt
2007; Parasuraman 1995), losing a parent or becoming separated from family members (Sapir 1993;
Sapir and Lechat 1986), and experiencing malnutrition and poor diet (Webster 1994; Young and
Jaspars 1995) or artificial feeding (i.e., bottle feeding) (Kelly 1993). Female youths are at higher
risk of death (Ramirez et al. 2005; Rivers 1982; Sapir 1993), at least in developing nations. However,
research by Zahran, Peek, and Brody (2008) shows that in disasters in the United States, the death
rate for male children is higher than the death rate for female children across all age cohorts. There
is no consensus in the literature on the age at which children are most at risk for death or injury in
disasters, largely because different types of disaster seem to differentially impact children of various ages. For example, Zahran, Peek, and Brody (2008) found that in the United States infants and
very young children age 0–4 are most likely to die of exposure to extreme heat, 5–14 year olds are
most likely to die in cataclysmic storms and flood events, and adolescents and young adults age
15–24 are most likely to die of excessive cold.

Increased rates of physical abuse may also contribute to children's vulnerability in the aftermath
of disaster. In one of the first attempts to empirically examine whether or not child abuse escalates
after natural disasters, Curtis, Miller, and Berry (2000) discovered statistically significant increases
in child abuse reports in the first six months following Hurricane Hugo and the Loma Prieta earthquake, but found no statistically significant change in abuse rates following Hurricane Andrew.
Keenan and colleagues (2004) examined whether there was an increase in traumatic brain injury
(TBI, commonly referred to as shaken baby syndrome) among children two years old or younger
after Hurricane Floyd. The results showed an increase in the rate of inflicted TBI in the most
affected counties for six months following the disaster, possibly reflecting increased injury risk due
to prolonged stress among caregivers.

Following the 2004 Indian Ocean tsunami, the media and advocacy organizations drew attention
to the risks of sexual violence and human trafficking that children, and especially girls, faced in

displaced person camps (Enarson, Fothergill, and Peek 2006). Drawing on interviews with women's advocacy organizations, Fisher (2005) documented incidents of rape, molestation, and physical abuse perpetrated against women and girls in the tsunami aftermath. Over 2000 sex offenders were lost in the chaos of the Hurricane Katrina evacuation, giving rise to reasonable fears about child predators in and around shelters (see Lauten and Lietz 2008). After Katrina, some efforts were enacted to identify children separated from their legal guardians, to help thwart abductions, and to prevent child physical and sexual abuse (Brandenburg et al. 2007; National Center for Missing and Exploited Children 2006). However, the mere size of the mass shelters that opened after Katrina—as many as 60,000 people sought refuge at the Louisiana Superdome, with up to 25,000 at the nearby New Orleans Convention Center—exposed children to potential violence and compromised the ability of parents to establish a sense of safety for their families (Garrett et al. 2007; Lauten and Lietz 2008). These security threats continued as Katrina evacuees were moved into trailer parks, where almost half of the residents did not feel safe walking in their community at night and 45% did not feel comfortable letting their children play in the trailer parks during the day (International Medical Corps 2006). These settings were enormously stressful for the parents as well as for the children themselves (Fothergill and Peek 2006).

The impact of disasters on children's academic progress and educational outcomes is another area that has received increasing, although still insufficient, attention in the research literature (see Peek 2008). Disasters often destroy school buildings, especially in locations where engineering standards and building codes are not enforced or where buildings are of less structural integrity: Hewitt (2007) inventoried tens of thousands of schools that collapsed in earthquakes over the past two decades in several developing countries. The loss of schools may leave surviving children with few alternatives for an adequate education. Following Katrina, displaced students, many of whom were already behind their peers in reading and math, suffered significant challenges (Casserly 2006; Children's Defense Fund 2006). Vital records were lost in the storm, which resulted in delayed enrollment for some youth (Picou and Marshall 2007). Although getting children back into school was a top priority among parents (Fothergill and Peek 2006), many families did not immediately enroll their children in new schools because they were unsure how long they would be staying in their new community, and others simply did not want to let their children out of their sight (Casserly 2006). Some students were forced to enroll in several different schools as families moved across state lines in search of employment and affordable housing (Abramson and Garfield 2006; Picou and Marshall 2007). One study found that children experienced between one and eleven school changes over a three-month period following the storm, with an average of three moves per child (Lauten and Lietz 2008).

7.5.3 CHILDREN—SHORT- AND LONG-TERM RECOVERY

Much of the literature available on children and recovery is geared toward adults and the ways that they can help children in the disaster aftermath. Parents are often recognized as the single most important source of social support for children following disaster (Prinstein et al. 1996). Parents provide material and emotional support, give comfort and nurturance, and offer a sense of physical safety. In addition to parents, other individuals such as teachers, peers, school counselors, psychologists, pediatricians, disaster relief volunteers, and shelter workers have been identified as playing key roles in re-establishing normalcy, allowing children to express their emotions, and assisting in coping efforts (Barrett, Ausbrooks, and Martinez-Cosio 2008; Johnston and Redlener 2006; Peek and Fothergill 2006; Peek, Sutton, and Gump 2008; Shen and Sink 2002; see also Figure 7.3). Indeed, Fothergill and Peek (2006, 122) argue that these various "support agents" play different, but vitally important, roles in the short- and long-term post-disaster recovery of children.

Some scholars have underscored the importance of encouraging traumatized children to express their feelings—verbally, in written form, through art, and play—to begin healing and recovery (Fothergill and Peek 2006; Looman 2006; Peek, Sutton, and Gump 2008; Raynor 2002). These

FIGURE 7.3 Walkaround Elmo entertains children in New York City as part of a FEMA Crisis Counseling session through the State of New York Office of Mental Health. *Source*: Photo by Andrea Booher/FEMA news photo.

different outlets may help children to articulate their sadness, fears, anxieties, most pressing needs, and hopes for the future. As Looman (2006) notes, however, the age of the child will likely determine the preferred mode of expression: younger children tend to want to draw about their experiences, while adolescents prefer to talk or write about what happened to them in a disaster.

The importance of reopening schools and day-care centers quickly after a disaster has also been highlighted as essential to the successful recovery of children, families, and communities (U.S. Government Accountability Office 2006; Wilson and Kershaw 2008). Indeed, schools are central to children's return to routine and normalcy. However, when a disaster causes widespread infrastructure damage and leads to the loss of teachers and other vital personnel, school reopening may be significantly delayed. Reopening schools may also be complicated by the presence of evacuated residents and emergency response personnel, since schools are often used as shelter facilities in disasters.

School-aged children who are displaced to new schools may face particular challenges in the recovery process. Picou and Marshall (2007) found that students who were displaced to Alabama following Katrina lacked reliable access to transportation and experienced unstable living situations, which led to attendance problems and negatively impacted academic performance. Moreover, families of displaced students suffered severe financial burdens that manifested in a lack of financial support for the daily needs of many displaced students. The rapid influx of new students also created challenges for teachers, school staff, and administrators. Teachers had to go to great lengths to ensure that evacuee children's emotional and academic needs were met, while also balancing the demands of the rest of the students in the class. Barrett, Ausbrooks, and Martinez-Cosio (2008) surveyed displaced middle and high school students who evacuated to Texas after Katrina. They found that nine months after the storm, there were few differences between the relocated Katrina evacuees and their peers in their new schools in terms of emotional well-being. However, evacuee youth were more prone to participate in risky behaviors and fewer protective behaviors (such as school sports or other extracurricular activities) than their non-evacuee peers. The findings indicate that the youths who built positive relationships with their new school, and those who had garnered positive support from adults (especially with their teachers), were managing better than those without a positive source of social support.

Children are at special risk for adverse psychological responses to disaster, but symptoms typically decrease rapidly and recovery is generally complete by 18 months to 3 years post-event (Vogel and Vernberg 1993). Some children suffer longer-term impairment, however. Children most at risk for protracted psychological reactions and delayed recovery include those who experienced highly stressful disasters that involved direct life threat; significant loss; separation from parents; and intense parental stress reactions (see Garrett et al. 2007; Vogel and Vernberg 1993). Chemtob, Nomura, and Abramovitz (2008) explored the long-term emotional and behavioral consequences of the September 11 terrorist attacks for 116 children who were five years old or younger and living or going to preschool in Manhattan at the time of the disaster. Nearly one fourth of the children in the study were exposed to high-intensity events, such as seeing the World Trade Center towers collapse, seeing injured people or dead bodies, or witnessing people jump out of buildings. The study found that children exposed to such traumatic events were nearly five times more likely to suffer from sleep problems and almost three times more likely to be depressed or anxious than children who were not exposed to the attacks. In a follow-up study to the Buffalo Creek flood, Green and colleagues (1991) evaluated child survivors 17 years post-event when they were adults (the subjects were first evaluated in 1974, two years after the disaster). The findings show that the survivors experienced a general decline in impairment over time, suggesting that most of the participants had indeed recovered from the disaster.

The long-term physical health effects for child disaster survivors are complex and not well understood. In the aftermath of September 11, children in Manhattan were exposed to high levels of contaminants in the air as a result of the dust and debris generated by the collapse of the twin towers and other surrounding buildings (Bartlett and Patrarca 2002). Experts testified that the clouds of dust contained benzene, mercury, dioxins, fiberglass, and asbestos, among other substances, and that children could potentially face long-term health issues as a result of exposure (Bartlett and Patrarca 2002, 9). Tens of thousands of Gulf Coast children who lived in FEMA-issued trailers after Katrina may experience lifelong health problems due to the formaldehyde present in the units (Gonzales 2008). Children, as well as adults, suffered ear, nose, and throat irritation; nausea; severe headaches; and asthma, and could potentially develop cancer as a result of the exposure to formaldehyde. The World Health Organization (2005) reports that an increasing number of children are becoming physically disabled due to an increase in sudden-onset disasters, malnutrition, chronic illness, war and other forms of violence, accidents, and environmental damage.

7.5.4   ELDERLY—WARNING/EVACUATION/RESPONSE

The ultimate goal of communicating warnings is to motivate individuals to take appropriate protective actions in the event of an impending threat. Yet few studies have explored ways to most effectively warn or communicate risk to the elderly. This means that we know very little about how older people prefer to receive warnings or how they interpret that information (Phillips and Morrow 2007). Mayhorn (2005) draws upon the literature on aging to illustrate how documented normative age-related changes in perception, attention, memory, text comprehension, and decision making all may affect the processing of hazard-related risk and warning messages. Based on this information, Mayhorn asserts that when developing messages for older adults, designers should tailor the characteristics of the messages to compensate for age-related declines in visual and auditory perception and should take account of different types of memory limitations. With the rapid advent of new communication technologies—such as email and other Web-based advancements, cell phone text messaging, and automatic telephone alert notification systems—it has become increasingly important to consider the ways that an older person's age and related physical and cognitive abilities, as well as their income, prior experience, social conditions, and educational backgrounds, might affect their capabilities to access and utilize these technologies.

Early studies on the elderly and disaster suggested that older persons are less likely to receive warnings than younger persons. Isolated living arrangements, diminished social networks, lower

rates of information-seeking behavior, and limited physical and mental capacities were all identified as possible obstacles to the receipt of warning messages among seniors (Friedsam 1962; Perry
1979). Klinenberg's (2002) research on the 1995 Chicago heat wave, where almost three fourths of
the fatalities were among the elderly, revealed that city agencies and the media delayed warning the
public about the imminent heat wave. Hundreds of the most vulnerable were dead before officials
activated the city's heat emergency plan. When volunteers and city workers began canvassing neighborhoods to warn people of the dangers of the heat, many Chicago seniors refused to open their
doors out of fear. Others were unable to engage in recommended protective actions (such as turning
on fans or air conditioners or walking to air conditioned public spaces) due to financial constraints
and physical limitations.

The research available on warning response among the elderly is conflicting. Some of the first
studies on this topic characterized older persons as a population in need of special attention among
emergency managers because of their noncompliance to warnings and unwillingness to cooperate
with authorities (see Perry 1990). Possible explanations for elderly warning noncompliance included
social isolation among some members of the population, inflexibility, a strong sense of independence, refusal to be separated from normal surroundings, limited mobility and higher degrees of
physical infirmity, and fears of being mistreated by authorities (Friedsam 1962; Turner 1976). More
systematic research by Perry and Lindell (1997), however, has challenged these assumptions about
the elderly (also see Hutton 1976). Specifically, Perry and Lindell (1997) evaluated warning response
among older persons across a variety of natural and technological disaster events, and found that
citizens aged 65 and older who received warning messages were no less likely to comply with warnings and evacuation orders than their younger counterparts. In some cases, the elderly were actually
more likely to comply. The authors conclude that while age alone is not a useful predictor of warning compliance, age is clearly important in the warning phase to the extent that related physical,
psychological, financial, and social conditions impact such things as the probability of receiving a
warning, understanding it, and taking action based upon it (p. 264).

Although evacuation—moving citizens from a place of danger to a place of relative safety—has
long been used as a protective mechanism when disasters threaten (Perry 1990, 94), seniors often
face additional challenges in the evacuation process. For instance, evacuation potentially entails significant financial (e.g., use of automobile, fuel, hotel stay, etc.), emotional (e.g., fear of the unknown;
reluctance to leave pets, property, or possessions; etc.), and social (e.g., reliance on relatives, stigma,
mistreatment, etc.) costs that may be exacerbated for elderly populations (International Federation
of Red Cross and Red Crescent Societies 2007; Mayhorn 2005). Low-income seniors, the home-
bound, and those with physical or cognitive disabilities face compounded barriers that often make
self-evacuation highly unlikely or impossible. For the frailest seniors, the risks of leaving must be
balanced with the risks of staying. For example, when Hurricane Rita threatened the Gulf Coast,
2.5 million people evacuated the region, largely motivated by fears of another Katrina-like catastrophe (Garrett et al. 2007). Of the 111 storm-related deaths in Rita, 90 were due to the evacuation
process itself as gridlock on the highway and oppressive heat took its toll on the chronically ill and
elderly (Garrett et al. 2007, 192). As Moody (2006, 14) notes, on the one hand, leaving the home in
which an elder has lived for years can provoke "transfer trauma" and even cause death. On the other
hand, simply leaving individuals alone to risk death is tantamount to abandonment of the weakest
members of our society.

Nine out of ten, or 90%, of elderly Americans live at home, and an increasing number of these
individuals live alone (U.S. Census Bureau 2006). Even when early warnings (as with a slow-rising
flood or hurricane) are issued hours or days before a disaster occurs, few communities have plans in
place to identify and reach out to older adults most likely in need of evacuation assistance (Wilson
2006). For many older adults, especially those with disabilities or who require special medical
equipment, exiting their homes can be a great challenge when evacuation is required (McGuire,
Ford, and Okoro 2007). Yet the responsibility to evacuate is placed on these individuals and their
loved ones, which is particularly problematic in the United States where people move frequently,

families are often spatially dispersed, and it is common for seniors to lose valuable sources of social support as they age (Klinenberg 2002). Seniors who live at home may be at even greater risk when a disaster strikes with little or no warning (as with an earthquake, industrial accident, and terrorist attack). After the September 11 attacks, a number of older adults and persons with disabilities were left for three days in buildings in lower Manhattan that had been evacuated, which highlights the pressing need to identify vulnerable people who are not in institutional settings or connected to community service agencies (O'Brien 2003).

Most emergency evacuation planning for seniors has actually been geared toward nursing homes and other assisted living facilities (Lafond 1987), although less than 10% of elderly adults in the United States live in these settings. Nursing home residents are generally frail and at risk of rapid medical decline in the absence of continuous care (Laditka et al. 2007), and thus the stresses of evacuation can be particularly challenging for this population. However, the burden to evacuate is not placed upon each resident because long-term care establishments ostensibly have disaster and evacuation plans. The facility decides whether to evacuate, selects and arranges the mode of transportation, and plans appropriate temporary lodging (McGuire, Ford, and Okoro 2007). Yet, this certainly does not guarantee the safety and survival of residents, as was widely acknowledged after Hurricane Katrina. The owners of St. Rita's Nursing Home in St. Bernard Parish, just outside of New Orleans, were charged with the deaths of 35 elderly patients who drowned after the owners decided not to evacuate the facility. What received less attention from the media, however, was that of the approximately 60 nursing homes directly affected by Katrina, only 21 evacuated before the storm (Hull and Struck 2005). A number of these nursing home facilities, which are obviously located in an extremely hazardous region, did not even have an evacuation plan on file (Wilson 2006).

Prior studies have identified numerous problems encountered in evacuating nursing home residents during emergencies and disasters, including (1) the absence of specific evacuation plans; (2) an insufficient number of vehicles that can accommodate walkers, wheelchairs, and other specialized medical equipment; (3) transportation delays and the resultant length of time required to move nursing home residents to their designated shelters; (4) elevated stress and discomfort among the elderly as they wait for transport; (5) staff not being permitted to pass through police checkpoints after being called in to assist with an evacuation; (6) lack of adequate staff and high staff–client ratios; (7) large numbers of frail elderly and persons in need of specialized medical attention; (8) communication system disruption; and (9) lack of water, food, medicine, and other essential supplies (Mangum, Kosberg, and McDonald 1989; Vogt 1991; Wilson 2006). Vogt (1991) discovered that preparing for emergencies is a low priority within most nursing homes and related health care organizations, and that too often these organizations utilize fire drills to prepare for all types of emergencies when the majority of events are non-fire related. There is some evidence, however, that the catastrophic consequences of Hurricane Katrina have caused at least some nursing home administrators to reconsider their disaster preparedness and evacuation plans (Laditka et al. 2007).

Most elderly, like other members of the population, do not evacuate to public shelters but instead relocate to the homes of relatives or friends (Tierney, Lindell, and Perry 2001). However, elderly adults who do utilize public shelters may encounter settings—such as churches and public schools—that are difficult to navigate because the facilities are located on more than one level (Vogt 1991). The elderly often evacuate without medications, eyeglasses, and other supplies, and thus may arrive at shelters without necessary provisions or knowledge of the whereabouts of their doctors (Ketteridge and Fordham 1998). Nursing home residents are frequently evacuated to other nursing homes or to hospitals, where the professional staff can relatively easily care for their needs. In some mass evacuations, however, nursing home residents end up in settings that were never intended to accommodate physically or mentally impaired persons. This creates numerous challenges related to feeding, cleaning, dressing, providing medications, and caring for these vulnerable individuals (Mangum, Kosberg, and McDonald 1989; Wilson 2006).

Sheltering in place during an emergency, either as a recommended action or because of a lack of other viable options, can lead to potentially life-threatening situations for the elderly. After

September 11, service personnel lacked access to older and frail residents living in the area sur-rounding Ground Zero where the twin towers collapsed. Essential services such as meals for the homebound and home health care were not delivered because staff had no official authorization to carry out their responsibilities. In some cases, elderly and disabled persons were left alone for days with no electricity (and therefore no television, lights, elevators, or refrigerators), no running water, and no information about what was happening (O'Brien 2003).

7.5.5 ELDERLY—IMPACTS

When disaster does strike, older adults are among those most likely to perish (Bourque et al. 2006). In the United States, the Centers for Disease Control and Prevention (2004) recorded 6108 deaths caused by natural disaster events between 1999 and 2003. Over 40% (2670) of those who died were persons 65 years of age and above, although the elderly represent only about 12% of the entire population. Research has also shown that the proportion of elderly injured in disasters is higher than would be expected based on the population distribution of this age group (see Eldar 1992).

A number of factors place the elderly at increased risk for disaster-related injuries, mortality, and morbidity. Many older adults, and especially elderly women of color, live in socially and economi-cally marginalized positions prior to a disaster. Low-income seniors may be unable to increase their preparedness for disasters—by storing food, purchasing emergency first-aid equipment, stockpil-ing medicines, or upgrading their dwellings—which puts them at special risk in times of disas-ter. Sensory impairment, resulting from vision or hearing loss, may reduce the likelihood than an older adult will receive, accurately perceive, or appropriately act on hazard warnings (Eldar 1992; Mayhorn 2005). Age-related mobility problems make it more difficult for some older adults to escape during times of disaster. For instance, some seniors are physically incapable of walking to an evacuation point in the event of a tsunami warning or hiking up a hillside in a flash flood, both of which are recommended protective actions obviously aimed at more able-bodied persons. Reduced thermoregulatory capacity in the elderly, combined with a diminished ability to detect changes in their body temperatures, may partly explain their higher susceptibility to death from extreme cold and extreme heat (Medina-Ramón et al. 2006).

For the growing number of older persons who suffer from chronic ailments, the shock of a disas-ter may further exacerbate poor overall health and could lead to premature death (Medina-Ramón et al. 2006). Seniors are also more vulnerable because they typically have a lower injury threshold and a decreased ability to survive injury once it has occurred (Eldar 1992). A disaster can force indi-viduals to go for extended periods of time without adequate food, water, shelter, or access to regular medications, and the elderly are among those who have the hardest time withstanding these sorts of conditions. Older adults who take refuge in public shelters may suffer additional trauma and stress from the lack of privacy, crowded and noisy environment, uncomfortable sleeping arrangements, and lack of assistance with activities of daily living (HelpAge International 2005). Older people with ailments such as diabetes or cancer may face difficulty in resuming life-sustaining treatment due to lost medical histories, lack of health insurance, or insufficient financial resources. Disasters can result in disabling conditions for some elderly, as they are forced to go without eyeglasses, hear-ing aids, walkers, and other devices that assist their daily living (Eldar 1992). These persons, who may have been relatively independent before the disaster, could become totally reliant on others.

Where the elderly live also puts them at risk for financial loss, death, or injury in disasters. A sub-stantial proportion of older adults in the United States are concentrated in some of the most hazard-prone states. In fact, the four states with the highest number of federal disaster declarations—Texas, California, Florida, and New York—also happen to be the four states with the largest number of elderly residents (FEMA 2008; U.S. Census Bureau 2006). Older persons who live in low-cost housing are exposed to greater risks because of the lower quality construction of these buildings, which may be particularly susceptible to floods, fires, tornados, or earthquakes (Fothergill and Peek 2004). Elderly persons who live in high-crime, high-poverty neighborhoods that are run down and lack viable public spaces are more likely to suffer from social isolation and to receive insufficient assistance in a disaster (Klinenberg 2002).

Increased rates of elder abuse may contribute to the physical and emotional vulnerability of some older persons in communities struck by disasters, although this is a largely unexplored topic. After the Exxon Valdez oil spill in Alaska, community leaders responding to a survey reported an 11% increase in elder abuse (Araji 1992). The stresses of living in a post-disaster environment often strain family relationships (Morrow 1997), and individuals may become overwhelmed as they attempt to cope with their own or their family members' traumatic reactions to disaster, the loss of material possessions and valued family memorabilia, financial difficulties, and increased demands for carework between adults and their elderly parents. All of these factors could contribute to a higher incidence of elder abuse in the aftermath of disaster.

Although older persons are at greater risk for death or physical injury, available research suggests that they are actually less likely than their younger counterparts to suffer adverse psychological impacts in the aftermath of natural and human-made disasters (Ngo 2001). In their extensive review of the disaster mental health literature, Norris and colleagues (2002) report that negative psychological responses to disaster decline with age, and that middle-aged adults are actually most likely to be adversely affected. Greater chronic stress and additional demands related to providing care and support for dependent relatives may explain why being middle-aged is a risk factor for post-disaster distress (Bolin and Klenow 1988; Thompson, Norris, and Hanacek 1993). The elderly seem to be more psychologically resilient because of the greater life experience, maturity, and fewer obligations and responsibilities that come with age (Ngo 2001; Norris et al. 2002). In addition, the lower psychological vulnerability of older adults might be attributed to previous disaster exposure and related improved preparedness and positive coping skills (Bell, Kara, and Batterson 1978; Huerta and Horton 1978; Lawson and Thomas 2007; Ngo 2001; Norris and Murrell 1988).

While older adults as a whole may exhibit lower rates of post-disaster distress, they are still at risk for adverse psychological outcomes after exposure to natural disaster. Indeed, a number of studies have confirmed that the elderly have suffered from anxiety, depressive symptoms, and considerable physical and mental distress for months or even several years in the aftermath of disaster (Krause 1987; Melick and Logue 1985; Ollendick and Hoffmann 1982; Phifer 1990). Furthermore, rates of psychological distress tend to vary significantly among the elderly, as some segments of the older adult population are more vulnerable than others to disaster. In particular, pre-disaster characteristics and conditions of the elderly (e.g., socioeconomic status, race, gender, marital status, family size, available support networks, prior traumatic experiences) and disaster impacts (e.g., severity of exposure, financial and material loss, displacement) all influence mental health outcomes in the immediate and longer-term aftermath of disaster (Bolin and Klenow 1988; Ngo 2001; Norris et al. 2002; Tracy and Galea 2006).

One consistent finding in the literature is that poor or low-income seniors are often most vulnerable to adverse psychological outcomes. This differential vulnerability may be directly related to associated deficits in coping tactics and low social support resources (Phifer 1990). While some research has found that men exposed to disaster exhibit higher rates of stress and may engage in negative coping behaviors (e.g., alcohol abuse) (Phifer 1990), numerous studies have shown that older women are more vulnerable to the effects of stress than older men (see Fothergill 1996; Ollenburger and Tobin 1999). Older women, and especially older minority women, are more likely to be unmarried, live alone, have more caretaking roles, and have fewer socioeconomic resources, which puts them at risk for stress-related illness after disaster (Ollenburger and Tobin 1999). However, older women typically have more social support, which suggests that their superior support networks may help them cope more effectively than men (Klinenberg 2002; Krause 1987; Tyler 2006).

Even though the elderly exhibit less post-impact psychological disruption than younger cohorts, they tend to experience greater proportional dollar losses (Bell 1978; Bolin and Klenow 1983; Kilijanek and Drabek 1979; Poulshock and Cohen 1975). These higher losses have been attributed to the elderly living in hazardous areas and residing in housing less resistant to forces of nature, although more systematic research across time, place, and disaster type is necessary to better understand the actual extent of losses suffered by the elderly (Ngo 2001). Early research by Friedsam (1961, 1962) and Bolin and Klenow (1983) discovered that older citizens were more likely to report greater material losses, despite indications that damages were evenly distributed across age groups. However, work by Huerta and Horton (1978) found no pattern of over-reporting among the elderly. One thing that is certain is that those who have lived the longest often are at the greatest risk of losing the accumulated assets of a lifetime. Indeed, as a group, the elderly tend to lose more irreplaceable items, and it is the loss of these possessions that often causes great distress among older persons (Huerta and Horton 1978; Ketteridge and Fordham 1998; Kilijanek and Drabek 1979).

7.5.6 ELDERLY—SHORT- AND LONG-TERM RECOVERY

The stress confronted by disaster victims is multifaceted, involving not only immediate loss and trauma but also a continuing requirement to adapt to a changing environment during the disaster recovery period (Norris and Hutchins 1989, 34). The research evidence available suggests that seniors often face financial, physical, and emotional obstacles as they struggle to recover and rebuild after a disaster. However, older adults who suffer less severe disruptions and have access to sufficient resources and sources of social support are able to cope effectively in the short- and longer-term aftermath of disaster.

As described previously, several studies have found that older citizens tend to experience greater proportional dollar losses in disasters. Yet many seniors, and especially elderly women, have inadequate savings or insurance coverage to help begin the process of disaster recovery (Bolin 1982; Childers 1999; Morrow-Jones and Morrow-Jones 1991). Moreover, relative to younger groups, the elderly are less likely to qualify for low-interest loans (Bolin 1982; Bolin and Klenow 1988). In an examination of the disaster loan process following the 1995 flooding in New Orleans, Childers (1999) found that poor elderly women were five times less likely than other elderly households, and almost six times less likely than younger people, to be approved for a loan. This is despite the fact that these low-income elderly women were over-represented in the population applying to FEMA for loans.

Many aid agencies assume—incorrectly—that generalized emergency and recovery aid will reach older people or that family members will look after their interests (International Federation of Red Cross and Red Crescent Societies 2007). This assumption is particularly problematic in light of past research that has documented that older adults are among those least likely to take advantage of aid (in the form of food, shelter, health care, or mental health services) or cash assistance from government or private sources (Poulshock and Cohen 1975). In their study of the long-term impacts of a tornado disaster on the elderly, Kilijanek and Drabek (1979, 559) argued that seniors and their families suffered from a "pattern of neglect." Of nine categories of potential help sources—(1) relatives, (2) friends, (3) religious organizations, (4) Red Cross, (5) Salvation Army, (6) other voluntary organizations, (7) governmental agencies, (8) strangers, and (9) employers—victims over 60 years of age received aid from all categories less frequently than did younger victims. Furthermore, nearly 20% of older citizens who suffered the most extensive damage received no aid whatsoever from any of the nine sources.

The elderly may not receive adequate recovery assistance for several reasons. First, discrimination against the elderly by government agencies, humanitarian organizations, and communities may limit their access to vital post-disaster aid (HelpAge International 2005; International Federation of Red Cross and Red Crescent Societies 2007). Second, overly bureaucratic agency procedures may discourage the elderly from applying for assistance. A number of scholars have noted that the elderly tend to feel confused, intimidated, and frustrated by complicated claim forms and procedural regulations (Bell, Kara, and Batterson 1978; Huerta and Horton 1978; Phillips and Morrow 2007). FEMA no longer requires that disaster victims travel to an application center and wait in line to fill out myriad forms (Childers 1999), a process that was particularly problematic for older persons who required additional support or transportation assistance to leave their homes (Poulshock and Cohen 1975). However, new technologies—such as voice-prompt telephone systems and Internet-based aid applications—may be similarly inaccessible to certain segments of the elderly population. Third, the elderly, especially those with limited social networks, may lack the necessary information and support mechanisms to navigate increasingly complex recovery aid application processes (Childers 1999). Fourth, a generational emphasis on self-sufficiency and independence may lead some elderly to fear that accepting aid will leave them dependent (Bell, Kara, and Batterson 1978; Ngo 2001). Fifth, and related to the previous point, the perceived stigma attached to accepting "welfare" may discourage elderly from requesting any type of assistance (Huerta and Horton 1978; Poulshock and Cohen 1975).

Some studies have found that the elderly tend to suffer serious long-term health effects after disaster, including persistent depressive symptoms and perceived deterioration of physical health (Friedsam 1962; Melick and Logue 1985; Phifer 1990; Takeda, Tamura, and Tatsuki 2003; Tyler and Hoyt 2000). Yet other research suggests that older persons do not suffer lasting negative physical or mental health impacts (Hutchins and Norris 1989; Kilijanek and Drabek 1979), and that they actually rebound at equal rates or more quickly than younger persons (Bell, Kara, and Batterson 1978; Bolin and Klenow 1988; Miller, Turner, and Kimball 1981). In fact, some research has shown that the elderly experience positive impacts such as strengthened familial relationships and an increase in civic mindedness (as evidenced by higher rates of volunteerism and community involvement) during the recovery period (Bell, Kara, and Batterson 1978; Takeda, Tamura, and Tatsuki 2003).

Resource and social support differentials may help explain these conflicting findings regarding the long-term effects of disasters for elders (Takeda, Tamura, and Tatsuki 2003; Tyler 2006). Following a major tornado in Paris, Texas, Bolin and Klenow (1988) compared the psychosocial recovery of black and white elderly and non-elderly disaster victims. They discovered that elders within each racial group were more likely to be psychosocially recovered than were the younger victim samples, although a significantly higher proportion of white elders were fully recovered at eight months post-impact than were black elders. A number of characteristics had a positive effect on psychosocial recovery for both black and white elderly disaster victims, including higher socioeconomic status, being married, having adequate insurance and sources of federal aid, and experiencing fewer post-disaster moves while in temporary housing. This study clearly indicates that the black and white elderly victims who recovered the fastest had more financial, social, and emotional resources available to help them in coping with the numerous demands of the post-disaster environment.

It is also important to acknowledge that the lasting effects of disaster and prospects for recovery among the elderly may be shaped by the severity of the event. Disasters that cause more severe losses, trauma exposure, and ongoing displacement seem to be particularly stressful for the elderly and subsequently lead to slower recovery (Miller, Turner, and Kimball 1981). For example, post–Hurricane Katrina, seniors suffered more serious health declines in much greater numbers than younger storm victims (Spiegel 2006). In addition, in the year following Katrina's landfall, Stephens and colleagues (2007) observed a significant increase in the proportion of deaths (43% increase over baseline) among current and former New Orleans residents. The researchers argue that the excess mortality, especially among the elderly and other vulnerable groups, demonstrates the enduring health consequences of a major natural disaster. They also suggest that the indirect deaths largely resulted from a virtually destroyed public health infrastructure. Sanders, Bowie, and Bowie (2003) interviewed elderly African American public housing residents who were forcibly relocated from their homes when Hurricane Andrew struck Florida. They found that the seniors suffered from various physical and mental health conditions, but only about one fourth of the older adults had their health care needs met during the relocation. The physical and emotional challenges that the elderly faced were exacerbated by their separation from family, friends, former health care providers, and various community support services.

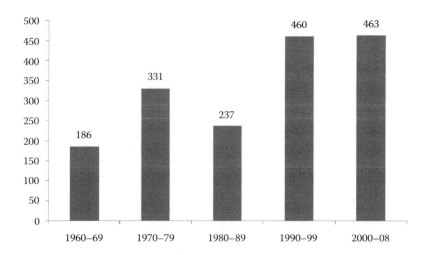

FIGURE 7.4 Number of U.S. federal disaster declarations, 1960–2008. *Source*: FEMA (Federal Emergency Management Agency). Declared disasters by year or state. http://www.fema.gov/news/disaster_totals_annual. fema (accessed February 4, 2008).

7.6 FUTURE RISK AND IMPLICATIONS FOR ACTION

Disaster risk is on the rise in the United States. Over the past five decades, the number of federal disaster declarations has increased substantially (Figure 7.4). The economic losses, damage to the built and natural environment, and human costs of these major disasters have been severe. Adjusting for inflation, natural disasters resulted in approximately $387 billion in property losses and over $85 billion in crop losses in the United States from 1960–2005. During the same time period, disasters claimed the lives of nearly 19,000 Americans and injured over 170,000 more (SHELDUS 2005).

Beyond better tracking and reporting, the increase in the number of disaster events may be attributed to various demographic, socioeconomic, environmental, and technological factors. The U.S. population more than tripled from 1900 to 2000, placing more people in harm's way. The growing population has been accompanied by greater diversity, longer life expectancies, and more significant gaps between high- and low-income populations. Climate change, coastal land loss, and environmental degradation have resulted in more extreme weather events and have impacted fragile ecosystems. In addition, increased urbanization, infrastructure decay, and unsustainable develop- ment in hazard-prone areas such as floodplains, coastal regions, and earthquake fault zones have contributed to rising disaster losses.

Most experts agree that the financial and human tolls of disasters will continue to increase throughout the 21st century (Mileti 1999). Without a significant change in practice and policy, children and the elderly will also continue to be among those most affected when disaster strikes. Therefore, this final section presents some possible approaches for addressing the vulnerability of children and the elderly before and after disaster.

7.6.1 Recognize the Vulnerability of Children and the Elderly

A first step in reducing the vulnerability of children and the elderly involves recognition that these groups often have fewer resources and limited capacity to prepare for disaster, may suffer dispro- portionate losses when disaster strikes, and tend to face barriers in the recovery process. Available research evidence in the United States and in international contexts shows that children and the elderly are among those most at risk for death and injury in disaster; they may experience both short- and longer-term psychological impairment in the aftermath of disaster; they often suffer increased risk in shelters due to poor design and planning decisions; and they may require additional emotional, financial, and/or educational support during the recovery period. Volunteers, emergency managers, and other professionals who assist with disaster preparedness, response, and recovery activities must be encouraged to consider the elevated risks that children and the elderly face across the disaster life cycle. Moreover, these professionals should be taught to recognize the root causes—from increased exposure to hazards to unequal access to resources—that contribute to the vulnerability of the very young and the very old.

A growing number of research studies, policy briefings, and field reports focus on the experiences and needs of children and older persons in disasters. This information should be integrated into higher education curriculum for emergency managers, disaster planning and training exercises, emergency response protocols, shelter planning activities, and community preparedness and education materials. A sustained focus on the special needs of children and the elderly will help to ensure that these groups are not rendered invisible in disaster planning and post-disaster resource allocation.

7.6.2   ACKNOWLEDGE DIFFERENTIAL VULNERABILITY AND TARGET RESOURCES ACCORDINGLY

In the United States, children and the elderly have very different pre- and post-disaster experiences on the basis of their age and stage of development, income and access to resources, race, gender, physical and mental abilities, geographic location, housing situation, and family structure. These critical social and demographic factors influence whether young people and older adults will prepare for disaster, receive warnings, take recommended protective actions, access aid, or recover fully from trauma. Thus, while it is important to recognize that children and the elderly are among the most vulnerable groups in emergency situations, it is also vital to acknowledge that not all children and not all elderly are equally vulnerable. Indeed, age intersects with many other factors to determine differential rates of vulnerability among children and older adults. For instance, a poor, elderly African American woman living alone in substandard rental housing is at increased risk for death or physical injury in a sudden-onset disaster. This is largely due to what Phillips and Morrow (2007, 63) refer to as the "clustering" of vulnerability factors that ultimately leads to amplified risk in disaster for the most marginalized members of society.

Resources for disaster preparedness, emergency response and sheltering, and long-term recovery should be allocated in such a way that acknowledges that some children and some older adults are more vulnerable to the harmful impacts of disaster and thus require greater assistance. Of course, determining the relative vulnerability of children and the elderly and identifying those most at risk before and after a disaster can be challenging. However, emergency management agencies and community organizations can work together to develop means to find and work with the most vulnerable groups of children and the elderly (Table 7.1).

7.6.3   MANDATE INSTITUTIONAL PREPAREDNESS

The limited research evidence available suggests that day-care centers, schools, nursing homes, and other institutions that serve the needs of children or the elderly are often not prepared for disasters. These institutions should be required to (1) stockpile food, water, medications, and other necessary emergency supplies; (2) upgrade their dwellings (for example, structures in earthquake zones should be retrofitted and heavy items such as bookcases should be bolted down); (3) develop emergency response guidelines and evacuation plans in consultation with local emergency management agencies; and (4) review emergency plans on a regular basis with staff and parents of children or family members of the elderly.

Private and public day-care centers and schools, nursing homes, senior living facilities, and other institutions may require financial support to carry out various preparedness activities that would help increase the safety of the populations they serve. This means that local, state, and federal government entities must commit the necessary resources to ensure that these organizations can appropriately prepare and can reopen in a timely manner in the aftermath of disaster.

TABLE 7.1
Indicators of Increased Vulnerability among Children and the Elderly

Children	Elderly
Very young (0–5 years of age)	Oldest old (85 years of age or older)
Live in a single-parent household	Frail elderly
Homeless	Poor
Poor	Chronically ill
Mentally or physically disabled	Mentally or physically disabled
Occupy older or less stable housing	Experience sensory or mobility limitations
Racial or ethnic minorities	Live alone
Pet owners	Socially isolated
Attend inadequately prepared day-care centers or schools	Renters
Lack access to social support	Occupy older or less stable housing
Have limited coping resources	Live in inadequately prepared nursing homes or senior
Reside in a hazard-prone area	living facilities
	Racial or ethnic minorities
	Pet owners
	Reside in a hazard-prone area

7.6.4 Build Capacities and Involve Children and the Elderly

Children and the elderly represent over one third of the entire U.S. population. Beyond their sheer numbers, both children and older adults have considerable strengths that could serve as a significant resource for families, communities, and organizations attempting to prepare for, respond to, and recover from disasters. Rather than excluding their voices, children and the elderly should be actively encouraged to participate in disaster planning and relief efforts. Below I offer just a few examples of ways that children and the elderly can, and have, contributed in meaningful ways to vulnerability reduction efforts.

An increasing number of children are learning about hazards in schools, on the Internet, and through popular media (Wachtendorf, Brown, and Nickle 2008; Wisner 2006). Children can draw on their newly acquired knowledge to help their families assemble emergency supply kits and develop household evacuation plans. Adolescents across the United States are becoming involved in Teen School Emergency Response Training (Teen SERT) programs, which help students to learn basic preparedness and response skills so they can handle emergency situations. Bilingual children may translate disaster warnings and other materials for non-English speaking adults in their families and communities (Mitchell et al. 2008). During the emergency response phase of disaster, children may actively engage in search and rescue activities and assist less able-bodied family members with evacuation (Kirschke and van Vliet 2005). Children often express a strong desire to be involved with post-disaster community rebuilding efforts, and have contributed to reconstruction planning and design, assisted with cleanup activities, and helped to rebuild houses and schools (see Peek 2008).

The elderly have a wealth of knowledge and experience accumulated over a lifetime. Older persons know the history of their community, and their experiences and memories of past disasters can assist in planning and risk mitigation activities. The elderly are aware of the unique needs of older adults, and they can articulate those needs to emergency managers and other professionals. Shelter planning committees and local emergency management agencies could include members of the elderly community on decision-making and advisory bodies such as disaster preparedness committees. Given that the elderly population of the United States is projected to double in coming decades, and that an increasing number of seniors live alone, the elderly can play an active role in identifying and reaching out to the most vulnerable members of the community. Building these types of social networks with elders could ultimately save the lives of those who are socially isolated

FIGURE 7.5   A Red Cross volunteer assists survivors at a recovery center. *Source*: Photo by Liz Roll/FEMA news photo

or have mobility impairments (Klinenberg 2002). The elderly already comprise a large percentage of volunteers in nongovernmental organizations and in disaster relief and recovery (Lafond 1987). They should be acknowledged for their myriad contributions and encouraged to continue serving in this important capacity (Figure 7.5).

7.7 SUMMARY

Although disasters occur across the United States, their impacts are distributed unevenly. As this chapter has demonstrated, children and the elderly are often among the most vulnerable to natural and human-made hazards. Yet the vulnerability of these groups is neither inherent nor inevitable. Because vulnerability is rooted in social, economic, and cultural processes, it is possible to reduce many of the risks that children and the elderly face in disasters. Like other forms of social change, however, reducing vulnerability among these groups will require a sustained commitment from families, communities, emergency management agencies, disaster relief organizations, and all levels of government.

7.8 DISCUSSION QUESTIONS

1. In what ways do race, class, gender, physical and mental ability, and age interact and influence the experiences of children and the elderly in disaster?
2. What challenges does growing diversity among both youth and elderly populations pose for disaster planning and response? What opportunities for reducing vulnerability may emerge as a result of increasingly diverse younger and older populations?
3. How does unequal access to resources influence the experiences of children and the elderly before and after disaster?
4. How can organizations active in disaster planning, emergency management, and long-term recovery be more responsive to the specific needs of children and the elderly?
5. How can families and communities be more responsive to the specific needs of children and the elderly?
6. In what ways could the research findings detailed in this chapter be applied to emergency preparedness, response, or recovery activities?

7. Although an increasing number of studies have focused on the experiences of children and the elderly in disaster contexts, important gaps in knowledge remain. What do you see as the most pressing research needs in this subfield of disaster research?
8. What do you view as the greatest strengths of children and the elderly, especially as they relate to potential contributions to disaster planning and response?
9. How could children and the elderly be more actively engaged in disaster planning and response?

ACKNOWLEDGMENTS

Dr. Alice Fothergill offered feedback on earlier drafts of this chapter, which is gratefully acknowledged. I would also like to thank Dr. Brenda Phillips for inviting me to write this chapter and for her helpful advice and continual support.

REFERENCES

Abramson, D., and R. Garfield. 2006. *On the edge: Children and families displaced by Hurricanes Katrina and Rita face a looming medical and mental health crisis.* New York: Columbia University Mailman School of Public Health.

Abramson, D., I. Redlener, T. Stehling-Ariza, and E. Fuller. 2007. *The legacy of Katrina's children: Estimating the numbers of hurricane-related at-risk children in the Gulf Coast states of Louisiana and Mississippi.* New York: Columbia University Mailman School of Public Health.

Adams, J. 1995. *Risk.* London: UCL Press.

Araji, S. 1992. The Exxon-Valdez oil spill: Social, economic, and psychological impacts on Homer. Unpublished final report to the community of Homer, Department of Sociology, University of Alaska.

Barrett, E. J., C. Y. B. Ausbrooks, and M. Martinez-Cosio. 2008. The school as a source of support for Katrina-evacuated youth. *Children, Youth and Environments* 18 (1): 202–36.

Bartlett, S., and J. Patrarca. 2002. *Schools of Ground Zero: Early lessons learned in children's environmental health.* Washington, DC: American Public Health Association and Healthy Schools Network, Inc.

Bell, B. D. 1978. Disaster impact and response: Overcoming the thousand natural shocks. *The Gerontologist* 18:531–40.

Bell, B. D., G. Kara, and C. Batterson. 1978. Service utilization and adjustment patterns of elderly tornado victims in an American disaster. *Mass Emergencies* 3:71–81.

Bolin, R. 1982. *Long-term family recovery from disaster.* Boulder: Institute of Behavioral Science, University of Colorado.

Bolin, R., and D. J. Klenow. 1983. Response of the elderly to disaster. *International Journal of Aging and Human Development* 16(4):283–96.

———. 1988. Older people in disaster: A comparison of black and white victims. *International Journal of Aging and Human Development* 26 (1): 29–43.

Bourque, L. B., J. M. Siegel, M. Kano, and M. M. Wood. 2006. Morbidity and mortality associated with disasters. In *Handbook of disaster research,* eds. H. Rodríguez, E. L. Quarantelli, and R. R. Dynes, 97–112. New York: Springer.

Boyden, J. 2003. Children under fire: Challenging assumptions about children's resilience. *Children, Youth and Environments* 13 (1). http://colorado.edu/journals/cye (accessed March 1, 2008).

Brandenburg, M. A., M. B. Ogle, B. A. Washington, M. J. Garner, S. A. Watkins, and K. L. Brandenburg. 2006. 'Operation Child-Safe': A strategy for preventing unintentional pediatric injuries at a Hurricane Katrina evacuee shelter. *Prehospital and Disaster Medicine* 21 (5): 359–65.

Brandenburg, M. A., S. M. Watkins, K. L. Brandenburg, and C. Schieche. 2007. Operation Child-ID: Reunifying children with their legal guardians after Hurricane Katrina. *Disasters* 31 (3): 277–87.

Carter, M. T., S. Kendall, and J. P. Clark. 1983. Household response to warnings. *International Journal of Mass Emergencies and Disasters* 9 (1): 94–104.

Casserly, M. 2006. Double jeopardy: Public education in New Orleans before and after the storm. In *There is no such thing as a natural disaster: Race, class, and Hurricane Katrina,* eds. C. Hartman and G. D. Squires, 197–214. New York: Routledge.

Centers for Disease Control and Prevention. 2004. *Compressed mortality file: Underlying cause of death.* http://wonder.cdc.gov/mortSQL.html (accessed February 8, 2008).

Chemtob, C. M., Y. Nomura, and R. A. Abramovitz. 2008. Impact of conjoined exposure to the World Trade Center attacks and to other traumatic events on the behavioral problems of preschool children. *Archives of Pediatrics and Adolescent Medicine* 162 (2): 126–33.

Childers, C. D. 1999. Elderly female-headed households in the disaster loan process. *International Journal of Mass Emergencies and Disasters* 17 (1): 99–110.

Children's Defense Fund. 2006. *Katrina's children: A call to conscience and action.* Washington, DC: Children's Defense Fund.

Curtis, T., B. C. Miller, and E. H. Berry. 2000. Changes in reports and incidence of child abuse following natural disasters. *Child Abuse and Neglect* 24:1151–62.

Dash, N., and H. Gladwin. 2007. Evacuation decision making and behavioral responses: Individual and household. *Natural Hazards Review* 8 (3): 69–77.

Edwards, M. L. 1993. Social location and self-protective behavior: Implications for earthquake preparedness. *International Journal of Mass Emergencies and Disasters* 11 (3): 293–303.

Eldar, R. 1992. The needs of elderly persons in natural disasters: Observations and recommendations. *Disasters* 16 (4): 355–58.

Enarson, E., A. Fothergill, and L. Peek. 2006. Gender and disaster: Foundations and directions. In *Handbook of disaster research,* eds. H. Rodríguez, E. L. Quarantelli, and R.R. Dynes, 130–46. New York: Springer.

Fass, S., and N. K. Cauthen. 2007. *Who are America's poor children? The official story.* New York: National Center for Children in Poverty, Columbia University Mailman School of Public Health.

FEMA (Federal Emergency Management Agency). 2008. *Declared disasters by year or state.* http://www.fema.gov/news/disaster_totals_annual.fema (accessed February 4, 2008).

Fischer III, H. W., G. F. Stine, B. L. Stoker, M. L. Trowbridge, and E. M. Drain. 1995. Evacuation behavior: Why do some evacuate while others do not? A case study of Ephrata, Pennsylvania (USA) evacuation. *Disaster Prevention and Management* 4 (4): 30–36.

Fisher, S. 2005. Gender based violence in Sri Lanka in the aftermath of the 2004 Tsunami crisis: The role of international organizations and international NGOs in prevention and response to gender based violence. PhD dissertation, University of Leeds.

Fothergill, A. 1996. Gender, risk, and disaster. *International Journal of Mass Emergencies and Disasters* 14 (1): 33–56.

Fothergill, A., E. Maestas, and J. Darlington. 1999. Race, ethnicity, and disasters in the United States: A review of the literature. *Disasters* 23 (2): 156–73.

Fothergill, A., and L. Peek. 2004. Poverty and disasters in the United States: A review of the sociological literature. *Natural Hazards* 32:89–110.

———. 2006. Surviving catastrophe: A study of children in Hurricane Katrina. In *Learning from catastrophe: Quick response research in the wake of Hurricane Katrina,* ed. Natural Hazards Center, 97–130. Boulder: Institute of Behavioral Science, University of Colorado.

Friedsam, H. J. 1961. Reactions of older persons to disaster-caused losses. *The Gerontologist* 1:34–37.

———. 1962. Older persons in disaster. In *Man and society in disaster,* eds. G. W. Baker and D. W. Chapman, 151–82. New York: Basic Books.

Garrett, A. L., R. Grant, P. Madrid, A. Brito, D. Abramson, and I. Redlener. 2007. Children and megadisasters: Lessons learned in the new millennium. *Advances in Pediatrics* 54:189–214.

Glass, R. I., J. J. Urrutia, S. Sibony, H. Smith, B. Garcia, and L. Rizzo. 1977. Earthquake injuries related to housing in a Guatemalan village. *Science* 197:638–43.

Gonzales, J. M. 2008. Kids in Katrina trailers may face lifelong ailments. *Denver Post,* May 28.

Green, B. L., M. Korol, M. C. Grace, M. G. Vary, A. C. Leonard, G. C. Gleser, and S. Smitson-Cohen. 1991. Children and disaster: Age, gender, and parental effects on PTSD symptoms. *Journal of the American Academy of Child and Adolescent Psychiatry* 30 (6): 945–51.

He, W., M. Sengupta, V. A. Velkoff, and K. A. DeBarros. 2005. *65+ in the United States: 2005.* U.S. Census Bureau, Current Population Reports. Washington, DC: U.S. Government Printing Office.

Heath, S. E., S. K. Voeks, and L. T. Glickman. 2000. A study of pet rescue in two disasters. *International Journal of Mass Emergencies and Disasters* 18 (3): 361–81.

HelpAge International. 2005. The impact of the Indian Ocean Tsunami on older people: Issues and recommendations. London: HelpAge International.

Hewitt, K. 2007. Preventable disasters: Addressing social vulnerability, institutional risk, and civil ethics. *Geographischs Rundschau International Edition* 3 (1): 43–52.

Houts, P. S., M. K. Lindell, T. W. Hu, P. D. Cleary, G. Tokuhata, and C. B. Flynn. 1984. The protective action decision model applied to evacuation during the Three Mile Island crisis. *International Journal of Mass Emergencies and Disasters* 2 (1): 27–39.

Huerta, F., and R. Horton. 1978. Coping behavior of elderly flood victims. *The Gerontologist* 18 (6): 541–46.

Hull, A., and D. Struck. 2005. At nursing home, Katrina dealt only the first blow: Nuns labored for days in fatal heat to get help for patients. *Washington Post,* September 23.

Hutchins, G. L., and F. H. Norris. 1989. Life change in the disaster recovery period. *Environment and Behavior* 21 (1): 33–56.

Hutton, J. R. 1976. The differential distribution of death in disaster: A test of theoretical propositions. *Mass Emergencies* 1:261–66.

Ikeda, K. 1995. Gender differences in human loss and vulnerability to natural disasters: A case study from Bangladesh. *Indian Journal of Gender Studies* 2 (2): 171–93.

International Federation of Red Cross and Red Crescent Societies. 2007. *World disasters report 2007: Focus on discrimination.* Bloomfield, CT: Kumarian Press.

International Medical Corps. 2006. *Displaced in America: Health status among internally displaced persons in Louisiana and Mississippi travel trailer parks.* Santa Monica, CA: International Medical Corps.

Jacobs, A. 2008. Parents grief turns to rage at Chinese officials. *New York Times,* May 28.

Jeney-Gammon, P., T. K. Daugherty, A. J. Finch Jr., R. W. Belter, and K. Y. Foster. 1993. Children's coping styles and report of depressive symptoms following a natural disaster. *The Journal of Genetic Psychology* 154 (2): 259–67.

Johnson, J. H. 1985. Role conflict in a radiological emergency: The case of public school teachers. *Journal of Environmental Systems* 15 (1): 77–91.

Johnston, C., and I. Redlener. 2006. Critical concepts for children in disasters identified by hands-on professionals: Summary of issues demanding solutions before the next one. *Pediatrics* 117 (5): 458–60.

Junn, E. N., and D. W. Guerin. 1996. Factors related to earthquake preparedness among child care professionals: Theory and policy implications. *International Journal of Mass Emergencies and Disasters* 14 (3): 343–59.

Keenan, H. T., S. W. Marshall, M. A. Nocera, and D. K. Runyan. 2004. Increased incidence of inflicted traumatic brain injury in children after a natural disaster. *American Journal of Preventive Medicine* 26 (3): 189–93.

Kelly, M. 1993. Infant feeding in emergencies. *Disasters* 17 (2): 110–21.

Ketteridge, A., and M. Fordham. 1998. Flood evacuation in two communities in Scotland: Lessons from European research. *International Journal of Mass Emergencies and Disasters* 16 (2): 119–43.

Kilijanek, T. S., and T. E. Drabek. 1979. Assessing long-term impacts of a natural disaster: A focus on the elderly. *The Gerontologist* 19 (6): 555–66.

Kirschke, J., and W. van Vliet. 2005. 'How can they look so happy?' Reconstructing the place of children after Hurricane Katrina: Images and reflections. *Children, Youth and Environments* 15 (2): 378–91.

Klinenberg, E. 2002. *Heat wave: A social autopsy of disaster in Chicago.* Chicago: University of Chicago Press.

Kozol, J. 1991. *Savage inequalities: Children in America's schools.* New York: Crown Publishers.

———. 2005. *The shame of the nation: The restoration of apartheid schooling in America.* New York: Crown Publishers.

Krause, N. 1987. Exploring the impact of a natural disaster on the health and psychological well-being of older adults. *Journal of Human Stress* 13 (12): 61–69.

La Greca, A. M., W. K. Silverman, E. M. Vernberg, and M. C. Roberts. 2002. Introduction. In *Helping children cope with disasters and terrorism,* eds. A. M. La Greca, W. K. Silverman, E. M. Vernberg, and M. C. Roberts, 3–8. Washington, DC: American Psychological Association.

La Greca, A. M., W. K. Silverman, and S. B. Wasserstein. 1998. Children's predisaster functioning as a predictor of post-traumatic stress following Hurricane Andrew. *Journal of Consulting and Clinical Psychology* 66 (6): 883–92.

Laditka, S. B., J. N. Laditka, S. Xirasagar, C. B. Cornman, C. B. Davis, and J. V. E. Richter. 2007. Protecting nursing home residents during emergencies and disasters: An exploratory study from South Carolina. *Prehospital and Disaster Medicine* 22 (1): 42–48.

Lafond, R. 1987. Emergency planning for the elderly. *Emergency Preparedness Digest* 14 (3): 15–21.

Larsen, J. 2006. *Setting the record straight: More than 52,000 Europeans died from heat in summer 2003.* Washington, DC: Earth Policy Institute.

Lauten, A. W., and K. Lietz. 2008. A look at the standards gap: Comparing child protection responses in the aftermath of Hurricane Katrina and the Indian Ocean Tsunami. *Children, Youth and Environments* 18 (1): 158–201.

Lawson, E. J., and C. Thomas. 2007. Wading in the waters: Spirituality and older Black Katrina survivors. *Journal of Health Care for the Poor and Underserved* 18:341–54.

Lengua, L. J., A. C. Long, K. I. Smith, and A. N. Meltzoff. 2005. Pre-attack symptomatology and temperament as predictors of children's responses to the September 11 terrorist attacks. *Journal of Child Psychology and Psychiatry* 46:631–45.

Lindell, M. K., J. Lu, and C. S. Prater. 2005. Household decision making and evacuation in response to Hurricane Lili. *Natural Hazards Review* 6 (4): 171–79.

Lonigan, C. J., M. P. Shannon, C. M. Taylor, A. J. Finch, Jr., and F. R. Sallee. 1994. Children exposed to disaster: II. Risk factors for the development of post-traumatic symptomatology. *Journal of the American Academy of Child and Adolescent Psychiatry* 33 (1): 94–105.

Looman, W. S. 2006. A developmental approach to understanding drawings and narratives from children displaced by Hurricane Katrina. *Journal of Pediatric Health Care* 20 (3): 158–66.

Maida, C. A., N. S. Gordon, and G. Strauss. 1993. Child and parent reactions to the Los Angeles area Whittier Narrows earthquake. *Journal of Social Behavior and Personality* 8:421–36.

Mandalakas, A., K. Torjesen, and K. Olness. 1999. How to help the children in complex humanitarian emergencies: A practical manual. http://www.ipa-world.org/programs/Children_in_Disasters.pdf (accessed May 30, 2008).

Mangum, W. P., J. I. Kosberg, and P. McDonald. 1989. Hurricane Elena and Pinellas County, Florida: Some lessons learned from the largest evacuation of nursing home patients in history. *The Gerontologist* 29 (3): 388–92.

Markenson, D., and I. Redlener. 2004. Pediatric disaster terrorism preparedness national guidelines and recommendations: Findings of an evidence-based consensus process. *Biosecurity and Bioterrorism* 2 (4): 301–14.

Mayhorn, C. B. 2005. Cognitive aging and the processing of hazard information and disaster warnings. *Natural Hazards Review* 6 (4): 165–70.

McFarlane, A. C. 1987. Family functioning and overprotection following a natural disaster: The longitudinal effects of post-traumatic morbidity. *Australian and New Zealand Journal of Psychiatry* 21:210–18.

McGuire, L. C., E. S. Ford, and C. A. Okoro. 2007. Natural disasters and older U.S. adults with disabilities: Implications for evacuation. *Disasters* 31 (1): 49–56.

Medina-Ramón, M., A. Zanobetti, D. P. Cavanagh, and J. Schwartz. 2006. Extreme temperatures and mortality: Assessing effect modification by personal characteristics and specific cause of death in a multi-city case-only analysis. *Environmental Health Perspectives* 114 (9): 1331–36.

Melick, M. E., and J. N. Logue. 1985. The effect of disaster on the health and well-being of older women. *International Journal of Aging and Human Development* 21 (1): 27–37.

Mileti, D. S. 1999. *Disasters by design: A reassessment of natural hazards in the United States*. Washington, DC: Joseph Henry Press.

Mileti, D. S., and J. D. Darlington. 1997. The role of searching in shaping reactions to earthquake risk information. *Social Problems* 44:89–103.

Mileti, D. S., and C. Fitzpatrick. 1992. Causal sequence of risk communication in the Parkfield earthquake prediction experiment. *Risk Analysis* 12 (3): 393–400.

Mileti, D. S., and P. W. O'Brien. 1992. Warnings during disaster: Normalizing communicated risk. *Social Problems* 39:40–57.

Miller, J. A., J. G. Turner, and E. Kimball. 1981. Big Thompson flood victims: One year later. *Family Relations* 30 (1): 111–16.

Mitchell, T., K. Haynes, N. Hall, W. Choong, and K. Oven. 2008. The role of children and youth in communicating disaster risk. *Children, Youth and Environments* 18 (1): 254–79.

Moody, H. R. 2006. The ethics of evacuation. *The Public Policy and Aging Report* 16 (2): 14–15.

Morrow, B. H. 1997. Stretching the bonds: The families of Andrew. In *Hurricane Andrew, ethnicity, gender, and the sociology of disaster,* eds. W. G. Peacock, H. Gladwin, and B. H. Morrow, 141–70. London: Routledge.

Morrow-Jones, H. A., and C. R. Morrow-Jones. 1991. Mobility due to natural disaster: Theoretical considerations and preliminary analysis. *Disasters* 15:126–32.

National Center for Missing and Exploited Children. 2006. National Center for Missing and Exploited Children reunites last missing child separated by Hurricanes Katrina and Rita. Press release. Alexandria, VA: National Center for Missing and Exploited Children.

Newman, K. S., and V. T. Chen. 2007. *The missing class: Portraits of the near poor in America.* Boston: Beacon Press.

Ngo, E. B. 2001. When disasters and age collide: Reviewing vulnerability of the elderly. *Natural Hazards Review* 2 (2): 80–89.

Norris, F. H., M. J. Friedman, P. J. Watson, C. M. Byrne, E. Diaz, and K. Kaniasty. 2002. 60,000 disaster victims speak: Part I. An empirical review of the empirical literature, 1981–2001. *Psychiatry* 65 (3): 207–39.

Norris, F. H., and G. L. Hutchins. 1989. Life change in the disaster recovery period. *Environment and Behavior* 21 (1): 33–56.

Norris, F. H., and S. A. Murrell. 1988. Prior experience as a moderator of disaster impact on anxiety symptoms in older adults. *American Journal of Community Psychology* 16:665–83.

O'Brien, N. 2003. *Emergency preparedness for older people.* New York: International Longevity Center-USA.

Ollenburger, J. C., and G. A. Tobin. 1999. Women, aging, and post-disaster stress: Risk factors. *International Journal of Mass Emergencies and Disasters* 17 (1): 65–78.

Ollendick, D. G., and M. Hoffman. 1982. Assessment of psychological reactions in disaster victims. *Journal of Community Psychology* 10:157–67.

Oxfam International. 2005. Back to work: How people are recovering their livelihoods 12 months after the tsunami. Oxfam briefing paper. London: Oxfam International.

Parasuraman, S. 1995. The impact of the 1993 Latur-Osmanabad (Maharashtra) earthquake on lives, livelihoods, and property. *Disasters* 19 (2): 156–69.

Peek, L. 2008. Children and disasters: Understanding vulnerability, developing capacities, and promoting resilience. *Children, Youth and Environments* 18 (1): 1–29.

Peek, L., and A. Fothergill. 2006. Reconstructing childhood: An exploratory study of children in Hurricane Katrina. Quick response report #186. Boulder: Natural Hazards Center, University of Colorado.

———. 2008. Displacement, gender, and the challenges of parenting after Hurricane Katrina. *National Women's Studies Association Journal* 20 (3): 69–105.

Peek, L., and L. M. Stough. Forthcoming. Children with disabilities in disaster. Under review at *Child Development.*

Peek, L., J. Sutton, and J. Gump. 2008. Caring for children in the aftermath of disaster: The Church of the Brethren Children's Disaster Services program. *Children, Youth and Environments* 18 (1): 408–21.

Perry, R. W. 1979. Evacuation decision making in natural disasters. *Mass Emergencies* 4:25–38.

———. 1990. Evacuation warning compliance among elderly citizens. *Disaster Management* 3 (2): 94–96.

Perry, R. W., and M. K. Lindell. 1997. Aged citizens in the warning phase of disasters: Re-examining the evidence. *International Journal of Aging and Human Development* 44 (4): 257–67.

Pfefferbaum, B., S. J. Nixon, P. M. Tucker, R. D. Tivis, V. L. Moore, R. H. Gurwitch, R. S. Pynoos, and H. K. Geis. 1999. Post-traumatic stress responses in bereaved children after the Oklahoma City bombing. *Journal of the American Academy of Child and Adolescent Psychiatry* 38:1372–79.

Phifer, J. F. 1990. Psychological distress and somatic symptoms after natural disaster: Differential vulnerability among older adults. *Psychology and Aging* 5 (3): 412–20.

Phillips, B. D., and P. L. Hewett. 2005. Home alone: Disasters, mass emergencies, and children in self-care. *Journal of Emergency Management* 3 (2): 31–35.

Phillips, B. D., and B. H. Morrow. 2007. Social science research needs: Focus on vulnerable populations, forecasting, and warnings. *Natural Hazards Review* 8 (3): 61–68.

Picou, J. S., and B. K. Marshall. 2007. Social impacts of Hurricane Katrina on displaced K–12 students and educational institutions in coastal Alabama counties: Some preliminary observations. *Sociological Spectrum* 27:767–80.

Poulshock, S. W., and E. S. Cohen. 1975. The elderly in the aftermath of a disaster. *The Gerontologist* 15 (4): 357–61.

Prinstein, M. J., A. M. La Greca, E. M. Vernberg, and W. K. Silverman. 1996. Children's coping assistance: How parents, teachers, and friends help children cope after a natural disaster. *Journal of Clinical Child Psychology* 25 (4): 463–75.

Ramirez. M., M. Kano, L. B. Bourque, and K. I. Shoaf. 2005. Child and household factors associated with fatal and non-fatal pediatric injury during the 1999 Kocaeli earthquake. *International Journal of Mass Emergencies and Disasters* 23 (2): 129–47.

Rath, B., J. Donato, A. Duggan, K. Perrin, D. R. Bronfin, R. Ratard, R. VanDyke, and M. Magnus. 2007. Adverse health outcomes after Hurricane Katrina among children and adolescents with chronic conditions. *Journal of Health Care for the Poor and Underserved* 18 (2): 405–17.

Raynor, C. M. 2002. The role of play in the recovery process. In *Children and disasters: A practical guide to healing and recovery,* eds. W. N. Zubenko and J. Capozzoli, 124–34. New York: Oxford University Press.

Reijneveld, S. A., M. R. Crone, A. A. Schuller, F. C. Verhulst, and S. P. Verloove-Vanhorick. 2005. The changing impact of a severe disaster on the mental health and substance misuse of adolescents: Follow-up of a controlled study. *Psychological Medicine* 35:367–76.

Rivers, J. P. W. 1982. Women and children last: An essay on sex discrimination in disasters. *Disasters* 6 (4): 256–67.

Sanders, S., S. L. Bowie, and Y. D. Bowie. 2003. Lessons learned on forced relocation of older adults: The impact of Hurricane Andrew on health, mental health, and social support of public housing residents. *Journal of Gerontological Social Work* 40 (4): 23–35.

Sapir, D. G. 1993. Natural and man-made disasters: The vulnerability of women-headed households and children without families. *World Health Statistics Quarterly* 46:227–33.

Sapir, D. G., and M. F. Lechat. 1986. Reducing the impact of natural disasters: Why aren't we better prepared? *Health Policy and Planning* 1 (2): 118–26.

Saylor, C. F., B. L. Cowart, J. A. Lipovsky, C. Jackson, and A. J. Finch, Jr. 2003. Media exposure to September 11: Elementary school students' experiences and post-traumatic symptoms. *American Behavioral Scientist* 46 (12): 1622–42.

Shannon, M. P., C. J. Lonigan, A. J. Finch Jr., and C. M. Taylor. 1994. Children exposed to disaster: I. Epidemiology of post-traumatic symptoms and symptom profiles. *Journal of the American Academy of Child and Adolescent Psychiatry* 33 (1): 80–93.

Sharkey, P. 2007. Survival and death in New Orleans: An empirical look at the human impact of Katrina. *Journal of Black Studies* 37 (4): 482–501.

SHELDUS (Spatial Hazards Events and Losses Database for the United States). 2005. *2005 U.S. hazards losses.* http://www.cas.sc.edu/geog/hrl/SHELDUS.html (accessed May 30, 2008).

Shen, Y., and C. A. Sink. 2002. Helping elementary-age children cope with disasters. *Professional School Counseling* 5 (5): 322–31.

Smith, F. 2008. The smallest victims of California wildfires are often forgotten. Crisis and Emergency Management Newsletter 14(1). http://www.seas.gwu.edu/~emse232/february2008_7.html (accessed February 18, 2008).

Spiegel, A. 2006. Katrina's impact on elderly still resonates. *National Public Radio,* March 1.

Stephens, K. U., D. Grew, K. Chin, P. Kadetz, P. G. Greenough, F. M. Burkle, Jr., S. L. Robinson, and E. R. Franklin. 2007. Excess mortality in the aftermath of Hurricane Katrina: A preliminary report. *Disaster Medicine and Public Health Preparedness* 1 (1): 15–20.

Stuber, J., S. Galea, B. Pfefferbaum, S. Vandivere, K. Moore, and G. Fairbrother. 2005. Behavior problems in New York City's children after the September 11, 2001 terrorist attacks. *American Journal of Orthopsychiatry* 75 (2): 190–200.

Swenson, C. C., C. F. Saylor, P. Powell, S. J. Stokes, K. Y. Foster, and R. W. Belter. 1996. Impact of a natural disaster on preschool children: Adjustment 14 months after a hurricane. *American Journal of Orthopsychiatry* 66 (1): 122–30.

Takeda, J., K. Tamura, and S. Tatsuki. 2003. Life recovery of 1995 Kobe earthquake survivors in Nishinomiya city: A total-quality-management-based assessment of disadvantaged populations. *Natural Hazards* 29:565–83.

Thompson, M. P., F. H. Norris, and B. Hanacek. 1993. Age differences in the psychological consequences of Hurricane Hugo. *Psychology and Aging* 8:606–16.

Tierney, K. J., M. K. Lindell, and R. W. Perry. 2001. *Facing the unexpected: Disaster preparedness and response in the United States.* Washington, DC: Joseph Henry Press.

Tracy, M., and S. Galea. 2006. Post-traumatic stress disorder and depression among older adults after a disaster: The role of ongoing trauma and stressors. *Public Policy and Aging Report* 16 (2): 16–19.

Turner, R. 1976. Earthquake prediction and public policy. *Mass Emergencies* 1 (3): 179–202.

Tyler, K. A. 2006. The impact of support received and support provision on changes in perceived social support among older adults. *International Journal of Aging and Human Development* 62 (1): 21–38.

Tyler, K. A., and D. Hoyt. 2000. The effects of an acute stressor on depressive symptoms among older adults: The moderating effects of social support and age. *Research on Aging* 22:143–64.

Udwin, O. 1993. Annotation: Children's reactions to traumatic events. *Journal of Child Psychology and Psychiatry* 34 (2): 115–27.

Unger, J. B., T. R. Simon, and T. L. Newman. 1998. Early adolescent street youths: An overlooked population with unique problems and service needs. *Journal of Early Adolescence* 18 (4): 324–48.

U.S. Census Bureau. 2006. *2006 American Community Survey data.* http://www.census.gov/ (accessed February 1, 2008).

U.S. Department of Health and Human Services, Administration on Aging. 2006. *A profile of older Americans: 2006.* Washington, DC.

U.S. Department of Health and Human Services. 2008. *The 2008 Health and Human Services poverty guidelines.* http://aspe.hhs.gov/poverty/08poverty.shtml (accessed February 1, 2008).

U.S. Government Accountability Office. 2006. *Lessons learned for protecting and educating children after the Gulf Coast hurricanes.* www.gao.gov/new.items/d06680r.pdf (accessed February 1, 2008).

Vernberg, E. M., A. M. LaGreca, W. K. Silverman, and M. J. Prinstein. 1996. Prediction of post-traumatic stress symptoms in children after Hurricane Andrew. *Journal of Abnormal Psychology* 105 (2): 237–48.

Vogel, J. M., and E. M. Vernberg. 1993. Part 1: Children's psychological responses to disasters. *Journal of Clinical Child Psychology* 22 (2): 464–84.

Vogt, B. M. 1991. Issues in nursing home evacuations. *International Journal of Mass Emergencies and Disasters* 9 (2): 247–65.

Wachtendorf, T., B. Brown, and M. C. Nickle. 2008. Big Bird, disaster masters, and high school students taking charge: The social capacities of children in disaster education. *Children, Youth and Environments* 18 (1): 456–69.

Warheit, G. J., R. S. Zimmerman, E. L. Khoury, W. A. Vega, and A. G. Gil. 1996. Disaster related stresses, depressive signs and symptoms, and suicidal ideation among a multi-racial/ethnic sample of adolescents: A longitudinal analysis. *Journal of Child Psychology and Psychiatry* 37 (4): 435–44.

Wasserstein, S. B., and A. M. LaGreca. 1998. Hurricane Andrew: Parent conflict as a moderator of children's adjustment. *Hispanic Journal of Behavioral Sciences* 20 (2): 212–24.

Webster, C. 1994. Saving children during the Depression: Britain's silent emergency, 1919–1939. *Disasters* 18 (3): 213–20.

Weissbecker, I., S. E. Sephton, M. B. Martin, and D. M. Simpson. 2008. Psychological and physiological correlates of stress in children exposed to disaster: Review of current research and recommendations for intervention. *Children, Youth and Environments* 18 (1): 30–70.

Wilson, N. 2006. Hurricane Katrina: Unequal opportunity disaster. *Public Policy and Aging Report* 16 (2): 8–13.

Wilson, S. L., and M. A. Kershaw. 2008. Caring for young children after a hurricane: Childcare workers reflect on support and training needs. *Children, Youth and Environments* 18 (1): 237–53.

Wisner, B. 2006. *Let our children teach us! A review of the role of education and knowledge in disaster risk reduction.* Bangalore, India: Books for Change.

World Health Organization (WHO). 2005. Disability, including prevention, management, and rehabilitation. Geneva, Switzerland: World Health Organization.

Young, H., and S. Jaspars. 1995. Nutrition, disease, and death in times of famine. *Disasters* 19 (2): 94–109.

Zahran, S., L. Peek, and S. D. Brody. 2008. Youth mortality by forces of nature. *Children, Youth and Environments* 18 (1): 371–88.

RESOURCES—CHILDREN AND DISASTERS

BOOKS

Gordon, N. *Children and disasters.* New York: Routledge, 1999.

LaGreca, A. M., W. K. Silverman, E. M. Vernberg, and M. C. Roberts, eds. *Helping children cope with disasters and terrorism.* Washington, DC: American Psychological Association, 2002.

Ronan, K. R., and D. Johnston. *Promoting community resilience in disasters: The role for schools, youth, and families.* New York: Springer, 2005.

Rosenfeld, L. B., J. S. Caye, O. Ayalon, and M. Lahad. *When their world falls apart: helping families and children manage the effects of disasters.* Washington, DC: NASW Press, 2005.

Zubenko, W. N., and J. A. Capozzoli, eds. *Children and disasters: A practical guide to healing and recovery.* New York: Oxford University Press, 2002.

KEY WEB SITES

American Red Cross Masters of Disaster Program
http://www.redcross.org/disaster/masters/

Children, Youth, and Environments. Special Issue on Children and Disasters. 18 (1), 2008.
http://www.colorado.edu/journals/cye/18_1/index.htm

Church of the Brethren Children's Disaster Services
http://www.brethren.org/genbd/BDM/CDSindex.html

FEMA for Kids
http://www.fema.gov/kids/index.htm

Ready Kids
http://www.ready.gov/kids/home.html

Save the Children
http://www.savethechildren.org/usemergency

RESOURCES—ELDERLY AND DISASTERS

BOOKS

Bolin, R. *Long-term family recovery from disaster.* Boulder: Institute of Behavioral Science, University of Colorado, 1982.
International Federation of Red Cross and Red Crescent Societies. *World disasters report 2007: Focus on discrimination.* Bloomfield, CT: Kumarian Press, 2007.
Klinenberg, E. *Heat wave: A social autopsy of disaster in Chicago.* Chicago: University of Chicago Press, 2002.

KEY WEB SITES

Administration on Aging
http://www.aoa.gov/

American Association of Retired People
http://aarpforemost.com/safety/preparefordisaster/disaster.htm

American Red Cross
http://www.redcross.org/services/disaster/0,1082,0_603_,00.html

Gray Panthers
http://www.graypanthers.org/

National Organization on Disability
http://www.nod.org/

8 Disability

Alan Clive, Elizabeth A. Davis,
Rebecca Hansen, and Jennifer Mincin

CONTENTS

8.1 CHAPTER PURPOSE

This chapter serves as an overview of disaster-related disability issues across the age spectrum from pediatric to geriatric. The chapter addresses existing mandates and challenges for integrating disability issues and populations into emergency planning. Strategies and solutions are proposed for use within an empowerment model that ensures full participation of the disability community. Resources are listed at the end of the chapter to further guide emergency managers and other professionals in the field.

8.2 OBJECTIVES

As a result of completing this chapter, the reader will be able to:

1. Identify specific factors that can contribute to increased vulnerability of people with disabilities as a result of disaster.
2. Recognize theoretical concepts and terms about disability in the context of emergency management.
3. Understand critical disability issues in the disaster life cycle including communications, sheltering, evacuation, and related planning concepts.
4. Utilize strategies and resources to increase resiliency within the disability community.

8.3 INTRODUCTION

Disability issues impact every aspect of emergency management and therefore must be incorporated and integrated into all phases, plans, response systems, and long-term recovery efforts in emergency management. Several factors may increase vulnerability of people with disabilities during disasters. At the head of any list are pre-existing disabling conditions, including impaired physical mobility, diminished sensory awareness and general health, and social and economic constraints (Tierney, Petak, and Hahn 1988). Existing attitudinal barriers and misconceptions within the emergency management community also contribute to inadequate planning for people with disabilities.

Often the disability population is either not thought of during disasters and emergencies, or organizations and agencies are not sure how to best work with and assist people with disabilities. Even with legislation and mandates, the concerns and unique needs of the disability population are still not fully and meaningfully integrated into all phases of emergency management. The consequences are dire. People with disabilities, as well as older people, are disproportionately affected by disasters with higher rates of loss of life and a longer period of time rebuilding their lives (Tokesky and Weston 2006).

It is important that emergency managers, health professionals, and first responders treat people with disabilities as people first, not as medical or disabling conditions with bodies attached. Such thinking marginalizes people with disabilities and may lead to inaccurate assumptions about abilities or perceived limitations.

8.4 DEMOGRAPHIC OVERVIEW IN THE UNITED STATES

Disabilities are prevalent across the United States. Consider these statistics:

- According to the U.S. Census's 2006 American Community Survey (ACS), approximately 15.2% of non-institutionalized Americans over the age of five reported having a disability, or over 41 million (U.S. Census Bureau ACS 2006). However, most disability organizations place the number higher, at closer to 54 million, because the census does not take into account unreported disabilities, those living in institutions, among other factors (National Organization on Disability n.d.).

- Disability rates increase with age: 41% of those over the age of 65 reported one or more disabilities. Nearly 14 million people over 60 have one or more disabilities (U.S. Census Bureau 2000).
- Just over 5.2 million American children between the ages of 5 and 20 have a disability (U.S. Census Bureau 2000).
- Veterans comprise a significant portion of people with disabilities; approximately 2.9 million veterans have one or more disability, a 30% increase since 2001 (Associated Press 2008). As of January 2008, over 30,000 soldiers have been wounded in the Iraq War with injuries including loss of limbs and post-traumatic stress syndrome (The Brookings Institution 2008; U.S. Equal Employment Opportunity Commission 2008).

Despite these numbers, thousands of Americans with disabilities have prospered and thrived in a variety of occupations. Too often, however, disability places an individual on a cruel downward slide into lowered socioeconomic status, which constrains the ability to respond effectively to disaster. To cite only one example, emergency management publications wisely emphasize the need to organize and keep an emergency supply kit, which should be periodically updated as needs change and various items age and expire. But how many persons living in poverty can afford to set aside extra food and medication when they are engaged in a daily struggle to put bread on the table (Davis 2006)? The following demographic data starkly outline the relationship between disability and lower socioeconomic status:

- People with disabilities are more likely to live at or below the poverty level and are nearly twice as likely as people without disabilities to have an annual household income of $15,000 or less (Disability Funders Network n.d.).
- Over 65% of working-age American adults with disabilities are unemployed. Of these working adults, nearly one third earn an income below the poverty level (Disability Funders Network n.d.).
- Those who are disabled, and for whom competitive work is an impossibility, rely on the benefits of Social Security Disability Insurance and Supplemental Security Income. Frequently, federal payments by themselves fall below the equivalent of minimum-wage employment, making the descent into poverty inevitable (Atkins and Guisti 2003).
- Assistive technology is essential for more than a third of disabled Americans to permit self-care at home. This technology can range from a walker to a sophisticated computer controlling many household functions. While social service agencies can provide some of this equipment at low or no cost, they usually cannot pay for its continued maintenance and repair. Obviously, a person's income affects the ability to purchase and keep such items in a functioning state (Disability Funders Network n.d.).

8.5   DEFINITIONS AND CONCEPTS

Although the legal system has clearly defined "disability" (see Box 8.1) the use and meaning of terms related to disability remain contentious within the emergency management profession. In addition to or instead of using the term "disability," many jurisdictions are using the term "special needs populations." This term usually encompasses the disability community, but also includes other vulnerable groups, such as the elderly, children, immigrants, disabled veterans, etc. The use and distinctions among these terms are important to consider. For instance, confusion over the definition of special needs during the 2007 California wildfires reportedly hindered response and recovery efforts because certain jurisdictions had different definitions of "special needs" (California

---

BOX 8.1   THE ADA DEFINITION OF DISABILITY

The Americans with Disabilities Act of 1990 (ADA) codified a legal definition for the term "disability," and created a protected class of persons with disabilities, who can use the statute as legal authority to enforce civil rights. According to the ADA, an individual is defined as someone with a disability if he or she:

1. Has a physical or mental impairment that substantially limits a major life activity,
2. Has a record of such an impairment
3. Is regarded as having such an impairment

Types of disabilities as defined under the ADA (including the age spectrum from pediatric to geriatric) are:

1. Physical (e.g., people with severe arthritis or spinal cord injuries, people who use wheelchairs, people with multiple sclerosis)
2. Sensory (e.g., people who are blind, deaf, hard of hearing)
3. Cognitive (e.g., people with mental illness, learning disabilities, mental retardation, developmental disabilities)

Office of Emergency Services 2008). While each jurisdiction will need to assess its community and identify special needs populations, it is important to clearly articulate the identified population. In addition, emergency managers need to ensure that people with disabilities, who are a protected class, receive reasonable accommodations.

8.5.1 DISABILITY AS A PROTECTED CLASS

The Americans with Disabilities Act of 1990 (ADA) defines disability, distinguishes disability as a protected class, and provides broad nondiscrimination protections and rights to people with disabilities. Though the ADA does not specifically discuss the issue of compliance in emergency planning and response, it mandates compliance with public and private sector facilities and programs (Davis and Sutherland 2005). In support of this interpretation of the ADA, the U.S. Department of Justice (DOJ) issued a guide for state and local governments (see *DOJ Best Practices Toolkit* in Resources) to assist them in making their emergency preparedness and response programs accessible to people with disabilities (Jones 2006).

The DOJ guidance declares that, essentially, people with disabilities must have access to and cannot be excluded from, emergency plans and programs. This interpretation is increasingly recognized in the emergency management community:

> While not specifically articulated within many of the authorities mentioned [in the ADA], in a post–September 11 United States, the interpretations are now shaped by a "big picture" approach and extend the rights of people with disabilities to share in access to services and programs, to include emergency preparedness planning and response (Davis and Sutherland 2005).

Access must be both physical (e.g., architectural barriers) as well as programmatic. For example, evacuation plans must include a means of safely assisting people with mobility impairments and other disabilities from home to shelter. Shelters must be accessible. People with disabilities should expect courteous treatment from a well-trained and skilled emergency response staff. Preparedness information distributed before or recovery information available after the disaster must be in alternate formats accessible to persons requiring such accommodations.

BOX 8.2 NRF DEFINES SPECIAL NEEDS

The National Response Framework defines the special needs concept as "[a] population whose members may have additional needs before, during, and after an incident in one or more of the following functional areas: maintaining independence, communication, transportation, supervision, and medical care. Individuals in need of additional response assistance may include those who have disabilities; who live in institutionalized settings; who are elderly; who are children; who are from diverse cultures, who have limited English proficiency, or who are non-English speaking; or who are transportation disadvantaged" (U.S. Department of Homeland Security n.d.).

The above refers to government functions and accessibility but the same is true for private business as well. In a case of first impression, the Circuit Court in Montgomery County, Maryland, endorsed the notion that the ADA Title III should be interpreted to mean that places of common access such as a department store and a mall need to take into account people with disabilities in their facility emergency plans (*Savage v. City Place Ltd. Partnership*, 2004 WL 3045404 [Md. Cir. Ct. 2004]).

8.5.2 SPECIAL NEEDS POPULATIONS TERMINOLOGY

Jurisdictions should identify populations that require specialized planning. Over the years, "special needs" planning has included people with disabilities and seniors and the frail elderly. In addition, special needs can include other important populations such as immigrants (including both documented and non-documented people), people who are non-English speaking or who have attained limited English proficiency, pregnant women, children (infants to late adolescence), homeless populations, individuals and families living in poverty, and those who cannot drive or do not own a car (transportation disadvantaged).

As noted above, the term "special needs populations" is widely used within the emergency management profession. However, whereas "disability," is defined in federal law and regulation, "special needs" has no such legal definition. Since "special needs" continues to be used as a term by emergency practitioners, a debate has continued for some years among professionals in the emergency management, health care, and disability advocacy communities as to its validity.

"Special needs populations" can range from a single group to multiple, even overlapping populations. Some disability advocates oppose the use of broad definitions, because the additional "special needs" groups that are included often far outnumber people with disabilities. Advocates also contend that this type of terminology overshadows the specific needs of people with disabilities, placing additional demands on already strained resources (Kailes 2005).

As a result of disability groups and advocates working with the emergency management field, the trend seems to be moving toward utilizing a concept of special needs that establishes a flexible framework, addressing a broad set of common function-based needs irrespective of specific diagnosis, status, or labels of an individual. This concept is demonstrated in the recently published special needs definition in FEMA's National Response Framework (NRF), which can be viewed in Box 8.2 (U.S. Department of Homeland Security n.d.).

8.5.3 PERSONS WITH MEDICAL CONDITIONS

Millions of people throughout the United States have one or more existing medical conditions, some more severe than others. Certain medical conditions are defined as disabilities, so persons with such disabilities are protected by the ADA. For more on health issues and related planning in emergencies, see Chapter 9.

8.6   CONCEPTUAL MODELS AND APPROACHES

Generally speaking, there are three prevalent "models" or frameworks for conceptualizing disability: the medical model, the socio-political model and the functional model. Each will be briefly discussed in this section.

8.6.1   THE MEDICAL MODEL

People with disabilities are not a homogeneous group. They encompass a wide range of abilities and types. Some people are born with disabilities, while others acquire them through illness, accidents, or because of inadequate access to social and health care services. Often, society makes assumptions about people with disabilities, assessing their level of independence or dependence on little or no evidence. For example, people with disabilities are often labeled "handicapped," based on visible characteristics, although these attributes may not, in fact, be disabling (Tierney, Petak, and Hahn 1988).

For centuries, people with disabilities suffered under the "medical model" of disability, which equated an individual's condition with sickness, no matter the root cause. As a result, the problems of people with disabilities are medically managed and handled by the health care system. Within the medical framework, however, we actually learn very little about the genuine capabilities or limitations of the individual. The information gleaned from this perspective does not allow a truly accurate determination of an individual's disaster-related "special need," nor indicate which emergency management component should provide a response.

8.6.2   THE SOCIO-POLITICAL MODEL

The socio-political model points out that society has created barriers and perceives disability focusing more on the abilities limitations and that ameliorative action is required (Tierney, Petak, and Hahn 1988). According to Hubbard,

> The sociopolitical model views disability as a policy and civil rights issue, not as a health impairment or a diagnosis-related funding issue. Individuals with disabilities are considered an oppressed minority faced with architectural, sensory, attitudinal, cognitive, and economic barriers, who are treated as second-class citizens, facing daily prejudice and discrimination (2004).

The socio-political model is more of an empowerment model. Rather than "blaming the victim," the socio-political model states that it is society and its barriers that adversely affect people with disabilities, not the disability itself (Hubbard 2004). For example, if a workplace is not wheelchair accessible, a person in a wheelchair, who may be highly qualified, will not be able to physically access the building, hence that person can not work there. This type of barrier is created by socially structuring the workplace to include some and exclude others (Hubbard 2004). According to Tierny, "Technology, law, public policies, organizational practices, and the attitudes of other members have an impact on the extent to which physical impairments limit activity and constrain role performance" (Tierney, Petak, and Hahn 1988, 11).

8.6.3   THE FUNCTIONAL MODEL

The medical model was used through the late decades of the 20th century, when the functional model began to replace it. This new paradigm discards the notion of disability as illness, viewing the disability population as heterogeneous rather than uniform. Each person with a disability is expected to have a particular level of capacity and may, but not necessarily will, have disaster-related needs requiring different levels of response from the emergency management community. Within this framework, planners will work with service providers and individuals with disabilities to identify both their probable disaster-related needs and realistic strategies to meet those needs. This approach helps to identify appropriate resources and practical solutions that will support individuals at each stage of the emergency. The best plans will emerge from a mutually respectful relationship among emergency managers, advocates, and members of the disability communities.

The following are two examples of how the functional model approach is applied in practice in juxtaposition with the medical model, which would instead assume need based on condition or medical term.

Example A

Individuals living with multiple sclerosis (MS) may require some level of assistance during emergencies. MS is a chronic condition that will impact people differently depending of the type of MS they have, and so the level of independence, need for assistance, etc., can vary greatly. But heat is something that aggravates the disease, creating a critical problem for people standing unprotected from sunlight or humid weather in long lines to obtain information, food, or other assistance at a recovery center. Therefore, it is more useful for a planner to utilize the functional model to identify the likely needs of individuals with MS, rather than to focus only on the fact that an individual is living with MS. It is the need beyond an individual's ability that is important in this model rather than the condition and medical label.

Example B

The same approach can be used in regard to people who are deaf or hard of hearing. Their capabilities and needs are clustered on a curve, with those who are totally self-sufficient in disaster at one end, and people who have a variety of specific needs at the other end. Working with this community, you can identify the actual needs as they relate to emergency situations, and appropriate solutions to the range of needs. In the case of emergency communications, it will be necessary to identify different means to ensure that emergency notifications and warnings are received and acted upon by individuals who need assistance to receive and understand those warnings. With the help of individuals in the deaf and hard of hearing community, you can select the appropriate modalities.

8.7   DISABILITY STEREOTYPES AND STIGMAS

A lack of awareness about and understanding of the disability community pervades American society. This is true despite decades of campaigning on the part of federal agencies and advocacy organizations to foster a more positive image (Shapiro 1994). Trapped by societal stereotypes and stigmas, it is no surprise that people with disabilities have received little attention from emergency managers until recent years. Below are a few examples of stereotypes or barriers that remain prominent in everyday thought. Each notion or myth is contrasted with information that contradicts each belief and presents a more realistic picture of people with disabilities.

- *Myth*: The person's disability or illness is perceived as the individual's dominant characteristic or so-called "master identity," relegating the individual to a marginal role in society as an "invalid" or "handicapped" person. *Reality*: The key concept of the disability rights movement, which supports the functional model, is the contention that individual differences, such as race, ethnicity, gender, religion, and the like, far outweigh disabling conditions as the defining component of the personality (Shapiro 1994). The movement has attempted to reconstruct the image of the person, using language to move disability from first to last in popular thinking (for example, using "woman who is blind" rather than "blind woman"). The idea is to place the person first in the view of society, emphasizing that the disability is a part, but not the total identity, of the person (Leeds 1990).

- *Myth*: Disabilities are assumed to make people totally dependent on others, supporting the view that people with disabilities must be taken care of, rather than seen as fellow contributing members of the community. *Reality*: Since disabilities vary widely in intensity and degree of impairment, the type of assistance a person with a disability may need also varies. The level of aid could range from none or very limited assistance to the need for many social services to maintain the individual at home. For example, many people with a disability may need only a few critical items of technology or adapted equipment, or perhaps the use of a service animal, to live and work independently. Last, compensatory abilities are likely to be developed utilizing resources and other elements in the environment.
- *Myth*: People with disabilities have medical conditions and/or are sick. *Reality*: Having a disability does not mean a person is sick or has a medical condition (Access Center n.d.). People with disabilities may be sick or not sick just as someone without a disability may be sick or not sick (Access Center n.d.). This myth perpetuates negative stereotypes about people with disabilities. According to the Access Center, "Mistaking a disability for sickness not only fails to respond to a person's needs, it perpetuates a negative stereotype and an assumption that the person can and should be cured" (Access Center n.d.).
- *Myth*: Accommodating people with disabilities is cost-prohibitive. *Reality*: Often, making accommodations is not expensive and the more expensive accommodations, such as retrofitting a building, can be funded through government programs if necessary. More often than not, accommodations can be simple and inexpensive. For example, students with dyslexia may need a simple tape recorder to record lectures or extra time on an exam. A person who is blind may request a reading program for the computer at work. According to the Access Center, "Simple inexpensive devices are often the most critical in helping people with a disability live independently. Assistive devices can be as affordable as an eating utensil or Velcro strap" (n.d.).

Many other misconceptions about disability shape our thinking, unconsciously or not, including:

- People bring their disabling condition upon themselves and are responsible for it.
- People with disabilities are "damaged goods."
- People with disabilities offer little to society and are nothing but a burden.
- Older people are slow and generally unproductive.

These societal stereotypes can be found in emergency management practices and policies as well. This is especially true in terms of planning and response. For example, Davis and Mincin cite a case study in which there was a fire at a senior care facility that housed 300 individuals, including people with disabilities (2003). Lack of understanding the needs of people with disabilities and not having inclusive plans caused additional chaos and resulted in inappropriate sheltering of the seniors and people with disabilities (initially, they were temporarily housed in a school gym without adequate equipment or facilities). Davis and Mincin state:

> [S]ince the senior housing facility technically fell under local government jurisdiction, it was the responsibility of local government to have plans in place for alternate relocation facilities and transportation to those pre-designated sites. In fact, none of the agencies involved in the incident were actually aware of whose primary responsibility it was to relocate and transport the seniors. Additionally, there was a severe lack of on-scene staff with expertise in the area of special needs and a communication failure as a result of the absence of pre-established protocol delineating roles and responsibilities (2005, 11).

8.8   RELEVANCE TO THE PRACTICE OF EMERGENCY MANAGEMENT

Stereotypical thinking about persons with disabilities can result in emergency managers ignoring this group before, during, or after the disaster event. Emergency managers and relief organizations often are not sure how to work best with and assist people with disabilities. Even with legislation and mandates in place (see Box 8.3), the concerns and unique needs of the disability population are still not fully and meaningfully integrated into all phases of emergency management. The consequences can be dire: people with disabilities, as well as older people, are disproportionately affected by disasters with higher rates of loss of life and a longer period of time rebuilding their lives, as we will see next.

BOX 8.3   RECENT LEGISLATIVE CHANGES IMPACTING SPECIAL NEEDS POPULATIONS

The catastrophic events of September 11 and Hurricanes Katrina and Rita in 2005 resulted in new federal legislation, which theoretically should bring about greater integration of disability and special needs issues into emergency planning. Activities in 2008, such as drafting of new guidance and terminology, together with revision of the National Response Framework (NRF), are expected to create a purposeful strategic approach to disability and special needs throughout the disaster cycle. Laws are now in effect that direct the emergency management community to implement a specific agenda, but these mandates are still too recent to have obtained the desired effect. Federal emergency managers continue to debate various planning components. As discussed above, the very definition of "special needs populations" remains contested. As local planners begin to utilize national guidance, familiarizing themselves with the latest opinions on these issues, they are bound to make major contributions with local solutions and resources.

Two major pieces of new policy and legislation are:

2004 EXECUTIVE ORDER AND CREATION OF INTERAGENCY COORDINATING COUNCIL

On July 22, 2004, President George W. Bush signed Executive Order 13347 to strengthen emergency preparedness with respect to individuals with disabilities in the federal arena (U.S. Department of Homeland Security 2006a). This executive order directs the federal government to address the safety and security needs of people with disabilities in emergency situations, including natural and man-made disasters. To this end, the executive order created an Interagency Coordinating Council on Emergency Preparedness and Individuals with Disabilities (ICC), chaired by the DHS and comprised of several federal agencies as members.

POST-KATRINA EMERGENCY MANAGEMENT REFORM ACT OF 2007

In the aftermath of Hurricane Katrina, Congress made significant changes to FEMA's enabling legislation, the Stafford Act, including the incorporation of disability and special needs issues. The new law, entitled the *Post-Katrina Emergency Management Reform Act of 2007*, included provisions for the following:

- The inclusion of people with disabilities in every phase of emergency management at all levels of government
- Requirements for plans for the provision of post-disaster case-management services to victims and their families
- Requirements for accessible temporary and replacement housing
- Non-discrimination in services on the basis of disability
- Establishment of a National Disability Coordinator within DHS (currently located within FEMA)

FIGURE 8.1 Reminders and remnants from an overpass in New Orleans, Hurricane Katrina. *Source*: Photo by Pam Jenkins and Barbara Davidson, with permission.

The disproportionate impact of disasters on people with disabilities and the elderly is well documented in data from Hurricane Katrina as well as information from earlier disasters, such as Hurricane Andrew in 1992 and the multiple hurricanes that struck Florida in 2004. Statistics indicate that of the estimated 1800 persons who died in Hurricane Katrina and its aftermath, 71% were older than 60, and 47% exceeded the age of 75 (Cahalan and Renne 2007). The proportion of persons over the age of 60 who died in each of the four Florida Hurricanes of 2004 ranged from 40% to 60% (Weston and Tokesky 2006). The most devastating natural event to strike the United States in a century, Hurricane Katrina was the impetus for new legislation requiring the inclusion of special needs populations in all aspects of emergency management, including mitigation, planning, response, and recovery efforts (Figure 8.1).

8.8.1 Federal Communications Commission Regulations, Section 79.2

The Federal Communications Commission (FCC) first exercised its enforcement authority in regard to Section 79.2 in February 2005, when the commission sanctioned three television broadcasters for failure during the 2003 southern California wildfires to comply with the rule requiring visual presentation of emergency information (FCC 2005). While broadcasters can meet the terms of Section 79.2 by ensuring emergency information is available in closed captioning, they can also make the information accessible through open captioning, crawls, scrolls that appear on the screen, prepared signs, charts or handwritten information on a whiteboard) (Hearing Loss Web 2006). In addition to ensuring that mainstream sources, such as television, radio, Internet, newspapers, and emerging 2-1-1 information centers are accessible, jurisdictions should utilize nontraditional sources available to people with disabilities. These might include social service agencies, ethnic newspapers, a local closed-loop radio station, disability groups' own newsletters, senior living announcement boards, and fliers and newsletters from faith-based organizations.

8.8.2 Section 508 of the Rehabilitation Act

Section 508 of the Rehabilitation Act, as amended, requires that the federal government's electronic and information technology be accessible. The law covers all types of electronic and information-retrieval devices in the federal sector, and is not limited to assistive equipment used by people with disabilities. It applies to all federal agencies when they develop, procure, maintain, or use such technology. Federal agencies must ensure that this technology is accessible to employees and the public to the extent that access does not pose an "undue burden" (Access Board n.d.).

Media coverage of Hurricanes Katrina and Rita in 2005 included many images of people with disabilities and medical conditions who were stranded on bridges, in nursing homes, and on rooftops, with little hope of rescue. Although many of the elderly affected by Katrina were disabled or mobility-restricted, most had lived independently. In New Orleans, 15% of the population consisted of those over the age of 60; 74% of known victims were in this same age group.

The failure to assist people with psychiatric disabilities had particularly severe consequences. Specifically, some of these individuals had difficulty comprehending evacuation messages and other essential communications because their needs were ignored (National Council on Disability 2006). Mismanagement of the evacuation of people with psychiatric disabilities resulted in residents being misplaced and mistreated. Officials physically lost residents of group homes and psychiatric facilities, many of whom are still missing. Others have not, or cannot, return home because essential support systems have not been restored, or because the cost of living has increased too much. Many among this population never reached evacuation shelters because they were inappropriately and involuntarily institutionalized. Some of these people still have not been discharged from these institutions, despite favorable evaluations (National Council on Disability 2006).

8.9   VULNERABILITY ACROSS THE DISASTER LIFE CYCLE

While disasters and emergencies affect everyone, their impact on people with disabilities is compounded by lack of access to critical information or services at key moments in the life cycle of the event. That inability to obtain the information or service, in turn, will usually be a function of an individual's disability. Below, we will look at some of these access issues.

8.9.1   WARNINGS

An individual's ability to respond with or without assistance to a warning depends fundamentally on whether or not it is received and understood. Like many concepts we will discuss, this issue is identical for persons with and without disabilities. The difference, however, is that emergency planning must include the requirement for accessible alternatives to allow access to the warning or alert for those who cannot hear or comprehend it. Doing so at least provides the opportunity to act upon the information where and when feasible.

However, standard methods of communicating emergency information, whether through mainstream media, or through notification systems such as sirens, alarms, or reverse 9-1-1 networks, and whether operated by local jurisdictions, building owners, or another entity, fall far short of providing information in multiple accessible formats. Evidence shows that government entities still struggle to provide accessible information to people with disabilities. For example, in 2005 just over four out of ten emergency management officials (42%) reported having conducted public information campaigns specifically targeted at people with disabilities. Of these, only 16% said the outreach campaign was available in accessible formats (National Organization on Disability 2005). Only slowly are jurisdictions working to improve notification systems (for a leading example, see Box 8.4 on the Oklahoma WARN system).

The FCC establishes requirements for and enforces standards of broadcasting accessibility of emergency information. These powers are granted in Section 79.2 of the Telecommunications Act (FCC n.d.), which will be discussed shortly. The FCC created a process for consumers to raise complaints regarding noncompliance. Jurisdictions and broadcasters are legally obligated to ensure that emergency-related messaging is provided in accessible formats. Too often, however, accessibility standards and requirements are adhered to partially or not at all. Governments and broadcasters must be aware of and meet these standards, while consumers, advocates, and planners must work toward full compliance before, during, and after the event.

BOX 8.4   OKLAHOMA WARN SYSTEM

The Oklahoma WARN (OK-WARN) is a pager weather notification system for Oklahomans who are deaf or hard of hearing. Created after the 1999 tornado season with funding from the state school for the deaf, it provides notification and warning, together with life-saving information on such quickly arising weather events as flash floods. It was created by meteorologist Vincent Wood, who recognized that people who are deaf or hard of hearing have limited access to emergency information. The OK-WARN requires that a person already have a vibrating pager, but this technology is relatively inexpensive and has been adopted enthusiastically throughout the nation by individuals who are deaf or hard of hearing. Participants receive alerts from the national weather service only a minute or two after they reach weather radios.

The program was piloted in 2001 and was so successful that it is still currently in place. In 2008, OK-WARN was awarded the prestigious Alan Clive Service and Spirit Award presented every year at the National Hurricane Conference. (See more in Chapter 15.)

Other standards, such as Section 508 of the Rehabilitation Act apply to the accessibility of all types of electronic and information technology in the federal sector. The 508 standards are generally applied in relation to accessibility of federal Web sites, but may be found at other levels of government and in the private sector.

Television and radio have demonstrably failed as avenues of warning for people with hearing loss, those who are blind or have low vision, and those having a variety of cognitive disabilities. Several methods have been developed to target and disseminate information to these populations. Let's look at some examples of accessible technologies and approaches that can be incorporated into emergency notification systems.

Below is a list of some methods for sharing information with people with disabilities:

- Technology: Closed or open captioning, video description, relay and video relay services, accessible Web sites and publications, and pagers and text messaging.
- Interpreters: Sign language interpreters (shown on television, on the Web, at press conferences), language interpreters (available by phone for rapid communication in many different languages).
- Written communications: Enlarged font and plain language styles in written and spoken language, communication boards that utilize pictorial illustrations of various words and phrases, and Braille.
- TTY/TDD (TeleTYpewriter Telecommunications Device for the Deaf): Many jurisdictions are starting to utilize automated telephone dialing services or reverse 9-1-1 systems that should include the capability for TTY/TDD messaging. Hotlines established by government or different agencies must include TTY/TDD numbers and operators, as well as relay messaging options.

Efforts to identify resources and methods for communication with different disability populations have been stepped up recently. For example, since 2004, the Carl and Ruth Shapiro Family National Center for Accessible Media at WGBH, through its Access Alerts grant funded by the U.S. Department of Commerce, has developed information requirements for accessible messaging that apply to every aspect of notification and has advocated for readily achievable accessible emergency technology and practices (see Box 8.5).

The unique circumstances of some people with disabilities make it likely that they will not receive emergency communications in a timely manner. The chances of contacting these often difficult-to-reach individuals can be improved by involving organizations working within the disability

---

BOX 8.5   ACCESS ALERTS PROJECT

The Carl and Ruth Shapiro National Center for Accessible Media at WGBH created the Access Alerts project to research and disseminate approaches to make emergency warning messages accessible. The project, funded by the U.S. Department of Commerce, Technology Opportunities Program, extends through October 2004–September 2008. In order to accomplish its work, the program brings together emergency alert providers, local information resources, telecommunications industry and public broadcasting representatives, and consumers. The project will deliver information requirements, an information repository, and recommendations (National Center for Accessible Media n.d.).

---

community, service providers, and community groups. These agencies can assist in content development to ensure that the message reaches the intended recipients. Many jurisdictions now rely on these agencies to share information with their existing client lists when an emergency strikes.

8.9.2   Evacuation

Once the issue of warning is resolved, the emergency manager turns to developing plans for the safe evacuation of the community. The timing of evacuation depends primarily on the type of disaster. An earthquake provides no warning, and all evacuation begins after the main event, as people leave unstable neighborhoods and relocate to identified shelters. A flood or hurricane may allow time, from several hours to one or two days, for evacuation. A hazardous materials release of lethal gas, for example, is one of the most difficult types of events to plan for, as the area to be evacuated may change from hour to hour, depending on winds that blow in unanticipated directions.

In planning the safe removal from danger of persons with disabilities, the emergency manager must consider both those who live independently in the community, and those who live in congregate care facilities. The scope of evacuation, of course, can vary from a few buildings or homes to a single neighborhood to one or several counties.

Many people with disabilities can evacuate on their own when given timely and accurate information. However, others, whether living alone or in a group setting, will require assistance. A 2005 survey conducted by the AARP found that 15% of adults age 50 or older, and 25% over the age of 75, require assistance from another person to evacuate from their home. This survey also revealed that of the approximately 13 million persons age 50 and older who will need help, about half will require aid from someone outside their household (Gibson and Hayunga 2006).

An evacuation requires resources from both public and private entities. People with mobility impairments must be moved in accessible vans or buses driven by knowledgeable staff. Critically ill people must be transported in ambulances or ambulettes. Many individuals with cognitive disabilities cannot drive but can ride in an ordinary vehicle. Organizations that deliver services to these populations, such as schools, nursing homes, hospitals, and day-care programs, rely on the same small number of providers. They often believe, mistakenly, that the limited resources available can meet all emergency needs. It is critical that these entities establish agreements among themselves and with companies supplying such resources, to work together to coordinate the use of available vehicles, establish priorities, and attempt to identify any additional resources from within or outside the jurisdiction. Several locations merit additional attention.

8.9.2.1   Congregate Care Settings

A jurisdiction may order an evacuation, but hospitals and nursing homes are sometimes exempted. In such cases, decision-making authority lies with the facility administrator to evacuate or shelter in place (U.S. Government Accountability Office 2006). Administrators have to consider in-house resources and arrival of potential assistance against the risks of moving large numbers of people, which can be especially dangerous for frail patients or residents. When administrators choose to evacuate, they must consider availability of alternate sites, transportation resources, and movement of equipment, records, and staff. Whenever feasible, communication throughout the operation with residents, families, and staff alleviates stress and promotes cooperation.

Most residents will fare better in a "like-to-like" transfer, in which they are relocated to a facility with the same or higher-skilled staffing and care capabilities. Unfortunately, too often residents are brought to shelter locations that do not have adequate care levels. This became such a significant problem in Florida during the 1990s that the state legislature enacted "anti-dumping" laws to prohibit nursing homes from using an established public shelter as part of their evacuation plan.

"Transfer trauma" may occur when moving individuals whose age, disability, or medical condition has left them particularly frail. The actual evacuation itself can result in both physical and emotional trauma. Trauma can present as disorientation, advancing if untreated to serious deterioration of health or condition, further injury, or even death. Nursing homes and other critical care facilities must be especially aware of transfer trauma, conducting evacuations carefully to avoid or reduce it (Fernandez et al. 2002).

8.9.2.2   Workplaces and Residential Units

While most buildings with multiple units, such as offices, apartments, or condominiums, have a fire safety plan, these plans often fail to specifically take into account people with disabilities. This deficiency creates a possibly dangerous environment for people with disabilities, others who work or live in the building, and rescuers. Both FEMA and the U.S. Fire Administration (USFA) offer excellent planning guides (see links in the Resources section of this chapter). Facility safety plans should include, at a minimum (Job Accommodation Network n.d.),

- Voluntary identification of people who may need assistance and the type of assistance required
- Accessible emergency notification and signage
- Purchase of and training on evacuation equipment designed for use by persons with disabilities
- Designation of areas of rescue assistance for people who cannot use the stairways or designated emergency exits
- Unobstructed paths of egress from the building
- Drills and exercises on procedures for all affected individuals

8.9.3   RESPONSE

Failure to plan effective notification and evacuation systems will greatly impact the disability population. Disconnection from support systems, including health care, can undermine an individual's ability to respond to the disaster, and restrict overall self-sufficiency and independence. Such catastrophic losses can result in deterioration of health, infliction of injury, or even in death. This section explores these and other impacts on the disability community.

8.9.3.1   Ineffective Notification System

Inaccessible or incomplete information can have a dire impact on people with disabilities. A building owner who is not fully compliant and installed only audible smoke alarms, creates the possibility that a person who is deaf or hard of hearing may not be aware that the alarm has sounded, and may lose the opportunity to evacuate safely. Even if alarms are audible/visual, a means must be found to alert persons with hearing disabilities who may work in an area outside of the direct sightline. Television stations that disregard FCC regulations for broadcast of emergency information in a visual format deny people with sensory or cognitive disabilities critical information about evacuation routes, shelter locations, and the like. This is illustrated when an evacuation route is reported, for example, without a map or other clear visual.

8.9.3.2 Ineffective Management and Mismanagement of Resources

All too often, the experience of individuals with disabilities is that plans fall short of identifying, coordinating, and appropriately matching critical resources to people. Effective management to provide resources can be a matter of life and death for this population. Individuals with disabilities have suffered needlessly for want of such items or services as condition-specific medication, durable medical equipment (DME), accessible transportation, sign-language interpreters, oxygen canister refill capability, dialysis equipment, and diabetic supplies, to name a few items on what is a very long list.

The following typical example occurs all too frequently: a nursing home administrator establishes a transportation agreement with a bus company to evacuate residents if an emergency so demands. When the time for evacuation arrives, it is discovered to the astonishment of all that the company did not supply vehicles with power lifts to accommodate electric wheelchairs (U.S. Government Accountability Office 2006). Such resource mismanagement will significantly impact the residents' ability to evacuate safely, and will endanger staff and transportation providers. Those who did not evacuate from certain areas prior to landfall of Hurricane Katrina were left stranded, requiring complex and dangerous rescue by helicopter or boat. Many residents bore great risks during the event and died as a result.

Another aspect of resource mismanagement is the absence of disability agencies in the planning process. Therefore, it becomes more difficult during emergencies for these agencies to access the system and offer resources. Simultaneously, emergency managers fail to integrate such valuable resources or even know of their existence. Such disconnects result in a lack of resources for people with disabilities.

The Special Needs Assessment for Katrina Evacuees report (National Organization on Disability 2005b) supports the reality of disengagement between and among agencies. In 2006, the National Organization on Disability (NOD) sent a team of special needs and emergency management experts to Texas, Louisiana, Alabama, and Mississippi in the aftermath of Hurricane Katrina. The team, referred to as the Special Needs Assessment for Katrina Evacuees (SNAKE), was sent to the affected areas to assess the degree of accessibility for people with disabilities; the capacity of service provider organizations to work with emergency management agencies; and the quality of sheltering for the disability and aging communities. The team soon discovered that disability organizations did not have relationships in place prior to Katrina, and as a result did not know how to contact or coordinate and integrate response services. The following are key findings from the SNAKE report:

- Fifty four percent (54%) of the respondents did not have a working agreement with disability and aging organizations prior to the event. Fifty percent (50%) made contacts with those organizations as a result of their Hurricane Katrina experience (National Organization on Disability 2005a).
- The gap between emergency management and disability- and aging-specific organizations widened when the organizations serving these populations tried to connect with the emergency management community; 85.7% of these community-based groups indicated that they did not know how to link with the emergency management system (National Organization on Disability 2005a).

8.9.3.3 Sheltering

During or after a disaster, a critical number of community residents, including people with disabilities, take refuge in a shelter. Traditionally, many jurisdictions have relied on and partnered with the American Red Cross, other volunteer groups, and faith-based organizations to manage and operate shelters. By long-standing American Red Cross policy, shelters are seen as a lifeboat on land, offering minimal provisions—food, water, a place to rest, and medical care equivalent to first aid. In addition to these so-called general population shelters, many jurisdictions have begun to establish special/medical needs shelters to provide a higher level of care, skilled staff, and equipment. Special/medical needs shelters may be co-located with general population shelters or may be stand-alone facilities. In this section, sheltering issues that impact people with disabilities will be addressed.

The ADA under Title II and III interpretation requires shelters to be accessible and to otherwise accommodate persons with disabilities. In July 2007, the U.S. Department of Justice (DOJ) released guidance to state and local governments establishing these standards (U.S. Department of Justice 2007). In the same year, the Department of Homeland Security (DHS) conducted a nationwide review of emergency plans. During this review, teams of emergency managers and ADA experts examined emergency management plans from jurisdictions throughout the United States. A select team assessed integration of special needs issues into these plans. The team concluded, among other things, that states should develop standards for the care of individuals with disabilities, emphasizing that a priority factor for shelter selection should be accessibility for persons with disabilities (U.S. Department of Homeland Seurity 2006). While governments are slowly but steadily becoming aware of these requirements, shelters still fall short of basic ADA standards (e.g., an accessible route into the site location and accessible bathrooms). It is much easier to remedy these deficiencies when shelters are preselected, and it becomes much more problematic during the spontaneous identification of shelters.

As a result, many people with disabilities, particularly those with mobility impairments, cannot use shelters safely, if at all. In fact, individuals with accessibility needs who otherwise do not require assistance or medical care, such as healthy wheelchair users, often are separated from friends and family, and are sent to an alternative shelter or a special/medical needs facility. This separation causes an unnecessary hardship on the individual, and is an inefficient use of resources. The person must be sent, possibly via accessible transportation, to a new location, and if at a medical needs shelter, will consume space and resources an individual with an actual medical condition may actually require. If general population shelters accommodate people with disabilities, they can involve family and friends familiar with the individual's needs, reduce their trauma, and provide valuable support.

Stakeholders can assist in the process of ensuring that shelters are selected with regard to accessibility. Accessibility experts can, for example, be familiar with a facility survey that includes specific criteria, and can join facility review teams.

One effective strategy begins with the identification by emergency managers of facilities that are both likely to be accessible and known by the community. The Senior Center Safe Center program is founded on this concept. Local governments either build new senior centers or retrofit existing facilities for dual use as shelters. These centers offer activities and services in the community every day, are outside the flood plain, and are built to withstand hurricane- and tornado-force winds. In addition to being accessible, they are equipped with a generator, extra wall outlets, and satellite telephones. The roofs of these facilities are painted bright colors for easy recognition during flyovers and rescue operations. As of early 2008, this shelter model is in place in Alabama and Florida.

Effective sheltering begins with registration at the door of the shelter. Without a shelter intake process that is sensitive to the needs of people with disabilities, many problems may go unidentified. The purpose of shelters is to capture information on how to meet functional needs. While the process must allow an individual the right not to divulge his or her status, a lack of inclusiveness can cause hardship to the individual and staff during the shelter stay. Therefore, if needs are acknowledged at intake, an opportunity is created early in what might become a prolonged stay to offer possible accommodations, or to determine the need to place the person in a different setting (e.g., medical needs shelter, hospital, or nursing home).

In an attempt to serve evacuees with more consideration, and to reduce stress on hospitals, many jurisdictions have established special/medical needs shelters. These shelters are intended for people who have medical and/or care requirements beyond those which can be met at a general population shelter facility. This approach has generated considerable debate; opponents criticize the methodology for separating or segregating disability and special needs populations from the larger community. However, harsh reality finds emergency planners struggling to find adequate resources, so it makes sense to pool assets to support this level of sheltering. An abundance of resources is required to support such a shelter, including skilled medical staffing, specialized equipment, uninterrupted power generation, abundant medication supplies, and the like. Emergency managers are increasingly attempting to co-locate special/medical needs shelters within or near general population shelters. Undoubtedly, they face a struggle, since many jurisdictions are encountering shortages in the very resources needed to support general population facilities.

In addition to being physically accessible, general population shelters should be equipped, and shelter staff trained to provide, accommodations for people with disabilities. These may include programmatic accommodations, using sign language interpreters, or providing minimal activities of daily living (ADL) assistance, such as help with eating, to individuals who require it. By law, service animals are allowed in shelters and should not be separated from their owners. Many might look upon this advice as a counsel of perfection, and would contend it is impossible to make shelters as accessible as advocates suggest. These changes will not come overnight to every city and county in America, but there must be a standard we can look to as we proceed to change the role of persons with disabilities in emergency management planning.

Resource allocation and distribution is a shelter issue that can adversely impact people with disabilities. As was mentioned above in the evacuation section, for a variety of reasons people may arrive at shelters without medication, assistive devices (eyeglasses, canes, walkers, etc.), and durable medical equipment (oxygen machines and tanks). Planning for this reality will minimize the impact of such losses, and permit individuals to maintain an equal or similar level of independence to that enjoyed before the event. First and foremost, jurisdictions should educate the public about the importance of bringing necessary items with them. Planners should also identify sources of DME and other assistive devices that are likely to be needed in a shelter (e.g., oxygen tank refills, manual wheelchairs, walkers). Establishing partnerships with medical equipment suppliers, pharmacies, disability agencies, and other related retailers will help tremendously in identifying supplies.

8.9.3.4 Continuity of Care

Continuity of care includes not separating people with disabilities from their caregivers and continuity of operations planning (COOP). Following these steps may not only save lives, it will make evacuations and re-entry smoother and impose less burden on responders, relief workers, and emergency managers.

Earlier, we discussed the negative impact of separating people with disabilities from friends, relatives, and caregivers. The importance of keeping disabled people together with their support network cannot be overemphasized. With the support network in place, an individual may be able to sustain more easily in either a general population shelter or in a medical needs facility. Often, individuals are separated due to circumstances or policy. People may have no time to evacuate together, and individuals who require accessible transportation often are unable to travel with others in their support network. It is only common sense to expect that, deprived of familiar assistance, their ability to sustain independently will decline.

Many people with disabilities rely on caregivers to provide various levels of support, from a few hours a week to round-the-clock service. Caregivers are a diverse group which, in any given community, will include family members or friends caring for other family members or friends in their homes, such as an older spouse caring for his or her spouse debilitated by stroke, family members caring for a child with a disability, or, increasingly common today, adult children caring for elderly parents. Caregivers come from outside the family/friend network as well, such as paid home healthcare providers, and personal care assistants or professional caregivers employed in hospice clinics, adult homes, senior day-care centers, and other residential and social facilities.

The increased vulnerability to disaster among people with disabilities and their caregivers became dramatically evident during the evacuation of New Orleans during Hurricane Katrina.

The Washington Post, Kaiser Family Foundation, and Harvard School of Public Health (2005) conducted interviews of displaced survivors in Houston, finding that over 40% of those who did not evacuate in a timely manner were either physically unable to leave for lack of transport, or were caring for a disabled person (Morin and Rein 2005). While the discussion thus far has focused on the individual with a disability, the reality is that many factors combine to make caregivers nearly or equally vulnerable in disaster. The very act of assisting their client may endanger the caregiver's safety. Paid helpers can be torn by obligation to their own family and the client, pressures that may push them to take unreasonable risks. These intersecting obligations have the power to sap their resilience precisely when it is most needed. Clearly, the role of caregivers during disaster is essential, and it is no overstatement to say that the caregiver may mean the difference for the client with a disability between life and death. Emergency managers have increasingly come to understand the importance of caregivers, and the need for strategies to ensure that they are considered and incorporated into plans.

Failure to establish emergency plans that include service providers (home health agencies, outpatient clinics, etc.) often creates a crisis for these providers. They may not be able to operate at full capacity or at all, interrupting critical treatments or service their clients must continue. Without establishing relationships between emergency managers and care providers, and between the care provider and the client, people who rely on these services may be left without alternatives. For example, after a disaster, dialysis clinics, meal service centers, or paratransit systems may not be functioning, making recovery and rebuilding very difficult, if not impossible, for some persons with disabilities. Some clients may be so isolated that service providers cannot reach them (Fernandez et al. 2002).

During evacuation, people with disabilities are all too often separated from individual critical equipment and support that they rely on daily. For example, after Hurricane Katrina, hundreds of persons with disabilities were separated from critical equipment, such as electric wheelchairs. As a result those authorizing moving and receiving evacuees had to provide individual support and replace highly specialized and expensive equipment, which was often not readily available (National Organization on Disability 2005b).

8.9.4 SHORT- AND LONG-TERM RECOVERY

This section will discuss some of the needs people with disabilities have after a disaster. This includes reentry issues, housing, and other types of longer-term disaster human services.

The recovery process of cleaning debris, restoring transportation routes and utilities, and repairing houses severely impacts people with disabilities and their capacity to return safely home. No one who relies on electricity to sustain life, such as people who use oxygen or ventilators, can return to an apartment or house without power. The lack of transportation services (especially accessible transportation), combined with the usual problems of road access post-event, can severely limit a person's ability to resume health care services, work, and school.

Lack of suitable accessible housing is a major obstacle to getting people with disabilities to return to the community. Many cities and towns have a shortage of accessible housing before a disaster event occurs. After a disaster occurs, demand for long-term, permanent housing rises, precisely as resources become even scarcer. As federal and state rebuilding programs are established during the recovery phase, emergency management and the disability community must advocate together for accessible housing and accommodation rights to be integral to these programs. Federally funded housing programs, such as those administered by the Department of Housing and Urban Development (HUD), include requirements in accordance with the ADA, Uniform Federal

Accessibility Standards (UFAS), and other regulations that a certain percentage of all construction meets accessibility standards. As homes are being repaired or rebuilt with federal money, it is vital to consider accessibility requirements for individual homeowners or potential renters. Further, jurisdictions should consider encouraging or mandating the utilization of universal design in all new construction and urban planning to ensure at least minimal accessibility, as this opportunity to design access can be a positive outcome from a devastating event.

Temporary housing, such as the travel trailers and mobile homes FEMA often provides, also falls short of meeting accessibility requirements (Advocacy Center 2007). In fact, the problem became so dire in Louisiana and Mississippi after Hurricanes Katrina and Rita that an advocacy organization filed and won a lawsuit against FEMA on behalf of 11 Katrina and Rita evacuees with disabilities (Advocacy Center 2007). After the hurricanes it was noted that, although approximately 25% of Katrina evacuees have disabilities, only 1%–2% of such people from Louisiana and Mississippi received accessible trailers. On September 26, 2006, the Federal District Court for the Eastern District of Louisiana approved a settlement to ensure that FEMA will provide accessible trailers to people with disabilities. FEMA has continued to work toward a more appropriate solution as evidenced in the release of the 2008 Disaster Housing Plan (FEMA 2008).

In addition to ensuring that temporary housing is accessible to people with disabilities, long-term (permanent) housing needs to be accessible as well. Retrofitting houses so that people with physical disabilities can have a permanent home is not only an important step in helping victims of disaster rebuild their lives, it is an important step in rebuilding the devastated community. When homes are rebuilt that are accessible, it encourages all buildings in the community to be rebuilt per laws and regulations. This can have an overall beneficial effect on the entire community in many ways. The National Council on Disability asserts,

> The entire community benefits as access to public works and structures will increase access to the employment, healthcare, and independence for people with disabilities. We must ensure that the federal, state, and local authorities who operate public buildings will fill their obligation to comply with the laws; the cost of complying with the relevant laws later will undoubtedly exceed that of getting it right the first time (2008).

Until services such as home-based care, health clinics, hospitals, and schools are restored, many people with disabilities may not be able to return. Without the proper support, they may not be able to function independently or safely. Service providers can also play a big role during recovery in helping clients to understand the aid available through federal and state government programs, private grants and foundations, and traditional disaster relief organizations, such as the American Red Cross. The National Council on Disability reported that many disability advocates believed that a majority of people with disabilities had not returned to New Orleans nearly three years after the storm because of lack of social and health services as well as accessible housing and other public facilities (2008).

Through coordination with aid organizations, service providers can communicate benefit opportunities and eligibility requirements to their clientele, as well as determine their own internal policy and items for which they may apply. Too often, services are duplicated among agencies, while others are ignored or forgotten. Through a more coordinated effort, the needs of disaster victims can be met with greater effectiveness and efficiency.

The National Council on Disability's January 2008 quarterly report, People with Disabilities and Emergency Management, outlined continued lessons learned after Hurricanes Katrina and Rita. Lessons learned included better coordination of both social and health care services as well as more emphasis on mental health (National Council on Disability 2008). An important aspect to coordination of services is ensuring there are enough resources and funding to provide services. Relationship building becomes even more valuable during the planning phase. According to the quarterly report:

It is critical that organizations and agencies, both NGOs and government entities, collaborate prior to, during and after a disaster. In addition, people with disabilities should be included in the collaborative efforts as volunteers, staff, planners, and organizations. For example, the Center for Independent Living (CIL) utilizes people with disabilities as staff, board members and volunteers. In addition, the CIL tries to recruit individuals with disabilities as AmeriCorps volunteers. Recommended organizations to collaborate with include: Centers for Independent Living (state and local if applicable), Departments of Rehabilitation Services, relief organizations, and government agencies (local and state) such as Aging, Disability, MRDD, etc. Some of these agencies assisted in locating consumers/clients, access to additional services and resources and equipment. Government agencies are especially helpful in terms of working with NGOs to gain access to areas where access would be prohibitive. For example, government entities can assist with ordering and loading trucks with necessary items, transportation of these items, and coordination. Since most government agencies are connected with emergency operations, they have direct access to many resources as well as the ability to deploy and coordinate as requested and necessary. Again, as mentioned earlier, VOAD organizations are also focused on greater collaboration among organizations in planning for disasters (National Council on Disability 2008).

8.9.5   IMPLICATIONS FOR ACTION

Understanding the needs of people with disabilities and overcoming bias is half the task for emergency managers; equally important is taking this information and putting it into action. This includes addressing vulnerability through planning and preparedness efforts, incorporating the Emergency Management Assistance Compact (EMAC), identification and assessment, exercises and drills, and outreach, building capacity, continuity of operations planning (COOP), and registry systems.

8.9.5.1   Addressing Vulnerability through Planning and Preparedness

Disability issues can be addressed effectively by joining together key stakeholders from the community (see Box 8.6 for recommended participants). The collaboration of emergency management and disability stakeholders brings to the planning table people with various levels of expertise, resources, refined skill sets, and problem-solving capabilities. It cannot be reasonably expected that one agency or organization can effectively address alone the large scope and complexity of these issues. In fact, emergency managers most often do not have the expertise in disability and special needs issues, nor the resources to deal with these issues without assistance. According to a 2005 poll, emergency planning officials are twice as likely to feel that the resources they have are inadequate (41%) than they are to say that resources are adequate (18%) (National Organization on Disability 2005a).

Below are three examples of special needs planning groups formed at the federal, state, and local levels. There are many more that have been working to meaningfully integrate special needs issues into the emergency management structure.

- The federal level: As a result of Executive Order 13347 (see Figure 8.3, Recent Legislative Changes), the Interagency Coordinating Council on Emergency Preparedness for People with Disabilities (ICC) was established (U.S. Department of Homeland Security 2006a). Comprised of several federal agencies, the ICC is responsible for developing strategies for incorporating disability issues into all federal emergency plans and guidance. The ICC works through designated subcommittees on topics such as emergency transportation, emergency communications, health, and others.
- The state level: The New Jersey Special Needs Advisory Panel is another example of the collaborative approach. This panel brings together emergency management, health, disability, and other groups from around the state to incorporate special needs issues into state plans. Meeting regularly, the group works on planning, training, and exercises, and has successfully encouraged the creation of local groups.

BOX 8.6   LIST OF RECOMMENDED PLANNING PARTICIPANTS

Below is a list of some of the stakeholders to be included in planning groups and other efforts to increase mutual understanding among emergency managers, disability advocates, and service providers.

- **Aging**: Area Agency on Aging, senior centers, aging advocacy organizations (AARP, etc.)
- **Voluntary organizations**: American Red Cross, Salvation Army, faith-based organizations, sheltering agencies (lead agency[s] responsible for disaster shelters), United Way, Voluntary Organizations Active in Disaster (VOAD)
- **Disability related**: Developmental Disabilities Networks, agencies serving specific disabilities and general disability populations, individuals with disabilities from the community (leadership), local independent living council/center, education department or staff from disability-specific schools
- **Health and care facilities**: Dialysis Treatment Network, home-based care industry (visiting nurse services, home health aides associations, etc.), hospice care providers, hospital associations, health departments, medical and health care organizations, mental health department, mental health providers, nursing organization/association, residential health care facilities (nursing homes, skilled care homes, assisted living facilities), day-care centers, durable medical equipment companies
- **Emergency management and first response**: Ambulance industry, emergency management agency/office, fire departments
- **Other**: Housing agency/authority, human services department, legal authority (jurisdiction's corporation counsel or general counsel), local media, transportation networks, Veterans Affairs (VA)

- The local level: The Illinois Public Health Association, the Illinois Department of Public Health, and the Illinois Emergency Management Agency support the creation of local special needs advisory panels throughout the state. Several groups have formed within counties with support from the state, which provides training and minimal funding.

Service providers in the disability community are key contacts prior to, during, and after a disaster. While many people with disabilities do not require or seek out any type of service or assistance, others receive a number of different services that allow them to maintain their status as independent, contributing members of the community. Service providers or advocacy agencies that work directly with disability populations have the best knowledge about the needs of the community, and have established and maintained trusted relationships. As a result, they are predictably expected to experience high call volumes and requests for assistance during disasters, because they already have connections to individuals, families, and the community at large. Emergency management agencies will look to service providers to assist with identifying populations and conducting needs assessments, coordinating resources, and, if at all possible, enhancing everyday services to include additional assistance or to incorporate more people who have been made eligible for their services because of disaster.

Emergency management planners can help such organizations to enhance assistance capabilities by helping organizations to identify hazard vulnerabilities; assisting them to develop a continuity of operations plan to improve their capability of continuing operations throughout the incident; and informing them of federal and state aid for which they may be eligible, and the details of the application process (Fernandez et al. 2002).

8.9.5.2   Incorporating the Emergency Management Assistance Compact

The Emergency Management Assistance Compact (EMAC) is a common agreement used in emergency management among states outlining emergency services and resources that can be extended from those states during disasters to a stricken area. Until 2005, EMAC was not applied to the disaster-related needs of people with disabilities. However, following Hurricane Katrina, the U.S. Administration on Aging utilized EMAC to bring in social workers, case managers, and service providers from other states into the Gulf Coast to assist elderly disaster victims (Weston and Tokesky 2006). Utilizing this approach built the capacity of the impacted area to address senior population needs. This approach can be replicated in future disasters, and expanded beyond seniors into the larger disability community.

8.9.5.3   Identification and Assessment

A thorough community assessment, targeted to identify disability populations and their disaster-related needs, will be a tremendous asset to disaster planning. This effort must be collaborative, incorporating multiple sources of information to obtain the most accurate picture. It will prove easier to identify people with disabilities who are affiliated with a service or advocacy agency, than those who are not. Working with an inclusive disabilities planning group, as mentioned above, will be an extremely helpful source of data, and will allow needs assessors to drill down beneath the standard demographic information provided in sources such as the U.S. Census. This project will address vulnerabilities within the communities and identify

- Individuals with disabilities who will require assistance during emergencies and what that level of assistance actually is required
- Resource capacities and limitations
- Locations of clusters of people with specific disabilities (e.g., School for the Blind or Deaf, congregate care facility, etc.)
- Targets for individual preparedness programs
- Community-based resources unknown or unavailable to emergency management before, such as private fleets of accessible vehicles

An example of a success story regarding the identification of a specific-needs group working together with first responders can be illustrated by both terrorist attacks on the World Trade Center (1993 and 2001). The Associated Blind, an advocacy organization that also has people who are blind and with other disabilities on staff, are located right near the World Trade Center. After the 1993 bombing, the Associated Blind worked closely with the Fire Department of New York (FDNY) on emergency preparedness, planning, and effective evacuation routes for staff as well as rescue techniques for the firefighters. The plans were tested and staff practiced drills. As a result, all staff safely evacuated their building during the 2001 terrorist attacks (National Organization on Disability n.d.). This is a powerful example of how identifying special needs populations and working with them before the disaster hits can save lives.

8.9.5.4   Exercises and Drills

Exercises and drills, which include key stakeholders representing disability populations as well as the individuals themselves, will provide valuable practical information to improve emergency plans. Persons with disabilities should be involved in all phases of this activity, including exercise and drill design, implementation, and evaluation. Experience has demonstrated that participation by people with disabilities brings out new and unexpected issues, which were either planned for inadequately or never considered seriously, if at all. Consider some of the findings from the 2005 Department of Homeland Security's (DHS) third national Top Officials (TOPOFF3) drill (Davis and Mincin 2003):

FIGURE 8.2 FEMA specialists work with a survivor to identify mitigation measures for a home. *Source*: Photo by Greg Henshall/FEMA news photo.

- Not all facilities utilized were accessible.
- Information should be provided in alternate formats and closed-captioned.
- People with disabilities were inadequately represented during play.
- Disability-related objectives should be included in the exercise plan.

Further, ponder the unexpected outcome from the Interagency Chemical Exercise in New York City in 1998 that showed without proper experience in decontaminating people with auxiliary aids (i.e., wheelchairs, walkers, canes, etc.), with service animals, and with attached medical supports such as insulin pumps and cochlear implants, the "cold zone" became compromised for the original victims, all aid workers, and the second wave of first responders (Byrne and Davis 2005).

8.9.5.5 Outreach

Outreach to people with disabilities must be conducted during the preparedness, response, recovery, and mitigation phases, since they are likely to receive incomplete or no information about emergency plans and preparedness messages (Figure 8.2). The following strategies have been used during all phases, some working more effectively when applied to preparedness, others producing better results during response and recovery. No one strategy will work alone; multiple approaches should be used to complement each other and to contact a larger percentage of this often hard-to-reach population.

- Coordinate community teams to go door-to-door, to senior centers, and to other known formal and informal gathering places. Teams can be composed of staff members from emergency management agencies, first responder units, service providers, voluntary organizations, and others who are well informed about the needs of people with disabilities. They receive training pre-event specifically for this task.
- Implement a reverse 9-1-1 system, which allows authorities to communicate key information to individuals via phone or TTY/TDD. Ensure that all 9-1-1 systems are accessible according to applicable standards.
- Utilize peer counselors (professionals or paraprofessionals) who have disabilities themselves.
- Establish fully accessible sites to disseminate information, and ensure that location(s) are readily available to public transportation and paratransit.

- Provide preparedness, response, or recovery information on Web sites, particularly those meeting 508 compliance standards.
- Involve schools, residential care facilities, community and senior centers, and similar organizations to relay information.
- Send information through utility bills, bank statements, or as a part of governmental mailings.
- Affirm that existing benefits will not be affected by accepting disaster relief funds.

8.9.5.6 Building Capacity

Building capacity within the disability community so that individuals are more prepared and better able to respond during disasters is a key concept that emergency managers should incorporate into planning and outreach efforts. There are several ways to accomplish this including working through networks and providing accurate and timely information.

One of the greatest resources any individual possesses is his or her ability to self-prepare. An increasing amount of emergency preparedness information is now available, more than ever being targeted to people with disabilities and seniors who frequently have disabling conditions. The primary source of this information is the Internet as there are several Web sites being dedicated to this issue. However, millions of Americans are still computer illiterate or do not own a system. Many who use computers may not be aware that the guidance is available. There are no filters to distinguish valid and useful information (see Resources section) from sites created essentially to sell a product. Further, some persons with disabilities will need assistance or assistive technologies to understand the necessary steps to be prepared for disasters.

In order to ensure that people with disabilities are aware of and have access to preparedness information, jurisdictions can work through social networks, community-based service organizations, and home health-care agencies. In addition to distributing the information, staff members of such organizations, when properly trained, can discuss the material with their clients or patients and assist them to take recommended steps for greater preparedness.

Persons who are blind, or who have mental retardation or mental illness will require accessible formats. In many cases, the issue of access has been resolved by the development of software that gives the computer the ability to read aloud text on the monitor screen. For those not yet comfortable with mouse and keyboard, brochures and pamphlets can be recorded on cassette tape or produced in Braille. Several organizations have created model preparedness information directed at people with cognitive disabilities or who can understand only very basic ideas or who benefit from pictorial and graphic representations.

8.9.5.7 Continuity of Operations Planning among Disability Service Agencies

Social service agencies should develop continuity of operations plans (COOP). All such agencies, private or public, struggle to find the funding and staff to develop such plans. At a minimum, the COOP plan should indicate a source of backup for essential functions and resources such as equipment, staffing, record keeping, facilities, and means of service delivery.

Congregate and residential care facilities must also develop COOP plans. The Joint Commission on Accreditation of Healthcare Organizations (JCAHO) accredits eight different types of health care facilities, the most relevant to emergency management being hospitals, long-term care facilities, behavioral health care clinics, and ambulatory care institutions. In early 2008 JCAHO released a detailed standard for business continuity planning for these facilities, including procedures for operational interruptions, developing a backup system, and testing of those systems.

8.9.5.8 Registries

To overcome the challenge of identifying those who require assistance (whether for notification or evacuation, etc.) and what form that assistance might take, some jurisdictions utilize a registry system. Though registries differ in purpose and operation, generally they comprise a database of people with various needs (eligibility determined by jurisdiction) who voluntarily register. Since registries are by legal interpretation voluntarily joined, it must be expected that they will not capture all those requiring assistance; the registry is instead one tool among many others for consideration.

Registries, when effectively in place, provide a variety of information, depending on the design by the jurisdiction. Common data found in a registry include the basic pedigree information, reason or level of assistance needs, and specific critical data, for example. Registries can assist managers to target preparedness materials and messages, and to streamline emergency communications. Florida has mandated the creation of a special needs registry by every county, while most other states leave such action to the discretion of local authorities. Registries can be of enormous help to the emergency manager, but come with a number of issues that should be carefully examined pre-implementation.

Registries are one of several possible tools a jurisdiction may use to identify people with disaster-related needs. That said, caution should be taken when planning a registry system. Emergency managers often become frustrated with the registry, because only a small percentage of the eligible population needing assistance actually give out their names and addresses (White et al. 2007).

Here are some of the other issues that raise doubts about registries:

- During the first few days of the 2003 California wildfires, the registry lists were locked in secure locations in local fire stations, and could not be used for the intended purpose. The state did not have a centralized dispatching system to coordinate efforts among the communities, which curtailed the ability to ensure that everyone was notified (California State Independent Living Council 2004).
- Due to the very nature of the types of people registered, death and relocation cause registries to quickly become outdated unless efficiently maintained, requiring financial and personnel resources few agencies possess.
- The creation of a registry usually creates unfounded expectations as well, which must be carefully managed. By virtue of having registered, people may believe that they will automatically receive assistance from the jurisdiction, which often is not the case. Managers must be firm and clear in describing exactly what individuals can expect as a result of returning the registration form.
- Residents may rely too much on having registered rather than taking the time to work up a personal preparedness plan. Those who refused to register prior to an emergency will clog the agency's phone lines at the last moment of a mandatory evacuation, expecting that they can register and be rescued.
- Confidentiality laws and obligations may impact the registry negatively, and should be fully explored and understood prior to taking any other action to implement such a list. For example, the Health Insurance Portability and Accountability Act (HIPAA), Public Law 104-191, and other privacy laws may affect the type of information or the collection method allowed. People often will refuse to sign up for the registry because they are unclear about how the information will be used or if it will be secured.

8.9.5.9 Training

Training press officers, outreach teams, shelter staff, and first responders on disability issues will help enhance communication with the disability community as well as increase awareness on better response methods during evacuations and rescues.

Disability service providers, in coordination with emergency management, can assist in the training of press officers and other outreach workers to ensure that they are attuned to disaster-related needs issues. Training should focus on modality, i.e., different methods for relaying information and content, evaluation of effectiveness, and coordination of dissemination.

Outreach teams working in the community to help people prepare or providing post-disaster recovery information should also be trained on disability issues. For example, after the World

Trade Center attacks in New York in September 2001, outreach teams were trained on general recovery information as well as on disability awareness. They learned to identify communication and service needs while working in the field, and received specific demographic information on the targeted area and guidance about interfacing with disability organizations (Mackert and Davis 2002).

Shelter staff, largely composed of volunteers, must receive training on how to work with people with disabilities. Minimally, this instruction should address sensitization to the issues, intake processes, and dealing with accommodation requests. Disability service agencies should be involved in the design and conduct of the training, whether held in advance of an occurrence or spontaneously just after an event.

Many first responders and other emergency management personnel are not trained in and lack basic understanding of emergency-related disability issues (White et al. 2007). Conversely, many disability organizations and individuals with disabilities know little about emergency management. Cross training that brings together these two distinct communities has proven to be highly effective. There are now free, cost sharing, and for-fee training packages available to states and localities. Examples such as the FEMA G197 Course, the Oklahoma Assistive Technology Program, and others will be found in the Resources section. Oftentimes, first responders welcome such relationships as they offer an opportunity for them to learn more and increase their skills base.

8.10   SUMMARY

In conclusion, anyone involved in emergency planning, response, and/or recovery issues and the disability community needs to keep several points in mind. The issues that present will be the most labor intensive, costly, and time consuming. They will be ongoing and are best approached in partnership with the stakeholders directly. This ensures appropriateness of the plans, includes community buy-in, brings new information and resources into the equation, and leads to sustainability over time.

In order to truly maximize efforts given the above points, the goal should be to "universalize" as often as possible. Just like the point made earlier about incorporating the concepts of universal design and access when redesigning or rebuilding a community post disaster, so can we borrow that term in other ways. The use of open captions at the bottom of the television image may have been done with the needs of the deaf and hard of hearing in mind, but the written word available to reinforce the spoken message can be a benefit to persons with learning disabilities or to those for whom English is not their proficient first language. Just as the assurance that the designated shelter or temporary housing unit have an access ramp leading into it may have been done with a wheelchair user in mind, so can that benefit an older person with an unsteady gait or even a mother of very young children in a stroller. If many types of needs for many people can be addressed simultaneously and with slight variations, the limited disaster resources will be maximized and leveraged. This will reduce individual needs as well as impacts on volunteers and staff.

Further, when an empowerment model is applied to the concept of emergency preparedness it is consistent with the social and political movements in the disability community. It enables people with disabilities to become active and informed consumers of emergency information and to take their survival into their own hands to the best of their abilities rather than be passive victims waiting for help from others. For all the reasons stated in this chapter, that has a lasting impact on the system as well as the community.

8.11   DISCUSSION QUESTIONS

1. What key agencies or organizations in your community need to be working together?
2. Is there a way to "universalize" solutions to meet the needs of the targeted populations and the general populations?

3. How can a community maximize limited resources and staff, and address them in the face of diminished funds?
4. What attitudes on both sides need to be addressed in order to move a partnership forward?
5. Are there creative funding streams or ways of work as a consortium to put certain more costly measures in place?
6. What nontraditional resources do both emergency planners and disability organizations bring to the table?

REFERENCES

Access Board. n.d. Electronic and information technology standards: An overview. http://www.access-board.gov/sec508/summary.htm (accessed February 13, 2008).

Access Center. n.d. Myths about disability. http://www.acils.com/acil/myths.html (accessed July 21, 2008).

Advocacy Center. 2007. FEMA trailer lawsuit update. http://www.advocacyla.org/news/fema/php (accessed May 5, 2008).

Associated Press. 2008. Amid smaller vet population, number of disabled U.S. veterans rising. *International Herald Tribune*, May 11. http://www.iht.com/articles/ap/2008/05/11/america/NA-GEN-US-Disabled-Veterans.php (accessed July 22, 2008).

Atkins, D., and C. Guisti. 2003. The confluence of poverty and disability. http://www.housingforall.org/rop0304%20poverty%20and%20disability.pdf (accessed February 20, 2008).

The Brookings Institution. 2008. Iraq index: Tracking variables of reconstruction and security in post-Saddam Iraq. January 28. http://www.brookings.edu/saban/iraq-index.aspx (accessed March 5, 2008).

Byrne, M., and E. A. Davis. 2005. Preparedness for all: Why including people with disabilities in drills is a learning tool: Interagency Chemical Exercise (I.C.E.). *IAEM Bulletin*, April.

Cahalan, C., and J. Renne. 2007. Safeguarding independent living: Emergency evacuation of the elderly and disabled. *Transition*, Spring.

California Office of Emergency Services. 2008. 2007 San Diego County firestorms after action report, February. http://www.sandiego.gov/mayor/pdf/fireafteraction.pdf (accessed May 27, 2008).

California State Independent Living Council. 2004. The impact of Southern California wildfires on people with disabilities. Sacramento, California (April).

Davis, E., and J. Mincin. June 26, 2005. *Incorporating special needs populations into emergency planning and exercises.* Research and Training Center on Independent Living, University of Kansas.

Davis, E., and D. Sutherland. 2005. It's the law: Preparedness and people with disabilities. *International Association of Emergency Managers Bulletin* 22 (3).

Davis, E. A. 2006. Are we prepared for the cost of preparedness? *Homeland Protection Professional*, April.

Disability Funders Network. n.d. Disability stats and facts. http://www.disabilityfunders.org/disability-stats-and-facts (accessed May 27, 2008).

FCC. 2005. Emergency access. http://ftp.fcc.gov/cgb/dro/emergency_access.html (accessed March 13, 2008).

FCC. n.d. Part 79—Accessibility of emergency information. http://www.fcc.gov/cgb/dro/emergency_info_regs.html (accessed March 11, 2008).

FEMA. 2008. 2008 housing plan. http://www.fema.gov/news/newsrelease.fema?id=43785 (accessed June 26, 2008).

Fernandez, L. S., D. Byard, C. Lin, S. Benson, and J. A. Barbera. 2002. Frail elderly as disaster victims: Emergency management strategies. *Prehospital and Disaster Medicine* April–June. http://www.gwu.edu/~icdrm/publications/67-74_fernandez.pdf (accessed January 28, 2008).

Gibson, M. J., and M. Hayunga. 2006. We can do better: Lessons learned for protecting older persons in disasters. AARP Public Policy Institute. http://www.aarp.org/research/health/disabilities/better.html (accessed April 11, 2008).

H.R. 5441 [109th] Department of Homeland Security Appropriations Act, 2007. http://thomas.loc.gov/cgi-binquery/z?c109:H.R.5441.

Hearing Loss Web. 2006. Public notice DA 06-2627: Obligation of video programming distributors to make emergency information accessible to persons with hearing disabilities using closed captioning, release December 29. http://www.hearinglossweb.com/Issues/Access/Captioning/Television/emrg/fcc.htm (accessed March 1, 2008).

Hubbard, S. 2004. Disability studies and health care curriculum: The great divide. *Journal of Allied Health* (Fall). http://findarticles.com/p/articles/mi_qa4040/is_200410/ai_n9460411 (accessed on July 21, 2008)

Job Accommodation Network (JAN). n.d. http://www.jan.wvu.edu/ (accessed on July 21, 2008).

Jones, N. 2006. CRS report for Congress: The Americans with Disabilities Act and emergency preparedness and response. http://www.ncseonline.org/NLE/CRSreports/06Jul/RS22254.pdf (accessed on May 27, 2008).

Kailes, J. I. April, 2005. *Disaster Services and "Special Needs" – Term of Art or Meaningless Term?* IAEM Bulletin, Vol. 22, No. 4.

Leeds, M. H. 1990. *Rights and responsibilities—People with disabilities in employment and public accommodations.* New York: Mark H. Leeds, Esq.

Mackert, R., and E. Davis. 2002. Report on special needs—Issues, efforts and lessons learned. FEMA (February).

National Center for Accessible Media (NCAM). n.d. Access to emergency alerts for people with disabilities. http://ncam.wgbh.org/alerts/ (accessed February 14, 2008).

National Council on Disability (NCD). 2006. The needs of people with psychiatric disabilities during and after Hurricanes Katrina and Rita: position paper and recommendations. http://www.ncd.gov/newsroom/publications/2006/peopleneeds.htm (accessed March 3, 2008).

National Council on Disability (NCD). 2008. Quarterly meeting: People with disabilities and emergency management. http://www.ncd.gov/newsroom/publications/2008/Proceedings_Monograph.html. (accessed July 21, 2008).

National Organization on Disability (NOD). 2005a. Emergency preparedness survey report, Nov. 30. http://www.benfieldhrc.org/disaster_studies/disability&disasters/episurvey_rpt.pdf (accessed March 3, 2007).

National Organization on Disability (NOD). 2005b. Report on special needs assessment for Katrina evacuees (SNAKE) project. September. http://www.nod.org/Resources/PDFs/katrina_snake_report.pdf (accessed January 26, 2008).

National Organization on Disability (NOD). n.d. Emergency preparedness initiative's guide on the special needs of people with disabilities for emergency managers, planners, and responders. http://www.nod.org/index.cfm?fuseaction=Feature.showFeature&FeatureID=1034 (accessed on July 21, 2008).

Savage v. City Place Ltd. Partnership, 2004 WL 3045404 (Md. Cir. Ct. 2004).

Shapiro, J. 1994. No pity: People with disabilities forging a new civil rights movement. New York: Three Rivers Press.

Tierney, K. J., W. J. Petak, and H. Hahn. 1988. *Disabled persons and earthquake hazards.* Boulder, CO: Institute of Behavioral Science, University of Colorado.

Tokesky, G., and M. Weston. 2006. Impacts and contributions of older persons in emergency situations: A case study of Hurricane Katrina in the United States of America. Unpublished report. Geneva: World Health Organization.

U.S. Census Bureau, Disability Status and the Characteristics of People in Group Quarters: A Brief Analysis of Disability Prevalence Among the Civilian Noninstitutionalized and Total Populations in the American Community Survey, http:/www.census.gov/hhes/www/disability/GQdisaility.pdf (accessed July 22, 2008).

U.S. Census Bureau. http://www.census.gov/ (accessed May 27, 2008).

U.S. Department of Homeland Security (DHS). 2006a. *About the Interagency Coordinating Council, Emergency Preparedness Now.* Issue 2: Spring. http://www.disabilitypreparedness.gov/news/spring2006/about.htm (accessed February 25, 2008).

U.S. Department of Homeland Security (DHS). 2006b. *Nationwide plan review: Phase two report.* June 16. Washington, DC: DHS.

U.S. Department of Homeland Security (DHS). n.d. *National response framework: Glossary/acronyms.* http://www.fema.gov/emergency/nrf/glossary.htm (accessed on May 27, 2008).

U.S. Department of Justice (DOJ). 2007. Seventh installment of the toolkit. *ADA Best Practices Toolkit for State and Local Governments.* http://www.ada.gov/pcatoolkit/toolkitmain.htm (accessed February 26, 2008).

U.S. Equal Employment Opportunity Commission. 2008. *Veterans with service-connected disabilities in the workplace and the Americans with Disabilities Act (ADA).* http://www.eeoc.gov/facts/veterans-disabilities.html (accessed July 22, 2008).

U.S. Government Accountability Office (GAO). 2006. *Disaster preparedness: Preliminary observations on the evacuation of hospitals and nursing homes due to hurricanes.* http://www.gao.gov/new.items/d06443r.pdf (accessed March 3, 2008).

U.S. Government Accountability Office (GA0). 2008. *National disaster response: FEMA should take action to improve capacity and coordination between government and voluntary sectors.* GAO Highlights. www.gao.gov/highlights/d08369high.pdf (accessed March 15, 2008).

The Washington Post, Kaiser Family Foundation, and Harvard University. 2005. Survey of Hurricane Katrina evacuees. www.kff.org/newsmedia/upload/7401.pdf (accessed March 2, 2008).

Weston, M., Tokesky, G. 2006. *Impacts and Contributions of Older Persons in emergency situations: A Case Study of Hurricane Katrina in the United States of America.*

White, G. W., M. H. Fox, C. Rooney, and J. Rowland. 2007. Final report findings of Nobody Left Behind: Preparedness for Persons with Mobility Impairments research project. Lawrence, KS: Research and Training Center on Independent Living. http://www.nobodyleftbehind2.org/~rrtcpbs/findings/ (accessed March 15, 2008).

RESOURCES

- The Access Center, a nonprofit service organization, also provides general advocacy information and a full list of myths that can be used for educational purposes. http://www.acils.com/index.html.
- The Community Emergency Preparedness Information Network (CEPIN) offers a course called Emergency Responders and the Deaf and Hard of Hearing Community: Taking the First Steps to Disaster Preparedness to provide deaf and hard of hearing individuals and emergency responders with the skills needed to prepare for, respond to, and recover from emergency situations involving people with hearing loss For more information visit http://www.cepintdi.org/default.aspx?pageid=41.
- The Communication Picture Board was designed to help bridge the communication gap between emergency first responders and people who are deaf. The picture board is proven to also effectively enhance the communications needs between first responders and non-English speaking populations, children, people with developmental disabilities, as well as those impacted by a traumatic event. These boards are helpful in a variety of settings: in the field, on an ambulance, in a shelter, at an assistance center, etc. Found at http://www.eadassociates.com/products.html#cpb
- Deaf and Hard of Hearing Consumer Advocacy Network and Northern Virginia Resource Center for Deaf and Hard of Hearing Persons, Emergency Preparedness and Emergency Communication Access: Lessons Learned Since 9/11 and Recommendation December 2004. Found at http://tap.gallaudet.edu/emergency/nov05conference/EmergencyReports/DHHCANEmergencyReport.pdf.
- EAD & Associates, LLC Readiness Wheels designed to help seniors and people with disabilities get better prepared for all kinds of disasters. The two-sided emergency preparedness wheels are sturdy, easy-to-use, and magnetized. They provide guidance on getting prepared and how to respond when a disaster occurs. Found at http://www.eadassociates.com/products.html#wheels.
- FEMA's Emergency Management Institute offers G197 and IS197, Emergency Planning and Special Needs Populations. This is a two and a half day course geared toward emergency planners and service providers and outlines key concepts and strategies for incorporating special needs populations issues into emergency plans. For more information, visit http://training.fema.gov/. There are a limited number of people qualified to present this course for certification credit, so contact your State Emergency Management Office or the EMI course manager about bringing the course to your area.
- Job Accommodation Network (JAN) is a service of the Office of Disability Employment Policy (ODEP) of the U.S. Department of Labor. It is a free consulting service designed to increase the employability of people with disabilities by providing individualized worksite accommodations solutions, providing technical assistance regarding the ADA and other disability related legislation, and educating callers about self-employment options. Found at http://www.jan.wvu.edu/.
- The National Organization on Disability Emergency Preparedness Initiative's Guide on the Special Needs of People with Disabilities for Emergency Managers, Planners, and Responders. This pamphlet can be found at http://www.nod.org/index.cfm?fuseaction=Feature.showFeature&FeatureID=1034.

- National Fire Protection Association (NFPA) is the world's leading advocate of fire prevention and an authoritative source on public safety. NFPA develops, publishes, and disseminates more than 300 consensus codes and standards intended to minimize the possibility and effects of fire and other risks. General Web site found at http://www.nfpa.org/index.asp?cookie%5Ftest=1. In addition, the NFPA has a newsletter, e-Access, designed to help reduce the worldwide burden of fire and other hazards on the quality of life for people with disabilities, which can be found at http://ebm.e.nfpa.org/r/regf2?aid=272412627&n=300&a=0.
- Nobody Left Behind Materials: Disaster Preparedness for People with Mobility Disabilities provides in depth research, information, and resources designed for both consumers and emergency planners http://www.nobodyleftbehind2.org/.
- Oklahoma Assistive Technologies http://www.ok.gov/abletech/ provides a variety of services and resources to people with disabilities and their advocates, caregivers and service providers and has emerged as a leader in offering disability information for first responders. Many states provide similar services as well.
- Oklahoma WARN: http://www.ok.gov/OEM/OK-WARN/index.html. OK Warn is a system that offers a variety of messaging options to deliver warnings to people that are deaf or hard of hearing.
- Project Safe EV-AC provides research and information on evacuation of people with disabilities during emergencies. http://evac.icdi.wvu.edu/.
- USFA Citizen Preparedness: http://www.usfa.dhs.gov/citizens/index.shtm.

9 Health

Deborah S. K. Thomas, Elizabeth A. Davis, and Alan Clive

CONTENTS

9.1 CHAPTER PURPOSE

As a fundamental human right, a healthy quality of life translates to safety and well-being throughout the disaster life cycle. In this chapter, health is treated as a broad concept that extends far beyond the existence of disease and considers its implications for emergency management. In one respect, health is a condition that is superimposed upon other characteristics, such as gender, age, race, or class, but it is also an indicator of vulnerability. Additionally, health status is also linked to the health care and public health systems, both of which also act as critical infrastructure and are directly relevant to a discussion of vulnerability. This chapter explores these relationships to further an understanding of the health aspects of vulnerability.

9.2   OBJECTIVES

As a result of reading this chapter, the reader should be able to:

1. Understand and identify issues specific to health related to vulnerability.
2. Define terms used by the health community and understand the relevance of those definitions in the context of emergency management and disasters.
3. Critically assess traditional emergency management approaches to addressing health.
4. Understand health as a factor of resiliency.
5. Describe strategies for integrating health concerns throughout all phases of emergency management.
6. Discuss ways to conduct community outreach with health stakeholders.

9.3   INTRODUCTION

Health as a condition is yet another factor contributing to and illuminating social vulnerability, both prior to and after an event. Health status reveals much about susceptible populations, as well as potential special-needs groups. Unlike many of the other characteristics discussed so far, however, it also has other dimensions that directly affect keeping people safe and increasing resilience. Disease can increase vulnerability, but as an agent can also act as an event causing an outbreak of a deadly infection (a public health emergency). Additionally, the heath care and public health systems are critical infrastructures, the viability of which directly increases or decreases people's vulnerability. As a consequence, this chapter will address a slightly broader set of issues than other topical chapters, still following the same overall format. After setting the context, the discussion will turn to health across the disaster cycle, followed by some ideas for strategies and solutions for increasing capacity and resilience.

9.4   DEFINITIONS AND CONCEPTS

Health is perhaps not as easy to define as one might at first assume. Consider for a moment how people would answer if asked whether they felt healthy and what it means to be healthy. Some people might respond that they are a little sick with a cold or even are extremely tired. Others might say they feel healthy even though they have a chronic illness, such as high blood pressure, arthritis, asthma, or diabetes. Still others might mention happiness. The wide range of potential interpretations captures the many facets of health and the challenges for assigning strict meaning related only to disease.

The World Health Organization's (WHO) definition adopted in 1948 stands as a comprehensive and accepted definition: "Health is a state of complete physical, mental and social well-being and not merely the absence of disease or infirmity" (WHO 1948). This encompasses many aspects of health in addition to sickness, illness, or injury and embodies a broad set of considerations, implying that treatment of the individual alone is not the only solution to achieve healthy people and communities. Yet, even until the late 1970s, the western paradigm emphasized the absence of disease and injury, a perspective that in some regards persists today when the focus does not extend beyond personal, clinical, or medical treatment.

Boorse (1977) argues that defining health by the absence of disease is particularly problematic because definitions of disease can be expanded almost infinitely so that everyone would really have some deficiency. Further, everyone will have some form of illness, probably numerous times, throughout a lifetime. However, this does not necessarily translate to a disability or even limited functionality. Having the common cold each year, or even multiple times a year, would not be considered a chronic illness, but certainly translates to a person being unhealthy for that period of time and possibly (or not) missing work or school and potentially requiring some medications. In other words, health as a condition encompasses both acute (rapid onset and progression) and chronic illness (persists for a long period of time and may have continued progression), as well as daily conditions of well-being. As a consequence, it is challenging to discern when everyday experiences transform from healthy to unhealthy.

In addition to taking an unnecessarily narrow view of absence of disease to mean health, its assessment based on averages or norms can be equally as limiting. Society determines what is normal, both cognitively and physically. As such, healthy versus unhealthy is commonly delineated by an average of occurrence or a judgment of what is functionally normal in a given setting or by a particular group (see Chapter 8 on disabilities, which emphasizes functional approach). While it is important to have culturally specific definitions of health, just because a certain condition is pervasive and common, does not mean that health should be measured from the statistical average. Janzen uses the example of malnutrition to illustrate this point: "If a society has widespread malnutrition the statistical norm for height and weight might not be healthy if a cross-society measure or norm is used" (2002, 69). Having said this, utilizing statistical measures with consideration for contextual issues is incredibly useful for evaluating and understanding health (see Section 9.5, which uses some measures to illustrate health status, especially as it relates to vulnerability).

In 1978, the WHO reaffirmed the 1948 broad definition of health in the Alma Ata Declaration, which extended health as a "fundamental human right" that is "a most important worldwide social goal whose realization requires the action of many other social and economic sectors in addition to the health sector" (WHO 1978, Article 1). Thus, health relates directly to a certain quality of life and a standard of living, not only to an individual's disease and injury characteristics or to biological considerations. While some argue this definition is too broad, it does capture vital aspects for appreciating how we come to understand health and health outcomes.

Not all health status is attributable to our genetic makeup, our individual characteristics, or even behavior; evidence and research increasingly point to social contributors and conditions as well. In other words, our health is a function of our individual traits along with the types of places and conditions in which we live, as well as our standing in society. In short, genetics and individual characteristics alone do not determine the likelihood of developing a particular disease; many contextual variables directly affect the level of health as well. For example, non-health infrastructure, such as transportation or garbage collection common in many communities across the United States, keeps people healthy. As an illustration, in most parts of the United States people can drink clean tap water delivered directly to homes, and sewage systems minimize human contact with wastewater. These basic services are not necessarily considered part of the health infrastructure, rather the urban infrastructure, yet they save thousands of lives and reduce illness significantly by decreasing the spread of disease that would otherwise occur through contaminated water supplies. In fact, health "is maintained by a cushion of adequate nutrition, social support, water supply, housing, sanitation, and continued collective defense against contagious and degenerative disease" (Feierman and Janzen 1992, xvii).

These relationships are captured by the ecological model of health, which acknowledges and incorporates the many dimensions, interrelationships, and influences that contribute to health, and health professionals, particularly in public health, require a fundamental understanding of this approach (Gebbie, Rosenstock, and Hernandez 2003). Biological risk factors, including the biology of disease and individual traits, are embedded within broader environmental, social, and behavioral factors and influences. In other words, we exist within a series of social, political, and economic networks and systems, all of which contribute to our well-being and health. Further, health requires treatment of individual conditions, but also attention to population and community health, as well as the social, economic, and political structures that directly affect health. According to Janzen (2002), understanding health should "include alongside the factors in the ecology of health the impact of household budget priorities, larger economic factors, and above all social and political institutions and forces" (2002, 80). While genetics, our immediate environment, and individual behavior and characteristics certainly contribute to our health status, social conditions and structural considerations also come to bear on how healthy we are (see Chapter 2 for a discussion of structure and agency).

9.5 DEMOGRAPHIC OVERVIEW

A brief review of some statistics begins to illuminate how health is a condition that should be considered in emergency management, as well as how disease can act as a disaster. Importantly, disease burdens are not the same among all groups of people or across social, economic, and environmental conditions, revealing disparity that is not only linked to biology or risk, but also a reflection of quality of life considerations linked to differential health and vulnerability status. Examining the leading causes of mortality worldwide provides a backdrop to delve into further detail about the United States and considerations about the quality and meaning of the data.

Globally, a distinct difference exists in the leading causes of death between high-income and low-income countries (Table 9.1). Overall, many more people die from infectious diseases and at younger ages in low-income counties. Surprising to some, the burden of chronic disease in low-income countries is also quite high with heart disease and stroke taking millions of lives. High-income countries, on the other hand, experience mortality primarily from chronic diseases and populations are often aging. While it is true that everyone will die of something, the stark differences in causes of death do speak to the realities of life in these places. Taking one example from the list to illustrate, according to the World Health Organization (2006), diarrhea kills more than 1.9 million children a year mostly from resulting dehydration. This is highly treatable with oral rehydration salts for a cost of only about 10 cents, and so while more than a million children are saved each year and programs are expanding, millions are still dying, mostly in low-income countries. An inexpensive treatment exists; thus, the reason millions still die cannot be attributed to that. Instead, the challenges revolve around availability, access, awareness and education, distribution, and acceptability, all of which are embedded in cultural and social systems as linked to health.

In the United States the leading causes of mortality are similar to high-income countries with some notable differences, partly due to consolidating all types of cancer into a single category (Table 9.2). However, a significant number of deaths are attributable to accidents, more aligned with the low-income countries. Importantly, the causes of death are not quite the same for all segments of the population. The numbers are presented by gender and for whites and blacks to illustrate the point that overall numbers can mask the experiences of subpopulations. The map of longevity across the United States also reveals stark regional variation (Figure 9.1) with shorter life expectancies for men and women in the Southeast and generally longer life expectancies in the West, upper Midwest, and Northeast. This varies for men and women, particularly in how long these groups will generally

TABLE 9.1
Worldwide Leading Causes of Mortality

Ranking	Low-Income Countries	High-Income Countries
1	Lower respiratory infections (2.94)	Coronary heart disease (1.33)
2	Coronary heart disease (2.47)	Stroke and other cerebrovascular diseases (0.76)
3	Perinatal conditions (2.40)	Trachea, bronchus, lung cancers (0.48)
4	Diarrheal diseases (1.81)	Lower respiratory infections (0.31)
5	HIV/AIDS (1.51)	Chronic obstructive pulmonary disease (0.29)
6	Stroke and other cerebrovascular diseases (1.48)	Alzheimer's and other dementias (0.28)
7	Chronic obstructive pulmonary disease (0.94)	Colon and rectum cancers (0.27)
8	Tuberculosis (0.91)	Diabetes mellitus (0.22)
9	Malaria (0.86)	Breast cancer (0.16)
10	Road traffic accidents (0.48)	Stomach cancer (0.14)

Source: WHO (World Health Organization). 2008. Fact sheet no. 310: Top 10 causes of death. http://www.who.int/mediacentre/factsheets/fs310/en/index.html (accessed October 31, 2008).

Note: The number in parentheses is the number of deaths in millions.

TABLE 9.2
CDC Leading Causes of Death, 2005

Cause of Death	All	Male	Female	White	Black
Diseases of heart	1 (26.6%)	1 (26.7%)	1 (26.5%)	1 (26.9%)	1 (25.3%)
Malignant neoplasms (cancer)	2 (22.8%)	2 (24.0%)	2 (21.7%)	2 (23.0%)	2 (21.6%)
Cerebrovascular diseases (stroke)	3 (5.9%)	5 (4.7%)	3 (7.0%)	3 (5.8%)	3 (6.0%)
Chronic lower respiratory diseases	4 (5.3%)	4 (5.3%)	4 (5.5%)	4 (5.8%)	7 (2.8%)
Accidents (unintentional injuries)	5 (5.3%)	3 (6.3%)	6 (3.3%)	5 (4.8%)	4 (4.7%)
Diabetes mellitus	6 (3.1%)	6 (3.0%)	7 (3.1%)	7 (2.8%)	5 (4.4%)
Alzheimer's disease	7 (2.9%)	10 (1.7%)	5 (4.1%)	6 (3.2%)	—
Influenza and pneumonia	8 (2.6%)	7 (2.3%)	8 (2.8%)	8 (2.6%)	—
Nephritis, nephrotic syndrome and nephrosis (kidney disease)	9 (1.8%)	9 (1.8%)	9 (1.8%)	9 (1.7%)	8 (2.8%)
Septicemia (blood poisoning)	10 (1.4%)	—	10 (1.5%)	—	10 (2.1%)
Intentional self-harm (suicide)	—	8 (2.1%)	—	10 (1.4%)	—
Assault (homicide)	—	—	—	—	6 (3.0%)
Human immunodeficiency virus (HIV) disease	—	—	—	—	9 (2.4%)

Source: Centers for Disease Control, National Center for Health Statistics, National Vital Statistics System. 2008. Deaths: Preliminary Data for 2005, Table B. http://www.cdc.gov/nchs/products/pubs/pubd/hestats/prelimdeaths05/prelim-deaths05.htm (accessed November 1, 2008).

Note: Percentages represent total deaths in that group due to the cause indicated.

live with a difference of about 12 years between the shortest life expectancy for men in Mississippi (70.4 years of age) and the longest for women in Hawaii (82.5 years of age). Biology certainly plays a role, but the regional patterns would indicate other factors of importance.

Focusing on the direct impacts of disasters as a cause of death also highlights variation in vulnerability. Stark regional patterns exist globally (Figure 9.2). Capturing a global pattern of vulnerability, the OFDA/CRED International Database compiles current and historical information on disaster impacts around the world based on a standardized data collection methodology (EM-DAT 2008). Importantly, these only represent relatively large events that kill more than 10 people, affect 100 people, require a declaration of a state of emergency, or call for international assistance. As such, this is not a complete depiction and is further limited because no details by gender, age, or minority status about the types of people affected are compiled, mostly because this information is not commonly reported. Still, general trends can be detected, giving some insights into vulnerability and establishing further questions for investigation.

From 1975–2007, earthquakes killed the most people (847,276), followed by drought (677,613), storms (310,341) and floods (204,706), and then epidemics (187,068). Asia and Africa have the highest numbers of deaths from natural disasters regionally, but the types of events are different. Focusing on the countries in the highest two categories, China, Indonesia (the 2000 tsunami), and Iran experience significant fatalities from earthquakes, with flooding also of importance in China. By contrast, in Sudan and Ethiopia in Africa, deaths stem from drought and epidemics. Indian disaster fatalities result from earthquakes and flooding, while in Bangladesh most people perish from storms (typhoons) and flooding, as well as epidemics. Overall, lower-income countries have much higher death rates than higher-income countries. Of the more than two million people who died from disasters during this period as recorded in the Emergency Events Database (EM-DAT), only 12,731 occurred in the United States, a figure in alignment with other high-income countries.

A different database allows a more detailed picture of hazard fatalities at the sub-national level for the United States (Figure 9.3). The Spatial Hazard Events and Losses Database for the United

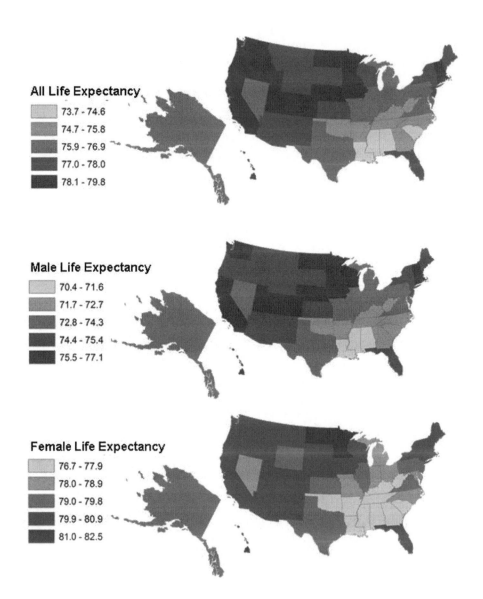

FIGURE 9.1   U.S. life expectancy, 2000. *Data source*: U.S. Census Bureau. Average life expectancy at birth by state for 2000. http://www.census.gov/population/projections/MethTab2.xls (accessed October 1, 2008). Map created by Deborah Thomas, with permission.

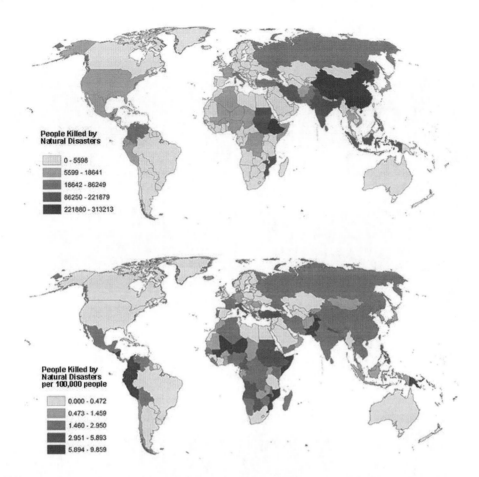

FIGURE 9.2 Worldwide disaster fatalities, 1975-2007. *Data source*: EM-DAT: The OFDA/CRED International Disaster Database – www.emdat.net – Université Catholique de Louvain – Brussels – Belgium. (accessed November 1, 2008). Map created by Deborah Thomas, with permission.

States (SHELDUS) contains information on 18 different types of natural hazards that caused more than $50,000 in property or crop loss or at least one death (Hazards and Vulnerability Research Institute 2008). Not surprisingly, deaths and injuries are not uniformly distributed, either regionally or by hazard type.

In terms of raw numbers, casualties are concentrated the South/Southeast, the Great Lakes, and California. When taken as a proportion of the population, the pattern shifts to the Midwest and Intermountain West, for deaths and injury rates are even further concentrated in the deep western Gulf States and along the Mississippi River Valley. When fatalities are viewed by county rates, rather than state, the distribution is somewhat more disperse, but still concentrated in the lower Mississippi River valley, the Great Plains, and the Intermountain West. Interestingly, tornadoes/wind, flooding, heat, and winter weather caused the most fatalities, distinctive from the international experience. One might assume the variation exists because particular hazards occur less frequently. However, the United States does not necessarily experience fewer hazard types or events per area, but rather the interaction of social vulnerability with hazards is different. For example, in the case of earthquakes, California did experience major events in populated areas in Loma Prieta in 1989 and again in Northridge in 1994, neither of which resulted in substantial deaths. Consequently, evidence again points to social vulnerability as the explanation for the disparity. This overview highlights some key issues around health and vulnerability, illustrating how they are intrinsically linked, both in terms of the direct effects on people's lives and the association between

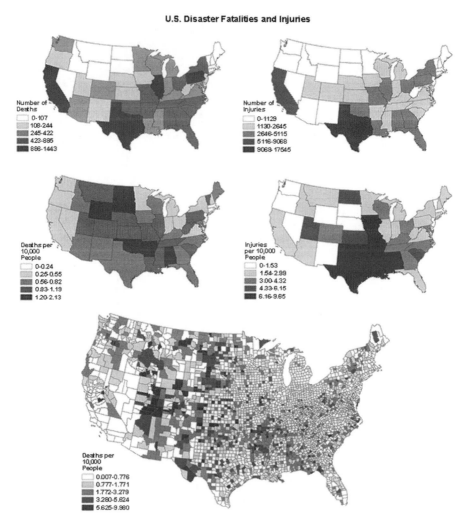

FIGURE 9.3   U.S. hazard fatalities, 1975-2007. *Data source*: Hazards and Vulnerability Research Institute. The spatial hazard events and losses database for the United States, version 6.2 [Online Database]. Columbia, SC: University of South Carolina, 2008. http://www.sheldus.org (accessed October 1, 2008). Map created by Deborah Thomas, with permission.

disparities in health outcomes and vulnerability. Additionally, while these data can suggest patterns and relationships, the importance of delving further into aggregate numbers is clearly illustrated; a pattern at the global level may or may not persist at finer scales or overall rates may not be applicable to subgroups or equivalent among groups. Monitoring and assessing health and vulnerability require standardized data collection in disaggregate form, but information is not always collected, recorded, and/or broken down by various groups. This brief review demonstrates the relevance and necessity of health into the emergency management planning and response process.

9.6   RELEVANCE

The discussion around health likely resonates with the constructs of social vulnerability presented in previous chapters, particularly Chapters 1 and 2. A stream of research in health, in fact, parallels that of vulnerability science, and is concerned with quite similar factors in the exploration

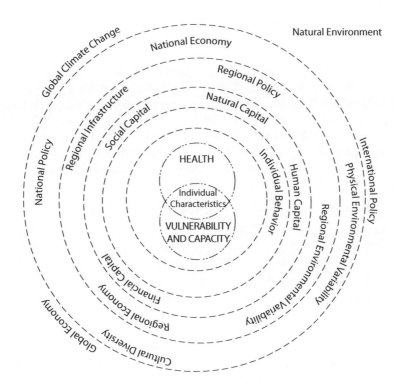

FIGURE 9.4 Model of Factors Contributing to Vulnerability and Health. *Source*: Thomas, D., J. Scandlyn, J. Brett, C. Simon, and K. Oviatt, with permission.

of the determinants of health, those underlying characteristics, circumstances, and situations that contribute to health outcomes (Lindsay 2003). Social determinants of health broadly include social, economic, and environmental conditions affecting health. Evidence points to a wide range of community characteristics that directly link to health status, such as the configuration of the built environment, access to quality and appropriate health care services, quality of transportation systems, accessibility to quality food sources, economic opportunities, environmental quality, among nearly every other condition that would translate to a quality of life (Berkman and Kawachi 2000).

Figure 9.4 illustrates the interplay between contextual factors and the individual that affect vulnerability as associated with disasters, as well as health status. Individual traits and characteristics contribute to health status and vulnerability, as does the capital (presented in Chapters 2 and 3) that supports and influences a person. In this way, a person who has individual characteristics that might suggest high vulnerability or poor health status may actually have access to resources and infrastructure that could improve overall level of health and increase resilience. Additionally, this model recognizes structural influences that exist at larger scales, often beyond an individual's control (see discussion of agency and structure in Chapter 2), but which affect one's circumstances. Health and vulnerability do not result from one single aspect of these interrelationships, but rather interactions among them at and between scales.

In essence, this all means that the social, economic, and environmental circumstances of a place have direct and indirect effects on individual and community health (Brennan Ramirez, Baker, and Metzler 2008). By extension, because these conditions vary significantly, they likely play a part explaining observed differences in health outcomes across various populations and places (Braveman and Gruskin 2003). Even though significant numbers of studies have started to establish the multi-level influences on health, these linkages and influences are not always well understood, requiring additional inquiry into these relationships.

Like vulnerability expressing itself differentially throughout subpopulations and, as a consequence, hazards impacting various groups disproportionately, the existence of health disparities is also well established (Ver Ploeg and Perrin 2004). Health disparity, or health inequity, is revealed through varying health status based on race and ethnicity, income status, gender, or age (Carter-Pokras and Baquet 2002). Unfortunately, as with data challenges for the examination of disaggregate effects and outcomes from disaster impacts, data limitations also exist in health records and surveillance systems for fully documenting and assessing inequities about health status and outcomes (Ver Ploeg and Perrin 2004). In order to reduce these, a research agenda must be established around detecting, understanding, and reducing disparities (Kilbourne et al. 2006), an approach also necessary for decreasing social vulnerability and increasing resilience as well.

9.7 VULNERABILITY ACROSS THE DISASTER LIFE CYCLE

Health and vulnerability are integrally related on many levels, including similarities in streams of research into underlying factors, disparities that exist between groups creating differential experiences, and the link between agency and structure. Keeping people healthy and safe during and after an event is crucial, which requires planning in advance and considering the current state of health. In addition, health itself can be the source of a disaster, such as a disease outbreak or through bioterrorism. Understanding and addressing the interrelationships between health and vulnerability is vital for emergency management. This part of the chapter directly addresses emerging issues related to health across the disaster life cycle, reviewing the following areas: (1) health as a reflection of vulnerability, (2) current challenges with health in the United States, (3) the integration of public health and health care sectors with emergency management, (4) health impacted by disasters and considerations for evacuation, warning, and response, (5) health as part of the recovery process.

9.7.1 Health as a Reflection of Vulnerability

Those characteristics and factors that create differential exposure to and experiences with hazards are often the very same as those identified in considering social determinants of health and health disparities. As a consequence, not only is health an overlay with other characteristics, such as gender, age, or income status, that must be considered for disaster planning, it is also a reflection of underlying factors that contribute to vulnerability. A portion of an assessment conducted in 2006 of patient needs and gaps in service for Salud Family Health Centers (Salud) illustrates this association (de Jesus Diaz-Perez, Thomas, and Farley 2007).

Salud is a federally qualified community and migrant health center system providing services in six counties in northeastern Colorado to indigent, uninsured, underinsured, migrant, and seasonal farm-worker populations. Part of the evaluation involved developing a description of health care need in the region based on a set of variables and approach defined by previous research (Wang and Luo 2005; Luo and Wang 2003). While this study is embedded within an evaluation of various aspects of health care access, the purpose here is to illustrate similarities between defining health care need and understanding vulnerability (see Chapter 14 for a more detailed discussion of vulnerability assessment).

To define populations with higher needs, data from the U.S. Census were compiled based on broad categories (Table 9.3), which were then statistically analyzed using a factor analysis, which combines data and condenses variables into similar groupings. The analysis condensed 13 variables into three broad categories, including socio-cultural barriers, socioeconomic disadvantages, and isolation (Figure 9.5). From these, a composite score was calculated to determine health care need based on output from the statistical analysis; a block group with no scores (factor loadings) for the three broad categories in the upper quartile was considered low need and block groups were defined as high if at least one score was in the upper quartile and none were in the lowest. The composite

TABLE 9.3
Data Included in the Analysis of Health Care Need

Category	Variable from 2000 U.S. Census at Block Group Level
Groups in high need of services	Seniors
	Children
	Women of reproductive age
Socioeconomic status	Poverty
	Female-headed households
	Home ownership
	Median income
Indicators of deprived environment	Households with more than one occupant per room
	Housing without basic amenities
Indicators of cultural and linguistic barriers and awareness	Population without high school diploma
	Linguistically isolated households
	Non-white minorities
Transportation mobility	Household without vehicles

Source: de Jesus Diaz-Perez, M., D. Thomas, and T. Farley. Assessing the gaps in service for a community health center system. 2007 Annual Meeting of the Association of American Geographers, San Francisco, California Online Program. http://communicate.aag.org/eseries/aag_org/program/AbstractDetail. cfm?AbstractID=13398 (accessed October 10, 2008).

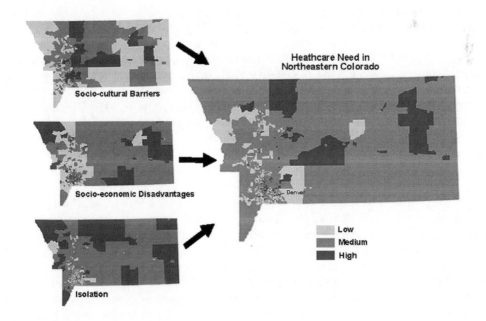

FIGURE 9.5   Health need in Northeastern Colorado. *Source*: de Jesus Diaz-Perez, M., D. Thomas, and T. Farley. *Assessing gaps in service for a community health center system.* 2007 Annual Meeting of the Association of American Geographers, San Francisco, California Online Program. http://communicate.aag. org/eseries/aag_org/program/AbstractDetail.cfm?AbstractID=13398 (accessed October 10, 2008).

map displays areas with an aggregate of conditions and characteristics, converging to reveal health need. The results can then inform health policy and even aid in locating additional health services.

Because the variables included in this analysis are quite similar to indicators of vulnerability, the results could equally highlight potential areas of concern to emergency management. Further, this also points to the necessity for utilizing health data to support public health and health care preparedness, response, and recovery (see Section 9.7.3 for discussion of these sectors), explicitly planning for those with existing conditions. For example, Holt et al. (2008) illustrate the use of the Centers for Disease Control and Prevention's (CDC's) Behavioral Risk Factor Surveillance System (BRFSS) to assess health status along with the American Hospital Association Annual Survey Database to establish health care resources in a geographic information systems environment for response planning (GIS; see Section 14.8 for a brief review of these technologies for vulnerability assessment). Established in 1984, the BRFSS is "a state-based system of health surveys that collects information on health risk behaviors, preventive health practices, and health care access primarily related to chronic disease and injury" (CDC 2008a), which can provide insights into community health not otherwise available. Thus, these data and the approach can aid in incorporating health concerns into emergency management and public health preparedness.

In essence, conducting vulnerability assessments that incorporate aspects of health during disaster planning enables effective public health and health care response, as well as ensuring that health is directly addressed in a systematic and meaningful way during recovery. In this way, baseline information is available for disaster planning and can then be monitored over time.

9.7.2 THE STATE OF HEALTH CARE IN THE UNITED STATES UNDERLYING DISASTER PLANNING

The previous section also alludes to several other relevant heath issues that directly affect vulnerability, including both access to health care and then by extension the complexity of the systems that address health in the United States. Access is a function of availability, both in terms of types of services and openings, in a reasonable proximity with appropriate transportation, as well as economically obtainable, either through payment or insurance. Unfortunately, both aspects pose challenges for many people in the United States. Figure 9.6 represents medically underserved areas and populations across the United States, which is a designation derived from a composite score ratio of primary medical care physicians per 1000 population, infant mortality rate, percentage of the population with incomes below the poverty level, and percentage of the population age 65 or over (HHS 2008b).

According to the CDC (2008b), 16.4% of people under the age of 65 (43 million) and 8.9% of children under 18 years of age were uninsured in 2007. The good news is that the number and percentage of uninsured children declined from 1996 to 2006, probably mostly from an increase in the numbers and percentages covered by public health insurance, which increased to 27.4% (Chu and Rhoades 2008). Health coverage is available through Medicaid for qualified low-income individuals and families through state administered programs, and Medicare health insurance is provided for people 65 years of age and older, people under 65 with certain disabilities, and all people with permanent kidney failure (CDC 2008c). Additionally, the federal government provides health services to higher need populations through the Community Health Centers program (Salud in the previous discussion is one of these), which supplied primary care to over 16 million individuals nationally each year (HHS 2008c). Universal health insurance does not exist in the United States and the mechanisms for gaining coverage are disparate.

The health care system is a complex configuration dominated by private insurance with additional care provided by nonprofit organizations, private and public health providers, and public health agencies. Additionally, advocacy groups also play a role. Hospitals, clinics, pharmacies, nursing homes, primary care physicians, specialty doctors, nursing, physical therapy, mental health services, ambulance response, fire and police, community organizations, among many others are components of the health system, one that has several exemplary elements to it, but also is not

FIGURE 9.6 Medically underserved areas and populations across the United States. *Source*: Generated on the Health Resources and Services Administration (HRSA) Web site (http://datawarehouse.hrsa.gov/)

equally accessible to all because of limited availability in many places and high cost. While the debates persist as to the cause and mechanisms for correcting it, there is little doubt that a health care crisis exists in the United States, where the U.S. infant mortality rate ranks 29th internationally (CDC 2008d) and the per capita expenditure in 2006 was $7,026 per person or 16% of the U.S. gross domestic product, more than any other nation (HHS 2008a).

This discussion of the health system and accessibility issues points to three major challenges for incorporating health into emergency management: (1) people without access prior to a disaster will not have improved opportunities for addressing health issues after an event; (2) a health care system in crisis will not perform better in the face of a disaster, which has many implications for disaster planning and response; and (3) the health care and public health systems are intricate and multifaceted, making linkages to emergency management necessary, while sometimes tricky.

9.7.3 INTEGRATION OF HEALTH CARE, PUBLIC HEALTH, AND EMERGENCY MANAGEMENT SYSTEMS

Health is an intricate arrangement of individual, community, and structural considerations. As a consequence, improving health ultimately requires a systems and policy approach, not just individual level interventions and treatment. Not surprisingly, multiple approaches exist for addressing health needs and improving health status. These models, as they relate to segments of the health system, also perform associated functions in U.S. disaster/emergency response and management systems.

Health care/medicine and public health differ in focus and approach, although they are clearly interrelated and inform one another. A medical model (reviewed in Chapter 8 with regard to disabilities) drives health care, which emphasizes the treatment of individuals for particular diseases, conditions, and/or injuries. In this way, a person is diagnosed and then appropriate treatment administered at an individual level. The ecological model of health (described in Section 9.4) guides public health, which focuses on populations (rather than individuals) drawing from multiple social science and natural science disciplines with prevention, rather than treatment, as an overarching goal. It consists of the established core areas of "epidemiology, biostatistics, environmental health, health services administration, and social and behavioral science, but … it also encompass eight critical new areas: informatics, genomics, communication, cultural competence, community-based participatory research, policy and law, global health, and ethics" (Gebbie, Rosenstock, and Hernandez 2005, 1). Major priorities include (1) prevention of epidemics, spread of disease, and injury; (2) protection against environmental hazards; (3) promotion of healthy behaviors; (4) responding to disasters and assisting communities in recovery; and (5) assuring the quality and accessibility of health services (Public Health Functions Steering Committee 1994).

Even though both approaches are concerned with improving health, divisions are not necessarily black and white (many studies, researchers, and practitioners bridging the two), and research from one area frequently informs the other, yet they are "distinct fields with separate infrastructures and financing mechanisms, unique perspectives, and a divergent, sometimes, tumultuous history" (Salinsky 2002, 3). Then, adding emergency management to the equation with a different history, emphasis, and approach, one that has tended to be top down, requires significant organizational and inter-agency planning and coordination. In fact, while medicine and public health have clearly interfaced with disasters for a long time, it has not been until recently that research and practice in these fields have become integrated into multidisciplinary disaster management and response (Shoaf and Rottman 2000). Just to illustrate this point, the American Academy of Disaster Medicine (AADM) was only organized in 2006 to promote education in disaster medicine and provide a mechanism for assessing physician qualifications in this area (American Academy of Disaster Medicine 2008), and the CDC's Centers for Public Health Preparedness (CPHP) program only came online in 2000 to "strengthen terrorism and emergency preparedness by linking academic expertise to state and local health agency needs" (CDC 2008e). Perhaps because of this recent coupling and the difference in historical development and frame of reference, improved integration of public health and emergency management remains a priority (Hooke and Rogers 2005).

9.7.3.1 Public Health and Medical Services Response System

The National Response Framework (NRF) identifies key principles, roles, and structures organizing the national response to all hazards, including natural and technological disasters, major transportation accidents, and acts of terrorism (U.S. Department of Homeland Security 2008). It is important to recognize that emergency response is a complex relationship of local, state, and federal agencies, with local jurisdiction retaining primary responsibility for response, the intricacies of which are not discussed here. Instead, the overview focuses on the relevance to health. The priorities for public health and medical services in the NRF include saving lives and protecting the health and safety of the public, respondents, and recovery workers, as well as protecting critical resources and facilitating the recovery of individuals, families, governments, and the environment (U.S. Department of Homeland Security 2008).

Emergency Support Function (ESF) #8 is specifically aimed at federal public health and medical services coordinated by the Department of Health and Human Services. These include

> behavioral health needs consisting of both mental health and substance abuse considerations for incident victims and response workers and, as appropriate, medical needs groups defined … as individuals in need of additional medical response assistance, and veterinary and/or animal health issues (U.S. Department of Homeland Security 2008).

In 2006, The Pandemic and All-Hazards Preparedness Act (PAHPA) was enacted into law to further define the role of public health and medical services. PAHPA's purpose is "to improve the Nation's public health and medical preparedness and response capabilities for emergencies, whether deliberate, accidental, or natural" and has attempted to streamline the federal public health response (U.S. Congressional Record 2006). The U.S. Department of Health and Human Services (HHS), under the Assistant Secretary for Preparedness and Response, is the lead agency and coordinates several national programs and efforts that support state and local efforts related health and disasters.

PAHPA addresses national surveillance methods and systems, surge capacity (personnel, facilities, and equipment), and vaccines.

In support of ESF #8, the National Disaster Medical System (NDMS) is in place to supplement medical response to a disaster and patient evacuation and includes Disaster Medical Assistance Teams (DMAT), Disaster Mortuary Operational Response Teams (DMORT), National Veterinary Response Team (NVRT), National Nurse Response Team (NNRT), National Pharmacy Response Teams (NPRTs), as well as Federal Coordinating Centers for recruitment and coordination of hospitals for receiving evacuated patients. All of these teams are comprised of people with expertise in defined specialty areas and are deployed in the event of a designated, declared disaster. Additionally, HHS oversees the Hospital Preparedness Program (HPP) as mandated by PAHPA, which focuses on the health care and hospital systems. Priority areas include interoperable communication systems, bed tracking, personnel management, fatality management planning, and hospital evacuation planning. Additionally, other activities involve bed and personnel surge capacity, decontamination capabilities, isolation capacity, pharmaceutical supplies, training, education, drills, and exercises.

Also a responsibility of HHS, the Healthcare and Public Health Sector-Specific Plan supplements the National Infrastructure Protection Plan for the protection of this critical infrastructure (HHS 2007a). The disruption of this sector has wide-ranging and extensive implications negatively affecting society and consequently requires particular attention for ensuring its function and operation. This document devises a plan for comprehensively identifying and prioritizing assets, risk, protective programs, and evaluation of these programs (HHS 2007a).

9.7.3.2 Public Health Functions

While medical care responsibilities predominantly revolve around primary care, emergency rooms, home care, acute and intensive care, and treatment, public health functions, while certainly interrelated, are somewhat distinct. According to Noji (2005), the role of public health in emergency response is

> to assess the needs of disaster-affected populations, match available resources to those needs, prevent further adverse health effects, implement disease control strategies for well-defined problems, evaluate the effectiveness of disaster relief programs, and improve contingency plans for various types of future disasters (2005, S29).

These are aligned with the public health core areas and functions presented previously. In essence, this corresponds to the following activities: disease surveillance, epidemiology, laboratory services, vaccination and vaccination programs, information sharing and communication, and environmental monitoring and remediation (HHS 2007b). Although somewhat oriented toward bioterrorism, the HHS's *Public Health Emergency Response: A Guide for Leaders and Responders* provides a detailed review of all of these activities (HHS 2007b). Without reviewing all of these, as it is somewhat beyond the scope of this chapter, some attention will be devoted to surveillance, environmental health, and communication (Section 9.8 addresses communication as a strategy for success).

One of the main roles that public health plays is disease surveillance, in other words, the collection and monitoring of health data (Gebbie, Rosenstock, and Hernandez 2003; PAHO 2000; Public Health Functions Steering Committee 1994). In this way, a disease outbreak can be detected and then investigated for confirmation, followed by containment activities. Or, surveillance systems can also be used to document, assess, and monitor the effects of a disaster event, including on chronic health conditions (not just acute occurrences) in order to formulate response activities and also for establishing long-term interventions or mitigation activities (Mokdad et al. 2005). Public health utilizes epidemiology, which is defined in simple terms by the National Cancer Institute (2008) as "the study of the patterns, causes, and control of disease in groups of people," to specific research design structures along with statistical analyses in order to understand the outbreak or the disaster impacts with some degree of confidence. Additionally and importantly, theories, models, and approaches from social and behavioral sciences are also utilized.

The association of emergency management, public health and environmental health, and safety may not at first blush be obvious, but in the most basic sense disasters are extreme environmental events (Logue 1996). Additionally, technological events have direct environmental health impacts and in the United Statets, the Environmental Protection Agency (EPA) is designated to prepare for and respond to oil, hazardous substance, pollutant, or contaminant emergencies, also working with other agencies within the context of a natural disaster. Natural events can cause contamination and affect water supply and waste disposal, solid waste handling, food handling, vector control, and/ or home sanitation (PAHO 2000). Additionally, occupational health and safety are also important aspects of environmental health and disasters, keeping workers safe. Hurricane Katrina demonstrates the connection; the environmental health impacts of Hurricane Katrina were far reaching, including unwatering, power, natural gas vector/rodent/animal control, underground storage tanks, food safety, drinking water, wastewater, road conditions, solid waste/debris, sediments/soil contamination (toxic chemicals), and housing (e.g., damage and mold) (CDC and EPA 2005). The EPA responded to chemical and oil spills, collected abandoned chemical containers, coordinated recycling of damaged appliances, and collected and recycled electronic waste (GAO 2007). In terms of environmental monitoring, the EPA also conducted air, water, sediment, and soil sampling; helped assess drinking water and wastewater infrastructures; and issued timely information to the public on a variety of environmental health risks. All of this points to the ways in which environmental health and disasters are intrinsically linked.

9.7.3.3 Considerations for Public Health Emergency Response

Because of the configuration of the public health system and the nature of dealing with health concerns, federalism, privacy, and fairness in allocating resources have implications for public health emergency response (Hodge, Gostin, and Vernick 2007). The previous discussion on the public health and medical services response system centered on national organization and coordination. However, much of public health practice (like emergency management) occurs at the state and local level, where funding and divisions of efforts among levels of government vary greatly (Hodge, Gostin, and Vernick 2007; Salinsky 2002). This has implications across the entire disaster life cycle in terms of quality, continuity, capabilities, and even resources. Ultimately, this translates to the need for significant interjurisdictional coordination, which is usually not easy. Additionally, high quality response and recovery are also linked to the strength of the public health infrastructure at the state and local level, a system that is understaffed and underfunded (Trust for America's Health 2008). Similar to the health care system generally, the public health system cannot realistically be expected to perform at a level higher than it exists at a baseline.

Another extremely sensitive topic of concern is information sharing. As required by the Health Insurance Portability and Accountability Act of 1996 (HIPAA), health care plans, clearinghouses, and providers must adhere to the Standards for Privacy of Individually Identifiable Health Information (the Privacy Rule; HHS 2002). Essentially this means that health information must be protected and treated as private unless an individual has consented to access, and information cannot be release or shared outside of the defined criteria and guidelines. In terms of disaster response, the guidance published by HHS (2005) with regard to Hurricane Katrina states that health care providers can share individual health information for treatment, notification as necessary, imminent danger to a person or the public, and release of information on whether a person is in a facility and general condition. Additionally, entities not covered by the Privacy Rule, such as the American Red Cross, can share patient information. So, for all intents and purposes, HIPAA does not really apply in the disaster context, but is not clearly defined, nor is there other legislation that covers this privacy protection (Hodge, Gostin, and Vernick 2007). The acquisition, analysis, and dissemination of public health information are extraordinarily necessary for quality public health preparedness and response, but privacy issues should be addressed.

In summary, emergency management and public health/medical systems must integrate and coordinate effectively in order to address both public health emergencies, as well as natural, technological, and human-induced events. National efforts offer a framework for defining roles and responsibilities, and both public health and medicine offer significant resources, foundations of knowledge, and opportunities for improving preparedness, response, recovery, and mitigation, protecting the well-being of individuals and communities across the United States.

9.7.4 Addressing Disaster Health Concerns

Nearly every chapter in this book has emphasized and highlighted the health impacts of disaster events and reflections of health in the recovery process as it relates to various groups. In a sense, health is the underpinning factor that captures our attention and concern; if disasters did not affect people's health, we might not be nearly as interested in them. Apart from the health impacts of disasters, pre-existing health conditions may not be nearly as recognizable or as discrete as other vulnerability considerations and so may not attract the same level of attention in preparedness activities. The previous sections directly addressed the systems that are in place for preparedness and response for the protection of the public's health. This section will highlight disaster health concerns and myths, and will then focus on some health considerations in evacuation warning and response.

9.7.4.1 Health Concerns

According to the Pan American Health Organization (PAHO 2000), all disasters have common health challenges, including social reactions, communicable diseases, population displacements, climatic exposure, food and nutrition, water supply and sanitation, mental health, and damage to the health infrastructure. However, many disaster myths are also perpetuated that are on the whole not true and are detrimental to preparedness and response efforts (Eberwine 2005; de Ville de Goyet 2000; de Ville de Goyet 1999). When an event occurs, it is entirely normal to have both individual and social reactions; however, this generally does not result in panic or shock, but rather people spontaneously organizing to address local needs. Additionally, disasters do not bring out the worst in human behavior and do not usually result in looting or rioting. It is important to recognize that people may have conflicting responsibilities, say, to children, family, and work, but this is not a deviant behavior. Any and all assistance is needed immediately in the affected area also does not hold true. Communities need support in areas where they do not have the resources.

In terms of health impacts, mass disease outbreaks and epidemics in the aftermath of an event are not inevitable. Most disease transmission can be attributed to fecal contamination of water and food, and so ensuring a source of clean drinking water and a mechanism for sanitation is essential; outbreaks are also attributable to population density and displacement. In short, disruptions to water supply and sanitation systems do pose serious health risk and so should be given consideration. Evacuation and population displacement require emergency response attention. In reality, climate exposure usually presents little threat to health. Food shortages can be quite common, resulting from destruction of the food supply or the food distribution system. For example, when the delivery truck cannot restock a grocery store during a blizzard, food supplies are temporarily interrupted, which can be problematic if people do not have a stock of food at home. Damage to the public health and health care infrastructure can have extensive and long-lasting impacts; a community cannot return to "normal" without these resources in place during the recovery process.

Mental health effects of disasters in the population are generally not acute, but this depends on the type of event and the experiences, and events can have long-lasting effects on various aspects of mental health. Norris et al. (2002a), in an analysis based on a review of 20 years of literature, found that youth more than adults, who were from developing rather than developed countries or experienced mass violence, were more likely to have adverse outcomes (posttraumatic stress, depression, and anxiety, as well as posttraumatic stress disorder, major depression disorder, generalized anxiety disorder, and panic disorder). For adults, more severe exposure, females, middle age, ethnic minority status, secondary stressors, prior psychiatric problems, and weak or deteriorating psycho-social resources increased the likelihood of adverse outcomes (Norris et al. 2002a). Interestingly in this study, rescue and recovery workers showed remarkable resilience, but this should not deter agencies from providing mental health services to responders. Based on the overall findings from the first phase of the study, the team recommended

> early intervention following disasters, especially when the disaster is associated with extreme and widespread damage to property, ongoing financial problems for the stricken community, violence that resulted from human intent, and a high prevalence of trauma in the form of injuries, threat to life, and loss of life (Norris et al. 2002b).

When planning for public health disaster response, addressing these broad public health concerns, while not falling for the myths, is vital for the best outcome.

9.7.4.2 Climate and Health

Increasing recognition and interest in the health effects of climate change have emerged in recent years and so necessitate at least mention of this topic, especially given the relationship to hazards, as well as public health preparedness activities. Broad consensus exists that the climate is warming, with many environmental, social, and economic implications. The relationship between climate and health is essentially related to weather-related climate events and shifting patterns of disease (Relman et al. 2008; Shea 2007). While there is little doubt that climate change has an effect on health, the complexity of the interaction is not well understood beyond generalizations and studies on specific types of hazards, for example, heat waves or droughts, but the full range of effects is only beginning to be established. Climate change will likely pose new health challenges, although many of the functions already performed by public health, particularly within the context of preparedness, are applicable to understanding the health effects of climate change (Frumkin et al. 2008). It will be incumbent on public health broadly and public health preparedness specifically to engage with this emerging topic.

9.7.4.3 Health Considerations for Evacuation, Warning, and Response

The health considerations for evacuation, warning, and response revolve around individual needs and then the extending effects on disaster operations. During both advance warning events as well as sudden impact events, individuals need to bring personal medications which should be labeled with the identified dosage and interval during any relocation. Additionally, a person should keep a backup prescription (although for some medications this is not possible) in order to obtain a refill in the event of lost medication or if the time away from home extends beyond the amount available. Ideally, an individual should have additional refills already in possession, but again there may be limitations placed on the amount that can be obtained at a given time, either because of the type of medication, insurance restrictions, or lack of money to pay for a double prescription. Complications further arise from medications that need refrigeration (such as insulin) and so this simple measure would require attention in shelters, or in the selection of a place to stay. Beyond medications, some people also require medical treatment, such as dialysis, radiation, chemotherapy, methadone maintenance, or mental health visits. Additionally, if the evacuation is longer term a person may not have access to a physician for continued treatment or prescription refill. Further, if the health care system itself is compromised because the effects of a disaster are so extensive, a person may not be able to continue treatment simply because the health resource is no longer available (see Box 9.1).

In short, a person who is dependent on a particular medication or treatment of a chronic (or acute) condition should carefully plan to the best degree possible in consultation with a health care provider prior to any event. This should also include support systems and networks (friends and family), as well as plans for home, work, and school.

In terms of hospitals, shelters, and other health care providers, health has implications for operations. Shelters can become quickly strained if they are responsible for continuum of care exceeding

---

BOX 9.1   HURRICANE KATRINA

Hurricane Katrina has had far-reaching health consequences, particularly on the most vulner-able, stemming from a compromised health care system, long-term displacement of people from their homes and communities, and environmental contamination. Not only was the health care system compromised, its fragility continues to affect recovery; hospital capacity remains diminished with some of the hospitals never reopened (Charity Hospital as a notable example), particularly those serving lower income, vulnerable populations (Eaton 2007). But it is not only about hospitals as institutions; the story includes individual people. Nurses, phy-sicians, pharmacists, among all others were also among the evacuees, some of whom have not returned and who were also among the populations who lost houses. Physicians have had to struggle to rebuild practices with little federal assistance and populations who have returned slowly, which has particularly affected pediatricians (Needle 2008). Further, without jobs people lose insurance, which also affects the ability of the health care system to rebound. However, without an intact and healthy infrastructure, how do people return, especially those who rely on this system for regular monitored treatment for any chronic condition, including mental health, diabetes, heart disease, or numerous other serious ailments? Ultimately, the result is a conundrum: many people cannot return without a functioning health system and resources, but the health care system needs human resources and patients to operate. The bot-tom line is that recovery depends on a functioning health infrastructure.

Women and children have particularly suffered. In one longitudinal study of 1082 ran-domly selected displaced Gulf Coast households, the Gulf Coast Child and Family Health (CAFH) study has reported some disturbing findings regarding the physical and mental health of children and mothers, as well as living conditions (CHF and NCDP 2008). For example, "[A]lmost half of parents reported that one or more of their children showed signs of new emotional or behavioral difficulties that did not exist prior to Hurricane Katrina" (CHF and NCDP 2008, 9). Mother's health status also directly affects her child's and is illustrated by another finding: "Symptoms of depression among mothers was high, and their children were two and a half times more likely to have an emotional or behavioral problem than children of mothers who did not show signs of depression" (CHF and NCDP 2008, 9). Given that other studies have found that women's (Jones-DeWeever 2008) and children's (Redlener, DeRosa, and Hut 2008) health has suffered severely in the aftermath of the hurricane as well (Jones-DeWeever 2008), this does not bode well for the suffering of people in post-Katrina Louisiana and Mississippi.

---

capabilities, but the reality is the population comes as it comes and will likely be reflective of the pre-existing vulnerable populations. The expectation is that hospitals will stay open, but they will likely not be able to provide elective services or even attend to non-priority cases; typical ailments still need treatment, but the capacity may not exist. And, in some instances, hospitals must be evacu-ated. Overall, hospitals must be reserved for care and not become unplanned shelters. Home health care can also become disrupted during a disaster. Cross-jurisdictional care can also be problematic. And so, the medical and public health response planning is extremely important, particularly for those with health conditions, and should include workforce emergency response training.

9.7.5   SHORT- AND LONG-TERM RECOVERY

In terms of short and long term recovery, this should involve ensuring that a recovery plan is in place with agreed-upon goals specific to health. The greatest challenge for health is likely ensuring that the public health and health care infrastructure is returned to a pre-event level. However, this returns to a point presented previously in the chapter; if the system was inadequate before the disaster, then it will likely still not meet the needs even if returned to that status. In this instance, aiming to improve the infrastructure would be a laudable goal. For example, if a clinic was deteriorated prior to an event and then incurred damage, would it be logical to rebuild it to previous conditions? Ensuring that health services returned and environmental conditions are safe (debris removal, contamination cleanup, road repair, utility repair, and sanitation and clean water availability) is a priority for recovery because it would be extremely difficult for individuals to return for the longer term without these resources, particularly if they had diminished health conditions. Additional recovery efforts include providing long-term follow-up to those affected, both the population and responders, and ensuring that post-event assessments on successes and failure are conducted that can guide future planning.

9.8 STRATEGIES FOR SUCCESS

Throughout the chapter, an emphasis was placed on integration and coordination between public health and emergency management planning and response; this remains central for successful disaster loss reduction and ensuring that vulnerable people are not hidden, but rather explicitly included in dialogue about disaster planning. In addition to coordinating, each of these systems has much to learn from one another due to the focus of each, but also historical development. Public health emphasizes prevention rather than response, while emergency management's purview is disasters.

Public health has a great deal of experience in the communication of health risks, which are generally focused at creating healthy behaviors and lifestyles. In many cases, this most directly aligns with mitigation due to the prevention orientation of the messages. Emergency communication, however, has a greater sense of urgency, may be more incomplete, and can change as an event unfolds (Hooke and Rogers 2005). The audience is of extreme importance when creating a message, and any risk communication should really be designed for multiple audiences to include diverse populations. Risk communication involves working with the media and having a lead spokesperson so that messages are not confused. The bottom line is that effective communication among all stakeholders will only improve emergency response efforts.

Community preparedness is essential for effectively addressing health issues in emergency management, and community-based approaches provide an effective mechanism for involving stakeholders and empowering communities (see Chapter 14 for a discussion of the use of a participatory, community-based approach for vulnerability assessment). This process establishes relationships and builds trust, in addition to giving the community a voice in setting priorities for disaster planning. Additionally, education occurs throughout as well.

Two examples derive from a focus on reducing health disparities and improving community health. Even though the focus is health specifically, the efforts can certainly inform vulnerability reduction efforts at the community level. The Toolkit for Health and Resilience In Vulnerable Environments (THRIVE) is a community assessment designed specifically to improve health outcomes and reduce disparities (Davis, Cook, and Cohen 2005). Using a resilience approach to community health in order to evaluate risk as well as resources, the assessment included built environment factors, services and institutions, and structural considerations in a community engagement process. The second example provides guidance for selecting from several models and approaches, simply laying out a process for helping communities address social determinants of health (Brennan Ramirez, Baker, and Metzler 2008). After presenting several case studies as examples of products from completed and ongoing processes, guidelines for adapting the social determinates of health to any neighborhood are supplied. The general elements include (1) enlisting participation, (2) methods for assessing the social determinants of health, (3) a process for building community capacity, (4) approaches for focusing the initiative, (5) development and implementation of an action plan, (6) assessment of progress, and (7) recommendations for maintenance. Both of these efforts present exciting opportunities for focusing on community assets as well as risk based on an action approach that can be an impetus for change.

9.9 SUMMARY

Health as considered a basic human right by extension equates to equal access to safety and well-being as the cornerstone to reducing vulnerability and increasing resilience. In its association with vulnerability, it is an overlay of other characteristics and it is also a reflection of the fragility or vitality of a community. In many ways, we are concerned with the effects of disasters because of the ways they impact people's well-being. As a consequence, health captures many elements that place it at the center of considering vulnerability, capacity, and resilience. An unhealthy community with a broken public health and health care system would likely not weather a disaster without significant loss.

9.10 DISCUSSION QUESTIONS

1. What types of non-health infrastructure directly affect the health status of a community?
2. In further consideration of the data tables and maps presented on disease and disaster mortality, what additional underlying factors may lead to the patterns? How are these related to vulnerability?
3. What is the relationship of individual characteristics and structural considerations? What contributes to your health?
4. In using health as an indicator of vulnerability, what types of variables would you like to examine?
5. What are the functions of public health and how do they contribute to an understanding of vulnerability and improve emergency management capabilities?
6. When considering the health care and public health systems, what considerations affect their functioning for emergency response?
7. Public health focuses on prevention. How does this relate to emergency management?
8. In terms of health, how can prevention be incorporated into emergency management as an overlay of vulnerability?
9. How does a community-based approach strengthen a community's resilience for addressing social determinants of both health and vulnerability?

ACKNOWLEDGMENTS

Sincere thanks go to Jean Scandlyn, Ronica Rooks, and Sharry Erzinger, who are not only dear friends, but also treasured colleagues who selflessly provided invaluable advice on this chapter. And my sincere gratitude goes to Brenda Phillips for her words of encouragement, insights, friendship, and patience. Alan Clive sadly passed away during the writing of the chapter. His tenacity and spirit will be remembered and it is with gratitude and fondness that we dedicate this to him.

REFERENCES

American Academy of Disaster Medicine. 2008. http://www.aapsga.org/academies/disaster-medicine/index.html (accessed December 4, 2008).

Berkman, L. F., and I. Kawachi, eds. 2000. *Social epidemiology*. New York: Oxford University Press.

Braveman, P., and S. Gruskin. 2003. Defining equity in health. *Journal of Epidemiology and Community Health* 57:254–58.

Brennan Ramirez, L. K., E. A. Baker, and M. Metzler. 2008. Promoting health equity: A resource to help communities address social determinants of health. Atlanta: U.S. Department of Health and Human Services, Centers for Disease Control and Prevention. http://www.cdc.gov/nccdphp/dach/chaps/ (accessed October 1, 2008).

Boorse, C. 1977. Health as a theoretical concept. *Philosophy of Science* 44:542–77.

Carter-Pokras, O., and C. Baquet. 2002. What is a health disparity? *Public Health Reports*, 117 (5): 426–34.

CDC (Centers for Disease Control and Prevention). 2008a. About the BRFSS. http://www.cdc.gov/BRFSS/about.htm (accessed November 30, 2008).

———. National Center for Health Statistics. 2008b. Health insurance coverage. http://www.cdc.gov/nchs/FASTATS/hinsure.htm (accessed November 17, 2008).

———. National Center for Health Statistics. 2008c. Topics: Medicare program—General information, and Medicaid program—General information. http://www.cms.hhs.gov/home/medicare.asp (accessed November 17, 2008).

———. National Center for Health Statistics. 2008d. Recent trends in infant mortality in the United States. NCHS Data Brief No. 9, October. http://www.cdc.gov/nchs/FASTATS/hinsure.htm (accessed November 17, 2008).

———. 2008e. Centers for public health preparedness. http://www.bt.cdc.gov/cotper/cphp/ (accessed December 18, 2008).

CDC and EPA (Centers for Disease Control and the U.S. Environmental Protection Agency), Joint Taskforce. 2005. Hurricane Katrina response, initial assessment. http://www.bt.cdc.gov/disasters/hurricanes/katrina/pdf/envassessment.pdf (accessed December 15, 2005).

CHF and NCDP (Children's Health Fund and the National Center for Disaster Preparedness). 2008. Legacy of shame: The on-going public health disaster of children struggling in post-Katrina Louisiana. Columbia University Mailman School of Public Health. http://www.childrenshealthfund.org/PDF/BR-WhitePaper_Final.pdf (accessed December 20, 2008).

Chu, M. C., and J. A. Rhoades. 2008. The uninsured in America, 1996–2007: Estimates for the U.S. civilian noninstitutionalized population under age 65. Statistical brief #214. Rockville, MD: Agency for Healthcare Research and Quality. http://www.meps.ahrq.gov/mepsweb/data_files/publications/st214/stat214.pdf (accessed November 18, 2008).

Davis, R., D. Cook, and L. Cohen. 2005. A community resilience approach to reducing ethnic and racial disparities in health. *AJPH* 95 (12): 2168–73.

de Jesus Diaz-Perez, M., D. Thomas, and T. Farley. 2007. *Assessing gaps in service for a community health center system.* 2007 Annual Meeting of the Association of American Geographers, San Francisco, California. Online program. http://communicate.aag.org/eseries/aag_org/program/AbstractDetail.cfm?AbstractID=13398 (accessed October 10, 2008).

de Ville de Goyet, C. 1999. Stop propagating disaster myths. *Prehospital Disaster Med* 14:213–14.

———. 2000. Stop propagating disaster myths. *Lancet* 356 (9231): 762–64.

Eaton, L. 2007. New Orleans recovery is slowed by closed hospitals. *New York Times*, July 24, 2007.

Eberwine, D. 2005. Disaster myths that just won't die. *Perspectives in Health* 10 (1) http://www.paho.org/English/DD/PIN/Number21_article01.htm (accessed November 1, 2008).

EM-DAT (*Emergency Events Database*). 2008. *EMDAT: The OFDA/CRED international disaster database. Université Catholique de Louvain—Brussels, Belgium. http://www.emdat.net (accessed October 1, 2008).*

Feierman, S., and J. M. Janzen, eds. 1992. *The social basis of health and healing in Africa.* Berkeley, CA: University of California Press.

Frumkin, H., J. Hess, G. Luber, J. Malilay, and M. McGeehin. 2008. Climate change: The public health response. *AJPH* 98 (3): 435–45.

GAO (U.S. Government Accountability Office). 2007. *Report to congressional committees, Hurricane Katrina, EPA's current and future environmental protection efforts could be enhanced by addressing issues and challenges faced on the Gulf Coast.* http://www.gao.gov/new.items/d07651.pdf (accessed December 15, 2008).

Gebbie, K., L. Rosenstock, and L. M. Hernandez, eds. 2003. *Who will keep the public healthy? Educating public health professionals for the 21st Century.* Committee on Educating Public Health Professionals for the 21st Century, National Academy of Sciences. Washington, DC: National Academies Press.

Hazards and Vulnerability Research Institute. 2008. The spatial hazard events and losses database for the United States, version 6.2 [online database]. Columbia, SC: University of South Carolina. http://www.sheldus.org (accessed October 1, 2008).

HHS (U.S. Department of Health and Human Services). 2002. *Modifications to the standards for privacy of individually identifiable health information—final rule.* http://www.hhs.gov/news/press/2002pres/20020809.html (accessed November 12, 2008).

———. 2005. *Hurricane Katrina bulletin #2: HIPAA privacy rule compliance guidance and enforcement statement for activities in response to Hurricane Katrina.* http://www.hhs.gov/ocr/hipaa/EnforcementStatement.pdf (accessed November 12, 2008).

————. 2007a. *Public health and healthcare: Critical infrastructure and key resources sector-specific plan as input to the National Infrastructure Protection Plan* (Redacted). http://www.hhs.gov/aspr/opeo/cip/healthssp_08_508.pdf (accessed December 4, 2008).

————. 2007b. *Public health emergency response: A guide for leaders and responders.* http://www.hhs.gov/emergency (accessed October 1, 2008).

————. Centers for Medicare and Medicaid Services. 2008a. *National health expenditure data highlights.* http://www.cms.hhs.gov/NationalHealthExpendData/02_NationalHealthAccountsHistorical.asp#TopOfPage (accessed November 30, 2008).

————. Health Resources and Services Administration. 2008b. *Interactive mapping site: Medically underserved areas and populations across the U.S.* http://datawarehouse.hrsa.gov/ (accessed December 1, 2008).

————. Health Resources and Services Administration. 2008c. *Primary health care: The Health Center Program.* http://bphc.hrsa.gov/ (accessed November 30, 2008).

Hodge, J. G. Jr., L. O. Gostin, and J. S. Vernick. 2007. The pandemic and all-hazards preparedness act: Improving public health emergency response. *JAMA* 297 (15): 1708–11.

Holt, J. B., A. H. Mokdad, E. S. Ford, E. J. Simoes, G. A. Mensah, and W. P. Bartoli. 2008. Use of BRFSS data and GIS technology for rapid public health response during natural disasters. *Prev Chronic Disease* 5 (3): A97.

Hooke, W., and P. G. Rogers, eds. 2005. *Public health risks of disasters: Communication, infrastructure, and preparedness.* Roundtable on Environmental Health Sciences, Research, and Medicine, National Research Council. Washington, DC: National Academies Press.

Janzen, J. M. 2002. *The social fabric of health: An introduction to medical anthropology.* Boston: McGraw-Hill.

Jones-DeWeever, A. A. 2008. *Women in the wake of the storm: Examining the post-Katrina realities of the women of New Orleans and the Gulf Coast.* Washington, DC: Institute for Women's Policy Research. http://www.iwpr.org/pdf/GulfCoastExecutiveSummary.pdf (accessed December 20, 2008).

Kilbourne, A. M., G. Switzer, K. Hyman, M. Crowley-Matoka, and M. J. Fine. 2006. Advancing health disparities research within the health care system: A conceptual framework. *American Journal of Public Health* 96 (12): 2113–21.

Lindsay, J. R. 2003. The determinants of disaster vulnerability: Achieving sustainable mitigation through population health. *Natural Hazards* 28:291–304.

Logue, J. N. 1996. Disasters, the environment, and public health: Improving our response. *AJPH* 86 (9): 1207–10.

Luo, W., and F. H. Wang. 2003. Measures of spatial accessibility to health care in a GIS environment: synthesis and a case study in the Chicago region. *Environment and Planning B-Planning & Design* 30 (6): 865–84.

Mokdad, A. H., G. A. Mensah, S. F. Posner, E. Reed, E. J. Simoes, and M. M. Engelgau. 2005. When chronic conditions become acute: Prevention and control of chronic diseases and adverse health outcomes during natural disasters. *Prev Chronic Dis* 2(Suppl 1):A04.

National Cancer Institute. 2008. Glossary: The nation's investment in cancer research. http://plan2005.cancer.gov/glossary.html (accessed December 1, 2008).

Needle, S. 2008. Pediatric private practice after Hurricane Katrina: Proposal for recovery. *Pediatrics* 122 (4): 836–42.

Noji, E. K. 2005. Public health issues in disasters. *Crit Care Med* 33(1 Suppl):S29–33.

Norris, F. H., M. J. Friedman, P. J. Watson, C. M. Byrne, E. Diaz, and K. Kaniasty. 2002a. 60,000 disaster victims speak: Part I. An empirical review of the empirical literature, 1981–2001. *Psychiatry* 65 (3): 207–39.

————. 2002b. 60,000 disaster victims speak: Part II. An empirical review of the empirical literature, 1981–2001. *Psychiatry* 65 (3): 240–60.

PAHO (Pan American Health Organization). 2000. *Natural disasters: Protecting the public's health.* Scientific publication no. 575. Washington, DC: Pan American Health Organization, Pan American Sanitary Bureau, Regional Office of the World Health Organization.

Public Health Functions Steering Committee. 1994. Healthy people in healthy communities. http://www.health.gov/phfunctions/public.htm (accessed November 6, 2008).

Relman, D. A., M. A. Hamburg, E. R. Choffnes, and A. Mack, Rapporteurs, Forum on Global Health. 2008. *Global climate change and extreme weather events: Understanding the contributions to infectious disease emergence: Workshop summary.* Washington, DC: National Academies Press. http://www.nap.edu/catalog/12435.html (accessed September 25, 2008).

Redlener, I., C. DeRosa, and R. Hut. 2008. Legacy of shame: The on-going public health disaster of children struggling in post-Katrina Louisiana. The Children's Health Fund and the National Center for Disaster Preparedness, Columbia University Mailman School of Public Health. http://www.childrenshealthfund.org/PDF/BR-WhitePaper_Final.pdf (accessed December 15, 2008).

Salinsky, E. 2002. Public health emergency preparedness: Fundamentals of the "system." National Health Policy Forum background paper. Washington, DC: NHPF.

Shea, K. M. 2007. Global climate change and children's health. *Pediatrics* 120 (5): e1359–67.

Shoaf, K. I., and S. J. Rottman. 2000. The role of public health in disaster preparedness, mitigation, response, and recovery. *Prehospital and Disaster Medicine* 15 (4). http://pdm.medicine.wisc.edu/Shoaf2.htm (accessed October 1, 2008).

Trust for America's Health. 2008. Issue report: Shortchanging America's health 2008, a state-by-state look at how federal public health dollars are spent. http://www.rwjf.org/files/research/shortchanging2008.pdf (accessed December 15, 2008).

U.S. Census Bureau. 2008. Census 2000 Gateway. http://www.census.gov/main/www/cen2000.html (accessed October 30, 2008).

U.S. Congressional Record. 2006. Pandemic and All-Hazards Preparedness Act (PAHPA). Public Law No. 109-417, 109th Congress. http://frwebgate.access.gpo.gov/cgi-bin/getdoc.cgi?dbname=109_cong_public_laws&docid=f:publ417.109.pdf (accessed August 26, 2008).

U.S. Department of Homeland Security. 2008. *National response framework: Overview.* http://www.fema.gov/emergency/nrf/ (accessed August 1, 2008).

Ver Ploeg, M., and E. Perrin, eds. 2004. *Eliminating health disparities: measurement and data needs.* Panel on DHHS Collection of Race and Ethnic Data, National Research Council. Washington, DC: National Academies Press.

Wang, F., and W. Luo. 2005. Assessing spatial and nonspatial factors for healthcare access: Towards an integrated approach to defining health professional shortage areas. *Health & Place* 11:131–46.

WHO (World Health Organization). 1948. Preamble to the constitution of the World Health Organization as adopted by the International Health Conference, New York, 19–22 June, 1946; signed on 22 July 1946 by the representatives of 61 States (Official Records of the World Health Organization, no. 2, p. 100) and entered into force on 7 April 1948.

———. 1978. Declaration of Alma Ata, Article 1. http://www.euro.who.int/AboutWHO/Policy/20010827_1 (accessed October 31, 2008).

———. 2006. Improved formula for oral rehydration salts to save children's lives. http://www.who.int/mediacentre/news/releases/2006/pr14/en/index.html (accessed October 15, 2008).

RESOURCES

American Academy of Pediatrics. Children's health topics: disaster preparedness. 2008. http://www.aap.org/healthtopics/disasters.cfm (accessed November 23, 2008).

American Journal of Disaster Medicine. http://www.pnpco.com/pn03000.html (accessed December 1, 2008).

Centers for Disease Control (CDC). Coping with a disaster or traumatic event, trauma and disaster mental health resources. http://www.bt.cdc.gov/mentalhealth/ (accessed October 9, 2008).

Centers for Disease Control (CDC). Public health preparedness: Mobilizing state by state, a CDC report on the public health emergency preparedness cooperative agreement. 2008. http://emergency.cdc.gov/publications/feb08phprep/ (accessed September 30, 2008).

Centers for Disease Control (CDC), Coordinating Office for Terrorism Preparedness and Emergency Response (COTPER). http://www.bt.cdc.gov/cotper/ (accessed September 30, 2008).

Centers for Disease Control (CDC), Emergency Preparedness and Response. http://emergency.cdc.gov/ (accessed September 30, 2008).

Centers for Public Health Preparedness (CPHP). http://www.bt.cdc.gov/cotper/cphp/ (accessed September 30, 2008).

Disaster Medicine and Public Health Preparedness (journal). http://www.dmphp.org/ (accessed December 5, 2008).

Environmental Protection Agency (EPA), Emergency Response. http://www.epa.gov/superfund/programs/er/index.htm (accessed September 30, 2008).

International Strategy for Disaster Reduction. ISDR-biblio 3: health, disasters and risk. Geneva: UN/ISDR-12-2008.

International   Journal   of   Disaster   Medicine.   http://www.informaworld.com/smpp/
    title~content=t713699767~db=all (accessed December 5, 2008).

Journal of Prehospital and Disaster Medicine. The official medical journal of the World Association for Disaster
    and Emergency Medicine. http://pdm.medicine.wisc.edu/ (accessed December 5, 2008).

Mayo Clinic. Managing your mental health during a disaster. http://www.mayoclinic.com/health/mental-health/
    MH00124 (accessed September 30, 2008).

U.S. Department of Health and Human Services, Agency for Healthcare Research and Quality (AHRQ), Public
    Health Emergency Preparedness. http://www.ahrq.gov/prep/ (accessed September 30, 2008).

U.S. Department of Health and Human Services, Assistant Secretary for Preparedness and Response, Office of
    Preparedness and Emergency Operations. http://www.hhs.gov/aspr/opeo/index.html (accessed September
    30, 2008).

U.S. Food and Drug Administration, Drug Preparedness and Response to Bioterrorism (FDA/CDER). http://
    www.fda.gov/cder/drugprepare/default.htm (accessed September 30, 2008).

World Health Organization. 2002. *Gender and health in disasters.* Geneva, Switzerland: World Health
    Organization.

10 Language and Literacy

Betty Hearn Morrow

CONTENTS

10.1 CHAPTER PURPOSE

Communication is a vital part of emergency management and response. In order to be effective the message must be understood clearly. This is especially crucial when this communication affects public safety and is received under conditions of stress and time pressure. An important first requirement in this process is knowledge about the language proficiency of targeted audiences.

10.2 OBJECTIVES

As a result of reading this chapter, the reader should be able to

1. Analyze disaster case studies where language or literacy factors hampered the delivery of emergency or disaster messages or services.
2. Use current data on U.S. immigration patterns and literacy levels to identify potential patterns of language and literacy isolation in various regions of the country.
3. Assess the reading level of disaster-related materials.
4. Locate and use national, state, and local resources to help translate or produce materials to deliver emergency-related messages that are appropriate to local language and literacy patterns.
5. Develop strategies for reaching isolated residents and communities with language-appropriate emergency and disaster-related messages.

10.3 INTRODUCTION

Vulnerability can be exacerbated by limited language proficiency, either oral or written. While the United States has one of the highest literacy rates in the world, it is still true that many citizens, both native and foreign born, have limited reading ability. An even more important factor in the context of emergency management is the growing number of people for whom English is a second language. While every region of the United States has foreign-born residents, they tend to be clustered in those urban and coastal regions most prone to natural hazards, such as earthquakes and coastal storms. While research indicates that recent immigrants are assimilating at a faster rate that ever before (Vigdor 2008), it can be assumed that many, particularly older immigrants and those from developing nations, are not fluent enough to understand most written and oral communication in English.

It is the responsibility of emergency managers and responders to take whatever measures necessary to reach everyone within their regions of responsibility. Any program receiving federal assistance must meet the requirements of an executive order that requires "meaningful access" to services for those with limited English proficiency (U.S. Department of Justice 2000). The Web site, *Limited English Proficiency: A Federal Interagency Website* (www.lep.gov), provides guidelines, tools, and materials for its implementation.

10.4 DEMOGRAPHIC OVERVIEW

In this section, we review how language and literacy issues may influence abilities to prepare for, respond to, and recover from disaster events. Numerous lessons can be learned from what has happened in previous disasters. This section reviews languages in the United States and demonstrates what happens when new immigrants, tourists, international business associates, and others do not receive emergency-time information. A subsequent section examines literacy issues for new immigrants as well as for U.S. citizens and outlines implications for the practice of emergency management.

10.4.1 LANGUAGE

Several examples of language difficulties related to disaster response have emerged from past events. An example of language impeding hazard warning occurred in 1987 when an F4 tornado came down in Saragosa, Texas (Aguirre 1988). Saragosa was a small, unincorporated town of agricultural workers with all but two families being of Mexican descent. The official tornado warnings from the National Weather Service were issued in English only. The local TV station broadcast the warnings in English, but the cable Spanish TV station did not provide weather information. The local Spanish radio station transmitted a warning, but the hastily translated message did not reflect the urgency of the situation. There were no sirens. In all, 29 people were killed, most of Mexican descent.

When Hurricane Andrew destroyed much of south Miami-Dade County, Florida, in 1992, thousands of the people most heavily impacted were of Latin or Haitian origin. Many agricultural workers, including migrants, were living in the hardest hit areas. There were also recent immigrants from Central and South America and the Caribbean. Response agencies, such as FEMA and the American Red Cross, were not prepared initially to communicate in Spanish and Haitian Creole. They lacked translators and most written materials were available only in English. As a result, information and assistance were often slow to reach these vulnerable groups. The assumption that all hurricane victims were English speakers prevented the distribution of food, medical supplies, and assistance information to some of the area's most needy residents and contributed to the slow utilization of the tent cities by homeless families (Yelvington 1997). Recovery information was eventually made available in other languages and locals were employed to go through the communities with flyers and loudspeakers (Phillips, Garza, and Neal 1994).

Similarly, many native English speakers living in the area hardest hit by Hurricane Andrew had low education levels, thus lacking English literacy skills. This may have affected the level of assistance they received. Residents of Florida City (a predominantly African American community) appeared to have greater needs, yet received fewer FEMA Individual Assistance and Individual and Family Grants per capita, than did those living in neighboring Homestead (Dash, Peacock, and Morrow 1997). There is no way of knowing the exact role language and literacy issues played, but it can be surmised that the complicated process of applying for assistance was harder for these groups. Applicants were first required to complete an application for a small business loan (even though they weren't asking for one) and be denied before they were eligible to apply for other funds. This process was particularly difficult to understand and negotiate for those with limited English proficiency.

People with hearing difficulties are at a distinct disadvantage when oral directions are given unaccompanied by American Sign Language and/or written information, or when there is no access to TTYs and open-caption television. The Special Needs Assessment for Katrina Evacuees Project reported that the most underserved group in shelters during the Katrina response were those who were deaf or had hearing problems (www.nod.org/Resource/PDFs/katrina_snake_report.pdf). A more complete discussion of this issue is found in Chapter 8.

The 1993 Northridge earthquake impacted a large immigrant population, many with limited English language ability. Most were Spanish, such as the agricultural workers in Ventura County, but dozens of other languages were found in the impacted areas. Los Angeles is a very segregated county, and there is ample evidence that many minority areas received far less attention from the media. A study comparing the level of print media coverage with the amount of damage incurred in communities found that "over-covered" communities (in relation to amount of damage incurred) were 61% non-Hispanic white while "under-covered" communities were only 22% non-Hispanic white (Rodriguez, Roval, and Place 1997). Early responders were not prepared to communicate with the "tens of thousands of non-English-speaking victims seeking help" (Bunting 1994, 1B). Another example: little attention was paid to Russian immigrants, many of who were elderly (Simon 1994). Relief agencies eventually adopted an aggressive outreach campaign using translators, but there were still misunderstandings about what qualified, how to deal with the bureaucratic structure of relief agencies, and how funds could be used (Bolin and Stanford 1998).

After Hurricane Katrina the tragic plight of New Orleanians captured national attention. Most people never realized that more than 5000 Vietnamese Americans lived in New Orleans and experienced loss of their homes and livelihoods. The local Catholic church serving the area with the highest concentration of Vietnamese became a focal point when two local priests provided necessary support and services. These priests managed the neighborhood evacuation, the experience of sheltering in the Convention Center, the relocation to refuge homes outside of the area, and most importantly, the return home. Given the large number of elderly Vietnamese who do not speak English, such a response mode likely saved lives because of the capacity of the leaders to communicate with the residents in their native language. The dedication of these local community leaders also resulted in a much faster rate of recovery and return than for most areas of New Orleans (Leong et al. 2007).

Similarly, until recently authorities had made few attempts to reach out to Spanish language residents. This lack of engagement was illustrated by a flyer that was developed without vetting the correct phrasing with the community. The need for Spanish language materials and workers has become more acute since Hurricane Katrina due to the influx of Spanish-speaking workers, many of whom are expected to remain in the community.

In summary, while English remains the primary spoken and written language in the United States, the extent to which other languages are primary is considerable, and increasing. According to the 2000 Census brief, *Language Use and English-Speaking Ability: 2000* (www.census.gov/prod/2003pubs/c2kbr-29.pdf), nearly 18% of the population speaks another language at home. For about 60% of these, the primary language is Spanish, but it should be noted that about 40 other languages have been officially recorded. Language patterns differ dramatically by region and it is imperative that emergency managers and responders examine the data related to the populations they serve. It should also be noted that American Sign Language is the primary language for many deaf people; by some estimates, it is the fourth most commonly used language in the United States, after English, Spanish, and Chinese (National Institute on Deafness and Other Communication Disorders 2000).

In fairness it should be said that many response agencies now have programs and materials targeting non-English speakers, especially during long-term recovery periods. FEMA, the American Red Cross, and the Centers for Disease Control have disaster-related Web sites in Spanish (see Resources section). During Hurricane Rita FEMA had translators available in 10 languages (FEMA 2005). Many emergency and disaster materials are now translated into multiple languages. The Red Cross has preparedness materials available on its Web site in 14 different languages including Arabic, Chinese, and Vietnamese (http://www.redcross.org/services/disaster/0,1082,0_504_,00.html). One example of material available in American Sign Language is a video available from the Centers for Disaster Control on handwashing after a disaster (http://www.bt.cdc.gov/disasters/psa/handwashing_asl.asp).

10.4.2 LITERACY ISSUES

There is less evidence of efforts to write printed materials at appropriate literacy levels. In some instances the use of "jargon" makes it more difficult for people who are already under stress to understand instructions. The following quotation provides an example from the *Plain Language at Work Newsletter* (Impact Information Plain-Language Services 2006).

Instructions from a post-Katrina State Web site:

> The Assistance Centers will help mitigate the potential for misunderstanding and abuse by providing standardized, structured, and guided relationships between homeowners and service providers. In addition, the Assistance Centers will maintain registries of professional service providers and building contractors. Through the Solicitation for Offer, Assistance Centers will be directed by the selected management firm and staffed by contracted experts, which may include non-profit organizations specializing in providing advisory services to homeowners (78 words, 39 difficult words, 16th-grade reading level).

This could be more easily put as

> Use the Assistance Centers if you have problems with builders or other services. These centers also keep lists of approved builders and services. We will attempt to select companies and non-profit groups who can best run these centers (38 words, 6 difficult words, 8th-grade reading level).

10.4.2.1 Literacy Rates among Immigrants

Literacy rates vary considerably by country. Table 10.1 provides literacy rates in their own languages for the countries of origin from which the United States received the most immigrants from 2000–2007. These figures are somewhat deceiving because immigrants in general tend to be more educated than the average person in their countries of origin. Most importantly, this does not include undocumented immigrants, many of whom are less educated. The important point is that it is important to know not just immigrant numbers, but also language and literacy patterns.

As shown in Table 10.1, women in immigrant populations are likely to be less literate. This is a serious issue for emergency managers considering that women usually have primary responsibilities for household preparedness and recovery, caring for family members throughout the process, often under difficult circumstances. Also, women in general tend to take hazard warnings more seriously, and thus are an important conduit to their families. Women also tend to have heavy responsibilities for seeking relief supplies and assistance for the household after an event. The language and literacy problems of immigrant or poorly educated women can increase the difficulties associated with getting help for their families from a system that tends to place women at a disadvantage.

TABLE 10.1
Illiteracy Rates for Countries with Most Legal Immigrants in the United States

Country of Origin	Number/Year[a]	Male Illiteracy (%)	Female Illiteracy (%)
Canada	18,207	1.0	1.0
Mexico	173,749	6.0	9.5
India	61,369	29.8	51.7
China	87,307	9.1	4.9
Philippines	74,606	7.5	7.3
El Salvador	31,780	17.2	22.3
Dominican Republic	38,068	15.4	15.2
South Korea	24,386	0.8	3.4
Cuba	45,614	2.8	3.1

Source: Department of Homeland Security (2004; 2009).
[a] Average number of legal immigrants/year immigrating from 2000–2007.

10.4.2.2 Literacy in the United States

There is a changing nature to what is called literacy in America. While concerns about inadequate literacy skills are not new, the nature of the concerns is evolving. In the past, literacy was considered the ability to read and use printed materials at an extremely basic level. Today adults need higher levels of basic skills to function effectively in many areas of their lives, and literacy is defined more broadly to include problem-solving and higher-level reasoning skills. Literacy is a range of tools that help people help themselves—and their families. It is not an end in itself, but a means to a better quality of life.

While very few adults in the United States are truly illiterate, there are many with low literacy skills that lack the foundation needed to find and keep decent jobs, participate actively in civic life, and support their children's education. According to the National Institute for Literacy, nearly one quarter of U.S. adults are considered functionally illiterate, that is, they lack a level of reading and writing needed to cope with everyday adult life. The National Assessment of Adult Literacy (NAAL 2006) does not classify people as merely "literate" or "illiterate," but measures prose, document, and quantitative components of literacy. Examples of skills that a person measuring at the lowest levels cannot perform are to locate eligibility from a table of benefits; to locate an intersection on a map; to locate two pieces of information in an article; to identify and enter background information on an application; and to calculate total costs of a purchase.

Most relevant to emergency and disaster materials are prose and document literacy. Prose is defined as the ability to use continuous texts such as reading brochures and instructional materials (Figure 10.1). Document literacy refers to the ability to complete forms such as job applications and understand maps (NAAL 2006). Figure 10.2 provides the results for prose and document literacy from the 2003 National Assessment of Adult Literacy.

These results are cause for concern with those scoring at basic or below basic totaling 43% for prose and 44% for document literacy. This currently translates to around 95 million adults. Additionally, it was noted that over four million would not be able to take the test because of language barriers. People in these circumstances are not likely to be able to read and understand emergency instructions. It follows that they will also experience problems with filling out assistance application forms and may require assistance and/or special materials. While it is important not to generalize to individuals, adults consistently scoring at the lowest literacy levels tend to be older, poorer members of an ethnic minority and/or less educated.

FIGURE 10.1 Written materials must take literacy levels into account. *Source*: George Armstrong/FEMA news photo.

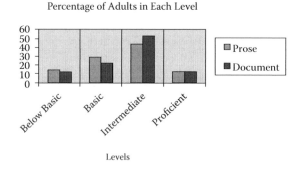

FIGURE 10.2 U.S. literacy scores. *Source*: Data from NAAL (National Assessment of Adult Literacy). A first look at the literacy of America's adults in the 21st century. 2006. http://nces.ed.gov/NAAL/PDF/2006470. pdf (accessed August 1, 2008)

Literacy scores are sometimes given in grade levels. For example,

This short sentence needs a reading age of less than nine years.
This longer sentence, which contains an adjectival clause and polysyllabic words, has a reading age of more than sixteen years.

As a general rule, it can be assumed that:

- Grade 3 or lower will not be able to read most low literacy materials and will need repeated oral instructions, materials composed primarily of illustrations, or audio or video messages.
- Grades 4–7 will need low literacy materials.
- Grades 7–8 will struggle with most materials, but will not be offended by low literacy materials.
- High school graduates will be able to read most materials (Doak, Doak, and Root 1996).

Several indicators of the extent to which the population of a given area may have language or literacy problems are available from the U.S. Census. As an example, Table 10.2 provides data for

TABLE 10.2
Adult Education and Population Data Related to Language and Literacy

	Foreign Born (%)	Language Other Than English (%)	Adults Without High School Education (%)
United States	11.9	18.4	19.6
California	26.5	40.8	23.2
Florida	17.6	24.2	20.1
Michigan	5.9	8.6	16.6
New York	20.8	27.5	20.9

Source: U.S. Census 2003a, 2003b, 2003c.

U.S. adults related to three factors associated with language and literacy problems for four states, as well as totals for the United States.

Based on national averages, it can be estimated that about 15%–20% of the residents in any community may have at least one of these characteristics. More importantly, the rates vary dramatically across states, and even more dramatically across counties. The best method is to look at county level statistics. For example, Miami-Dade County, Florida, has 50.9% foreign born, 67.9% with language other than English spoken at home, and 32.1% with less than a high school education. While many of these people will be literate and fluent in English, it can be assumed that large numbers will have problems reading most materials and completing basic writing tasks in English.

10.4.3 COMPOUNDED VULNERABILITIES

Groups who have problems with English are likely to have other characteristics limiting their ability to respond to an emergency or disaster. Over-represented in the Below Basic category in the NAAL are people with multiple disabilities, the elderly, blacks and Hispanics, and those with less than a high school education (NAAL 2006). As previously mentioned, female immigrants are more likely to lack literacy, thus compounding other gender inequalities. Even documented workers may be wary of government authorities due to negative experiences with authorities in their home countries. Both recent immigrants and foreign workers are liable to have limited education and low literacy rates in their own languages. Tourists, international business representatives, and foreign exchange students may not speak English or be familiar with the area.

The same people who have language and literacy issues are likely to be unfamiliar with U.S. culture. They may be relatively new to the area such as recent immigrants, migrants, foreign or guest workers, and be unfamiliar with local hazards and conditions. They are more likely to be located in rural or isolated areas. They often lack resources, including transportation, to respond without assistance. They may not have family and social connections in the community to consult in an emergency. Other vulnerability factors likely to be associated with limited language proficiency are poverty, race, and ethnicity (discussed in other chapters). Young children may only know their native language. These high-risk groups will be especially dependent upon emergency managers and responders, making it essential that disaster professionals collect data on their conditions and location.

10.5 SOLUTIONS AND STRATEGIES

Effective emergency managers know the populations they serve and plan their programs accordingly. Paying special attention to those at highest risk is not only altruistic, it is good management practice. As examples, General Electric, Federal Express, and Banco have reported considerable financial gain from rewriting materials in plain language (DuBay 2004). In the end it can make the job easier. The time spent learning about their situations and needs—and tailoring educational and response plans accordingly—can produce outstanding results. In disasters these groups tend to be hit the hardest, have the most serious relief needs, and recover last. Steps taken to prevent these results can pay big dividends.

10.5.1 KNOWING YOUR COMMUNITY

A critical point made throughout this book is that emergency professionals need to know their communities, including the levels of education and literacy. For immigrants and foreign-born workers, it would be useful to know the average age- and gender-specific literacy rates in their countries of origin. If migrant labor is used, it is important to know what the population census is likely to be at various times of the year. Resort areas tend to have patterns of tourism in terms of countries of origin and seasons.

The primary source of population data is the U.S. Census (www.census.gov), where estimates are available down to census block level according to such attributes as foreign-born and English as a second language. American FactFinder reports some aggregated census data in easy-to-use format (http://factfinder.census.gov). Other relevant data sources include the National Center for Educational Statistics (http://nces.ed.gov), the United Nations (www.un.org), and International Marketing Data and Statistics (usually available in libraries). Data on agricultural workers, tourists, and other relevant groups are often collected at the state level.

10.5.2 READING LEVEL ASSESSMENT

Emergency and disaster-related materials tend to be written at high reading levels. In many communities they need to be adapted to the lower language and literacy skills of some residents. In order to determine whether materials are appropriate and prepare original materials at appropriate levels, it is important to know how to make assessments. A number of methods have been developed for determining the reading level of text materials. Before using any of these methods to determine readability, a caution is in order. Many factors affect the readability of text, including sentence length, word choice, layout, tone, organization, use of illustrations, and appeal to the reader (Osborne 2000). While formulas are useful for a rough assessment, it is important to look at the material as a whole. It is important to use plain language. "Plain Language means writing in a way that is easy-to-understand, looks good, is organized logically, and is understandable the first time you read it" (DuBay 2004, 1).

Two of the most common methods for rough estimates of readability are the Flesch-Kincaid Formula used by the U.S. Department of Defense and the Simplified Measure of Gobbledygook (SMOG) developed by McLaughlin (1969). The Flesch-Kincaid Formula was created by Rudolf Flesch in the 1940s, and later enhanced by John P. Kincaid (Kincaid et al. 1975). It is used by the U.S. Department of Defense as a standard test. It rates text on a 100-point scale; the higher the score, the easier it is to read the document. For most standard documents, a score of approximately 60 to 70 is desirable. However, for many target groups it should be higher. The Flesch-Kincaid formula is as follows:

1. Calculate L—average sentence length (number of words/number of sentences).
2. Calculate N—average number of syllables per word (number of syllables/number of words).
3. Calculate grade level with formula $(L \times 0.39) + (N \times 11.8) - 15.59$.
4. Calculate reading age with formula $(L \times 0.39) + (N \times 11.8) - 10.59$.

TABLE 10.3
SMOG Conversion Table

Total Polysyllabic Word Count	Approximate Grade Level (+/– 1.5 Grades)
0–2	4
3–6	5
7–12	6
13–20	7
21–30	8
31–42	9
43–56	10
57–72	11
73–90	12
91 or more	Above high school level

Source: *Making health communication programs work, a planners guide.* U.S. Department of Health and Human Services, 1992.

Microsoft Word has a version of the Flesch-Kincaid in its software. It can be accessed through the Spelling and Grammar function.

The SMOG formula provides a very simple way to assess the reading level of text. The formula is as follows:

1. Select three samples of 10 consecutive sentences from different sections of the test (at least 100 words total).
2. Count the total number of words that have three or more syllables in the 30 sentences.
3. Using a calculator, find the square root of that number.

To test text that has fewer than 30 sentences using the SMOG,

1. Count all the polysyllabic words (i.e., more than three syllables).
2. Count the number of sentences.
3. Find the average number of polysyllabic words per sentence: Average = Total # polysyllabic words/total # sentences.
4. Multiply that average by the number of sentences short of 30.
5. Add that figure to the total number of polysyllabic words.
6. Find the square root and add the constant of three.

A quick version of SMOG using a reference table is often used to get a rough assessment. Count the number of polysyllabic words (three or more syllables) in a chain of 30 sentences. Look up the approximate grade level on the SMOG Conversion Table (Table 10.3).

These same readability formulas can be used to roughly estimate the readability of non-English documents.

Before using any emergency and disaster materials available from state and national sources, it is a good idea to check their readability. Most disaster information, such as that found on Web sites, is written at high levels. For example,

Food and Water in an Emergency. American Red Cross. 8th grade level
Fact Sheet: Earthquakes. Federal Emergency Management Agency. 12th grade level
Chemical Emergencies Overview. Centers for Disease Control. 12th grade level

10.5.3   REACHING TARGET POPULATIONS

Experts recommend that most text be written at about an 8th grade level. In order to be understood by the majority, however, it is best to write educational materials at no higher than 5th grade level. In some cases materials may need to be adjusted even lower for target audiences.

Many materials are now available in other languages, particularly Spanish. For more than 20 years, researchers have been calling for the development of a standardized vocabulary to convey emergency and disaster messages, such as tornado warnings (Aguirre 1988). Common words used in warning messages do not always have direct translations. As examples, the historical lack of Spanish-language degreed meteorologists allowed news writers, reporters, and anchors to alternatively translate "warning" as either *alerta* or *aviso*, and "watch" as either *alerta* or *aviso*. In contrast the National Weather Service Weather Forecast Office in Puerto Rico uses the term *vigilancia* for watch and *aviso* for warning (J. Toohey-Morales, May 2008, personal communication).

Nearly all the major response agencies, governmental and non-governmental, now have Spanish materials and Web sites. Others are available on the Web sites of international agencies, such as the Pan American Health Organization. FEMA has a Spanish Web site, and also provides information on its Web site in 15 different languages. However, these other-language materials also need to be checked for literacy levels.

Often, available materials will not suit local needs, so materials will need to be developed or adapted. Rather than considering this a burden, managers can seize this opportunity to engage people in these communities in the process of developing materials and programs for their neighbors. This topic is covered in more detail in the other chapters, but many materials are available to provide guidelines for dealing with cultural and language diversity. (See, for example, materials available on the Canadian Emergency Preparedness Web site). Another advantage is that they will be more appropriate for the area in terms of hazard risk, geography, and living situations. One way to begin this process is to have local people map the vulnerabilities of their neighborhoods. Materials are available to assist in this process, including Working With Women, which provides workshop guidelines to train local women to do vulnerability analysis (available in English and Spanish from the Gender and Disaster Network (http://gdnonline.org).

It is essential that emergency management agencies have the capacity to communicate with those they serve in their native language. Ideally, this means having personnel who can speak, at least rudimentary phrases, in the relevant language either through recruitment or in-service training. Understanding the dedication the latter requires, it remains an important recommendation. An interesting example is firefighters in Australia learning enough Turkish to communicate with the migrant community in Victoria (Mitchell 2003).

Getting the message prepared in a format that is easily understood by its targeted audience is only the beginning. Now the message must reach the audience—it must be marketed. A "social marketing" approach that combines working for the social good with using good commercial marketing techniques is now promoted by many agencies, including the Centers for Disease Control (http://www.social-marketing.org/success/cs-hpylori.html). According to the Social Marketing Institute (n.d.), this involves creating an enticing "product," minimizing the "price" the audience believes it must pay, making it available in places that reach the audience and fits its lifestyles, and promoting the exchange opportunity with creativity and through channels and tactics that maximize desired responses. It should be emphasized that the best way to know what marketing techniques will work in a specific community is to engage people from the targeted groups in the emergency planning and response process, such as within the emergency operations center or in community emergency response teams. Local community-based organizations and advocacy groups are excellent sources of information.

Providing simple messages on flyers at stores, printed on retail store bags, and leaflets and posters throughout communities such as in churches, restaurants, laundromats, emergency rooms, and gas stations has been successful in communities with literacy and/or language problems. Children are excellent conveyors of safety messages, such as hurricane and earthquake protection information.

This "reverse socialization" can be an effective way to reach adults through the children in their lives. Many programs for children and schools are available, such as FEMA for Kids in English and Spanish.

Written materials are only one way to reach high-risk groups. There is ample evidence that the best way is through mass media outlets, particularly when radio or television is available in their native languages. These are often small stations that are open to providing emergency educational and response programs and messages if engaged as part of the emergency management team. Some messages can be pre-prepared in relevant languages.

New technologies, such as text messages on cell phones and personal data assistants, are becoming standard in the communication of weather and emergency-related information. While it might seem that these technologies would not be available to immigrant and lower income groups, there is mounting evidence that cell phones are now used to replace landlines, even among more marginal populations. As the use of these technologies grows, it will be important that messages be produced and transmitted in other languages, according to the needs of the region. The moving text or trailers across the bottom of television screens have been found very effective to relay warning messages. National systems are now in place for their use. It is important that they be developed in appropriate languages for local areas.

In the rush to develop and use new technologies, it is important not to throw away more simple solutions. In many cases the most effective way to communicate with high-risk populations is to drive through the neighborhood, or go door to door, providing messages in local languages. Similarly, sirens are commonly used in California and Hawaii as methods of delivering emergency messages to communities where there are multiple languages. In order to reach all the diverse populations within most communities it is important to have redundancy, using a variety of methods and messages.

10.6   SUMMARY

The United States is an increasingly diverse nation. Hispanic and Asian populations are expected to triple, and non-Hispanic whites will make up only one half of the total population by 2050 (U.S. Census 2004). While some regions are impacted more than others, it would be rare to find a community in which there were not some people without English language proficiency, whether resulting from English not being their first language or from limited education, and thus low reading ability.

This has critical implications for emergency management and disaster planning. Those with English problems are also likely to have other qualities that can lead to response difficulties. It can be said that a community is only as resilient as its weakest link. These high-risk populations are likely to suffer disproportional impact from a hazard and to have the most difficulty during recovery. They consume an inordinate amount of resources throughout the response cycle. It is essential that emergency managers

* Know their communities, including the locations of high-risk groups.
* Use their communities, including local leadership of both genders.
* Develop programs and materials to reach targeted populations in effective ways.

Spending time and effort up front can have a large payoff from a management perspective. The result will be better communication, better relationships, more effective partners, and safer communities. And from a social justice standpoint, it's the right thing to do.

10.7   DISCUSSION QUESTIONS

1. What are some specific case studies from past disasters where literacy or language barriers hampered access to emergency or disaster information and services? Are they still occurring?

2. How can formal and informal sources of information about limited English proficiency populations in local communities be used to improve safety and services?

3. What are some common trends in literacy rates related to gender and countries of origin? What are the implications for your community?

4. Find an example of disaster or emergency text that is difficult to read and/or understand. Rewrite it in plain English.

5. Explain one way to analyze the reading level of text materials. Practice with materials from the Web sites of major response agencies or from your own community.

6. What are some strategies for delivering messages to targeted audiences that may have limited English proficiency? What can be done to be sure that high-risk populations are not left out with increased use of new technologies?

7. How can the development of special materials for those with limited language and literacy skills also enhance emergency management programs in other ways?

8. How can this argument be used to argue for increased funding of mitigation and educational programs?

REFERENCES

Aguirre, B. E. 1988. The lack of warnings before the Saragosa tornado. *International Journal of Mass Emergencies and Disasters* 6(1):65–74.

Bolin, R., and L. Stanford. 1998. *The Northridge earthquake: Vulnerability and disaster.* London: Routledge.

Bunting, G. F. 1994. Earthquake: The long road back. *Los Angeles Times.* February 4, 1B. Available through Lexis-Nexis.

Dash, N., W. G. Peacock, and B. H. Morrow. 1997. And the poor get poorer: A neglected black community. In *Hurricane Andrew: Ethnicity, gender, and the sociology of disasters,* eds. W. G. Peacock, B. H. Morrow, and H. Gladwin, 206–25. London: Routledge.

Doak, C., L. Doak, and J. Root. 1996. *Teaching patients with low literacy skills.* 2nd ed. Philadelphia: Lippincott Infosoft International, Inc.

Dubay, W. H. 2004. What is Plain Language? Report prepared for the Plain Language Ad-Hoc Committee of the Productivity and Quality Commission, July 19. http://qpc.co.la.ca.us/cms1_033658.pdf (accessed August 1, 2008).

FEMA (Federal Emergency Management Agency). 2005. FEMA helps Texas disaster victims in any language. http://www.fema.gov/news/newsrelease.fema?id=20526 (accessed August 1, 2008).

Impact Information Plain-Language Services. 2006. Post-Katrina jargon: Just what hurricane victims don't need. *Plain Language at Work Newsletter* 27, September 7. http://impact-information.com/impactinfo/newsletter/plwork27.htm (accessed May 25, 2008).

Kincaid, J. P., R. P. Fishburne Jr., R. L. Rogers, and B. S. Chissom. 1975. Derivation of new readability formulas (Automated Readability Index, Fog Count, and Flesch Reading Ease Formula) for Navy enlisted personnel, Research Branch Report 8-75, Millington, TN: Naval Technical Training, U. S. Naval Air Station, Memphis, TN.

Leong, K. J., C. A. Airriess, L. Wei, A. C.-C. Chen, and V. M. Keith. 2007. Resilient history and the rebuilding of a community: The Vietnamese American community in New Orleans East. *The Journal of American History* 94 (3). www.historycooperative.org (accessed August 1, 2008).

Mitchell, Louise. 2003. "Guidelines for Emergency Managers Working with Culturally and Linguistically Diverse Communities". *The Australian Journal of Emergency Management.* 18 (3): 13-18. http://search.informit.com.au/documentSummary;dn=376944415766551;res=IELHSS. (Accessed April 30, 2009)

McLaughlin, H. 1969. SMOG grading—A new readability formula. *Journal of Reading* 22:639–46.

NAAL (National Assessment of Adult Literacy). 2006. A first look at the literacy of America's adults in the 21st century. http://nces.ed.gov/NAAL/PDF/2006470.pdf (accessed August 1, 2008).

National Institute on Deafness and Other Communication Disorders. 2000. American Sign Language. http://www.nidcd.nih.gov/health/hearing/asl.asp (accessed July 21, 2008).

Osborne, H. 2000. In other words … Assessing readability … Rules for playing the numbers game. *Boston Globe. On Call.* December.

Phillips, B., L. Garza, and D. Neal. 1994. Intergroup relations in disasters: Service delivery barriers after Hurricane Andrew. *The Journal of Intergroup Relations* 3:18–27.

Rodriguez, C. M., E. Roval, and S. E. Place. 1997. Construction of the 'Northridge earthquake in Los Angeles' English and Spanish print media. Paper presented to the Southern California Environment and History Conference. September 19. http://www.csulb.edu/~rodrigue/scehc97.html (accessed May 25, 2008).

Simon, R. 1994. Quake aid requests near half million mark. *Los Angeles Times* April 2. NewsBank NewsFile Collection.

Social Marketing Institute. n.d. Social marketing. www.social-marketing.org/sm.html (accessed May 1, 2009).

U.S. Census Bureau. 2003a. *American Community Survey.* "Percent of Population that is Foreign Born." www.census.gov/acs/www/Products/Ranking/2003/R15T040.htm (accessed May 1, 2009).

U.S. Census Bureau. 2003b. *American Community Survey.* "Percent of People 5 Years and Over Who Speak a Language Other Than English at Home." www.census.gov/acs/www/Products/Ranking/2003/R03T040.htm (accessed May 1, 2009).

U.S. Census Bureau. 2003c. *Educational Attainment 2003.* "Educational Attainment of the Population 25 years and Over for the United States." Pp. 3–4. www.census.gov/prod/2003pubs/c2kbr-24.pdf.

U.S. Census Bureau. 2004. U.S. Census Bureau News. CB04-44. http://www.census.gov/Press-Release/www/releases/archives/population/001720.html. Accessed April 30, 2009.

U.S. Department of Homeland Security. 2004. *2004 Yearbook of Immigrant Statistics.* http://www.dhs.gov/xlibrary/assets/statistics/yearbook/2004/Yearbook2004.pdf (accessed April 30, 2009).

U.S. Department of Homeland Security. 2009. *U. S. Legal Permanent Residents: 2008.* www.dhs.gov/xlibrary/assets/statistics/publications/lpr_fr_2008.pdf (accessed April 30, 2009).

U.S. Department of Justice. 2000. *Executive order 131661: Improving access to services for persons with limited English proficiency.* http://www.usdoj.gov/crt/cor/Pubs/eolep.htm (accessed May 25, 2008).

Vigdor, J. L. 2008. Measuring immigrant assimilation in the United States. *Civic Report* 53, May. The Manhattan Institute. http://www.manhattan-institute.org/html/cr_53.htm (accessed May 25, 2008).

Yelvington, K. 1997. Coping in a temporary way: The tent cities. In *Hurricane Andrew: Ethnicity, gender, and the sociology of disasters,* eds. W. G. Peacock, B. H. Morrow, and H. Gladwin, 92–115. London: Routledge.

RESOURCES

American Red Cross materials in Spanish (http://www.cruzrojaamericana.org/index.asp).

Andreasen, A. R. *Social Marketing in the 21st Century.* New York: Sage, 2005.

Centers for Disaster Control materials in Spanish (http://www.bt.cdc.gov/preparedness/).

Dubay, W. H. The principles of readability. 2004. http://www.impact-information.com/impactinfo/readability02.pdf.

FEMA Educational materials in Spanish (http://www.fema.gov/spanish/index_spa.shtm).

Mitchell, L. Guidelines for emergency managers working with culturally and linguistically diverse communities. Emergency Management Australia. 2007. www.ema.gov.au/agd/EMA/emaInternet.nsf/Page/Communities_Research_Research.

National Institute for Literacy. www.nifl.gov (accessed May 1, 2009).

11 Households and Families

Lynn Blinn-Pike

CONTENTS

11.1   CHAPTER PURPOSE

The purpose of this chapter is to help the reader understand how disasters affect households and families. By understanding those impacts, it is possible to build household and family capacity, thereby reducing vulnerability. This chapter thus addresses how households and families, along with emergency managers, social service providers, and disaster organizations, can better prepare for, respond to, recover from, and mitigate disaster impacts.

11.2   OBJECTIVES

As a result of reading this chapter, readers should be able to:

1. Define and explain key terms that are used to understand household and family composition.
2. Describe current household and family composition patterns in the United States.
3. Identify the household and family composition patterns present in a given community and analyze the implications for local emergency response.

4. Understand the relationship between household and family characteristics and the ability to mitigate, prepare for, respond to, and recover from emergencies and disasters.
5. Explain ways in which a household's social resources, including relatives and social networks, are tied to disaster response.
6. Identify factors likely to be associated with high-risk households and families.
7. Understand how family stress and coping theory can be applied to explain reactions to disaster.
8. Develop strategies for reaching high-risk households and families, including renters, with emergency and disaster information and programs.
9. Develop effective strategies to protect, assist, and utilize family ties and strengths in emergency and disaster response.

11.3   INTRODUCTION

This chapter is divided into five parts. The first defines terms and concepts such as household and family. This is followed by a demographic section covering the relationship between household composition, family and social networks, and the ability to respond to and recover from disasters, and describing the status of households and families in the United States today. The third part explains the relevance of understanding family and disaster research for the practice of vulnerability reduction. This is followed by a section on how families deal with stress and cope with the trauma and hardship across the life cycle of disasters. The fifth section gives implications for action and outlines strategies for reducing vulnerability in disaster contexts, particularly looking at ways to reach high-risk households.

11.4   DEFINITIONS

What is a household? What is a family? Most people respond to hazards and experience disasters as members of households. It is typically at the household level that decisions are made related to insurance, housing mitigation, preparation, evacuation, response, and recovery. A household may be composed of a person living alone, or two or more persons living together. Most households are composed of families—people related by blood or marriage (or those who consider themselves to be family).

Although less true today, the U.S. family has typically consisted of a nuclear family, that is, one or both parents and their children. Three-generation families that include an elder adult are not uncommon, particularly among minorities, where families with more than one nuclear unit, such as two brothers and their families, are also sometimes found. A non-family household can be defined as someone who lives alone or shares a home with non-relatives, such as roommates or boarders. Male migrant workers, as one example, often share housing at their work locations.

For purposes of disaster response and emergency management, the issue is whether those living under the same roof are able and willing to pool their resources and make important decisions together. On the other hand, family networks often extend beyond the household to include other relatives. These non-household kin networks and resources can play a role in how a household copes with emergencies and disasters. Table 11.1 shows the percent of different types of households in the United States according to the 2006 census. It shows that of U.S. households, about half are made up of married couples with or without children (53%); 25% are made up of adults living alone; 16% are made up of individuals who are related; and 6% contain members who are not related.

11.5   IMPORTANT TRENDS AMONG HOUSEHOLDS
AND FAMILIES IN THE UNITED STATES

Government data show six recent trends that point to the importance of considering both households and families when dealing with disasters (U.S. Census Bureau 2002, 2003, 2004):

TABLE 11.1
Percentages of Different Types of Households and Families in the United States

Type of Household/Family	Percent
Married couples without children	28.7
Married couples with children	24.1
Women living alone	14.8
Men living alone	10.7
Other family households (i.e., single parents)	16.0
Other (i.e., non-family households)	5.7

Source: U.S. Census Bureau. Washington, DC, 2006.

- First, the popularity of marriage is declining. In 1970, 68% of adults were married; in 2002 that number had declined to 60%.
- Second, the age when people marry is increasing. In 1960, the median age for marriage was 22.8 years for men and 20.3 years for women. In 2002, the numbers changed to 27.1 and 25.3 years, respectively.
- Third, there is growing acceptance of couples living together without being married. Approximately half of all couples cohabit prior to marriage, and 40% of children will live in cohabiting families before they are 16 years of age.
- Fourth, census data appear to undercount lesbian and gay families. The 2000 census listed 601,209 individuals as lesbian or gay. Other estimates suggest that these numbers represent an undercount (Smith and Gates 2001). Most studies indicate a range from 2%–10% of the U.S. population as lesbian or gay. Assuming a conservative 5%, the total number of individuals would total 10,456,405 of the U.S. population. It is further estimated that approximately 30% of those individuals are in committed partnerships (Smith and Gates 2001).
- Fifth, the rate of divorce remains high. Approximately 50% of all U.S. marriages will end in divorce.
- Sixth, there is an increase in the number of minority groups in the United States, many of whom have patterns of marriage and family structures that are different from those of whites. For example, the following are the percentages of married couples by ethnic group: white (81%), Asian (80%), Hispanic (55%), and African American (48%). Minority families may be more likely to live in multi-generational households.
- And seventh, delayed childbearing, as well as increased longevity, resulted in many couples living in households or families without children. Increased rates of divorce and unmarried parenthood have resulted in many single parent households. Persons living alone, or with non-related persons, now make up about 30% of the total. The bottom line is that only about one quarter of U.S. households now include nuclear families, i.e., parents and their children.

Emergency managers, social service agencies, and disaster organizations must consider the diversity of households and family structures in order to address and reduce vulnerability. To illustrate briefly, consider these scenarios:

- Rates of later marriage and divorce mean that more people live alone. Isolation tends to be associated with slower warning receipt and inclination to evacuate.
- People in committed partnerships and marriages appear to be more likely to prepare for disaster, to want to mitigate their risks, and to evacuate.

- Sheltering experiences may be difficult for lesbian, gay, bisexual, or transgendered individuals and couples. Because of a lack of acceptance still present in U.S. society, it may be difficult or even dangerous for people to comfort each other in a public setting. Loss of a home is difficult; loss of social support increases trauma.
- Multi-generational households are more likely to evacuate as a unit. Gathering family members takes time. Consequently, advance warning and assistance with evacuation resources may be necessary.
- Divorce rates and single parenthood mean reduced incomes for many families. Lower-income households and families are less likely to be able to mitigate, prepare for, or recover from disasters.

Additional diversity exists even within these brief examples, with significant implications for a disaster context. For example, multi-generational households may also contain elderly members. Senior citizens do respond to evacuation messages when they are received but may require transportation assistance. Because disabilities increase with age, households with people who are disabled may not be able to evacuate easily. In households and families where a caregiver is present, that person may delay or resist evacuation because of the difficulties in doing so. Conversely, households and families represent ready units for outreach. Because many people tend to live in these collective units, it is possible to maximize public funds for public education efforts. Understanding household and family situations enables practitioners to design specific efforts for their respective risks.

Another concern stems from family and household income and assets. In general, it can be assumed that, other things being equal, households and families with fewer material and human resources will be at greater risk. Units that typically report lower incomes include single parents, elderly couples, people with disabilities, and lesbian couples. To safeguard a household or family against disaster, money helps with purchasing insurance, being able to evacuate, and affording recovery.

Yet households and families also generate other resources helpful in a disaster context. Multiple household and family members increase the number of people available to mitigate disaster, such as putting up storm shutters. Families also embed members in social networks that provide practical links to sources of warning information, evacuation resources, and recovery assistance. Psychological studies clearly demonstrate that social support systems foster greater resiliency to disaster impacts (Norris, Friedman, and Watson 2002; Norris et al. 2002). In short, families and households—our friends, significant others, partners, spouses, parents, and children—can help us through an event and provide a basic unit on which emergency management can build capacity and resilience.

It is important to note that these factors are not mutually exclusive and tend to overlap. In fact, they often co-exist in the same household or family, making them especially vulnerable. Examples include (1) poor elderly minority women living alone, (2) extended migrant farm worker families, and (3) minority grandparent(s) raising grandchildren. In the next section, we address this complex set of circumstances that can engender higher levels of social vulnerability and merits attention.

11.6   HIGH-RISK HOUSEHOLDS AND FAMILIES

Types of households that are more likely to be vulnerable include those who are poor, female-headed, and have members with disabilities or who are elderly. Minority households and families with lower incomes are also at higher risk for injury, death, or property loss. Renters, which include households and families, also represent a particular concern. We turn our attention to these issues next.

11.6.1   Situational Concerns

According to the U.S. Census Bureau (2006) (Table 11.2), a number of situations can be identified as of concern in disaster situations. Of particular concern, at least 10% of households and families fall

---

TABLE 11.2
Percentages of Different Types of At-Risk
Households and Families in the United States

Type of Household/Family	% of Total
Renters	34
Racial minority	33
Non-family	33
Disabled	15
Non-English speaking	19
Foreign born	12
Poor (below poverty level)	10
Elderly (over 65)	9
No vehicle	8
No phone service	5

Source: U.S. Census Bureau. Washington, DC, 2006.

---

below the governmental poverty level and qualify for federal entitlements. Income levels are often associated with particular households and families, such as single parents, recent immigrants, and senior citizens, as noted earlier. Income also creates situations where households and families lack resources for disasters. For example, at least 8% of all households and families do not own a vehicle. For those living in urban areas and dependent on public transportation, evacuation is very difficult. At least 120,000 residents in New Orleans (based on 2.4 persons × 51,000 housing units) did not have a vehicle available for evacuation purposes (Laska 2004). The census data also indicate that within U.S. households and families, approximately 34% are renters. Renting is often associated with lower incomes, which suggests heightened risks for these households and families. The topic of renters will be addressed separately later in this section.

Next, approximately 33% of all U.S. households and families are racial and ethnic minorities. Studies suggest that when coupled with income issues, minority units experience heightened risks (Fothergill, Maestas, and Darlington 1999). One third of households include non-family members, which presents challenges when applying for and receiving assistance. At least 15% of all households and families include a person with one or more disabilities. Nearly one fifth of U.S. units are non-English speaking and 12% are foreign born. What do these numbers suggest?

- Poverty increases vulnerability. With 10% of the population already below the poverty line, disasters will decrease their abilities to provide for members of their households and families. Disasters may also push those above the poverty line into impoverished situations.
- Families and households are likely to evacuate as units and it is important to keep them together. The evacuation of New Orleans resulted in hundreds of children being separated from family members. People with disabilities also lost not only their social support networks during the diaspora, but also their assistive devices and durable medical equipment. By understanding the situational realities of today's households and families, we can design improved evacuation protocols.
- The increasing numbers of minority families and households across the United States require attention to social, political, and cultural complexities associated with their disaster experiences (for specific details on racial and ethnic minorities, see Chapter 5).
- Immigration has always been the norm in the United States, a nation founded by those from foreign shores. Recent immigrants in particular require outreach because of unfamiliarity with new types of disasters and appropriate protective measures. Coupled with

20% of households and families that include non-English speaking members, outreach to educate and assist must be multi-lingual. After September 11th, for example, FEMA issued disaster information in dozens of languages across the New York area.

Good emergency management practice involves knowing the extent to which high-risk households and families live in each community, as well as the situations in which they tend to be concentrated. Resources that can be used to identify these units include geographic information system (GIS)-based community vulnerability mapping (Morrow 1999; Cutter, Mitchell, and Scott 2000; see also Chapter 14). By revealing the locations of specific household and family units, it is possible to initiate planning, launch preparedness efforts, assign response resources, and target recovery initiatives. By knowing who is in a given location, it is also possible to identify the resources and strengths that households and families may bring to a disaster context and design interventions that build on those capacities. In the next section, we learn about the value of those social networks.

11.6.2   THE VALUE OF SOCIAL NETWORKS

Families often reach out to networks of relatives and friends for assistance and such assistance is an important factor in household response (Bolin 1985). About three fourths of the 130,000 impacted households affected by Hurricane Andrew in south Florida were family units, and family ties were a very important coping factor (Morrow 1997). Relatives often lived together, especially in minority households, and three out of four households had other relatives living in the area. These relatives were an important source of assistance in cleanup and repairs: 44% of those heavily impacted and with relatives in the area reported receiving major help from them. Of those who had to move out of their homes, one third moved in with relatives. However, because relatives often live in close proximity, many victims also had relatives who were homeless and, therefore, not in positions to help.

Interviews with families who were impacted by massive flooding in Denver in 1965 showed that families evacuated as units and took refuge in homes of relatives rather than in official centers. Interaction between relatives during the warning period increased the likelihood that relatives' homes would be selected as evacuation points. Younger and older families, compared to middle-aged families, were more likely to seek help from and to evacuate with extended family members. Likewise, minority households were more likely to seek help from and evacuate with extended family members (Drabek and Boggs 1965). Clearly, the family and household units provide the potential for considerable assistance in a disaster situation. Though the circumstances of the event may be trying and overwhelming, those close to us can provide critical sources of support.

11.6.3   STRAIN AND STRESS

Although there is good news about households and families and the support they can bring to us during crisis, it is also true that events can cause strain and stress on us too. As might be expected, strained family relationships are common during disasters and long-term recovery periods (Davis and Ender 1999; Cohan and Cole 2002). For example, a number of persistent psychosocial effects have been identified among tornado victims, including strained family relationships, separation anxieties among children, sleep disturbances, and anxieties over disaster recurrence (Bolin 1982). The temporary housing of dislocated victims tends to be crowded, and they often feel socially isolated and vulnerable in strange surroundings. Not surprisingly, levels of stress are associated with the number of moves necessary before reestablishing permanent housing, and by the length of time spent in temporary shelters. The more moves (three moves was the critical number above which stress effects were clear), and the greater the amount of time spent in temporary shelters, the greater the incidence of persistent psychosocial effects. Living in FEMA trailers appears to be a particularly stressful experience, one that delays emotional recovery and may increase stress to the point where some households and families experience difficulty in reaching a full recovery.

As another example, bushfires devastated a major part of Southeast Australia in 1983. Fourteen people died, including a mother and her four children who were trapped in their car as they tried to reach safety. McFarlane (1987) assessed the long-term impact of the bushfires on the patterns of interaction in families by comparing a group of disaster-affected families with families who had not been exposed to the disaster. Eight months after the disaster, the disaster-affected families showed increased levels of conflict, irritability, and withdrawal compared to the non-affected families. Maternal overprotection and negative changes in parenting behaviors were also common in the affected families. Individuals who are sources of support can also be sources of stress, particularly if there are intense frequent contacts and inequality in the relationships. In a study after Hurricane Andrew, people were asked how much more stress they felt in their relationships with others. The results showed that they felt increased stress, in decreasing order, with their partners (56%), among other adults in the household (47%), between adults and children (46%), among children (43%), with relatives (30%), with neighbors (30%) and with friends (16%) (Morrow 1997).

Another trend that appears in responses to disasters stems from pre-existing conditions. Harvey (2005) studied people's accounts of loss and recovery from the 1993 flooding in the states of Illinois, Iowa, and Missouri. Forty-five individuals who had experienced very serious losses including homes, jobs, and property provided extensive written narratives about their losses and how they coped. Respondents reported in their narratives that marriages and close relationships that were problematic before the flooding often became more problematic as the flooding worsened. The presence of a pre-existing condition suggests how important it is to work on personal relationships prior to an event in order to prove more resilient afterwards. Similarly, professionals designing intervention programs for families and households would want to identify and assess pre-disaster roles, relationships, and issues.

It may be valuable to work with families on their internal coping mechanisms in addition to providing community resources. Vigil and Geary (2008) researched how adolescents were impacted by the ways in which their families coped with the effects of Hurricane Katrina. They studied 50 adolescents who were displaced by Katrina and were living in a relocation camp. The results showed that adolescents whose parents depended more on non-familial and community-provided support had lower self-esteem and more symptoms of distress and depression, thereby increasing stress in family relationships. Although utilizing community resources may be necessary for families, it also tended to make adolescents (1) more aware of their homelessness, (2) have more frequent memories of the hurricane experience, and (3) feel socially stigmatized. Clearly, it is necessary to provide private programs for families and to offer alternatives for family members of varying ages.

11.6.4 RESPONSE TO DISASTERS

Just as households and families are different and are affected by disasters in different ways, they also respond in different ways. What determines the degree of continuing vulnerability from a disaster? What accounts for two families from the same area, both left homeless, responding very differently? Family #1 may experience increased family stress, depression, and child behavioral problems, while family #2 may keep an optimistic outlook and draw on family, friends, and spiritual beliefs to get through this critical time. The first is described as more vulnerable, while the second is described as more resilient. Some factors associated with more difficult recoveries and greater stress include:

- Inadequate economic and material resources
- Physical and mental limitations
- Age, gender, race or ethnicity discrimination

- Large ratio of dependents (children, elderly) to productive adults (e.g., single parent households, large families)
- Lack of knowledge about how to cope due to lack of prior disaster experiences
- Illiteracy or inadequate language proficiency
- Unique cultural differences and beliefs
- Lack of integration into the community (i.e., new residents, migrants, recent immigrants, isolated households and families)
- Lack of community social services to assist households and families in need

Various theories have been developed to explain the factors associated with positive adjustment to a family crisis. One family stress model has been used to explain how individual families adjust to various crises, including physical disabilities (Florian and Dangoor 1994), dementia (Rankin, Haut, and Keefover 1992), divorce (Crosbie-Burnett 1989; Plunkett et al. 1997), and autism (Bristol 1987). The model, called the Double ABCX model, was founded in family stress theory and was adapted by McCubbin and Patterson (1983) from Hill's ABCX family crisis model (Hill 1949, 1958). It is based on the premise that how a family adapts to a particular crisis is the result of the sum of multiple factors. The model looks like this:

$$aA + bB + cC + BC = xX$$

where
   aA = the severity of the event causing the stress and the pile-up of problems
   bB = the resources (physical, social, and psychological) available to the family
   cC = the meaning the family attributes to the overall crisis
   BC = the way in which the family uses the other parts of the model to cope
   xX = how well the family adapts to the crisis and achieves a new balance

In applying this model to the disaster context, it is important to consider the severity of the event causing the stress and the pile-up of problems within a family (aA) because no one event occurs in isolation. A family dealing with relocation after a catastrophe may also be dealing with the stress related to normal life changes (i.e., an elderly member who needs to receive in-home or nursing home care, a young adult getting married or leaving for college, retirement), and pre-event problems such as financial losses, marital problems, abuse (Handmer 1985).

The resources available for the family (bB) can be described as existing and expanded. Existing resources include those from the individuals within the family (i.e., talents, orientations, and communication skills), the family unit (i.e., togetherness, role flexibility, shared values), and the community (i.e., friendships, social support, spirituality). The expanded resources are those that are new or that have not previously been used to deal with life situations. They may include establishing new supportive relationships with kin or neighbors, learning a new skill that is needed to repair damage, or attending community-based counseling groups for the first time.

The meaning that a family attributes to the disaster (cC) or the way they view it includes how they perceive the event itself, as well as the pile-up of stress, old and new resources, and estimates of what they think needs to be done to reestablish a balance in the family. When families are able to redefine the disaster and its related impacts in healthy ways, they are better able to make decisions, reduce emotional burdens, and view the situation as a challenge and opportunity to grow. Blinn-Pike, Phillips, and Reeves (2007) studied individuals and families who were living in evacuation shelters following Hurricane Katrina (see Box 11.1). One 18 year old viewed the crisis negatively and said that reading the newspaper made her feel "sad" because Katrina "ruined her life" and she "did not want to remember but she would always remember it." On the other hand, a 50-year-old father with a serious health condition provided the following quotation illustrating a more positive view of his situation:

BOX 11.1   SHELTER LIFE AFTER HURRICANE KATRINA

Blinn-Pike, Phillips, and Reeves (2007) asked nine survivors of Hurricane Katrina to take a total of 90 Polaroid photographs of their lives in their respective shelters and to participate in individual interviews about their photos. The results showed that they had four particular mental health needs:

Solitude: The residents sought solitude where they could process the devastation and stress they had recently experienced, as well as think about rebuilding their lives. They found this need was met by being able to shut out the world in private spaces and by walking around the facilities by themselves.

Social Relationships: The residents formed friendships with Red Cross volunteers, community members, and other shelter residents and often referred to them as "family." The photos included the friends themselves, as well as where they met to talk and "share a few laughs" including in the community volunteers' homes.

Security: Many of the residents had experienced near death events in the hurricane and felt insecure about their physical safety in the shelter. Photos were taken of the locked doors and security desks at their shelters. The photos also included supply closets, stocked shelves, boxes of MREs or "meals ready to eat," crates of bottled water, and food delivery trucks.

Outreach: When they moved to their current shelters, they were without "contact with the outside world" for more than two weeks while the shelters were set up. When the construction was completed, they took photos of televisions, telephones, and computers to show their relief in finally being able have contact with others, determine the condition of their homes, and apply to government agencies for assistance.

This is a lady who works next door. She is not a part of the shelter. She just comes through and always speaks and asks you how you are doing. … This lady is a diabetic and I am a diabetic. We talk about our diabetes. She has been a diabetic since she was a child and she has had a heart attack. She talks so uplifting so it helps you to be uplifted too. You get depressed. Your sugar be going up and your blood pressure be going up and at least you are safe in being with people. You can always get more furniture.

Families can cope with the impacts of a disaster (BC) in both problem-focused and emotion-focused ways. Problem-focused coping involves using strategies to change the source(s) of stress (i.e., seeking sources of financial and housing assistance). Emotion-focused coping involves both passively avoiding dealing with a situation (inactivity and denial) and actively viewing the situation in healthy ways. By responding to the event with resilience, a family might focus on the positive energies present in the community—the volunteers arriving to help rebuild; the faith-based sector that provides furniture, clothing, and prayer; the local emergency managers and elected officials deferring sleep to plan and implement; and the neighbors who ask after their well-being and bring food. Families can also look into the source of strain and stress and search for resources across the community from mental health agencies, social networks, the faith-based sector, work-based benefit programs, and newly developed disaster programs.

How well the family adapts to the crisis and achieves a new balance (xX) is the sum of the other parts of the model and has been measured in several ways. Researchers have assessed family adaptation to crisis by examining physical and mental health, feelings of well-being, level of family unity, and quality of marital and parenting relationships (Pakenham 2005).

While the discussion above has been about high-risk and vulnerable families, not all families have the characteristics that result in more serious implications from disasters. Resilient families will have fewer problems and may emerge even stronger. Families that are more resilient may

- Be well informed about hazards
- Have stable family and/or social networks
- Be well integrated into the community
- Have a high ratio of productive adults to dependents
- Have greater beliefs in gender equality and share household tasks
- Have a sound economic base
- Have a strong and healthy emotional base, illustrated by
  - Commitment
  - Mutual appreciation and respect
  - Close communication
  - Frequent time together
  - Effective coping abilities
- Nonviolent conflict management skills

These qualities of resiliency can be developed even if they are not present currently in a family or household unit. One means to do so is to link the family to the broader community and to build relationships external to the family or household unit. Social integration, on which resiliency may depend, refers to ties with the larger social world. People who have lived in a community longer often have ties to people and organizations that can provide assistance. More resilient families are likely to have friendships and connections that are sources of information, advice, physical assistance, financial assistance, and emotional comfort. They may feel that they belong in the community and have positive connections with neighbors, friends, clubs and organizations, religious groups, schools, and businesses. In short, they are part of something larger—that is, they are well integrated into the community.

11.6.5   DIFFERENTIAL VULNERABILITY

Just as households and families differ in their vulnerability to the affects of disaster, so do the individuals within them. The relative power of members of a given household and family can be an important factor in whether they get needed help and resources. For example, the post-disaster needs of women, children, and the elderly may be neglected in households and families with controlling male heads of household, particularly if disaster responders do not have specific outreach mechanisms and services in place for them, or do not involve women in decision making at all levels. Women who are victims of domestic violence may not assert their opinions or express their needs for fear of escalating physical harm to them or their children. The elderly may feel that they have few resources to help the family cope, may feel like a burden, and fear they will be left behind during evacuation and relocation (for additional details, see previous chapters on these social groups). In the next section, we profile concerns about another often-overlooked group: those who rent their homes.

11.6.5.1   Renters

Former renters make up a high proportion of displaced families ending up in tent cities and FEMA trailers after an event. Renters have less control over (1) damage-prevention initiatives such as installing storm shutters; (2) property maintenance and upkeep; (3) housing insurance; and (4) repairs and reconstruction. In addition, they have been found to have less experience with hazards and be less likely to be prepared for a hazardous event (Burby and Steinburg 2002). Most renters do not have insurance on their personal property even though such policies are relatively inexpensive. A very important factor affecting the number of homeless families after a disaster is whether there was mitigation, such as shutters and earthquake minimizing measures, on public and subsidized housing units. Families were dislocated from every public housing unit in south Miami-Dade County after Hurricane Andrew. Most of these families spent the next year or more in tent cities and FEMA trailers (Morrow 1997).

Renters are at risk for being displaced from their homes if the

- Housing has no hazard mitigation such as shutters, elevations, tie-downs, or retrofitting for seismic hazards
- Owner does not have funds for repairing or rebuilding the rental unit
- Owner decides not to use insurance payouts for rebuilding the rental property
- Owner decides to improve the property and raise the rent to above pre-event levels
- Property becomes part of a government "buyout" mitigation program
- Property owner(s) cannot be located (such as when all owners of a multi-owner condominium property cannot be located to give permission for rebuilding)

Most homeowners are insured and insurance companies are anxious to reduce losses. Disaster policies and assistance programs tend to help homeowners rather than renters and renters often believe they do not qualify for federal assistance. For example, both renters and homeowners may apply for federal disaster assistance. The first place to start is to apply for a Small Business Administration (SBA) loan. Renters may apply for the personal property loan, which cannot exceed $40,000. Acceptable items that can be covered include furniture, clothing, and cars damaged by the disaster. Homeowners may apply for real property loans of up to $200,000 (these numbers are from 2008 FEMA dollar limits).

The SBA loans seem reasonable at first glance. However, because renters live in buildings owned by someone else, they are at risk for long-term displacement in a disaster situation. The 1994 Northridge earthquake, for example, impacted renters hard. Los Angeles County declared that 27,000 multi-family buildings, or 84% of the damaged homes, were uninhabitable. Many renters went into other nearby rental units. However, a number of initiatives and partnerships were required to rebuild rental units (Comerio 1998). The economic recession, coupled with few apartment owners holding earthquake insurance, meant that funds would be meager for rental recovery. Many apartment buildings were owned by multiple landlords. The recession meant that there would be minimal cash flow for their collective efforts to rebuild and also undermined abilities to secure Small Business Administration disaster loans.

The Federal Emergency Management Agency (FEMA) provides other kinds of assistance for renters and homeowners. Coverage includes costs associated with debris removal, crisis counseling, medical services, funeral costs, transportation, and fuel, among other items. People must apply for that assistance, be confirmed by FEMA inspectors, and then document their expenses. In previous disasters, such as the 1989 Loma Prieta, California, earthquake, renters and others sued FEMA successfully over head-of-household issues. In some cases, the first person to apply for federal assistance within the rental unit affected secured the funds. Similar situations have been observed in households where domestic violence is present. In such circumstances, the abusive partner typically controls any federal disaster assistance. Finally, renters may believe that they do not qualify for federal assistance.

11.6.5.2 Assisting Renters

A number of disaster organizations assisted Northridge renters. Up to 160,000 residents received help from approximately 450 voluntary organizations. For renters, applying for assistance through voluntary organizations may be a particularly helpful route. However, even experienced disaster organizations tend to favor homeowners over renters. Disaster organizations that focus on rebuilding, for example, typically select low-income homeowners to assist. Renters who live in multi-family households, public housing, or in rental homes usually remain at the mercy of landlords or governmental agencies. Displacement can be considerable, as is the case in Louisiana after Hurricane Katrina. Public housing units have been condemned across multiple parishes. New units are being rebuilt in mixed-income units. Concern has arisen that low-income households and families will experience permanent displacement as a result.

To rebuild rental units after the Northridge earthquake, the city of Los Angeles secured $10,641,000 in funding for both single- and multi-family housing. Housing and Urban Development (HUD) provided funds from its Community Development Block Grants (CDBG) and HOME Investment Partnership Funds. The state convinced some lenders to forgive loans and late payments. Los Angeles donated funds to repair 12,000 rental units. By 1997, three fourths of the units were repaired to some degree (Comerio 1998). Meanwhile, renters had relocated to new places, farther away from friends, social resources, and work than before.

Communities can assist renters in several ways. After the Loma Prieta earthquake, for example, Santa Cruz, California, built the Neary Lagoon Housing Cooperative with a mix of pre-disaster and disaster funds. The co-op set aside 25% of its units for earthquake victims, to ensure that those directly affected did not lose rental housing permanently. The city also sustained damage to three of four single-room occupancy (SRO) hotels that provided affordable, convenient rentals to seniors and low-income households. Efforts were put into place to ensure that the rebuilt units remained affordable. Temporary housing was secured in a previously abandoned nursing home. Some SRO residents stayed there until able to return to the downtown SROs. Rental prices in those units increased less than $100. After Hurricane Katrina, though, rental prices have increased as much as 25% in rental units. Public officials can make a difference in retaining a diverse residential community for all income levels and types of households by mandating rent controls. In Mississippi, Lutheran Disaster Services has taken on the task of advocating for renters.

Additional activities that would benefit renters include

- Developing mitigation programs that target landlords and renters
- Developing local ordinances regarding landlord responsibilities
- Planning targeted hazard educational campaigns
- Promoting community land use planning that protects affordable rental housing
- Launching campaigns promoting renters' insurance
- Developing disaster recovery plans anticipating that many renters will likely be homeless after a major event

11.7   HOUSEHOLD AND FAMILY RESPONSES ACROSS THE DISASTER LIFE CYCLE

In this section, we follow the format developed in previous chapters to organize both research and ideas about household and family responses across the disaster life cycle. The purpose is both to demonstrate what we know and to recommend practical advice that can be used to strengthen families and household responses and build more resilient units that spur community recovery as well.

11.7.1   WARNING/EVACUATION/RESPONSE

In the first phase of disasters, households and families respond to warnings, seek information and advice, and decide how to prepare and/or evacuate. There is some evidence that they make their preparation and evacuation decisions as a unit (Figure 11.1). In general, groups with children are more prone to evacuate, and those with elderly are less likely to leave (Heath et al. 2001; Gladwin, Gladwin, and Peacock 2001).

There is further evidence that households and families prefer to evacuate as a group and will wait for all members before leaving. It is unusual for more than 20% of evacuees to actually go to shelters, *as most prefer to stay with family members or friends.* As early as 1968, Drabek and Boggs reported on a study of Denver families who experienced relocation as a result of the massive flood

FIGURE 11.1 A family commences evacuation through the New Orleans Union Passenger Terminal (NOUPT) prior to Hurricane Gustav in 2008. *Source*: Jacinta Quesada/FEMA news photo.

of 1965. They described (1) their responses to initial warnings as disbelief, (2) their preferences to evaluate as a unit, and (3) their tendencies to take refuge in the homes of relatives rather than in official shelters. These findings were confirmed by Mikami and Ikedo (1985) when they studied a devastating flood in 1982 in Nagasaki, Japan. The Japanese families tended to underestimate the possibility of a disaster and then made every effort to contact and be with their family members. According to Mikami and Ikedo (1985), in both pending floods and earthquakes, Japanese would return to their homes to check on the well-being of other family members. If this was not possible, they would make so many telephone calls that it was necessary to regulate private calls in Nagasaki so that communication lines would be open for public emergency use. In a coastal Louisiana post-Katrina survey respondents ranked being able to keep family members together as the third most important factor in future evacuation decisions. Only being able to track the hurricane and knowing its intensity were rated as more important (Morrow and Gladwin 2006). As households and families increasingly go their separate ways each day to jobs, schools, and other activities, this issue becomes important to emergency managers.

Several studies have examined how minority families go through the early stages of disaster response. Perry and Greene (1982) studied the responses of Mexican American families when they were warned of a pending flood in the western United States in 1978. The flood eventually resulted in over \$6 million in damages and the evacuation of 1200 people. They reported that the Mexican American families, compared to white families who lived in the same danger zone, were more skeptical about the warnings and perceived themselves to be in less danger. Consequently, they were less likely to evacuate and continued with their daily routines.

Based on Hurricane Katrina, Eisenman et al. (2007) and Fothergill and Peek (2004) suggested that minority groups living in the United States are at greater risk for not responding to disaster warnings due to language barriers, distrust of governmental authorities, preferences for seeking information from family or relatives, and lack of transportation and economic resources (see also Chapter 5 and Perry, Mushkatel 1986; Peguero 2006).

There is some evidence that the more pets in a household or family, the higher the risk of household evacuation failure. In a study by Hall et al. (2004), many residents explained that they failed to evacuate because they owned multiple pets. This study reinforced that human–pet bonds influence family emergency evacuation. The conclusion was that pre-disaster planning should place a high priority on facilitating pet evacuation through pre-disaster education of pet owners and emergency management personnel. In addition, it is important for mental health professionals who work in disaster preparation and response to comprehend the importance of this bond.

11.7.2 IMPACTS

While is important to keep in mind that household and family arrangements can be complex, it is also important to understand that disasters can affect them in different ways. Table 11.3 shows that disasters can impact households and families in four ways: economic, emotional/psychological, physical, and/or social.

No household or family is impacted in exactly the same way by a disaster. One group may suffer severe physical or mental health problems but have the economic resources to seek professional help. A second group may experience increased emotional problems that lead to increased marital

---

TABLE 11.3
Four Ways Disasters Can Impact Households and Families

Economic	Uninsured home and property losses
	Temporary or permanent loss of employment
	Higher living costs, including transportation
Emotional/psychological	Role overload, conflict, or inadequacy
	Overworked parents and bored children
	Stress in intimate and partner relationships
	Family violence
	Behavioral problems in children
Physical	Loss of family members and/or friends
	Destroyed or damaged homes
	Loss of possessions including personal treasures
	Loss of environment and tools for everyday living
	Temporary or permanent dislocation
	Longer commutes to work or school
	Loss of local businesses, services, schools, recreational programs, etc.
Social	Loss of neighborhood
	Loss of social networks, institutions, and services

Source: FEMA. A social vulnerability approach to disasters. FEMA Emergency Management Institute, Higher Education Project, 2003. http://www.training.fema.gov/EMIWeb/edu/sovul.asp.

problems, substance abuse, and/or domestic violence as a result of the economic strain of losing their jobs and home. And a third may find that their biggest concerns have to do with the impact on their children. Depending on the ages of the children, the loss of their neighborhood, friends, school, and relatives can result in aggressive or risky behaviors, loss of interest in school, and depression. There is mounting evidence that family violence increases in the aftermath of major disasters. It is important for communities be prepared to deal with this, and for officials to be alert to the possibilities (see Chapter 12 for further details).

Research on the impact of living in evacuation shelters immediately following a disaster, which families prefer not to do, is limited (Nigg et al. 2006). Blinn-Pike, Phillips, and Reeves (2007, see Box 11.1) found that Katrina evacuees formed bonds with the other residents in their shelters and formed "family" units that provided important temporary support. One resident was in the shelter with her two children, ages 9 and 11 years. She took a photo of one of the community volunteers and titled it "my friend" and described her as "an angel and she brought me over to her house one day. We are family now." The residents took photos of group gathering areas that became informal places to tell their disaster stories, listen to others' stories, and find solace that they were not alone in their trauma. Several residents described the individuals at these gatherings as "family." The gathering places included dining areas, lounge areas, outdoor picnic tables, and entrances to the shelters.

An 18-year-old resident took a picture of an empty picnic table and titled it "memories." She stated that she took the photo because "everybody sits there and talks about the bad stuff that's going on. ... It makes me feel comfortable—almost like family because we always sit there and talk about stuff." A middle aged man took a picture of the dining room and said, "The dining room is where we eat ... and I think the dining room is where we all get a chance to all be together and talk to each other ... if you have a problem then you can tell the guy next to you."

The impact of disaster can be as diverse as the families and households that go through the event. As explained earlier in this chapter, the personal strengths that families and household members bring to an event can help. Pre-existing experiences may also provide some degree of inoculation from the experience, although researchers have also discovered that unresolved traumas (disasters, interpersonal violence) can significantly increase stress levels, including the potential for post-traumatic stress disorder (Norris, Friedman, and Watson 2002; Norris et al. 2002). The extent of the event is also important to consider. Disasters that cause widespread disruption to social networks and result in significant or even permanent displacement have the potential to cause serious problems. Although the cases of catastrophic events in the United States are rare, it may be that disasters such as Hurricane Katrina cause significant impacts on family and household members. The 1972 loss of an entire community in West Virginia led to increases in personal trauma, higher rates of job loss, increased alcohol and drug abuse, as well as interpersonal violence escalation and increased stress in children (Erikson 1976; Newman 1976).

11.7.3 RECOVERY

The research on disasters points to the role of both community-level and family-level factors in determining the effectiveness of short- and long-term recovery efforts. At the community level, one of the most important factors in short-term family recovery is the perceived availability of assistance and resources which family and friends often provide (Figure 11.2; and see Bolin 1981). Variables found to affect a household's or family's recovery from a disaster include:

- Family demographic characteristics (age, gender, and race)
- Housing needs
- Kinship support
- Pre-disaster socioeconomic status
- Impact and losses incurred in the disaster
- Employment continuity

FIGURE 11.2   Friends and family help with cleanup after a seven-foot flood reached into a Cedar Rapids, Iowa, home in 2008. *Source*: Photo by Greg Henshall /FEMA news photo

Bolin (1981) studied families one year after two tornados hit Wichita Falls, Texas. The tornados left more than 18,000 people homeless, 900 injured, and 47 dead. He concentrated on predictors of emotional and economic recovery. The best predictors of emotional recovery included:

- Fewer housing and relocation issues
- More informal aid from kin and community
- Younger age of adult(s) in the family
- Less damage to the home
- More and better insurance coverage

While the predictors of economic recovery are similar to those listed for emotional recovery, two additional predictors of economic recovery were revealed:

- Religiosity
- Previous disaster experience

Religiosity may reflect more active church involvement and therefore more access to formal and informal aid from the church and church members. Faith-based structures also offer a means to explain crisis through their belief system and an organized framework within which to deliver services. There may also be an acceptance-of-fate factor involved, allowing more religious families to deal better with crisis. Household or family members with previous disaster experience may be more knowledgeable about how to obtain the assistance that can shorten their recovery times. Previous disaster experience in other studies is also associated with greater resilience, whether that disaster might be a house fire, an economic crisis, a serious illness or death in the family, or a disaster. By learning from the events that we go through, we may be able to strengthen our personal resistance to disaster impacts.

The experience of a disaster will vary from one community to another and from one family to another. Displacement may differ as well for some family and household members. As described in Chapter 8, people with disabilities and seniors may linger in shelters and temporary shelters as they seek appropriate and accessible accommodations. Larger family units may experience delays as well, as they seek homes that avoid overcrowding, which is associated with stress, increased interpersonal tension and violence, and conflict. The experience of living in temporary settings may be challenging as well, because of now living at a distance from schools, work, and familiar locations like health care facilities, grocery stores, and pharmacies. Adapting to these new locations and the associated impacts on the household budget (such as transportation costs) may be particularly stressful.

Being away from one's home can be difficult on everyone, particularly seniors, children, and people with disabilities who need access to familiar locations, resources, health providers, and schools. The recovery process, including rebuilding, can be short or long. Renters may be able to relocate quickly—or may face elongated displacement as described earlier. Rebuilding may be able to commence quickly but could also take considerable time (see Box 11.2 and Dash et al. 2007).

BOX 11.2   REBUILDING AFTER DISASTERS

Depending on one's income level, insurance, amount of damage, and understanding of the (re) building process, getting back to permanent housing can occur quickly or it can take years, assuming you are fortunate enough to own your own home. Think about the steps that have to be undertaken before that happens:

- Debris must be sorted, piled, and removed including hazardous materials like household and vehicular chemicals, pesticides, and painting supplies.
- Insurance and/or federal and state funds for rebuilding must be secured.
- Homeowners will need to secure grants or loans for rebuilding. FEMA provides grants and loans. Based on income, the homeowner will either receive a loan (maximum of $200,000, in 2009 dollars) or be referred to individual assistance programs for a grant. The maximum grant in 2009 was $30,300. Homeowners (and renters) may also qualify for other assistance including room furnishings, appliances, educational materials including computers and school books, tools used for a job, cleanup items, damage to a vehicle, and moving and storage expenses.
- For a single-family home the building site must be cleared and prepared. A concrete slab may need to be removed and re-poured.
- Blueprints for a new home must be designed and approved and the homeowner must secure a contractor, subcontractors, and building permits.
- The next step is to purchase building supplies, which may be in short supply due to the disaster.
- Many elderly living on social security—who own their homes outright, but cannot afford sufficient insurance coverage (or perhaps any at all)—may be relying exclusively on the FEMA grant of $30,300. Most communities establish a Long Term Recovery Committee or Unmet Needs Committee that aids families through volunteer labor.

Imagine staying in a travel trailer, hotel room, or with family while rebuilding. You may be living out of suitcases, unable to cook the kinds of food that you want, and traveling out of your way to take children to now-distant schools or to your own worksite. The time spent in someone else's home may become stressful. You are trying to stay on top of the rebuilding, to schedule contractors, subcontractors, and inspectors; to deal with the FEMA and insurance paperwork; and to remain optimistic that you will get home again. You are away from neighbors and social support networks. What coping mechanisms might you use to survive the rebuilding process?

Source: Adapted from Phillips, B. *Disaster recovery*. Boca Raton, FL: CRC Press, 2009.

Minimal research has been conducted to date on the long-term experiences of families and house-holds during the recovery period. What does exist suggests that social vulnerability varies across family and household units and that a diverse set of recovery planning efforts must take that into account.

11.8 IMPLICATIONS FOR ACTION

Hazard mitigation means taking action to reduce or prevent future damage, preferably before a disaster strikes. As the losses from recent hurricanes have mounted, state and federal authorities have directed more attention to hazard mitigation initiatives, such as developing and advertising materials and methods to strengthen homes; providing funding for low-income families to purchase hurricane shutters; working with households and families, neighborhoods, and communities, to improve flood plain management; strengthening building codes and compliance; and improving levee protection.

A number of agencies, such as FEMA and the American Red Cross, have developed Web sites and materials to help households and families reduce their vulnerability. Some strategies that can be used by emergency managers and disaster professions to reach households and families include (see previous chapters for specific content on race, ethnicity, age, gender, and disability, and also see the Resources section at the end of this chapter):

- Designing preparedness materials and training programs that link to the diverse array of families and households
- Distributing free pamphlets and materials in public places, such as schools and supermarkets
- Making full use of the public media, including ethnic radio stations
- Placing information in local newsletters and tabloids
- Working with community agencies and organizations
- Developing materials targeting special needs, such as large print pamphlets, materials in appropriate languages, and materials at appropriate reading levels

11.8.1 USING HOUSEHOLD AND FAMILY STRENGTHS

An important lesson from the research on groups and disasters is that family and kin networks are valued and important sources of support during disaster, particularly among minority households and families. They can be an important asset to communities and should be encouraged.

Strategies to assist households and families through a disaster crisis while effectively utilizing family ties and strengths include

- Reopening schools and childcare programs quickly. Children will be bored and parents stressed. Schools are often used as shelters but should be avoided as temporary housing in the aftermath. Child-care operators and family caregivers provide a valuable service that needs support in order to get parents back to work and to keep children safe, yet they rarely are considered part of the recovery effort.
- Giving high priority to parks and recreational programs. Children and youth need to be kept occupied during long recovery periods to avoid boredom, depression, and behavioral problems.
- Expanding the definition of family or household to include culturally diverse models when designing assistance programs. There have been many examples in past disasters where nontraditional families, such as two families living together, have experienced difficulty getting appropriate assistance.
- Keeping families together throughout evacuation including evacuation of seniors and peo-ple with disabilities, particularly children with disabilities.

- Keeping family and social groups together when assigning shelter space or temporary housing. Serious problems, including violence, have occurred as the result of cultural and ethnic differences not being taken into account when assigning households and families to temporary housing. Grouping households and families together enables them to provide each other emotional and physical support, such as child care.
- Facilitating family communication channels during the crisis period by providing access to telephones and e-mail in shelters and temporary housing areas (to the extent possible including accessible communication devices).
- Anticipating and planning for increased needs for family services, including counseling services, teen programs, child abuse caseworkers, and domestic violence shelters.
- Providing diverse temporary housing that is accessible and located as close as possible to familiar neighborhoods and schools.
- Offering programming in temporary housing that enables families to cope with stress and strain.
- Developing family and household conflict resolution and mediation programs.
- Offering respite care for caretakers, child care and recreational programs in temporary housing parks and apartment units, and senior center programming.
- Launching a case management process for recovery planning among low-income, single-parent, and senior families and households, and others deemed to be at risk.
- Connecting volunteer resources to families seeking to rebuild but lacking resources to do so, through the case management process.
- Developing programs that target the particular problems of renters including displacement and advocate for their needs and rights. Work with landlords to expedite rebuilding of multi-family housing.

11.9 SUMMARY

This chapter addressed a complex question: How do households and families prepare for, respond to, and recover from disasters? As this chapter revealed, the answer requires that the following group and individual factors be taken into consideration at each stage of the disaster life cycle: (1) composition of households and families; (2) composition and utilization of social networks; (3) composition, availability, and utilization of resources; (4) risk status of households and families; and (5) ability to mitigate and handle family stress. It is clear that families and households bring social networks, personal relationships, and resources that can help them to prepare for and move through a disaster experience. It is equally clear that differential vulnerability exists across those units, including the potential for significant effects on seniors, children and teens, minority families and households, renters, and those at risk for interpersonal violence. Building capacity within families and households strengthens their resilience in the face of what may seem like overwhelming obstacles to survival and recovery. Working at and nurturing personal relationships is a primary action that can be taken to strengthen family and household resilience, particularly before disaster strikes.

11.10 DISCUSSION QUESTIONS

1. What does the fact that differences in households and families exist in a community mean to an emergency manager?
2. What are the implications for emergency managers seeking to design preparedness, response, and recovery programs?
3. What are some types of households and families that are likely to be found in rural communities, coastal communities, and urban centers?
4. What can a community do to assist renters to mitigate and respond to disasters?

5. What things can emergency managers and responders do to help households and families cope and reduce stress?
6. How can the Family Stress Model be used to help emergency managers provide better services to families and households?
7. If you were a local mental health professional, what kinds of programs might you design before and after disaster to support different variations of family and household units?
8. If you were a school administrator, what might you do to build capacity and foster resiliency within the next generation?

REFERENCES

Aguirre, B. E. 1980. The long term effects of major natural disasters on marriage and divorce: An ecological study. *Victimology* 5:298–307.
Blinn-Pike, L., B. Phillips, and P. Reeves. 2006. Shelter life after Hurricane Katrina: A visual analysis of evacuee perspectives. *Journal of Mass Emergencies and Disasters* 24:303–31.
Bolin, R. C. 1981. Family recovery after disaster: A discriminant function analysis. Paper presented at the annual meeting of the American Sociological Association, San Antonio, TX.
———. 1982. *Long-term family recovery from disaster*. Boulder: University of Colorado.
———. 1985. Disasters and long-term recovery policy: A focus on housing and families. *Policy Studies Review* 4:709–15.
Bristol, M. M. 1987. Mothers of children with autism and communication disorders: Successful adaptation and the double ABCX model. *Journal of Autism and Developmental Disorders* 17:469–86.
Burby, R., and L. Steinburg. 2002. In the shadow of a refinery: Preparedness of vulnerable populations exposed to natech disasters. Paper presented at the International Sociological Association, Brisbane, Australia.
Cohan, C. L., and S. W. Cole. 2002. Life course transitions and natural disaster: Marriage, birth, and divorce following Hurricane Hugo. *Journal of Family Psychology* 16:14–25.
Comerio, M. 1998. *Disaster hits home: New policy for urban housing recovery*. Berkeley: University of California Press.
Crosbie-Burnett, M. 1989. Application of the family stress theory to remarriage: A model for assessing and helping stepfamilies. *Family Relations* 38:323–31.
Cutter, S. L., J. T. Mitchell, and M. S. Scott. 2000. Revealing the vulnerability of people and places: A case study of Georgetown County, South Carolina. *Annals of the Association of American Geographers* 90:713–37.
Dash, N., B. H. Morrow, J. Mainster, and L. Cunningham. 2007. Lasting effects of Hurricane Andrew on a working class community. *Natural Hazards Review* 8:13–21.
Davis, K. M., and M. G. Ender. 1999. The 1997 Red River Valley flood: Impact on marital relationships. *Applied Behavioral Science Review* 7:181–88.
Drabek, T. E., and K. S. Boggs. 1968. Families in disaster: Reactions and relatives. *Journal of Marriage and the Family* 30:443–51.
Eisenman, D. P. K., K. M. Cordasco, S. Asch, J. F. Golden, and D. Glik. 2007. Disaster planning and risk communication with vulnerable communities: Lessons from Hurricane Katrina. *American Journal of Public Health* 97:S109–15.
Erikson, K. 1976. *Everything in its path*. New York: Penguin.
Florian, V., and N. Dangoor. 1994. Personal and familial adaptation of women with severe physical disabilities: A further validation of the double ABCX model. *Journal of Marriage and the Family* 56:735–46.
Fothergill, A., E. Maestas, and J. D. Darlington. 1999. Race, ethnicity and disasters in the United States: A review of literature. *Disasters* 23:156–73.
Fothergill, A., and L. Peek. 2004. Poverty and disasters in the United States: A review of recent sociological findings. *Natural Disasters* 32:89–110.
Gladwin, C., H. Gladwin, and W. G. Peacock. 2001. Modeling hurricane evacuation decisions with ethnographic methods. *International Journal of Mass Emergencies and Disasters* 19:117–43.
Hall, M. J., A. Ng, R. J. Ursano, H. Holloway, C. Fullerton, and J. Casper. 2004. Psychological impact of the animal–human bond in disaster preparedness and response. *Journal of Psychiatric Practice* 10:368–73.
Handmer, J. 1985. Local reaction to acquisition: An Australian study. Working paper #53, Centre for Resource and Environmental Studies, Australian National University.

Harvey, J. H., S. K. Stein, N. Olsen, R. J. Roberts, S. K. Lutgendorf, and J. A. Ho. 1995. Narratives of loss and recovery from natural disaster. *Journal of Social Behavior and Personality* 10:313–30.

Heath, S. E., P. H. Kass, A. M. Beck, and L. T. Glicksman. 2001. Human and pet-related risk factors for household evacuation failure during a natural disaster. *American Journal of Epidemiology* 153:659–66.

Hill, R. 1949. *Families under stress.* New York: Harper and Row.

———. 1958. Generic features of families under stress. *Social Casework* 49:139–50.

Laska, S. 2004. "What if Hurricane Ivan Had Not Missed New Orleans." Natural Hazards Review, published at http://www.colorado.edu/hazards/o/nov04/nov04c.html. (November 2004, retrieved last May 11, 2009).

McCubbin, H. I., and J. M. Patterson. 1983. The family stress process: The double ABCX model of adjustment and adaptation. In *Social stress and the family: Advances and development in family stress theory and research,* eds. H. I. McCubbin, M. B. Sussman, and J. M. Patterson, 7–37. New York: Haworth.

McFarlane, A. C. 1987. Family functioning and overprotection following a natural disaster: The longitudinal effects of post-traumatic morbidity. *Australian and New Zealand Journal of Psychiatry* 21:210–18.

Mikami, S., and K. Ikedo. 1985. Human response to disasters. *International Journal of Mass Emergencies and Disasters* 3:107–32.

Morrow, B. H. 1997. Stretching the bonds: The families of Andrew. In *Hurricane Andrew: Ethnicity, gender and the sociology of disasters,* eds. W. G. Peacock, B. H. Morrow, and H. Gladwin, 141–70. New York: Routledge.

———. 1999. Identifying and mapping community vulnerability. *Disasters: The Journal of Disaster Studies, Policy and Management* 23:1–18.

Morrow, B. H., and H. Gladwin. 2006. Coastal Louisiana post-Katrina evacuation planning survey. Final report submitted through Dewberry and Davis and URS to FEMA.

Newman, J. 1976. Children of disaster. *American Journal of Psychiatry* 133:306–12.

Nigg, J. M., J. Barnshaw, and M. R. Torres. 2006. Hurricane Katrina and the flooding of New Orleans: Emergent issues in sheltering and temporary housing. *Annals of the American Academy of Political and Social Science* 604:113–28.

Norris, F. H., M. J. Friedman, and P. J. Watson. 2002. 60,000 disaster victims speak: Part II. Summary and implications of the disaster mental health research. *Psychiatry* 65 (3): 240–60.

Norris, F. H., M. J. Friedman, P. J. Watson, C. M. Byrne, E. Diaz, and K. Kaniasty. 2002. 60,000 disaster victims speak: Part I. An empirical review of the empirical literature, 1981–2001. *Psychiatry* 65 (3): 207–39.

Pakenham, K. I., C. Samios, and K. Sofronoff. 2005. Adjustment in mothers of children with Asperger syndrome: An application of the double ABCX model of family adjustment. *Autism* 9:191–212.

Peguero, A. A. 2006. Latino disaster vulnerability: The dissemination of hurricane mitigation information among Florida's homeowners. *Hispanic Journal of Behavioral Sciences* 28:5–22.

Perry, R. W., and M. R. Greene. 1982. The role of ethnicity in decision making process. *Sociological Inquiry* 52:306–34.

Perry, R. W., and A. H. Mushkatel. 1986. *Minority citizens in disasters.* Athens: University of Georgia Press.

Phillips, B. 2009. *Disaster recovery.* Boca Raton, FL: CRC Press.

Plunkett, S. W., M. G. Sanchez, C. S. Henry, and L. C. Robinson. 1997. Double ABCX model and children's post-divorce adaptation. *Journal of Divorce and Remarriage* 27:17–37.

Rankin, E. D., M. W. Haut, and R. W. Keefover. 1992. Clinical assessment of family caregivers in dementia. *The Gerontologist* 32:813–21.

Smith, D. M., and G. Gates. 2001. Gay and lesbian families in the United States. Washington, DC: Urban Institute. http://www.urban.org/publications/1000491.html (accessed August 1, 2008).

U.S. Census Bureau. 2002. Washington, DC.

———. 2003. Washington, DC.

———. 2004. Washington, DC.

———. 2006. *Selected social characteristics in the United States: 2006.* Washington, DC.

Vigil, J. M., and D. C. Geary. 2008. A preliminary investigation of family group coping styles and psychological well-being among adolescent survivors of Hurricane Katrina. *Journal of Family Psychology* 22:176–80.

RESOURCES

ORGANIZATIONS (ACCESSED AUGUST 2008)

- Gender and Disaster Network, www.gdnonline.org. The Gender and Disaster Network is an educational project initiated by women and men interested in gender relations in disaster contexts.

- National Council on Family Relations, www.ncfr.org. The National Council on Family Relations provides an educational forum for family researchers, educators, and practitioners to share in the development and dissemination of knowledge about families and family relationships, establishes professional standards, and works to promote family well-being.
- Cooperative State Research, Education, and Extension Service, www.csrees.usda.gov. The Cooperative State Research, Education, and Extension Service provides programs through partnerships with land-grant universities and cooperative extension faculty in every state. Programs that are supported include communities at risk, housing and environment, leadership and volunteer development, financial security, public policy, and rural and community development.

Resource Sites (Accessed August 2008)

- Family Emergency Preparedness Plan from Ready America (www.ready.gov), http://www.ready.gov/america/_downloads/familyemergencyplan.pdf
- Basic Emergency Supply Kit, http://www.ready.gov/america/_downloads/checklist2.pdf
- Protecting Your Family's Property from Disaster, http://www.fema.gov/plan/prevent/howto/index.shtm#4
- Pets and Disasters Emergency Preparedness Kit, http://www.hsus.org/hsus_field/hsus_disaster_center/

12 Violence and Disaster Vulnerability

Brenda D. Phillips, Pam Jenkins, and Elaine Enarson

CONTENTS

12.1   CHAPTER PURPOSE

How does living with violence and fear impact someone's vulnerability to disaster? How should emergency managers, caseworkers, shelter providers, child and elder care workers, and community advocates respond to problems of general violence before, during, and after disaster? How extensive is domestic violence in the aftermath of disaster, in particular? The purpose of this chapter is to examine concerns about all kinds of violence in a disaster context and recommend practical strategies to reduce injuries and deaths from all forms of violent behavior.

12.2   OBJECTIVES

As a result of reading this chapter, readers will be able to

1. Understand how different kinds of violence impact social groups in the United States.
2. Outline explanations for rates of violence in American culture and describe counter-trends.
3. Understand differential effects of disasters on various populations and groups.
4. Identify trends in exposure to violent situations.
5. Explain the relevance of understanding violence in disaster situations.
6. List the implications of violence for the practice of emergency management and related professions.
7. Explain practical steps that can be taken to mitigate violence as a factor in disaster vulnerability.

12.3   INTRODUCTION

In most disasters the crime rate drops, a reality that often surprises people. For example, looting, defined as the theft of people's possessions in a disaster, is unusual, although media reports suggest otherwise (Fischer 1998). In reality, people who are arrested in a disaster area are often local residents going back for a pet, medicines, or possessions (Tierney, Lindell, and Perry 2001). Despite the drop in the crime rate, it also appears that some violent acts go unrecognized and unrecorded in disaster contexts. Researchers have begun to uncover and reveal concerns about domestic violence in disaster. This chapter reviews those studies and also goes further by examining a wide set of issues about violence of all kinds. Violence remains one of the least examined and least understood behaviors in disaster contexts, particularly after the alarming and largely untrue media reports during Hurricane Katrina (see Box 12.1). What has not been widely told about those days is the considerable level of pro-social behavior that saved lives, prevented harm, and demonstrated remarkable resiliency (Rodriguez, Trainor, and Quarantelli 2006). Despite the general good news about disaster and crime, it remains true also that those at risk for violence remain so during and after an event. The deeply embedded societal problem of violence, of all kinds, still needs to be dealt with even in a disaster context.

The purpose of this chapter is to explore the full spectrum of violent events that might affect people or actually occur in disaster and to explore ways to reduce such risks. We begin by examining the presence and prevalence of violence in American culture and society.

12.3.1   VIOLENCE AND AMERICAN CULTURE AND SOCIETY

Advocates for those affected by violence suggest that American culture and history demonstrate a high degree of tolerance for violence (for examples of this debate, see Box 12.2). From childhood on, Americans are socialized to live, play, and even work in a culture that does not acknowledge the pervasiveness or influence of violence. Those concerned point to toy and game producers that

---

BOX 12.1   HURRICANE KATRINA: MYTH AND REALITY

A cliché in any disaster is that the event brings out the best and worst in people. As portrayed in the media, those affected by Hurricane Katrina appeared among the worst. We heard that they "were raping babies in the Superdome and Convention Center, guns were blazing in the Superdome, and helicopters were shot out of the sky as they tried to rescue people from roof tops." Very little of that proved to be true (Rodriguez, Trainor, and Quarantelli 2006). And the many acts of heroism, especially by African American men, went unnoticed and undocumented.

Yet all violence did not disappear during Katrina. Gretna sheriffs shot their guns in the air to keep New Orleanians from crossing the Crescent City Bridge to higher ground. Seven New Orleans police officers were charged with first-degree and attempted first-degree murder in a shooting of unarmed storm victims on the Dandbridge Bridge in Eastern New Orleans. A local jazz singer was raped on a rooftop as she waited for rescue. People lacking transportation were left to die in their homes and on bridges and overpasses.

Efforts to evacuate women and children in domestic violence shelters began on Friday before the storm came ashore late Sunday and early Monday (Jenkins and Phillips 2008). When the director of one shelter went to the bus station, the police had commandeered the station and no buses were leaving. The director eventually found keys to a church van and drove the residents to Baton Rouge herself. The storm and levee failures subsequently destroyed or severely damaged shelter locations across three parishes. Police and other rescue services normally involved in providing protection were compromised as well; nearly three years later, many police continue to work out of temporary trailers with insufficient staff.

In Louisiana, those who work to protect those at risk have been forced to reconfigure and reconceptualize the safety net not only for battered women and their children, but for those at risk for child and elder abuse as well. Crime rates in New Orleans have risen including homicide, domestic violence, and rape. Hurricane Katrina and the levee failures there flooded 80% of the city, destroyed important social networks and displaced social service organizations that would normally provide protection and support, and fostered a climate where violence has become a heightened concern.

Source: Pam Jenkins. With permission.

---

advertise violent options ranging from guns, bayonets, and tanks to graphic gaming software that awards points for brutal slayings and degrading interactions, particularly with women as the targets. Proponents of gun control legislation face an uphill battle to stem the sale of automatic and concealed weapons, even despite mass murders in university and school settings. To illustrate, the 2008 Oklahoma legislature launched an effort to *allow* students to carry concealed weapons on the state's higher education campuses; interestingly, they did not include authorization for faculty members to do so (the measure failed but continues to garner support). To ensure the safety of citizens from harm, legal reform has also produced legislation to secure protective orders, anti-stalking laws, and hate crime legislation, all of which serve as indicators that violence remains problematic across the nation.

Violence in American society is so significant that debates rage about how best to afford protection, particularly through easing or restricting access to violent weapons. Parenting and educators' organizations have worked to label toys, music, and software with warnings of violent content. Even television programs can be blocked by those who are concerned. In short, violence and related concerns permeate American culture. In contrast, other nations stand appalled at what appears to be acquiescence to the violent messages embedded in American lives from childhood forward. Sweden, for example, incarcerates parents who so much as spank a child. Even corporal punishment is believed to send the wrong message about proper interaction.

BOX 12.2   INTERPERSONAL VIOLENCE IN AMERICA

In this box, note the intersecting patterns of vulnerability to violence based on gender, social class, physical ability, race and ethnicity, and age. While in some cases rates of reported violence declined in the last decade (1990–2000), particularly among men, the overall patterns are consistent and exposure to violence remains high.

- Americans' easy access to firearms is reflected in homicide statistics. In 1996, handguns were used to murder 30 people in Great Britain, 106 in Canada, 15 in Japan, and 9390 in the United States.
- Between 1992 and 1998, 72% of the average annual 21,232 homicide victims over the age of 12 were killed with a firearm.
- In 1998, there were 30,708 deaths by firearms in the United States. Over 80% (26,189) of those who died were male.
- Gun death disproportionately affects young people. Among those aged 15–24, firearms are the second leading cause of death.
- The annual death toll from gunfire (mainly handguns) in recent years exceeds 30,000. Firearm fatalities grew by 24% between 1985 and 1994.
- Intentional violence against another person accounts for a third of all deaths due to injury, disproportionately involving young people. Homicide has been the leading cause of death among young (age 15–23) African American males and females for the past decade.
- Homicide is the second leading cause of death on the job among Americans. These deaths are three times higher among men than women, but homicide is the leading cause of workplace deaths among employed women.
- More often than homicide, Americans die from suicide, 57% of which are committed with firearms.
- Suicide rates increase with age and are highest among men over 65 (83% of suicides among older Americans in 1998). But suicide is the third leading cause of death among young people (age 15–24). Young white males are especially at risk of suicide, though rates among young black males are increasing. Suicide among lesbian and gay teenagers remains high.
- African American males (aged 15–24) have a homicide victimization rate substantially higher (185.1 per 100,000) than Hispanic males (97.3) and non-Hispanic whites (10) of the same age. Gun homicide is the leading cause of death for black males aged 15–34.
- Youth are three times more likely than adults to be victims of violence. One quarter of youth violent victimizations involved the use of a firearm.
- Adolescents have higher rates than younger children and adults for minor and serious forms of violence. In 1992, the rate of violent crime victimization per 1000 for juveniles (aged 12–17) and young adults (aged 18–24) was nearly twice the victimization rate for persons 25–34 and five times the rate for those over 35.
- Of all violent crimes measured by the National Crime Victimization Survey, many more were perpetrated by intimate partners (48%) or family members (32%) than by strangers (20%).
- In 70% of all homicides committed by intimate partners, the victims are women.
- The greatest risk of violence and injury women face is from male intimates. Three of every four (78%) rapes and aggravated and simple assaults committed against

women are committed by an intimate partner, compared with 4% of non-lethal violence experienced by men.

- People with disabilities are at higher risk than other Americans for sexual violence, especially women with physical and/or cognitive disabilities such as mental retardation.
- Rates of sexual violence against women with disabilities (as reported in 18 surveys conducted in the 1990s) ranged from 51% to 79%. Adults with mental retardation and learning disabilities reported lifetime experiences of sexual violence ranging from 25% to 67%. Among male and female victims, most (88%–98%) perpetrators are male and known to the victim.

Sources: National Center for Injury Prevention and Control (www.cdc.gov/ncipc/fact-steets); U.S. Department of Justice Statistics (www.ojp.usdoj.gov/bjs); National Institute for Occupational Health and Safety (www.cdc.gov/niosh/violfs); Center for the Study and Prevention of Violence, University of Colorado (www.colorado.edu/cspv/factsheets/violence), citing academic studies as well as data from government agencies; Jointogether report citing data from *National Vital Statistics Reports* 48 (11), 2000, www1.jointogether.org/gv/issues/impact. Compiled by Elaine Enarson.

12.3.2 COUNTERTRENDS

Counter influences can certainly be identified, though. American public opinion is "strongly supportive of measures to register firearms, promote firearm safety and keep criminals from acquiring guns" by "large majorities" (Smith 2003, 2). Those most at risk seem most likely to support antiviolence efforts; for example, there is a gender gap, with women less likely to support military spending and more likely to encourage gun control.

As another countertrend, social movements for peace and nonviolence have appeared throughout U.S. history. For example, an anti-child abuse effort developed in the early 1960s, which paved the way to safeguard other populations. In the 1970s, campaigns called Take Back the Night emerged to protest rape and sexual assault. Stronger laws against domestic violence arose at the same time from the battered women's shelter movement (Schechter 1982). Efforts continue to this day to strengthen protective orders for women at risk. In the 1980s, outcry arose over elder abuse including sexual, physical, and financial forms of violence and exploitation. Concern for lesbians, gay men, bisexual, and transgendered (LGBT) people emerged from the gay rights movement. Penalties for hate crimes have stiffened, in part as a response to the gay rights movement as well as increased response to hate crimes based on race. Most recently, countertrends to violence have included protesting the war in Iraq as well as capital punishment, hate crimes, gang violence, and terrorism. Web sites proclaim that "we are not afraid" and efforts have been launched by multiple faith traditions to foster peace in the Mideast. As a sign of resilience to the power of violence over our lives, tens of thousands of people turn out every year in Oklahoma City to remember those lost in the attack on the Murrah Federal Building and vow, through participation in the Oklahoma City Memorial Marathon, to never forget and never allow a repeat occurrence.

12.4 THE EFFECTS OF VIOLENCE ON AMERICAN SOCIETY

Americans experience violence in several different ways. In this section, we review the three forms of violence that can be distinguished and how people are affected by those different forms. We then turn to how fears of violence are often misplaced and how exposure to violence changes over time.

12.4.1 THREE FORMS OF VIOLENCE

Violence can be separated into three general categories that can be experienced. First, intentional violence includes that experienced at the individual level. Suicide serves as an example, although even this highly personal act may be influenced by social, economic, psychological, or other medical conditions (Durkheim 1897/1997). More Americans are harmed by self-inflicted injury than by others, including suicide and suicide attempts, accidental firearm injury, and harmful practices fostering violent death, such as drunk driving (Litaker 1996).

Other forms of intentional violence stem from interpersonal acts, including assault, hate crimes, abuse, and homicide. Intentional violence can occur at any age or in any population. Child, adult, or elder abuse can take multiple forms as well, including physical, psychological, verbal, sexual, or economic attack.

A second form of violence is termed structural violence, wherein corporate and/or government policies make people less safe, secure, and healthy. Also described as "organized violence" or economic violence, structural assault occurs when social policies operate to increase poverty, reduce life spans, and/or put people in dangerous spaces and situations. Corporate downsizing or federal policies for deinstitutionalization of mental health facilities, for example, put people on the street where the risk of violence increases dramatically (Wisner et al. 2005).

Political violence comprises the third form of violence experienced in American society. Such violence has historically included armed uprisings and riots or the response to protests, terrorist attacks (domestic and international), and even conscripted military service. A number of civil disturbances and riots occurred in the 1960s, many in protest of racism and discrimination. In 1968, Chicago police used tear gas on demonstrators at a national political convention. Two years later, National Guard troops opened fire on protesting students at Kent State University in Ohio, killing four of them. Most recently, terrorism represents a form of political violence experienced in the United States. In Oklahoma City, for example, 168 people including children in a day-care center, perished under a domestic attack. In 2001, over 3000 people representing 23 nations died in the externally generated terrorist attacks on New York City and Washington, DC. Historically, a mandatory draft in the United States sent tens of thousands of Americans to fight in wars they did not support—pacifists, including Quakers, Mennonites, and Amish men, have been forced to choose between military conscription or prison. Conscientious objectors to military initiatives have fared similarly.

12.4.2 DIFFERENTIAL EFFECTS OF VIOLENCE

A number of trends have been identified for the various forms of violence, often undermining multiple myths and beliefs about how violence occurs. For example, racist groups often assumed, and subsequently targeted, African American men for attacks on women. Such an untrue instance led to the murder of 14-year-old Emmitt Till in rural Mississippi in 1955 (Morris 1983), though his case was only one of thousands of similar, still-unsolved homicides. In fact, most intentional violence (e.g., rape, murder) occurs within rather than between racial and ethnic groups (South and Felson 1990).

Age also matters. Youth tend to be more affected by violence than other age groups, as victims and perpetrators, a trend especially true among males. Violence tends to decline as men age, although exceptions to that pattern do occur. Senior citizens experience other forms of violence at higher levels than those at younger ages, for example, forms of economic exploitation—often being targeted in scams designed for trusting elders including post-disaster roof repairs and building construction (Choi and Mayer 2000).

Violence is also differentially affected by gender. Within the family, women and children are most often subjected to violence by family members and acquaintances. The range of violence to which women are exposed can be considerable including physical attack, rape, forced prostitution, labor exploitation, and neglect (Watts and Zimmerman 2002). Young men, particularly African American men in low-income neighborhoods, have higher rates of exposure suggesting that a link of age, race, and income increases exposure to violence. Such exposure has been linked to increased rates of post-traumatic stress disorder (PTSD), which can be further aggravated in disaster contexts (Fitzpatrick and Boldizar 1993).

People with disabilities bear disproportionate risk of violence including sexual assault and financial exploitation. The American Bar Association (2000, see Petersilia 2000) reports that "studies from the U.S., Canada, Australia and Great Britain consistently confirm high rates of violence and abuse in the lives of persons with disabilities." Assault is particularly of concern for people with cognitive disabilities, with rates that may be four to ten times higher than for people without such circumstances. Children with disabilities are nearly twice as likely to experience both physical and sexual abuse as nondisabled children. Legal experts indicate that prosecution for people with disabilities, particularly those with cognitive or developmental disabilities, is particularly difficult.

Occupations and workplaces also expose some people to violence on a regular basis, such as service in the military, law enforcement agencies, and even first responders including firefighters, ambulance drivers, and paramedics. Political violence often affects occupational or social groups such as peace officers and political demonstrators, physicians and staff involved in reproductive services, and visible minorities subject to racial and ethnic profiling. After September 11, for example, young Muslim women feared wearing a traditional hijab or head covering for fear of misplaced reprisals (Peek 2003). Women in the military have begun to report assaults with as many as one in four women reporting sexual harassment, rape, and unwanted sexual advancement (Sadler et al. 2003). Rates of intimate partner violence appear to have increased in the workplace as well (Swanberg, Logan, and Macke 2005).

U.S. residents in highly stigmatized social groups may not be able to report violence to authorities. Homeless adults and teens living on the streets may fear encounters with the police or not merit local recognition as credible sources. Women, men, and youth working as prostitutes will not report crimes, assuming that they will be blamed for the assault due to the nature of their work. Undocumented workers fail to report crimes against them as well, out of fear of deportation, an anxiety that also affects legal immigrants as well.

Income also obscures the realities of violence. Interpersonal violence can take place at all socioeconomic levels; high incomes do not afford protection. In contrast, higher incomes mean that abusers may be more likely to hide their actions or to avoid prosecution or jail time. Studies clearly indicate that the lower the income or socioeconomic level of the neighborhood, the more likely that a crime will come to the attention of the police, and that the perpetrator will go to jail and spend more time there and be more likely to face capital punishment. The death penalty in particular has been critiqued as disproportionately affecting African American men (Free 1996). Economic levels thus obscure violence through privileging those with higher incomes who can afford good lawyers and avoid prosecution.

12.4.3 Trends in Exposure to Violence over Time

Violence trends vary over time. Since 2000, several notable trends have emerged in all three forms of violence. First, let's examine interpersonal violence. Since 2000, homicide rates overall have decreased as have rates of assault, in part because of a population that has been slowly aging. However, sexual violence rates (rape and battery) have remained at high numbers without much variation. Further, such crimes are believed to be under-reported, particularly date and marital rape. Workplace violence has increased as have school-based shootings from elementary levels through institutions of higher education. Hate crimes, which have not been recorded efficiently or until recently, have increased—most likely because of a greater willingness to report such violence as a result of legislation (for a general overview on violence worldwide, see Krug et al. 1998; for the United States, see the U.S. Department of Justice 2005). A hate crime is defined by the FBI as a "traditional offense like murder, arson, or vandalism with an added element of bias." Congress defines hate crime as a "criminal offense against a person or property motivated in whole or in part

BOX 12.3   FBI STATISTICS ON HATE CRIMES

In 2007, the Federal Bureau of Investigation released these statistics:

- Of 7621 noted bias incidents
  - 50.8% were motivated by racial bias and 13.2% by ethnicity or national origin bias.
  - 18.4% stemmed from a religious bias.
  - 16.5% originated from a sexual orientation bias.
  - 1% resulted from bias against a disability.
- There were 5408 hate crimes considered crimes against persons, which included
  - Intimidation, 47.4%
  - Simple assault, 31.1%
  - Aggravated assault, 20.6%
  - Nine murders
- There were 3579 crimes against property:
  - 81.4% were acts of destruction, damage, or vandalism.
  - 18.6% were burglary, larceny-theft, motor vehicle theft, arson, and other offenses.
- Of the known offenders
  - 62.9% were white.
  - 20.8% were black.
- Locations of hate crimes:
  - 30.5% took place in or near the victim's home.
  - 18.9% happened on roadways or alleys.
  - 11.3% occurred at schools or colleges.
  - 6% happened in parking lots or garages.
  - 4.1% happened in churches, synagogues, or temples.
  - The remaining percentages took place at other locations or unknown locations.

Source: Federal Bureau of Investigation. 2008. Hate crime statistics 2007. http://www.fbi.gov (accessed November 21, 2008).

by an offender's bias against a race, religion, disability, ethnic origin or sexual orientation" (FBI 2008, see Box 12.3).

Second, structural violence proves more difficult to measure. However, indicators of such violence have been collected by the Manchester College Peace Studies Institute (www.manchester. edu/connect/pr/files/news/violence2htm). Using governmental and corporate data from the years 1995–1998, those indicators show several trends of concern. Given the recession of 2008 that is expected to linger, a number of these trends are expected to increase.

- Complaints of civil rights violations to the Department of Justice have increased by 34%.
- Rising numbers of Americans were incarcerated for nonviolent offenses, especially young African American and Hispanic men.
- Deaths by police intervention have increased, especially among minority male youths.
- Deaths by capital punishment have increased.
- Rates of hunger in American households have escalated.
- Homelessness has risen.
- Exposure to air pollution, and subsequently risks to one's health, has increased in counties where industries exceeded government standards.

- The numbers of women, and their children, at or near the poverty line have risen.
- Gang membership has increased.
- Deaths from both legal and illegal drugs have increased.
- Smoking-related deaths, despite increasing bans on smoking locations, have risen.

Third, political and military violence since the turn of the last century demonstrates considerable impacts. As noted earlier, over 3000 died in the September 11 attacks and 168 perished in the Oklahoma City bombing. Other domestic attacks have included the 1996 bomb explosion at the Atlanta Olympics and the 2001 anthrax attacks. Dozens of Americans have been killed in politically motivated attacks against the United States. The U.S. marine barracks were attacked at Khobar Towers in Saudi Arabia in 1996; two years later the U.S. embassies in Kenya and Tanzania were bombed. In 2000, the U.S.S. Cole carrier ship survived a terrorist explosion off the coast of Yemen. In late 2008, Americans and others were targeted in an attack on a hotel in India. Military members routinely face intentional explosive devices (IEDs) and suicide attacks while serving abroad in the fight against terrorism.

12.5   RELEVANCE TO DISASTERS

The various forms of violence noted, along with the fear of such violence, can affect people's capacity to prepare for and respond to disasters. Violence can both enhance the likelihood of preparedness and limit potential response to and recovery from disasters. Some research suggests (e.g., Rubin and Renda-Tanali 2002) that the September 11 attacks and exposure to biological toxins (anthrax) increased Americans' confidence and trust in the federal government, though that trust appears to have declined over time (Sacks, Flattery, and Hut 2004). Extensive amounts of funding have fueled preparedness efforts for terrorist attacks through the new Department of Homeland Security. However, critics point out that the heavy emphasis on this form of political violence reduced capacity to respond to social groups at risk in disaster, a situation revealed through the number of people on the rooftops of Louisiana and Mississippi when Katrina hit.

The terrorist attacks did prompt some additional preparedness among Americans and certainly a willingness to endure airport security procedures. Although there is a difference between what people expect and actually do in disasters, it appears they are more likely to follow government guidelines about self-protection, suggesting that by understanding violence it may be possible to enhance individual levels of safety (Phillips, Metz, and Nieves 2006). Self-protection and preparedness initiatives may extend to

- Information-seeking from emergency management authorities
- Attending to emergency warnings
- Making emergency plans at home
- Increasing workplace emergency planning
- Assessing personal vulnerabilities to threats of all kinds
- Increasing vigilance about perceived threats to safety, for example, through neighborhood watch groups, storm-ready communities, and the like

Conversely, fear and violence may increase the vulnerabilities of some groups. An individual on the street exposed to violence, or a child fleeing a predator, may not know of a safe location. People may refuse a job because of concern over workplace safety, whether from interpersonal violence or from unsafe conditions on the job site. Employers may hire those most economically desperate in such locations, decreasing the life safety of those already marginalized by violence. Landlords and officials who abandon women and children to face disasters without providing a means of protection increase structural violence (Morrow and Enarson 1996). Those affected by domestic or partner violence may face a hard choice between living with a perpetrator or being homeless after a disaster.

Without policies to guide the rights of individuals living in federal-provided disaster housing, those at risk for violence remain unprotected.

People already living in violent situations may focus exclusively on the daily threat to their lives and lack time or the means to prepare for disaster. Further, those experiencing interpersonal violence are likely to be isolated from others and thus unable to access resources for evacuation, sheltering-in-place, or other forms of self-protection. Because social networks and family support are so critical in times of disaster, isolation from those sources may increase exposure to violence. For more examples, see Box 12.4.

12.6   FAMILY AND PARTNER VIOLENCE IN A DISASTER CONTEXT

In this section we profile violence against women, elder abuse, child abuse, sexual abuse, and partner (LGBT) violence. The purpose of this section is to reveal areas of concern for those involved in preparedness, response, and recovery efforts and to introduce solutions specific to a particular population. A section that follows outlines general strategies for reducing vulnerabilities and exposure to violence before, during, and after a disaster event.

12.6.1   WOMEN, VIOLENCE, AND DISASTER VULNERABILITY

At any point in the emergency management life cycle, women may be in danger of losing their lives or sustaining serious injuries. Homicide is one of the leading causes of death among American women, and workplace violence against women has increased, nearly always the result of interpersonal relationships. Violence and homelessness are also related. For example, nearly half of women in homeless shelters are fleeing domestic violence. Violence also impoverishes women. Full shelters and lack of affordable housing before, during, and after disasters may force women back into dangerous living conditions. Poor women are much more likely to rely on overcrowded domestic violence shelters than middle-class women with more resources, leaving them in even riskier environments as emergency preparedness is generally not a priority in shelters. These circumstances render many women far less able to withstand the effects of disasters. Moreover, disasters often create economic difficulties for families in the short and long term. The result of the economic difficulty is that victims may find themselves unable to leave a situation or take legal action to keep themselves and their children safe. In other words, the disruption caused by the disaster can exacerbate potentially violent situations (for an illustration, see Box 12.5).

The aftermath of any large-scale disaster may increase the vulnerability of many who would be victims of interpersonal violence. First, evacuating from an area will place families and friends in housing situations that may create the opportunity for domestic violence, rape, and sexual assault. After Katrina, for example, extended family members would stay with the one relative or friend who was in an evacuee city such as Baton Rouge, Dallas, or Atlanta. Sometimes, this would mean that there would be 30 people or more in a single-family dwelling. The evacuation also meant that people lacked access to familiar support systems including shelters, social service providers, health care workers, and others who often observe and stand between those at risk and those who offend.

It is not clear whether rates of domestic violence increase after a disaster, but some data and anecdotal evidence suggest that such is the case. What is clear is that violence against women has been and remains an issue before, during, and after disaster. The prevalence of the problem is so severe that it is shocking that emergency management has largely failed to address the problem. To illustrate the problem, consider that a Santa Cruz battered women's shelter reported a 50% increase in temporary restraining orders after the 1989 earthquake. That same year, the *Exxon Valdez* oil spill was associated with increased domestic violence including child neglect, elder and spouse abuse, child abuse, child sexual abuse, and rape. In 1992, post–Hurricane Andrew telephone calls for spouse abuse increased by 50% to the local community helpline. After the 1997 Grand Forks

BOX 12.4 FEAR, VIOLENCE, AND DISASTERS

What are you afraid of? How would these fears affect your feelings, choices, and decisions in the aftermath of a disastrous event in your city?

- Imagine being 14 and living on the streets of San Francisco because you ran away from a father, brother, or uncle who abused you. Would you go home for help after an earthquake? Who on the streets would help you learn how to protect yourself?
- Imagine working in a South Dade County, Florida, nursery all day knowing that without "papers" lost in the hurricane you can be deported and your family at home in El Salvador will not eat. Would you approach people in uniforms even if you desperately needed water after a hurricane?
- Imagine being a young African American man confronting white police officers barricading streets in an emergency. Would you ask for help from them? If they approached you, would you run?
- Imagine leaving your home in the dead of night with only your children and a few items of clothing for the safety of a women's shelter. If the floodwaters rise and the shelter is evacuated to the local high school gym, would you feel safe there? Would you go? Where would you live later?
- Imagine living "in the closet" with a same-sex partner because other gays and lesbians have been harassed, assaulted, and even killed in your state. Would you declare your living arrangements honestly and completely to FEMA, the Red Cross, or other private agencies? What is at stake?
- Imagine using medication and supportive friends to keep a mental illness under control—until a tornado made your doctor and hospital inaccessible and your friends were evacuated to different locations. Would you be at risk of suicide?
- Imagine being a low-income senior residing in the public housing unit in Lower Manhattan damaged in the September 11 attack. Would you be more likely to join the new self-help group residents formed after the attack? Would you be more likely to turn to authorities for advice about self-protection?
- Imagine being a visibly "Arab" (Middle-Eastern, or Islamic) resident subject to greater scrutiny by neighbors (for example, by neighborhood watch groups extending their surveillance from property theft to perceived terrorist threat). Immediately following the September 11 attack, an immigrant from Pakistan was shot to death in front of his own store by an Arizona man proclaiming himself to be a "patriotic American." Over a thousand men of Middle-Eastern origin were detained by U.S. law enforcement authorities after the September 2001 attacks. How comfortable would you be approaching either your neighbors or law enforcement officials for help in an emergency?
- Imagine being an 80-year-old African American man in an urban ghetto with high rates of street assault and theft. How easy would it be for you to leave your apartment and walk the streets in search of a cooler space during a heat wave?
- Imagine a bioterrorist attack on your city exposing you and others to biological or chemical weapons. How could your fears impinge on your ability to protect yourself? Are many residents in your community armed? Are there high levels of fear between neighbors or neighborhoods? What difference would it make?

Source: FEMA *Social Vulnerability to Disasters* course materials, lead developer Elaine Enarson.

BOX 12.5   ONE WOMAN'S STORY

In a study of women's experiences in Hurricane Andrew, Betty Morrow and Elaine Enarson (1996) interviewed an African American woman, a newcomer to Miami whose husband was a disabled police officer, where she was living in a shelter for battered women.

We were in the house, we stayed. But our landlord went to apply for FEMA—some of our things got waterlogged, but not bad. Then the landlord that owned the condo applied for FEMA government assistance, so he came and told us that we had to move out. So we said, Well, let's just go to Chicago, because there's no electricity here, there were crabs—literally crabs, and mosquitoes, because there was no way to shelter, eating us up. So we went to Chicago. Our parents sent for us. When we were in Chicago, our landlord took everything out of the apartment—everything. He just threw it out. The people went crazy! People was ripping off people, people was shooting at people, people were stealing really bad. And of course the shock of just losing things that got broke in the hurricane—my husband went crazy. He couldn't take the pressure—being used to everything, and then coming down to no eating (because we could not find food) … The car got destroyed in the hurricane and I tried to talk to the owner. … I said, "Look, I just lost everything in this hurricane. I'm not even working." Of course the school where I was working got destroyed, it was in Cutler Ridge. And my husband, of course he wasn't working because his business got destroyed. And it was just terrible. And I went outside—I found a job about six months later at the Keys, pumping gas. At this point, my husband's like, just berserk. He was fighting me. I'm trying to work at a gas station pumping gas. Then, luckily—the school didn't get hit that bad. … So I was subbing during the day, two hours rest in between, pumping gas at night from 5 until 9—and a husband sitting home that was too great and too grand to work for a little $7 or $10 an hour. And then he was beating me up, taking my money—there was just so much going on that I just couldn't—he was really going berserk! I was getting beat up pretty bad. So I decided—we were on our way from the Keys here to Homestead in this beat-up car that we did have running a little bit when he jumped on me. I ended up calling the police at a little wayside place, because nothing was really open. You can go miles and miles and don't find anything—no gas, no food, no nothing. But finally—like I'd say about six months later, Homestead got one gas station, so we made it there and I was able to call the police, and I ended up here at the shelter. And things just changed. I didn't have a job, I didn't have any clothes, because I was fleeing for my life. I came here with one shoe, ended up going to the hospital, the emergency room. … He really went crazy. Before, I would get beat up maybe once a month if I was lucky. Afterwards it was like every other day … I was getting tired of it, but I was scared to leave him, because where was I going to go? Who did I know? … But then, after the hurricane it all got worse. … I ran across a lot of women suffering, too, with their children— husbands beating them up and leaving them. It was pretty bad.

flood, counseling of domestic violence clients climbed 59%. Internationally, Hurricane Mitch (1998) also increased violence rates for both women and men. After the Indian Ocean tsunami in 2004, reports of domestic violence and assault in refugee camps came into nongovernmental organizations (NGOs) attempting to support survivors (Enarson 2006).

What is clear is that domestic violence has been and remains a problem across time, jurisdiction, and national borders. The type of disaster does not make a difference because the patterns are clear. Emergency managers, police, social service providers, community organizers and activists, and concerned citizens must take action to safeguard those at risk. Unfortunately, few jurisdictions and domestic violence providers take such action. Emergency managers and others that routinely plan for disaster also routinely exclude domestic violence providers. Those same providers often fail to prepare for disaster contexts including evacuation of residents and staff, continuity of operations, and resumption of services. A significant disconnection exists between the two communities with the information, resources, and expertise needed to address the issue (Enarson 1998).

Further, as often happens with disasters, routinely awarded grants are redirected toward disasters, meaning that local social service providers struggle to meet local need. One study that examined 77 domestic violence programs found considerable evidence that increased service demand was not met with adequate funding, staff time, volunteers, space, or equipment (Enarson 1999). A clear problem exists when those at risk for violence continue to experience vulnerability as a result of disaster and, because of a lack of planning for such circumstances, emergency managers and social service providers fail to reduce that risk. As discussed in a later section, something can be done about that service gap.

12.6.2 Age, Violence, and Vulnerability

As described in Chapter 7 on age, children and seniors may be at particular risk during disasters. Individuals separated from family members, children, and seniors with disabilities or frail medical conditions are likely to be particularly vulnerable. As a result of Hurricane Katrina, it became clear that children could become separated from family and guardians, rendering them potentially vulnerable to exploitation, abuse, or neglect. Though shelters established programs to assist children alone, the experience was undoubtedly something that must be avoided at all costs in the future. Further, children were taken by parents with only limited custodial authority. Difficulties in reuniting children with primary custodial parents have lingered for years, putting children at risk for neglect and/or abuse. It should be noted, though, that much of the violence that children experience occurs within their family units. Consequently, even if families remain intact during a disaster it is wise to train staff and volunteers working with survivors to identify children who may be in danger.

A number of key organizations should be considered as partners for working on issues of children's risk to violence. Those organizations include child protective services, homeless providers, organizations that address street violence including child prostitution, disability organizations, law enforcement, educators, and recreational program staff. Careful cross-training should take place in order to prepare these organizations for the disaster time period. Organizations likely to become involved in disaster response should be trained in the language, content, and procedures common to response and even recovery time periods. Similarly, disaster response and recovery organizations should cross-train with children's advocate organizations in order to understand and benefit from their knowledge and perspectives. Pre-disaster programs designed to identify children at risk and move them into safe environments need to be designed including those for children with prior abuse (such as screening for previous traumas likely to resurface during disaster), children separated from their families (e.g., shelter programs), and children with disabilities (who have a higher risk of exposure to violence). Key to assisting children, beyond providing a safe environment, is restoring structure and stability to their lives. Teachers, social service providers, and recreational staff can pre-design programs that reintegrate children into social and educational opportunities that provide a framework in which children can rebound (as described in Chapter 7).

Senior citizens are considered at risk for several forms of violence and abuse outside of the context of disasters. Those risks include sexual and physical violence, neglect (nutritional, medical, psychological), and financial exploitation. Frail elderly are particularly vulnerable because of being unable to easily access, manage, or control their health or resources. Even seniors in nursing homes have been exposed to assault and theft. Family members, friends, and even strangers may take advantage of their circumstances. Care must be taken, therefore, to insure that appropriate planning and preparedness has taken place along with building adequate partnerships among relevant senior care agencies and organizations.

Adult protective service organizations serve as a primary resource for assisting and supporting seniors at risk and should be brought in as key partners. Home health care agencies and health providers that work with homebound seniors or frail elderly can be tasked to assess risk. Shelter providers must be trained to conduct careful intake procedures to determine if social support (family, friends) exists for elderly residents. Training of shelter workers should include teaching them to recognize signs of abuse or exploitation and how to report concerns. State legal offices, such as the attorney general, can develop task forces to safeguard the interests of seniors involved in rebuilding their homes so as to reduce the risk for fraud. Because disability prevalence increases with age, disability organizations should be integrated into a planning team as well.

12.6.3 Race, Ethnicity, Violence, and Vulnerability

Historic patterns of segregation and discrimination, as well as repetitive threats and acts of violence, have resulted in higher vulnerability among racial and ethnic minorities. Segregation patterns since emancipation, for example, have marginalized minority housing into floodplains and other hazardous areas (Cutter 2006). In Princeville, North Carolina, for example, freed slaves established the first town incorporated by African Americans in the United States. Originally known as "Freedom Hill" this location was along the Tar River that repeatedly flooded. In the late 1990s after a series of rain events, Princeville (named after a mayor who rescued people during a flood in the 1800s) flooded again, this time up to the rooftops. Princeville residents chose not to move despite a federal buyout offer. As described by locals, the community represented—among other things—a safe haven against the threat of attack by the Ku Klux Klan. Flood risk occurred because of a hazardous location and people stayed in part because of violent threats. The threat of violence thus perpetuated risk, this time in a disaster context.

Similar circumstances lay behind patterns of neighborhood development in New Orleans, with the consequence that historically African American areas flooded (Cutter 2006). Racial and ethnic vulnerability in disasters includes disproportionate loss of life. This trend was seen as a result of Hurricane Katrina where more African Americans died than individuals from other races, even when controlling for original population numbers. Such deaths were also disproportionately older and male (Sharkey 2007).

Violence remains a concern throughout many minority communities to this day. Young African American males are far more likely to be exposed to violence than other races, with the consequence that symptoms of post-traumatic stress disorder (PTSD) rates are higher (Fitzpatrick and Boldizar 1993). Disasters produce further stress, though in general PTSD rates are lower than expected among most populations. The exception is among those exposed to trauma prior to the disaster. If that trauma has not been treated, the potential for PTSD among disaster survivors is much higher (Norris, Friedman, and Watson 2002; Norris et al. 2002). Racial and ethnic minorities that have sustained previous trauma, then, are more likely to be traumatized by a disaster event.

In an electronic discussion of the impacts of disasters on minority communities in the United States, FEMA's former associate director in the 1990s, Kay Goss (n.d.), said, "FEMA will do all it can to empower the African American community to fundamentally change the vulnerability of Black America to disasters." Doing so will require considerable attention from disaster managers and others dedicated not only to reducing the threat of disasters but of violence, economic discrimination, housing segregation, and political marginalization. Social problems lie behind many of the forms of violence described in this chapter, and require social solutions in which disaster managers and others concerned with vulnerability reduction must participate; "the more fundamental lesson of disasters, however, is that the social disadvantages that our society treats as ordinary and unremarkable become deadly in dramatic ways in the course of a disaster" (Farber, n.d.).

12.6.4 DISABILITY, VIOLENCE, AND DISASTER VULNERABILITY

Despite the decrease in crime over the past several decades, people with disabilities (especially developmental disabilities) "have not experienced greater safety" (American Bar Association 2000, see Petersilia 2000). There's no doubt that the idea of someone with a disability suffering violent attacks, abuse, or exploitation is stunning. Further, the same social characteristics that predict violence in general exist for individuals with disabilities as well. Poverty rates are higher among people with disabilities; consequently, protection of those living in dangerous areas, who use public transportation, or are dependent on those who might exploit them is of concern (American Bar Association 2000, see Petersilia 2000). As another example, children with disabilities (especially developmental disabilities) bear an alarming risk of sexual abuse (Wilgosh 1993).

Similarly, one study found that 13% of women with physical disabilities reported physical or sexual abuse in the year preceding the survey. Perpetrators included husbands, partners, attendants, health care providers, and strangers. Sexual abuse was more likely to be committed by strangers (Young et al. 1997), suggesting that leaving familiar settings to go to shelters or temporary locations might be of concern. The Center for Research on Women with Disabilities (2000) reports that the disability type most likely to receive services from domestic violence providers was an individual with mental illness; far fewer women with physical disabilities, developmental disabilities, or visual or hearing disabilities received services. It is clear that many individuals with disabilities remain under the radar for antiviolence services despite their risks (Young et al. 1997).

People with disabilities would benefit from pre-planning that increases their safety in an unfamiliar environment. In addition, it is clear that individuals with cognitive disabilities "often feel powerless to avoid painful or harmful experiences. When a person is dependent on another for food, clothing, shelter, and all social interaction, that dependency prevents him or her from resisting abuse" (American Bar Association 2000, see Petersilia 2000). Consequently, outreach and efforts to assess and protect individuals in shelters, temporary housing, or other locations used in a disaster context would be crucial. Part of that would need to involve safety training (American Bar Association 2000, see Petersilia 2000) that should include disaster preparedness. As with other areas of concern, it is necessary to build and work with a broad set of partners to address the issues of disabilities, disasters, and vulnerability. Likely partners would include judges, associations that work with and for people with disabilities, law enforcement, domestic violence protection services, and social service providers. For example, Safe Place in Austin, Texas, provides free and confidential services, including staff who use American Sign Language and also offer a Disability Services Safety Awareness Program (www.safeplace.org).

12.6.5 SEXUAL ORIENTATION, VIOLENCE, AND DISASTER VULNERABILITY

Stigmatized groups of all kinds, including sexual minorities, migrant workers, transients, faith groups, marginalized ethnic groups, sex workers, homeless men and women, and the many Americans who must seek out protected space "below the radar screen" for some reason (among them battered women), are clearly at risk of not receiving potentially lifesaving support in the wake of disasters. Lesbians, gay men, and bisexual or transgendered individuals are among those whose survival, safety, and well-being may be contingent upon finding safe space and low-key emergency social services. Interpersonal violence like hate crimes, including murders, rape, and physical assault, are particular concerns. Structural forms of violence include an "epidemic of homeless" among LGBT youth (Ray 2006). Intentional violence that occurs because of stigmatization, isolation, and marginalization includes higher rates of teen suicide.

In the only study of this diverse population in a disaster context, Eads (2002) found that the needs of the LGBT community were not well met after September 11. For example, supporting organizations reported knowing of individuals whose same-sex partner had been killed or injured. Yet they were denied information about their partner because they were not legal kin. Some reported fear of requesting services, despite losing a job or experiencing damage to their home. Some who did attempt access reported traumatizing experiences related to their sexual identity. Fear of hate crimes, reprisals, and being singled out or denied aid all prevent people qualified for aid from seeking it out. The American Red Cross did provide funds and programming to same-sex partners from donated monies.

A number of organizations exist to provide support to LGBT individuals and to disaster managers seeking to create a safer, more humane environment before, during, and after disasters. PFLAG (Parents and Friends of Lesbians and Gays), for example, has chapters in many areas. Antiviolence initiatives, gay rights organizations, faith-based communities, and others have stood by LGBT populations and can serve as sources of information, conduits for aid and relief, and as partners in planning and in aid distribution systems.

12.6.6 SUICIDE

Post-disaster suicide rates among both sexes and all age groups were found to have increased four years after a major disaster had been declared (1982–1989) in a sample of U.S. counties, while rates in non-impacted counties during the same time period did not increase (Krug et al. 1998). U.S. Department of Justice figures suggest that Americans are at higher risk of suicide than of interpersonal violence. For example,

- In 1998, there were 1.7 times as many suicides as homicides.
- Suicide is the third leading cause of death for young people (aged 15–24).
- Suicide rates increase with age and are higher among men; older men are especially at risk.
- From 1980–1995, suicide rates increased most rapidly among young black males.

Though mental health rates do not rise considerably after most disasters, there is potential for suicide to increase under some circumstances. For example, the magnitude and scope of the disaster could matter. Catastrophic events that tear apart the social fabric of a community produce isolating conditions that are associated with suicide (Durkheim 1897/1997). An event that involves loss of neighborhoods, social networks, and social support systems could increase the potential for suicide. Hurricane Katrina represents one example of an event of this magnitude; suicide rates appear to have risen since then. Local social and mental health service providers indicated that one year after the storm, suicide rates had risen from 9 per 100,000 to 26 per 100,000 in New Orleans (Penix 2006).

12.7 THE IMPACT OF VIOLENCE ON EMERGENCY MANAGEMENT PLANNING, RESPONSE, AND RECOVERY

Violence and associated emotional reactions can interfere with people's willingness to listen to and follow those in authority positions. Those who have arrived in the United States from nations of political repression or communities with historically poor relations with police may not trust law enforcement or others in a crisis. The Loma Prieta earthquake of 1989 illustrates the unanticipated consequences of emergency management planning when "participation by citizens was missing" (Phillips 1993, 104). Fear of the uniformed National Guard troops, there to provide support, kept recent immigrants from moving to better shelters with food, medical care, and tents. Their fear stemmed from multiple negative, even deadly, encounters with the military in their countries of origin including nations where missing family members became known as "los desparecidos" or "the disappeared" who never returned (Phillips 1993). Political refugees found the military-support option terrifying to the point of refusing to accept aid (Phillips 1993, 102–103):

> Victims' prior experience also hindered some outdoor sheltering attempts. To accommodate the outdoor campers, city and county officials persuaded the ARC to open Ramsey Park as an official shelter. To expedite this process, the National Guard erected tents inside fenced off areas of the park. However, Central American refugee families apparently found this image terrifying. Immigrants who had fled military and government-backed death squads in their native countries now faced similar imagery after disaster. What city, county, and ARC officials hoped would become appropriate shelter now became transformed into a symbolic concentration camp. Approximately three hundred campers refused to leave Callaghan Park for Ramsey Park—in part because of this horrific reminder.

Recent immigrants who experienced the 1994 Northridge earthquake avoided seeking assistance out of fears of deportation and possible violence (Bolin and Stanford 1998, 27):

> Indeed, an abrasive anti-immigrant discourse was (and continues to be) a prominent feature of the California political scene. FEMA, as part of a new federal law, requires all relief applicants to declare their residency status, a declaration subject to auditing by the Immigration and Naturalization Service. As one community worker in Ventura reported, "many Latinos around here think the federal government can just load them up in box cars and ship them off to Mexico, no matter how long they've lived here."

In subsequent disasters, immigrants also declined to visit relief centers despite promises from the federal government that basic humanitarian aid was free and did not require documentation. The risk of violence, exposure, or deportation due to having lost papers in the disaster overshadowed basic human needs for food, water, medical aid, clothing, and shelter.

After Hurricane Katrina, domestic violence shelter providers observed new problems as a result of the disaster. First, all of the shelters in three parishes were destroyed. Anticipating the destruction, shelter providers had to secure their own resources to transport women and children to safety in Baton Rouge and other locations. Second, at least half of the staff lost their own homes and had to relocate, resulting in considerable loss of key support for the previously sheltered women and children. Third, FEMA, which provided trailers to tens of thousands of evacuees, lacked a policy denying access to those who engaged in abuse. Women with few housing options returned to their abusers, further exposing themselves and their children to risk. In other instances, abusers tracked down and moved in with their victims (Jenkins and Phillips 2008). New Orleans three years after the 2005 storm remained an environment with serious safety issues. Police still operated out of temporary trailers with few officers assigned specifically to domestic violence. Rates of homicide, assault, and rape rose as well as mental illness and suicide rates. Friends and other sources of social support remained in faraway cities, trying to rebuild their own lives. The city's public hospital and most of the public housing units have not reopened; these historically safer havens have fared badly, with serious consequences for those experiencing interpersonal violence (Jenkins and Phillips 2008).

12.7.1 Disasters May Increase Exposure to Violence

As the cases above illustrate, disasters may increase people's exposure to violence and heighten the fearful context in which they try to survive, live, and provide for their families. The picture, though, is not clear because, as the New Orleans case illustrates, the context in which people experience violence is influenced by multiple, complex causes. It is possible, for example, that the catastrophic context of Hurricane Katrina increased a number of factors that led to increased interpersonal violence.

These factors include overcrowding in available housing and, on the other hand, isolation in areas where re-population is slow.

Disasters may also permit a context that increases other kinds of risk. After the 1994 Northridge, California, earthquake, household survey data did not find an increase in victimization across Los Angeles County, but did uncover a continuing risk for younger minority males and others already at risk (Siegel, Bourque, and Shoaf 1999). After the Exxon Valdez oil spill along the Alaskan coast-line, native men were much more likely than others to report both increased substance abuse and "fighting" in their community, among their friends, and in their own family. Researchers reported that the spill, the response, and the recovery periods all created conflicts, including the distribution of cleanup jobs, increased concerns over threats to the subsidence life on which the local economy and culture were based, and undermined abilities to feed their families (Palinkas, Petterson, and Russel 1993). Spousal and child abuse also appeared to increase in some areas affected by the oil spill. Elders in the community of Homer, Alaska, for example, reported an increase in violence (Aranji 1992). Similarly, domestic and sexual violence appear to increase in the wake of other disasters, sometimes as long as one year later (Enarson 1998). Reasons believed to influence those rates include

- Threats to identity such as the loss of a family protector and provider role
- Loss of control over powerful others
- Increased frequency due to increased contact (such as during mandatory relocation), inability to find a safer space (a lack of affordable housing, displacement during reconstruction, loss of transportation resources, reduced financial circumstances)
- Direct and indirect impacts on existing shelters and help systems such as reduced access to courts for protective orders

To summarize, there are several areas of concern. One concern is the prevalence of various kinds of violence already pre-existing in American culture before disaster. Because interpersonal, structural, and political violence disproportionately affect some social groups more than others, disaster managers and others need to understand their impact on the ability to prepare for, respond to, and recover from disasters. Disasters may also reveal violence or increase exposure. Regardless of whether increased exposure is associated with higher stress, ineffective policies, or a lack of understanding, we must be ready to protect children, people with disabilities, the elderly, racial and ethnic minorities, lesbians, gays, and others at risk. By working with law enforcement, social and health service providers, domestic violence shelter staff, antiviolence programs, and advocates for social groups at risk, emergency managers and others involved in post-service disaster delivery can design appropriate and effective interventions. This is the topic we turn to next.

12.8   PRACTICAL STEPS FOR EMERGENCY MANAGERS AND OTHERS

How can emergency managers, case managers, advocates, police, shelter providers, and others take steps to mitigate violence as a risk factor in disasters? In this section, we review practical strategies that can make a difference in the well-being of those at risk, including enhancing both personal and community resilience to disasters.

12.8.1   RESEARCH LOCAL PATTERNS OF VIOLENCE

A first step requires researching local patterns of violence as a part of vulnerability assessments. Patterns of violence, the types, extent, and impact on certain groups, should be identified histori-cally in the community. Even violence that occurred decades past, particularly if politically moti-vated, can linger to affect those living in the community today. Which social groups are likely to be fearful of violence and which kinds? How will those historic patterns affect people's willingness to listen to those in authority, to follow emergency recommendations, or to trust outside of their familiar social networks?

Personal and written accounts can be obtained by visiting community centers and speaking with those who serve groups vulnerable to violence. Violence data can also be obtained through local sources such as police and domestic violence programs, as well as through national clearinghouses. Most community agents prepare regular reports about violence, victims and survivors, trends, concerns, and patterns over time. With the passage of the Violence Against Women Act (VAWA), many communities now keep statistics on both civil and criminal proceedings as well as on service provision. Other communities utilize annual quality of life surveys that provide an overview of safety and risk.

12.8.2 Increase Knowledge about Barriers

A second step involves increasing the knowledge of the emergency manager or caseworker about barriers that limit residents' abilities to address risk in their lives. What kinds of barriers, for example, impede the ability of those at risk to move freely and safely about their community and at various times of the day? How, when, and where can those at risk—the homeless, children walking home from school, a mobility disabled individual waiting for public transportation, seniors living independently—access safe space? What kinds of barriers interfere with drawing on supportive interpersonal networks? By identifying those whom social groups trust, such as home health care workers, pastors, neighborhood leaders, and educators, it may be possible to identify routes through which information can be transmitted about personal safety and disasters. Further, efforts to safeguard those at risk for increased violence can be developed at a programmatic level such as a neighborhood watch type of program. By creating this program in a non-disaster environment, it can operate during and after disasters as well as reduce risks of violence.

In a disaster, the issues of safety and risk from violence will often take on a less important role in the immediate necessity to seek safety literally from the impending rapid-onset disaster. Yet the risks to interpersonal violence do not go away during this time, and emergency managers need to prepare shelter workers, transportation providers, and first responders about how the issues of interpersonal violence may impede an individual's or family's ability to seek safety.

For example, during Hurricane Katrina some mothers felt compelled to evacuate with abusers in order to keep their children safe. In a number of cases formerly abusive partners, who had custody for the weekend, evacuated with their children. Cross-jurisdictional custody battles remained unresolved as long as three years later.

How can existing resources such as emergency preparedness information, shelters, relief assistance, and recovery assets be used to protect those at risk and facilitate their protection not only from violence but also recovery? Suggestions include the following:

- Key emergency preparedness materials should include information on where to seek safety from threats of violence and how to report such violence to authorities.
- Evacuation resources should be prioritized to include those at risk such as residents in domestic violence, congregate care settings, residential locations for those with developmental disabilities, or homeless shelters.
- Shelters can designate staff as liaisons to groups within a shelter and to their advocacy groups. While those at risk may not interact with shelter staff, they may do so with an advocacy group that visits the shelter on a regular basis. Care should be taken to accord confidentiality and privacy. Intake procedures could allow people to self-identify issues of concern or to request that a particular organization be notified of their presence in the shelter.
- Transportation systems should include people present to monitor for violence, fraud, and exploitative behaviors.

- Law enforcement personnel and other first responders should understand that they may represent danger to some populations and to dress, act, and interact with people with sensitivity. By working with advocacy groups and locally trusted leaders, it may be possible to provide support and assistance to those experiencing violence.
- Relief centers should widely disseminate information on how to reach safe locations should an individual be experiencing violence of any kind.
- Staff and personnel can be trained on how to watch for suicide, to monitor for hate crimes, and to work sensitively with traumatized (but often silent) populations.
- Web sites can include links to advocacy and support organizations; information about violence, suicide, and hate crimes; and to places of safety.

12.8.3   KNOW YOUR COMMUNITY'S RESOURCES

Local networks and resources can assist and support the emergency management community about those at risk and help disseminate disaster information. A number of local or state agencies and organizations can become new partners in efforts to reduce violent exposure. Examples of such organizations might include

- Institutional safe homes, victim services, community outreach programs
- Domestic violence shelters
- Child and adult protective services
- Judicial systems and advocates for victims of violence or intimidation
- Government agencies with antiviolence initiatives
- Nonprofit service and advocacy agencies
- Advocacy groups for those at risk including seniors, people with disabilities, lesbian, gay, bisexual, and transgendered individuals
- Community networks, neighborhood collaboratives, self-help groups

First steps would include initiating local consultations with advocacy groups to increase capacity and reduce hazards in facilities or organizations serving people who routinely live with fear and violence: street children, the homeless, battered women, gays and lesbians, undocumented immigrants, gang members, and seniors in high-crime areas. By inviting representatives from these groups or their representative organizations or advocates to the emergency management planning table, fresh perspectives and insights can be generated. The harsh realities of violence can be revealed, understood, and planned for with an eye to reducing the threat of assault, abuse, or exploitation. Next steps would invite these new partners to emergency management cross-training and exercises so that partners build relationships, learn each others' perspectives and language, and design practical plans that link well to create a new kind of safety net.

These agencies can serve as productive partners in new efforts to address fear and violence as vulnerability factors in disaster education including professional training, community education, and cross-training of human services. For example,

- After the 1989 Loma Prieta earthquake, the city of Santa Cruz, California, distributed "Holiday Help Lines" flyers alerting residents that holidays in the wake of a disaster can be extremely stressful and providing contact information for seven community-based antiviolence groups.
- Interagency networks with managers and residents in group shelters such as domestic violence shelters, group homes for runaways, and halfway homes for ex-convicts can ensure their access to emergency assistance. The Emergency Network of Los Angeles is a community-based collaborative representing the needs and interests of recent immigrants and works closely with local emergency management authorities (see downloads at www.enla.org).

- After Hurricane Katrina, many nonprofits dealing with interpersonal violence created emergency plans. The New Orleans' Mayor's Task Force on Domestic Violence brought in disaster and domestic violence speakers to inform and support efforts to rebuild the local safety net for those at risk. The state of Louisiana provided training on maintaining rape crisis programs in the context of disasters.

12.8.4 Make Those at Risk a Priority

Both before and after disaster, make those at risk a priority. Include community agencies and organizations serving those affected by violence in all outreach efforts. Prioritize hazard mitigation, emergency preparedness outreach, assistance during evacuation, utility restoration, and financial relief to shelters housing people whose safety depends on these facilities. Homeless shelters, domestic violence shelters, and children's services all merit priority status.

By learning from previous events, we can improve future response. What Hurricane Katrina taught us is that the services for victims of domestic violence need to be mobile during evacuation, response, and recovery. Shelter residents need transportation resources and police protection during evacuation, shelter, and interim housing. People who are homeless or who work in occupations that place them at risk (e.g., prostitution) need to receive assistance to reach secure shelter as well. The traditional methods of helping victims of violence will not necessarily work after a disaster, especially if the agencies are impacted themselves. For example, Crescent House, the only shelter in Orleans Parish, was flooded and then caught fire.

It is also clear from studies that elderly residents underuse relief and recovery aid. Their reduced connection to resources and advocates may increase their exposure to exploitation or their risk of entering an abusive situation. Agencies must construct outreach programs, particularly through senior programs that connect seniors with seniors.

Agencies and organizations that provide antiviolence training, places of refuge, alternative school programs to keep kids off the streets, senior centers, home health care providers, and others in routine contact with those at risk must receive attention and priority for restoration of utilities, facilities, and funding.

12.8.5 Enhance Credibility among Authority Figures

Researchers make it clear that credibility is key to motivating people at risk to heed warning messages and access aid. Efforts might avoid unnecessarily intimidating symbolism, including appearance, language, demeanor, and signage. After Hurricane Andrew, employees removed the word "Federal" from a FEMA sign in south Dade County (Phillips, Neal, and Garza 1994). The U.S. Army set up mobile kitchens, brought in Spanish-speaking soldiers, and invited immigrant women into the kitchens to prepare culturally familiar meals. All types of shelters and agencies need to think carefully about how they let victims know that there are services. For example, after Katrina, Crescent House provided brochures, which featured Catholic Charities (their home agency) rather than services for domestic violence. Then, when someone would visit their table they could pick up information without arousing suspicion from an offender. Often, the workers would meet with the women in the bathroom of the center to make a safety plan. Disasters, for those exposed to violence, are not business as usual. Practicing flexibility in the delivery of services and information may be necessary rather than attempting to re-integrate standard outreach strategies.

12.8.6 Publicize

Emergency managers, social service providers, antiviolence agencies, and advocates can capitalize on local or national disaster events to integrate violence concerns into all aspects of local emergency management, for example, by

- Initiating student internships with local colleges and universities to study and analyze violence issues in disasters at the local level.
- Recruiting volunteers, students, and staff from groups at risk of violence, e.g., minority families in low-income neighborhoods.
- Disseminating preparedness, transportation, evacuation, protective action, and recovery information through agencies, organizations, program offices, and advocates to reach those historically at risk for violent exposure.
- Conducting emergency preparedness training at places where those at risk may congregate including homeless shelters, senior centers, recreational facilities, school programs, and domestic violence shelters.
- Involving civic and community organizations in developing emergency evacuation kits, first aid, and communication resources to be used during an event. For examples of items in such kits, visit www.ready.gov, www.fema.gov, or www.redcross.org.
- Increasing outreach to social groups at heightened risk of violence by publicizing updated contact information for relevant local and regional organizations (e.g., those working against intolerance and hate crimes, gang violence, violence against people with disabilities, and senior exploitation, as well as women's shelters).
- Participating in events to distribute information and enhance credibility among at-risk populations including Domestic Violence Month, Sexual Assault Awareness Week, Take Back the Night marches, Disability Awareness Week, Hispanic Heritage Month, African American History Month, Women's History Month, Gay Pride/Coming Out Day, Grandparents' Day, ethnic festivals, and other local events.

12.8.7 Planning

Planning for resumption of services to those at risk after a disaster is key. Every jurisdiction should have a functional annex dedicated to violence issues and should integrate key partners from across the community in order to build a working partnership. Central to any planning effort are

- Training social service providers on local hazards and assisting them with developing evacuation procedures, security needs, communication resources during disasters, and strategies for ensuring that services remain in place as needed during and after disaster. Appointing a staff member to be in charge of such training and planning is a first step (Louisiana Foundation Against Sexual Assault, n.d.).
- Training emergency management staff on local issues of violence within the community.
- Getting to know the service providers and key staff that take on the issue of violence, of all kinds, within the community.
- Integrating key community leaders into planning efforts in order to identify places where they can be of assistance and where they may need assistance themselves.
- Critiquing the existing plan for areas where violence issues have not been considered (for example, in disaster shelters or temporary housing) and, in concert with central partners, identifying solutions.
- Developing and maintaining updated phone call lists of organizations that are active participants in all phases of disasters from education through evacuation and relocation.
- Designing a communication system for participating organizations to stay in touch before, during, and after a crisis.
- Setting out a clear division of labor to identify and respond to those at risk for violence.
- Writing a formal memorandum of understanding regarding relationships and responsibilities.
- Examining short- and long-term recovery scenarios from other disasters in order to identify potential places where recovery planning is needed to aid those at risk for violence,

particularly service provision, temporary housing, temporary protection orders, hotlines, incarceration of offenders, and safe places.

12.9   SUMMARY

Violence in American culture and society remains unresolved, subsequently increasing risks in disaster situations. Some groups, such as senior citizens, children, survivors of domestic violence or hate crimes, homeless persons, people with disabilities, lesbians, gays, and others experience higher rates of exposure to violence outside the context of disaster; studies suggest that exposure may increase after disaster as well. It is the work of emergency managers, social service providers, health care workers, community and civic organizations, and advocates to partner with each other to educate and cross-train in each others' areas of expertise. By working together to understand the problem of violence and disaster vulnerability, it is possible to collaboratively share resources and address violence. Care must be taken to influence every dimension of the life cycle of emergency management including reaching out to affected groups through providing preparedness information, emergency response period resources, and recovery aid.

12.10   DISCUSSION QUESTIONS

1. How do the forms of violence discussed in this chapter relate to disasters through the disaster cycle?
2. What do you think are the most important issues raised by violence for emergency practitioners?
3. How does violence intersect with other patterns of vulnerability?
4. What emergency management policies could help to build strong human communities with reduced levels of violence and fear?
5. What is the role of the emergency manager in reducing vulnerabilities deeply rooted in the fabric of American society?
6. Briefly explain how hate crime, elder abuse, *or* domestic violence affects people's ability to anticipate, cope with, resist, and recover from a disaster.
7. Identify two patterns of violence in America you think call for special attention by emergency managers. Using a disaster event you have experienced or studied, illustrate how and why these patterns were significant.
8. What is meant by "structural violence"? How do you think it puts people at increased risk in disasters? Support your answer with concrete references to assigned readings.
9. Design a job for researchers by drafting a "request for proposal" in the area of disasters and violence. What do you want to learn more about and why? What methodologies would you encourage and why? How do you expect the findings would impact your work as an emergency manager?
10. In your view, how does violence relate to other forms of social vulnerability? Provide concrete examples from assigned readings.

REFERENCES

Aranji, S. 1992. *The Exxon-Valdez oil spill: Social, economic, and psychological impacts on Homer.* Anchorage, Alaska: University of Alaska.

Bolin, R., and L. Stanford. 1998. Cultural diversity, unmet needs, and disaster recovery: The Northridge earthquake. *Disasters* 22 (1): 21–38.

Center for Research on Women with Disabilities. 2000. Facts about programs delivering battered women's services to women with disabilities. http://www.bc.medu/crowd/abuse_women/progfact1.htm (accessed November 21, 2008).

Choi, N., and J. Mayer. 2000. Elder abuse, neglect and exploitation risk factors and prevention strategies. *Journal of Gerontological Social Work* 33 (2): 5–25.

Cutter, S. 2006. The geography of social vulnerability: Race, class and catastrophe. http://understandingka-trina.ssrc.org/ (accessed November 17, 2008).

Durkheim, E. 1897/1997. *Suicide*. New York: The Free Press.

Eads, M. 2002. Marginalized groups in times of crisis: Identity, needs and response. Quick Response Report #152, Natural Hazards Research and Applications Information Center. http://www.colorado.edu/hazards/ (accessed November 21, 2008).

Enarson, E. 1998. Battered women in disaster: A case study of gendered vulnerability. EIIP Virtual Library Online Presentation. http://www.emforum.org/vlibrary/libchat.htm (accessed November 15, 2008).

———. 1999. Violence against women in disaster. *Violence Against Women* 5 (7): 742–68.

———. 2006. Violence against women in disasters. http://www.gdnonline.org (accessed November 15, 2008).

Farber, D. n.d. Disaster law and inequality. http://risk.berkeley.edu/papers/Disaster_Law_and_Inequality_Farber.pdf (accessed November 21, 2008).

FBI (Federal Bureau of Investigation). 2008. Hate crime—overview. http://www.fbi.gov/hq/cid/civilrights/overview.htm (accessed November 21, 2008).

Fischer, H. W. 1998. *Response to disaster*, 2nd ed. Lanham, MD: University Press of America.

Fitzpatrick, K., and J. Boldizar. 1993. The prevalence and consequences of exposure to violence among African-American youth. *Journal of the American Academy of Child & Adolescent Psychiatry* 32 (2): 424–30.

Goss, K. n.d. EIIP virtual forum. http://www.emforum.org/pub/eiip/lc991110.txt (accessed November 20, 2008).

Jenkins, P., and B. Phillips. 2008. Battered women, catastrophe, and the context of safety after Hurricane Katrina. *NWSA Journal* 20 (3): 49–68.

Litaker, D. 1996. Preventing recurring injuries from violence: The risk of assault among Cleveland youth after hospitalization. *American Journal of Public Health* 86 (11): 1633–36.

Louisiana Foundation Against Sexual Assault. n.d. *Sexual violence in disasters*. Hammond, LA: Louisiana Foundation Against Sexual Assault.

Morris, A. 1984. *Origins of the civil rights movement*. New York: Free Press.

Morrow, B., and E. Enarson. 1996. Hurricane Andrew through women's eyes: Issues and recommendations. *International Journal of Mass Emergencies and Disasters* 14 (1): 1–22.

Norris, F. H., M. J. Friedman, and P. J. Watson. 2002. 60,000 Disaster victims speak: Part II. Summary and implications of the disaster mental health research. *Psychiatry* 65 (3): 240–60.

Norris, F. H., M. J. Friedman, P. J. Watson, C. M. Byrne, E. Diaz, and K. Kaniasty. 2002. 60,000 Disaster victims speak: Part I. An empirical review of the empirical literature, 1981–2001. *Psychiatry* 65 (3): 207–39.

Palinkas, L., M. Downs, J. Petterson, and J. Russel. 1993. Social, cultural and psychological impacts of the Exxon Valdez oil spill. *Human Organization* 52:1–13.

Peek, L. 2003. Community isolation and group solidarity: Examining Muslim student experiences after September 11th. In *Beyond September 11th*, ed. J. Monday, 333–54. Boulder, CO: Natural Hazards Center.

Penix, M. 2006. Post-Katrina depression triples suicide rate in New Orleans. *New Orleans City Business*. http://findarticles.com/p/articles/mi_qn4200/is_20060703/ai_n16512267 (accessed November 18, 2008).

Petersilia, J. 2000. Invisible victims: Violence against persons with developmental disabilities. American Bar Association. http://www.abanet.org/irr/hr/winter00humanrights/petersilia.html (accessed November 21, 2008).

Phillips, B. 1993. Cultural diversity in disasters: Sheltering, housing, and long-term recovery. *International Journal of Mass Emergencies and Disasters* 11:99–110.

Phillips, B., W. Metz, and L. Nieves. 2006. Disaster threat: Preparedness and potential response of the lowest income quartile. *Environmental Hazards* 6:123–33.

Phillips, B., D. Neal, and L. Garza. 1994. Intergroup relations in disasters: Service delivery barriers after Hurricane Andrew. *Journal of Intergroup Relations* 21:18–27.

Ray, N. 2006. *An epidemic of homelessness*. Washington, DC: National Gay and Lesbian Task Force Policy Institute and National Coalition for the Homeless.

Rodriguez, H., J. Trainor, and E. L. Quarantelli. 2006. Rising to the challenge of catastrophe: Emergent and prosocial behavior following Hurricane Katrina. *Annals of Political and Social Science* 604 (1): 82–101.

Rubin, C., and I. Renda-Tenali. 2002. Disaster terrorism timeline. http://www.disaster-timeline.com/terror-ismtl.html (accessed November 21, 2008).

Sacks, R., J. Flattery, and R. Hut. 2004. Crisis of confidence. http://www.childrenshealthfund.org/media/medi-akit/Maristsurvey_824.pdf (accessed November 19, 2008).

Sadler, A., B. Booth, B. Cook, and B. Doebbeling. 2003. Factors associated with women's risk of rape in the military environment. *American Journal of Industrial Medicine* 43:262–73.

Schechter, S. 1983. *Women and male violence.* Boston: South End Press.

Sharkey, P. 2007. Survival and death in New Orleans. *Journal of Black Studies* 37 (4): 482–501.

Siegel, J., L. Bourque, and K. Shoaf. 1999. Victimization after a natural disaster: Social disorganization or community cohesion? *International Journal of Mass Emergencies and Disasters* 17 (3): 265–94.

Smith, T.W. 2003. *Public opinion on gun control.* University of Chicago: National Opinion Research Center.

South, S., and R. Felson. 1990. The racial patterning of rape. *Social Forces* 69 (1): 71–93.

Swanberg, J., T. Logan, and C. Macke. 2005. Intimate partner violence, employment and the workplace. *Trauma, Violence and Abuse* 6 (4): 286–312.

Tierney, K., M. Lindell, and R. Perry. 2001. *Facing the unexpected.* Washington, DC: Joseph Henry Press.

U.S. Department of Justice. n.d. Crime and victims statistics. http://www.ojp.usdog.gov/bjs/cvict.htm (accessed November 15, 2008).

Watts, C., and C. Zimmerman. 2002. Violence against women: Global scope and magnitude. *The Lancet* 359:1232–37.

Wilgosh, L. 1993. Sexual abuse of children with disabilities: Intervention and treatment issues for parents. *Developmental Disabilities Bulletin* 21 (2). http://www.ualberta.ca/~jpdasddc/bulletin/articles/wilgosh 1993.html (accessed November 21, 2008).

Wisner, B., P. Blaikie, T. Cannon, and I Davis. 2005. *At risk*, 2nd ed. London: Routledge.

Young, M., M. Nosek, C. Howland, G. Chanpong, and D. Rintala. 1997. Prevalence of abuse of women with physical disabilities. *Archives of Physical Medicine and Rehabilitation* 78 (Suppl): S34–38.

RESOURCES

- *Community Oriented Policing Services* (COPS) office promotes community policing through hiring grants, promoting innovative approaches to solving crime, and through training and technical assistance to implement and sustain community policing. The COPS site lists publications and multimedia products on topics of interest to communities, such as community partnerships, crime prevention, problem solving, school safety, and many more.

- *Gender and Disaster Network*, see the searchable Gender Sourcebook at http://www.gdnonline.org. The Gender and Disaster Network remains the single best source of information on issues and resources for women experiencing violence in a disaster context.

- *Project Safe Neighborhoods: America's Network Against Gun Violence.* This is described as "a nation-wide commitment to reduce gun crime in America by networking existing local programs that target gun crime and providing those programs with additional tools to be successful. Under Project Safe Neighborhoods, newly appointed United States Attorneys will establish strategic partnerships between federal, state and local law enforcement agencies in an intensive offensive against gun crime."

- *The Safe Cities Network*, which was "established to help communities reduce gun violence through direct collaboration and the coordinated support of the federal government. Under the initiative, ten communities from across the country formed a network for sharing successful strategies, working with federal law enforcement and other agencies, and gaining access to experts in gun violence reduction."

- The *Weed and Seed program* is described as "the Department of Justice's premier community development initiative. This community-based initiative is an innovative and comprehensive multi-agency approach to law enforcement, crime prevention, and community revitalization. Communities work with their local U.S. attorneys to develop a Weed and Seed strategy which aims to prevent, control, and reduce violent crime, drug abuse, and gang activity in targeted high-crime neighborhoods across the country."

Section III

Building Capacity

13 The Nature of Human Communities

Eve Passerini

CONTENTS

13.1 CHAPTER PURPOSE

This chapter provides an overview of historic understandings of community and the role that strong networks and social capital play in improving a community's ability to mitigate and respond to disasters. The chapter explores the effects that disasters have on communities—from pulling communities closer together and fostering positive policy change in the "therapeutic community" effect to destroying community ties and deepening existing conflict in the "corrosive community" effect. The chapter also reviews the goals of sustainable development and notes barriers and incentives for action toward a community's common good. This chapter suggests that disaster professionals must be involved in the work of community building if they are to be successful at fostering long-term disaster resiliency.

13.2   OBJECTIVES

As a result of reading this chapter, the reader should be able to

1. Explain the complex nature of the term "community."
2. Note examples of how disasters can strengthen a community structure (the "therapeutic community" and positive policy change), but more often exacerbate existing community conflict (the "corrosive community").
3. Describe the characteristics of a sustainable, resilient community and the barriers and incentives to community decisions for the common good.
4. Explain why investing in strong communities is essential work for disaster professionals and give examples of nontraditional areas in which disaster professionals could be involved.

13.3   INTRODUCTION

In 2008, when an 8.0 earthquake in China disproportionately killed schoolchildren in collapsed classrooms, classic reactions included blaming faulty structures, lax building codes, and lack of code inspections. Certainly structural and regulatory issues were a problem, however, if we really want to know the cause of these children's unnecessary and untimely deaths, we need to dig deeper—into community. What caused the shoddy building and lax codes in the first place? Why were smaller beams and few inspectors seen as appropriate fiscal savings—in schools but not in government buildings? The reason so many children died in this earthquake was a combination of local government corruption, lack of social capital and networks, lack of voice and power of local people, and an acceptance of institutions that were unresponsive to true community needs.

In 2005, what made the U.S. hurricane in New Orleans so devastating? Obviously Katrina was a large storm and the levees failed—in fact meteorologists and engineers had predicted the New Orleans disaster for decades. But the shocking level of disruption and misery was not an inevitable result of the storm. Instead, a variety of social conditions and public policy choices turned a storm into a national nightmare. Although the city evacuation plan was one of the few in the country to include public transportation in its evacuation plans, officials (for a wide variety of reasons) failed to deploy public transportation before the storm (Litman 2005), even though 35% of African Americans in New Orleans did not own a car. A disaster at the end of the month (on the 29th) meant that poor people working for minimum wage, living paycheck-to-paycheck, or dependent on WIC, Social Security, disability, or Medicaid, had run out of money for that month and could not afford gas or a hotel. As then Senator Barack Obama noted (2005), "Whoever was in charge of planning was so detached from the realities of inner city life in New Orleans … that they couldn't conceive of the notion that they couldn't load up their SUVs, put $100 worth of gas in there, put some sparkling water [in] and drive off to a hotel and check in with a credit card … this other America was somehow not on people's radar screen." Also, decades of failing infrastructure (schools, hospitals, health care, etc.), contributed to an uninformed and ill population, with few resources to protect themselves. Distrust between races contributed to delinquent and slow aid after the storm. Extreme poverty, racism, classism, and few social safety nets made this disaster much worse than it needed to be.

In addition, many policy choices contributed to the disaster. For example, choices were made before the storm not to invest in building communication among emergency planning, response, and recovery groups. Choices were made to create an evacuation plan based on middle class assumptions. Choices were made to develop wetlands, rather than protect them as insurance against storm surges. Choices were made to deploy National Guard troops and equipment to Iraq, so they were not available to help. Choices not to implement national and global restraints on carbon dioxide emissions may have made the intensity or frequency of storms more likely. Natural events like hurricanes, floods, fires, tornadoes, and earthquakes are inevitable, but devastating disasters that destroy the fabric of communal lives are the result of the relationships between community values and the institutions they create (Hartman and Squires 2006; Brunsma, Overfelt and Picou 2007, and South End Collective 2005). Disaster professionals have traditionally focused on improving physical structures, but if you are looking for the root causes of disaster, it is important to also understand community structures.

13.4 WHAT IS A COMMUNITY?

Community is an important source of social, political, and economic support before and after a disaster. Community is a term that is often used, but difficult to define. We may all "know it when we see it," but … what is it? Traditionally, community has been defined as a group of individuals united by one or more of the following (which often overlap):

- Geography—floodplain, town, neighborhood
- Culture and interests—religion, ethnicity, family, class, politics, hobbies
- Organizations—business, professional, institutions, service, politics

In this section we explore the idea of a community and the assets that communities may offer in a disaster context. We look at classic and contemporary understandings of community and highlight the importance of networks and social capital to a well-functioning community.

13.4.1 CLASSIC THEORIES

Over time, theorists have described two main forms of community. The first form is represented by Tonnies' "*gemeinschaft*" (1887/1963), and Durkheim's "mechanical solidarity" (1893/1964), and Putnam's "communitarianism" (2000), which all broadly describe small pre-industrial villages and towns, or small pockets within a larger industrial or post-industrial city. This type of community is characterized by

- Emphasis on the group over the individual.
- Action toward a collective, common good.
- A common language, culture, and tradition.
- Social bonds that rely on similarities in tradition and geography.
- The glue holding this community together is that everyone is "the same."

In contrast, the second form of community is represented by Tonnies' "*gesellschaft*" (1887/1963), Durkheim's "organic solidarity" (1893/1964), and Mill's "social liberalism" (1856/1985), which all broadly describe the kind of society frequently seen in modern industrialized (or post-industrialized) cities. Community is characterized by

- Emphasis on the individual (freedom/self expression) over the group.
- No common language, culture, tradition, or even geography.
- Social bonds that rely on voluntary associations and contracts.
- Sometimes negatively associated with the disunity, conflict, narrow self-interest, and alienation of modern cities.
- Also associated, more positively, with the richness of multiculturalism and liberation from oppressive norms and traditions.
- The glue holding this community together is a commitment to broad common values, even though individuals may be from different groups with dissimilar values. So, you may have a Muslim, a Jew, and a Christian all sharing values of democracy, respect for others, or support for floodplain management, while having substantial differences in other values, language, or culture.

13.4.2 Mosaic of Communities

Recently, disaster scholars have noted that while we often make sweeping generalizations about "the community," there is rarely one single, unified, identifiable community—instead, multiple communities coexist and overlap in a "mosaic of communities" (Marsh and Buckle 2001). People living in the same geographic area can have vastly different values, sense of community, access to services, interests, religions, or sense of obligation to others. Even when people do share characteristics of a community, they may not realize that they are a community or act like a community. Community solidarity certainly does not emerge from simple geographical closeness, or even from shared interests or needs. Prior to effective community disaster work (education, risk analysis, mitigation, response training, etc.), a sense of community bonding and obligation must exist. Disaster professionals can help build a sense of community (agency, civic participation, communal obligations) within the "mosaic" through education, negotiation, and conflict resolution (Marsh and Buckle 2001).

The idea that disaster professionals should be working directly on the task of community building is relatively new. In the past, a community was assumed to be present and static. Knowing that it is a "mosaic" and that it may be loosely bonded suggests that working to build community could be valuable for much of the work that disaster professionals do. For example, Scillo (2001–2002) points out a number of reasons to be involved in community building:

- To get support for a project
- To legitimate the process
- To create "buy-in" and "ownership" of the project
- To educate and provide information
- To gather community input (risk perception, views, expectations, etc.)
- To use community input (local knowledge) to help make decisions
- To encourage communities to take responsibility for the work of risk reduction
- To encourage widespread participation in decision making
- To get people to change their risky behavior

13.4.3 Networks

Shared geography is not a necessary part of the definition of community if social networks exist. Large-scale communities (like a city) are made up of a variety of smaller groups knit together with networks of interdependence, communication, values, trade, and conflict. When networks exist, members are more likely to produce new information, find new opportunities for solving problems, and obtain needed resources (Granovetter 1973). Weak ties to colleagues such as the grocer, colleagues from organizations, or "a friend of a friend" can be as important as the strong ties of family and religious community in terms of community strength and potential for recovery (Granovetter 1973). The more networks there are between groups, the better able a community is to recover from a disaster—emotionally, financially, socially, and environmentally.

New technologies like Facebook, Twitter, blogs, and Google Earth can be used to disseminate warnings and information about danger, as well as to provide vital information during an event. During a California wildfire that destroyed more than 1500 homes, social networking sites (like Facebook, Myspace, etc.) were used to keep the community apprised of the situation in real time (instead of waiting for daily press reports), and allowed anyone with information to share, instead of relying on official media. These new technologies have many implications for disaster response coordination. According to Eric Rasmussen, president and CEO of the nonprofit organization Innovative Support to Emergencies, Diseases, and Disaster:

> We can send an SMS [short message service/texting] message onto Google Earth in an emergency center, and it sees a dot with a color-coded response, with my name and date. Right underneath that,

there's a button that says reply, and aid workers can send a note that we have the resources you need 2 miles north … Suddenly there's a two-way conversation using nothing but a cell phone with one bar (Olson 2008).

The potential for the electronic enhancement of networks once thought impossible or impractical appears vast (see Box 13.1 and Figure 13.1).

13.4.4 Social Capital

Social capital is the value of all networks and ties between people and groups. Social capital includes the trust, norms, and networks that affect social and economic activities. Social capital determines a community's capacity to plan for disaster, evacuate, respond, and recover. Isolated communities, or communities that only interact with other communities just like themselves, or communities in which groups are not networked with each other, have low social capital. Communities that have

---

BOX 13.1   GREATER NEW ORLEANS COMMUNITY DATA CENTER

An example of new and innovative networks:

This organization builds sustainable sources of data and information to support non-profit planning in a rapidly changing post-catastrophe environment. It helps the nonprofit sector access information and interpret data, and then act on it to eliminate obstacles to recovery, identify needed reprioritizations, and advocate for equity in rebuilding activities. The Web site includes easy-to-read interactive maps, spreadsheets, slideshows, census data, and news releases comparing pre- and post-Katrina data on almost everything, including poverty, racial segregation, day-care centers, schools, medical clinics, neighborhood boundaries, extent of flooding, repopulation, etc.

Source: The Greater New Orleans Community Data Center. www.gnocdc.org.

FIGURE 13.1   Neighbors helping neighbors. FEMA's Community Relations Program puts on a Neighbor Helping Neighbor workshop to empower community leaders and leverage community networks for recovery purposes. *Source*: Photo by Robert Kaufmann/FEMA news photo.

many networks of mutually supporting relationships have high social capital. Norms of social capital built through networks include:

- Mutual trust
- Shared values, commitments, cooperation
- Reciprocity (returning the favor, doing things for each other)
- Sharing information
- Civic involvement

Social capital comes in many forms. For example, Woolcock (2000) and Nakagawa and Shaw (2004) note three categories:

- *Bonding* social capital—ties among family, friends, neighbors, business associates. For example, sports programs, cultural events, trust in local leaders, participation in local events and community decision making, community-based groups and informal networks.
- *Bridging* social capital—ties between people from different ethnic, geographic, or occupational backgrounds who share similar economic status and political influence. For example, interaction with various stakeholders such as city planners, academics, activist groups, neighborhood associations, and networks between neighborhoods.
- *Linking* social capital—ties between the community and those in positions to influence public policy such as banks, schools, housing authorities, police, and agricultural extension offices. For example, interaction between government officials and community through civic or development activities.

The poor have strong bonding social capital, and some bridging social capital, but little linking social capital—which is critical to creating a disaster-resilient community. The most vulnerable populations have the least of all types of bonding. Building the social capital of the most vulnerable populations empowers them with voice and the ability to implement interpersonal connections and policy change that can reduce their vulnerability. High social capital in a community can enable it to:

- Bridge social divisions and share empathy and care across race, religion, age, etc.
- Be responsive to diverse needs and opinions
- Prevent or respond to corruption
- Be flexible in times of change
- Absorb stress and bounce back from disasters through resistance or adaptation
- Manage and maintain basic functions after a disaster
- Build social infrastructure (good schools, fair criminal justice, etc.)
- Expand and share networks of power, influence, wealth, prestige

Collective unity and social capital after a disaster can be built through mutual assistance with exchanges of labor, child care, tools, shelter, and dinners. In addition, charitable actions by volunteer groups offer materials, skills, resources, and hope. Commercial cooperation is fostered when stores reopen and show a commitment to community, and social capital is also built when public services such as schools, transportation, hospitals, and parks are re-established and well-funded (Chamlee-Wright 2006). Social capital is strongest when networks cross traditional social boundaries of race, class, gender, age, interest, etc.

13.5   HOW DOES A COMMUNITY RESPOND TO DISASTERS?

The effect that disasters have on community structure is not static and can be both positive and negative. In some cases disasters can strengthen a community structure (the "therapeutic community") but more often disasters exacerbate existing community conflict (the "corrosive community"). Community conflict can be undesirable; however, conflict can sometimes increase social interaction and social capital, and push stakeholders to implement positive policy change.

13.5.1 THE THERAPEUTIC COMMUNITY

Disasters are often thought to pull communities together, although this shared unity is usually short-lived. The idea of the "therapeutic community" is that after a disaster the collective imagination of a community is activated like never before. A community once fractured by diverse interests and historic rifts can be turned into a united community of survivors with a shared history—because the process of response and recovery breaks old ways, promoting innovation and improvisation, changing traditional norms and roles, creating new communication across once static social boundaries, and focusing diverse groups on common goals. Disasters can increase feelings of social bonding and group culture, and be "therapeutic" for a community. "The shared trauma of a disaster can create community … in the same way that common language and common cultural backgrounds can … [creates] a common culture, a source of kinship" (Erikson 1994, 231; see also Quarantelli and Dynes 1976; Barton 1970; Fritz 1961, 685). The therapeutic community may exist for a short time after a disaster. (Recall the solidarity of New Yorkers after September 11th, or the immediate local response to the Chinese earthquakes. Or, recall how everyone suddenly talks to each other on the streets or on the bus after a huge snowstorm.) It may last longer for some subgroups within a community (for example, a particular neighborhood). But the collective mind of the "therapeutic" community does not last through the initial response phase. Soon after a disaster the ordinary ways of thinking and interacting creep back, and life goes back to normal. In some cases a "corrosive community" process replaces the "therapeutic community," wherein existing inequalities are exacerbated, different agendas and perceptions emerge, blame is assigned, and groups fight for resources.

13.5.2 THE CORROSIVE COMMUNITY

The "corrosive community" is characterized by a loss of trust in community—a perceived loss of charity, concern, empathy, and recovery resources; a fragmentation of community groups; and a breakdown of social relationships, both personal and institutional. As victims and survivors fight for scarce resources and debate recovery options, community conflict emerges.

Disasters do not create conflict; they amplify previously existing inequality within a community. Poor, young, elderly, and minority populations are most vulnerable every day—including disaster days. Disaster "tears the scab off" a community to expose the persistent wound of conflict and vulnerability underneath. Some examples of community conflict and corrosion include

- Inadequate social infrastructure (health care, housing, education, etc.)—Before Katrina, one third of New Orleans lived in poverty. The city had the highest murder rate in the United States, an infant mortality rate twice as high as Beijing's, and a bankrupt education system with the lowest paid teachers in the nation. Thirty-five percent of African Americans did not own a car. The vulnerability of the population was very high before, during, and after the storm.
- Race and class divisions—The Chicago heat wave of 1995 killed African Americans at a higher rate than whites, because of higher social isolation in depopulated parts of town. Of all disaster deaths worldwide, 2% come from developed countries, and 98% come from less developed and developing countries. Hate crimes against Arab Americans increased after the World Trade Center was bombed. Racial tension soared after Hurricane Katrina with victims blamed for their loss. Conflict can also emerge when some groups receive more aid or faster aid than others.

- Corruption—After the Chinese Earthquake in 2008, locals protested shoddy school construction and rampant government corruption. Similar charges were made after Hurricane Andrew in Florida when newer houses failed and older ones remained standing.
- Tension between outsiders and locals—Tension can occur when local organizations are ignored or under funded compared to outside organizations, when local businesses are undermined by overabundance of relief supplies, and when non-local urban planners have more voice than local citizens or planners. Concerns emerge that outside contractors, builders, and volunteer "trauma tourists" take recovery jobs of locals.
- Land use planning—Conflict arises about the value of developing or restoring beaches, wetlands, floodplains, high wild land fire areas, earthquake faults, etc. What is the "highest" or "best use" of the land? And, without careful planning rules, gentrification can occur in the rebuilding phase, leaving poor people nowhere to live in the community.
- Looting—Social behavior after a disaster is overwhelmingly pro-social. However, a persistent stereotype of large-scale disasters is of rampant looting and lawlessness. In fact, "the mass media played a significant role in promulgating erroneous beliefs about disaster behavior" (Tierney, Bevc, and Kuligowsi 2006). For example, after Hurricane Katrina there were reports of riots, murders, babies with their throats slit, an epidemic of rape, looting, carjacking, and shooting at rescue helicopters. Most of these reports turned out to be false or grossly inflated—few bodies, witnesses, survivors, or survivors' relatives could be found. In most cases there were other explanations. Most "looting" was of perishable food and drink. Most deaths were natural. People reported they fired shots to get noticed and be rescued. "Pro-social behavior (much of it emergent) was by far the primary response to Katrina, despite widespread media reports of massive antisocial behavior" (Rodriguez, Trainor, and Quarantelli 2006). However, when lawlessness does occur after a disaster, it is most likely when the local police force is seen as corrupt or inefficient, people are extremely disadvantaged compared to others, unemployment is high, and high gang membership and crime rates existed before the disaster (Dynes and Quarantelli 1968; Quarantelli and Dynes 1970, 1976).

Conflict is usually viewed as a negative thing in a community. However, conflict can also have positive outcomes. Without conflict the United States wouldn't have women's suffrage or the Voting Rights Act of 1965, as two examples among many. Conflict can push groups of people to form alliances, articulate concerns, and push for change. Organizations—from antiviolence against women groups to affordable housing groups to immigrant advocates to environmentalists to senators—can find new room and voice for political mobilization of the marginalized, and disasters can create a new forum to critique the status quo (Olson and Drury 1997; Passerini 2000) (see Box 13.2).

13.6 SUSTAINABILITY AND THE COMMON GOOD: BARRIERS AND INCENTIVES

Many disaster managers and city planners now work toward the goal of sustainable, resilient communities. A sustainable community meets the needs of the present without compromising the ability of others (in other communities, or in future generations) to meet their own needs. A sustainable community is one that balances:

- Social equality and equity
- Economic vitality
- Environmental responsibility and health

Such a balance requires a community with shared values and vision working for the common good. It sounds good in theory, but it does not come easily. There are many barriers to a community

---

BOX 13.2   CONFLICT CAN BE POSITIVE

Disasters can spark *long-term policy change* by triggering increased interaction, issue formation, blaming, and framing. The experience of a disaster can renew and enhance the building of social capital as new networks form. Examples include the following:

- The Johnstown Flood of 1897 disproportionately affected the poor, spurred public outrage, and fueled the progressive political movement of the era.
- The Mississippi flood of 1927 expanded opinions of what the federal government owed people, hastened the move of African Americans from South to North, helped elect Herbert Hoover, and turned African Americans away from allegiance to the Republican Party (Barry 1998).
- The *Exxon Valdez* disaster changed laws and increased watchdog organizations.
- Hurricane Katrina reminded America that racism and poverty are stark realities in the 21st century, and led to significant changes in federal disaster response.

---

coming to consensus around the common good, but there are also conditions that can be fostered that make such consensus more likely.

13.6.1   Sustainable, Disaster Resilient Community

The more sustainable a community is, the better able it is to both mitigate disasters before they happen and bounce back after a disaster with minimum impact. *Disasters by Design* (Mileti 1999) and *Holistic Disaster Recovery: Ideas for Building Local Sustainability After a Natural Disaster* (Natural Hazards Research and Application Information Center 2001, 1–3) identify six principles of community sustainability (see Box 13.3). First, resident's *quality of life* is maintained and enhanced. For example, proactive initiatives to help the most vulnerable are secured; social safety nets are in place; venues exist for civic, sport, and artistic events; homeownership is high; and the community has agency and awareness of hazards and mitigation. Second, local *economic vitality* is enhanced through reliable jobs, a diversified business pool, and a stable tax base. However, environmental interests are never subservient to business interests. In the best cases, business realizes it can save money and attract customers by not damaging the environment. Third, *social and intergenerational equity* is ensured so that everyone is treated fairly in the current generation, and so that future generations do not pay for the mistakes and inaction of the current generation. This is often done by protecting the environment, the economy, and moving toward a more inclusive community of vast opportunities for everyone. Fourth, *environmental systems* that protect a community from the impacts of disasters are maintained and enhanced by replacing local practices that are detrimental

---

BOX 13.3   SIX PRINCIPLES OF COMMUNITY SUSTAINABILITY

1. Maintain and enhance resident's quality of life.
2. Enhance local economic vitality.
3. Ensure social and intergenerational equity.
4. Maintain and enhance environmental systems.
5. Incorporate disaster resilience and mitigation.
6. Use a consensus-building, participatory process when making decisions.

Source: Adapted from *Holistic Disaster Recovery,* 2006. With permission from the Natural Hazards Center and the Public Entity Risk Institute.

---

with those that allow ecosystems to continuously renew themselves. Sometimes this means protecting areas and creating parks and open space, and other times it means changing long-held patterns such as reductions in driving, sprawl, and pollution. Protecting environmental systems includes reducing CO_2 emissions to reduce the impact of global climate change. Fifth, *disaster resilience and mitigation* are incorporated into everyday community decisions, which necessitates good coordination and networking between groups and organizations, as well as effective government that can coordinate across jurisdictions. Sixth, a *consensus-building, participatory process* is used to make decisions. Overt efforts to improve racial, class, or religious barriers to communication, cooperation, and compassion are implemented. Government represents diverse voices of the community and there is strong leadership for building common goals.

13.6.2   THE COMMON GOOD

A sustainable, resilient community can effectively plan for, and recover well from, a disaster. So why aren't there more such communities? Because building a sustainable, resilient community involves creating "common goods"—public services or resources for which access is shared equally and regulated by community—and creating common good can be controversial. The "commons" has traditionally been used to refer to a common pool of resources for which access is shared equally and governed, not by government and not by individuals, but by a community of users. The "community of users" can include a wide range of stakeholders including landowners, residents, citizens, interest groups, and various local, state, and federal (and even global) representatives. Access is shared and regulated among stakeholders, but is not necessarily free to non-stakeholders. Examples of resources that have traditionally been considered commons include wildlife, fish, oil, groundwater, soil, lakes, streams, farming or grazing land, outer space, Antarctica, and the atmosphere. While natural disasters are not a physical entity (like a lake), they do, like other commons, represent dynamic systems of human–natural interactions. Just as the nature of groundwater changes according to human interactions and demands, so do floodways, wildfire–urban interfaces, earthquake zones, and hurricane-prone coastal areas. Just as our concern with the quality of the oceans and the atmosphere grows with increased population and industrialization, increased population also increases our concerns with the frequency of disasters and the state of disaster-prone areas. The physical property vulnerability of disasters can be regarded as commons property—and a resource. In Boulder, Colorado, for example, a wide array of parks, pedestrian paths, wetlands, and open-space areas have been established in the floodplain. An extensive system of land acquisition and home buyouts has helped clear the hazardous land of residents, and has created a long-term response to flash floods. These protected areas are now places of recreation, which make the city more attractive to citizens, tourists, and businesses. They reduce human and economic losses after a large flood, and make the city less vulnerable to extreme weather. The money and lives saved by not inhabiting the floodplain constitute a community resource.

The common good can also include safety, education, health care, public transportation, parks, quality of life, building codes, land use codes, and insurance requirements. One of the roles of community is to provide for the common good. The challenge for a community is to create a collective consciousness in which common social goals take priority over individual goals. Only collective values and debate can decide whether the community good is better served by protecting or developing wetlands, investing in public transportation or private, or creating better opportunities for health, employment, or education. The political will to commit adequate resources for changes that support a resilient, sustainable community are often based on moral arguments—what and who should be helped, saved, protected, restricted, enhanced … and why? "The problem of the commons is one of how society creates superordinate allegiance to something—the commons or the communal—that transcends people's immediate and everyday sense of reality" (McCay and Acheson 1987, 24). "Superordinate allegiance" does not mean complete, homogeneous agreement, but rather a new form of collective consciousness which embodies openness to difference, and which finds ways to bring different identity groups together without suppressing or subsuming those differences (Young 1990). We must acknowledge, and constructively deal with, conflict over resources, power, and influence, paying close attention to the process of decision making. Solidarity among group members leads them to attach value to others' outcomes, as well as their own (Fireman and Gamson 1977). When cultures that act for the common good and ones that do not are compared, the distinguishing factor is "the locus and nature of authority," in other words, the power of the community (McCay and Acheson 1987, 27).

Disasters are often the result of a failure of a community to plan for the common, long-term good. Barriers to providing for the common good include

- Disproportionate allocation of burden: Those who feel they will not be affected by a disaster (because of location, wealth, or influence) may be hesitant to expend resources for those who will be affected. Questions arise around how much risk (and risk prevention) should be shared by the community and how much should be individual responsibility.
- Short time horizons: We tend to make short-term plans. Politicians think in terms of the political cycle (four years), businesses in terms of the business cycle (six months or a year). How do you get people to forego short-term benefits for future long-term benefits?
- Biased reward structure: Not all voices have equal power. Economic interests are often weighed heavier than social or ecological interests. Affluent, mainstream people have more influence than poor or marginalized people. Future generations have no political power. Thus, pollution laws are lax, zoning and code regulations are not implemented or enforced, and social programs are often the last to be funded. Are there ways to change the system so that a wider diversity of voices, including future generations, have a role in decision making?

Some people argue that we will always look out for our own interests first, and common interests second. The "common good" is a dream, they say—maybe possible in pre-industrialized "gemeinschaft" communities, but not possible in today's more complex communities. Scholars of the common good have found that under conditions where people have little connection to each other, the common good is very difficult to achieve. However, they have also found that cooperation and long-term planning for the common good in a community is not a dream and can, in fact, be fostered. Groups are more likely to agree on the common good and make choices that enhance the common good when (Ostrom 1990; Berke, Kartez, and Wenger 1993):

- Groups share a common interest.
- Groups have many ties to each other.
- Groups have a voice in making and enforcing their own rules.
- Groups interact often with each other.
- Groups expect future interaction with each other (reciprocity).
- Structural incentives encourage commons decisions (unbiased reward structure).

In a nutshell, stronger social capital makes decisions for the common good more likely.

13.7 STRENGTHENING SOCIAL CAPITAL

Disaster professionals have long understood that the root causes of disasters are social as well as physical. And yet their work continues to be largely focused on physical infrastructure, and less on community infrastructure (as described in Chapter 1). Addressing inequality of resources, power, and voice within a community—strengthening a community's social capital and thus capacity for sustainable resiliency—must be a part of a disaster professional's daily work (Geis 2000; Wisner 2000; Mileti 1999). Disaster professionals must consider stepping out of their traditionally defined roles

BOX 13.4   LADDER OF COMMUNITY
PARTICIPATION (FROM LOW TO HIGH)

1. Community has no participation – organization tells community nothing.
2. Community receives information – organization makes plan and announces it. The community is told and expected to comply.
3. Community is consulted – organization promotes plan and seeks to develop the support that will facilitate acceptance or give sufficient sanction to the plan so that administrative compliance can be expected.
4. Community advises – organization presents plan and invites questions. It is prepared to modify the plan only if absolutely necessary.
5. Community plans jointly – organization presents a tentative plan subject to change and invites recommendations from those affected. Expects to make changes to plan.
6. Community has delegated authority – organization identifies and presents a problem to community, defines the limits, and asks community to make a series of decisions that can be embodied in a plan that it will accept.
7. Community has control – organization asks community to identify the problem and make all of the key decisions regarding goals and means. It is willing to help the community at each step to accomplish its own goals, even to the extent of administrative control of the program.

Sources: Adapted from Scillio 2006, and Smithies and Webster 1998

to create new roles that help build community capacity. There are many levels of engagement with community—from no contact to the community in full control (Scillo 2001–2002; see Box 13.4).

The level of engagement depends, in part, on the nature of the project and goals, but the more communities can share in the power and responsibility, the more integrated changes will be in the fabric of the community. A few examples of nontraditional roles for disaster professionals before and after disasters include the ideas addressed in the following sections, which resonate well with those from other chapters, suggesting a consistency in approach is warranted.

13.7.1   BUILDING NETWORKS

Disaster work should no longer be separate from everyday community work. Disaster professionals can help build emergency management into existing community organizations and everyday routines by developing policies and practices that facilitate families and communities assisting each other. They can organize neighborhoods around hazard mitigation and helping coordinate communication between community groups. You can help create networks where none existed before and build capacity of local organizations to do the work of outside organizations. You can work to facilitate partnerships between all stakeholders (e.g., levels of government, nongovernmental organizations [NGOs], grassroots organizations, faith-based organizations, and local citizens) and encourage general volunteerism as well as emergency preparedness volunteerism, as it increases networks and social capital. When possible, invest in local people rather than outside helping agencies.

13.7.2   DIVERSIFYING VOICES

Marginalized groups should be empowered by including them in open and diverse dialogue, and respecting their unique and valuable insights. In the past some communities have been ignored or manipulated so that the powerful could meet their own needs, but all people deserve a place and a power at the table. Emergency response teams and planning committees, for example, should be actively diversified by race, class, religion, ethnicity, gender, etc. Those who currently have power and voice must become advocates for those who don't—and we should always ask … whose voice is missing, what are the barriers to their participation, and what can I do to make sure that voice is heard?

13.7.3 FOSTERING DEMOCRATIC PARTICIPATION

Including multiple voices, and having a wide cross-section of the population in the decision-making process, means that unique and valuable ideas will be included, and the interests of all parties will be protected. Disaster professionals should be vigilant to make sure political or economic interests do not dominate the discussion and decision. Don't be afraid to bring the social, environmental, and moral issues to the table and encourage the framing of values around the common good, rather than individual good. Encourage equitable distribution of costs and benefits. Improve the ability of all people to advocate for their needs. Provide opportunities for discussion and participation. Increased participation builds trust in leaders, and legitimates the idea that government decisions reflect community desires.

13.7.4 ERASING SOCIAL VULNERABILITY

Poverty, racism, and gender inequality create disaster vulnerability. One sure way for disaster professionals to increase the odds that a community will recover quickly would be to address unemployment, underemployment, bad health care, unsafe housing, poor skills and schools, unfair lending policies, poor public transportation, and high crime, rape, and domestic abuse rates. If you can identify and target the most vulnerable and build lasting safety nets and capacity for self-advocacy and self-sufficiency, you will create a disaster-resilient community.

13.7.5 PARTICIPATING IN LAND USE AND ENVIRONMENTAL DECISIONS

Disaster professionals do not often participate in civic conversations about the hydrocarbon economy, but they should. No particular storm is caused by climate change, but increased climate change increases the frequency and/or intensity of storms, floods, and droughts. Changes in behavior that lead to reductions in carbon emissions (building bike paths, taxing emissions, supporting national renewable energy policy and international treaties)—in the long term—contribute to less vulnerable communities. Likewise, the work of arguing in favor of protecting hazardous areas and natural ecosystem protections should not be the proprietary role of environmentalists—disaster professionals should be involved, too. Be advocates, experts, and allies in conflicts that have secondary impacts on disaster vulnerability (for example, tax breaks to oil companies to cut canals, which then puts salt water in freshwater marshes, killing flora and resulting in erosion and greater storm surge potential). Insist on a voice in land use decisions.

13.7.6 BUILD TRUST IN INSTITUTIONS

When communities have a shared understanding and perception that institutions (like law enforcement, emergency management, etc.) are fair and effective—trust is built in a community. Trust is a major component of social capital. Participation in community activities and decisions helps build trust in institutions (Miller 2007). Thus, when we do community work, we increase disaster resiliency. It is a cycle, a circle, a self-fulfilling prophecy. For example, a community invests in creating a more effective, unbiased law enforcement and legal system (or emergency response system, etc.). That process brings people together in dialogue. Then, when a disaster happens, groups have both stronger ties with each other and they trust law enforcement to respond appropriately. Because of those ties and trust, community members will cooperate and volunteer with law enforcement (or

FIGURE 13.2 Greensburg recovery meeting. Lions Clubs from Kansas organized a recovery meeting after the 2007 tornado that destroyed Greensburg, Kansas. Participants included residents, business owners, and government leaders. *Source*: Photo by Greg Henshall/FEMA news photo.

shelters, etc.) during the disaster. That helping behavior, in itself, increases trust and social ties even more, making the community even stronger for the next disaster. All disaster work should have a double-function—one that serves the community during a disaster, and one that serves the community everyday in the absence of a disaster.

13.8   SUMMARY

The work of disaster professionals has traditionally focused on building and protecting structures, designing warning systems, and developing response and recovery plans—a necessary but somewhat antiquated set of roles. Today, we understand that communities will continue to be vulnerable if the community structure itself is weak. Disaster professionals should play a central role in building networks and social capital that improve a community's ability to respond to stress—every day, as well as during extreme natural events. This chapter reviewed classic understandings of the term "community" and the role that networks and social capital play in community well-being. Disasters can have therapeutic and/or corrosive effects on a community, and the best way to ensure positive effects is to build the capacity for community self-advocacy and self- sufficiency. Such goals are often described as "sustainable development" and action toward the long-term common good. Disaster professionals must be involved in this work of community building if they are to be successful at fostering long-term, sustainable disaster resiliency. Understanding the different forms of community and social networks and the ways in which disaster can strengthen or weaken community ties can help identify the underlying barriers and incentives to building sustainable, resilient communities. The work of investing in strong communities should be a primary goal of disaster professionals.

13.9   DISCUSSION QUESTIONS

1. The romantic image of "community" is *"gemeinschaft"*—where everyone at the table has similar backgrounds and values. How can strong ties and social capital be built in a diverse community (*"gesellschaft"*)? Choose two unrelated groups in your area and brainstorm ways you could work to increase networks and shared values to create greater social capital.

2. Use Google Images and search for "Looting vs. Finding." Compare the two pictures and captions from the 2005 Katrina hurricane. In what ways did community turn "corrosive" during this disaster? Can you imagine ways in which disaster professionals could have prevented much of the conflict of Katrina, or, once it happened, could have worked constructively with the conflict to build future social capital?

3. What are the public goods associated with disasters in your community? What conflicts arise over managing them? Whose interests, over what time period, should have priority? What are possible conflicting interests? Using your knowledge of how social capital can influence action toward the common good, suggest ways that disaster professionals could help build capacity within a community for commons decisions.

4. Consider the preparedness, response, and recovery phases of disasters in your area. As a disaster professional, what nontraditional actions could you take to build social capital to increase sustainability and resiliency?

REFERENCES

Barry, J. 1998. *Rising tide: The great Mississippi flood of 1927 and how it changed America.* New York: Simon & Schuster.

Barton, A. 1970. *Communities in disaster: A sociological analysis.* Garden City, NY: Anchor Books.

Berke, P., J. Kartez, and D. Wenger. 1993. Recovery after disaster: Achieving sustainable development, mitigation, and equity. *Disasters* 17 (2): 93–109.

Brunsma, D., D. Overfelt, and S. Picou. 2007. *The sociology of Katrina: Perspectives on a modern catastrophe.* New York: Rowman & Littlefield Publishers.

Chamlee-Wright, E. 2006. After the storm: Social capital regrouping in the wake of Hurricane Katrina. Global prosperity initiative working paper. Arlington, VA: Mercatus Center, George Mason University.

Durkheim, E. 1893/1964. *The division of labor in society.* New York: Free Press.

Dynes, R., and E. L. Quarantelli. 1968. What looting in civil disturbances really means. *Trans-action* 5 (6): 9–14.

Erickson, K. 1994. *A new species of trouble: The human experience of modern disasters.* New York: WW Norton & Company.

Fritz, C. 1961. Disaster. In *Contemporary social problems*, eds. R. Merton and R. Nibet, Ch. 14. New York: Harper & Row.

Geis, D. 2000. By design: The disaster resistant and quality of life community. *Natural Hazards Review* 1 (3): 151–60.

Granovetter, M. 1973. The strength of weak ties. *American Journal of Sociology* 78 (6): 1360–1380.

Hartman, C., and G. D. Squires. 2006. *There is no such thing as a natural disaster: Race, class, and Hurricane Katrina.* New York: Routledge Press.

Litman, T. 2005. *Lessons from Katrina and Rita: What major disasters can teach transportation planners.* Victoria Transportation Policy Institute.

Marsh, G., and P. Buckle. 2001. Community: The concept of community in the risk and emergency management context. *Australian Journal of Emergency Management* 16 (1): 5–7.

McCay, B., and J. Acheson. 1987. *The question of the commons: The culture and ecology of communal resources.* Tucson: University of Arizona Press.

Mileti, D. 1999. *Disasters by design: A reassessment of natural hazards in the United States.* Washington, DC: Joseph Henry Press.

Miller, L. 2007. Collective disaster responses to Katrina and Rita: Exploring therapeutic community, social capital, and social control. *Southern Rural Sociology* 22 (2): 45–65.

Mill, J. S. 1856/1985. *On liberty.* Ed. G. Himmelfarb. United Kingdom: Penguin.

Nakagawa, Y., and R. Shaw. 2004. Social capital: A missing link to disaster recovery. *International Journal of Mass Emergencies and Disasters* 22 (1): 5–34.

Natural Hazards Research and Application Information Center. 2001. *Holistic disaster recovery: Ideas for building local sustainability after a natural disaster.* Boulder, CO. www.colorado.edu/hazards (accessed December 11, 2001).

Obama, B. 2005 (Sept. 11). Interview with George Stephanopoulos on ABC's *Meet the Press.*

Olson, R. S., and A. C. Drury. 1997. Un-therapeutic communities: A cross-national analysis of post-disaster political unrest. *International Journal of Mass Emergencies and Disasters* 15 (2): 221–38.

Olson, S. 2008. Twitter, Facebook called on for higher purpose. *News Blog.* http://news.cnet.com/8301-10784_3-9852369-7.html (accessed December 10, 2008).

Ostrom, E. 1990. *Governing the commons: The evolution of institutions for collective action.* Cambridge: Cambridge University Press.

Passerini, E. 2000. Disasters as agents of social change in recovery and reconstruction. *Natural Hazards Review* 1 (2): 67–72.

Putnam, R. D. 2000. *Bowling alone: The collapse and revival of American community.* New York: Simon & Schuster.

Quarantelli, E. L., and R. R. Dynes. 1976. Community conflict: Its absence and its presence in natural disasters. *Mass Emergencies* 1:139–52.

Rodriguez, H., J. Trainor, and E. Quarentelli. 2006. Rising to the challenge of catastrophe: The emergent and pro-social behavior following hurricane Katrina. *Annals of the American Academy of Political and Social Science* 604 (1): 82–101.

Scillio, Mark. 2001-2002 (Summer). "Working with the community in emergency management." Australian Journal of Emergency Management 16 (4): 59–61. Accessed May 12, 2009 at http://www.ema.gov.au/www/emaweb/rwpattach.nsf/VAP/(3A6790B96C927794AF1031D9395C5C20)~Working_with_the_community_in_emergency_risk_management.pdf/$file/Working_with_the_community_in_emergency_risk_management.pdf.

Smithies, J., and G. Webster. 1998. *Community involvement in health: From passive recipients to active participants.* Ashgate Arena, UK: Aldershot.

South End Press Collective. 2005. *What lies beneath: Katrina, race, and the state of the nation.* Cambridge, MA: South End Press.

Tierney, K., C. Bevc, and E. Kuligowsi. 2006. Metaphors matter: Disaster myths, media frames, and their consequences in hurricane Katrina. *Annals of the American Academy of Political and Social Science* 604 (1): 57–81.

Tonnies, F. 1887/1963. *Gemeinschaft und gesellschaft. (Community and society).* New York: Harper and Row.

Wisner, B. 2000. Capitalism and the shifting spatial and social distribution of hazard and vulnerability. *Australian Journal of Emergency Management* 16 (2): 44–50.

Woolcock, M. 2000. Managing risk and opportunity in developing countries: The role of social capital. In *The Dimensions of Development,* ed. Gustav Ranis, 197–212. Yale: Center for International and Area Studies.

Young, I. M. 1990. The idea of community and the politics of difference. In *Feminism/Postmodernism,* ed. Linda Nicholson, 300–23. New York: Routlege.

RESOURCES

ONLINE ARTICLES AND BOOKS

Bankoff, G. The tale of the three pigs: Taking another look at vulnerability in the light of the Indian Ocean tsunami and hurricane Katrina. 2006. http://understandingkatrina.ssrc.org/Bankoff/ (accessed December, 11, 2008).

Fussell, E. Leaving New Orleans: Social stratification, networks, and hurricane evacuation. 2006. http://understandingkatrina.ssrc.org/Fussell/ (accessed December, 11, 2008).

Geis, D. By design: The disaster resilient and quality-of-life community. *Natural Hazards Review* 1, no. 3 (2000): 151–60. http://www.benfieldhrc.org/resources/Build_Sus_Comm/dis_res_qual_life.pdf (accessed December, 11, 2008).

Miller, L. Collective disaster responses to Katrina and Rita: Exploring therapeutic community, social capital, and social control. Southern Rural Sociology 22, no. 2 (2007): 45–65. http://www.ag.auburn.edu/auxiliary/srsa/pages/Articles/SRS%202007%2022%202%2045-63.pdf (accessed December, 11, 2008).

Nakagawa, Y., and R. Shaw. Social capital: A missing link to disaster recovery. *International Journal of Mass Emergencies and Disasters* 22, no. 1 (2004): 5–34. http://www.iedm.ges.kyoto-u.ac.jp/publication/papers/2005/25%20Social%20Capital%20A%20missing%20link%20to%20disaster%20recovery.pdf (accessed December, 11, 2008).

Natural Hazards Research and Application Center. *Holistic disaster recovery: Ideas for building local sustainability after a natural disaster.* Boulder, CO, 2001. http://www.colorado.edu/hazards/publications/holistic/holistic2001.html (accessed December 11, 2008).

14 Measuring and Conveying Social Vulnerability

Deborah S .K. Thomas, Pamela K. Stephens,
and Jennifer Goldsmith

CONTENTS

14.1 CHAPTER PURPOSE

Having a mechanism for understanding a community's vulnerabilities and capacities in a systematic fashion is necessary for fully translating the concepts of social vulnerability into research and practice. Community vulnerability assessments (CVA) can put valuable information into the hands of all decision makers, including the public, policy makers, emergency managers, and numerous other members of a community, with the goal of vulnerability reduction. Most importantly, CVA can incorporate community voices along with the traditional "official" data sources, providing a mechanism for participation and a basis for action for all who are potentially affected. This chapter focuses on community vulnerability assessment approaches, particularly emphasizing the evaluation of social vulnerability and capacity.

14.2 OBJECTIVES

As a result of reading this chapter, readers should be able to:

1. Understand the value of community vulnerability assessments (CVA).
2. Define and explain the basic elements of CVA.
3. Describe participatory capacity and vulnerability assessment (PCVA) and what it can offer vulnerability assessments.
4. Describe levels of sophistication in conducting various approaches to CVA/PCVA.
5. Appreciate the link to sustainable livelihoods approach.
6. Understand the relevance of carefully identifying indicators and the importance of establishing criteria for assessing vulnerability.
7. Identify various data sources and mechanisms for collection.
8. Understand how geographic information system (GIS) mapping technologies and related tools are utilized to conduct CVA.
9. Discuss the steps needed for communities and governments to move beyond the information-gathering stage of identifying social vulnerability issues to incorporate into preparedness and mitigation plans.

14.3 INTRODUCTION

Previous chapters explored a range of social vulnerability topics in detail, examining how individual and social conditions interplay with hazard events throughout the emergency management cycle. People within a community are rarely affected uniformly by a disaster and their ability to recover and rebuild their lives also varies widely depending on economic status, race, gender, age, and education level. Having an appreciation of how and why these factors come to bear on social vulnerability and capacity to handle natural and human-induced events is vital to reducing death and destruction. But, we must move beyond just acknowledging these issues to incorporating these concepts directly into the decision-making process in meaningful ways throughout the emergency management cycle.

Vulnerability assessments provide a means for systematically identifying, analyzing, monitoring, and explicitly integrating social vulnerability into all aspects of preparedness, response, recovery, and mitigation. These essential tools inform every aspect of emergency management, revealing who may need additional assistance in the face of an event, who might struggle with recovery, and identifying the necessity and prioritization for mitigation activities. Additionally and importantly, vulnerability assessments also establish what strengths and resources exist in communities, incorporating valuable information for developing strategies for resiliency.

This chapter explores the concept of vulnerability assessment and examines mechanisms for conducting them. The first section of the chapter presents the relevance of vulnerability assessments with a presentation of various models and approaches, along with general elements of a CVA. Then, a discussion of indicators, data needs, and collection mechanisms follows, including an emphasis on community-based, participatory processes. Next, the relevance of mapping technologies (GIS, geographic information systems) is presented. The last section provides a discussion of various models and approaches to CVA, as well as strategies for implementation and inclusion in planning processes.

14.4 IMPORTANCE OF VULNERABILITY ASSESSMENT

Although there is no established single approach, fundamentally vulnerability assessments are mechanisms for measuring and conveying how social conditions, the built environment, and political/economic structures relate to the hazard risk in a community. They play an important role in establishing a knowledge base of information about the unique hazard and social context of a particular place, revealing the interplay in human–environment interactions at a given location (Turner et al. 2003). Importantly, assessments can be conducted at a variety of scales, at the community level, regionally, or even nationally, to evaluate the level of susceptibilities to natural and human-induced events. Much of the following discussion applies at broader scales, but the primary emphasis is placed on community-level assessment activities due to the fact that so much of mitigation, preparedness planning, recovery, and response is local.

The most basic function of vulnerability assessments establishes a systematic inventory of data about hazards, risk, vulnerability, and capacity/resources. By bringing together information on hazard risk and social vulnerability, results reveal hazardous places in relation to populations, people, and neighborhoods along with physical risk, explicitly illuminating the relationship between hazard risk and social condition. In this way, social vulnerability and capacity are not hidden pieces of the risk equation, but rather included directly enmeshed in the formal emergency management process. Additionally, a community inventory ensures that an appraisal of assets and needs is already in position should an event occur to inform response and recovery efforts. For example, this information can be integrated into preparedness plans to identify in advance who might need assistance for evacuation, to estimate sheltering needs, to distribute materials to those not speaking the primary language, or to request state or federal aid.

Once an inventory is generated, it establishes a baseline for comparison across space and time, supplying guidance for evaluating mitigation strategies and preparedness activities. In other words, the output is useful for identifying successes and the need for adjustment in these activities. Ideally, an assessment is a process, unfolding over time and creating community dialogue. Places are not static; communities' compositions (built environment, as well as social, political, and economic structures) change over time. The inventory alters, but so too do the voices that set priorities. People move into a community who may not be familiar with local hazards or risks. Further, elected officials, with varying knowledge of vulnerability, change office. A vulnerability assessment, then, can increase community awareness, especially if the process (and conversation) continues, and establishes a line of communication among all stakeholders.

Ultimately, vulnerability assessments can influence policy changes that address the root causes of social vulnerability, as well as evaluating hazards, by linking disaster loss reduction to other community priorities in social services, public and environmental health, and urban/regional/rural planning, among others. Vulnerability assessments are extremely relevant and necessary for understanding disaster risk in communities. They can offer a way of prioritizing mitigation strategies, developing aid interventions, increasing protection and enhancement of economic structures, assisting in the creation of self-protective measures, and supporting institutions in their role of disaster prevention (Cannon, Twigg, and Rowell 2003). In order to reach any of these goals, it is incumbent for loss reduction that assessments are conducted with as much integrity as possible and results are utilized to inform emergency management decision making, while avoiding pitfalls, such as too much focus on simply identifying indicators or in data collection activities.

14.5 MODELS FOR HAZARD VULNERABILITY ASSESSMENT

Capturing community vulnerability and capacity within an assessment process is no easy task, requiring careful consideration up front about what community characteristics will be represented and how they will be incorporated into an evaluation. There is not a single accepted set of indicators or approach or even set of terminology, and so initial planning with relevant stakeholders is essential. Fundamentally, criteria should be established at the onset of any vulnerability assessment assuring that (1) the purpose, goals, and objectives are clearly defined; (2) data elements are selected that align with these; (3) a process (rules, guidance, scoping, definitions, evaluation) is delineated and a vulnerability assessment model adopted that realistically acknowledges data, time, and resource considerations; and (4) mechanisms for disseminating findings and incorporating into planning and decision-making processes are identified. This section presents a general overview of assessment models, along with basic steps, including a focus on community-based, participatory processes and a link to sustainable livelihoods. Subsequent sections elaborate on the use of mapping technologies and discussion of establishing indicators along with data considerations and collection methods.

In terms of the factors and specific steps to include in a community vulnerability assessment, many models exist, both theoretically based and applied, at all scales, local to national. Birkmann (2006) offers a review of frameworks that inform vulnerability assessments. Some focus exclusively on hazard risk (FEMA 1997; Coburn, Spence, and Pomonis 1994), while others emphasize social, political, and/or economic vulnerability (Cutter, Boruff, and Shirley 2003; Cutter and Finch 2008). Still others extend into capturing capacity and assets in order to discern resilience. More sophisticated approaches endeavor to systematically bring all of these contributors to vulnerability together, merging physical and social sciences and engineering approaches. Effectively taking structural and agency considerations into account is also particularly challenging. Further, vulnerability and capacity are particularly local in nature. As a consequence, community-based approaches are incredibly relevant for capturing the forces that contribute to risk. Additionally, mapping and geographic information technologies are commonly embedded in nearly all vulnerability assessment processes (see Section 14.8 for further discussion of mapping).

Approaches to vulnerability assessment can be summed up broadly and practically for comparative purposes by considering outcomes, data requirements, and special considerations (Table 14.1). A single hazard assessment represents the most basic approach for understanding risk, requiring the least resources (in terms of time, money, and human resources) and data inputs. Although a single modeling technique can be quite sophisticated and reveal critical hazard risk, the output is linear in the sense it only provides information about a single hazard, not multiple hazards, and commonly neglects the entire human dimension. Earthquake modeling, for example, is highly technical and necessary, as is the monitoring and detection of floods or severe weather. However, the output can only go so far for understanding the total risk and disaster equation. As such, vulnerability assessments must move further along the continuum to more sophisticated approaches that address the social condition, more thoroughly capturing human–environment interactions. The results become much more insightful and richer, informing vulnerability and risk reduction efforts. But at the same time, the reality is that as the approach becomes more extensive and inclusive, data needs are more intensive, the time commitment and human resources required increase and the overall process becomes more expensive.

The "simplest" models involve the inventory and collection of hazard risk data. The term is in quotes because, in fact, physical models that adequately capture and convey hazard risk are by no means easy, requiring highly researched and developed detection and modeling techniques. These vary by specific hazard, and a choice of models may even exist for one specific hazard type. For example, earthquake detection, modeling, and prediction approaches are quite different than models for flooding. The major challenge is that no single person will be completely versed in all of these topical areas, but fortunately, for many areas of the United States much data and information exist on hazard risk including historical hazard data (Thomas, Wilhemi and Hayes 2006; Mileti 1999; Cova 1999). FEMA's Multi-Hazard Identification and Risk Assessment (1997), for example, guides communities through a hazard assessment approach. While it does not speak to issues of social vulnerability in any significant way, it does provide direction for initial steps in a more robust process. For the purposes of this book, the emphasis is not on the methods and mechanisms for processing hazard risk, but the attention is focused on measuring and understanding social vulnerability. Numerous models move beyond hazard assessment to examine contextual factors, including populations, the economy, and the environment (Cannon, Twigg, and Rowell 2003).

TABLE 14.1
Broad Vulnerability Assessment Approaches

Approach	Outcomes	Data Requirements	Considerations
Single hazard assessment	Documentation and/or models of risk for a particular hazard	Hazard risk information for a single hazard Historical event and impact data Monitoring data to generate models or already generated model output	In localities with extreme risk from a particular hazard an important first step A somewhat limited view of hazard risk Socioeconomic conditions are commonly excluded, but sometimes included in impact modeling and in a rather simplistic fashion
Multi-hazard assessment	Inventory of all hazards in a given location Mapping and analysis of multiple hazards risk	Hazard risk information for a single hazard Historical event and impact data Requires monitoring data to generate models or already generated model output	Provides a more comprehensive picture of hazard risk throughout a community Challenges of combining and weighting the risk from different hazards Same issues as the single hazard assessment with socioeconomic conditions
Basic CVA	Includes multi-hazard risk Explicit attention to socioeconomic conditions in relation to hazard risk	Existing secondary data sources for social analysis (and likely hazards) Relying primarily on readily available U.S. Census data (in U.S. context) for socioeconomic considerations May include some additional locally derived datasets	Often focus on potential structural impacts without a refined approach to understanding social vulnerability A start to understanding human–environment interactions when limited resources are available for conducting the analysis Challenges of how to weight and/or express various indicators of vulnerability
Intermediate CVA/VCA	A more advanced treatment of vulnerability, using additional databases beyond U.S. Census for social and economic analysis Includes information on capacity	Moves beyond a simple U.S. Census analysis to include other local-level sources of data Includes indicators of capacity, including neighborhood and community resources May begin to include some primary data collected from surveys or focus groups	Additional locally derived secondary databases are housed in numerous agencies and so require being inquisitive and creative Challenges of integrating data collected for a variety of purposes
Community-based, participatory VA	Expand societal analysis substantially to include both top-down and bottom-up information A process that involves capturing local knowledge and perceptions and incorporating into the assessment	Collection of primary data through various participatory techniques, such as personal interviews, community information sessions, focus groups, surveys, etc. In the most advanced process, involves stakeholders of all types Capturing institutions and networks within the community relevant to disaster resilience as well as vulnerability	Provides extremely rich information about socioeconomic conditions and resources/capacity in a community A single model for conducting CBPVA does not exist, as numerous approaches exist Intensive process if conducted with full potential in mind

14.5.1 ELEMENTS OF A BASIC COMMUNITY VULNERABILITY ASSESSMENT

This section will begin by presenting broad steps in a basic CVA approach in order to set the groundwork for presenting a more robust approach to vulnerability assessment. While these are certainly a good start, they are not necessarily the only way to proceed through the process, but do capture many of the most essential elements. The categories of information generated are similar among most place-based studies with the overarching themes of (1) identifying and analyzing hazards, (2) identifying and analyzing vulnerability and capacity of society, and finally (3) identifying high-risk areas, those areas that have both high hazard potential and vulnerability. For example, Cutter, Mitchell, and Scott (1996) established a process of vulnerability assessment at the local scale in Georgetown County, South Carolina, and Dao and Peduzzi (2003) performed a generally similar analysis at the global level, using different indicators and weighting schemes (see Section 14.6), but nonetheless attempting to capture these broad categories of information.

Much of this particular section builds from NOAA's Risk and Vulnerability Assessment Tool (NOAA 2008), which offers a tangible approach developed as guidance to local communities undertaking a CVA, mostly involving identifying and inventorying a variety of community characteristics for the purpose of selecting mitigation opportunities. Once a place is clearly defined (location, geographic boundaries) and an evaluation of end-user needs is established, the general steps include (1) hazard identification, (2) hazard analysis, (3) critical facilities analysis, (4) economic analysis, (5) environmental analysis, and (6) mitigation opportunity analysis. All of these incorporate mapping in order to ultimately identify high-risk areas, those places that have both a high hazard potential and high vulnerability.

14.5.1.1 Hazard Identification and Hazard Assessment

These two steps correspond to the multi-hazard assessment described previously. A community identifies all of the hazards that exist in that particular area. Depending on the geographic location, these may range from the full range of natural hazards (such as earthquakes, hurricanes, flooding, or even disease), human-induced hazards (such as toxic chemical or hazardous materials accidents, or oil spills), or a variety that fall somewhere in the middle (such as wildfires or global climate change). Once a "laundry-list" of all potential hazards is created, these should be prioritized based on likelihood of occurrence combined with the level of impact. A community may decide from the onset that a particular subset of hazards should be included. However, hazard assessment also informs setting priorities because this signifies which hazards rank highest in terms of potential threat and effect. The hazard assessment step identifies areas of high potential impact (both structural and non-structural) using probability, magnitude, historical event and/or loss information, and hazard risk modeling.

14.5.1.2 Critical Facilities Analysis

Moving into the arena of critical facilities in the CVA directly attends to the focus of this book. Critical facilities and infrastructure are those resources in a community that are essential and vital to its well-being and operation. No single defined set exists, but generally includes entities like fire, police, hospitals, shelters, utilities (clean water, sewer, electric/gas, waste disposal), and communication networks, as well as the transportation system, including roads, bridges, and tunnels. In other words, these are resources that a community would not want compromised during a hazard event. The first requirement is to create an inventory generated at the local level, including information and location about each facility or piece of infrastructure. Once these are identified, critical infrastructure and facilities can be examined in relation to the hazard risk from the second step in order to set planning and mitigation priorities.

14.5.1.3 Societal Analysis

The goal is to move beyond a basic assessment of the total populations that are potentially affected by various hazards to a more comprehensive understanding of differential experiences with hazards. While it is important to estimate numbers affected, say, downstream from a dam if it were to fail,

**BOX 14.1   CASE STUDY: A REFLECTION ON SEEKING
DATA FOR ASSESSING DISABILITY**

As part of a county-level vulnerability assessment, I was tasked with capturing populations with disabilities. I was able to locate basic demographic information related to total population, as well as information associated with age groups, which may identify older community members and could be used to estimate potential mobility-connected barriers. Unfortunately, when searching for information related to medical conditions or specific disabilities, I found very little data pertaining directly to disabilities. The information I was able to locate on Web sites such as the Employment and Disability Institute at Cornell University, the Kaiser Family Foundation State Health Facts (ND), and Colorado Department of Health and Environment (ND) was generally several years old. Additionally, much of the listed information provided little benefit to this endeavor. For example, death records listed mortality from specific conditions rather than exact numbers of persons currently living with those conditions. Further, when some disability information was located, it listed total percent of disabled populations, but did not provide statistics related to specific disabilities. In addition, estimates rather than actual figures were common. Even the data provided by the 2006 Disability Status Reports for Colorado developed by the Rehabilitation Research and Training Center on Disability Demographics and Statistics (StatsRRTC) at Cornell University offered demographic information only on the non-institutionalized population with disabilities, which would not provide accurate data for the total disabled population in the identified area, nor the statistical data by specific disability needed for special needs shelter planning.

Even after hours and days of searching, I was still unable to locate the data needed to identify the accurate numbers of people with disabilities to inform shelter planning. In the end, after much discussion with local emergency managers and disaster planners, I used 15% to 20% of the total county population as an estimated number of potential candidates for special needs sheltering, knowing that these numbers would result in a wide variance and offer only an educated guess for planning purposes. When developing plans for special needs shelters, accurate data is needed for the effective planning of staffing, supplies, and equipment, yet little exists. Without the ability to access up-to-date information, identifying community members with medical, mobility, and cognitive issues presents a significant challenge for emergency managers when developing effective special needs sheltering plans.

appreciating that various subgroups and neighborhoods have varied abilities to prepare, respond, mitigate, or recover is extraordinarily vital information, ensuring that all people have an equal opportunity for safety and security. Many of the previous chapters identified indicators or variables that reveal aspects of social vulnerability, such as minority populations, poverty status, age distribution, gender, educational attainment, public assistance, rental housing, disability, or a lack of transportation resources (see Box 14.1). Ultimately, the idea is to identify high need/high vulnerability areas and neighborhoods and then account for these in relation to high hazard risk zones. A basic analysis can rely on readily available secondary data (already collected data) from the U.S. Census to compile and analyze the information (U.S. Census Bureau 2008a, 2008b). While this does act as a good first step, the product is somewhat limited by the quality of the data (Skerry 2000). Importantly, many local governments collect and maintain other types of secondary data that are incredibly useful for more fully evaluating social characteristics because they are more current than the census data, contain different types of information, and are also potentially more accurate. Examples of these locally derived datasets include property tax/parcel records, school records (free/reduced lunch programs, enrollment, graduation rates), special needs registries, health registries (birth/death records), among many others. Apart from relying on secondary sources of data, collecting information directly (primary data collection) through implementing surveys, conducting focus groups, or even performing a series of interviews to capture local knowledge, ascertain people's perceptions, and/or clarify priorities most certainly improves the quality of the social analysis step. Additionally, incorporating information on community resources as well as vulnerabilities provides a more robust picture. Once data are compiled and integrated into a common format, the next challenge is defining "fragile" or vulnerable neighborhoods and combining the data in such a way to inform this. Then the results of this step are combined with output from the other steps to determine high vulnerability or hazard risk.

14.5.1.4   Economic Analysis

This phase of the CVA explicitly focuses on the economic sector. While not directly incorporating many of the individual topics covered in this book, economic strength is directly related to the vulnerability/capacity of a community. A diverse and healthy economic sector certainly contributes to employment, a tax base, and the overall vitality of a community. Thus, understanding the relationship of businesses, industry, and government facilities to hazard risk is central to vulnerability reduction, ensuring these can function efficiently and effectively. First, the major sectors of the economy are identified and inventoried (agriculture, mining, construction, manufacturing, transportation, wholesale and retail, services, finance, insurance, real estate, small businesses, or even home-based businesses), including largest employers, keeping in mind that small businesses are also extremely important to the economy of many communities. The zones of particular activity should then be analyzed in conjunction with the other phases of the CVA.

14.5.1.5   Environmental Analysis

In reality, this step aligns with the hazard assessment piece and ensures that the potential for secondary hazards is captured, as well as where ecologically sensitive areas and natural resources exist. Again, as in all other steps, this requires an inventory and evaluation, but in this case focusing on environmental considerations where the initial (primary hazards) event could cause additional incidents (secondary hazards). For example, an earthquake could cause a gas line to rupture with an ensuing explosion, or could cause damage to a dam and flooding downstream areas. Accounting for facilities and infrastructure that store, transport, or dispose of hazardous and toxic materials is also essential for understanding a community's vulnerability. Additionally, this step can include ecologically sensitive areas and natural resources. Understanding these risks in relation to the other hazards and social conditions is critical for setting risk reduction priorities.

14.5.1.6   Mitigation Opportunities Analysis

Without a doubt, going through all of the previous steps is extremely informative for reducing loss through preparedness and response activities. As important, however, is formulating strategic mitigation opportunities. Thus, this step examines all of the combined output from previous steps to identify where mitigation measures (either structural or nonstructural) would have the greatest potential for loss reduction, examining costs versus benefits. For example, this may take the form of starting a program to retrofit schools for earthquakes or ensuring new schools are not built in flood zones. Ultimately, mitigation undertakes reducing or eliminating loss if an event occurs, prevention rather than reaction. Still, unlimited funds are not available and so priorities must be set; CVA provides a mechanism for understanding where and what activities would be most beneficial.

14.5.2   Community-Based Participatory Research for Disaster Risk Reduction

> We will not succeed in advancing the agenda of the Hyogo Framework for Action if we
> do not engage local communities in all aspects of strategies for disaster risk reduction.
>
> **—Surajana Gupta at opening plenary of the First Global Platform on Disaster
> Risk Reduction, GROOTS, 2007**

The Hyogo Framework for Action adopted by 168 countries during the World Conference on Disaster Reduction in 2005 calls attention to the role of the community in disaster loss reduction activities (UN ISDR 2005) and the UN ISDR's *Words Into Action: A Guide for Implementing the Hyogo Framework* (2007) emphasizes the importance of community-based and participatory processes. The most sophisticated approach to assessing vulnerability is not just top-down, utilizing "scientific" and "objective" secondary data, but also bottom-up, incorporating information derived from the community in a multi-methods approach. The terms objective and scientific are in quotes, not because they are unimportant or uninformative, but because assumptions and uncertainty are embedded within them. Locally derived knowledge can add significant value to understanding local risk. Further, if decisions are made about a community, it stands to reason that members of that community should have a say in priority setting.

While experts may have vast knowledge about hazards and disaster risk reduction, they frequently do not have the same understanding of a local community as someone who is part of it. For example, residents may have a better sense of where most vulnerable populations are located, including home-bound, elderly, sick, tourists, the car-less, among others, than is reflected in formal databases. Further, residents likely have a better sense of local resources and assets, such as religious institutions, community-based organizations, businesses, and governmental structures, and how these do, or do not, serve the community. For instance, in creating an inventory of first responders, police stations would likely be identified as an asset in a top-down, "objective" assessment. However, many local community members may not utilize or even view this as a positive resource, depending on experiences with, and perceptions of, police. In short, including community-derived information ensures that cultural customs, local wisdom, and prior knowledge about disasters bolster and strengthen other conventional information sources. These insights can be captured through systematic survey and interview techniques in a more advanced vulnerability and capacity assessment, but extending to participatory approaches enriches both information and process significantly and likely improves chances for sustainable mitigation (Pearce 2003).

Although a "gold standard" model for conducting or implementing community-based vulnerability assessments does not exist, variations of these processes are applied in numerous locations globally (Pelling 2007). Sometimes known as "community vulnerability assessment" or "community-based vulnerability assessment" or "community capacity and vulnerability assessment" or "participatory community-based capacity and vulnerability assessment," or even "participatory vulnerability and risk assessments," they all attempt to give voice to the communities most directly affected by hazards and disasters and reveal the power that communities themselves have to address risk. For the purposes of this section, the term participatory community-based capacity and vulnerability assessment (PCVA) is used to capture the idea of stakeholder involvement at the community scale incorporating both capacity and vulnerability.

Pelling (2007) divides PCVA into three broad categories, within which variation in application also exists, including (1) procedural, (2) methodological, and (3) ideological. Procedural approaches generally focus on where the ownership of the process resides, either with local stakeholders themselves or with officials seeking to gain input from those stakeholders. Methodological approaches emphasize data transfer to and from stakeholders, deriving data from the community (quantitative and qualitative) and then also providing information to the community. Lastly, taking an ideological view, approaches range from extractive to emancipatory. Extractive processes emphasize information flow, deriving data from the community, whereas emancipatory processes accentuate community self-empowerment to generate change embedded in theoretical origins promoting *conscientizacão* (awareness or consciousness) as a means of community participation in learning and adaptation of technology (Freire 1973; see also Chapter 2). These broad categories are not necessarily mutually exclusive, but they do at least reveal the necessity of carefully and consciously choosing a participatory approach that matches the intended outcome in order to ensure goals are adequately met. Ultimately, the benefit of a variety of approaches is that the program can be tailored to fit the community and the goals of the assessment (see also Chapter 13 on the nature of communities and Chapter 16 on community empowerment for a more in-depth treatment of these ideas).

Keeping in mind that these are not the only approaches nor the most ideal in every context, several well-developed and documented processes for participatory disaster loss reduction activities exist, including Oxfam's Participatory Capacity and Vulnerability Assessment (de Dios 2002), the IFRC's Vulnerability and Capacity Assessment (IFRC 2006), and ADPC's Community-Based Disaster Risk Management (Abarquez and Murshed 2004). The community is emphasized in all of these approaches as active in the assessment process. Other common characteristics include deriving community-based data for informing risk reduction activities, community involvement and engagement throughout the process, and open knowledge transfer and communication. Although details vary, some generalized steps convey overarching and guiding themes for participatory disaster loss reduction (see Table 14.2).

As one can imagine, conducting a participatory assessment requires significant background work. Careful planning and preparation are absolutely necessary for producing successful and meaningful outcomes. In fact, the preparation phase probably requires the greatest amount of time commitment; neglecting any aspect will most likely result in less meaningful results and potentially even negative experiences. Once a community is selected, the preparation phase concentrates on clearly defining and preparing for the participatory activities. Significant effort and attention is required for building relationships and rapport in the community so that the participatory process has the greatest chance of success through stakeholder support, additionally ensuring representation from relevant and potentially marginalized, vulnerable groups. For example, incorporating a gendered approach could translate to having separate working groups for all or part of the session for men and women, or could mean focusing on women's groups for train-the-trainer meetings (Enarson 2003). Children are yet another extremely important group often overlooked, but when possible and appropriate should be part of the participatory process. Through education, inclusion, and self-empowerment, they hold the key for disaster loss reduction from the present into the future. Representation at the table, as it were, will directly affect any findings and so must be vigilantly considered (Beierle and Cayford 2002).

Beyond thorough preparation, the actual implementation phase includes working session(s) by which community-derived data are collected through a variety of mechanisms in a comfortable and open setting. This is followed by a compilation of the findings, analyzing where information converges in common themes or ideas. Ideally, any results should be presented to the participants for comment and evaluation. Lastly, those involved build consensus around findings and priority setting for mitigation and preparedness activities, developing an action plan for implementation, including evaluation. In theory, the process would be continuous with adjustments made to the data, priorities, and action plan over time in response to evaluation activities. However, the reality is that this often does not happen because the process is so intensive, limited financial and human resources exist, and it is difficult to maintain active involvement by members of the community. Still, even if a participatory assessment goes through the steps one time, the information generated and the benefits of the process are enormous.

14.5.3   LINK TO SUSTAINABLE LIVELIHOODS

Sustainable livelihood analysis (SLA) is not entirely distinct from PCVA; in fact, each phase of PCVA can incorporate primary SLA considerations, and conversely SLA could incorporate issues of risk. However, the focus of the analyses is slightly different. SLA stresses the complex set of characteristics (individual, household, and community) that affect people's livelihoods, focusing entirely on the human condition, where PCVA considers hazard risk along with social conditions. Along with the difference in emphasis, the scale of analysis is also somewhat finer, with SLA centering on the inter-relationships at an individual and household level that give rise to vulnerability or, from the SLA perspective, reduce capacity. In general, PCVA does not necessarily assess individuals or

TABLE 14.2
Generalized PCVA Process

Phase	Sample Activities
Planning and preparation	Identify community based on some criteria (hazard risk, local interest, political stability, etc.)
	Choose a conceptual framework to guide designing the process
	Build rapport with and understanding of the community
	Identify key stakeholders, groups, leaders to ensure representation from a variety of populations, including children, women, etc.
	Meet with relevant stakeholders to define the process, goals, and objectives
	Determine a timeline
	Identify what information will be collected and select appropriate data collection method
	Determine the number and type of event(s)
	Gain approvals
	Organize the event
	Begin the analysis of secondary sources of risk information
	Conduct a pre-test (a test run) of the event and selected methods
Implementation	Share the secondary data analysis conducted with existing sources, reviewing with the community
	Facilitation of dialogue, creating a comfortable, open, and flexible atmosphere
	Data collection through a variety of methods (pre-selected), including visual, oral, written, and/or facilitation
	Learning and knowledge sharing
	Creating a comfortable, open, and flexible atmosphere
Analysis	Systematically organizing and compiling the data
	Bringing together all of the various pieces of information, documenting where they converge and diverge
	Return to the community with the analysis for input and evaluation
Priority setting and action planning	Build consensus around priorities of the findings from the analysis
	Identify and design an action plan for mitigation and/or preparedness activities, including opportunities for vulnerability reduction and drawing on and building capacities
	Evaluation of the implementation of action plan items

Source: Compiled and derived from de Dios, H. B. *Participatory capacities and vulnerabilities assessment: Finding the link between disasters and development.* Great Britain: Oxfam, 2002; IFRC (International Federation of Red Cross and Red Crescent Societies). *What is VCA? An introduction to vulnerability and capacity assessment.* Geneva, Switzerland: IFRC, 2006. http://www.ifrc.org/Docs/pubs/disasters/resources/preparing-disasters/vca/whats-vca-en.pdf (accessed October 30, 2008); Abarquez, I., and Z. Murshed. 2004. *Community-based disaster risk management: Field practitioners' handbook.* Thailand: Asian Disaster Preparedness Center (ADPC).

even individual households, but rather emphasizes the community and variations throughout and so usually operates from a divergent starting point.

In SLA, social vulnerability is far more than the potential for loss and an interaction with hazard risk. Instead, it is intrinsically linked to people's livelihoods, which in turn affects their capabilities for reducing risk through preparedness, mitigation, response, and recovery to hazard risk. According to Cannon, Twigg, and Rowell (2003), social vulnerability encompasses (1) a person's initial well-being (nutritional status, for example); (2) livelihood and resilience related to economic resources; (3) self-protection; (4) social protection; and (5) social and political networks and institutions. Thus, in this framework vulnerability reduction activities should attempt to expand income and resources, self-empower households and communities, expand access to basic services, and directly address root causes of poverty (CARE 2002; Twigg 2001).

Although useful as a way to observe an overall picture of vulnerability, utilizing descriptive data from conventional sources to offer a baseline for vulnerability assessment does not necessarily capture the complexity of individual and social characteristics. In CVA (basic or intermediate), for example, low-income households, the elderly, and female-headed households are commonly identified as highly vulnerable populations. However, in order to obtain an accurate assessment, factors related to social structures and social networks should also be considered. For example, a family with a low income level might be prevented from evacuation or relocation after a disaster due to limited resources unless extended family or friends live nearby, in which case evacuation or relocation now become possible. In this instance, the social network reduces vulnerability. Social capital (as defined and described in Chapter 13 on community) has the potential to increase capacity for emergency response, although the relationship is complex (Murphy 2007). In fact SLA, and PCVA to a lesser extent, very explicitly captures data on the full range of individual and community capital, including financial (monetary economic means), physical (basic infrastructure), human (individual characteristics, including health and education), natural (environmental resources), social (social networks and links to institutions), and political (ability to use power) (CARE 2002). As an extension, vulnerability reduction revolves around linking to development, food security, poverty reduction, safe housing, improvements in infrastructure, and effective governance. Either PCVA or SLA vulnerability reduction approaches fundamentally speak to basic human rights and improving the human condition.

14.6   ESTABLISHING CRITERIA AND MEASUREMENT APPROACHES

Throughout this chapter, the significance of consciously and carefully designing every element of a vulnerability assessment is emphasized in order to achieve the most meaningful outcomes. This is particularly true of establishing an assessment process, but also for determining measurement criteria for social conditions in an attempt to quantify vulnerability. In some ways, this may seem contrary to the PCVA, but in fact, can be used in conjunction with it; a quantitatively driven vulnerability assessment does not replace PCVA. Instead, they serve different purposes with slightly unique outcomes. PCVA emphasizes the process and the learning and understanding that emerge along with producing extremely rich and informative data at a local level, drawing extensively on qualitative methods. Neither the process nor the information is generalizable to a broader population, but rather is specific to that locale, revealing complex interactions and in-depth associations that give rise to vulnerability. In fact, because of the nature of the participatory process, even comparisons from place to place are limited. On the other hand, more quantitative CVAs provide a means for measuring, comparing, and monitoring over time. Additionally, communities may not be ready or well suited for a PCVA, yet understanding social vulnerability is still necessary, and so conducting even a simple CVA is a start.

A fundamental component of any data-driven vulnerability assessment requiring careful consideration is identifying and choosing the indicators for inclusion. Indicators are measures that characterize key elements of a complex system to reflect the current situation and establish rate and direction of change. The indicators themselves or compilations of multiple indicators can be used to set priorities and guide policy. In order to adequately quantify and communicate, indicators should be clearly defined, reproducible, understandable, and practical, reflecting the interests of all relevant stakeholders.

Over the last decade or more, numerous groups have undertaken work on the development of sustainability and vulnerability indicators (SOPAC 2005; UN-DESA 2007). Even so, a single defined set of indicators for social vulnerability does not exist and the types of data included vary by scale of analysis. For example, global and even regional assessments tend to focus on population numbers, impact, and limited social vulnerability indicators (Peduzzi, Dao, and Herold 2005; Dao and Peduzzi 2003), which at this scale at least provides a broad-brushed depiction of disaster risk. At the regional or local level, more refined indicators are desirable. Thus, it is incumbent for the person or group conducting such an assessment to carefully judge which set of indicators best applies to a particular locality through a review of literature and preferably some type of consensus-building activity. Community leaders and/or government officials may decide, but this is also ideal for the use of community-based, participatory approaches.

Determining measurement variables begins with choosing a conceptual framework as applied to a particular scale with clearly defined outcomes that tie to the goals and objectives. This in turn guides a selection of categories for which individual indicators can be identified and selected. For example, accounting for health status, the choices for indicators may include infant mortality, life expectancy, number of doctors per 1000 people, or even number of hospitals per 1000 people. In considering education, literacy rates, percentage of adults with a high school diploma, or percentage of females completing high school reflect a slightly different aspect of vulnerability. Additionally, some indicators measuring the same observation have opposite interpretations for a vulnerability assessment. Median house value could signify poverty, but it can also reflect the amount of potential property loss. A corner convenience shop could be considered an asset by residents because of the easy access to some food products, while in other situations it might be a blight because of loitering and no real available resources. Likewise, a high percentage of rental property could be deemed negative in terms of real estate values, but may mean affordable housing in a cohesive neighborhood. Ultimately, relevance, accuracy, and availability of data serve as primary drivers for the selection of indicators.

Once indicators are collected, they can be examined independently across a community, but will often also be combined in some fashion into a composite index (Birkmann 2006). This can be calculated through a normalization process, by categorical scales, or even using statistical methods. Normalizing involves translating data into a common unit for averaging into a composite index. Median house value and percent female-headed households have different units and so would be placed on the same scale often based on the average of that particular dataset. Categorical scaling groups data within a single indicator that can then be expressed, for example, as low, average, and high (median household income, for instance). These groups are then combined over all vulnerability indicators. The challenge is that cut-points must be determined for categories, determining what is high and what is average. Lastly, indicators can be combined statistically to condense the data (e.g., Cutter, Boruff, and Shirley 2003) or as a multivariate modeling attempting to explain some variable—loss, for instance—through vulnerability indicators (e.g., Dao and Peduzzi 2003). The most ideal approach to vulnerability assessments is to incorporate mixed methods that combine both qualitative and quantitative information, in other words, both measured indicators along with qualities derived from surveys, interviews, focus groups, and other participatory approaches.

14.7   DATA CONSIDERATIONS

Vulnerability assessments are data driven, whether derived from existing sources or primary collection and rely on quality data sources (NRC 1999). The selected conceptual model with corresponding goals and objectives along with the scale of analysis will guide the type of data desired. At the same time the quality and type of data will directly affect the output. Much information already exists or can be collected, revealing various aspects of vulnerability and capacity (Table 14.3). In reality, data collection is a function of availability, time, and money, as compiling datasets requires significant resources and attention. All data are simplifications and generalizations of reality and produce both benefit and limitations.

In terms of secondary data, these are already collected and existing; however, the organization or entity that compiled the data did so for a purpose. Consequently, the data may or may not appropriately capture elements of vulnerability and capacity of interest. For example, even when considering post-disaster fatality information, which at first glance seems like a reliable source, several serious issues exist. Accounting for fatalities and death estimates can actually be challenging, especially

TABLE 14.3

Sample Information for Vulnerability Assessment Focusing on Social Conditions in U.S. Context

Broad Categories	Sample Information	Potential Source
Demographic	Minority populations	1, 3, 4
	Population over age 65	1, 3, 4
	Population under age 5	1, 3, 4
	Female-headed households	1, 3, 4
	English spoken at home	1
Education	Adults with no high school diploma	1
	Educational programs and initiatives	2, 3, 4
	Preschool programs and enrollment	2
Health	Birth and death records	2
	Health services (hospitals, clinics)	2
	Disease registries	2
	Special needs registries	2
	Nursing homes	2
	Accessibility	2, 3, 4
Economic	Households below poverty	1
	Households with public assistance income	2
	Rental housing	1
	Children on reduced/free lunch programs	2
Social services	Private and public social service agencies	2
	Support services to individuals and families that are relevant to disaster response and recovery	2, 3, 4
Political	Sector political representation (or lack thereof)	2, 3, 4
	Efficacy of municipality or local government	2, 3, 4
	Voting levels	2
	Political participation in civic affairs, including building and zoning matters	2, 3, 4
	Governmental organization and coordination around disaster-related issues	2
Infrastructure	Housing units with no vehicle available	1
	Hospitals	2
	Schools	2
	Public transportation	2
Social groups	Neighborhood organizations, such as homeowners' associations, civic clubs	2, 3, 4
	Religious organizations and groups	2, 3, 4
	Special interest groups	2
Social networks	Family and friend networks	3, 4
	Networks and coordinating groups	3, 4
	Communication networks (newspapers, newsletters, radio stations)	2, 3, 4
Secondary sources	U.S. Census	1
	Other state or local government agency or organization	2
Primary sources	Surveys, focus groups, key informant interviews	3
	Participatory process	4

when large numbers of people are involved. How precise is saying 220,000 people perished after the 2004 Indian Ocean Tsunami? If someone dies from a heart attack immediately following an earthquake is this attributable to the event? What if the overall rates for an area are significantly higher than usual? Beyond the accounting issue, even the numbers are frequently not disaggregated in a way that reveals vulnerability. In other words, deaths by gender, age, race or ethnicity, or even income level are not easily available, if in existence at all, for examining differential impacts. In sum, data may simply not be collected, have various standards (what is collected and how) for collection across political or organizational units, lack completeness (missing data), contain some level of error, or lack precision (either geographically or in terms of breakdowns). Further, even if data are collected, they may not be readily accessible.

Most countries have some type of census, but the level of analysis, method for collection, and types of socioeconomic data included varies. Many developing countries do not have a detailed resource at the local level, while many developed countries have country-specific versions that are quite detailed, with many countries falling somewhere in the middle. In the United States, the census data are a common source of secondary data for conducting a basic CVA or even as a component of more advanced assessments because of the vast amount of information on population and housing included. However, even with the large numbers of variables easily accessible on a local scale, this source also has many limitations and so should be used with caution (U.S. Census Bureau 2008a, b). Because it is collected only every 10 years and communities can change significantly during this time, the information may not reflect the actual configuration of the locality. In addition, many quality issues are also embedded within the data because of the collection process. For example, certain subpopulations are undercounted, such as minorities or homeless, among others (Skerry 2000). As a consequence, supplementing census data with other secondary sources is advantageous. These could include immigration data, public school records, property tax records, special needs registries, land use and zoning, service agencies, Medicaid and Medicare recipients, subsidized housing, community directories, religious organizations, special interest groups, among numerous others. The point is that local agencies and organizations maintain a variety of useful information; it is a matter of spending time seeking it out and evaluating the relevance and quality. In the United States, the local and/or regional planning office is often a good place to start. But even all of these sources, with all they can add to a vulnerability assessment, contain errors and biases.

Primary data collection methods involve those where information is acquired firsthand. These include surveys, interviews, focus groups, and numerous other tools utilized in the participatory process (Stallings 2002). Each of these approaches has advantages and disadvantages to the types of information obtained. Additionally, each requires vigilant planning, implementation, and analysis in order to appropriately and adequately obtain desired results. For example, if implemented correctly, data from surveys can be generalized to an entire population. A survey instrument must be carefully designed, pilot tested, and then administered to a representative sample of the population. The sampling process ensures that the appropriate number of people are included and from relevant geographic areas and subpopulations. The findings can then reflect characteristics, views, and perceptions of the entire group from which the sample was drawn. Interviews, on the other hand, are not generalizable, but provide greater detail of information. Focus groups, small groups of people (approximately 6–15 individuals) brought together to discuss a defined set of topics, give people the opportunity to interact, express views, possibly form consensus, and increase awareness. Like interviews, the data are quite detailed, cannot be generalized, and can be quite challenging to analyze.

Surveys, interviews, and/or focus groups can all be used as part of an advanced community-based vulnerability assessment, but may or may not be incorporated into a participatory process. Surveys, for instance, could be utilized to derive community-generated data, but not using a participatory approach. In this case, experts design and administer the instrument. On the other hand, community members may conduct the surveys or interviews within a participatory framework. An additional set of tools, including participatory mapping, timelines, seasonal calendars, ranking, transects (walking through a community making observations), and social network analysis, to name some, are all mechanisms for capturing information in a participatory process (Stoecker 2005). The bottom line is that the most sophisticated and advanced vulnerability assessment approaches will incorporate both primary and secondary data (beyond the census) and will utilize both quantitative and qualitative methods.

14.8   MAPPING APPROACHES

Nearly all vulnerability assessments now rely on geographic information systems (GIS) for understanding how hazard risk and vulnerability/capacity interact at a location and vary across space. GIS technologies are essentially computer mapping systems with analytical capabilities that are widely utilized throughout the emergency management cycle in a variety of ways (Thomas, Ertugay and Kemec 2006). As examples, GIS tools are used for risk assessment and communication, damage assessment, coordination and monitoring of cleanup efforts, and even evaluation of mitigation alternatives (Tobin and Montz 2004; Radke et al. 2000). While there are certainly many examples of modeling physical events with geotechnologies, their application to social vulnerability is no less relevant for preparedness, response, recovery, and mitigation, ensuring that vulnerability/capacity are represented and included along with hazard risk. Morrow (1999) emphasizes that knowing where vulnerable neighborhoods exist and understanding their circumstances is a critical step in effective emergency management. Additionally, Cutter, Mitchell, and Scott (2000) take a multi-hazard place-based approach to vulnerability assessment. Although focusing on impact assessment and only for earthquakes, floods, and wind, FEMA's HAZUS toolbox, explicitly designed for informing mitigation, does incorporate some elements of social vulnerability (FEMA 2008). Unfortunately, the data and methods are not nearly as developed for depicting a community's social vulnerability and capacities as for the modeling of physical events or damage assessment. Still, representing social conditions on a map along with hazard risk reveals the intersection in a powerful way.

Along with the possibilities, geographic modeling of social vulnerability poses many unique challenges, not the least of which is attempting to capture the multifaceted and complex aspects of social systems and human behavior. People utilize communities in different ways. For instance, the distribution of daytime and nighttime populations throughout an urban area is quite different. Further, social, economic, and political systems are not necessarily easy or even possible to record, calculate, and predict in a quantitative manner for inclusion into mathematically based models. Thus, the future of GIS for social vulnerability assessment will undoubtedly involve exploring mechanisms for incorporating qualitative along with quantitative information. Once on a map, information on social vulnerability and capacity has a strong potential for gaining legitimacy alongside the scientifically measured data.

Figure 14.1 depicts GIS output from a hazard and social vulnerability assessment. Without going into the complexity of the GIS processes or the specifics of the community, it illustrates how informative data displayed in this fashion can be, easily showing where high-risk locations exist. The map is a composite delineation of hazards in a small mountain community, representing wildfires, landslides, avalanches, hazardous materials spills, mines, and flooding on this single graphic, which is extraordinarily useful for preparedness and mitigation planning. At the same time, it also demonstrates challenges with conducting a comprehensive hazard and vulnerability assessment. For instance, questions should arise around what is actually displayed. What is the time period for the map? What were the data sources? How was the risk area for each hazard derived? How were the hazards zones combined and weighted? Further, social vulnerability, in this instance, is not incorporated in the map for several reasons. This resort community has few permanent residents, instead having tens of thousand of tourist visitors and homes predominantly bought as vacation residences, a situation not uncommon in numerous locations across the United States and internationally in resort, recreation, and tourist communities. Additionally, hundreds of service workers are employed, but they must commute to work because they cannot afford local housing. None of these populations is captured in the U.S. Census. Even if they were, this area represents only a single

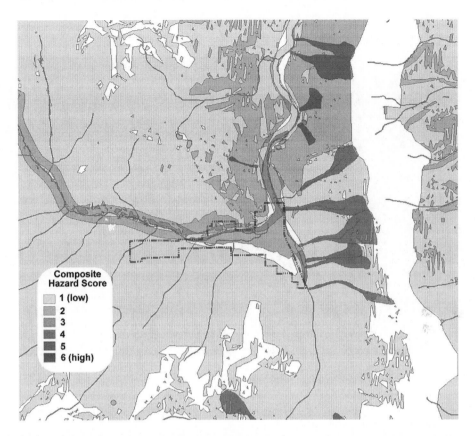

FIGURE 14.1 Sample GIS hazard assessment for a local U.S. community. *Map created by*: Deborah Thomas, with permission.

Census Tract (a U.S. Census geographic division by which data are compiled and released). As a consequence of this socio-demographic configuration, evaluating the nature of social vulnerability requires utilizing approaches beyond a basic CVA to account for these characteristics. Even though this example illuminates the necessity of using GIS and maps with care (in all instances, not only this case), they can form the basis for further discussion and future directions, certainly conveying information in a useful format.

Another example of utilizing GIS for preparedness planning and setting mitigation priorities involves generating hazard scenarios and estimating impacts. Figure 14.2 illustrates a potential earthquake event in Salt Lake City using FEMA's HAZUS-MH (FEMA 2008). In this case, only one possible 7.0 magnitude earthquake event at a time when children would likely be in school is represented; the scenario does not embody all possible earthquakes or all possible outcomes. Additionally, defining the parameters of the earthquake requires significant geo-technical scientific and engineering knowledge and high-quality data (physical, built environment, social) for this particular area to model a probable and possible event and the ensuing impacts. Again, as with the first example, even though many limitations exist and the output should be viewed critically, the maps and information do inform and guide emergency preparedness and mitigation activities, in this case showing where schools would be affected and estimating casualties.

Participatory GIS, in particular, has huge potential for social vulnerability assessments. As described previously, mapping is already utilized as a data-capturing tool in PCVA. This approach acknowledges that the vulnerability assessment (and emergency management by extension) is not just top-down, but also bottom-up. Input from residents is absolutely vital and the maps become a basis for dialogue, enhancing two-way communication between experts and communities. Additionally,

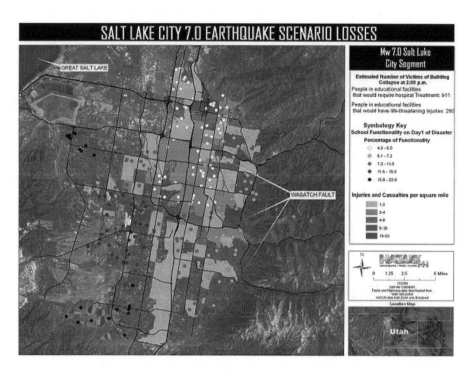

FIGURE 14.2 Example of estimated loss from an earthquake scenario. *Data and Modeling Source*: Federal Emergency Management Agency (FEMA). 2008. HAZUS: FEMA's Software Program for Estimating Potential Losses from Disasters. http://www.fema.gov/plan/prevent/hazus/ (accessed October 30, 2008). Map created by Jennifer Goldsmith, with permission.

maps can increase education about risk through the process and people's knowledge and perceptions can be recorded, adding or refining data. In other words, verifying secondary social data becomes possible through local involvement and priority setting can occur by those most affected.

Nearly all vulnerability assessments incorporate GIS into the process because of the extensive information they integrate and convey. Even though they should be applied with a great deal of care for many of the reasons discussed previously, mapping technologies capture, analyze, and convey data in an extremely accessible manner, one that appeals to the numerous stakeholders in a vulnerability assessment process.

14.9 FINAL CONSIDERATIONS

Just attempting to assess any one aspect of vulnerability can be a daunting process, considering the data, modeling, and analytical complexities, much less adequately combining integrating disciplines that inform the process. Terminology, data needs, and methods vary dramatically for every aspect of a vulnerability assessment, and expansive expertise is needed to bridge all of these subtopics. The physical modeling, even by hazard type, is a specialty unto itself. Then, there are specialists in social networking, survey methods, GIS technologies, participatory processes, and the list continues. Clearly, vulnerability assessment requires interdisciplinary approaches, or at a minimum a willingness to draw on information from multiple subject areas. Although it is an involved and intricate process and may be beneficial to assemble a team of experts, this may not often be possible, and so partnering with universities, consultants, or individuals in other agencies can be a viable alternative.

Even when conducting a simple CVA, a constant flow of information should occur. However, once an assessment is completed, it is equally important to publicize and to ensure translation of the results through a final report, presentations, new releases, community meetings, a Web site, and other outlets customized to that location. Ideally, a mechanism for feedback and/or submitting questions would also be desirable. By working with teachers and school districts, appropriate aspects of the vulnerability assessment can even be incorporated into school curriculums. These are but a few ideas of how to ensure results are disseminated and inform decision making.

Because a vulnerability assessment is fundamentally about people and the places where they live, a heavy responsibility resides with those undertaking the analysis. Mitigation and preparedness are laudable goals, but model outputs could have negative impacts on communities as well. Results from any loss estimation model could become the basis for geographical insurance ratings, for instance. Another illustration involves portraying vulnerable places. The indices rank neighborhoods and communities based on rather negative criteria. So, while the ultimate goal is to identify pockets of vulnerability to target resources and ultimately reduce loss, this is also a reflection of people's communities, a place where residents consider home, not necessarily vulnerable. Data ownership is also relevant. Do residents have a say in what is revealed about their community, especially from a PCVA process where the data are derived from them? Do they continue to have access to the data? The answer to both of these questions should be yes. Ethical considerations point to a need for particular sensitivity when collecting, maintaining, and analyzing data about people, not objects.

14.10 SUMMARY

Vulnerability assessments inform all phases of the emergency management cycle and offer a way to prioritize mitigation activities and increase the efficiency of response. Recognizing from the onset that conducting a vulnerability assessment is not a simple process and requires sufficient resources to achieve goals increases the potential for a successful outcome. The process should be informative, open, carefully designed, flexible, and proactive, not just after a disaster, but also as a preventative measure. Most importantly, results should be translated into decision making. CVA/PCVA, while extremely valuable and necessary, is really only part of the solution, not an entire answer unto itself.

14.11 DISCUSSION QUESTIONS

1. Why is a vulnerability assessment useful and what are its functions?
2. How does a basic CVA reveal community vulnerability?
3. What would the challenges be for implementing a PCVA in your community? What benefits might result?
4. Why do individual and household level livelihoods matter when considering social vulnerability and capacity?
5. How does a quantitatively driven social vulnerability assessment complement a PCVA? How are the outcomes similar? Different?
6. What are some characteristics of a disaster-resistant community? What indicators would be used to capture this?
7. What types of additional data would be useful for understanding social vulnerability beyond some of the types and sources listed in the chapter?
8. Why is mapping such a powerful tool for vulnerability assessment?
9. What are some challenges to the translation of CVA or PCVA to policy? How might these be overcome?
10. Why are ethical considerations so important both through the CVA/PCVA process and in any final results?

REFERENCES

Abarquez, I., and Z. Murshed. 2004. *Community-based disaster risk management: Field practitioners' hand-book*. Thailand: Asian Disaster Preparedness Center (ADPC).

Beierle, T. C., and J. Cayford. 2002. *Democracy in practice: Public participation in environmental decisions*. Washington, DC: Resources for the Future.

Birkmann, J., ed. 2006. *Measuring vulnerability to natural hazards: Toward disaster resilient societies*. New York: United Nations University Press.

Cannon, T., J. Twigg, and J. Rowell. 2003. *Social vulnerability, sustainable livelihoods and disasters*. Report to DFID, Conflict and Humanitarian Assistance Department (CHAD) and Sustainable Livelihoods Support Office. Natural Resources Institute, Department of International Development, University of Greenwich, UK.(pp. 1–63).http://www.proventionconsortium.org/themes/default/pdfs/CRA/DFIDSocialvulnerability. pdf, www.livelihoods.org/info/docs/vulnerability.doc (accessed October 30, 2008).

CARE. 2002. Household livelihood security assessments: A toolkit for practitioners. Prepared for the PHLS Unit by TANGO International Inc., Tucson, Arizona.

Coburn, A. W., R. J. S. Spence, and A. Pomonis. 1994. *Vulnerability and risk assessment*, 2nd ed. Cambridge, UK: UNDP Disaster Management Training Program, Cambridge Architectural Research Limited.

Cova, T. J. 1999. GIS in emergency management. In *Geographical information systems, vol. 2: Management issues and applications,* eds. P. A. Longley, M. F. Goodchild, D. Maguire, and D. Rhind, 845–58. New York: John Wiley & Sons, Inc.

Cutter, S. L., B. J. Boruff, and W. L. Shirley. 2003. Social vulnerability to environmental hazards. *Social Sciences Quarterly* 84:2.

Cutter, S. L., and C. Finch. 2008. Temporal and spatial changes in social vulnerability to natural hazards. *PNAS* 105 (7): 2301–2306. www.pnas.org_cgi_doi_10.1073_pnas.0710375105 (accessed October 30, 2008).

Cutter, S. L., J. T. Mitchell, and M. S. Scott. 2000. Revealing the vulnerability of people and places: A case study of Georgetown County, South Carolina. *Annals of the Association of American Geographers* 90:713–37.

Dao, H., and P. Peduzzi. 2003. Global risk and vulnerability index trends per year (GRAVITY). Geneva: UNDP/BCPR. http://www.grid.unep.ch/product/publication/download/ew_gravity4.pdf (accessed October 30, 2008).

de Dios, H. B. 2002. *Participatory capacities and vulnerabilities assessment: Finding the link between disasters and development*. Great Britain: Oxfam.

Enarson, E. 2003. Working with women at risk: Practical guidelines for assessing local disaster risk. Florida International University: International Hurricane Center.

FEMA (Federal Emergency Management Agency). 1997. Multi-hazard identification and risk assessment: A cornerstone of the National Mitigation Strategy. USA: FEMA.

FEMA (Federal Emergency Management Agency). 2008. HAZUS: FEMA's software program for estimating potential losses from disasters. http://www.fema.gov/plan/prevent/hazus/ (accessed October 30, 2008).

Freire, P. 1973. *Education for critical consciousness*. New York: Seabury.

Gupta, S. 2007. Opening plenary: First global platform on disaster risk reduction (GROOTS). http://www. groots.org/events/june_07_ISDR.html (accessed October 30, 2008).

IFRC (International Federation of Red Cross and Red Crescent Societies). 2006. *What is VCA? An introduction to vulnerability and capacity assessment.* Geneva, Switzerland: IFRC. http://www.ifrc.org/Docs/pubs/ disasters/resources/preparing-disasters/vca/whats-vca-en.pdf (accessed October 30, 2008).

Mileti, D. S. 1999. *Disasters by design: A reassessment of natural hazards in the United States*. Washington, DC: Joseph Henry Press.

Morrow, B. H. 1999. Identifying and mapping community vulnerability. *Disasters* 23:1.

Murphy, B. 2007. Locating social capital in resilient community-level emergency management. *Natural Hazards* 41:297–315.

NOAA (National Oceanic and Atmospheric Association) Coastal Services Center. 2008. Risk and vulnerability assessment tool (RVAT). http://www.csc.noaa.gov/rvat (accessed October 30, 2008).

NRC (National Research Council), Board on Natural Disasters, Commission on Geosciences, Environment, and Resources. 1999. *Reducing natural disasters through better information*. Washington, DC: National Academy Press.

Pearce, L. 2003. Disaster management and community planning, and public participation: How to achieve sustainable hazard mitigation. *Natural Hazards* 28:211–28.

Peduzzi, P., H. Dao, and C. Herold. 2005. Mapping disastrous natural hazards using global datasets. *Natural Hazards* 35:265–89.

Pelling, M. 2007. Learning from others: the scope and challenges for participatory disaster risk assessment. *Disasters* 31 (4): 373–85.

Radke, J., T. Cova, M. F. Sheridan, A. Troy, M. Lan, and R. Johnson. 2000. Application challenges for GIScience: Implications for research, education, and policy for risk assessment, emergency preparedness and response. *Journal of the Urban and Regional Information Systems Association* 12:15–30.

Skerry, P. 2000. *Counting on the census?: Race, group identity, and the evasion of politics.* Washington, DC: Brookings Institution Press.

SOPAC (South Pacific Applied Geoscience Commission). 2005. Measuring vulnerability in Small Island Developing States (SIDS): The environmental vulnerability index (EVI). http://www.un.org/esa/sustdev/sids/sidsvind.htm (accessed October 31, 2008).

Stallings, R. A., ed. 2002. *Methods of disaster research.* Xlibris Corporation: International Research Committee on Disasters.

Stoecker, R. 2005. *Research methods for community change.* Newbury Park, CA: Sage.

Thomas, D. S. K., K. Ertugay, and S. Kemec. 2006. The role of geographic information systems/remote sensing in disaster management. In *Handbook of disaster research,* eds. H. Rodriguez, E. L. Quarantelli, and R. Dynes. New York: Springer.

Thomas, D. S. K., O. V. Wilhelmi, and M. J. Hayes. 2006. Disaster reduction, drought, and the mountain resort community. In *Mountain resort planning and development in an era of globalization,* eds. T. Clark, A. Gill, and R. Hartmann. Elmsford, NY: Cognizant Communication Corp.

Tobin, G. A., and B. E. Montz. 2004. Natural hazards and technology: Vulnerability, risk, and community response in hazardous environments. In *Geography and technology,* eds. S. D. Brunn, S. L. Cutter, and J. W. Harrington, Jr. Boston: Kluwer Academic Publishers.

Turner II, B. L., P. A. Matson, J. J. McCarthy, R. W Corell, L. Christensen, N. Eckley, G. K. Hovelsrud-Broda, J. X. Kasperson, R. E. Kasperson, A. Luers, M. L. Martello, S. Mathiesen, R. Naylor, C. Polsky, A. Pulsipher, A. Schiller, H. Selin, and N. Tyler. 2003. Illustrating the coupled human–environment system for vulnerability analysis: Three case studies. *Proceedings of the National Academy of Sciences of the United States of America* 100:14.

Twigg, J. 2001. Sustainable livelihoods and vulnerability to disasters. Hazard Research Centre Working Paper 2. London: Benfield Greig. http://www.bghrc.com (accessed October 30, 2008).

UN-DESA (United Nations, Department of Economic and Social Affairs). 2007. Indicators of sustainable development: Guidelines and methodologies. Third edition. New York: United Nations. http://www.un.org/esa/sustdev/natlinfo/indicators/guidelines.pdf (accessed April 2, 2009).

UN ISDR (U.N. International Strategy for Disaster Reduction) 2005. Hyogo framework for action 2005–2015: Building the resilience of nations and communities to disasters. http://www.unisdr.org (accessed October 30, 2008).

UN ISDR (U.N. International Strategy for Disaster Reduction). 2007. Words into action: A guide for implementing the Hyogo framework. http://www.unisdr.org (accessed October 30, 2008).

U.S. Census Bureau. 2008a. Census 2000 gateway. http://www.census.gov/main/www/cen2000.html (accessed October 30, 2008).

U.S. Census Bureau. 2008b. United States Census 2010. http://www.census.gov/2010census/ (accessed October 30, 2008).

RESOURCES

Bangladesh Urban Disaster Mitigation Project (BUDMP). Hazard mapping and vulnerability assessment for flood mitigation. Bangkok: Asian Disaster Preparedness Center/AUDP, n.d. http://www.proventionconsortium.org/themes/default/pdfs/CRA/Bangladesh.pdf (accessed October 30, 2008).

Burby, R. Involving citizens in hazard mitigation planning. *Australian Journal of Emergency Management* (2001) 16:3. http://www.ema.gov.au/agd/ema/emainternet.nsf/Page/RWP09887172D1F56BE2CA256C75007EA6B9 (accessed on November 10, 2008).

California Seismic Hazards Mapping Program. http://gmw.consrv.ca.gov/shmp/index.htm (accessed October 30, 2008).

Cape Fear Council of Governments. Town of Holden Beach, North Carolina, community-based hazard mitigation plan. 2003. http://149.168.212.15/mitigation/Library/HoldenBeach_VulAssessment.pdf (accessed October 30, 2008).

Caribbean Hazard Mitigation Capacity Building Programme (CHAMP). http://www.cdera.org/projects/champ/mitiplcy/vulnerb.shtml (accessed October 30, 2008).

Center for Research on the Epidemiology of Disasters (CRED). http://www.cred.be/ (accessed October 15, 2008).

Comprehensive Emergency Management Plan 2005. Livermore, California. http://www.ci.livermore.ca.us/Livermore_Recovery_Plan/ANNEX-D-Livermore.pdf (accessed October 30, 2008).

EPA ReVa. http://www.epa.gov/reva/about.htm (accessed October 30, 2008).

Greenwood, D., and M. Levin. *Introduction to action research: Social research for social change.* Thousand Oaks, CA: Sage, 1998.

Hazard Mitigation Planning Committee (HMPC), Yuba City-Sutter County, California multi-hazard mitigation plan. 2007. http://www.yubacity.net/documents/News-Events/Multi-Hazard-Mitigation/MultiHazardSection42Vulnerability.pdf (accessed October 30, 2008).

Humanitarian Practice Network. http://www.odihpn.org/report.asp?id=2888 (accessed October 30, 2008).

ISDR. Global network of NGOs for community resilience to disasters. International Strategy for Disaster Reduction (ISDR). October 2006.

ISDR. Let our children teach us!: A review of the role of education and knowledge in disaster risk reduction. United Nations International Strategy for Disaster Risk Reduction (ISDR). July 2006.

Michigan Department of State Police. Local hazard mitigation planning workbook. EMD-Pub 207. 2003. http://www.michigan.gov/documents/7pub207_60741_7.pdf (accessed October 30, 2008).

MunichRe. http://www.munichre-foundation.org/StiftungsWebsite/ (accessed October 30, 2008).

Odeh Engineers, Inc. Statewide hazard risk and vulnerability assessment for the State of Rhode Island. North Providence Rhode Island. 2001. http://www.csc.noaa.gov/rihazard/pdfs/rhdisl_hazard_report.pdf (accessed October 30, 2008).

Oregon Partnership for Disaster Resilience: Showcase State Program. http://www.oregonshowcase.org/index.cfm?mode=about (accessed October 30, 2008).

Pacific Disaster Center (PDC). http://www.pdc.org/ (accessed October 30, 2008).

ProVention Consortium. http://www.proventionconsortium.org/ (accessed October 30, 2008).

Reason, P. Three approaches to participative inquiry. In *Handbook of qualitative research*, eds. N. K. Denzin and Y. Lincoln. Newbury Park, CA: Sage, 1994.

U.S. Center for Disease Control, Committee on Community Engagement. Principles of community engagement. http://www.cdc.gov/phppo/pce/part1.htm (accessed October 30, 2008).

Von Kotze, A., and A. Holloway. *Reducing risk: Participatory learning activities for disaster mitigation in Southern Africa.* Oxfam/IFRC, 1996.

Vrolijks, L. Guidelines for community vulnerability analysis: An approach for Pacific Island communities, South Pacific Disaster Reduction Programme (SPDRP) Organisation. 1996. http://www.proventionconsortium.org/themes/default/pdfs/CRA/SPDRP1998.pdf (accessed October 30, 2008).

15 New Ideas for Practitioners

Elaine Enarson, Eve Gruntfest, Brenda D. Phillips,
*and Deborah S. K. Thomas**

CONTENTS

15.1 CHAPTER PURPOSE

This book represents a major shift in hazards research and practice. The shift results from numerous long-term obstacles being directly and persistently confronted over many decades by a dedicated and growing cadre of hazard researchers and practitioners, and a recognition, particularly in the post-Hurricane Katrina landscape, that we are *not* learning from experience. This group, including many of the authors of this volume, represents the social science core of researchers who have progressed the field so that gender, race, class, and other social elements are valued as part of the vulnerability equation equally with physical characteristics of vulnerability. Their work has laid a strong foundation to transform the practice of disaster management, informing the new ideas that are included in chapter sections. To illustrate the benefits of such an integration of social and

---

* Chapter co-authors are listed alphabetically; we are indebted to Elaine Enarson and the FEMA Higher Education project for permission to use original content from the Social Vulnerability to Disasters course materials. All conclusions and suggestions in this chapter are the responsibility of the coauthors and do not necessarily reflect those of FEMA.

physical science with disaster management, this chapter describes concepts, strategies, and useful tools that are and can be used for immediate practical application.

15.2 OBJECTIVES

At the conclusion of this chapter, readers should be able to:

1. Describe the value of interdisciplinary social and physical science research for vulnerability reduction.
2. Identify new ideas for warning, evacuation, response, and other areas of disaster management that are supported with sound social science research.
3. List necessary next steps for integrating further social and physical science research with the practice of disaster management.
4. Appreciate the value of education and training in the area of social vulnerability.
5. Generate transformative change within the profession of emergency management and related fields.

15.3 INTRODUCTION

As described in the early chapters of this book, trying to control nature as the primary means to reduce natural hazards losses has been extremely expensive and frankly has not worked. In the 1970s, hazard researchers believed that assessing risks and understanding how risks were changing in floodplains, earthquake zones, volcanic areas, and elsewhere would bring knowledge of how to reduce vulnerability. But as White, Kates, and Burton note in their sobering 2001 article, vulnerability continues to increase.

It is clear from the chapters in this book and the extant literature that an integration of social science research with physical science understanding of hazards is the path that leads to minimizing risk. The case presented in this volume is more than compelling; without an understanding of the social nature of vulnerability, the transformative culture that must be cultivated to reduce risks will not evolve. Further, not linking scientific research with disaster management and vulnerability reduction efforts will elongate the time necessary to put effective policies and practices into place. For those who linger in harm's way, our first duty is to push beyond the separation of the sciences and the under-utilization of research. This chapter works toward that end by describing emerging ideas that have improved our abilities to reduce risk. Though much work remains to be done, it is equally clear that we stand on the edge of an important moment in time when understanding vulnerability and doing something about it is more than possible.

15.4 USING SOCIAL SCIENCE CONCEPTS AND TOOLS TO REDUCE VULNERABILITY

Gone (nearly?) are the days when the promise of new, expensive technologies is expected to make "all the difference," whether new radars, new computer programs, or new structural control works. There is no technological panacea. Rather, progress requires an end-to-end-to-end approach engaging all partners from individuals, households, local officials, first responders, researchers, and others rather than a top-down approach (Downton et al. 2005; Morss et al. 2005). This understanding has stemmed from, and reflects well, the overarching theme of previous chapters in this book: to reduce social vulnerability, we must engage all those affected by disasters in a collaborative risk-reduction process.

Social science has contributed significantly to this understanding by providing concepts, theories, and tools that assess and inform practice to help achieve the goal of life safety.

Social science has earned its place in the research and practice of hazard mitigation. It is no longer a marginalized add-on in research projects or in public policies. For example, growing demand for participation in grassroots efforts, including WAS*IS (Weather and Society * Integrated Studies) is transforming meteorology and hydrology as early career professionals demand more balanced training and experience with socially relevant projects (Demuth et al. 2007, www.sip.ucar.edu/wasis).

WAS*IS originated as an idea for a workshop to introduce meteorologists, who are enthusiastic about the societal impacts of weather but do not know how to begin pursuing such efforts, to social science. However, the interface of weather and society is interdisciplinary by nature so, as the idea evolved, the targeted audience was broadened to include meteorologists (and other physical scientists), social scientists, and practitioners to work jointly at this crossroads. The WAS*IS vision is to change the weather enterprise by comprehensively and sustainably integrating social science into meteorological research and practice. The WAS*IS mission for achieving this vision is to establish a framework for (1) building an interdisciplinary community of practitioners, researchers, and stakeholders—from the grassroots up—who are dedicated to the integration of meteorology and social science, and (2) providing this community with a means to learn about and further examine ideas, methods, and examples related to integrated weather–society work.

Developing a community of people who realize the value of and need for integrated studies is the best way to create change. Furthermore, by growing the community from the grassroots up, WAS*IS is a capacity-building movement that is energized and reinforced by the passions, experiences, and ideas of its people. This group will generate long-term collaborative efforts on integrated weather–society research and applications, and will provide career mentoring and support. The interdisciplinary community will also grow beyond the group of WAS*IS participants, as each person propagates the WAS*IS vision and creates new connections with friends and colleagues.

Regarding the second part of the framework, WAS*IS provides opportunities to learn about integrating meteorology and social science, as well as opportunities to undertake such work. There are few formal paths for focusing on these issues in traditional settings. Without a formal means for focused learning, people have to rely on ad hoc methods to learn and implement new tools and concepts, which can be frustrating and ineffective.

The primary mechanism for implementing WAS*IS currently is through workshops. The WAS*IS workshops provide participants with the initial, focused interaction with peers as well as a forum to explore ideas, methods, and examples related to integrated weather–society work. Bringing together people for several days to develop relationships, to learn, and to brainstorm together is invaluable for fostering energy and making WAS*IS sustainable. Following the workshops, participants then continue to interact and collaborate. The resultant knowledge and relationships garnered through WAS*IS are key to better serving society's weather-related needs.

As of December 2008, there are 172 WAS*ISers and the movement is growing. WAS*ISers are finding that putting their commitment to societal impacts on their resumes has helped them get new positions and promotions. New courses in "Weather and Society" have been developed at the University of Oklahoma, the University of Colorado Denver, and at the University of North Carolina Asheville. The U.S. National Weather Service is considering a new position for each forecast office dedicated to societal impacts. The next step is to develop similar capacity in social science. We need a cadre of social scientists interested in working across disciplines within social science and who know something about physical science concepts, methods, and policies.

It is clear from decades of work by dedicated disaster and hazards researchers that disasters are not "natural" events. Rather, they result from a misfit between the built environment, the impact of physical events, and the ways in which human systems are constructed (Mileti 1999). Vulnerabilities result as a reflection of the ways in which societies are constructed. Disproportionate risk reflects power structures in any society, and life safety is compromised when structural and situational inequalities interact. Non-sustainable development decisions increase risk. Thus, it is the goal of emergency management and other practitioners working in the field to reduce vulnerabilities.

Such reduction efforts imply a variety of strategies. Non-structural or social mitigation must be included as part of any reduction effort. For example, risk can be reduced by increasing disaster resilience and resistance. As written about so consistently and clearly in this volume, the root causes of vulnerability must be addressed. To do so, social change and empowerment are essential (see more in Chapter 16). Capacity building serves as a foundational element of non-structural mitigation or risk reduction efforts, in which practitioners must play a central role. That work starts with vulnerability assessment and mapping, as described in Chapter 14, and leads to disaster planning and preparedness efforts that build local capacity. In this approach, local knowledge and resources are a key part of building a resilient set of social networks that thwart the effects of disaster.

In order to build a strong grassroots-based effort, new relationships between professionals and the local community are needed. Grassroots risk reduction building requires that emergency managers and others influence community organizations and vice versa. By working with those at risk and the organizations that represent them, risk reduction efforts can be based on and emanate from those most at risk. People's own resources can be leveraged for self-protection, ultimately reducing the impact on emergency management agencies as well.

Historically, emergency management and civil defense agencies have resisted such a community organizing and grassroots approach despite the clear empirical evidence that it can work. Resistance stems from social constructions as well, as demonstrated well in Chapter 6 on gender. As von Kotze says (1999, 57), "the hazard-centered approach of the mainstream is dominated by men who are economically and often educationally advantaged, and who make decisions and arrangements from their 'malestream' point of view." Fordham (1998) agrees that the dominant hazards command and control approach is grounded in part in gender norms, for example, when emergency managers assign helper roles to women or view people with disabilities as helpless. From a gendered perspective, gender hierarchies privilege mainstream approaches while discouraging alternative views (Fordham 1998, 31):

> The dominant masculine engineering values and culture favour the rational over the emotional and can lead to the exclusion of subordinated groups and values. Even the language used in science and engineering is indicative of this androcentric dominance: masculine/objective, feminine/subjective; masculine science is "hard" science while feminine knowledge is subjective and "soft" … what is sought here is not necessarily a replacement of a masculine science and practice with a feminine paradigm but to acknowledge the legitimacy of alternative discourses.

Though the gender perspective is used here, it is easy to imagine alternative perspectives in which privilege is influenced by patterns of race and ethnic relations, able-ism, age-ism, and certainly by economic status. The latter is seen easily in the ways in which indigenous people's ideas and practices, both in the United States and internationally, have been undermined. In Peru, Maskrey (1989, 66) traced the root causes of a massive landslide in a Peruvian town to "the founding of a colonial town by the Spanish in a vulnerable location and the gradual abandoning of traditional agricultural practices." White settlement has dominated aboriginal cultures and sustainable living patterns and economic practices in Australia and Canada (Skertchly and Skertchly 1999; Buckland and Rahman 1999). In Bangladesh, Blaikie et al. (1998, 138–39) question how World Bank–funded "tech fixes" interface with local people's long-standing ways of living with floods (see Chapter 3 for more on sustainable development practices and issues). Within the United States, Native Americans respected the power of the Red River of the North and placed their settlements far from the flood plain. White communities that displaced indigenous populations led to extensive flooding in the 1990s. In short, respect for local knowledge and approaches from those vulnerable to disaster impact have been lost throughout the history of emergency management. This volume and this chapter encourage a return to not only more sustainable development approaches but also to the insights and perspectives that have historically been sidelined.

American disaster researcher E. L. Quarantelli (1998, 272) was optimistic about changing dominant ways of thinking about and researching disasters:

> [T]he more revolutionary we are in our thinking, the more likely we are to generate a new paradigm for disaster research. At least some of us ought to be revolutionaries rather than reformers. As a long time student of collective behavior and social movements, I am very well aware that the overwhelming majority of revolutions end in failure. But now and then one succeeds and transforms the behavior in the societies in which they occur, often in unexpected ways. So the more venturesome and imaginative among us should be encouraged to see if they can develop different paradigms for disaster research.

Indeed, researchers have reached conclusions challenging entrenched ideas in the hazards paradigm. As found throughout this volume, it is clear that disasters are not equal opportunity events; they are not social "levelers." Technical expertise and outside intervention have not prevented disasters. Jegillos (1999, 8) notes that in the Philippines, experts concur that community-based initiatives are needed rather than a long and failed "history of often uneven, inequitable and unsustainable results from 'top-down' interventions."

The transformative value of this volume is reflected in the words of Ben Wisner (personal communication), an original contributor to the FEMA Social Vulnerability to Disaster course materials and noted scholar-practitioner:

> How I learned to think differently ... I began with a fairly conventional approach to famine and rural development. But the conventional approach just didn't work in Eastern Kenya. I heard that from dozens of farmers, women and men. And the numbers didn't add up. The more in need of famine relief (measured as a percentage of children under three who were at 80% or below their standard weight for age), the less relief people got! Puzzled, I sought alternative explanations. ... Then a year or so later, I discovered that people about my age had been finding similar things in West Africa (e.g., cotton exports from Mali going up during the drought and famine there, 1968–1973). ... Pieces of the puzzle began to fall into place. My own acceptance of an alternative paradigm was born.

Outside of the United States and many First World nations, the idea of social vulnerability is respected. In Australia, experienced practitioner and scholar Philip Buckle (2000) notes that sociopolitical and even cultural contexts enabled a more rapid adoption of vulnerability analysis. In Australia, a stronger public sector with more state support of social services led the way. A more collective orientation to political culture, coupled with a formal commitment to egalitarianism and racial justice, supported the change to a "new idea." National identity as a leader in Asia and resistance to outside ideas and practices also compelled Australians to adopt vulnerability approaches and to work with communities to organize at the grassroots level (see Chapter 13 as well).

Could such a transformation be wrought here in the United States? Some features of our own culture and history support a vulnerability paradigm. For example, democratic norms promote participatory processes such as those urged in a number of chapters in this volume. The basis of this nation on resistance to oppression also lays a foundation for empowering those outside of traditional domains of power. Grassroots organizing traditions, including the effectiveness of the Obama campaign to place the first African American into the presidency, hold a long history here as well. Social transformation and social movements, as described in Chapter 1, serve as models for empowering women, racial and ethnic minorities, people with disabilities, and the elderly. Environmental justice movements that have exposed structural inequalities and revealed differential risk have led to significant policy and environmental change. And, in a post-Katrina world, the nation is ready for dramatic and profound changes that mean no one has to climb onto a roof or die on an overpass. The foundation exists for the acceptance of an alternate vision.

To illustrate further the ways in which social science concepts and tools have transformed disaster management and provided new ideas, the remainder of this chapter is divided into sections corresponding to the previous chapters. Next, we address social science contributions and new ideas for warning/evacuation/response, impacts, and recovery.

15.5 KNOWLEDGE, SKILLS, AND ABILITIES

What does an emergency manager or practitioner need to know in order to implement a vulnerability perspective? In this section we look at guiding principles, examples, and resources for moving toward a vulnerability approach.

15.5.1 GUIDING PRINCIPLES

Blaikie et al. (1998, 222–33) identify some guiding principles for moving toward a vulnerability approach. Those principles include

- A willingness and ability to connect with local people and local knowledge of how to live with hazards. To illustrate, the ways in which an individual with a disability is affected by mitigation measures or the local information provided by a Native American community regarding their environment could produce practical insights.
- Monitoring trends and anticipating vulnerabilities and capacities. This would include understanding how vulnerabilities change. Accessibility standards, for example, have transformed shelter environments. Newly vulnerable groups, such as veterans with disabilities, have been created.
- Understanding how to use participatory approaches and knowledge generated through it. Low-income households can be empowered to identify risk and educate those around them; for new immigrant households in particular, the social networks among the poor can be a means to reach those at risk.
- Knowing your community. By getting to know the social groups and social organizations present, a foundation is laid for more effective partnerships.
- Professional commitment to grassroots organizing as an integral part of non-structural mitigation. By leveraging the social capital of organizations and neighborhoods (see Chapters 13 and 16), warnings can be issued more thoroughly and evacuations can commence more effectively.
- Ability to network bureaucracies usually working in isolation. By bringing in other organizations and advocates, a fuller array of partnerships can be focused on the problem at hand. Post-disaster recovery has never been possible without voluntary organizations. By integrating this approach into other phases (preparedness, response, mitigation), a stronger set of practices can influence the full life cycle of disaster management.
- Commitment to working with citizen activists to reduce vulnerability. Significant progress has been made through citizen action, from the Boston Tea Party to recent social movements that have transformed society. The power and potential of people, through citizen participation, can profoundly influence disaster and hazard management.
- Understanding and appreciating people's struggle for basic human rights. Unless we spend time with those at risk, those who struggle to feed their families, avoid domestic violence, deal with hate crimes, labor to access basic services, and worry about mortgages, we will not understand how difficult it can be to prepare for and respond to disasters.
- Be accountable. Inform those at risk of what is being done, why things are or are not working, and what lies ahead. Accept responsibility for the differential risks that exist in society as part of the responsibility of the emergency manager or disaster practitioner. Accept that it is our duty, as fellow citizens, to address those differential risks in disaster and non-disaster contexts.

- Commit to change. Work with those at risk not only on disaster situations but also in areas that can make a difference: public and affordable housing; accessible public transportation; antiviolence programs and hate crime legislation; affordable health care; entitlement programs for seniors, people with disabilities, single parents and veterans; sustainable development policies and practices; and environmental justice for racial and ethnic minorities.

15.5.2 SENSITIVITY TO POWER RELATIONS

In order to move toward and adopt a vulnerability approach, practitioners must develop and practice sensitivity to gender, class, ethnicity, and power relations. To illustrate, a gender-sensitive practice might be guided by (Enarson and Morrow 1998; Morrow and Phillips 2008; Enarson and Phillips 2008):

- Using gender analysis in designing and evaluation projects
- Identifying gender bias in organizational culture and practice
- Advocating for gender equity in the planning, implementation, and evaluation of all initiatives to assess and reduce risk
- Working collaboratively and as equals with women
- Working with leading women's groups and organizations at the local level
- Relating relief and reconstruction to the reduction of gender vulnerabilities

Race-conscious practices can also be identified to reduce sources of bias and promote reduction of risk (see Aguirre 1998; Perry and Mushkatel 1986; Bolin with Stanford 1998; Fothergill, Maestas, and Darlington 1999). Strategies for doing so might include:

- Communicating across language barriers to reach diverse groups
- Using culturally appropriate and diverse media to reach racial and ethnic groups including alternative language stations
- Communicating with community leaders, advocacy groups, and faith-based organizations in all ethnic groups, particularly with locally respected leaders and those organizations that connect to recent immigrants
- Following culturally sensitive guidelines to tailor work to different communities, respecting and following cultural norms within various communities and groups
- Working collaboratively with and empowering ethnic community-based organizations that represent marginalized social groups
- Identifying with marginalized racial and ethnic communities through well-trained professionals, particularly those from within the communities at risk

Practitioners should also work at recognizing and being able to transcend class bias that tends to separate and divide people. Significant social capital exists within all socioeconomic classes including low-income levels. Based on previous chapters it is advisable to (Peacock, Gladwin, and Morrow 1997; Bolin with Stanford 1999):

- Advocate for the interests of low-income groups.
- Learn about the living conditions of poor people in their areas of responsibility.
- Identify economic differences between neighborhoods within communities.
- Be sensitive to class-biased assumptions about household structure, employment, and resources.
- Be sensitive to potential class-based barriers to government and nongovernmental relief and recovery services.

In short, Lindell and Prater (2000, 326) urge that

> emergency managers [should] get to know the residents of their communities to identify the ways in which potential implementation barriers affect different segments of the population. Frequent, personally delivered communications about inexpensive hazard adjustments that are targeted to specific segments of the risk area population may be the most effective means of reducing community vulnerability to earthquake hazard.

15.5.3 Transforming Practice through Professionalization

During the last two decades the field of emergency management has increasingly professionalized through the adoption of credentials, professional organizations, and both training and degree work. The FEMA Higher Education Project, which served as the source for this volume, has led many efforts to encourage the growth of emergency management and related degree programs. Well over 100 colleges and universities now offer degrees (both traditional and online) that are helping to build the next generation of emergency managers. A number of those degree programs include course content or even stand-alone courses on vulnerability. Courses can also be found in a number of social science programs, such as a department of sociology, on populations at risk (many of them offered by authors in this volume). Recently, Hesston College in Kansas developed a curriculum focused primarily on vulnerability reduction. Their efforts represent a stellar step toward transforming practice by using a vulnerability program. Unfortunately, social vulnerability is not necessarily at the core of many of these programs, but at least has become increasingly recognized; ultimately all programs should integrate some social vulnerability core education and training, even if it is not the entire emphasis of a program.

Dozens of workshops and conferences also exist both in support of training and higher education as well as for practice. Increasingly, vulnerability topics can be seen as workshop panels, presentations, and keynote speeches. Professional journals and organizations have promoted a greater understanding of vulnerability, such as the International Association of Emergency Managers, which has featured the topic in its bulletin and on the Listserve.

These trends reflect a larger national pattern of increasing specialization and the demand for formal credentials (Wilson 2000; Neal 2000; Darlington 2000), which should have vulnerability grounded in cutting-edge social science as a fundamental component. Employers also are increasingly expecting that those they hire will possess abilities to think across disciplines and fields of work, engage in effective community relations, interact with a diverse public, and collaborate with local citizens. Some suggest that emergency managers today represent "a new generation of emergency planners" rather than the old-school approach of top-down management styles (Dynes 1994, 156). Hurricane Katrina spurred on new approaches as well, with progress occurring at the federal level. FEMA, for example, has revised the National Response Framework to incorporate disability concerns. The National Housing Strategy (January 2009) recognizes the complexity of post-disaster housing given income and other issues. A state level housing task force that incorporates disability organizations is proposed and a special needs annex to the strategy is under development, as well as a Comprehensive Planning Guide (#301) on special needs and (#302) on service animals.

15.5.4 Integrating At-Risk Populations into Emergency Management Workplaces

Although some movement toward a vulnerability perspective can be identified, the process will reveal its greatest integration when the occupations of emergency management and related fields truly reflect the populations they seek to support. Yet there are clear indicators that only limited movement and progress has been made. For example, male students tend to dominate populations in most emergency managed and related degree programs (Neal, 2000). One explanation is that students tend to be drawn from first-responder-type occupations, which have historically been male. In a study of Florida county-level emergency management offices, Wilson (2000) found that only

FIGURE 15.1   Emergency Management Ontario (Canada) staff fostered and socialized a service animal that came to work and sensitized staff. Photo by Emergency Management Ontario. With permission.

15% of the directors and 13.5% of the assistant directors were female. As of late 2008, women had not led FEMA, although President-Elect Obama tapped Janet Napolitano to serve as secretary of the Department of Homeland Security.

A number of barriers exist to limit the increased participation of women, racial and ethnic minorities, and others to participate in emergency management practice (see also Chapter 6). Under-representation tends to stem from historic patterns of gender roles or from able-ism or racism. With gender, for example, it may be possible to hire from or recruit students from fields that women tend to dominate such as social work, women's studies, psychology, and health care, rather than an over-reliance on the male-dominated first responder and military professions. Job descriptions can adver-tise more widely than just traditional fields in order to recruit a diverse set of candidates with skills commensurate with those named above, particularly sensitivity to a wide range of circumstances (poverty, age-related situations, disabilities) and well-versed with interpersonal skills. Alternative arrangements can be made as well, such as hiring female or minority-owned consultants and busi-nesses that support the practice of emergency management.

Racial barriers compound overt and covert resistance to women and men of color in profes-sions related to emergency management and in employment, retention, and promotion practices in emergency management agencies. Cultural diversity programs and mentoring efforts can make a difference. It is clear that we have a long way to go even to sensitize workplaces to the needs of diverse populations. The Emergency Management Ontario (Canada) office has taken this on to sensitize staff to disability concerns. They offer lunchtime sign language classes. Their other efforts include raising a prospective service animal from puppy to adult. Staff members indicate they have raised their awareness to disability issues and express commitment to rescuing service animals in a disaster. For additional ideas, see Box 15.1.

15.6   WARNING/EVACUATION/RESPONSE

In this section, we describe some new ideas for the pre-disaster phase of warnings, evacuation, and response in order to encourage and urge readers toward change. Though space limits the full array

---

**BOX 15.1   STRATEGIES FOR INCREASING DIVERSITY
IN EMERGENCY MANAGEMENT**

To diversify the emergency management workplace, encourage transformation in degree programs in order to fuel a pipeline of diverse applicants:

- Conduct outreach to diversify the student body within emergency management and related degree programs.
- Connect with women's organizations, minority organizations, and student clubs to attract them to emergency management and related degree programs.
- Develop emergency management and related programs in historically black colleges and universities, tribal colleges, and those serving heavily Hispanic populations and women's colleges and universities.
- Integrate vulnerability perspectives across related fields including development studies, urban studies, environmental science and policy, women's studies, ethnic studies, disability studies, community studies, social work, urban planning, international relations, and the social sciences.
- Within the profession, consider efforts that:
  - Raise funds to support low-income students.
  - Create scholarships through professional associations.
  - Offer internships to individuals from historically marginalized and vulnerable groups.
  - Create workshop sessions at professional conferences and invite speakers with expertise to speak on vulnerability.
  - Invite community-based groups working with vulnerable groups and other advocacy groups to participate in identifying and interviewing candidates for open positions.
  - Develop brochures profiling successful nontraditional practitioners.
  - Offer educational materials that support broad outreach including Web sites, posters, flyers, and picture-based materials.
  - Interact with alternative media (e.g., African American–owned newspapers, Hispanic radio stations, women's newsletters, tribal publications, disability Web sites, environmental justice groups) to profile new approaches to risk management and new opportunities for nontraditional practitioners.
  - Connect with and support advocacy groups within the profession such as the Women Emergency Management Association in Australia or the Gender and Disaster Network.
  - Stay in tune with changing initiatives at relevant organizations such as the National Disability Council.

Source: FEMA Social Vulnerability course materials and authors.

---

of what can be described here, we refer the reader to previous chapters that contained useful ideas as well. In these upcoming sections, we focus on an integration of social science concepts as the basis for the tools described here.

15.6.1   KNOW YOUR COMMUNITY

Throughout this volume, it is clear that authors and practitioners recommend knowing your community as the one key guiding principle that governs effective practice. A good starting point is to simply open the yellow pages and identify social service organizations within the community. These organizations will typically fall into a number of categories relevant to socially vulnerable populations, including those that work with senior citizens, home-bound and medically fragile populations, women and children, those at risk for violence, the homeless, and people with disabilities. A savvy emergency manager will get to know each of these agencies, their personnel, and their capabilities in order to build a cadre of potential partners. Many of them can be brought into the emergency management arena by inviting them to participate in an existing Voluntary Organization Active in Disaster (VOAD) in the city or state. If such a VOAD does not yet exist, creating one can serve to organize and facilitate the creation of a useful network and provide disaster-relevant training to member organizations (for more, see the National Voluntary Organizations Active in Disaster or www.nvoad.org).

The networked organizations can provide insight into the numbers and kinds of populations that may be at risk locally and offer a valuable connection to them. Though census data can give a general overview (as described in previous chapters), those data remain limited to 10-year snapshots and annual estimates. Such data often miss emerging populations including recent immigrants, veterans disabled by recent wars, or individuals living in newly created facilities (e.g., prisons, nursing homes, state schools, workshops for the developmentally disabled). Organizations, including the faith-based sector, provide critical services to many at risk. For example, though the poverty rate remains fairly constant, what is clear is that people move into and out of poverty all the time. Similarly, homelessness seems constant but people move into and out of homelessness daily. Organizations that provide transitional facilities serve as a means to contact and inform those who are homeless about disaster preparedness, evacuation, and recovery. The transitional nature of such populations means that although the social problems of poverty and homelessness will always influence the practice of emergency management, the people we will try to reach will change. Local organizations provide useful ties to such dynamic populations. In the next sections, we offer some of the latest ideas that are working to transform vulnerability. The intent of the coming sections is not to cover thoroughly all new ideas, but rather to provide sources of inspiration for readers.

15.6.2 WARNINGS

As an example of getting to know your community and the value that it provides, consider the efforts of Jim Davis, the emergency coordinator for Pittsylvania County in Virginia. Davis first contacted a local community college regarding his concern for local residents who are deaf. He worked with the college to write a grant proposal to a local Lions Club, which provided some funding to purchase weather radios. Davis worked to adapt those radios so that they would vibrate pillows when he issued a warning. The devices were then given out to local residents who are deaf. One individual responded exactly as Davis had hoped, by becoming increasingly concerned about the risks faced by residents who are deaf. Davis then offered local Community Emergency Response Training (CERT) through local trainers and a certified sign language interpreter. Now, rather than being dependent on others for assistance during a disaster, local residents who are deaf can assist and support using their newly acquired skills. Davis transformed a formerly vulnerable population into one with capacities helpful to their families, neighborhoods, and community. For his efforts, Davis received the 2007 Clive Award at the National Hurricane Conference (for more, see Box 15.2). Davis' efforts worked because he (1) built a partnership among local organizations; (2) provided accessible equipment at no cost to recipients who tend to experience low incomes; (3) empowered local residents to work at their own preparedness; and (4) transformed vulnerability into resilience.

It is clear from Chapter 8 on disability that people who are deaf or hard of hearing do not get warning messages as easily as those who can, literally, hear warning sirens. In Oklahoma, a program called OK-Warn was developed out of the State Office of Emergency Management. Participants, accumulated on a database through the state agency, receive pager or e-mail warnings. What is important about OK-Warn is that it allows individuals to select the type of warning

BOX 15.2   THE ALAN CLIVE SERVICE AND SPIRIT AWARD

Alan Clive, blind since the age of 22, held a PhD in history, taught at the university level, published numerous articles, and was the director of a disability advocacy office in Massachusetts prior to joining FEMA in 1983. As a staff member of the Office of Equal Rights (ERO) for more than 22 years and in about 24 states on disaster assignment during that time, Dr. Clive was involved in almost every aspect of FEMA's disability program. His primary focus was on the needs of people with disabilities and elderly people in preparing for, responding to, and recovering from disaster. He taught this subject to the emergency management community through courses at FEMA and by television in a series of innovative videoconferences. Dr. Clive also supervised a cadre of disaster reservists who represented the ERO office at disaster sites, both attempting to resolve employee issues and ensuring that FEMA assistance is delivered with fairness and equity. Dr. Clive began to chair the National Hurricane Conference (NHC) Special Needs/Health Care Topic Committee in 1990, a role he held for nearly 18 years. He led efforts to feature workshops and sessions at the NHC on social vulnerability. In 2007, Alan Clive (a coauthor of Chapter 8 on disability, see Figure 15.2), received the first-ever International Association of Emergency Managers (IAEM) Career Excellence Award. The award "recognizes a national/international leader who has made significant contributions throughout his/her career to promote and improve the emergency management profession" (IAEM 2007, 1). Dr. Clive received the award for his efforts to "advocate for vulnerable populations" and "for the strong convictions and spirit he brought to his work" (IAEM 2007).

The Alan Clive Service and Spirit Award is presented at the National Hurricane Conference to "honor an individual or organization who has demonstrated outstanding leadership in the past years toward meeting the goal that all aspects of emergency management shall be accomplished in an equitable and impartial manner without discrimination, and with the inclusion of all people who can make a contribution."

In 2006, the Clive Award was first given to the Advocacy Center, as described by Dr. Clive: "the Advocacy Center is the designated protection and advocacy agency for the state of Louisiana. The Advocacy Center has four offices throughout the state. The New Orleans office was destroyed by Hurricane Katrina and operations were centralized in the Baton Rouge office. The Advocacy Center staff immediately began visiting the shelters throughout the state to ascertain the numbers of persons with disabilities in the shelters and their needs for a variety of services. Despite the lack of resources and the fact that 16 staff of the agency lost most if not all of their possessions, the staff went to work immediately with existing resources. In addition to the immediate response, the Advocacy Center developed resource materials on a variety of service programs for Katrina victims such as Medicaid, food stamps, housing, and unemployment insurance. The Advocacy Center also raised funds to assist not only their employees but also people with disabilities across the state who were affected by the storm. In the late fall, NDRN, a parent organization, obtained FEMA/UMCOR support for a case management project. As a result, hundreds of Katrina victims are receiving case management services from a legally based advocacy organization. At the same time, the Advocacy Center also filed a class action law suit against FEMA over a lack of accessible modified trailers."

In 2006, the Clive Award went to Jim Davis, an emergency coordinator in Pittsylvania County, Virginia, who secured funding to purchase weather radios in his county through a partnership with a local community college. Jim worked with the manufacturer to modify the radios to vibrate pillows and distribute them to area residents who are deaf. Jim then continued on and organized CERT training for this same group in his area, resulting in a higher level of independence and initiative among those who historically were "vulnerable" by virtue of a lack of effort to link them into the same information and notification flows available to others. This created the ability for all residents to take self-sustaining action and make emergency decisions in real time.

Jim's efforts all originated from a class assignment. In a statement to nominate Jim for this award, his former professor stated, "It is always the hope and dream of educators that their efforts will make a difference. In Jim's case, he went above and beyond such hope. He initially took a class project to only design an intervention effort and actually found a way to implement it. He took his conceptual ideas about building partnerships and reached out to make them happen. He picked up on notions of empowering those at risk to participate in their own response and recovery and made it possible. He embraced the idea of sustainability by creating a group of people to continue to care for the community. He made a difference because he didn't just pick up a text book and read it—he decided to make it real to his community."

In 2008, the Clive Award went to OK-WARN, the Oklahoma Weather Alert Remote Notification program for emergency weather/situation notification service via alphanumeric pagers and/or e-mail addresses. The free hazardous weather pager program gives deaf and hard-of-hearing Oklahomans better access to important severe weather information. Mr. Vincent Wood, NOAA National Severe Storms Laboratory research meteorologist and one of the program founders, accepted the award on behalf of a consortium of individuals and organizations behind the project. Following the May 3, 1999, tornado outbreak, Wood conducted a nine-month survey that revealed 81% of deaf and hard-of-hearing people experienced fear about being unprepared for weather emergencies and have relatively limited ways of knowing severe weather is imminent. When Wood presented the study results and pager idea to Jim Purpura, then–Warning Coordination Meteorologist with the National Weather Service Norman Forecast Office, Mr. Purpura suggested using an automated computer system to initiate pages of products from the NWS.

Representatives from the Oklahoma Department of Civil Emergency Management recommended using their Emergency Management Paging Alert System (EMPAS) to send weather alerts to the deaf community. EMPAS developer Weather Affirmation, LLC, of Oklahoma City, agreed to adapt the system with the understanding that its use would be limited to individuals who are deaf or hard-of-hearing. The Oklahoma School for the Deaf in Sulphur, a division of the Oklahoma Department of Rehabilitation Services, agreed to oversee and finance the pilot program. They purchased a computer system, equipment, phone lines, and a one-year software license at a cost of $13,000. Approximately 50 people selected to participate purchased pagers and paid monthly airtime charges. Mr. Purpura, with the help of Wood, interpreters, and School for the Deaf staff, provided weather safety training for program participants, helping them know what to do once they receive hazardous weather alerts, such as severe thunderstorm and tornado warnings. Further expansion of the program was made possible by a federal mitigation grant from FEMA.

Dr. Clive died in December, 2008, shortly before publication of this volume. His work lives on in those he inspires including readers such as yourself.

Source: Friends and family of Alan Clive and the International Association of Emergency Managers (2007, news release). See Figure 15.2.

FIGURE 15.2 Dr. Alan Clive at work in the Federal Emergency Management Agency Office of Equal Rights. FEMA News Photo.

they wish to receive. By understanding that people acquire information in different ways and by designing a warning system to meet that preference, it is possible to enhance warning receipt and interpretation and to motivate compliance with protective action instructions. OK-Warn received the 2008 Clive Award. OK-Warn's efforts worked because they (1) respected the ways in which a local population preferred to receive information; (2) provided an affordable means to receive warnings; (3) offered accessible devices; and (4) networked among state agencies to connect information to affected populations.

15.6.3 EVACUATION

Previous chapters demonstrate clearly that evacuation is problematic for socially vulnerable populations for a number of reasons. Institutionalized discrimination, for example, means that warning messages reflect the dominant culture and fail to integrate understanding of local cultural practices, literacy levels, and languages. Poverty levels render people vulnerable due to limited means for transportation. Failure at the highest levels to build a public transportation or infrastructure system that is available, affordable, and accessible exacerbates the problems with evacuation. Further, not grasping why people fail to leave familiar environments (with nearby health care, prescription availability, and family) or underestimate the current risk vis-à-vis their previous experience means that people remain vulnerable. Hurricane Katrina revealed these social problems clearly in 2005. Three years later, some important lessons had been transformed into enlightened practice.

For example, people felt they could not afford to evacuate for Katrina, which occurred at the end of the month. Because so many low-income households lived from check to check, the end of the month was a particularly difficult time financially. Lacking the means to evacuate, many stayed in place. A more sophisticated understanding of how to spur evacuation thus led the U.S. Postal Service to send out entitlement checks (e.g., Social Security, veterans' benefits, disability supplements) prior to the expected dislocation from Hurricanes Gustav and Ike in 2008 (Social Security Administration 2008). By releasing entitlement checks early, people reluctant to use meager resources for leaving could make the decision to do so.

The United States Fire Administration offers a detailed guide, *Orientation Manual for First Responders on the Evacuation of People with Disabilities,* which integrates people with disabilities into first responder training. The principle of inclusion resonates throughout the research on socially vulnerable populations. By demonstrating how to physically move and communicate with someone at risk, such as a person with a disability, that individual shares expertise and insight with those seeking to be of assistance. By allowing the socially vulnerable person to be the expert, power changes the nature of the relationship. A victim becomes actively engaged in his or her own evacuation and response, reduces the impact on the responding agency, and maintains functional independence.

As another example, Project Safe EV-AC (*Sound, Accessible, Free, Effective*) focused on the fear and anxiety that many feel when faced with developing emergency plans for evacuation. The Safe EV-AC Web site offers downloadable brochures that reflect recommendations from Chapters 5 and 10 to reflect cultural diversity by offering information in both English and Spanish (see http://evac.icdi.wvu.edu/library/). As their mission, SAFE EV-AC focused on "accommodation of individuals with cognitive, psychiatric, respiratory, hearing, vision, motor, and temporary impairments such as pregnancy." Materials have been developed to "assist with safely evacuating people with disabilities from locations such as places that care for the aged, prisons and jails, educational facilities, hospitals, public assembly properties, homes, hotels and motels, stores, manufacturing facilities, eating and drinking establishments, lodgings, and office buildings." Project Safe EV-AC works because it targets populations that need information, understands why people may be reluctant to prepare, and offers a means to overcome that barrier. Project Safe EV-AC empowers and transforms.

15.6.4 RESPONSE

Encouraging evacuation and compliance with instructions may be challenging. An individual or child with a significant psychological or cognitive disability may have difficulty comprehending instructions. Consequently, it is critical to ensure that those involved in response procedures can accurately and effectively communicate with a wide range of potential evacuees or victims. The Western Pennsylvania School for the Deaf in Edgewood, Pennsylvania, created a sign language booklet that includes the universal sign language alphabet. An increasing number of ambulance services also include pictorial signboards that include the sign language alphabet, locally spoken languages, and pictures that convey essential information between victim and first responder. In Australia, local firefighters realized that local Turkish immigrants were experiencing higher fire rates, resulting in injuries, deaths, and property damage. A small set of firefighters contacted a local immigrant center as well as a cultural organization. They learned about Turkish customs and basic language skills. By working with the organizations, they were able to communicate more effectively with the local community and became more known, trusted, and credible. The result? Fewer fires (Mitchell 2003).

Response planning requires an understanding of the population and its particular characteristics. Argonne National Laboratory has designed software (http://www.dis.anl.gov/projects/spp.html) that enables planners to use GIS for the purposes of:

- Establishing registries with personal information
- Mapping locations to registered persons using GIS information
- Creating reports and maps
- Analyzing information vis-à-vis response zones specific to area hazards
- Organizing emergency response plans for rapid retrieval

Argonne National Laboratory indicates that because the Special Populations Planner connects to a registry, care should be taken. Registries are lists of people who may require assistance with evacuation. Registries have not yet been researched to assess their viability, but anecdotal evidence suggests that lists may be difficult to develop and maintain, expensive for staff to update, inaccessible during times of emergency, and involve issues of confidentiality that need to be addressed. For Hurricane Ike, which approached the Texas coast in 2008, a 2-1-1 call-in system was used for those at risk to self-identify and request assistance as an alternative to a pre-established registry. It is fortunate that Ike was smaller numerically in comparison to the evacuation needs of Katrina because the 2-1-1 call-in system worked fairly effectively.

15.7 PROTECTIVE ACTION DURING RESPONSE

Alabama is creating a "Safe Center for Senior Citizens" through the state Department of Senior Services. The effort uses a senior center in concert with a safe center area, built to FEMA standards, to be used should a disaster strike this state, which is prone to tornadoes, hurricanes, and high wind events. The Guin Safe Center includes generator power and additional wall outlets for light medical equipment. The center specifies a location for those with Alzheimer's or dementia. Communications facilities have been enhanced through a satellite phone. Staff and volunteers are trained for disasters. The location also offers shelf-stable meals, and shower and laundry facilities so that the facility can function as a shelter. Additional safe centers will be constructed in coming years and will feature a light blue roof color. The color designates a safe location not only for local seniors but for those who may be visiting. Because the safe center is also a senior center, the facility maintains continual use and serves as a multi-function location (Alabama Department of Senior Services 2008).

In late 2008, FEMA provided a grant of $3.2 million to the Association for Retarded Citizens in Baldwin County, Alabama, to build a special needs safe room. The purpose is to build a safe location, built to FEMA 361 safe room standards and able to withstand winds of 200 miles per hour. The grant will also assist with retrofits to the laundry and life skills training center to increase the wind load standard up to 200 miles per hour. The training center is a 13,000 square foot facility. By creating these safer locations, it is now possible for those at risk to take protective action immediately in a familiar environment. The facility is the first of its kind in the nation and serves as a model for other communities.

The U.S. Department of Justice has issued recommendations regarding accessibility standards for local shelters. Based on the Americans with Disabilities Act, the standards provide guidance on a number of issues from aisles and doorway widths to cot heights for various kinds of disabilities to kitchen access for people with diabetes. A helpful checklist and guidebook can be downloaded to assess local shelters for accessibility and can be found at http://www.ada.gov/pcatoolkit/chap7shel-terchk.pdf (accessed December 30, 2008).

15.8 RECOVERY

After most disasters, social service and civic organizations step in to assist with recovery needs, particularly rebuilding the homes of low-income families and households. However, there is considerably more to recovery than just homes. Temporary housing units, which are funded or provided by FEMA to qualified survivors, have historically lacked accessible standards. In a post-Katrina lawsuit (*Brou v. FEMA*, also named DHS), a settlement provided for a process to identify applicants of accessible FEMA trailers. A local advocacy organization assisted with identifying those in need and FEMA worked to provide such units. As another example, Louisiana domestic violence organizations discovered that FEMA lacked any policy regarding trailer occupancy or resident protection should a resident be subject to domestic violence. The recovery period remains an area of particular need.

In the aftermath of a disaster, recovery planners often look to the general needs of the community rather than considering the particular needs of socially vulnerable populations and how the community could be transformed to create a safer, more affordable, and increasingly accessible location. Consider, for example, if a community might:

- Convene recovery meetings in the laundry rooms of public housing units so that low-income families could attend and participate.
- Redesign damaged public transportation to be accessible for seniors, children, and people with disabilities.

- Refuse to take lands of historically disenfranchised groups in order to rebuild.
- Cast a wider net with economic redevelopment by offering micro-loans for home-based work, creating a city wide free Internet to encourage telecommunicating and greener recovery, and encouraging loans to small businesses. After Katrina, the Mennonite Economic Development Association offered micro-loans to such small businesses in order to help retain the racial and ethnic diversity of the coast.
- Incorporate local concerns with environmental damage, such as those espoused by Native American tribes along Louisiana's Gulf Coast, into restoration efforts that would stem storm surge in future events.
- Maintain the quality of indigent health care and specialized health care for seniors, children, and people with disabilities.
- Link housing, work, transportation, and health care facilities so that movement among these different critical locations is easier, accessible, and more affordable.
- Incorporate local cultural heritage into the rebuilt architecture.
- Mitigate future risks without undue impact on those who might be displaced by some measures such as elevations that affect seniors and people with disabilities.
- Incorporates features like elevators to allow people with mobility disabilities to avoid displacement from familiar locations.

After Hurricane Ike, the U.S. Department of Homeland Security Office for Civil Rights and Civil Liberties (2008) conducted an impact report for special needs populations. As noted in the report,

> [E]ngaging the perspectives of special needs populations during the recovery process can help the community to become more supportive, inclusive, accessible, and resilient for everyone. Effective recovery creates opportunities for families to support their elderly members, provide advancement for children with special needs, foster independence of adults with disabilities, and celebrate the richness of cultural heritage. Experience shows that if people are to remain and invest in their community, the community needs to build its capacity to support its special needs population (p. 5).

It is clear that Katrina taught a number of lessons regarding social vulnerability. By heeding that call to action and incorporating new ideas, future consequences can be avoided.

15.9 CHALLENGES AND RECOMMENDATIONS FOR THE USE OF SOCIAL SCIENCE CONCEPTS AND TOOLS

While the serious integration of social science as a sustainable component of natural hazard research and practice, rather than as a one-time add-on, has great promise for long-term loss reduction. The road to a complete acceptance and use of social science concepts and tools, however, is not a smooth one. Two currently divergent roads must meet: collaboration of social scientists with physical scientists, and integration of social science research with emergency management.

15.9.1 Social and Physical Science Research

Presently, other than notable exceptions including the authors of this volume, there is limited capacity within the social sciences to competently collaborate with physical scientists on natural hazard mitigation. Three main obstacles to successful collaboration include the following:

- Like physical scientists, most social scientists operate within narrow disciplinary stovepipes.
- Most social scientists, even if they want to collaborate with physical scientists and engineers, have very limited knowledge of the physical scientist's concepts and tools related to natural hazards.

- A strong tendency for physical scientists exists to underestimate the social science effort that is necessary to understand how best to incorporate a fair understanding of human behavior in the face of risk and natural hazards. Once physical scientists accept that reducing losses from tornadoes, for example, has at least as much to do with human response to warnings as it does to increasing lead time, often they will look for human behavior modelers or human factor engineers.

The process of predicting human behavior is at least as complicated as predicting the weather that results from changing atmospheric conditions. Yet billions of dollars in research funding has advanced the state of physical science in predicting volcanic eruptions, tsunamis, hurricanes, tornadoes, and many other hazards. Achieving parallel progress on the human behavior side will also require years of research and, as is accepted in science, it will not be a direct route to success. A considerable shift in funding social science disaster research is a necessary means to accomplishing this parallel but joint research agenda.

Another means for introducing this shift can occur through professional researchers interacting through workshops. For example, the WAS*IS workshops aimed primarily at physical scientists have had major impacts in changing practices in the National Weather Service and elsewhere. Societally relevant metrics, new ways to communicate uncertainty, and major progress in increasing collaboration across the public and private sectors are only a few examples. For instance, in the United States the National Weather Service is starting to incorporate societal impacts in its forecasts. Previously in severe summer weather conditions the forecasters were concerned mostly with predictions of the size of the hail. Hail stones three-quarter inch size and 58 mile-per-hour wind speeds were required to meet the criteria for a severe thunderstorm. Now their forecasts also take into account whether the storm will affect rush hour traffic or have other impacts that will affect large numbers of people.

There also are numerous new ways to communicate uncertainty and a growing recognition that effective warnings are not a one-size-fits-all commodity (Hayden et al. 2007). Probabilistic information is essential for many businesses. For example, businesses that pour concrete cannot operate if the temperatures are below freezing. Probabilistic forecasts provide windows of opportunity for when it will be most likely that the temperatures will be above freezing within a five-day or three-day window.

Key to increasing understanding within this core of physical scientists is the extension of social vulnerability research into their areas of expertise. Meteorologists who warn the public must understand the significance of and content required to deliver meaningful messages to people with disabilities, seniors, children home alone, or administrators of congregate care facilities. Engineers who design structural features to mitigate risk must couple that effort with accessibility standards. Safe rooms (such as the FEMA 361 standard), for example, must be redesigned to permit wheelchair access both above and below ground.

However, participating in a workshop does not transform physical scientists into social scientists or vice versa. A new capacity of social scientists must be built in order to foster meaningful research. Social scientists must understand how the agencies work, as well as what field techniques, data, tools, and concepts are most useful for physical understanding of hazards. This interdisciplinary cross-fertilization is required in order to accelerate the change that will allow the research and stakeholder communities to learn from experience and reduce losses overall. This new community of scientists and practitioners could aid in cross-hazard work extending to issues related to climate change, increasing losses from the most common hazard in the United States (floods) and, most importantly, the effects of any hazard on a socially vulnerable population.

15.9.2 Social Science Research and Emergency Management Practice

Research suggests that knowledge transfer from researchers to practitioners occurs in a slow and unwieldy fashion (Mileti 1999; Fothergill 2000). Academic research tends to move into the public domain faster than that governed by proprietary or private interests (though it can be bought through consulting contracts). However, academic researchers must work within a framework that demands certain standards, including publication in top-notch scientific journals and presentations at professional conferences. Annual reviews, salary increments, and tenure all ride on these accomplishments. These venues, however, are not the place where most emergency managers glean their information. Thus, a disconnect exists between these two unfortunately separated communities.

Emergency managers tend to prefer information sources that include emergency management conferences, Listservs, courses available through FEMA or state agencies, and professional networks (Mileti 1999; Fothergill 2000). Direct experience is also valued, often above and beyond that acquired through research sources or academic degree programs. Though the field is changing continually, the research-based discipline of emergency management can truly be said to be in its early years with only a handful of bachelor's degree programs across the nation (though there are dozens of minors and certificate programs in emergency management, security studies, or similar fields). Fewer graduate programs exist and at present only two doctoral programs deliver research-based content or inspire the next generation of researchers. In short, the mechanisms to link researchers and practitioners tend to be distant and not overlap. There are also few structural rewards for academics who engage in applied disaster work or for emergency managers who secure degrees (especially those who lack practical experience).

To foster a better dialogue between these communities—both of which are dedicated to life safety and motivated to make their work relevant to today's society—we offer these recommendations:

- Participate in each other's Listservs and engage in dialogue with each other over issues relevant to socially vulnerable populations.
- Attend and present at emergency management conferences.
- Contact academic researchers to acquire copies of their research and invite them to give local presentations at emergency management agencies.
- Involve academic researchers, and social and physical scientists both, in consulting contracts designed to develop, for example, special needs emergency operations plans, evacuation protocol, shelter arrangements, and recovery programs.
- Attend workshops that involve both social scientists and emergency managers working on common problems, for example, those found at the National Hurricane Conference.

15.10 SUMMARY

The chapters of this new volume are a "must-read" for all of the hazards community, including all brands of scientists (social and physical) and practitioners. Ultimately, it is our hope that every academic program will have at least a class that concentrates entirely on social vulnerability and the potential that increasing capacity and building resilience from a social science perspective has for reducing disaster loss. Ideally, social vulnerability and social science approaches would be embedded throughout entire programs, including an emphasis on the relevance and active role of community and the necessity of integrating social and physical science, along with engineering. The vision for mainstreaming social vulnerability extends to the credentialing of professionals.

15.11 DISCUSSION QUESTIONS

1. What are the structural barriers to the use of social science research by physical scientists?
2. Why is there a disconnect between researchers and practitioners?
3. What are some characteristics of our society that make a shift to a vulnerability way of thinking about hazards and disasters difficult?

4. Which groups of people active in managing risk are least likely to accept a new view? Why?

5. What are some characteristics or trends in contemporary U.S. society that make a vulnerability paradigm appealing? To which social groups particularly? Why?

6. How would you recruit a woman of color into an emergency management workplace and ensure that you retain her as a valued employee of the organization?

7. Your aunt has been active in organizing others to resist the tribe's plan to license a nearby waste treatment plant. She is a single parent who has been saving money to return to college and complete her education but isn't sure what profession she wants to enter. What would she bring to emergency management? How could her success be nurtured?

8. Describe the knowledge, skills, and abilities needed for an emergency manager developing a community education plan for Miami, Florida. What would a professional trained to use a social vulnerability perspective bring to the job that others might not?

REFERENCES

Aguirre, B. 1988. The lack of warnings before the Saragosa tornado. *International Journal of Mass Emergencies and Disasters* 6 (1): 65–74.

Alabama Department of Senior Services. 2008. Alabama safe center for senior citizens. http://www.aoa.gov (accessed December 30, 2008).

Blaikie, P., T. Cannon, I. Davis, and B. Wisner. 1998. *At risk*. London: Routledge.

Bolin, R., with L. Stanford. 1998. *The Northridge earthquake: Vulnerability and disaster*. New York: Routledge.

Buckland, J., and M. Rahman. 1999. Community-based disaster mitigation during the 1997 Red River flood in Canada. *Disasters* 23 (2): 174–91.

Buckle, P. 1998. Redefining community and vulnerability in the context of emergency management. *Australian Journal of Emergency Management* Summer:21–26.

Darlington, J. 2000. The profession of emergency management: Educational opportunities and gaps. Presentation to the Natural Hazards Workshop, Boulder, CO. www.fema.gov/emi/edu/prof_em.pdf (accessed November 21, 2008).

Demuth, J., E. Gruntfest, S. Drobot, R. Morss, and J. Lazo. 2007. Weather & Society*Integrated Studies (WAS*IS): Building a community for integrating meteorology and social science. *Bulletin of the American Meteorological Society* 88 (11): 1729–37.

Downton, M., R. Morss, E. Gruntfest, O. Wilhelmi, and M. Higgins 2005. Interactions between scientific uncertainty and flood management decisions: Two case studies in Colorado. *Environmental Hazards* 7:134–46.

Dynes, R. 1994. Community emergency planning: False assumptions and inappropriate analogies. *International Journal of Mass Emergencies and Disasters* 12 (2): 141–58.

Enarson, E., and B. Morrow, eds. 1998. *The gendered terrain of disaster*. Westport, CT: Praeger.

Enarson, E., and B. Phillips. 2008. Invitation to a new feminist disaster sociology: Integrating feminist theory and methods. In *Women and disasters: From theory to practice*, eds. B. Phillips and B. Morrow, 41–74. Philadelphia, PA: Xlibris, International Research Committee on Disasters.

Fordham, M. 1998. Participatory planning for flood mitigation: Models and approaches. *Australian Journal of Emergency Management* Summer:27–33.

Fothergill, A. 2000. Knowledge transfer between researchers and practitioners. *Natural Hazards Review* 1 (2): 92–98.

Fothergill, A., E. Maestas, and J. Darlington. 1999. Race, ethnicity and disasters in the United States: A review of the literature. *Disasters* 23 (2): 156–73.

Hayden, M., S. Drobot, E. Gruntfest, C. Benight, S. Radil, and L. Barnes. 2007. Information sources for flash flood warnings in Denver, CO, and Austin, TX. *Environmental Hazards* 7:211–19.

Jegillos, S. 1999. Fundamentals of disaster risk management: How are Southeast Asian countries addressing this? In *Risk, sustainable development and disasters: Southern perspectives*, ed. A. Holloway, 7–16. Cape Town, South Africa: Periperi Publications.

Lindell, M., and C. Prater. 2000. Household adoption of seismic hazard adjustments: A comparison of residents in two states. *International Journal of Mass Emergencies and Disasters* 18 (2): 317–38.

Maskrey, A. 1989. *Disaster mitigation: A community-based approach*. United Kingdom: Oxfam.

Mileti, D. 1999. *Disasters by design*. Washington, DC: Joseph Henry Press.

Mitchell, L. 2003. Guidelines for emergency managers working with culturally and linguistically diverse communities. *Australian Journal of Emergency Management* 18 (1): 13–18.

Morrow, B., and B. Phillips. 2008. What's gender got to do with it? In *Women and disasters: From theory to practice*, eds. B. Phillips and B. Morrow, 27–40. Philadelphia, PA: Xlibris, International Research Committee on Disasters.

Morss, R., O. Wilhelmi, E. Gruntfest, and M. Downton. 2005. Flood risk uncertainty and scientific information for decision-making: Lessons from an interdisciplinary project. *Bulletin of the American Meteorological Society* 86 (11): 1594–1601.

Neal, D. 2000. Developing degree programs in disaster management: Some reflections and observations. *International Journal of Mass Emergencies and Disasters* 18 (3): 417–37.

Peacock, W., H. Gladwin, and B. H. Morrow, eds. 1997. *Hurricane Andrew*. London: Routledge.

Perry, R., and A. Mushkatel. 1986. *Minority citizens in disasters*. Athens, GA: University of Georgia Press.

Quarantelli, E. L. 1998. Epilogue: Where have we been and where might we go? In *What is a disaster?* ed. E. L. Quarantelli, 234–73. New York: Routledge.

Skertchly, A., and K. Skertchly. 1999. Traditional Aboriginal knowledge and sustained human survival in the face of severe natural hazards in the Australian monsoon region: Some lessons from the past for today and tomorrow. *Australian Journal of Emergency Management* Summer:42–50.

Social Security Administration. 2008. Release of entitlement checks. http://www.ssa.gov/pressoffice/pr/hurricanegustav-pr.htm (accessed December 23, 2008).

U.S. Department of Homeland Security. 2008. Special needs populations impact assessment source document. Emergency support function #14 Long-term community recovery. Washington, DC: Department of Homeland Security Office for Civil Rights and Civil Liberties.

von Kotze, A. 1999. A new concept of risk? In *Risk, sustainable development and disasters: Southern perspectives*, ed. A. Holloway, 33–40. Cape Town, South Africa: Periperi Publications.

White, G. F., R. W. Kates, and I. Burton. 2001. Knowing better and losing even more: The use of knowledge in hazards management. *Environmental Hazards* 3:81–92.

Wilson, J. 2000. The state of emergency management 2000: The process of emergency management professionalization in the United States and Florida. Unpublished doctoral dissertation. Department of Sociology and Anthropology, Florida International University, Miami.

RESOURCES

The following free downloads can be currently accessed as of December 23, 2008:

- Special Populations Planner, Argonne National Laboratory: http://www.dis.anl.gov/projects/spp.html.
- Firefighter Etiquette: http://www.ok.gov/abletech/Fire_safety/Fire_Safety_Solutions_Grant_Etiquette_guide.html.
- Project Safe EV-AC: http://evac.icdi.wvu.edu/library/.
- The FEMA Higher Education Project with links to college and university programs: http://www.training.fema.gov/EMIweb/edu/collegelist/.

16 Promoting Empowerment: Social Change in Disasters

William E. Lovekamp

CONTENTS

16.1 CHAPTER PURPOSE

This chapter defines and examines sources of social change and empowerment, and addresses how disasters can influence social change. Also, this chapter examines the importance of nongovernmental and community-based organizations in promoting social change at the grassroots level. The chapter concludes with case studies of September 11th, 2001 and Hurricane Katrina that serve as examples of empowerment and social change within communities.

16.2 OBJECTIVES

As a result of reading this chapter, you should be able to

1. Recognize and develop a critical understanding of the processes of social change and empowerment.
2. Understand the importance of nongovernmental and community-based organizations for promoting empowerment and creating social change.
3. Acquire knowledge about the history of disaster research and theory.
4. Assess how disasters can influence social change.
5. Identify change in disaster stricken communities after September 11th, 2001 and Hurricane Katrina.

16.3 INTRODUCTION TO SOCIAL CHANGE

The history of virtually all societies is marked by social change. Social change is defined as "the significant alteration of social structure and cultural patterns through time" (Harper and Leicht 2002, 5). The first component of social change, social structure, refers to the patterns of interaction among persons or groups that have become routine and repetitive. These routine and repetitive patterns of interaction create social institutions or systems. The structure of any society is somewhat specific to that society, depending on the patterns of interaction of social institutions. The second component of change, culture, is often called the "roadmap of life" within a society and contains values, norms, symbols, and material culture. The key to understanding social change is to examine and identify how structural issues (economy, demographic distribution and/or change, complexity of political systems, etc.) and their relationship to cultural issues (values, how people in society think, what they hope for, how they live). Social change can occur when one or both of these are altered.

There are also several sources of social change. Changes in technology, such as the agricultural and industrial revolutions, account for some of the most dramatic and historical social change ever witnessed. Some scholars suggest that humans have recently seen a third technological revolution with the introduction of the microchip, which has resulted in computers and, subsequently, the "information age." Technology not only changes how humans work, but also changes how people interact with one another. Hence, the information age and the use of the Internet, cell phones, iPods, text messaging, Facebook, etc., have altered the way we communicate with others and live. Ideologies, similar to technology, can promote the status quo or promote social change. Ideologies are cultural beliefs such as democracy, communism, multiculturalism, etc., that justify social arrangements. An ideological change in our society, such as the emphasis on multiculturalism, has transformed education. For example, there is a great emphasis on English–Spanish bilingualism, English–Spanish public signs in areas with large Hispanic populations, and some states, such as California, allow drivers to take exams in a number of languages. Competition can also cause social change by "forcing individuals to adopt new forms of behavior to attain desired goals" or be an effect of social change because "a changing society has more goals open to competition than a static society" (Vago 2004, 19). Conflict between different groups has also been identified as an agent of social change. While competitors usually have the same goal and are subject to rules of competing, parties in conflict often have different and incompatible goals and may threaten or coerce each other, leading to social change. Economic forces also shape individuals' lives. For example, Karl Marx argued that organization of the economic system determines how other social institutions (religion, politics, family, education, etc.) would be structured. Large corporations increasingly create and control markets and determine what members of society "shall eat, drink, wear, and smoke, and how their homes shall look, and what price they shall pay for what they buy" (Vago 2004, 33). With corporations controlling markets, economic power is centralized. Resistance or conflict with these corporations and economic conditions can often lead to social change. Finally, globalization has more recently been identified as a source of social change. In fact, it could even be argued that globalization is a form of social change with expanding economic markets, divisions of labor, and the dissemination of culture within and across societies.

Finally, empowerment or the ability to make choices is also a key component of social change. According to Naila Kabeer (1999), empowerment refers to "the expansion in people's ability to make strategic life choices in a context where this ability was previously denied to them" (p. 437). And in examining empowerment, we need to examine "how the matrix of domination is structured along certain axes—race, gender, class, sexuality, and nation—as well as how it operates through interconnected domains of power—structural, interpersonal, disciplinary, and hegemonic" (Collins 2000, 288–89). Empowerment is providing power to those who have been historically marginalized, usually on the basis of race and ethnicity, social class, and gender, and providing them with the ability to make choices that are beneficial to them in the future, to allow them to create change. In what follows, this chapter examines how disasters can alter the social structure or culture of communities or societies, influence social change, and empower historically disadvantaged groups (Figure 16.1).

16.4   DISASTERS AND SOCIAL CHANGE

Researchers have long debated whether disasters can produce large-scale social change. Most research that discusses social change is situated within the recovery literature, and it is generally agreed that major change rarely results from disasters. Disasters do not cause growing and

FIGURE 16.1   Evidence of empowerment efforts as well as resilience and recovery after Hurricane Katrina. Photo by Pam Jenkins and Barbara Davidson. With permission.

prosperous communities to decline nor do they cause communities on the decline to rise up and become prosperous. Research argues equally for the two positions that (1) disasters contribute to change only by accelerating trends that were already under way prior to impact; and (2) disasters rarely have noticeable impacts on communities beyond the change caused during and immediately after the disaster occurrence, what would be considered the short-term recovery period (Nigg and Tierney 1993). Dynes (1975) adds to this debate by identifying three types of societies, their vulnerability to disasters, and the likelihood that disasters will produce social change. Type I societies are characterized by small populations, organized in terms of family, kin, and clan or tribal relationships, and have a fragile economic base. Disasters can produce considerable disruption and social change in these societies. Type II societies have larger populations and more stable economies where disasters typically produce moderate disruption and social change. Type III societies have large populations and a complex and integrated social structure, such as nation-states, and are most resistant to social change and disruption. They have considerable resources and established institutional structures, such as the Federal Emergency Management Agency (FEMA), the Department of Homeland Security (DHS), Red Cross, etc., to cope. So, research tends to demonstrate that while the relationship between social change and disasters is mixed, more developed societies are more likely to experience very little social change and disruption.

Social change has also been an area of interest from the beginning of disaster research as a field of study. Samuel Prince's investigation of the town of Halifax, Nova Scotia, after the explosion of a munitions ship in 1917 is credited as the first study of the social characteristics of a disaster and social change. He noted that "catastrophes" were not isolated events, but part of the fabric of the community. Because catastrophes interfered with the equilibrium of the social institutions within a given society, they are critical to social change. In his study of Halifax, Prince (1920) found that the community grew more rapidly after the explosion than it ordinarily might have. More specifically, the explosion prompted increases in building permits, bank clearings, postal and tramway revenues, and generated a renewed interest in voting, city planning and civic improvement, health, education, and recreation. He states that "Halifax has been galvanized into life through the testing experience of a great catastrophe. She has undergone a civic transformation, such as could hardly otherwise have happened in fifty years" (Prince 1920, 139). In this instance, the disaster created positive social change in Halifax in a way that otherwise would have been impossible or, at the very least, improbable.

Pitrim Sorokin (1942) wrote the first theoretical book on "calamities" where he focused on the effects of the calamities on "behavior, social organization and cultural life of the populations involved" (p. 9). Formal organizational activities and control (especially by government) increases in the post-disaster period and attempts to re-establish equilibrium. Such calamities increase the competitiveness for resources between social groupings of individuals in society where there is an imbalance, which can lead to social change. He also notes that "when [a disaster] overtakes a given society, it becomes the focal point of attention in science and art, religion and morals, and other fields" (Sorokin 1942, 156). It can change the entire socio-cultural landscape.

Gideon Sjoberg (1962) suggested that disasters are a "key variable in altering social structures of industrial–urban societies" (p. 356). Disasters create channels for mobility and create demographic shifts within a society that in "normal" times might not exist or may bring to light structural changes that were already in motion prior to the catastrophe. Sjoberg contended that many of the dramatic social changes in the 20th century within industrial societies were brought about by social structure responding to catastrophe. Whenever hope is perceived and people are permitted access to mechanisms of social and political power, efforts to bring about social change will be made. Marginalized groups who are already dissatisfied with the social order may seek change through reform or revolution. Similar to Sorokin, he contends that:

> actors will struggle to re-establish equilibrium in the system if they see hope for its attainment in a reasonable period. But when they hold little confidence in the utility of their efforts, people will passively accept the disaster's consequences, distasteful though this may be (Sjoberg 1962, 374).*

Hence, disasters can influence social change, but this is often dependent on the stability of the social structure and characteristics of the culture, as well as the ability of groups to mobilize resources and power to fight for change.

16.5   HOW DO MEMBERS OF A SOCIETY BRING ABOUT SOCIAL CHANGE?

While disasters can create opportunities for social change, it is also important to understand the mechanisms that facilitate that change. In this section, I discuss how members of a society can bring about change in disaster times, define something as a problem, mobilize and take action, and the importance of nongovernmental organizations and community-based, grassroots groups.

The application of the social constructionist perspective to disasters has been very useful. This theoretical perspective was originally developed to explain the existence of social problems and how groups define conditions as problems and how they eventually address them. Spector and Kitsuse (1973) define social problems as "the activities of groups making assertions of grievances and claims with respect to some putative conditions" (p. 415). When people make claims that a condition is a problem, which is inherently socially constructed and defined, and respond to the claims, the condition is then regarded as a social problem. Hence, most social constructionist research focuses on claims-making activities and examines how these claims come to be accepted as legitimate and worthy of action (Best 1990). This perspective has been applied to the field of disaster research and arguably has made the largest theoretical contribution to disaster research in the United States (Mileti 1999, 211). This perspective "views disasters as socially produced through the formation of a common and shared definition ... and that disasters do not exist in and of themselves but are the products of how

---

* For an excellent summary of disasters and social change literature up to 1993, see Nigg, Joanne M., and Kathleen J. Tierney. 1993. "Disasters and Social Change: Consequences for Community Construct and Affect." Unpublished paper presented at the American Sociological Association Annual Meeting, Miami, Florida. http://www.udel.edu/DRC/preliminary/195.pdf

people agree to define them" (Mileti 1999, 210–11). Hence, this perspective is used to "examine the meanings of disasters for community residents, reflected in the claims-making activities through which they define the disaster and translate their understandings into claims for action" (Aronoff and Gunter 1992, 346). Others add that disasters are best conceptualized as nonroutine social problems and adopt a social constructionist perspective (Kreps and Drabek 1996; Kreps 1998). In one of the best examples to date, Stallings used the social constructionist perspective to examine an earthquake threat as a social problem for it involves "people a) reacting to past earthquakes [condition is problematic], b) to press for change in the present, c) in order to avoid an otherwise more negative future [actions will influence social change]" (1997, 3). This perspective clearly enables researchers to examine the mechanisms that create change within disaster-affected communities.

Furthermore, researchers have examined connections of disasters and involvement in social movements, which clearly have the ability to influence social change. Most movements literature investigates the relationship between technological or human-induced disasters and movements activity, while relatively little research explores the relationship between natural disasters and movements. This is primarily because natural disasters are often incorrectly viewed as "acts of God" where blame is not assigned, reducing the likelihood of mobilization to fight for change. In contrast, an examination of social movement participation after the Three Mile Island disaster reveals how the construction of shared grievances, established social networks, previous activism, and existing friendship networks all serve as catalysts for social movement involvement (Cable, Walsh, and Warland 1988; Walsh and Warland 1983). Furthermore, following an examination of the two different paths of activism present in the Three Mile Island disaster, the researchers concluded "recruitment and commitment patterns appear to depend on complex interactions between and among grievances, existing networks, and prevailing ideologies" (Cable, Walsh, and Warland 1988, 966). In technological disasters, blame is often assigned and communities are much more likely to mobilize and fight for social change that will protect them in the future.

In another example, Blocker, Rochford, and Sherkat (1991) examine elements of protest movements during a large metropolitan flash flood on Memorial Day weekend in 1984 in Tulsa, Oklahoma. Many people believed the flood resulted from inadequacies of their city to maintain their flood control system. When blame is assigned in a natural disaster rather than dismissing it as an "act of God," mobilization is much more likely. As a result, hundreds of citizens targeted their city government through protests. While not all community members participated, many with similar background characteristics, a strong sense of solidarity, and shared grievances were much more likely to participate (Blocker, Rochford, and Sherkat 1991). Therefore, if people are able to recognize the social structural and political causes of disasters and not dismiss them as "acts of God," mobilization, movement participation, and change are much more likely.

Finally, it is important to examine the role of nongovernmental and community-based organizations as resources for people and communities in disasters. Nongovernmental organizations are "independent, flexible, democratic, secular, non-profit people's organizations working for and/or assisting in the empowerment of economically and socially marginalized people" (Cousins 1991). They can be (1) charitable organizations, which typically take a top-down approach to helping others; (2) service organizations, which provide health, family planning, and/or educational services and in which people are expected to participate; (3) participatory organizations, which comprise self-help activities in which local people are involved in the implementation of a project; or (4) empowering organizations, which help people help themselves by teaching them an understanding of the social, political, and economic forces that shape their lives (Cousins 1991).

Community-based organizations are a type of nongovernmental organization arising from efforts by local citizens that usually adopts a grassroots approach to helping others or helping others to help themselves and may include religious organizations, women's organizations, social clubs, etc. Community-based organizations are often important in disasters because they provide services that traditional emergency service providers do not, or cannot, provide. Some nongovernmental organizations and many government-based emergency service providers are bound by formalized criteria or regulations in the type of services they can provide and/or the populations they can serve. Community-based organizations may have less stringent criteria and/or can be flexible enough that they can meet unique needs of specialized populations. Community-based organizations are often influential in establishing "unmet needs committees" after disasters to provide services to people who otherwise would "fall between the cracks." They can also provide day-to-day services for specialized populations, such as the disabled, elderly, poor, immigrant, homeless, or special health needs communities. They can also help reduce vulnerability to disasters because they know the specialized needs of their clients or community and can bring those needs to the attention of emergency managers and disaster planners. They also engage in coalition building where they are developing partnerships with each other in collaborative efforts to reduce vulnerabilities of specialized populations and/or promote social change. Hence, participation in social movements, making collective claims that disasters are social problems, and participation in nongovernmental, community-based organizations are all key components to facilitate social change and empowerment both in normal times and in disaster situations. What follows are two "case studies" of recent disasters, the September 11, 2001, terrorist attacks and Hurricane Katrina, both of which have significantly impacted America and our cultural landscape, and illustrate the concepts of community mobilization, empowerment, and social change.

16.5.1 September 11th, 2001 Terrorist Attacks

We all remember the tragic events that unfolded on September 11th, 2001. The terrorist attacks and the collapse of the World Trade Center towers will forever be etched into the collective memory of the United States. Approximately 2749 people died and more than 7000 of the World Trade Center population were injured or hospitalized (Foner 2005). These events were defining moments that are intrinsically connected in complex ways to social and policy changes in the aftermath.

Some of the most visible policy changes since September 11th, 2001, are the creation of the Department of Homeland Security (DHS), the Transportation Security Administration (TSA), and the Homeland Security Advisory System. The September 11th, 2001, terrorist attacks serve as what Birkland (2004) calls a "focusing event" and provide policy makers with a window of opportunity. It is important to note, however, that many social processes were present before the terrorist attacks. For instance, the militaristic focus of government response after the terrorist attacks has been present in disaster management since its creation.

Since the terrorist attacks there has been a resurgence in support for military involvement in disaster response and a de-emphasis on community-based preparedness and mitigation, as evidenced by the elimination of Project Impact (Tierney and Bevc 2007). It has also been argued that FEMA has disinvested in and de-emphasized its role in natural disasters and now primarily focuses on homeland security issues since the terrorist attacks, even though disasters pose much greater and more consistent risks than terrorism (Birkland 2004). The creation of the Department of Homeland Security, the focus on airline security and terrorism, and the absorption of FEMA into DHS to fight the "war" on terrorism are all consistent with this militaristic view (for additional thoughts on disasters and conflict, see Box 16.1).

Not only did the terrorist attacks usher in numerous policy changes, the attacks also had significant impacts on many communities across the United States. One such community, Manhattan, has the largest Chinese ethnic community in the United States. Chinatown is home to some 56,000 Asian residents, 33,000 workers, and 4000 businesses that are Chinese owned and operated (Akbar and Sims 2008). Also, Chinatown is located less than 10 blocks from "ground zero"—the name that came to be associated with the site where the World Trade Center towers fell, and was partially declared a "frozen zone," part of the disaster area that was cordoned off by police and National Guard troops.

Also, garment work is the largest industry in Chinatown. Before September 11th, there were approximately 246 garment factories in Chinatown employing nearly 14,000 garment workers

---

BOX 16.1   DISASTERS AS "WAR" AND MILITARISTIC RESPONSE

The view of disasters as similar to "war" and a military style of response was promoted in the 1950s from anxiety over the Cold War and incorporated into classic definitions of disaster. In the 1960s, Charles Fritz emphasized the following two reasons for the study of disasters: "first, to secure more adequate protection of the nation from the destructive consequences and potential atomic, biological, and chemical attack; and second, to produce the maximal amount of disruption to the enemy in the event of a war" (Fritz 1961, 653). Much of the early disaster research evolved as a response to the institutional demand for understanding how people would react in the face of danger, specifically how communities would react to dangerous events to gain insight into potential reactions to other destructive external agents, such as war. This conflict-oriented approach views disaster as a duplication of war, an expression of social vulnerabilities, an entrance into a state of uncertainty, and as attacks on groups or communities. Furthermore, this approach focuses on the destructive external agents of disasters and promotes a militaristic response. This militaristic command style of administration was further emphasized when, prior to the creation of the Federal Emergency Management Agency (FEMA) in 1979, most disaster programs were under the Office of Civil Defense and later the Defense Civil Preparedness Agency. After the Cold-War era, disaster preparedness and mitigation became more grassroots and community-based and continued through the President Clinton era with the creation of Project Impact, a community-based effort at disaster preparedness and mitigation.

(Akbar and Sims 2008). In the year following the terrorist attacks, Chinatown's garment industry lost an estimated $490 million with the shutdown of approximately 65 garment factories (Akbar and Sims 2008). It is now estimated that approximately 100 garment factories closed, eliminating about 8000 Chinese garment worker jobs (Sim 2002). When the work was still available, many had trouble getting to their homes and to work. Even more, Chinese who work in Chinatown but live in Brooklyn and Queens had even more difficulties getting into the frozen zone. "Those lucky enough to have kept an old pay stub with the factory address were allowed in; others had to walk around the perimeter until they found a breach in security" (Chin 2005, 195).

Furthermore, the only work remaining for the garment industry was work that was left over from before the terrorist attacks. No new work came into the majority of factories until January 2002 (Chin 2005). Also, while living in the enclave community, many women working in the garment factories were unable to find other work, which was only available outside the community. The networks women had established were often with other women garment workers who knew very little about other jobs available for women outside of Chinatown (Chin 2005). Also, women did not work outside of the community; all of the family members who worked outside of the community were men. As a result, many Chinese women have started to leave Chinatown to look for work; many who traveled to Chinatown from other areas have since found other work in their communities; and many more are learning to speak English as a way of broadening their social networks to ensure that they are more marketable when looking for work. Chin (2005) concludes that garment workers are in the midst of "producing their own sea change" in both the garment industry and community by changing the way they look for work. The old way of finding jobs through family networks are no longer effective. Garment workers no longer have the right connections, and the old connections they once had no longer point them to secure jobs. The effects of September 11th on the local Chinatown economy have transformed the community in numerous ways. Time will continue to tell the story of change in Chinatown.

In a second example of change after September 11th, 2001, it has been well documented that Muslims experienced many forms of overt and covert prejudice and discrimination after the terrorist attacks. Public perception was that anyone who looked Muslim must have been tied to the terrorists or been part of the attack. This story was solidified with heightened media publicity in Jersey City after the attacks. Jersey City is within a few miles of Manhattan, is racially and ethnically diverse, and is home to a very large Muslim population. The media and the nation focused on Jersey City with hostility partially because of the link the community had with Sheik Omar Abdel-Rahman, who spoke in the community years ago and was convicted of planning the 1993 World Trade Center Attack (Bryan 2005). This was also an area of intense FBI infiltration. The FBI, under the order of General John Ashcroft, was ordered to interview some 5000 male Muslims between the ages of 18 and 33 in their homes or at their workplaces for information relating to terrorism (Bryan 2005; Nabeer 2006). Also, approximately 800 of a total of 1200 INS detainees were housed in two New Jersey jails located just outside of Jersey City (Bryan 2005).

Muslims across America became the target of hate crimes and discrimination as a result of these events. Many women were harassed or beaten for wearing the hijab, a head scarf that has great religious significance, in public. If they choose not to wear the hijab in public, they risk not being true to their faith. Muslims were assaulted and scorned on the streets and in banks, coffee shops, grocery stores, etc., by random passers-by, neighbors, and police. The attacks ranged from "children throwing rocks at Muslim women to teenagers throwing beer cans to adult men and women punching Muslim women in the face while attempting to rip off their clothes and tear their veils" (Bryan 2005, 143). In her study of Muslim students, Peek (2003) demonstrates how students did not feel like a part of the larger community because they were portrayed as "the enemy" or "the other"; were excluded from the process of mourning, social bonding, and helping behaviors; and were very concerned about their safety and discrimination.

Despite the severity of the scorn, prejudice, and discrimination following the terrorist attacks, the events led to positive social change for many in the Muslim community in Jersey City and in Muslim communities across the United States. In response to the hostility experienced, many Muslims chose not to blend in or downplay their Arab or Muslim identity (Bryan 2005; Peek 2003). Many believed this to be a critical time to change the way Islam was represented and to educate the media, political leaders, and the larger society about their religion. Muslims began spending more time together reading and discussing the Qur'an; learning Arabic and attending religious services, some for the first time; and paid much closer attention to Islamic rules. The result was that community ties were heightened and Muslim identity and culture were reaffirmed for many after September 11th. Muslim women and men stated that after September 11th "they gained a renewed sense of purpose in their roles as strong sisters and brothers of Islam" (Bryan 2005, 155). Muslim students in the New York City area believed that "people were genuinely interested in learning about Islam and understanding them and their faith" (Peek 2003, 345). And since September 11th, many American Muslim organizations, both secular and religious, have spoken out publicly and contributed to the national conversation on conflict prevention and terrorism (Huda 2006). As we can see from the aforementioned examples, while many social processes or changes were already taking place prior to September 11th, such as the move of garment factories out of Chinatown and hostility toward Muslim Americans, the terrorist attacks had a direct and significant impact on each of these communities and facilitated policy and social change in a variety of ways.

16.5.2 Hurricane Katrina

Hurricane Katrina struck the Mississippi/Louisiana coast, covering approximately 90,000 square miles, as a category 3 storm on August 29, 2005. Damages were easily in excess of $160 billion with more than 1800 deaths, several hundred people missing, and almost one million area residents forced to evacuate (Gill 2007). This was one of the largest shifts in a single population in this country since the Dust Bowl of the 1930s and one of the worst disasters to ever impact the United States (see Box 16.2). The general consensus is that while Katrina caused sudden and widespread changes

---

BOX 16.2   REPOPULATION OF NEW ORLEANS

With a pre-Katrina population of approximately 455,000, New Orleans experienced a dramatic population loss after the disaster, but the population had been declining since its peak of 600,000 in 1960 (Jervis 2008). Recent population estimates show that the population is growing and by December 2008, the number of households actively receiving mail (a crude indicator of repopulation) reached 73.7% of pre-storm levels in New Orleans, compared to 50% one year after Katrina and 69% in August 2007 (Greater New Orleans Community Data Center 2009). The larger metro area of New Orleans had reached 88.1% repopulation by December 2008 (Greater New Orleans Community Data Center 2009).

While the population is beginning to reach pre-Katrina totals, reoccupation is much slower in areas that were impoverished before the storm, particularly in areas such as the Lower Ninth Ward of New Orleans. For example, by September 2008, the Lower Ninth Ward had only recovered 19% of its July 2005 resident population while the Central Business District/French Quarter and English Turn, areas least affected by flooding and less impoverished, contain 103% and 107% of their pre-Katrina resident populations, respectively (Greater New Orleans Community Data Center 2009).

Source: Liu, A., and A. Plyer. The New Orleans Index: Tracking recovery of New Orleans and the metro area. 2008. http://www.gnocdc.org/NOLAIndex/NOLAIndex.pdf (accessed November 21, 2008 and May 7, 2009). With permission.

TABLE 16.1
Total Population Estimates for New Orleans

	Jefferson	Orleans	Plaquemines	St. Bernard	St. Charles	St. John	St. Tammany	MSA
Census 2000	455,466	484,674	26,757	67,229	48,072	43,044	191,268	1,316,510
July 2005	449,640	453,726	28,588	64,683	50,164	45,602	217,551	1,309,954
July 2006	420,891	210,198	21,625	13,875	51,969	47,693	224,227	990,478
July 2007	423,520[a]	239,124[a]	21,540[a]	19,826[a]	52,044	47,684	226,625	1,030,363

Source: U.S. Census Bureau (*The New Orleans Index*, August 2008).

Note: 2005 and 2006 estimates were revised with the release of the 2007 census estimates.

[a] Orleans Parish, Jefferson Parish, St. Bernard Parish, and Plaquemines Parish have officially challenged their July 2007 census estimates.

---

to the physical and social fabric of the area, many changes were already taking place; Katrina simply sped up the process.

Green, Bates, and Smyth (2007) state that the most important issues impeding recovery and repopulation are levee construction, flood insurance, labor shortages, and an overwhelmed service sector. Generally, people in New Orleans parish do not believe that current levees will protect them from another Katrina, particularly those living below sea level, and Gulf Coast reports are consistent in claiming that the city remains at significant risk of re-flooding even after more than $7 billion was spent to repair and improve the levees (Green, Bates, and Smyth 2007; Katz 2008). While confidence in levees to protect people and their homes is lacking, there are other factors contributing to slow recovery. For instance, home insurance premiums have skyrocketed. The State Insurance Rating Commission approved increases in premiums of 16%–35% for 2007, some of which had already increased by 40% in 2006 (Warner 2007). Labor shortages have also hampered recovery efforts. *Help wanted* signs are still posted all over the Gulf Coast region for tourist and hospitality jobs traditionally filled by residents of the lower income neighborhoods. Also, since there are so few residents to fill many of the day labor positions, the debris removal and the repair and rebuilding of flood-damaged buildings is being carried out by migrant workers (Green, Bates, and Smyth 2007). This was partially due to the suspension of the Davis-Bacon Act immediately after the hurricane. The act requires federal contractors to pay the prevailing wage in the area. Once this was suspended, it encouraged many Mexican and Latino immigrants to move to the Gulf Coast area as day laborers helping with debris removal and disaster restoration industries. This has resulted in an immigrant labor market that is becoming institutionalized in New Orleans where many are settling and becoming long-term residents, often living in extremely difficult conditions and subject to exploitation (Donato et al. 2007). The overwhelmed service sector is another impediment to recovery. Hospitals, supermarkets, cafes, convenience stores, and schools have been slow to reopen and often operate short staffed and for shorter hours. Charity Hospital, which opened in 1939 with nearly 2700 beds and had a long-standing tradition of serving poor people in New Orleans despite federal and state disinvestments in health care provision and subsidization, will not reopen (Katz 2008). Also, the Louisiana State University Health Sciences Center University Hospital reopened in November 2006 but in a significantly limited capacity, only having 200 beds available (Katz 2008).

Many educational institutions in the Gulf Coast have also struggled to rebuild, redefine themselves, and change their focus. Two years after Katrina there are widespread teacher shortages with very few primary and secondary schools reopened, long waiting lists, and long commutes to out-of-neighborhood schools (Green, Bates, and Smyth 2007). As Katz (2008) notes, schools anchor communities are at the heart of social reproduction—"social practices and forces associated with sustaining production and social life" (p. 18). By December 2008 in Orleans Parish, 65 (70%) of private schools had reopened and 89 (70%) of public school facilities had reopened- 48 as charter schools, 4 as non-charter selective admission schools, 3 as alternative schools, and 34 as non-charter schools run by the Recovery School District-while eight additional public and two private schools opened in the fall of 2008 (Greater New Orleans Community Data Center 2009). Most of the schools that remained closed were in the most devastated and impoverished areas. This does not seem to be empowering the poor, minority communities that bore the brunt of the storm. Without schools, how can communities be socially reproduced? Conversely, a new report conducted at the Scott S. Cowen Institute for Public Education Initiatives at Tulane University indicates that while there are still many obstacles, most parents, teachers, and citizens believe that public schools have improved over the last year, better than they were before Katrina, and that the large number of charter schools that have opened since the storm has boosted community involvement in education (Maxwell 2008). New Orleans is experiencing a new model of education that is decentralized and multidistrict, traditional, and chartered instead of an Orleans Parish School Board characterized as one of financial mismanagement and corruption, academic failure, and administrative dysfunction and an urban school district that was characterized as one of the worst in the country before Hurricane Katrina (Akbar and Sims 2008; Johnson 2008).

Institutions of higher education have also had to overcome their own obstacles and have had to redefine themselves. For example, Esmail, Eargle, and Das (2007) analyzed *Chronicle of Higher Education* articles and coverage of Katrina's impact on colleges and universities and documented changes in location of instruction, programs, teaching methods, learning outcomes, funding, and policy. Tulane and Southern University, among others, fired faculty and staff and reduced their degree program offerings. Tulane instituted a community service component and Delgado Community College has moved more toward vocational learning and expanded offerings for high demand fields such as construction and nursing. Hurricane Katrina accelerated the growth of the "virtual university" where more courses are offered online in lieu of the traditional classroom setting. Also, with fewer resources universities and colleges have been forced to use fewer faculty members to teach more students, a trend that was already in progress.

FEMA instituted changes in funding so that private colleges and universities are able to more adequately receive funding in the event of disasters. Previously, private institutions could not receive funding if they had been awarded a small business loan or sustained operating losses. There are a few relevant examples of New Orleans area's Historically Black Colleges and Universities (HBCUs) using these funds to change in positive ways and move forward. For example, Xavier University will be receiving a $165 million low-interest federal loan to retire a significant amount of its debt incurred from Katrina, and Southern University, which previously never had residence halls, received a $44 million federal loan at 1% interest to be used to build a dormitory complex for 700 students (Mangan 2008). However, Louisiana's higher education commissioner, E. Joseph Savoie, said despite the promise of funding, FEMA still owes the state's colleges and universities $350 million for damages from Katrina and an additional $37 million from Hurricane Rita's destruction while private colleges have dipped into endowments and taken out loans (Mangan 2008). On a positive note, by fall 2007, New Orleans' colleges and universities had recovered 74% of their pre-Katrina enrollment, which will significantly help their financial situations and in their more general recovery efforts (Greater New Orleans Community Data Center 2008). While there are still many obstacles for education in the coming years, there are signs of hope and change.

Another example of social change after Katrina has been well documented in the New Orleans Jewish community. In the years following Hurricane Katrina, they have been able to develop a solid plan for changing their community in very positive ways. It is estimated that the pre-Katrina Jewish population was approximately 10,000, down from a Jewish population of nearly 13,000 25 years ago, and about 6000 in the summer of 2006, a year after Katrina (Chalew 2007; Nolan 2008). After Katrina, the community established an online database that was updated daily on the Jewish Federation's Web site with current contact information for members of the community. This made it possible for people to contact one another from within the community that had been displaced by the storm. The federation publicized meetings to be held in communities where Jewish New Orleanians had resettled and shared information about insurance issues and other resources to assist them in recovery (Chalew 2007). Some $20 million was donated from the United Jewish Communities and hundreds of synagogues, federations, and private donors, from around the country. These funds were allocated directly to every Jewish agency, organization, and synagogue in New Orleans (Chalew 2007).

As a way to rebuild their community, the Jewish Federation of Greater New Orleans developed a "newcomers" plan to attract new, young Jewish people to the community. Newcomers are offered incentives such as a moving grant of up to $3000, interest-free housing or business loans of up to $15,000 each, rental assistance of up to $2500, job search and business networking, reduced tuition in the New Orleans Jewish Day School, and free synagogue membership for a year (Chalew 2007). It is currently estimated that the program has generated approximately 850 newcomers to New Orleans (Nolan 2008). As Micheal Weil, executive director of the Jewish Federation of Greater New Orleans, stated, "There is no sense in going back to where we were before the storm. We have the opportunity now to make past dreams and new dreams of a vibrant Jewish New Orleans come true" (Chalew 2007). This is a clear example of social change that is community based and community defined.

In yet another example, the historically marginalized Vietnamese American community in New Orleans East experienced a high rate of return, rapid rebuilding, and high levels of community involvement while receiving little city government support and being absent from the national post-Katrina discussions about race, class, and social justice. Shared migration experiences and strong commitment to and leadership in the Catholic Church were at the center of the community's mobilization and reemergence after Hurricane Katrina (Leong et al. 2007). They also established themselves very quickly as active stakeholders in their community and the city. They organized successfully with African American community members, environmentalists, and other justice advocates in the Coalition for a Strong New Orleans East to oppose a landfill for hurricane debris to be located two miles from their community (Leong et al. 2007). People were very well connected with other members of their community, became well connected with other minority groups to create a more extended form of community, mobilized to oppose larger structural barriers to recovery, and used a community-based model of recovery that can serve as a model for other communities.

Inspirational models of local, community-based leadership, and community-based advocacy and activism have also emerged after Katrina by strong women activists who themselves were victims. While men have dominated the cleanup and construction efforts, the work of rebuilding communities and the social service sector and reopening schools will rely heavily on women and their skills and draw extensively from their indigenous knowledge of the local community. One example of these emergent, women-led groups, Women of the Storm, was created predominantly by a privileged group of white women in New Orleans who have actively mobilized a socially and economically diverse group of white, Vietnamese, Latina, and African American women to educate American governmental leaders about the needs of the people affected by Hurricanes Katrina and Rita for developing safe and secure neighborhoods and communities. They have been successful through advocacy and lobbying in Washington, DC, challenging congressional leaders to visit New Orleans, and offering educational tours, data, and personal narratives of survivors (Pyles and Lewis 2007).

The New Orleans Regional Alliance Against Abuse (NORAA) is another local, women-led, community-based group. This group is comprised of women social workers who are advocates from various programs and parishes that formed in the weeks following Katrina in Baton Rouge to serve survivors of sexual and domestic abuse in Katrina-affected areas. This group was able to establish new networks across these diverse programs and parishes and effectively create an umbrella group of domestic violence services to meet the needs of women survivors of domestic violence and sexual assault in the service area impacted by the hurricanes (Pyles and Lewis 2007).

The third example is a group of women advocating the right for citizens who were public housing residents, mostly poor people and people of color, to return to their homes. They have developed specific keys to recovery such as "a) fair treatment of residents by the U.S. Department of Housing and Urban Development (HUD) and the Housing Authority of New Orleans (HANO) in accordance with federal regulations, b) responding to the needs of residents who have returned, and c) keeping in touch with residents who want to return but are still living away from New Orleans" (Pyles and Lewis 2007). They have organized many activities, including public demonstrations at HUD and HANO offices, leadership-training workshops, job fairs, summer youth programs, and bringing health and mental health services to affected neighborhoods. These are all excellent examples of community-based activism and mobilization by strong woman leaders that can serve as models for other disaster-stricken communities across the United States.*

16.6 SUMMARY

This chapter examined the relationship between disasters and social change; how members of a community can create change; the importance of empowerment, mobilization, and community-based organizations; and presented examples of September 11, 2001 and Hurricane Katrina (Figure 16.2).

As demonstrated in this chapter, disasters often contribute to change by accelerating trends that were already in progress, such as a focus on militarism after the September 11, 2001, terrorist attacks, a decline in population, and the presence of racial and ethnic tensions in southern communities impacted by Hurricane Katrina. Also, disasters can facilitate or provide opportunities for empowerment of traditionally marginalized groups. For instance, Muslim community members after September 11 have been able to use the attacks to redefine themselves as Muslims, build stronger social connections in their communities, and educate the larger public about Islam in an effort to bring about more tolerance for their religion. Also, the New Orleans Jewish community was able to recreate their identity and recruit "newcomers" to their faith and community, the New Orleans

---

* For a comprehensive report of women leaders in the Gulf Coast, see Vaill, Sarah. 2006. "The Calm in the Storm: Women Leaders in Gulf Coast Recovery." A report by the Women's Funding Network AND the Ms. Foundation for Women. http://www.ms.foundation.org/user-assets/PDF/WFNMFWkatrina_report_1.pdf

FIGURE 16.2 Community resistance and organizing in New Orleans after Hurricane Katrina. Photo by Pam Jenkins and Barbara Davidson. With permission.

Vietnamese community was able to reclaim, redefine, and rebuild their community using community-based models of recovery, and strong women activists were able to mobilize and promote empowerment of marginalized women after Hurricane Katrina. It is clear that disasters have the ability to foster social change that is community based that empowers traditionally disadvantaged groups, and recovery and reconstruction can be arranged so that the people within those communities have the ability to rebuild their communities so that they best serve their needs.

To that end, we must recognize that disasters are opportunities for policy and social change, and we have a responsibility as researchers, policy advocates, emergency managers, and civically engaged human beings to ensure that disasters do not further marginalize groups that have historically been disadvantaged. We need to promote policy and social changes that empower these communities, particularly those historically disadvantaged and disempowered, that have been affected by disasters. We cannot allow people in positions of power who have little or no vested interest in or indigenous knowledge of affected communities to define policy and social changes that will take place within these communities. We must also ensure that disaster preparedness, mitigation, response, and recovery are community based and that people in disaster-impacted communities have the ability to define what is important to them and to determine what changes are in their own best interest. Nongovernmental, community-based organizations and groups are critical to incorporating indigenous knowledge. We must listen to and incorporate the voices of these groups to promote holistic and equitable disaster recovery.

REFERENCES

Akbar, R., and M. J. Sims. 2008. Surviving Katrina and keeping our eyes on the prize. *Urban Education* 43 (4): 445–62.

Aronoff, M., and V. Gunter. 1992. Defining disaster: Local constructions for recovery in the aftermath of contamination. *Social Problems* 39 (4): 345–65.

Best, J. 1990. *Threatened children*. Chicago: University of Chicago Press.

Birkland, T. A. 2004. The world changed today: Agenda-setting and policy change in the wake of the September 11 terrorist attacks. *Review of Policy Research* 21 (2): 179–200.

Blocker, T. J, E. B. Rochford Jr., and D. E. Sherkat. 1991. Political responses to natural hazards: Social movement participation following a flood disaster. *International Journal of Mass Emergencies and Disasters* 9 (3): 367–82.

Bryan, J. L. 2005. Constructing the true Islam in hostile times: The impact of 9/11 on Arab Muslims in Jersey City. In *Wounded city: The social impact of 9/11*, ed. N. Foner, 133–59. New York: Russell Sage Foundation.

Cable, S., E. J. Walsh, and R. H. Warland. 1988. Differential paths to political activism: Comparisons of four mobilization processes after the Three Mile Island accident. *Social Forces* 66 (4): 951–69.

Chalew, G. N. 2007. A community revitalized, a city rediscovered: The New Orleans Jewish community two years post-Katrina. *Journal of Jewish Communal Service* 83 (1): 84–87.

Chin, M. M. 2005. Moving on: Chinese garment workers After 9/11. In *Wounded city: The social impact of 9/11*, ed. N. Foner, 184–207. New York: Russell Sage Foundation.

Collins, P. H. 2000. *Black feminist thought*. New York: Routledge.

Cousins, W. 1991. Non-governmental initiatives. In *The urban poor and basic infrastructure services in Asia and the Pacific*. Manila: Asian Development Bank.

Donato, K. M., N. Trujillo-Pagan, C. L. Bankston III, and A. Singer. 2007. Reconstructing New Orleans after Katrina: The emergence of an immigrant labor market. In *The sociology of Katrina*, eds. D. L. Brunsma, D. Overfelt, and J. S. Picou, 217–34. Maryland: Rowman & Littlefield Publishers, Inc.

Dynes, R. R. 1975. The comparative study of disaster: A social organizational approach. *Mass Emergencies* 1:21–31.

Esmail, A. M., L. A. Eargle, and S. K. Das. 2007. Hurricane Katrina and its impact on education. In *The sociology of Katrina*, eds. D. L. Brunsma, D. Overfelt, and J. S. Picou, 191–202. Maryland: Rowman & Littlefield Publishers.

Foner, N. 2005. The social effects of 9/11 on New York City. In *Wounded city: The social impact of 9/11*, ed. N. Foner, 3–27. New York: Russell Sage Foundation.

Fritz, C. 1961. Disaster. In *Contemporary social problems*, eds. R. K. Merton and R. A. Nisbet, 651–94. New York: Harcourt Press.

Gill, D. A. 2007. Disaster research and Hurricane Katrina: Guest editor's introduction. *Sociological Spectrum* 27 (6): 609–12.

Greater New Orleans Community Data Center. 2008. The New Orleans index: Tracking the recovery of New Orleans and the metro area. http://www.gnocdc.org (accessed August 11, 2008).

Green, R., L. K. Bates, and A. Smyth. 2007. Impediments to recovery in New Orleans Upper and Lower Ninth Ward: One year after Hurricane Katrina. *Disasters* 31 (4): 311–35.

Harper, C. L., and K. T. Leicht. 2002. *Exploring social change: America and the world*. 4th ed. New Jersey: Prentice Hall.

Huda, Q. 2006. Conflict prevention and peace-building efforts by American Muslim organizations following September 11. *Journal of Muslim Minority Affairs* 26 (2): 187–203.

Jervis, R. 2008. New Orleans may have hit plateau. *USA Today*, August 4, p. 1A.

Johnson, K. A. 2008. Hope for an uncertain future: Recovery and rebuilding efforts in New Orleans's schools. *Urban Education* 43 (4): 421–44.

Kabeer, N. 1999. Resources, agency, achievement: Reflections on the measurement of women's empowerment. *Development and Change* 30 (3): 435–64.

Katz, C. 2008. Bad elements: Katrina and the scoured landscape of social reproduction. *Gender, Place and Culture* 15 (1): 15–29.

Kreps, G. A. 1998. Disaster as systemic event and social catalyst: A clarification of subject matter. In *What is a disaster? Perspectives on the question*, ed. E. L. Quarantelli, 31–55. New York: Routledge.

Kreps, G. A., and T. E. Drabek. 1996. Disasters as nonroutine social problems. *International Journal of Mass Emergencies and Disasters* 14 (2): 129–53.

Leong, K. J., C. A. Airriess, W. Li, A. Chia-Chen Chen, and V. M. Keith. 2007. Resilient history and the rebuilding of a community: The Vietnamese American community in New Orleans East. *The Journal of American History* 94 (3): 770–79.

Mangan, K. 2008. New Orleans colleges slog toward recovery from Katrina. *Chronicle of Higher Education* 54 (18): A1–22.

Maxwell, L. A. 2008. New Orleans schools. *Education Week*, April 30:5.

Mileti, D. S. 1999. *Disasters by design*. Washington, DC: Joseph Henry Press.

Nabeer, N. 2006. The rules of forced engagement: Race, gender, and the culture of fear among Arab immigrants in San-Francisco post-9/11. *Cultural Dynamics* 18 (3): 235–67.

Nigg, J. M., and K. J. Tierney. 1993. Disasters and social change: Consequences for community construct and affect. Paper presented at the Annual Meeting of the American Sociological Association. 1–50.

Nolan, B. 2008. Revitalizing the Jewish community. *The Times-Picayune*, May 25, p. 1A.

Peek, L. 2003. Community isolation and group solidarity: Examining the Muslim student experience after September 11th. In *Beyond September 11th: An account of post-disaster research*, ed. J. Monday, 333–54. Boulder: Institute of Behavioral Science, University of Colorado.

Prince, S. H. 1920. *Catastrophe and social change*. New York: Longmans, Green & Co.

Pyles, L., and J. S. Lewis. 2007. Women of the storm: Advocacy and organizing in post-Katrina New Orleans. *Affilia* 22 (4): 385–89.

Sim, S. 2002. Chinatown one year after September 11th: An economic impact study. Asian American Federation of New York. http://www.aafny.org/research/dl/911study/001WholeRpt.pdf (accessed December 23, 2008).

Sjoberg, G. 1962. Disasters and social change. In *Man and society in disaster*, eds. G. W. Baker and D. W. Chapman, 356–84. New York: Basic Books, Inc.

Sorokin, P. A. 1942. *Man and society in calamity*. New York: Greenwood Press.

Spector, M., and J. I. Kitsuse. 1973. Toward a sociology of social problems. *Social Problems* 20:407–49.

Stallings, R. A. 1997. Sociological theories and disaster studies. Paper presented at Disaster and Risk Conference: Disaster Research Center University of Delaware.

Tierney, K., and C. Bevc. 2007. Disaster as war: Militarism and the social construction of disaster in New Orleans. In *The sociology of Katrina*, eds. D. L. Brunsma, D. Overfelt, and J. S. Picou, 35–49. Maryland: Rowman & Littlefield.

Vago, S. 2004. *Social change*. 5th ed. New Jersey: Prentice Hall.

Walsh, E. J., and R. H. Warland. 1983. Social movement involvement in the wake of nuclear accident: Activists and free riders in the TMI Area. *American Sociological Review* 48 (6): 764–80.

Warner, C. 2007. Insurance rate increases Ok'd: Coastal parishes to bear bulk of higher charges. *Times-Picayune*, May 25:1.

Biographies of Contributors

Lynn Blinn-Pike is a professor in the Department of Sociology at Indiana University–Purdue University, Indianapolis. Her teaching and research focus on visual sociology, death and dying, and social problems. Her work includes giving emergency shelter residents cameras and having them document their lives after Hurricane Katrina. She is currently studying how women with breast cancer perceive artistic photographs of other women with the same disease. She earned her doctorate from the Ohio State University.

John Brett received his PhD in medical anthropology from the University of California San Francisco and Berkeley and is on the faculty in the Department of Anthropology, University of Colorado Denver. He conducts research in the United States and Bolivia around questions of microfinance and sustainable livelihoods.

Alan Clive (deceased) served for 22 years as civil rights program manager for the headquarters office of FEMA in Washington, DC. His area of responsibility included implementation of policy to ensure that disaster-related needs of people with disabilities are included in all levels of emergency planning. With Elizabeth Davis, Jane Kushma, and Jennifer Mincin, he is the author most recently of "Identifying and Accommodating High-Risk and High-Vulnerability Populations," in Tener Goodwin Veenema, ed., *Disaster Nursing and Emergency Preparedness for Chemical, Biological, and Radiological Terrorism and Other Hazards* (2007). He received his doctorate from the University of Michigan.

Nicole Dash is an associate professor and undergraduate program director of sociology at the University of North Texas. Her teaching and research interests focus on emergency evacuation, disaster recovery, and vulnerable populations. She has been published in a variety of journals including the *International Journal of Mass Emergencies and Disasters* and *Natural Hazards Review*. In addition, she has worked on GIS (Geographic Information Systems) for FEMA after both Hurricanes Andrew and Fran. She earned her doctorate from Florida International University in 2002.

Elizabeth A. Davis is managing director and founder of EAD & Associates, LLC, and consults for public jurisdictions and agencies, private businesses, home-based care agencies, and residential health care organizations. She retired as the first director of the National Organization on Disability's Emergency Preparedness Initiative but remains an advisor to DHS and FEMA and sits on several national advisory boards. Prior to founding EAD & Associates, she was an advocate for many years and worked in the NYC Mayor's Office for People with Disabilities as assistant to counsel and senior policy advisor and at the NYC Office of Emergency Management. She received her JD from Boston University School of Law and her EdM from Boston University School of Education with a degree in the socio-bicultural study of deafness and American Sign Language. She received her BA from Barnard College at Columbia University.

Elaine Enarson is an independent disaster sociologist in the Denver area. She writes widely on gender and disaster risk reduction based on U.S. and international field studies and is coeditor of the forthcoming international reader *Women, Gender and Disaster: Global Issues and Initiatives*. Before returning to Colorado, Elaine taught in the Applied Disaster and Emergency Studies Department of Brandon University in Brandon, Manitoba, Canada, where she worked with provincial women's organizations to build disaster resilience. Elaine earned her PhD in sociology from the University of Oregon.

Maureen Fordham has been researching disasters since 1988. She has a particular interest in marginalized groups in disaster including women and children. She was a founding member of the Gender and Disaster Network in 1997 and is the keeper of the Web site (www.gdnonline.org). She is also the joint founder and editor, with Ben Wisner, of Radix: Radical Interpretations of Disaster (www.radixonline.org). She was the editor of the *International Journal of Mass Emergencies and Disasters* between 2002 and 2006. She teaches at Northumbria University, United Kingdom, where she is the leader of the master of science program in Disaster Management and Sustainable Development and associate director of the Disaster and Development Centre.

Jennifer Goldsmith graduated with a bachelor's degree in geography from the University of Colorado Denver in 2003. She is currently a candidate for the master of integrated science degree from the University of Colorado Denver. For her capstone project, she will conduct a potential losses avoided study for a 7.0 earthquake scenario in a portion of the Wasatch Front, whereby the level of structural mitigation measures taken in the area had been increased. Jennifer is also working for FEMA as a disaster assistance employee in support of the Hazard Mitigation Division.

Eve Gruntfest is director of the Social Science Woven into Meteorology (SSWIM) initiative at the University of Oklahoma. She is also codirector of the WAS*IS (Weather and Society Integrated Studies) movement. She is an internationally known expert in flash floods, natural hazard warnings, and integrating social science into physical science and engineering. After 27 years on the faculty, Eve Gruntfest is now professor emeritus of geography and environmental studies at the University of Colorado at Colorado Springs. She earned her master's degree and PhD in geography at the University of Colorado.

Rebecca Hansen is senior project manager at EAD & Associates, LLC, and works nationwide with clients including governments, nonprofits, and private entities. Her professional emphasis is the integration of special needs and human services issues into emergency management standards, planning, and practices. In her field she has developed and conducted several training sessions for public health and emergency management professionals. During Hurricanes Katrina and Rita, she worked as a subject matter expert on one of four rapid assessment teams deployed by a national disability organization as well as serving on a select special needs advisory group to the Road Home Program in Louisiana. She received her BA from the State University of New York at Albany and earned a master's degree in social work from the Hunter College School of Social Work.

Alison Herring earned her bachelor of science degree in applied psychology and sociology at the University of Surrey, England and her master of arts in sociology at the University of North Texas. She is currently a doctoral student in sociology at the University of North Texas. Her research interests include disasters and collective behavior.

Pamela Jenkins is a professor of sociology and faculty in the Women's Studies Program at the University of New Orleans. She is a founding and associate member of UNO's Center for Hazard Assessment, Response, and Technology. Her research interests include documenting the response to Katrina as part of a national research team on Hurricane Katrina evacuees. She has published on first responders, faith-based communities, response to the storm, and the experiences of elderly during and after Katrina.

William E. Lovekamp is an assistant professor of sociology at Eastern Illinois University. His research examines disaster preparedness and recovery; how vulnerability is influenced by race, ethnicity, gender, and social class; perceptions of risk; and environmental racism. He is currently researching perceived risk and preparedness of college students and the capacity of universities to integrate various elements of the FEMA Disaster Resistant University Initiative as well as the negotiation of women's work roles in floods in Bangladesh. He earned a doctorate from Southern Illinois University.

Brenda G. McCoy is an assistant professor and program coordinator for sociology at the University of North Texas Dallas campus. Her teaching and research interests include health disparities in vulnerable populations, health care organizations, and gender. She earned a doctorate in sociology from the University of North Texas in 2005.

Jennifer Mincin has served as a senior project manager at EAD & Associates, LLC, and adjunct professor at Hunter College School of Social Work. She focuses on disaster, special needs, human services, community rebuilding, and recovery nationally and internationally. She has developed and conducted several training sessions for emergency management professionals as well as having served on a select special needs advisory group to The Road Home recovery program in Louisiana. She has also served as director of human services at the Nassau County Office of Emergency Management and was manager for Project Liberty in New York City during 9/11. She has two degrees from Columbia University including a master's in public policy and is ABD at the Graduate Center City University of New York with a focus in social policy, vulnerable populations, and disaster human services. Ms. Mincin is now with the International Relief Committee where she works with refugee services.

Betty Hearn Morrow is professor emeritus at Florida International University and former director of the Laboratory for Social and Behavioral Research at the International Hurricane Research Center. Her research focuses on the effects of human and social factors on the ability of individuals, families, and communities to respond to hazards. She is coeditor of *The Gendered Terrain of Disaster,* as well as *Women and Disasters* and *Hurricane Andrew: Ethnicity, Gender and the Sociology of Disaster.* Retired from academia, she continues an active research agenda as a consulting sociologist, primarily focusing on issues related to warning messages, evacuation, social vulnerability, and community resilience.

Katie Oviatt earned her BA in anthropology from the University of Nebraska at Lincoln in 2004. She is currently pursuing a master's degree in anthropology from the University of Colorado Denver. Her emphasis is on sustainable development and political ecology. Her current research is on the perception of disasters and disaster vulnerability in Bolivia.

Eve Passerini is associate professor and chair of the Sociology Department at Regis University in Denver, Colorado. Her teaching and research interests include sustainable development/redevelopment, environmental sociology, gender, and community-based research. She has been published in *American Sociologist, Sociological Forum, Environmental Professional, Mathematical Sociology,* the *Natural Hazards Review,* and the *International Journal of Mass Emergencies and Disasters.* She earned her doctorate from the University of Colorado Boulder.

Lori Peek is an assistant professor in the Department of Sociology at Colorado State University. She is also associate chair for research projects for the Social Science Research Council Task Force on Hurricane Katrina and Rebuilding the Gulf Coast. Peek's research examines the experiences of vulnerable populations in disaster, and she conducted field research in New York City after the September 11th, 2001 terrorist attacks and in New Orleans following Hurricane Katrina. She earned her doctorate from the University of Colorado Boulder.

Brenda D. Phillips is a professor in the Fire and Emergency Management Program and a senior researcher with the Center for the Study of Disasters and Extreme Events at Oklahoma State University. Her teaching and research focuses on disaster recovery, at-risk populations, and community relations. She has been published in the *International Journal of Mass Emergencies and Disasters, Disaster Prevention and Management, Disasters*, the *Journal of Emergency Management*, and *Humanity and Society*, and is the author of *Disaster Recovery* and coeditor of *Women and Disasters*. She earned a doctorate from Ohio State University.

Jean Scandlyn is research assistant professor in anthropology and health and behavioral sciences at the University of Colorado Denver and a visiting assistant professor at Colorado College. Her teaching and research focus on medical anthropology, global and community health, and migration with an emphasis on the health and well-being of adolescents and young adults in the United States and Latin America.

Carrie N. Simon received her BA in biology and studio art from Kenyon College in 2002. She will complete her master's degree in public health at the Colorado School of Public Health in 2009 with her thesis that looks at neighborhood environments and physical activity. Her passion for environmental science and health has taken her all over the world from the Turks and Caicos Islands to Bolivia. Her future plans include international traveling and pursuing an interdisciplinary doctorate in environmental/resource management and public health.

Pamela Stephens is completing her graduate degree at the University of Colorado Denver in public administration with a focus on emergency management and homeland security, and she is currently working on her thesis project developing an evacuation and sheltering plan focused on high-risk populations for a local county health department. Pamela is also working as a contracting consultant developing emergency response plans for a statewide community health organization, as well as volunteering as a government services liaison for the Mile High Red Cross and a senior advocate for the Colorado State Long Term Care Ombudsman Office.

Deborah S. K. Thomas is an associate professor in the Department of Geography and Environmental Sciences at the University of Colorado Denver. Her interests include hazards and health, as well as social science applications of GIS, both in the United States and internationally with current projects in Bolivia and Tanzania. Collaborating with people in various disciplines and local/state agencies defines her work, resulting in numerous publications and presentations.

Index